Lecture Notes in Computer Science   3952

Commenced Publication in 1973
Founding and Former Series Editors:
Gerhard Goos, Juris Hartmanis, and Jan van Leeuwen

Aleš Leonardis   Horst Bischof
Axel Pinz (Eds.)

Computer Vision – ECCV 2006

9th European Conference on Computer Vision
Graz, Austria, May 7-13, 2006
Proceedings, Part II

 Springer

Volume Editors

Aleš Leonardis
University of Ljubljana
Faculty of Computer and Information Science
Visual Cognitive Systems Laboratory
Trzaska 25, 1001 Ljubljana, Slovenia
E-mail: alesl@fri.uni-lj.si

Horst Bischof
Graz University of Technology
Institute for Computer Graphics and Vision
Inffeldgasse 16, 8010 Graz, Austria
E-mail: bischof@icg.tu-graz.ac.at

Axel Pinz
Graz University of Technology
Institute of Electrical Measurement and Measurement Signal Processing
Schießstattgasse 14b, 8010 Graz, Austria
E-mail: Axel.Pinz@tugraz.at

Library of Congress Control Number: 2006924180

CR Subject Classification (1998): I.4, I.3.5, I.5, I.2.9-10

LNCS Sublibrary: SL 6 – Image Processing, Computer Vision, Pattern Recognition, and Graphics

ISSN	0302-9743
ISBN-10	3-540-33834-9 Springer Berlin Heidelberg New York
ISBN-13	978-3-540-33834-5 Springer Berlin Heidelberg New York

Springer is a part of Springer Science+Business Media

springer.com

© Springer-Verlag Berlin Heidelberg 2006
Printed in Germany

Typesetting: Camera-ready by author, data conversion by Scientific Publishing Services, Chennai, India
Printed on acid-free paper   SPIN: 11744047   06/3142   5 4 3 2 1 0

Preface

These are the proceedings of the 9th European Conference on Computer Vision (ECCV 2006), the premium European conference on computer vision, held in Graz, Austria, in May 2006.

In response to our conference call, we received 811 papers, the largest number of submissions so far. Finally, 41 papers were selected for podium presentation and 151 for presentation in poster sessions (a 23.67% acceptance rate).

The double-blind reviewing process started by assigning each paper to one of the 22 area chairs, who then selected 3 reviewers for each paper. After the reviews were received, the authors were offered the possibility to provide feedback on the reviews. On the basis of the reviews and the rebuttal of the authors, the area chairs wrote the initial consolidation report for each paper. Finally, all the area chairs attended a two-day meeting in Graz, where all decisions on acceptance/rejection were made. At that meeting, the area chairs responsible for similar sub-fields thoroughly evaluated the assigned papers and discussed them in great depth. Again, all decisions were reached without the knowledge of the authors' identity. We are fully aware of the fact that reviewing is always also subjective, and that some good papers might have been overlooked; however, we tried our best to apply a fair selection process.

The conference preparation went smoothly thanks to several people. We first wish to thank the ECCV Steering Committee for entrusting us with the organization of the conference. We are grateful to the area chairs, who did a tremendous job in selecting the papers, and to more than 340 Program Committee members and 220 additional reviewers for all their professional efforts. To the organizers of the previous ECCV 2004 in Prague, Vaclav Hlaváč, Jiří Matas and Tomáš Pajdla for providing many insights, additional information, and the superb conference software. Finally, we would also like to thank the authors for contributing a large number of excellent papers to support the high standards of the ECCV conference.

Many people showed dedication and enthusiasm in the preparation of the conference. We would like to express our deepest gratitude to all the members of the involved institutes, that is, the Institute of Electrical Measurement and Measurement Signal Processing and the Institute for Computer Graphics and Vision, both at Graz University of Technology, and the Visual Cognitive Systems Laboratory at the University of Ljubljana. In particular, we would like to express our warmest thanks to Friedrich Fraundorfer for all his help (and patience) with the conference software and many other issues concerning the event, as well as Johanna Pfeifer for her great help with the organizational matters.

February 2006

Aleš Leonardis,
Horst Bischof,
Axel Pinz

Organization

Conference Chair

Axel Pinz   Graz University of Technology, Austria

Program Chairs

Horst Bischof   Graz University of Technology, Austria
Aleš Leonardis   University of Ljubljana, Slovenia

Organization Committee

Markus Brandner	Local Arrangements	Graz Univ. of Technology, Austria
Friedrich Fraundorfer	Local Arrangements	Graz Univ. of Technology, Austria
Matjaž Jogan	Tutorials Chair	Univ. of Ljubljana, Slovenia
Andreas Opelt	Local Arrangements	Graz Univ. of Technology, Austria
Johanna Pfeifer	Conference Secretariat	Graz Univ. of Technology, Austria
Matthias Rüther	Local Arrangements	Graz Univ. of Technology, Austria
Danijel Skočaj	Workshops Chair	Univ. of Ljubljana, Slovenia

Conference Board

Hans Burkhardt   University of Freiburg, Germany
Bernard Buxton   University College London, UK
Roberto Cipolla   University of Cambridge, UK
Jan-Olof Eklundh   Royal Institute of Technology, Sweden
Olivier Faugeras   INRIA, Sophia Antipolis, France
Anders Heyden   Lund University, Sweden
Bernd Neumann   University of Hamburg, Germany
Mads Nielsen   IT University of Copenhagen, Denmark
Tomáš Pajdla   CTU Prague, Czech Republic
Giulio Sandini   University of Genoa, Italy
David Vernon   Trinity College, Ireland

Area Chairs

Michael Black   Brown University, USA
Joachim M. Buhmann   ETH Zürich, Switzerland

Rachid Deriche	INRIA Sophia Antipolis, France
Pascal Fua	EPFL Lausanne, Switzerland
Luc Van Gool	KU Leuven, Belgium & ETH Zürich, Switzerland
Edwin Hancock	University of York, UK
Richard Hartley	Australian National University, Australia
Sing Bing Kang	Microsoft Research, USA
Stan Li	Chinese Academy of Sciences, Beijing, China
David Lowe	University of British Columbia, Canada
Jirí Matas	CTU Prague, Czech Republic
Nikos Paragios	Ecole Centrale de Paris, France
Marc Pollefeys	University of North Carolina at Chapel Hill, USA
Long Quan	HKUST, Hong Kong, China
Bernt Schiele	Darmstadt University of Technology, Germany
Amnon Shashua	Hebrew University of Jerusalem, Israel
Peter Sturm	INRIA Rhône-Alpes, France
Chris Taylor	University of Manchester, UK
Bill Triggs	INRIA Rhône-Alpes, France
Joachim Weickert	Saarland University, Germany
Daphna Weinshall	Hebrew University of Jerusalem, Israel
Andrew Zisserman	University of Oxford, UK

Program Committee

Motilal Agrawal	Stan Birchfield	Octavia Camps
Jörgen Ahlberg	Laure Blanc-Feraud	David Capel
Miguel Alemán-Flores	Nicolas P. de la Blanca	Barbara Caputo
Yiannis Aloimonos	Volker Blanz	Stefan Carlsson
Amir Amini	Rein van den Boomgaard	Vicent Caselles
Arnon Amir	Patrick Bouthemy	Tat-Jen Cham
Elli Angelopoulou	Richard Bowden	Mike Chantler
Adnan Ansar	Edmond Boyer	Francois Chaumette
Helder Araujo	Yuri Boykov	Rama Chellappa
Tal Arbel	Francois Bremond	Tsuhan Chen
Antonis Argyros	Thomas Breuel	Dmitry Chetverikov
Karl Astrom	Lisa Brown	Ondrej Chum
Shai Avidan	Michael Brown	James Clark
Vemuri Baba	Thomas Brox	Bob Collins
Subhashis Banerjee	Alfred Bruckstein	Dorin Comaniciu
Aharon Bar-Hillel	Andres Bruhn	Tim Cootes
Kobus Barnard	Roberto Brunelli	Joao Costeira
Joao Pedro Barreto	Antoni Buades	Daniel Cremers
Chiraz Ben Abdelkader	Michael Burl	Antonio Criminisi
Marie-Odile Berger	Brian Burns	James Crowley
Marcelo Bertalmio	Darius Burschka	Kristin Dana
Ross Beveridge	Aurelio Campilho	Kostas Daniilidis

Trevor Darrell
James W. Davis
Fernando DelaTorre
Herve Delingette
Frank Dellaert
Frederic Devernay
Michel Dhome
Sven Dickinson
Zachary Dodds
Ondrej Drbohlav
Mark S. Drew
Zoran Duric
Pinar Duygulu
Charles Dyer
Alexei Efros
Jan-Olof Eklundh
James Elder
Ahmed Elgammal
Mark Everingham
Aly Farag
Paolo Favaro
Ronald Fedkiw
Michael Felsberg
Rob Fergus
Cornelia Fermüller
Vittorio Ferrari
Frank P. Ferrie
James Ferryman
Mario Figueiredo
Graham Finlayson
Bob Fisher
Patrick Flynn
Wolfgang Förstner
Hassan Foroosh
David Forsyth
Friedrich Fraundorfer
Daniel Freedman
Andrea Fusiello
Xiang Gao
Nikolas Gebert
Yakup Genc
Guido Gerig
Jan-Mark Geusebroek
Christopher Geyer
Georgy Gimel'farb

Joshua Gluckman
Jacob Goldberger
Dmitry Goldgof
Venu Govindaraju
Etienne Grossmann
Frederic Guichard
Yanlin Guo
Allan Hanbury
Horst Haussecker
Eric Hayman
Tamir Hazan
Martial Hebert
Bernd Heisele
Anders Heyden
R. Andrew Hicks
Adrian Hilton
Jeffrey Ho
Tin Kam Ho
David Hogg
Ki-Sang Hong
Anthony Hoogs
Joachim Hornegger
Kun Huang
Slobodan Ilic
Atsushi Imiya
Sergey Ioffe
Michael Isard
Yuri Ivanov
Allan D. Jepson
Hailin Jin
Peter Johansen
Nebojsa Jojic
Mike Jones
Fredrik Kahl
J.K. Kamarainen
Chandra Kambhamettu
Yoshinari Kameda
Kenichi Kanatani
Qifa Ke
Daniel Keren
Renaud Keriven
Benjamin Kimia
Ron Kimmel
Nahum Kiryati
Josef Kittler

Georges Koepfler
Vladimir Kolmogorov
Pierre Kornprobst
Jana Kosecka
Danica Kragic
Kiriakos Kutulakos
InSo Kweon
Shang-Hong Lai
Ivan Laptev
Erik Learned-Miller
Sang Wook Lee
Bastian Leibe
Christophe Lenglet
Vincent Lepetit
Thomas Leung
Stephen Lin
Michael Lindenbaum
Jim Little
Yanxi Liu
Alex Loui
Brian Lovell
Claus Madsen
Marcus Magnor
Shyjan Mahamud
Atsuto Maki
Tom Malzbender
R. Manmatha
Petros Maragos
Sebastien Marcel
Eric Marchand
Jorge Marques
Jose Luis Marroquin
David Martin
Aleix M. Martinez
Bogdan Matei
Yasuyuki Matsushita
Iain Matthews
Stephen Maybank
Helmut Mayer
Leonard McMillan
Gerard Medioni
Etienne Memin
Rudolf Mester
Dimitris Metaxas
Krystian Mikolajczyk

Majid Mirmehdi
Anurag Mittal
J.M.M. Montiel
Theo Moons
Philippos Mordohai
Greg Mori
Pavel Mrázek
Jane Mulligan
Joe Mundy
Vittorio Murino
Hans-Hellmut Nagel
Vic Nalwa
Srinivasa Narasimhan
P.J. Narayanan
Oscar Nestares
Heiko Neumann
Jan Neumann
Ram Nevatia
Ko Nishino
David Nister
Thomas O'Donnell
Masatoshi Okutomi
Ole Fogh Olsen
Tomáš Pajdla
Chris Pal
Theodore Papadopoulo
Nikos Paragios
Ioannis Pavlidis
Vladimir Pavlovic
Shmuel Peleg
Marcello Pelillo
Francisco Perales
Sylvain Petitjean
Matti Pietikainen
Filiberto Pla
Robert Pless
Jean Ponce
Rich Radke
Ravi Ramamoorthi
Deva Ramanan
Visvanathan Ramesh
Ramesh Raskar
Christopher Rasmussen
Carlo Regazzoni
James Rehg

Paolo Remagnino
Xiaofeng Ren
Tammy Riklin-Raviv
Ehud Rivlin
Antonio Robles-Kelly
Karl Rohr
Sami Romdhani
Bodo Rosenhahn
Arun Ross
Carsten Rother
Nicolas Rougon
Mikael Rousson
Sebastien Roy
Javier Sanchez
Jose Santos-Victor
Guillermo Sapiro
Radim Sara
Jun Sato
Yoichi Sato
Eric Saund
Hanno Scharr
Daniel Scharstein
Yoav Y. Schechner
Otmar Scherzer
Christoph Schnörr
Stan Sclaroff
Yongduek Seo
Mubarak Shah
Gregory Shakhnarovich
Ying Shan
Eitan Sharon
Jianbo Shi
Ilan Shimshoni
Ali Shokoufandeh
Kaleem Siddiqi
Greg Slabaugh
Cristian Sminchisescu
Stefano Soatto
Nir Sochen
Jon Sporring
Anuj Srivastava
Chris Stauffer
Drew Steedly
Charles Stewart
Tomáš Suk

Rahul Sukthankar
Josephine Sullivan
Changming Sun
David Suter
Tomáš Svoboda
Richard Szeliski
Tamas Sziranyi
Hugues Talbot
Tieniu Tan
Chi-keung Tang
Xiaoou Tang
Hai Tao
Sibel Tari
Gabriel Taubin
Camillo Jose Taylor
Demetri Terzopoulos
Ying-li Tian
Carlo Tomasi
Antonio Torralba
Andrea Torsello
Panos Trahanias
Mohan Trivedi
Emanuele Trucco
David Tschumperle
Yanghai Tsin
Matthew Turk
Tinne Tuytelaars
Nuno Vasconcelos
Olga Veksler
Svetha Venkatesh
David Vernon
Alessandro Verri
Luminita Aura Vese
Rene Vidal
Markus Vincze
Jordi Vitria
Julia Vogel
Toshikazu Wada
Tomáš Werner
Carl-Fredrik Westin
Yonatan Wexler
Ross Whitaker
Richard Wildes
Chris Williams
James Williams

Lance Williams	Jie Yang	Cha Zhang
Richard Wilson	Ming-Hsuan Yang	Song-Chun Zhu
Lior Wolf	Ruigang Yang	Todd Zickler
Kwan-Yee K. Wong	Jingyi Yu	Michael Zillich
Ming Xie	Ramin Zabih	Larry Zitnick
Yasushi Yagi	Changshui Zhang	Lilla Zöllei
Hulya Yalcin	Zhengyou Zhang	Steven Zucker

Additional Reviewers

Vitaly Ablavsky	Chi-Wei Chu	Leo Grady
Jeff Abrahamson	Andrea Colombari	Kristen Grauman
Daniel Abretske	Jason Corso	Ralph Gross
Amit Adam	Bruce Culbertson	Nicolas Guilbert
Gaurav Aggarwal	Goksel Dedeoglu	Abdenour Hadid
Amit Agrawal	David Demirdjian	Onur Hamsici
Timo Ahonen	Konstantinos Derpanis	Scott Helmer
Amir Akbarzadeh	Zvi Devir	Yacov Hel-Or
H. Can Aras	Stephan Didas	Derek Hoiem
Tamar Avraham	Miodrag Dimitrijevic	Byung-Woo Hong
Harlyn Baker	Ryan Eckbo	Steve Hordley
Patrick Baker	Christopher Engels	Changbo Hu
Hynek Bakstein	Aykut Erdem	Rui Huang
Olof Barr	Erkut Erdem	Xinyu Huang
Adrien Bartoli	Anders Ericsson	Camille Izard
Paul Beardsley	Kenny Erleben	Vidit Jain
Isabelle Bégin	Steven Eschrich	Vishal Jain
Ohad Ben-Shahar	Francisco Estrada	Christopher Jaynes
Møarten Björkman	Ricardo Fabbri	Kideog Jeong
Mark Borg	Xiaodong Fan	Björn Johansson
Jake Bouvrie	Craig Fancourt	Marie-Pierre Jolly
Bernhard Burgeth	Michela Farenzena	Erik Jonsson
Frédéric Cao	Han Feng	Klas Josephson
Gustavo Carneiro	Doug Fidaleo	Michael Kaess
Nicholas Carter	Robert Fischer	Rahul Khare
Umberto Castellani	Andrew Fitzhugh	Dae-Woong Kim
Bruno Cernuschi-Frias	Francois Fleuret	Jong-Sung Kim
Ming-Ching Chang	Per-Erik Forssén	Kristian Kirk
Roland Chapuis	Ben Fransen	Dan Kushnir
Thierry Chateau	Clement Fredembach	Ville Kyrki
Hong Chen	Mario Fritz	Pascal Lagger
Xilin Chen	Gareth Funka-Lea	Prasun Lala
Sen-ching Cheung	Darren Gawely	Michael Langer
Tat-Jun Chin	Atiyeh Ghoreyshi	Catherine Laporte
Mario Christhoudias	Alvina Goh	Jean-Marc Lavest

Albert Law
Jean-Pierre Lecadre
Maxime Lhuillier
Gang Li
Qi Li
Zhiguo Li
Hwasup Lim
Sernam Lim
Zicheng Liu
Wei-Lwun Lu
Roberto Lublinerman
Simon Lucey
Gian Luca Mariottini
Scott McCloskey
Changki Min
Thomas Moeslund
Kooksang Moon
Louis Morency
Davide Moschini
Matthias Mühlich
Artiom Myaskouvskey
Kai Ni
Michael Nielsen
Carol Novak
Fredrik Nyberg
Sang-Min Oh
Takahiro Okabe
Kenki Okuma
Carl Olsson
Margarita Osadchy
Magnus Oskarsson
Niels Overgaard
Ozge Ozcanli
Mustafa Ozuysal
Vasu Parameswaran
Prakash Patel
Massimiliano Pavan
Patrick Perez
Michael Phelps

Julien Pilet
David Pisinger
Jean-Philippe Pons
Yuan Quan
Ariadna Quattoni
Kevin Quennesson
Ali Rahimi
Ashish Raj
Ananath Ranganathan
Avinash Ravichandran
Randall Rojas
Mikael Rousson
Adit Sahasrabudhe
Roman Sandler
Imari Sato
Peter Savadjiev
Grant Schindler
Konrad Schindler
Robert Schwanke
Edgar Seemann
Husrev Taha Sencar
Ali Shahrokni
Hong Shen
Fan Shufei
Johan Skoglund
Natalia Slesareva
Jan Sochman
Jan Erik Solem
Jonathan Starck
Jesse Stewart
Henrik Stewenius
Moritz Stoerring
Svetlana Stolpner
Mingxuan Sun
Ying Sun
Amir Tamrakar
Robby Tan
Tele Tan
Donald Tanguay

Leonid Taycher
Ashwin Thangali
David Thirde
Mani Thomas
Tai-Peng Tian
David Tolliver
Nhon Trinh
Ambrish Tyagi
Raquel Urtasun
Joost Van-de-Weijer
Andrea Vedaldi
Dejun Wang
Hanzi Wang
Jingbin Wang
Liang Wang
Martin Welk
Adam Williams
Bob Woodham
Stefan Wörz
Christopher Wren
Junwen Wu
Wen Wu
Rong Yan
Changjiang Yang
Qing-Xiong Yang
Alper Yilmaz
Jerry Yokono
David Young
Quan Yuan
Alan Yuille
Micheal Yurick
Dimitrios Zarpalas
Guoying Zhao
Tao Zhao
Song-Feng Zheng
Jie Zhu
Loe Zhu
Manli Zhu

Sponsoring Institutions

Advanced Computer Vision, Austria
Graz University of Technology, Austria
University of Ljubljana, Slovenia

Table of Contents – Part II

Multiview Geometry and 3D Reconstruction

Statistical Models and Visual Learning

Low-Level Vision, Image Features

Face/Gesture/Action Detection and Recognition

Segmentation and Grouping

Object Recognition, Retrieval and Indexing

Segmentation

Comparison of Energy Minimization Algorithms
for Highly Connected Graphs

Vladimir Kolmogorov[1] and Carsten Rother[2]

[1] University College London
vnk@adastral.ucl.ac.uk
[2] Microsoft Research Ltd., Cambridge, UK
carrot@microsoft.com

Abstract. Algorithms for discrete energy minimization play a fundamental role for low-level vision. Known techniques include graph cuts, belief propagation (BP) and recently introduced tree-reweighted message passing (TRW). So far, the standard benchmark for their comparison has been a 4-connected grid-graph arising in pixel-labelling stereo. This minimization problem, however, has been largely solved: recent work shows that for many scenes TRW finds the global optimum. Furthermore, it is known that a 4-connected grid-graph is a poor stereo model since it does not take occlusions into account.

We propose the problem of stereo with occlusions as a new test bed for minimization algorithms. This is a more challenging graph since it has much larger connectivity, and it also serves as a better stereo model. An attractive feature of this problem is that increased connectivity does not result in increased complexity of message passing algorithms. Indeed, one contribution of this paper is to show that sophisticated implementations of BP and TRW have the same time and memory complexity as that of 4-connected grid-graph stereo.

The main conclusion of our experimental study is that for our problem graph cut outperforms both TRW and BP considerably. TRW achieves consistently a lower energy than BP. However, as connectivity increases the speed of convergence of TRW becomes slower. Unlike 4-connected grids, the difference between the energy of the best optimization method and the lower bound of TRW appears significant. This shows the hardness of the problem and motivates future research.

1 Introduction

Many early vision problems can be naturally formulated in terms of energy minimization where the energy function has the following form:

$$E(\mathbf{x}) = \sum_{p \in \mathcal{V}} D_p(x_p) + \sum_{(p,q) \in \mathcal{E}} V_{pq}(x_p, x_q) . \tag{1}$$

Set $\mathcal{V}$ usually corresponds to pixels; x_p denotes the label of pixel p which must belong to some finite set. For motion or stereo, the labels are disparities, while for image restoration they represent intensities. This energy is often derived in the context of Markov Random Fields [1]: unary terms D_p represent data likelihoods, and pairwise terms V_{pq} encode a prior over labellings. Energy minimization framework has been applied with great success to many vision applications such as stereo [2,3,4,5,6,7],

A. Leonardis, H. Bischof, and A. Pinz (Eds.): ECCV 2006, Part II, LNCS 3952, pp. 1–15, 2006.

image restoration [2], image segmentation [8], texture synthesis [9]. Algorithms for minimizing energy E are therefore of fundamental importance in vision. In this paper we consider three different algorithms: Graph Cut, belief propagation (BP) and tree-reweighted message passing (TRW). For the problem of stereo matching these methods are among the best performing optimization techniques [10]. A comparison of their advantages and disadvantages is at the end of this section.

So far, comparison studies of these optimization methods have been rather limited in the sense that they only consider energy functions with a particular graph structure [11, 12, 13, 14]. The algorithms have been tested on the energy function arising in stereo matching problem [2]. This energy is defined on a graph with a 4-neighborhood system, where nodes correspond to pixels in the left image. Occlusion are not modeled since this gives a more complex and highly connected graph structure. The comparison studies consistently concluded that the lowest energy is obtained by TRW, graph cuts come second and BP comes third [11, 12, 13, 14]. Very recently, it has been shown [13] that TRW even achieves the global optimum for standard benchmark stereo pairs [10]. Consequently, this problem, which was considered to be very challenging a decade ago, has now largely been solved. The comparison studies also showed that the proposed energy gives large error statistics compared with state-of-the art methods, and consequently progress in this field can only be achieved by improving the energy formulation itself, as stated in [11, 13].

The main goal of this paper is to test how different optimization methods perform on graphs with larger connectivity. Our study has two motivations. First, such energy functions are becoming increasingly important in vision [3, 4, 5, 6, 7, 15]. They typically arise when we need to match two images while imposing regularization on the deformation field. Pixels (or features) in one image can potentially match to many pixels (features) in the other image, which yields a highly connected graph structure.

Our second motivation is to understand better intrinsic properties of different algorithms. One way to achieve this is to consider a very difficult problem: Algorithm's weaknesses then become more apparent, which may suggest ways of improving the method. It is known that the presence of short cycles in the graph makes the problem harder for message passing techniques. From this point of view, the problem that we are considering is much more challenging than 4-connected grid graphs. Another indicator of the difficulty of our problem will be shown by our experiments.

We choose the energy function arising in the problem of stereo with occlusions [4]. In this case there are nodes corresponding to pixels in the left and right image, and each node has $K + 4$ neighbors where K is the number of disparities. We propose this problem as a new challenging test bed for minimization algorithms. Our experiments also show that modeling occlusions gives a significantly better stereo model, since the energy of the ground truth is close to the energy of the best optimization method, and the value of the energy correlates with the error statistics derived from ground truth.

When applying BP or TRW to this energy, we immediately run into efficiency problems. There are K labels and $O(NK)$ edges, so a straightforward implementation would take $O(NK^2)$ memory and time for one iteration, even with the distance transform technique in [16]. By exploiting a special structure of the energy we show that both quantities can be reduced to $O(NK)$. Thus, we get the same complexity as that of message passing for the simple stereo problem without occlusions.

We have tested the three different optimization methods on six standard benchmark images [10]. The findings are different to the scenario of a 4-connected grid-graphs. For our problem graph cut clearly outperforms message passing techniques, i.e. TRW and BP, both in terms of lower energy and lower error rates wrt to ground truth.

It is worth mentioning that energy functions with similar graph structure were used in other methods for stereo with occlusions [6, 7]. In both approaches each pixel is connected to $O(K)$ pixels in the other image. The former uses graph cuts as a minimization algorithm, as the latter uses BP. However, [7] does not attempt to apply message passing to the original function. Instead, an iterative technique is used where in each iteration the energy function is approximated with a simpler one, and BP is then applying to a graph with 4-neighborhood system.

Let us compare the three optimization methods.

Graph cuts were introduced into computer vision in the 90's [17, 2] and showed a major improvement over previously used simulated annealing [1]. The strength of graph cuts is that for many applications it gives very accurate results, i.e. it finds a solution with very low energy. In fact, in some cases it even finds a *global* minimum [17, 18]. A major drawback of graph cuts, however, is that it can be applied only to a limited class of energy functions. There are different graph cut-based methods: Expansion move [2], swap move [2] or jump move [19]. Each has its own restrictions that come from the fact that binary minimization problems used in the "inner loop" must be *submodular*. Expansion move algorithm is perhaps the most powerful technique [14], but can be applied to a smaller set of functions than swap move. Following [4], we use expansion move version of the graph cut algorithm for the problem of stereo with occlusions.

The class of functions that graph cuts can handle covers many useful applications, but in some cases the energy falls outside this class, for example, in the super-resolution problem [20] This may also occur when parameters of the energy function are learned from training data [21]. In this case one can either approximate a non-submodular function with a submodular one [15], or use more general algorithms. Two of such algorithms are described below.

Belief propagation (BP). Max-product loopy belief propagation (BP) [22, 16] is a very popular technique for approximate inference. Unlike graph cuts, BP can be applied to any function of the form 1. Unfortunately, recent studies have shown that for a simple stereo problem it finds considerably higher energy than graph cuts [11, 23, 12, 13].

Tree-reweighted message passing (TRW) was recently introduced by Wainwright et al. [24]. Similar to BP it can be applied to any function of the form 1. However, there are several important differences. First, on a simple stereo problem it finds slightly lower energy than graph cuts [12]. Second, it maintains a lower bound on the energy that can be used to measure how close we are to the energy of an optimal solution. Third, there is a variant of TRW algorithm, called TRW-S, with certain convergence properties [12]. In contrast, no convergence guarantees are known for BP algorithm. For our comparison we use this variant of the TRW algorithm introduced in [12].

2   Background

We begin by introducing our notation. Let $\mathcal{G} = (\mathcal{V}, \mathcal{E})$ be an undirected graph with the set of vertices $\mathcal{V}$ and the set of edges $\mathcal{E}$. We assume that for each $p \in \mathcal{V}$ variable x_p takes values in some discrete set $\mathcal{L} = \{0, \ldots, K - 1\}$ where K is the number of labels[1].

Function $D_p(\cdot)$ in energy 1 is determined by K values. It is convenient to treat D_p as a vector of size $K \times 1$. Later we introduce other vectors of size $K \times 1$ (in particular, messages m). Notation $D' = D + m$ denotes the usual sum of two vectors, i.e. $D'(k) = D(k) + m(k)$ for any $k \in \mathcal{L}$.

2.1   Overview of Message Passing Algorithms

We now give an overview of BP and TRW algorithms. They both maintain messages m_{pq} for directed edges $p \to q$, which are vectors of size $K \times 1$. The basic operation of the algorithms is *passing a message* from node p to its neighbor q. The effect of this operation is that message m_{pq} gets updated according to a certain rule (which is different for BP and for TRW).

An important choice that we have to make is the schedule of updating messages. There are many possible approaches; for example, [11] uses parallel (or synchronous) and *accelerated* schedules, and [12] uses *sequential* schedule. In this paper we use the latter one. One advantage of this schedule is that it requires half as much memory compared to other schedules. For TRW algorithm sequential schedule also has a theoretical advantage described in the end of this section.

---

0. Set all messages to zero.
1. For nodes $p \in \mathcal{V}$ do the following operation in the order of increasing $i(p)$:
   (a) Aggregation: compute $\widehat{D}_p = D_p + \sum_{(q,p) \in \mathcal{E}} m_{qp}$
   (b) Propagation: for every edge $(p, q) \in \mathcal{E}$ with $i(p) < i(q)$ update message m_{pq} as follows:
      - Compute $D_{pq} = \gamma_{pq}\widehat{D}_p - m_{qp}$
      - Set $m_{pq}(x_q) := \min_{x_p}\{D_{pq}(x_p) + V_{pq}(x_p, x_q)\}$
2. Reverse the ordering: set $i(p) := |\mathcal{V}| + 1 - i(p)$.
3. Check whether a stopping criterion is satisfied; if yes, terminate, otherwise go to step 1.

Fig. 1. Sequential message passing algorithm. Function $i : \mathcal{V} \to \{1, 2, \ldots, |\mathcal{V}|\}$ gives the ordering of nodes. Weighting coefficient γ_{pq} is 1 for BP and a value in $(0, 1]$ for TRW (see text).

Sequential schedule is specified by some ordering of nodes $i(p), p \in \mathcal{V}$ (which can be chosen arbitrarily). During the forward pass, we process nodes in the order of increasing $i(p)$, and we send messages from node p to all its forward neighbors (i.e. nodes q with $i(q) > i(p)$). After that we perform similar procedure in the reverse direction (backward pass). A precise description of the algorithm is given in Fig. 1. Note that the operation of computing the minimum in step 1(b) can be computed efficiently, for many interaction potentials $V_{p,q}$, in time O(k) using distance transforms [16].

---

[1] To simplify notation, we assumed that number of labels is the same of all nodes. Note that in general this is not required.

Memory requirements. An important property of the sequential schedule is that for each edge (q, r) it is enough to store message in only one direction. Namely, suppose that $i(q) < i(r)$ and p is the node being processed. Then we store message m_{qr} if $i(q) < i(p)$, and message m_{rq} otherwise. The reverse messages are not needed since we update them before they are used. The same space in memory can be used for storing one of the two messages. The exact moment when m_{qp} gets replaced with m_{pq} is when edge (p, q) is processed in step 1(b).

The fact that memory requirements of message passing can be reduced by half was first noted in [16] for a special case (bipartite graphs and simulation of parallel schedule of updating messages). It was generalized to arbitrary graphs and larger class of schedules in [12].

Weighting coefficients. Both BP and TRW algorithms have the structure shown in Fig. 1. The difference between the two is that they use difference coefficients γ_{pq}. For BP algorithm we set $\gamma_{pq} = 1$. Next we describe how to choose these coefficients for TRW algorithm.

First we select set $\mathcal{T}$ of trees in graph $\mathcal{G}$ such that each edge is covered by at least one tree. We also select probability distribution over $\mathcal{T}$, i.e. function $\rho : \mathcal{T} \to (0, 1]$ such that $\sum_{T \in \mathcal{T}} \rho(T) = 1$. Set $\mathcal{T}$ and distribution ρ define coefficients γ_{pq} as follows: $\gamma_{pq} = \rho_{pq} / \rho_p$ where ρ_p and ρ_{pq} are the probabilities that tree T chosen under ρ contains node p and edge (p, q), respectively.

TRW and lower bound on the energy. As shown in [24], for any set of messages $\mathbf{m} = \{m_{pq} \mid (p \to q) \in \mathcal{E}\}$ it is possible to compute a lower bound on the energy, denoted as $\Phi_\rho(\mathbf{m})$. In other words, for any $\mathbf{m}$ and for any configuration $\mathbf{x}$ we have $\Phi_\rho(\mathbf{m}) \leq E(\mathbf{x})$. Function $\Phi_\rho(\mathbf{m})$ serves as a motivation for TRW: the goal of updating messages is to maximize $\Phi_\rho(\mathbf{m})$, i.e. to get the tightest bound on the energy.

In general, TRW algorithms in [24] do not always increase the bound - function $\Phi_\rho(\mathbf{m})$ may go down (and the algorithm may not converge). In contrast, sequential schedule proposed in [12] does have the property that the bound never decreases, assuming that the following condition holds: trees in $\mathcal{T}$ are *monotonic* chains, i.e. chains $T = (p_1, \ldots, p_m)$ such that sequence $(i(p_1), \ldots, i(p_m))$ is monotonic. The algorithm in Fig. 1 with this selection of trees is referred to as *sequential tree-reweighted message passing* (TRW-S).

Choosing solution. An important question is how to choose solution $\mathbf{x}$ given messages $\mathbf{m}$. The standard method is to choose label x_p for node p that minimizes $\widehat{D}_p(x_p)$ where $\widehat{D}_p = D_p + \sum m_{qp}$ and the sum is over edges $(q, p) \in \mathcal{E}$. However, it is often the case that $\widehat{D}_p(x_p)$ has several minima. In the case of TRW algorithm this is not surprising: if upon convergence all nodes had unique minimum, then it would give the *global* minimum of the energy, as shown in [24]. Clearly, we cannot expect this in general since otherwise we could solve arbitrary NP-hard problems.

To alleviate the problem of multiple minima, we use the same technique as in [12]. We assign variables to nodes p in the order given by $i(p)$. We select label x_p that minimizes $D_p(x_p) + \sum_{i(q)<i(p)} V_{qp}(x_q, x_p) + \sum_{i(q)>i(p)} m_{qp}(x_p)$.

2.2 Stereo with Occlusions

In this section we review the energy function used in [4], adopting it to our notation. For simplicity we restrict our attention to the case of two rectified cameras.

The set of nodes contains pixels $\mathcal{V}^L$ in the left image and pixels $\mathcal{V}^R$ in the right image, so $\mathcal{V} = \mathcal{V}^L \cup \mathcal{V}^R$. Label x_p for pixel p denotes its disparity. We assume that $x_p \in \mathcal{L} = \{0, \ldots, K - 1\}$ where K is the number of disparities. Pixel p with label k corresponds to some pixel q in the other image which we denote as $q = \mathcal{F}(p, k)$. Formally, coordinates of q are defined as follows:

$$(q_x, q_y) = \begin{cases} (p_x - k, p_y) & \text{if } p \in \mathcal{V}^L \\ (p_x + k, p_y) & \text{if } p \in \mathcal{V}^R \end{cases}$$

Note that $q = \mathcal{F}(p, k)$ implies $p = \mathcal{F}(q, k)$, and vice versa.

The energy function in [4] does not use unary data terms D_p; instead, all information is contained in pairwise terms V_{pq}. In order to describe them, first we need to define the set of edges $\mathcal{E}$. It contains edges of two types: *coherence* edges $\mathcal{E}^C$ and *stereo* edges $\mathcal{E}^S$ discussed below.

Coherence edges. These edges encode the constraint that disparity maps in the left and right images should be spatially coherent. Set $\mathcal{E}^C$ contains edges (p, q) where p, q are neighboring pixels in the same image defined, for example, using 4-neighborhood system.

For the purpose of comparison of minimization algorithms we used Potts terms V_{pq}:

$$V_{pq}(x_p, x_q) = \lambda_{pq} \cdot [x_p \neq x_q]$$

where $[\cdot]$ is 1 if its argument is true, and 0 otherwise. This term prefers piecewise constant disparity maps. To get better results, however, it might be advantageous to use terms that allow smooth variations, especially when the number of disparities is large. A good choice could be truncated linear term.

Stereo edges. Each pixel p (except for pixels at image boundary) has K incident edges connecting it to pixels $\mathcal{F}(p, 0), \ldots, \mathcal{F}(p, K - 1)$ in the other image. To simplify notation, we denote edge (p, q) with $q = \mathcal{F}(p, k))$ as either (p, k) or (k, q).

Terms V_{pk} combine data and visibility terms defined in [4]. They can be written as

$$V_{pk}(x_p, x_q) = \begin{cases} M_{pk} & \text{if} \quad x_p = x_q = k \\ \infty & \begin{array}{l} \text{if } x_p = k, x_q < k \\ \text{or } x_q = k, x_p < k \end{array} \\ 0 & \text{otherwise} \end{cases} \tag{2}$$

where $q = \mathcal{F}(p, k)$ (see Fig. 2). Constant M_{pk} is the *matching score* between pixels p and q. The expansion move algorithm in [4] can only be applied if all scores are non-positive. Therefore, M_{pk} can be defined, for example, as $M_{pk} = \min\{\|Intensity(p) - Intensity(q)\|^2 - C, 0\}$ where C is a positive constant.

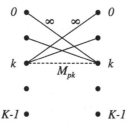

Fig. 2. Structure of term $V_{pk}(\cdot, \cdot)$ for stereo edge (p, q) with $q = \mathcal{F}(p, k)$. Left column represents pixel p, right column pixel q. Costs $V(k', k'')$ are shown on links from label k' to k''. The dashed link $k - k$ has cost M_{pk}, solid links have infinite costs. Links that are not shown have cost zero.

3   Efficient Message Passing for Stereo with Occlusions

In this paper we apply sequential message passing algorithm in Fig. 1 to the energy function defined in the previous section. However, a naive implementation is extremely inefficient. Indeed, consider first the memory requirements. We have $O(NK)$ edges where N is the number of pixels. For each edge we need to store a message which is a vector with K components. This results in $O(NK^2)$ memory requirements.

We now show how this number can be reduced to $O(NK)$. Consider message m_{pk} from pixel p to pixel $q = \mathcal{F}(p, k)$. It is obtained as the result of applying distance transform to vector D_{pk} via edge term V_{pk} (step 1(b) of the algorithm). Inspecting the structure of V_{pk} we conclude that

$$m_{pk}(k') = \begin{cases} A_{pk} = \min\{\widetilde{A}_{pk}, \widetilde{C}_{pk}\} & \text{if } k' < k \\ B_{pk} = \min\{\widetilde{B}_{pk} + M_{pk}, \widetilde{C}_{pk}\} & \text{if } k' = k \\ C_{pk} = \min\{\widetilde{A}_{pk}, \widetilde{B}_{pk}, \widetilde{C}_{pk}\} & \text{if } k' > k \end{cases}$$

where

$$\widetilde{A}_{pk} = \min_{0 \le k' < k} D_{pk}(k') \; ; \quad B_{pk} = D_{pk}(k) \; ; \quad \widetilde{C}_{pk} = \min_{k < k' < K} D_{pk}(k') \tag{3}$$

Therefore, although m_{pk} is a vector with K components, it can be stored using only three numbers - A_{pk}, B_{pk} and C_{pk}. (In fact, even two numbers are sufficient. The messages are defined only up to an additive constant. Thus, it is enough to store $A_{pk} - C_{pk}$ and $B_{pk} - C_{pk}$, for example.)

To summarize, messages can be stored using $4NK$ numbers, ignoring effects at image boundaries ($2NK$ numbers for coherence edges and $2NK$ numbers for stereo edges[2]). We also need NK numbers to store matching scores M_{pk}.

Now let us consider the complexity of one iteration. If we are not careful, we may get $O(NK^2)$ running time even with the trick described above. Next we show how to implement the algorithm so that we get $O(NK)$ complexity for one iteration.

---

[2] Recall that in the sequential message passing algorithm for each edge we need to store a message only in one direction.

Aggregation. Let us consider the aggregation step for pixel p. We need to sum $K + 4$ vectors of size K corresponding to K stereo edges and 4 coherence edges. A naive implementation would take $O(K^2)$ time. However, it is possible to reduce it to $O(K)$ using ideas from dynamic programming.

Summing messages in coherence edges is not a problem since their number is constant. Thus, we focus on summing messages corresponding to stereo edges, i.e. computing $D = \sum_{k=0}^{K-1} m_{kp}$. Suppose that message m_{kp} is described by numbers A_k, B_k, C_k (we drop subscript p for brevity). We can write

$$D = \begin{pmatrix} B_0 \\ C_0 \\ \dots \\ C_0 \\ C_0 \end{pmatrix} + \begin{pmatrix} A_1 \\ B_1 \\ \dots \\ C_1 \\ C_1 \end{pmatrix} + \dots + \begin{pmatrix} A_{K-2} \\ A_{K-2} \\ \dots \\ B_{K-2} \\ C_{K-2} \end{pmatrix} + \begin{pmatrix} A_{K-1} \\ A_{K-1} \\ \dots \\ A_{K-1} \\ B_{K-1} \end{pmatrix}$$

To compute D, we first compute sums $\bar{A}_k = \sum_{k'=k+1}^{K-1} A_{k'}$ and $\bar{C}_k = \sum_{k'=0}^{k-1} C_{k'}$ for $k = 0, 1, \dots, K-1$ (by definition, $\bar{A}_{K-1} = \bar{C}_0 = 0$). This can be done in $O(K)$ time using recursions

$$\bar{A}_{k-1} = \bar{A}_k + A_k \ , \quad \bar{C}_{k+1} = \bar{C}_k + C_k \ .$$

Now computing D is easy: $D(k) = \bar{A}_k + B_k + \bar{C}_k$.

Propagation. Now consider the propagation step 2(b) for pixel p. Updating messages in coherence edges can be done in $O(K)$ time using distance transform techniques in [16]. We focus on updating messages m_{pk} in stereo edges for disparities $k \in \mathcal{L}$ with $i(\mathcal{F}(p,k)) > i(p)$. In order to update message m_{pk}, we need to compute numbers $\widehat{A}_{pk} = \min_{0 \le k' < k} D_{pk}(k')$ and $\widehat{C}_{pk} = \min_{k < k' < K} D_{pk}(k')$ (eq. 3). Direct calculation of these minima would take $O(K)$ time, resulting in $O(K^2)$ complexity for $O(K)$ stereo edges. To improve the running time, we do the following precalculation. For vector $\widehat{D}_p$ obtained after aggregation step 2(a), we compute values $\widehat{A}_{pk} = \min_{0 \le k' < k} \widehat{D}_p(k')$ and $\widehat{C}_{pk} = \min_{k < k' < K} \widehat{D}_p(k')$ (by definition, $\widehat{A}_{p0} = \widehat{C}_{p,K-1} = \infty$). This can be done in $O(K)$ time using recursions

$$\widehat{A}_{p,k+1} = \min\{\widehat{A}_{pk}, \widehat{D}_p(k)\}, \ \widehat{C}_{p,k-1} = \min\{\widehat{C}_{pk}, \widehat{D}_p(k)\}.$$

Now values $\widetilde{A}_{pk}$, $\widetilde{B}_{pk}$, $\widetilde{C}_{pk}$ can be computed in constant time as follows:

$$\widetilde{A}_{pk} = \gamma_{pk}\widehat{A}_{pk} - A_{kp} \ ; \quad \widetilde{B}_{pk} = \gamma_{pk}\widehat{D}_p(k) - B_{kp} \ ; \quad \widetilde{C}_{pk} = \gamma_{pk}\widehat{C}_{pk} - C_{kp} \quad (4)$$

where A_{kp}, B_{kp}, C_{kp} describe message m_{kp} in the reverse direction.

4   Experimental Results

We tested the methods on four benchmark stereo images, which were used in the stereo survey paper [10] and also two ground truth data sets with large disparity range [25]. All data sets are available online[3]. Fig. 3-4 show left disparity maps produced by different

[3] http://cat.middlebury.edu/stereo/

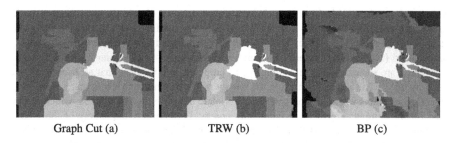

| Graph Cut (a) | TRW (b) | BP (c) |

Fig. 3. Tsukuba image. The left disparity map produced by (a) graph cuts, (b) TRW, and (c) BP, which is clearly the worst result.

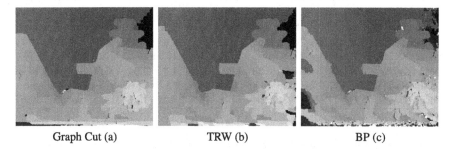

| Graph Cut (a) | TRW (b) | BP (c) |

Fig. 4. Teddy image. The left disparity map produced by (a) graph cuts, which has the lowest error statistics, (b) TRW, and (c) BP.

methods. More disparity maps can be found in [26]. Visually BP performed worse than graph cut and TRW, and also the results of BP were always less smooth. Numerical results for all six data sets are summarized in table 1. All experiments give a concise and clear message: Graph cut consistently outperforms TRW and BP, both in terms of lower energy and smaller error rate wrt ground truth ($B_{\bar{\mathcal{O}}}$ and $B_{\mathcal{D}}$). For smaller number of labels ($K < 30$) TRW clearly outperforms BP, otherwise TRW performs only marginally better. For all examples the quality of the results is correlated with the obtained energy, i.e. low energy corresponds to a low error statistics ($B_{\bar{\mathcal{O}}}$ and $B_{\mathcal{D}}$). Also, the energy of the ground truth (last column table 1) lies within the range of the energy computed by graph cut and TRW. For stereo without occlusions these two observations could not be established: The energy of the ground truth is considerably larger than graph cut and BP, and low energy did not necessarily correspond to a good result [11, 13]. Therefore, we can conclude that modeling occlusions gives a better stereo model. The fact that the ground truth energy is larger than the best method does not contradict to this: The problem is inherently ambiguous, which means that it is impossible to design an energy function whose global minimum always gives a correct solution.

Plots of energy vs. runtime are shown in Fig. 5. For instance, one iteration of TRW takes about 3.26 sec. for teddy (image size 450×375 and $K = 54$) on a Pentium IV 3.2 GHz processor. For all examples the discrete curve for graph cut is always below the curve of TRW and BP. An interesting observation is that the relative performance of TRW and BP depends on the number of labels: Larger connectivity makes TRW

Table 1. Comparison table for six benchmark stereo pairs applied to the optimization methods: Graph cut, TRW and BP. Both TRW and BP were run for 10.000 iterations, and graph cut until convergence. The values for $B_{\bar{O}}$ and B_D correspond to the percentage of pixels in non-occluded ($B_{\bar{O}}$) and textureless (B_D) areas with a disparity error greater than 1 wrt ground truth. These are standard error measurements as proposed in [10]. Note that all energies E are scaled by 10^{-3}. The last column gives the energy of the ground truth. Note that a very small percentage of pixels in the ground truth image violate the visibility constrained, which are ignored for the computation of the ground truth energy. Furthermore, the energy of the ground truth can only be computed for three data sets since for Tsukuba only one ground truth disparity map is available and Teddy and Cones have undefined areas in the disparity map. (see text for discussion).

Image	Graph Cut			TRW			BP			Ground Truth
	$B_{\bar{O}}$	B_D	E	$B_{\bar{O}}$	B_D	E	$B_{\bar{O}}$	B_D	E	E (violation)
Tsukuba (K=16)	1.84	6.50	-1536	2.62	7.15	-1534	7.52	16.10	-1495	not available
Sawtooth (K=19)	0.56	6.26	-2071	0.65	7.12	-2065	3.43	10.39	-2020	-2027 (0.16%)
Venus (K=21)	1.20	6.11	-2118	1.55	8.12	-2109	10.31	14.88	-2021	-2069 (0.47%)
Map (K=29)	0.38	5.32	-3460	0.58	7.20	-3407	1.21	9.64	-3374	-3410 (0.40%)
Teddy (K=54)	13.14	23.35	-10273	14.88	26.95	-9889	15.25	27.63	-9834	not available
Cones (K=56)	5.16	11.99	-13936	6.04	14.16	-13648	9.25	15.14	-13455	not available

algorithm much slower, while the speed of BP is affected less significantly. Note, however, that when TRW is run long enough, it always outperformed BP (see table 1). It is worth noting that neither TRW nor BP converged. BP gets into a loop after typically $50 - 200$ iterations. In case of TRW the lower bound never decreases with time. Since it is bounded from above, the lower bound must converge to a fixed number. In our experiments, however, the lower bound of TRW continued increasing slowly even after 50000 iterations (for Tsukuba), which means that the algorithm still did not converge.

In order to understand how difficult our problem is, we looked at how close the energy E_{min} of the best method is to the lower bound E_{bound} given by TRW. Since absolute numbers are not very meaningful, we can consider the ratio $\frac{E_{min}-E_{bound}}{E_{bound}}$. If all energy values are non-negative, then this ratio gives an upper bound on the approximation factor. In our case, however, the energy can be negative due to numbers $M_{pq} \leq 0$. To solve this problem, we added constant NC to the energy where N is the number of pixels and C is defined in section 2.2. Since there are at most N terms M_{pq} in the energy and $M_{pq} \geq -C$, this ensures that energy is always non-negative. Furthermore, absolute energy values of the two models: stereo with and without occlusions are related, if we use same matching costs and similar smoothness parameters. This is confirmed by our experiments: E_{min} differ by about 3 times for the two models and Tsukuba data set, i.e. they are of the same order of magnitude. For stereo without occlusions ratios $\frac{E_{min}-E_{bound}}{E_{bound}}$ were as follows [12]: Tsukuba (0.0037%), Map (0.055%), Sawtooth (0.096%), and Venus(0.014%). For our model the corresponding values are: Tsukuba (3.09%), Map (3.28%), Sawtooth (1.27%), and Venus(2.26%). These values are in average two to three orders of magnitude larger for our model. Consequently, we may conclude that our problem is considerably harder than stereo without occlusions.

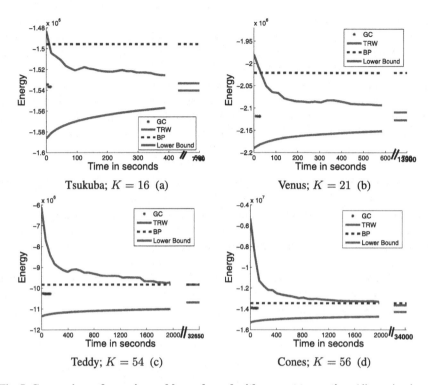

Fig. 5. Comparison of energies and lower bound with respect to runtime (discussion in text)

4.1   Settings for TRW

In order to implement TRW-S algorithm we need to make several choices. First, we need to select the ordering of nodes $i(p)$. In our implementation we used row-major order for both left and right images, and nodes of the left images had smaller ordering than nodes of the right image. Next, we need to choose the set of trees $\mathcal{T}$. As described in sec. 2, these trees must be chains that are monotonic with respect to ordering $i(p)$. We selected each horizonal and vertical line in the two images as a single chain; we call them *coherence chains*[4]. In addition, every stereo edge was declared to be a chain. It can be seen that with this choice every edge in the graph is covered by exactly one tree. Finally, we need to select probability distribution ρ^T over trees $T \in \mathcal{T}$. As our experiments show, this distribution affects the results of the algorithm significantly.

Intuitively, coherence and stereo chains are quite different, therefore they should be assigned different probabilities. The difference between coherence and stereo chains, however, is not the only source of asymmetry. Indeed, consider some node p and an incident stereo edge (p,q) where $q = \mathcal{F}(p,k)$. Term V_{pk} for this edge has a very special structure; in particular, there is one preferred label, namely label k. Recall that if labels of pixels p and q are k then this edge contributes matching cost M_{pq} to the energy function, otherwise the penalty is either 0 or ∞. Thus, it could be beneficial to select

---

[4] There are $2(W + H)$ such chains where W is the width of the image and H is the height.

probabilities that would favor label k over other labels $k' \in \mathcal{L} - \{k\}$ for the chain corresponding to edge (p, q), and we will show that this improves the performance of TRW. Since the scheme described in sec. 2 does not allow this (each tree has a single probability which does not depend on labels), we now extend the tree-reweighted algorithm to allow probabilities that depend on labels. Consider the case when each edge is covered by exactly one chain. Let us define a probability distribution over trees *for each node* $p \in \mathcal{V}$ *and label* $k \in \mathcal{L}$. We denote it as $\rho(T; p, k)$. We require that $\sum_{T \in \mathcal{T}} \rho(T; p, k) = 1$ for all p, k. In addition, $\rho(T; p, k)$ must be positive if tree T contains node p, and zero otherwise. Using these probabilities, we define coefficients $\gamma_{pq}(k)$ as follows: $\gamma_{pq}(k) = \rho(T; p, k)$ where T is the tree containing edge (p, q). The algorithm in Fig. 1 is then modified as follows: In step 1(b) vector D_{pq} is computed as $D_{pq}(k) = \gamma_{pq}(k)\widehat{D}_p(k) - m_{qp}(k)$ for all $k \in \mathcal{L}$. We claim that the modified algorithm has the same properties properties as the sequential tree-reweighted message passing method in [12]. In particular, the lower bound is guaranteed not to decrease, and there exists a limit point satisfying the weak tree agreement condition [26].

Let us apply this scheme to the problem of stereo with occlusions. Consider node $p \in \mathcal{V}$ and label $k \in \mathcal{L}$. This node is contained in $K + 2$ trees (unless it is a pixel near the image boundary): vertical coherence chain, horizontal coherence chain and K stereo chains. We set probabilities $\rho(T; p, k)$ as follows:

$$\rho(T; p, k) = \begin{cases} \rho^C & \text{if } T \text{ is a coherence edge} \\ \rho^{S1} & \text{if } T = (p, \mathcal{F}(p, k)) \\ \rho^{S2} & \text{if } T = (p, \mathcal{F}(p, k')) \text{ for } k' \neq k \end{cases} .$$

Note that there must hold $2\rho^C + \rho^{S1} + (K - 1)\rho^{S2} = 1$. Due to this constraint we are left with two degrees of freedom for the choice of the tree probabilities: ρ^C and β^S = ρ^{S1}/ρ^{S2}. Note that in the TRW algorithm the γ_{pk} in eqn. 4 has to be replaced by: $\gamma_{pk} = \rho^{S1}$ for $\widetilde{B}_{pk}$ and $\gamma_{pk} = \rho^{S2}$ for $\widetilde{A}_{pk}$ and $\widetilde{C}_{pk}$.

We examined different settings of ρ^C and β^S for three data sets. We discovered that the settings depend on the number of labels. For a thorough investigation we re-scaled the teddy image with a factor of 1.5 and 3 ("Teddy Small"), which correspond to a maximum disparity of 36 and 18 respectively. Fig. 6 shows the energy of TRW for a large range of values for ρ^C and β^S, where TRW was run for a fixed amount of 700 iterations. An obvious observation is that for extreme settings, e.g. β^S very close to 1 or below 0.4, the results are worse. The first conclusion we can draw is that the energy is more sensitive to parameters settings for larger disparities. For "Teddy Small" the range of comparable low energies for ρ^C is [0.4, 0.9] whereas for teddy it is [0.7, 0.8]. The second observation is that parameters which give the lowest energy differ, depending on the number of disparities. The optimal setting of ρ^C is 0.76 ($K = 54$) and 0.9 ($K = 36$ and 18). The optimal probability for different stereo edges β^S is less sensitive to the number of disparities. For these three examples a value of $\beta^S = 3.0$ gives low energy. Taking this into account we chose the settings as follows: $\rho^C = 0.9(K < 40)$; otherwise 0.78; and $\beta^S = 3.0$. We do not claim that this is the optimal setting for TRW for this type of energy, however, we believe that it is sufficient for a comparison to other methods. We believe that further testing of these probabilities might improve the

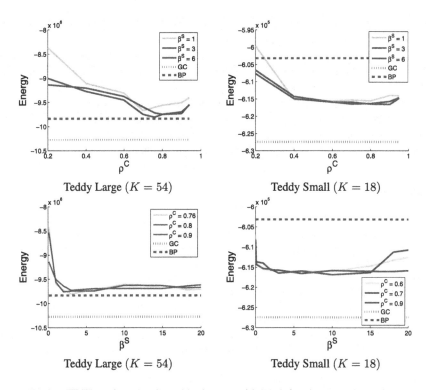

Fig. 6. Testing TRW settings for the teddy data set with 54 (left column) and 18 (right column) disparities (discussion in text)

performance of TRW only marginal. A more significant improvement might come from changing the structure of the trees, e.g. choosing longer stereo chains.

5   Conclusions

We have presented an experimental comparison of three optimization techniques: Graph cut, BP and TRW for highly connected graphs. We have chosen the energy of the stereo with occlusions problem. Despite high connectivity of the graph, we have shown that message passing techniques can still be applied efficiently.

In the past comparisons have only been carried out for relatively simple 4-connected grid-graphs, in particular for stereo without occlusions. Our findings are different to 4-connected graphs where TRW outperforms graph cut, and even achieves the global optimum for some problems. For highly connected graphs, graph cut clearly outperforms TRW and BP, both in terms of lower energy and lower error rates with respect to ground truth. We found that for all examples TRW is capable of obtaining lower energy than BP. However, as the connectivity increases, the speed of convergence for TRW becomes slower and slower, while the speed of BP is affected less significantly. This suggests that a future direction of research is to try improving the speed of TRW, like by choosing trees in a different way or using a different schedule of updating messages. We believe that if the speed is improved then TRW may still outperform graph cuts.

The experiments show that modeling occlusions gives a better stereo model. Another finding is that the difference between the lower bound of TRW and the minimum energy of the best method is significant compared to 4-connected graphs. This indicates the hardness of the problem, at least for algorithms based on solving LP relaxation (such as TRW). Consequently we propose this energy as new test bed for optimization techniques and hope that it will motivate future research in this area. Furthermore, we also plan to analyse other vision problems with highly connected graphs such as [15].

References

1. Geman, S., Geman, D.: Stochastic relaxation, Gibbs distributions, and the Bayesian restoration of images. IEEE Trans. Pattern Anal. Machine Intell. 6 (1984) 721–741
2. Boykov, Y., Veksler, O., Zabih, R.: Fast approximate energy minimization via graph cuts. IEEE Transactions on Pattern Analysis and Machine Intelligence 23(11) (2001)
3. Kolmogorov, V., Zabih, R.: Computing visual correspondence with occlusions using graph cuts. In: IEEE International Conference on Computer Vision. (2001)
4. Kolmogorov, V., Zabih, R.: Multi-camera scene reconstruction via graph cuts. In: Proc. Europ. Conf. Comp. Vision. Volume 3. (2002) 82–96
5. Sun, J., Zheng, N., Shum, H.: Stereo matching using belief propagation. IEEE Transactions on Pattern Analysis and Machine Intelligence 25(7) (2003) 787–800
6. Lin, M., Tomasi, C.: Surfaces with occlusions from layered stereo. IEEE Transactions on Pattern Analysis and Machine Intelligence 26(8) (2004) 710–717
7. Sun, J., Li, Y., Kang, S.B., Shum, H.: Symmetric stereo matching for occlusion handling. In: IEEE Conf. on Comp. Vis. and Pat. Recog. (2005)
8. Boykov, Y., Jolly, M.P.: Interactive graph cuts for optimal boundary and region segmentation of objects in N-D images. In: Proc. Int. Conf. Comp. Vision. (2001)
9. Kwatra, V., Schödl, A., Essa, I., Turk, G., Bobick, A.: Graphcut textures: Image and video synthesis using graph cuts. ACM Transactions on Graphics, SIGGRAPH 2003 (2003)
10. Scharstein, D., Szeliski, R.: A taxonomy and evaluation of dense two-frame stereo correspondence algorithms. Int. J. Computer Vision 47 (2002) 7–42
11. Tappen, M.F., Freeman, W.T.: Comparison of graph cuts with belief propagation for stereo, using identical MRF parameters. In: Proc. Int. Conf. Comp. Vision. (2003)
12. Kolmogorov, V.: Convergent tree-reweighted message passing for energy minimization. In: Artificial Intelligence and Statistics. (2005)
13. Meltzer, T., Yanover, C., Weiss, Y.: Globally optimal solutions for energy minimization in stereo vision using reweighted belief propagation. In: Proc. Int. Conf. Comp. Vision. (2005)
14. Szeliski, R., Zabih, R., Scharstein, D., Veksler, O., Kolmogorov, V., Agarwala, A., Tappen, M., Rother, C.: A comparative study of energy minimization methods for markov random fields. In: Proc. Europ. Conf. Comp. Vision. (2006)
15. Rother, C., Kumar, S., Kolmogorov, V., Blake, A.: Digital tapestry. In: IEEE Conf. on Comp. Vis. and Pat. Recog. (2005)
16. Felzenszwalb, P., Huttenlocher, D.: Efficient belief propagation for early vision. In: IEEE Conf. on Comp. Vis. and Pat. Recog. (2004)
17. Greig, D., Porteous, B., Seheult, A.: Exact maximum a posteriori estimation for binary images. Journal of the Royal Statistical Society, Series B 51 (1989) 271–279
18. Ishikawa, H.: Exact optimization for Markov Random Fields with convex priors. IEEE Trans. Pattern Anal. Machine Intell. 25(10) (2003) 1333–1336

19. Veksler, O.: Efficient graph-based energy minimization methods in computer vision. PhD thesis, Cornell University, Dept. of Computer Science, Ithaca, NY (1999)
20. Freeman, W.T., Pasztor, E.C., Carmichael, O.T.: Learning low-level vision. Int. J. Computer Vision **40** (2000) 25–47
21. Kumar, S., Herbert, M.: Discriminative fields for modeling spatial dependencies in natural images. In: Advances in Neural Information Processing Systems. (2004)
22. Pearl, J.: Probabilistic Reasoning in Intelligent Systems: Networks of Plausible Inference. Morgan Kaufmann Publishers Inc. (1988)
23. Barbu, A., Yuille, A.L.: Motion estimation by Swendsen-Wang cuts. In: CVPR. (2004)
24. Wainwright, M., Jaakkola, T., Willsky, A.: MAP estimation via agreement on (hyper)trees: Message-passing and linear-programming approaches. IEEE Transactions on Information Theory **51(11)** (2005) 3697–3717
25. Scharstein, D., Szelsiki, R.: High-accuracy stereo depth maps using structured light. In: IEEE Conf. on Comp. Vis. and Pat. Recog. (2003)
26. Kolmogorov, V., Rother, C.: Comparison of energy minimization algorithms for highly connected graphs. Technical Report MSR-TR-2006-19 (2006)

A Comparative Study of Energy Minimization Methods for Markov Random Fields

Richard Szeliski[1], Ramin Zabih[2], Daniel Scharstein[3],
Olga Veksler[4], Vladimir Kolmogorov[5], Aseem Agarwala[6],
Marshall Tappen[7], and Carsten Rother[1]

[1] Microsoft Research
{szeliski, carrot}@microsoft.com
[2] Cornell University
rdz@cs.cornell.edu
[3] Middlebury College
schar@middlebury.edu
[4] University of Western Ontario
olga@csd.uwo.ca
[5] University College London
vnk@adastral.ucl.ac.uk
[6] University of Washington
aseem@cs.washington.edu
[7] MIT
mtappen@mit.edu

Abstract. One of the most exciting advances in early vision has been the development of efficient energy minimization algorithms. Many early vision tasks require labeling each pixel with some quantity such as depth or texture. While many such problems can be elegantly expressed in the language of Markov Random Fields (MRF's), the resulting energy minimization problems were widely viewed as intractable. Recently, algorithms such as graph cuts and loopy belief propagation (LBP) have proven to be very powerful: for example, such methods form the basis for almost all the top-performing stereo methods. Unfortunately, most papers define their own energy function, which is minimized with a specific algorithm of their choice. As a result, the tradeoffs among different energy minimization algorithms are not well understood. In this paper we describe a set of energy minimization benchmarks, which we use to compare the solution quality and running time of several common energy minimization algorithms. We investigate three promising recent methods—graph cuts, LBP, and tree-reweighted message passing—as well as the well-known older iterated conditional modes (ICM) algorithm. Our benchmark problems are drawn from published energy functions used for stereo, image stitching and interactive segmentation. We also provide a general-purpose software interface that allows vision researchers to easily switch between optimization methods with minimal overhead. We expect that the availability of our benchmarks and interface will make it significantly easier for vision researchers to adopt the best method for their specific problems. Benchmarks, code, results and images are available at http://vision.middlebury.edu/MRF.

A. Leonardis, H. Bischof, and A. Pinz (Eds.): ECCV 2006, Part II, LNCS 3952, pp. 16–29, 2006.
© Springer-Verlag Berlin Heidelberg 2006

1   Introduction

Many problems in early vision involve assigning each pixel a label, where the labels represent some local quantity such as disparity. Such pixel labeling problems are naturally represented in terms of energy minimization, where the energy function has two terms: one term penalizes solutions that are inconsistent with the observed data, while the other term enforces spatial coherence. One of the reasons this framework is so popular is that it can be justified in terms of maximum a posteriori estimation of a Markov Random Field [1, 2]. Despite the elegance and power of the energy minimization approach, its early adoption was slowed by computational considerations. The algorithms that were originally used, such as ICM [1] or simulated annealing [3], proved to be extremely inefficient.

In the last few years, energy minimization approaches have had a renaissance, primarily due to powerful new optimization algorithms such as graph cuts [4, 5] and loopy belief propagation (LBP) [6]. The results, especially in stereo, have been dramatic; according to the widely-used Middlebury stereo benchmarks [7], almost all the top-performing stereo methods rely on graph cuts or LBP. Moreover, these methods give substantially more accurate results than were previously possible. Simultaneously, the range of applications of pixel labeling problems has also expanded dramatically, moving from early applications such as image restoration [1], texture modeling [8], image labeling [9], and stereo matching [3, 4], to applications such as interactive photo segmentation [10, 11] and the automatic placement of seams in digital photomontages [12].

Relatively little attention has been paid, however, to the relative performance of various optimization algorithms. Among the few exceptions are [14], which compared the efficiency of several different max flow algorithms for graph cuts, and [13], which compared graph cuts with LBP. [13] also noted a particulary impressive demonstration of the effectiveness of modern energy minimization methods: for the stereo problems in the Middlebury benchmarks, both graph cuts and LBP produced results whose energy is lower than the ground truth solution. We will return to this issue at the end of this paper.

While it is generally accepted that algorithms such as graph cuts are a huge improvement over older techniques such as simulated annealing, less is known about the efficiency vs. accuracy tradeoff among more recently developed algorithms. Concurrently with our work, [15] compared tree-reweighted message passing, LBP and graph cuts for highly connected graphs.

In this paper, we evaluate a number of different energy minimization algorithms for pixel labeling problems. We propose a number of benchmark problems for energy minimization and use these benchmarks to compare several different energy minimization methods. Since much of the work in energy minimization has been motivated by pixel labeling problems over 2D grids, we have restricted our attention to problems with this simple topology. (The extension of our work to more general topologies, such as 3D, is straightforward.)

This paper is organized as follows. In section 2 we give a precise description of the energy functions that we consider, and present a simple but general software interface to describe such energy functions and to call an arbitrary energy minimization algorithm. In section 3 we describe the different energy minimization algorithms that we have implemented, and in section 4 we present our set of benchmarks. In section 5 we provide our experimental comparison of the different energy minimization methods, and we conclude in section 6.

2   Problem Formulation and Experimental Infrastructure

We define a pixel labeling problem as assigning to every pixel p a label, which we write as l_p. The collection of all pixel-label assignments is denoted by l, the number of pixels is n, and the number of labels is m. The energy function E, which can also be viewed as the log likelihood of the posterior distribution of a Markov Random Field [2, 16], is composed of a data energy E_d and smoothness energy E_s, $E = E_d + \lambda E_s$. The data energy is simply the sum of a set of per-pixel data costs $d_p(l)$, $E_d = \sum_p d_p(l_p)$. In the MRF framework, the data energy comes from the (negative) log likelihood of the measurement noise.

We assume that pixels form a 2D grid, so that each p can also be written in terms of its coordinates $p = (i, j)$. We use the standard 4-connected neighborhood system, so that the smoothness energy is the sum of spatially varying horizontal and vertical nearest-neighbor smoothness costs, $V_{pq}(l_p, l_q)$, where if $p = (i, j)$ and $q = (s, t)$ then $|i - s| + |j - t| = 1$. If we let $\mathcal{N}$ denote the set of all such neighboring pixel pairs, the smoothness energy is

$$E_s = \sum_{\{p,q\} \in \mathcal{N}} V_{pq}(l_p, l_q). \tag{1}$$

Note that in equation 1, the notation $\{p, q\}$ stands for an unordered set, that is the sum is over *unordered* pairs of neighboring pixels.

In the MRF framework, the smoothness energy comes from the negative log likelihood of the prior. In this paper, we consider a general form of the smoothness costs, where different pairings of adjacent labels can lead to different costs. This is important in a number of applications, ranging from stereo matching (§8.2 of [4]) to image stitching and texture quilting [12, 17, 18].

A more restricted form of the smoothness energy is $E_s = \sum_{\{p,q\} \in \mathcal{N}} w_{pq} \cdot V(|l_p - l_q|)$, where the smoothness terms are the product of spatially varying per-pairing weights w_{pq} and a non-decreasing function of the label difference $V(\Delta l) = V(|l_p - l_q|)$. While we could represent V using an m-valued look-up table, for simplicity, we instead parameterize V using a simple clipped monomial form $V(\Delta l) = \min(|\Delta l|^k, V_{\max})$, with $k \in \{1, 2\}$. If we set $V_{\max} = 1.0$, we get the Potts model, $V(\Delta l) = 1 - \delta(\Delta l)$, which penalizes any pair of different labels uniformly (δ is the unit impulse function).

While they are not our primary focus, a number of important special cases have fast exact algorithms. If there are only two labels, the natural Potts model smoothness cost can be solved exactly with graph cuts (this was first applied to images by [19]). If the labels are the integers starting with 0 and the smoothness cost is an arbitrary convex function, [20] gives a graph cut construction. An algorithm due to [21] can be used with $V(\Delta l) = \Delta l$ (L_1 smoothness) and convex data costs. However, the NP-hardness result proved in [4] applies if there are more than two labels, as long as the class of smoothness costs includes the Potts model. This, unfortunately, implies that the vast majority of MRF-based energy functions are intractable.

The class of energy functions we are considering is quite broad, and not all energy minimization methods can handle the entire class. For example, acceleration techniques based on distance transforms [22] can significantly speed up message-passing algorithms such as LBP or TRW, yet these methods are only applicable for certain smoothness costs V. Other algorithms, such as graph cuts, only have good theoretical guarantees for certain choices of V (see section 3 for a discussion of this issue). We will assume that any algorithm can run on any benchmark problem; this can generally be ensured by reverting to a weaker or slower of the algorithm if necessary for a particular benchmark.

2.1   Software Interface for Energy Minimization

Now that we have defined the class of energy functions that we minimize, we need to compare different energy minimization methods on the same energy function E. Conceptually, it is easy to switch from one energy minimization method to another, but in practice, most applications are tied to a particular choice of E. As a result, almost no one in vision has ever answered questions like "how would your results look if you used LBP instead of graph cuts to minimize your E?" (The closest to this was [13], who compared LBP and graph cuts for stereo.) In order to create a set of benchmarks, it was necessary to design a standard software interface (API) that allows a user to specify an energy function E and to easily call a variety of energy minimization methods to minimize E.

The software API is available at http://vision.middlebury.edu/MRF, as are all of our benchmarks and implementations of most of the energy minimization methods discussed in this paper. The API allows the user to define any energy function described above. The data cost energy can be specified implicitly, as a function $d_p()$ or explicitly as an array. The smoothness cost likewise can be specified either by defining the parameters k and $V_{\max}$, or by providing an explicit function or array. Excerpts from an example program that uses our API to call two different energy minimization algorithms on the same energy function are given below.

```
// Abstract definition of an energy function E
EnergyFunction *E = (EnergyFunction *) new EnergyFunction(data,smooth);
// Energy minimization of E via ICM
solver = (MRF *) new ICM(width,height,num_labels,E);
// To use graph cuts to minimize E instead, substitute the line below
// solver = (MRF *) new Expansion(width,height,num_labels,E);
// Run one iteration, store the amount of time it takes in t
solver->optimize(1,&t);
// Print out the resulting energy and running time
print_stats( solver->totalEnergy(), t);
```

Note that the interface also has the notion of an iteration, but it is up to each energy minimization method to interpret this notion. Most algorithms have some natural intermediate point where they have a current answer. By supporting this, our API allows us to plot the curve of energy versus time. This is particularly important because a number of powerful methods (such as TRW and graph cuts) make very small changes in the last few iterations.

2.2   Evaluation Methodology

To evaluate the quality of a given solution, we need the final energy E along with the computation time required, as a function of the number of iterations. For every benchmark, we produce a plot that keeps track of the energy vs. computation time for every algorithm tested. We implemented the algorithms in C or C++, and ran the benchmarks on a modern Pentium 4. Most of the experiments used the same machine (3.4 GHz, 2GB RAM), while a few used a fairly similar computer.

Of course, not all authors spent the same amount of effort tuning their implementation for our benchmarks. Note that while the natural way to compare energy minimization algorithms is in terms of their energy and speed, it is not always the case that the lowest energy solution is the best one for a vision problem. (We return to this issue at the end of section 6.)

3   Energy Minimization Algorithms

In this section, we describe the optimization algorithms that we have implemented and included in our interface. Most of the energy minimization algorithms were implemented by their original inventors; the exceptions are ICM and LBP, which we implemented ourselves (for LBP, we received help from several experts).

Iterated conditional modes (ICM) — Iterated conditional modes [1] uses a deterministic "greedy" strategy to find a local minimum. It starts with an estimate of the labeling, and then for each pixel it chooses the label giving the largest decrease of the energy function. This process is repeated until convergence, which is guaranteed to occur, and in practice is very rapid.

Unfortunately, the results are extremely sensitive to the initial estimate, especially in high-dimensional spaces with non-convex energies (such as arise in vision) due to the huge number of local minima. In our experiments, we initialized ICM in a winner-take-all manner, by assigning each pixel the label with the lowest data cost. This resulted in significantly better performance.

Graph cuts — The two most popular graph cuts algorithms, called the *swap move* algorithm and the *expansion move* algorithm, were introduced in [4]. These algorithms rapidly compute a strong local minimum, in the sense that no "permitted move" will produce a labeling with lower energy.

For a pair of labels α, β, a swap move takes some subset of the pixels currently given the label α and assigns them the label β, and vice-versa. The swap move algorithm finds a local minimum such that there is no swap move, for any pair of labels α,β, that will produce a lower energy labeling. Analogously, we define an expansion move for a label α to increase the set of pixels that are given this label. The expansion move algorithm finds a local minimum such that no expansion move, for any label α, yields a labeling with lower energy.

The criteria for a local minimum with respect to expansion moves (swap moves) are so strong that there are many fewer minima in high dimensional spaces compared to standard moves. In the original work of [4] the swap move algorithm was shown to be applicable to any energy where V_{pq} is a semi-metric, and the expansion move algorithm to any energy where V_{pq} is a metric. The results of [5] imply that the expansion move algorithm can be used if for all labels α,β,and γ, $V_{pq}(\alpha,\alpha) + V_{pq}(\beta,\gamma) \leq V_{pq}(\alpha,\gamma) + V_{pq}(\beta,\alpha)$. The swap move algorithm can be used if for all labels α,β $V_{pq}(\alpha,\alpha) + V_{pq}(\beta,\beta) \leq V_{pq}(\alpha,\beta) + V_{pq}(\beta,\alpha)$. (This constraint comes from the notion of regular, i.e. submodular, binary energy functions, which are closely related to graph cuts.)

If the energy does not obey these constraints, graph cut algorithms can still be applied by "truncating" the violating terms [24]. In this case, however, we are no longer guaranteed to find the optimal labeling with respect to swap (or expansion) moves. In paractice, the performance of this version seems to work well when only relatively few terms need to be truncated.

Max-product loopy belief propagation (LBP) — To evaluate the performance of LBP, we implemented the max-product LBP version, which is designed to find the lowest energy solution. The other main variant of LBP, the sum-product algorithm, does not directly search for a minimum energy solution, but instead computes the marginal probability distribution of each node in the graph. The belief propagation algorithm was originally designed for graphs without cycles [25], in which case it produces the exact result for our energy. However, there is nothing in the formulation of BP that prevents it from being tried on graphs with loops.

In general, LPB is not guaranteed to converge, and may go into an infinite loop switching between two labelings. Felzenszwalb and Huttenlocher [22] present a number of ways to speed up the basic algorithm. In particular, our LBP implementation uses the distance transform method described in [22], which significantly reduces the running time of the algorithm.

Tree-reweighted message passing (TRW) — Tree-reweighted message passing [30] is a message-passing algorithm similar, on the surface, to LBP. Let $M_{p \to q}^t$ be the message that pixel p sends to its neighbor q at iteration t; this is a vector of size m (the number of labels). The message update rule is:

$$M_{p \to q}^t(l_q) = \min_{l_p} \left(c_{pq}\{d_p(l_p) + \sum_{s \in \mathcal{N}(p)} M_{s \to p}^{t-1}(l_p)\} - M_{q \to p}^{t-1}(l_p) + V_{pq}(l_p, l_q) \right).$$

The coefficients c_{pq} are determined in the following way. First, a set of trees from the neighborhood graph (a 2D grid in our case) is chosen so that each edge is in at least one tree. A probability distribution ρ over the set of trees is then chosen. Finally, c_{pq} is set to ρ_{pq}/ρ_p, i.e. the probability that a tree chosen randomly under ρ contains edge (p,q) *given* that it contains p. Note that if c_{pq} were set to 1, the update rule would be identical to that of standard LBP.

An interesting feature of the TRW algorithm is that it computes a lower bound on the energy. The original TRW algorithm does not necessarily converge, and does not, in fact, guarantee that the lower bound always increases with time. In this paper we use an improved version of TRW due to [23], which is called sequential TRW, or TRW-S. In this version, the lower bound estimate is guaranteed not to decrease, which results in certain convergence properties. In TRW-S we first select an arbitrary pixel ordering function $S(p)$. The messages are updated in order of increasing $S(p)$ and at the next iteration in the reverse order. Trees are constrained to be chains that are monotonic with respect to $S(p)$. Note that the algorithm can be implemented using half as much memory as standard BP [23].

4   Benchmark Problems

For our benchmark problems, we have created a representative set of low-level energy minimization problems drawn from a range of different applications. As with the optimization methods, we were fortunate enough to persuade the original authors of the problems to contribute their energy functions and data.

Stereo matching — For stereo matching, we followed in the footsteps of [13] and used a simple energy function for stereo, applied to images from the widely-used Middlebury stereo data set [7]. We used different energy functions for different images, to make the optimization problems more varied. For the "Tsukuba" image we used the truncated L_1 distance $V_{\max} = 2, k = 1$, with $\lambda = 20$ and $m = 16$ labels. For "Venus" we used the truncated L_2 distance $V_{\max} = 2, k = 7$, with $\lambda = 50$ and $m = 20$ labels. For "Teddy" we used the Potts model $V_{\max} = 1, k = 1$, with $\lambda = 10$ and $m = 60$ labels. The default smoothness weight was $w_{pq} = 1$ at all pixels. For "Tsukuba" and "Teddy" we increased the weight at locations where the intensity gradient g_{pq} in the left image is small: we used $w_{pq} = 2$ if $|g_{pq}| \leq 8$ for "Tsukuba," and $w_{pq} = 3$ if $|g_{pq}| \leq 10$ for "Teddy."

Photomontage — The Photomontage system [12] seamlessly stitches together multiple photographs for a variety of photo merging applications. We formed benchmarks for two such applications, panoramic stitching and group photo merging. The input is a set of aligned images $S_1, S_2, \ldots, S_m$ of equal dimension; the labels are the image indexes, i.e. $1, 2, ..., m$; the final output image is formed by copying colors from the input images according to the computed labeling. If two neighbors p and q are assigned the same input image, they should appear natural in the composite and so $V_{pq}(i,i) = 0$. If $l_p \neq l_q$, we say that a seam exists between p and q; then V_{pq} measures how visually noticeable the seam is in the composite. The data term $d_p(i)$ is 0 if pixel p is in the field of view of image i, and ∞ otherwise.

The first benchmark stitches together the panorama in Fig. 8 of [12]. (See the project web page for all images.) The smoothness energy, derived from [18], is

$V_{pq} = |S_{l_p}(p) - S_{l_q}(p)| + |S_{l_p}(q) - S_{l_q}(q)|$. This energy function is suitable for the expansion algorithm without truncation.

The second benchmark stitches together the five group photographs shown in Fig. 1 of [12]. The best depiction of each person is to be included in a composite. Photomontage itself is interactive, but to make the benchmark repeatable the user strokes are saved into a data file. For any pixel p underneath a drawn stroke, $d_p(l_p) = 0$ if l_p equals the user-indicated source image, and ∞ otherwise. The smoothness terms are modified from the first benchmark to encourage seams along strong edges. The expansion algorithm is applicable to this energy only after truncating certain terms, but it continues to work well in practice.

Binary image segmentation — Binary MRF's are also widely used in medical image segmentation [10], stereo matching using minimal surfaces [27, 28], and video segmentation using stereo disparity cues [29] As previously mentioned, for the natural Ising model smoothness costs, the global minimum can be computed rapidly via a graph cuts [19]; this result has been generalized to other smoothness costs by [5].) Nevertheless, such energy functions still form an interesting benchmark, since there may well be other heuristic algorithms that perform faster while achieving nearly the same level of performance.

Our benchmark consists of a segmentation problem, inspired by the interactive segmentation algorithm of [10] or its more recent extensions [11]. As with our Photomontage stitching example, this application requires user interaction; we handle this issue as above, by saving the user interactions to a file and using them to derive the data costs.

The data cost is the log likelihood of a pixel belonging to either foreground or background and is modeled as two separate Gaussian mixture models as in [11]. The smoothness term is a standard Potts model which is contrast sensitive: $V_{pq} = || \exp(-\beta \|x_i - x_j\|^2)|| + \lambda_2$, where $\lambda = 50$ and $\lambda_2 = 10$. The quantity β is set to $(2\langle \|x_i - x_j\|^2 \rangle)^{-1}$ where the expectation denotes an average over the image, as motivated in [11]. The impact of λ_2 is to remove small and isolated areas that have high contrast.

Image restoration and inpainting — We experimented with the "penguin" image, which appears in figure 7 in [22]. We added random noise to each pixel, and also obscured a portion of the image. The labels are intensities, and the data cost for each pixel is the squared difference between the label and the observed distance. However, pixels in the obscured portion have a data cost of 0 for any intensity. The smoothness energy was the truncated L_2 distance with uniform w_{pq}'s (we used $V_{\max} = 200, k = 2, w_{pq} = 25$).

5   Experimental Results

The experimental results from running the different optimization algorithms on these benchmarks are given in figure 1 (stereo), figure 2 (Photomontage), and figure 3 (binary image segmentation). The images themselves are provided on the project web page. The x-axis of these plots shows running times, measured

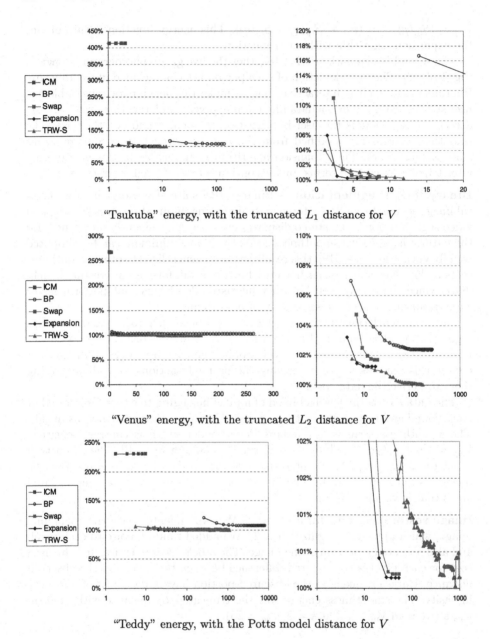

"Tsukuba" energy, with the truncated L_1 distance for V

"Venus" energy, with the truncated L_2 distance for V

"Teddy" energy, with the Potts model distance for V

Fig. 1. Results on stereo matching benchmarks. Each plot shows energies vs. run time in seconds. Energies are given relative to the largest lower bound provided by the TRW-S method. The plots on the right are zoomed versions of the plots on the left. Note that some of the horizontal (time) axes use a log scale to better visualize the results. ICM is omitted in the right plots, due to its poor performance. Depth map images are available at http://vision.middlebury.edu/MRF.

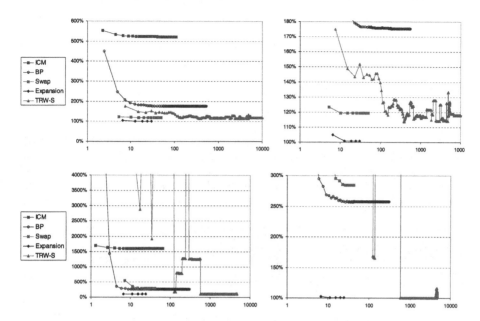

Fig. 2. Results on the Photomontage benchmarks, "Panorama" is at top and "Family" is below. Each plot shows energies vs. run time in seconds, using a log scale for time. The plots on the right are zoomed versions of the plots on the left. ICM is omitted in the right plots, due to poor performance. The associated color images can be found on the project web page.

in seconds. Note that some figures use a log scale for running time, which is necessary since some algorithms perform very poorly. For the y-axis, we made use of TRW's ability to compute a lower bound on the energy of the optimal solution. We normalized the energy by dividing it by the best known lower bound given by any run of TRW-S. Due to space limitations we had to omit the plots for the image restoration benchmark; they can be found on the project web page.

For all of these examples, the best methods achieved results that are extremely close to the global minimum, with less than 1 percent error. For example, on "Tsukuba", expansion moves and TRW-S got to within 0.27% of the optimum, while on "Panorama" expansion moves was within 0.78%. These statistics may actually understate the performance of the methods; since the global minimum is unknown, we use the TRW-S lower bound, which (of course) can underestimate the optimal energy.

The individual plots show some interesting features. In figure 1, TRW-S does extremely well, but in the "Teddy" energy it eventually oscillates. However, during the oscillation it achieves the best energy of any algorithm on any of our stereo benchmarks, within 0.018% of the global minimum. The same oscillation is seen in figure 2, though this time without as good performance. On the binary image segmentation problems, shown in figure 3, graph cuts are guaranteed to

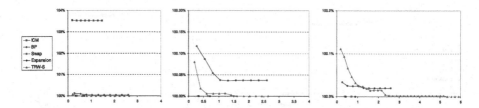

Fig. 3. Results on binary image segmentation benchmarks. Graph cuts are guaranteed to compute the global minimum, as is TRW-S. (In fact, this minimum is found by the first iteration of the swap move algorithm, which is equivalent to a single max flow computation.) Note that LBP comes extremely close (under 0.04% error), but never actually attains it.

Fig. 4. Results on "Panorama" benchmark. LBP output is shown at left, TRW-S in the middle, and expansion moves at right. Larger versions of these images are available on the project web page.

compute the global minimum, as is TRW-S (but not the original TRW [30]). LBP comes extremely close (under 0.04% error), but never actually attains it.

For reasons of space, we have omitted most of the actual images from this paper (they are available at `http://vision.middlebury.edu/MRF`). In terms of visual quality, the ICM results looked noticeably worse, but the others were difficult to distinguish on most of our benchmarks. The exception was the Photomontage benchmarks. On "Panorama", shown in figure 4, LBP makes some major errors, leaving slices of several people floating in the air. TRW-S does quite well, though the some of its seams are more noticeable than those produced by expansion moves (which gives the visually best results). On "Family" (not shown), LBP also makes major errors, while TRW-S and expansion moves both work well.

6   Discussion

The strongest impression that one gets from our data is of how much better modern energy minimization methods are than ICM, and how close they come to computing the global minimum. We do not believe that this is purely due to flaws in ICM, but simply reflects the fact that the methods used until the late 1990's performed poorly. (As additional evidence, [4] compared the energy produced by graph cuts with simulated annealing, and obtained a similarly large improvement.) We believe that our study demonstrates that the state of the art in energy minimization has advanced significantly in the last few years.

There is also a dramatic difference in performance among the different energy minimization methods on our benchmarks, and on some of the benchmarks there are clear winners. On the Photomontage benchmark, expansion moves perform best, which provides some justification for the fact that this algorithm is used by various image stitching applications [12, 26]. On the stereo benchmark, the two best methods seem to be TRW-S and expansion moves. There are also some obvious paired comparisons; for instance, there never seems to be any reason to use swap moves instead of expansion moves. In terms of runtime, the expansion move algorithm is clearly the winner among the competitive methods (i.e., all except ICM), but as noted not all methods have been optimized for speed equally.

There is clearly a need for more research on message-passing methods such as TRW-S and LBP. While LBP is a well-regarded and widely used method, on our benchmarks it performed surprisingly poorly (the only method it consistently outperformed was ICM). This may be due to a quirk in our benchmarks, or it may reflect issues with the way we scheduled message updates (despite the help we were given by several experts on LBP). TRW-S, which has not been widely used in vision, gave consistently strong results. In addition, the lower bound on the energy provided by TRW-S proved extremely useful in our study. For a user of energy minimization methods, this lower bound can serve as a confidence measure, providing assurance that the solution obtained has near-optimal energy. Another area that needs investigation is the use of graph cut algorithms for wider classes of energy functions than the limited ones they were originally designed for. The benchmarks that were most challenging for the expansion move algorithm (such as "Venus") use a V that is not a metric.

Another important issue centers around the use of energy to compare energy minimization algorithms. The goal in computer vision, of course, is not to compute the lowest energy solution to a problem, but rather the most accurate one. While computing the global minimum was shown to be NP-hard [4], it is sometimes possible for special cases. For example, the energy minimization problem can be recast as an integer program, which can be solved as a linear program; if the linear program's solutions happen to be integers, they are the global minimum. This is the basis for the approach was taken by [31], who demonstrated that they could compute the global minimum for several common energy functions on the Middlebury images. The global minimum has only slightly lower energy than that produced by graph cuts or LBP. In addition, [31] points out that the globally minimum is no more accurate than the results achieved with graph cuts or LBP. More precisely, according to [31] at best graph cuts produces an energy that is 0.018% over the global minimum, while at worst the energy is 3.6% larger; at best LBP gives an energy that is 3.4% higher, and at worst 30%.

In light of these results, it is clear that for the models we have considered, better minimization techniques are unlikely to produce significantly more accurate labelings. For the Middlebury stereo benchmarks this is particularly clear: the best methods produce energies that are extremely close to the global minimum; the global minimum, when known, is no more accurate than the ground truth; and, in fact, the ground truth has substantially higher energy. However, it is still important to compare energy minimization algorithms using the energy they produce as a benchmark. Creating more accurate models will not lead to better results if good labelings under these models cannot be found. It is also difficult to gauge the power of a model without the ability to produce low energy labelings.

7 Conclusions and Future Work

There are many natural extensions to our work that we are currently pursuing, including energy minimization algorithms, classes of energy functions, and selection of benchmarks. While most of the energy minimization algorithms we have implemented are fairly mature, there is probably room for improvement in our implementation of LBP, especially in terms of the schedule of message updates. We also plan to implement several other modern algorithms, as well as additional benchmarks. We are particularly interested in [31], whose method could potentially achieve the global minimum on some of our benchmarks, and [32], who generalize the expansion move algorithm so that (like TRW) it also computes a lower bound on the energy.

We also plan to increase the class of energy functions we consider. We hope to investigate different grid topologies (such as the 8-connected topology for 2D, or 26-connected for 3D), as well as non-local topologies such as those used with multiple depth maps [15]. Finally, we will expand our set of benchmarks to include both more images and more applications, and continue to update our project web page to include the latest results in this rapidly evolving area.

References

1. Besag, J.: On the statistical analysis of dirty pictures (with discussion). Journal of the Royal Statistical Society, Series B **48** (1986) 259–302
2. Geman, S., Geman, D.: Stochastic relaxation, Gibbs distributions, and the Bayesian restoration of images. IEEE Trans Pattern Anal Mach Intell **6** (1984) 721–741
3. Barnard, S.: Stochastic stereo matching over scale. Intern Journ Comp Vis **3** (1989) 17–32
4. Boykov, Y., Veksler, O., Zabih, R.: Fast approximate energy minimization via graph cuts. IEEE Trans Pattern Anal Mach Intell **23** (2001) 1222–1239
5. Kolmogorov, V., Zabih, R.: What energy functions can be minimized via graph cuts? IEEE Trans Pattern Anal Mach Intell **26** (2004) 147–59
6. Yedidia, J.S., Freeman, W.T., Weiss, Y.: Generalized belief propagation. In: NIPS. (2000) 689–695
7. Scharstein, D., Szeliski, R.: A taxonomy and evaluation of dense two-frame stereo correspondence algorithms. Intern Journ Comp Vis **47** (2002) 7–42
8. Geman, S., Graffigne, C.: Markov Random Field image models and their applications to computer vision. In: Intern Cong of Mathematicians. (1986) 1496–1517
9. Chou, P.B., Brown, C.M.: The theory and practice of Bayesian image labeling. Intern Journ Comp Vis 4 (1990) 185–210

10. Boykov, Y., Jolly, M.P.: Interactive graph cuts for optimal boundary and region segmentation of objects in N-D images. In: ICCV. (2001) I: 105–112
11. Rother, C., Kolmogorov, V., Blake, A.: "GrabCut" - interactive foreground extraction using iterated graph cuts. SIGGRAPH **23** (2004) 309–314
12. Agarwala, A., et al.: Interactive digital photomontage. SIGGRAPH **23** (2004) 292–300
13. Tappen, M.F., Freeman, W.T.: Comparison of graph cuts with belief propagation for stereo, using identical MRF parameters. In: ICCV. (2003) 900–907
14. Boykov, Y., Kolmogorov, V.: An experimental comparison of min-cut/max-flow algorithms for energy minimization in vision. IEEE Trans Pattern Anal Mach Intell **26** (2004) 1124–1137
15. Kolmogorov, V., Rother, C.: Comparison of energy minimization algorithms for highly connected graphs. In: ECCV. (2006)
16. Li, S.: Markov Random Field Modeling in Computer Vision. Springer-Verlag (1995)
17. Efros, A.A., Freeman, W.T.: Image quilting for texture synthesis and transfer. SIGGRAPH (2001) 341–346
18. Kwatra, V., Schodl, A., Essa, I., Turk, G., Bobick, A.: Graphcut textures: Image and video synthesis using graph cuts. SIGGRAPH (2003)
19. Greig, D., Porteous, B., Seheult, A.: Exact maximum a posteriori estimation for binary images. Journal of the Royal Statistical Society, Series B **51** (1989) 271–279
20. Ishikawa, H.: Exact optimization for Markov Random Fields with convex priors. IEEE Trans Pattern Anal Mach Intell **25** (2003) 1333–1336
21. Hochbaum, D.S.: An efficient algorithm for image segmentation, Markov Random Fields and related problems. Journal of the ACM (JACM) **48** (2001) 686–701
22. Felzenszwalb, P.F., Huttenlocher, D.P.: Efficient belief propagation for early vision. In: CVPR. (2004) 261–268
23. Kolmogorov, V.: Convergent tree-reweighted message passing for energy minimization. In: AISTATS. (2005)
24. Rother, C., Kumar, S., Kolmogorov, V., Blake, A.: Digital tapestry. In: CVPR. (2005)
25. Pearl, J.: Probabilistic reasoning in intelligent systems: networks of plausible inference. Morgan Kaufmann (1988)
26. Agarwala, A., et al.: Panoramic video textures. SIGGRAPH **24** (2005) 821–827
27. Snow, D., Viola, P., Zabih, R.: Exact voxel occupancy with graph cuts. In: CVPR. (2000) 345–352
28. Buehler, C., et al.: Minimal surfaces for stereo vision. In: ECCV. (2002) 885–899
29. Kolmogorov, V., Criminisi, A., Blake, A., Cross, G., Rother, C.: Bi-layer segmentation of binocular stereo video. In: CVPR. (2005) 407–414
30. Wainwright, M.J., Jaakkola, T.S., Willsky, A.S.: MAP estimation via agreement on (hyper)trees: Message-passing and linear-programming approaches. IEEE Trans Info Theory **51** (2005)
31. Meltzer, T., Yanover, C., Weiss, Y.: Globally optimal solutions for energy minimization in stereo vision using reweighted belief propagation. In: ICCV. (2005)
32. Komodakis, N., Tziritas, G. A new framework for approximate labeling via graph cuts In: ICCV. (2005)

Measuring Uncertainty in Graph Cut Solutions - Efficiently Computing Min-marginal Energies Using Dynamic Graph Cuts*

Pushmeet Kohli and Philip H.S. Torr

Department of Computing,
Oxford Brookes University, Oxford
{pushmeet.kohli, philiptorr}@brookes.ac.uk

Abstract. In recent years the use of graph-cuts has become quite popular in computer vision. However, researchers have repeatedly asked the question whether it might be possible to compute a measure of uncertainty associated with the graph-cut solutions. In this paper we answer this particular question by showing how the min-marginals associated with the label assignments in a MRF can be efficiently computed using a new algorithm based on dynamic graph cuts. We start by reporting the discovery of a novel relationship between the min-marginal energy corresponding to a latent variable label assignment, and the flow potentials of the node representing that variable in the graph used in the energy minimization procedure. We then proceed to show how the min-marginal energy can be computed by minimizing a *projection* of the energy function defined by the MRF. We propose a fast and novel algorithm based on dynamic graph cuts to efficiently minimize these energy projections. The min-marginal energies obtained by our proposed algorithm are exact, as opposed to the ones obtained from other inference algorithms like loopy belief propagation and generalized belief propagation. We conclude by showing how min-marginals can be used to compute a confidence measure for label assignments in labelling problems such as image segmentation.

1 Introduction

Researchers in computer vision have extensively used graph cuts to compute the maximum a posteriori (MAP) solutions for various discrete pixel labelling problems such as image restoration, segmentation and stereo. Graph cuts are preferred over other inference algorithms like Loopy Belief Propagation (LBP), Generalized Belief Propagation (GBP) and the recently introduced Tree Re-weighted message passing (TRW) [1, 2] primarily because of their ability to find globally optimal solutions for an important class of energy functions (sub-modular) in polynomial time [3]. Even in problems where they do not guarantee globally optimal solutions, they can be used to find solutions which are strong local minima of the energy [4]. These solutions for certain problems have been shown to be better than the ones obtained by other methods [5].

* This work was supported by the EPSRC research grant GR/T21790/01(P) and the IST Programme of the European Community, under the PASCAL Network of Excellence, IST-2002-506778.

A. Leonardis, H. Bischof, and A. Pinz (Eds.): ECCV 2006, Part II, LNCS 3952, pp. 30–43, 2006.

Graph cuts however do suffer from a big disadvantage. Unlike other inference algorithms, they do not provide any uncertainty measure associated with the solution they produce. This is a serious drawback since researchers do not have any information regarding the probability of a particular latent variable assignment in a graph cut solution. Inference algorithms like LBP, GBP, and TRW provide the user with marginal or min-marginal energies associated with each latent variable. However, these algorithms are not exact. Note that for tree-structured graphs, the simple max-product belief propagation algorithm gives the exact max-marginal probabilities/min-marginal energies[1] for different label assignments in $O(nl^2)$ time where n is the number of latent variables, and l is the number of labels a latent variable can take.

This paper addresses the problem of efficiently computing the min-marginals associated with the label assignments of any latent variable in a Markov Random Field (MRF). Our method can work on all MRFs that can be solved using graph cuts. First, we show how in the case of binary variables, the min-marginals associated with the labellings of a latent variable are related to the *flow-potentials* (defined in section 3) of the node representing that latent variable in the graph constructed in the energy minimization procedure. The exact min-marginal energies can be found by computing these *flow-potentials*. We then show how flow potential computation is equivalent to minimizing *projections* of the original energy function[2].

Minimizing a *projection* of an energy function is a computationally expensive operation and requires a graph cut to be computed. In order to obtain the min-marginals corresponding to all label assignments of all random variables, we need to compute a graph cut $O(nl)$ number of times. In this paper, we present an algorithm based on dynamic graph cuts [6] which solves these $O(nl)$ graph cuts extremely quickly. Our experiments show that the running time of this algorithm i.e. the time taken for it to compute the min-marginals corresponding to all latent variable label assignments is of the same order of magnitude as the time taken to compute a single graph cut.

Overview of Dynamic Graph Cuts. Dynamic computation is a paradigm that prescribes solving a problem by dynamically updating the solution of the previous problem instance. Its hope is to be more efficient than a computation of the solution from scratch after every change in the problem. A considerable speedup in computation time can be achieved by this procedure especially when the problem is large scale and changes are few. Dynamic algorithms are not new to computer vision. They have been extensively used in computational geometry for problems such as range searching, intersections, point location, convex hull, proximity and many others [7].

Boykov and Jolly [8] were the first to use a *partially* dynamic st-mincut algorithm in a vision application, by proposing a technique with which they could update capacities of *certain* graph edges, and recompute the st-mincut dynamically. They used this

---

[1] We will explain the relation between max-marginal probabilities and min-marginal energies later in section 2. To make our notation consistent with recent work in graph cuts, we formulate the problem in terms of min-marginal energies (subsequently referred to as simply min marginals).

[2] A projection of the function $f(x_1, x_2, ..., x_n)$ can be obtained by fixing the values of some of the variables in the function $f(.)$. For instance $f'(x_2, ..., x_n) = f(0, x_2, ..., x_n)$ is a projection of the function $f(.)$.

method for performing interactive image segmentation, where the user could improve segmentation results by giving additional segmentation cues (seeds) in an online fashion. However, their scheme was restrictive and did not allow for general changes in the graph. In one of our earlier papers, we proposed a new algorithm overcoming this restriction [6], which is faster and allows for arbitrary changes in the graph. The running time of this new algorithm has been empirically shown to increase linearly with the number of edge weights changed in the graph. In this paper, we will use this algorithm to compute the exact min-marginals efficiently. To summarize, the key contributions of this paper include:

- A novel relationship between min-marginal energies and node flow-potentials in the residual graph obtained after the graph cut computation.
- A method to compute min-marginals by minimizing energy function projections.
- An extremely fast algorithm based on dynamic graph cuts for efficiently minimizing these energy projections.
- A method to obtain confidence maps for different assignments in labelling problems such as image segmentation.

Organization of the Paper. A brief outline of the paper is given next. We discuss MRFs and min-marginal energies in section 2. In section 3, we formulate the st-mincut problem, define terms that would be used in the paper, and describe how certain energy functions can be minimized using graph cuts. In section 4, we show how min-marginals can be found by minimizing projections of the original energy function. We then propose a novel algorithm based on dynamic graph cuts to efficiently compute the minima of these energy projections. In section 5, we show some experimental results of our algorithm.

2   Notation and Preliminaries

We will now describe the notation used in the paper. We will formulate our problem in terms of a *pairwise* MRF[3]. Note that the pairwise assumption does not affect the generality of our formulation since any MRF involving higher order interaction terms can be converted to a *pairwise* MRF by addition of auxiliary variables in the MRF [9].

Consider a random field consisting of a set of discrete random variables $\{x_1, \ldots, x_n\}$ defined on the set $\mathcal{V}$, such that each variable x_v takes values from the label set $\mathcal{X}_v$. We represent the set of all variables $x_v, \forall v \in \mathcal{V}$ by the vector $\mathbf{x}$ which takes values from the set $\mathcal{X}$ defined as $\mathcal{X} = \mathcal{X}_1 \times \mathcal{X}_2 \times \ldots \times \mathcal{X}_n$. Unless noted otherwise, we use symbols u and v to denote values in $\mathcal{V}$, and i and j to denote particular values in $\mathcal{X}_u$ and $\mathcal{X}_v$ respectively. Further, we use $\mathcal{N}_v$ to denote the set consisting of indices of all variables which are neighbours of the random variable x_v in the graphical model. The random field is said to be a MRF with respect to a neighborhood $\mathcal{N} = \{\mathcal{N}_v | v \in \mathcal{V}\}$ if and only if it satisfies the positivity property $\Pr(\mathbf{x}) > 0 \ \forall \mathbf{x} \in \mathcal{X}$, and the Markovian property

$$\Pr(x_v | \{x_u : u \in \mathcal{V} - \{v\}\}) = \Pr(x_v | \{x_u : u \in \mathcal{N}_v\}) \qquad \forall v \in \mathcal{V}. \qquad (1)$$

---

[3] Pairwise MRFs have cliques of size at most two.

The MAP-MRF estimation problem can be formulated as an energy minimization problem where the energy corresponding to the configuration $\mathbf{x}$ is the negative log likelihood of the joint posterior probability of a MRF configuration and is defined as

$$E(\mathbf{x}|\theta) = -\log \Pr(\mathbf{x}|\mathbf{D}) - \text{const.} \qquad (2)$$

Here θ is the energy parameter vector defining the MRF [1]. The energy of a configuration for such a pairwise MRF can be written in terms of unary and pairwise energy terms as:

$$E(\mathbf{x}|\theta) = \sum_{v \in \mathcal{V}} \left(\phi(\mathbf{x}_v) + \sum_{u \in \mathcal{N}_v} \phi(\mathbf{x}_u, \mathbf{x}_v) \right) + \text{const.} \qquad (3)$$

In the paper, $\psi(\theta)$ is used to denote the value of the energy of the MAP configuration of the MRF and is defined as:

$$\psi(\theta) = \min_{\mathbf{x} \in \mathcal{X}} E(\mathbf{x}|\theta). \qquad (4)$$

The term *optimal solution* will be used to refer to the MAP solution in the paper.

Min-marginal Energies. A min-marginal is a function that provides information about the minimum values of the energy E under different constraints. Following the notation of [1], we define the min-marginal energies $\psi_{v;j}, \psi_{uv;ij}$ as:

$$\psi_{v;j}(\theta) = \min_{\mathbf{x} \in \mathcal{X}, x_v = j} E(\mathbf{x}|\theta), \quad \text{and} \quad \psi_{uv;ij}(\theta) = \min_{\mathbf{x} \in \mathcal{X}, x_u = i, x_v = j} E(\mathbf{x}|\theta). \qquad (5)$$

In words, given an energy function E whose value depends on the variables $(x_1, \ldots, x_n)$, $\psi_{v;j}(\theta)$ represents the minimum energy value obtained if we fix the value of variable x_v to j and minimize over all remaining variables. Similarly, $\psi_{uv;ij}(\theta)$ represents the value of the minimum energy in the case when the values of variables x_u and x_v are fixed to i and j respectively.

2.1   Computing the Likelihood of a Label Assignment

Now we show how min-marginals can be used to compute a confidence measure for a particular latent variable label assignment. Given the function $\Pr(\mathbf{x}|\mathbf{D})$, which specifies the probability of a configuration of the MRF, the max-marginal $\mu_{v;j}$ gives us the value of the maximum probability over all possible configurations of the MRF in which $x_v = j$. Formally, it is defined as:

$$\mu_{v;j} = \max_{\mathbf{x} \in \mathcal{X}; x_v = j} \Pr(\mathbf{x}|\mathbf{D}) \qquad (6)$$

Inference algorithms like max-product belief propagation produce the max-marginals along with the MAP solution. These max-marginals can be used to obtain a confidence measure σ for any latent variable labelling as:

$$\sigma_{v;j} = \frac{\max_{\mathbf{x} \in \mathcal{X}, x_v = j} \Pr(\mathbf{x}|\mathbf{D})}{\sum_{k \in \mathcal{X}_v} \max_{\mathbf{x} \in \mathcal{X}, x_v = k} \Pr(\mathbf{x}|\mathbf{D})} = \frac{\mu_{v;j}}{\sum_{k \in \mathcal{X}_v} \mu_{v;k}} \qquad (7)$$

where $\sigma_{v;j}$ is the confidence for the latent variable x_v taking label j. This is the ratio of the max-marginal corresponding to the label assignment $x_v = j$ to the sum of the max-marginals for all possible label assignments.

We now proceed to show how these max-marginals can be obtained from the min-marginal energies computed by our algorithm. Substituting the value of $\Pr(\mathbf{x}|\mathbf{D})$ from equation (2) in equation (6), we get $\mu_{v;j} = \max_{\mathbf{x}\in\mathcal{X};x_v=j} (\exp(-E(\mathbf{x}|\theta) - \text{const}))$ or $\mu_{i;j} = \frac{1}{Z}\exp(-\min_{\mathbf{x}\in\mathcal{X};x_v=j} E(\mathbf{x}|\theta))$, where Z is the partition function. Combining this with equation (5a), we get $\mu_{i;j} = \frac{1}{Z}\exp(-\psi_{v;j}(\theta))$. As an example consider a binary label object-background image segmentation problem, where there are two possible labels i.e. object ('ob') and background ('bg'). The confidence measure $\sigma_{v;ob}$ associated with the pixel v being labelled as object can be computed as:

$$\sigma_{v;ob} = \frac{\mu_{v;ob}}{\mu_{v;ob} + \mu_{v;bg}} = \frac{\frac{1}{Z}\exp(-\psi_{v;ob}(\theta))}{\frac{1}{Z}\exp(-\psi_{v;ob}(\theta)) + \frac{1}{Z}\exp(-\psi_{v;bg}(\theta))}, \tag{8}$$

$$\text{or} \quad \sigma_{v;ob} = \frac{\exp(-\psi_{v;ob}(\theta))}{\exp(-\psi_{v;ob}(\theta)) + \exp(-\psi_{v;bg}(\theta))} \tag{9}$$

Note that the Z's cancel and thus we can compute the confidence measure from the min-marginal energies alone without knowledge of the partition function.

2.2 Computing the M Most Probable Configurations

Another important use of min-marginals has been to find the M most probable configurations (or labellings) for latent variables in a Bayesian network [10]. Dawid [11] showed how min-marginals on junction trees can be computed, which was later used by [12] to find the M most probable configurations of a probabilistic graphical network. Note that the method of [11] is guaranteed to run in polynomial time for tree-structured networks. However, for arbitrary graphs, its worst case complexity is exponential in the number of the nodes in the graphical model.

3 The st-Minimum Cut Problem

In this section we will give a brief overview of graph cuts and show how they can used to minimize energy functions such as the one defined in equation (3). A cut is a partition of the node set V of a graph G into two parts S and $\overline{S} = V - S$, and is defined by the set of edges (i, j) such that $i \in S$ and $j \in \overline{S}$. The cost of a cut $(S, \overline{S})$ is equal to: $C(S, \overline{S}) = \sum_{(i,j)\in E; i\in S; j\in\overline{S}}(c_{ij})$ where c_{ij} is the cost associated with the edge (i, j). For a weighted graph $G(V, E)$ with two special nodes, namely the source s and the sink t, collectively referred to as the terminals, the st-mincut problem is that of finding a cut with the smallest cost satisfying the properties $s \in S$ and $t \in \overline{S}$.

By the Ford-Fulkerson theorem [13], the st-mincut problem is equivalent to computing the maximum flow from the source to the sink with the capacity of each edge equal to c_{ij}. Specifically, while passing flow through the network, a number of edges become saturated. When the maximum amount of flow is being passed in the network, there remains no path from the source to the sink that does not have a saturated edge. In effect, these saturated edges separate the source from the sink and thus by the Ford-Fulkerson theorem, constitute the minimum cut.

Computing the Maximum Flow. The Max-flow problem for a capacitated network $G(V, E)$ with a non-negative capacity c_{ij} associated with each edge is that of finding the maximum flow f from the source node s to the sink node t subject to the edge capacity and flow balance constraints:

$$0 \leq f_{ij} \leq c_{ij} \quad \forall (i, j) \in E, \quad \text{and} \tag{10}$$

$$\sum_{i \in N(v)} (f_{vi} - f_{iv}) = 0 \quad \forall v \in V - \{s, t\} \tag{11}$$

where f_{ij} is the flow from node i to node j, and $N(v)$ is the neighbourhood of v.

Residual Graphs, Augmenting Paths and Flow Potentials. Given a flow f_{ij}, the residual capacity r_{ij} of an edge $(i, j) \in E$ is the maximum additional flow that can be sent from node i to node j using the edges (i, j) and (j, i). The residual capacity r_{ij} has two components: the unused capacity of the edge (i, j): $c_{ij} - f_{ij}$ and the current flow f_{ji} from node j to node i which can be reduced to increase the flow from i to j. A residual graph $G(f)$ of a graph G consists of the node set V and the edges with positive residual capacity (with respect to the flow f). The topology of $G(f)$ is identical to G. $G(f)$ differs only in the capacity of its edges and so for zero flow i.e. $f_{ij} = 0 \; \forall (i, j) \in E$, $G(f)$ is same as G.

An augmenting path is a path from the source to the sink along unsaturated edges of the residual graph. Augmenting path based algorithms for solving the max-flow problem work by repeatedly finding augmenting paths in the residual graph and saturating them. When no more augmenting paths can be found i.e. the source and sink are disconnected in the residual graph, the maximum flow is obtained.

We define the *flow potentials* of a graph node as the maximum amount of flow that can be pumped between it and the two terminals without invalidating the flow balance (11) and edge capacity (10) constraints of the weighted graph. For a node i, we refer the maximum amount of flow that can be pumped from it is as the source flow potential f_i^s and that into it as the sink flow potential f_i^t. The computation of flow potential is not a trivial process and in essence requires a graph cut to be computed as shown in figure 2. The flow potentials of a particular graph node are shown in figure 1(a). Note that in a residual graph $G(f_{\max})$ where $f_{\max}$ is the maximum flow, all nodes on the sink side of the st-mincut are disconnected from the source and thus have the source flow potential equal to zero. Similarly, all nodes belonging to the source have the sink flow potential equal to zero. We will show later that the flow-potentials we have just defined are intimately linked to the min-marginals.

3.1   Minimizing Energies Using Graph Cuts

The basic procedure for energy minimization using graph cuts comprises of building a graph in which each cut defines a configuration $\mathbf{x}$, and the cost of the cut is equal to the energy value associated with $\mathbf{x}$ i.e. $E(\mathbf{x}|\theta)$. Kolmogorov and Zabih [3] showed under what conditions energies like (3) can be minimized exactly using st-mincuts. They also described how to construct the graph for this particular class of energy functions. Their

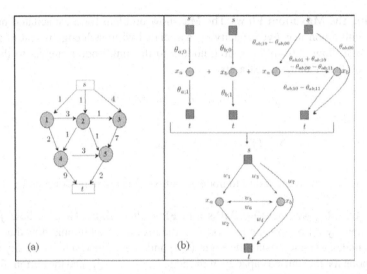

Fig. 1. a) Illustrating the flow potentials of graph nodes. The figure shows a directed graph having seven nodes, two of which are the terminal nodes, the source s and the sink t. The number associated with each directed edge in this graph is a capacity which tells us the maximum amount of flow that can be passed through it in the direction of the arrow. The flow potentials for node 4 in this graph when no flow is passing through any of the edges are $f_4^s = 2$ and $f_4^t = 11$. b) Energy minimization using graph cuts. The figure shows how individual unary and pairwise terms of an energy function taking two binary variables are represented and combined in the graph. The cost of a st-cut in the final graph is equal to the energy $E(\mathbf{x})$ of the configuration $\mathbf{x}$ the cut induces. The minimum cost st-cut induces the least energy configuration $\mathbf{x}$ for the energy function.

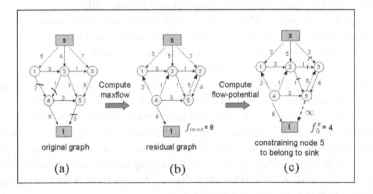

Fig. 2. Computing min-marginals using graph cuts. In (a) we see the graph representing the original energy function. This is used to compute the minimum value of the energy $\psi(\theta)$ which is equal to the max-flow $f_{\max} = 8$. The residual graph obtained after the computation of max-flow is shown in (b). In (c) we show how the flow-potential f_5^s can be computed in the residual graph by adding an infinite capacity edge between it and the sink and computing the max-flow again. The addition of this new edge constrains node 5 to belong to sink side of the st-cut. A max-flow computation in the graph (c) yields $f_5^s = 4$. This from theorem 1, we obtain the min-marginal $\psi_{5;c} = 8 + 4 = 12$, where T(c) = source(s).

work dealt with energy functions involving binary random variables. The conditions and graph construction corresponding to the multiple label case was later given in [14].

The basic graph construction for the minimization procedure works by decomposing the energy function into unary and pairwise energy terms. The MRF energy (3) can be written as:

$$E(\mathbf{x}|\theta) = \theta_{\text{const}} + \sum_{v \in V, i \in \mathcal{X}_v} \theta_{v;i}\delta_i(x_v) + \sum_{(s,t) \in E, (j,k) \in (\mathcal{X}_s, \mathcal{X}_t)} \theta_{st;jk}\delta_j(x_s)\delta_k(x_t), \quad (12)$$

where $\theta_{v;i}$ is the penalty for assigning label i to latent variable x_v, $\theta_{st;ij}$ is the penalty for assigning labels i and j to the latent variables x_s and x_t, and each $\delta_j(x_s)$ is an indicator function which is defined as:

$$\delta_j(x_s) = \begin{cases} 1 \text{ if } x_s = j, \text{where} j \in \mathcal{X}_s \\ 0 \text{ otherwise} \end{cases},$$

These individual energy terms are represented by weighted edges in the graph. Multiple edges between the same nodes are merged into a single edge by adding their weights. Finally, the st-mincut is found in this graph, which provides us with the MAP solution. The cost of this cut corresponds to the energy of the MAP solution. The labelling of a latent variable depends on the terminal it is disconnected from by the minimum cut. If the node is disconnected from the source, we assign it the value zero and one otherwise. The graph construction for a two node MRF is shown in figure 1(b).

4   Computing Min-marginals Using Graph Cuts

We will now explain how min-marginal energies can be computed using graph cuts. The total flow f_{total} flowing from the source s to the sink t in a graph is equal to the difference between the total amount of flow coming in to a terminal node and that going out i.e.

$$f_{\text{total}} = \sum_{i \in N(s)} (f_{si} - f_{is}) = \sum_{i \in N(t)} (f_{it} - f_{ti}). \quad (13)$$

We know that the cost of the st-mincut in an energy representing graph is equal to the energy of the optimal configuration. From the Ford-Fulkerson theorem, this is also equal to the maximum amount of flow $f_{\max}$ that can be transferred from the source to the sink. Hence from the minimum energy (4) and total flow equation (13) for a graph in which maxflow has been achieved i.e. $f_{\text{total}} = f_{\max}$, we obtain:

$$\psi(\theta) = \min_{\mathbf{x} \in \mathcal{X}} E(\mathbf{x}|\theta) = f_{\max} = \sum_{i \in N(s)} (f_{si} - f_{is}). \quad (14)$$

Note that flow cannot be pushed into the source i.e. $f_{is} = 0, \forall i \in V$. Thus, we get $\psi(\theta) = \sum_{i \in N(s)} f_{si}$. The MAP configuration $\mathbf{x}^*$ of a MRF is the one having the least energy and is defined as $\mathbf{x}^* = \arg\min_{\mathbf{x} \in \mathcal{X}} E(\mathbf{x}|\theta)$. The min-marginals corresponding to the optimal label assignments for the latent variables are equal to the minimum energy i.e.

$$\psi_{v;x_v^*}(\theta) = \min_{\mathbf{x} \in \mathcal{X}, x_v = x_v^*} E(\mathbf{x}|\theta) = \psi(\theta) \quad (15)$$

where x_v^* is the label given to the latent variable x_v in the MAP configuration $\mathbf{x}^*$. Thus the maximum flow equals the min-marginals for the case when the latent variables take their respective MAP labels. The min-marginal energy $\psi_{v;x_v^-}(\theta)$ corresponding to a non-optimal label x_v^- can be computed by finding the minimum value of the energy function projection E' obtained by constraining the value of x_v to x_v^- as:

$$\psi_{v;x_v^-}(\theta) = \min_{\mathbf{x} \in \mathcal{X}, x_v = x_v^-} E(\mathbf{x}|\theta) = \min_{(\mathbf{x} - x_v) \in (\mathcal{X} - \mathcal{X}_v)} E(x_1, .., x_v^-, x_{v+1}..x_n|\theta). \quad (16)$$

In the next paragraph, we will show that this constraint can be enforced in the original graph construction used for minimizing $E(x|\theta)$ by modifying certain edge weights which make sure that the latent variable x_v takes the label x_v^-. The exact modifications needed in the graph for the binary label case are given first while those required in the graph for the multi-label case are discussed later.

Min-marginals and Flow potentials. We now show how in the case of binary variables, flow-potentials in the residual graph $G(f_{\max})$ are related to the min-marginal energy values. We will use a and b to represent the MAP and non-MAP label respectively.

Theorem 1. *The min-marginal energy of a binary latent variable x_v is equal to the sum of the max-flow and the flow-potential of the node representing it in the residual graph corresponding to the max-flow solution $G(f_{\max})$ i.e.*

$$\psi_{v;j}(\theta) = \min_{x \in \mathcal{X}, x_v = j} E(\mathbf{x}|\theta) = \psi(\theta) + f_v^{T(j)} = f_{\max} + f_v^{T(j)} \quad (17)$$

where $T(j)$ is the terminal corresponding to the label j, and $f_{\max}$ is the value of the maximum flow in the graph G representing the energy function $E(\mathbf{x}|\theta)$.

Proof. The proof is trivial for the case where the latent variable takes the optimal label. We already know that the value of the min-marginal $\psi_{v;a}(\theta)$ is equal to the lowest energy $\psi(\theta)$. Further, the flow potential of the node for the terminal corresponding to the label assignment is zero since the node is disconnected from the terminal $T(a)$ by the minimum cut[4].

We already know from (16) that the min-marginal $\psi_{v;b}(\theta)$ corresponding to the non-optimal label b can be computed by finding the minimum value of the function E under the constraint $x_v = b$. This constraint can be enforced in our original graph (used for minimizing $E(x|\theta)$) by adding an edge with infinite weight between the graph node and the terminal corresponding to the label a, and then computing the st-mincut on this updated graph[5]. It can be easily seen that the additional amount of flow that would now

---

[4] The amount of flow that can be transferred from the node to the terminal $T(a)$ in the residual graph is zero since otherwise it would contradict our assumption that the max-flow solution has been achieved.

[5] Adding an infinite weight edge between the node and the terminal $T(a)$ is equivalent to putting a hard constraint on the variable x_v to have the label b. Please note that the addition of an infinite weight edge can be realized by using an edge whose weight is more than the sum of all other edges incident on the node. This condition would make sure that the edge is not saturated during the max-flow computation.

flow from the source to the sink is equal to the flow potential $f_v^{T(b)}$ of the node. Thus the value of the max-flow now becomes equal to $\psi(\theta) + f_v^{T(b)}$ where $T(b)$ is the terminal corresponding to the label b. The whole process is shown graphically in figure 2.

We have shown how minimizing an energy function with constraints on the value of a latent variable, is equivalent to computing the flow potentials of a node in the residual graph $G(f_{\max})$. Note that a similar procedure can be used to compute the min-marginal $\psi_{uv;ij}(\theta)$ by taking the projection and enforcing hard constraints on pairs of latent variables.

Extension to Multiple Labels. Graph cuts can also be used to optimize certain specific energy functions which involve variables taking multiple labels [14]. Graphs representing the projections of such energy functions can be obtained by incorporating hard constraints in a fashion analogous to the one used for binary variables. In the graph construction for multiple labels proposed by Ishikawa [14], the label of a discrete latent variable is found by observing which data edge is cut. The value of a variable can be constrained or 'fixed' in this graph construction by making sure that the data edge corresponding to the particular label is cut. This can be realized by adding edges of infinite capacity from the source and the sink to the tail and head node of the edge respectively as shown in figure 3. The cost of the st-mincut in this modified graph will give the exact value of min-marginal energy associated with that particular labelling.

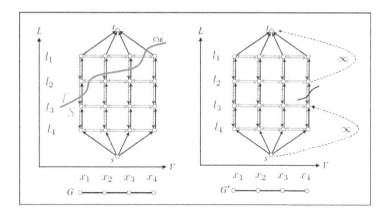

Fig. 3. Graph construction for projections of energy functions involving multiple labels. The first graph G shows the graph construction proposed by Ishikawa [14] for minimizing energy functions representing MRFs involving latent variables which can take more than 2 labels. All the label sets $\mathcal{X}_v \ \forall v \in V$, consist of 4 labels namely l_1, l_2, l_3 and l_4. The MAP configuration of the MRF induced by the st-mincut is found by observing which data edges are cut (data edges are depicted as black arrows). Four of them are in the cut here (as seen in graph G), representing the assignments $x_1 = l_2$, $x_2 = l_3$, $x_3 = l_3$, and $x_4 = l_4$. The graph G' representing the projection $E' = E(x_1, x_2, x_3, l_2)$ can be obtained by inserting infinite capacity edges from the source and the sink to the tail and head node respectively of the edge representing the label l_2 for latent variable x_4.

4.1 Minimizing Energy Function Projections Using Dynamic Graph Cuts

Having shown how min-marginals can be computed using graph cuts, we now explain how this can be done efficiently. As explained in the proof of theorem 1, we can compute min-marginals by minimizing projections of the energy function. It might be thought that such a process is extremely computationally expensive as a graph cut has to be computed for each min-marginal computation. While modifying the graph in order to minimize the projection E' of the energy function, we observed that only a few edge weights have to be changed in the original graph[6] as seen in figure 2, where only one infinite capacity edge had to inserted in the graph. In our earlier work [6], we had showed that the st-mincut can be recomputed rapidly for such minimal changes in the problem by using the dynamic graph cut algorithm. The dynamic graph cut algorithm works by updating the residual graph obtained from the previous minimization procedure to reflect the changes in the problem. It then recomputes the st-mincut on this updated residual graph. This scheme enables extremely fast computation of the st-mincut when the number of changes in the problem are few. Our proposed algorithm is given in Table 1.

Table 1. Algorithm for computing min-marginal energies using dynamic graph cuts

1. Construct graph G for minimizing the MRF energy E.
2. Compute the maximum s-t flow in the graph. This induces the residual graph G_r consisting of unsaturated edges.
3. If a label assignment is included in the MAP solution obtained in step 2, then the corresponding min-marginal is equal to the energy of the MAP solution.
4. For computing each remaining min-marginal, perform the following operations:
(a) Obtain the energy projection E' corresponding to the latent variable assignment.
(b) Construct the graph G' to minimize E'.
(c) Use dynamic updates as given in [6] to make G_r consistent with G', thus obtaining the new graph G_r'.
(d) Compute the min-marginal by minimizing E' using the dynamic st-mincut algorithm [6] on G_r'.

4.2 Algorithmic Complexity and Experimental Evaluation

We now discuss issues related to the complexity of the algorithm shown in Table 1. Note that in step (4d) of the algorithm, the amount of flow computed is equal to the difference in the min-marginal $\psi_{v;j}(\theta)$ of the particular label assignment and the minimum energy $\psi(\theta)$. Let $\mathcal{Q}$ be the set of all label assignments whose corresponding min-marginals have to be computed. Then the number of augmenting paths to be found during the whole algorithm is bounded from above by: $U = \psi(\theta) + \sum_{q \in \mathcal{Q}}(\psi_q(\theta) - \psi(\theta))$. For the case of binary random variables, assuming that we want to compute all latent variable min-marginals i.e. $\mathcal{Q} = \{(u;i) : u \in V, i \in \mathcal{X}_v\}$ and $q_{max} = \max_{q \in \mathcal{Q}}(\psi_q(\theta) - \psi(\theta))$, the complexity of the above algorithm becomes $O((\psi(\theta) + nq_{max})T(n, m))$, where

---

[6] The exact number of edge weights that have to be changed is of the order of the number of variables whose value is being fixed for obtaining the projection.

Table 2. Times (in seconds) taken for min-marginal computation for binary random variables. For a sequence of randomly generated MRFs of a particular size and neighbourhood system, a pair of times is given in each cell of the table. On the left is the average time taken to compute the MAP solution using a single graph cut while on the right is the average time taken to compute the min-marginals corresponding to all latent variable label assignments.

MRF size	10^5	2×10^5	4×10^5	8×10^5
4-neighbourhood	0.18, 0.70	0.46, 1.34	0.92, 3.156	2.17, 8.21
8-neighbourhood	0.40, 1.53	1.39, 3.59	2.42, 8.50	5.12, 15.61

$T(n, m)$ is the complexity of finding an augmenting path in the graph with n nodes and m edges and pushing flow through it. Although the worst case complexity $T(n, m)$ of the augmentation operation is $O(m)$, we observe experimentally that using the dual search tree algorithm of [5], we can get a much better amortized time performance. The average time taken by our algorithm for computing the min-marginals in random MRFs of different sizes is shown in Table 2.

5 Applications of Min-marginals

Min-marginal energies have been used for a number of different purposes. One of the most important of these has been to compute the M most probable configurations of a MRF [10]. Prior to this work, the use of min-marginals was severely restricted because they were computationally expensive to compute for MRFs having a large number of latent variables. However, our new algorithm is able to handle a MRF of far larger size which opens up possibilities for many new applications. For instance, in the experiments shown in figure 4, the time taken for all min-marginal computations for a MRF consisting of 2×10^5 binary latent variables was 1.2 seconds which is roughly four times the time taken for a single graph cut. Next, we show how min-marginals can be used to obtain a confidence value for any pixel label assignment in the image segmentation problem.

Min-marginals as a Confidence Measure. We have shown in section 2.1 how min-marginals can be used to compute a confidence measure for any latent variable assignment in a MRF. Figure 4 shows the confidence values obtained for a MRF used for modeling the two label (foreground and background) image-segmentation problem as defined in [8]. Note that ideally we would like the confidence map to be black and white showing extremely 'low' or 'high' confidence for a particular label assignment. However, as can be seen from the result, the confidence map contains regions of different shades of grey. Such confidence maps can be used to direct user interaction in the context of interactive image segmentation. In order to remove the ambiguity in the solution, the user could give additional cues in the grey regions.

Recently, a number of image segmentation method have been proposed which couple MRFs with prior information about the shape of the object being segmented. In a separate work within this volume [15], we describe how a shape prior generated using an articulated human model can be integrated with the MRF used to solve the image

Fig. 4. Image segmentation with max-marginal probabilities. The first image is a frame of the movie Run Lola Run. The second shows the binary foreground-background segmentation where the aim was to segment out the human. The third and fourth images shows the confidence values obtained by our algorithm for assigning pixels to be foreground and background respectively. In the image, the max-marginal probability is represented in terms of decreasing intensity of the pixel. Our algorithm took 1.2 seconds for computing the max-marginal probabilities for each latent variable label assignment. The time taken to compute the MAP solution was 0.3 seconds.

Fig. 5. Effect of incorporating a shape prior on the confidence values. The first column shows the original image from which we intend to segment out the human. The images in the first row are the result of using only colour information for the segmentation problem. The images in the second row correspond to using a shape prior along with the colour information. In the second column, we see the images representing the difference of the unary penalties $\theta_{v;bg} - \theta_{v;fg}$ for every pixel v. The MAP segmentation is shown in the third column, while the images in the fourth column show the confidence values obtained by our algorithm for labelling pixels as foreground.

segmentation problem. The effect of incorporating a shape prior on the confidence values of the pixels can be seen in figure 5. Our analysis of uncertainty shows that the incorporation of the shape prior in the image segmentation problem gives better results, and reduces the ambiguity in the solution.

6 Conclusions

In this paper we addressed the long-standing problem of computing the exact min-marginals for graphs with arbitrary topology in polynomial time. We propose a novel algorithm based on dynamic graph cuts [6] that computes the min-marginals extremely efficiently. Our algorithm makes it feasible to compute exact min-marginals for MRFs with large number of latent variables. This opens up many new applications for min-marginals which were not feasible earlier. We have presented one such application in the form of obtaining confidence values for pixel label assignments in the image segmentation problem.

References

1. Kolmogorov, V.: Convergent tree-reweighted message passing for energy minimization. In: AISTATS05. (2005) 182–189
2. M. J. Wainwright, T.S.J., Willsky, A.S.: Map estimation via agreement on (hyper)trees: Message-passing and linear-programming approaches. Technical Report UCB/CSD-03-1269 (2003)
3. Kolmogorov, V., Zabih, R.: What energy functions can be minimized via graph cuts? In: ECCV02. (2002) III: 65 ff.
4. Boykov, Y., Veksler, O., Zabih, R.: Markov random fields with efficient approximations. In: CVPR98. (1998) 648–655
5. Boykov, Y., Kolmogorov, V.: An experimental comparison of min-cut/max-flow algorithms for energy minimization in vision. PAMI **26** (2004) 1124–1137
6. Kohli, P., Torr, P.: Eficiently solving dynamic markov random fields using graph cuts. In: ICCV05. (2005)
7. Chiang, Y.J., Tamassia, R.: Dynamic algorithms in computational geometry. Technical Report CS-91-24 (1991)
8. Boykov, Y., Jolly, M.: Interactive graph cuts for optimal boundary and region segmentation of objects in n-d images. In: ICCV01. (2001) I: 105–112
9. Weiss, Y., Freeman, W.T.: On the optimality of solutions of the max-product belief-propagation algorithm in arbitrary graphs. IEEE Transactions on Information Theory (2001)
10. Yanover, C., Weiss, Y.: Finding the m most probable configurations in arbitrary graphical models. In: Advances in Neural Information Processing Systems 16. MIT Press (2004)
11. Dawid, P.: Applications of a general propagation algorithm for probabilistic expert systems. Statistics and Computing. **2** (1992) 25–36
12. Nilsson, D.: An efficient algorithm for finding the m most probable configurations in bayesian networks. Statistics and Computing **8** (1998) 159–173
13. Ford, L., Fulkerson, D.: Flows in Networks. Princeton University Press, Princeton (1962)
14. Ishikawa, H.: Exact optimization for markov random fields with convex priors. PAMI **25** (2003) 1333–1336
15. Bray, M., Kohli, P., Torr, P.: Posecut: Simulataneous segmentation and 3d pose estimation of humans using dynamic graph cuts. In: ECCV06. (2006)

Tracking Dynamic Near-Regular Texture Under Occlusion and Rapid Movements

Wen-Chieh Lin[1] and Yanxi Liu[2]

[1] College of Computer Science, National Chiao-Tung University, Taiwan
wclin@cs.nctu.edu.tw
[2] School of Computer Science, Carnegie Mellon University, USA
yanxi@cs.cmu.edu

Abstract. We present a dynamic near-regular texture (NRT) tracking algorithm nested in a lattice-based Markov-Random-Field (MRF) model of a 3D spatiotemporal space. One basic observation used in our work is that the lattice structure of a dynamic NRT remains invariant despite its drastic geometry or appearance variations. On the other hand, dynamic NRT imposes special computational challenges to the state of the art tracking algorithms: including highly ambiguous correspondences, occlusions, and drastic illumination and appearance variations. Our tracking algorithm takes advantage of the topological invariant property of the dynamic NRT by combining a global lattice structure that characterizes the topological constraint among multiple textons and an image observation model that handles local geometry and appearance variations. Without any assumptions on the types of motion, camera model or lighting conditions, our tracking algorithm can effectively capture the varying underlying lattice structure of a dynamic NRT in different real world examples, including moving cloth, underwater patterns and marching crowd.

1 Introduction

Real-world examples of near-regular texture (NRT) are numerous, especially in man-made environment, such as fabric patterns, decorated surface of architectures, floor patterns, and wallpapers. Effective computational algorithms to handle NRTs, however, are scarce. Although texture analysis and synthesis have been studied in computer vision and computer graphics for years, the geometric and photometric regularity of NRT have not been fully exploited in existing algorithms. Liu et al.[1, 2] first utilized the idea of departures from regularity to analyze and manipulate a static NRT.

An NRT $\mathcal{P}$ is defined as a geometric and photometric deformation of a regular texture $\mathcal{P} = d(\mathcal{P}_r)$, where $\mathcal{P}_r$ is a congruent wallpaper pattern formed by 2D translations of a single tile and d is the deformation mapping [1]. Dynamic NRTs are NRTs under motion. Correspondingly, we define the basic unit of a dynamic NRT *texton*, as a geometrically and photometrically varying tile, moving through a 3D spatiotemporal space. Topologically, the structure of an NRT can be modeled as a network of statistically varied springs. Photometrically, the appearance of different textons are similar but not exactly identical. The

A. Leonardis, H. Bischof, and A. Pinz (Eds.): ECCV 2006, Part II, LNCS 3952, pp. 44–55, 2006.
© Springer-Verlag Berlin Heidelberg 2006

Tightly coupled textons

Loosely coupled textons

Lattice model

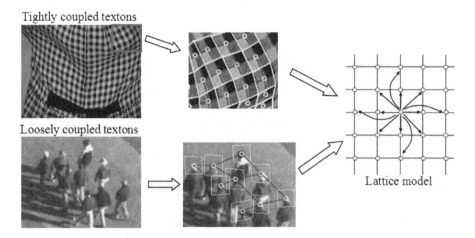

Fig. 1. Lattices (red lines) and textons (yellow quadrilaterals) of different types of NRTs. We model the lattice of an NRT as an MRF where each node represents a texton. The state of a node statistically depends on its twelve neighbors (pointed by arrows).

tracking of dynamic NRT is to treat the deformation field d as a function of time $d(t)$ while maintaining its topological relations. Figure 1 shows the lattice and textons of different types of dynamic NRTs.

In this paper, we further exploit texture regularity to track a dynamic NRT under rapid motion and self-occlusions. One fundamental observation in our work is that the topological structure of a dynamic NRT remains invariant while the NRT going through geometric and photometric variations. Tracking a dynamic NRT, however, is challenging computationally. Because textons of an NRT have similar appearance, a tracking algorithm can easily mistake one texton for another. Furthermore, the tracking problem becomes very difficult when textons move rapidly or occlude each other. Due to these difficulties, tracking textons of a dynamic NRT remains an unsolved problem.

Seeking for an effective computational tool and an in-depth understanding of dynamic NRTs, we propose a lattice-based tracking algorithm based on a spatiotemporal inference formulation. We treat textons of an NRT as multiple targets with a topological constraint while allowing individual textons to vary flexibly in geometry and appearance. Inspired by the physics-based cloth simulation[3], we model the lattice topology as a network of springs and implement it as a Markov Random Field (MRF). We use a Lucas-Kanade-registration-based observation model to handle the appearance and geometry variations of individual textons in the tracking process. Under such a computational modeling of the topology and appearance of a dynamic NRT, we solve the spatiotemporal inference problem using the belief propagation and the particle filtering algorithms. The main contribution of this paper is a framework to track the global structure as well as individual textons of a dynamic NRT, which may undergo rapid motion, occlusion, large geometric and photometric deformations.

2   Related Work

Our work is related to three types of tracking problems: deformable object tracking, cloth motion capture, and multi-target tracking. Image alignment is adopted in many deformable object tracking algorithms where different models are used to confine the deformation space, such as PCA[4, 5], finite element mesh[6], or subdivision surface[7]. These models are not suitable for tracking textons on a folded surface as they assume the surface to be tracked is smooth and non-folded. Recently, Pilet et al. track a non-rigid surface by repeatedly detecting and matching features in an image sequence[8]. They do not handle NRT tracking in which repeated patterns can cause a serious feature correspondence problem.

The goal of cloth motion capture is to capture the 3D motion of cloth. Special calibrated multi-camera systems[9, 10, 11], color-coded patterns[9, 10], or controlled lighting[9] are required to reduce the tracking difficulties due to ambiguous feature correspondences or occlusion problems. Guskov[12] developed an algorithm that can detect and track a black-white chess board pattern on cloth. His algorithm does not work on general NRTs since the black-white chess board pattern is assumed in the detection and image alignment process. Our tracking algorithm can serve as the front end of a cloth motion capture system where no special purpose color-coded pattern or camera calibration is required.

Tracking textons of a dynamic NRT can also be considered as a special case of multi-target tracking. The main difference between NRT tracking and multi-target tracking is that the connection topology among targets does not change in NRT tracking. Modeling the spatial relation among tracked targets using an MRF has been applied to ant tracking[13], sports player tracking[14] and hand tracking[15]. These algorithms may not track dynamic NRTs effectively since topology regularity is not explicitly modeled and utilized.

Existing algorithms for deformable object tracking, cloth motion capture, or multi-target tracking succeed in their respective domains, but none of them deals with general NRT tracking problem under various types of motion and occlusion conditions as treated in this paper. Our approach combines techniques used in multi-target tracking (MRF) and deformable object tracking (image alignment). Therefore, we can track various types of dynamic NRTs under different motion and conditions in a unified framework.

3   Approach

Dynamic NRTs can be categorized into two types based on the spatial connectivity between textons. If the textons of a dynamic NRT are located on a deforming surface where there is no gap between textons, we call this type of texture a *dynamic NRT with tightly coupled textons*. On the other hand, if two neighboring textons are allowed to move with a loosely connected constraint, there might be a gap or overlap between two neighbor textons. We call this type of texture a *dynamic NRT with loosely coupled textons*. Figure 1 illustrates these two types of dynamic NRTs.

Our NRT tracking algorithm consists of four components: 1)**texton detection, 2)spatial inference, 3)temporal tracking, and 4)template update**

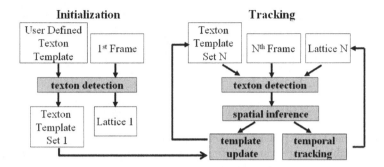

Fig. 2. Tracking approach overview

(Figure 2). In the **initialization stage**, the texton detection algorithm finds all textons in the first frame based on a given template for textons. All detected textons are then geometrically aligned. We call these aligned textons from the first frame *texton templates*. A quadrilateral lattice is constructed by connecting the centers of detected textons. In the **tracking stage**, texton detection is performed at each frame to include any additional texton entering the scene. We handle the texton tracking problem through a statistical inference process consisting of spatial inference and temporal tracking, where the states of a texton (position, shape, and visibility) are sampled and its distribution is modeled by a particle filter in the tracking process. In each frame, a set of sampled states is drawn and a dynamic model generates the predicted states for the next frame. Belief propagation (BP)[16, 17] is then applied to these predicted states to find the most likely lattice configuration based on an MRF-based lattice model and image data. BP also provides the probability of each texton state, which is used to refine the approximation of the distribution of texton states through particle filtering. The above process iterates until the whole image sequence is tracked. In addition, the texton template set is updated to handle the variation of image intensities of textons in the tracking process.

3.1 Tracking Initialization and Texton Detection

In the initialization stage, the user identifies a texton in the first image frame by specifying two vectors t_1 and t_2 that form a parallelogram (Figure 3(a)). Once the first texton is identified, the second, third, and fourth textons are obtained by translating the first texton by t_1, $-t_1$ and t_2. A texton template T^1 is constructed by transforming the parallelogram region in the image to a rectangular region $[1, w] \times [1, h]$, where $w = length(t_1)$, $h = length(t_2)$, and the affine transformation matrix A_1 is parameterized by the image coordinates of texton vertices $(c^{1x}, c^{1y}), (c^{2x}, c^{2y}), (c^{3x}, c^{3y}), (c^{4x}, c^{4y})$,

$$A_1 = \begin{bmatrix} c^{1x} & c^{3x} & \frac{c^{2x}+c^{4x}}{2} \\ c^{1y} & c^{3y} & \frac{c^{2y}+c^{4y}}{2} \\ 1 & 1 & 1 \end{bmatrix} \begin{bmatrix} w & 1 & w \\ 1 & h & \frac{h}{2} \\ 1 & 1 & 1 \end{bmatrix}^{-1} \tag{1}$$

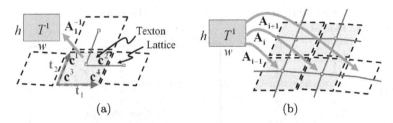

Fig. 3. (a)Initial texton (yellow parallelogram formed by t_1 and t_2) and lattice (red lines). The neighboring textons are estimated by translating the first texton by t_1, $-t_1$ and t_2. (b)Spatial prediction of the position of a new texton.

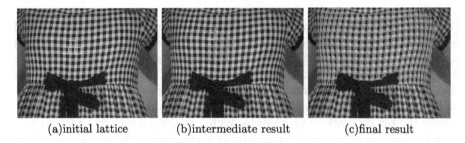

    (a)initial lattice   (b)intermediate result   (c)final result

Fig. 4. Temporal tracking initialization via spatial tracking

Using the first four textons as the basis for the initial lattice, the lattice grows by repeating the spatial prediction and the validation steps. In the spatial prediction step, the vertices of a texton are estimated from existing textons. Let A_i be the affine transformation matrix that maps pixels of the texton template T^i to the texton i in the image. Suppose texton $i-1$, i, and $i+1$ are on the same lattice row or column, and A_{i-1} and A_i are known, A_{i+1} is predicted by $A_{i+1} = A_i \cdot A_{i-1}^{-1} \cdot A_i$[18]. In the validation step, we verify if the texton is valid by checking its associative topology constraints, area and side length difference with the neighboring textons. Additionally, the vertex positions of all valid textons are refined through an image alignment process where a global optimization that involves the whole lattice is performed[18]. The spatial prediction and validation process are repeated until no new texton is detected. A texton template set $T_1 = \{T_1^i\}_{i=1}^N$ is constructed by collecting all valid texton template T_t^i, where T_t denotes the template set at frame t. The initial configuration of lattice is obtained by connecting all the centers of textons. Figure 4 shows texton detection results at different stages of tracking initialization.

3.2 Spatial Inference

Let $X_t = (x_t^1, x_t^2, ..., x_t^N)$ be the configuration of the lattice and $Z_t = (z_t^1, z_t^2, ..., z_t^N)$ the image observation at frame t, where N is the number of textons, and x_t^i, z_t^i represent the state and the image intensities of texton i respectively. The spatial inference problem is modeled as a Markov network[17]:

$$p(X_t|Z_t) \propto \prod_{(i,j)\in\mathcal{E}} \varphi(x_t^i, x_t^j) \prod_{i=1}^{N} \phi(x_t^i, z_t^i) \tag{2}$$

where $x_t^i = (c_t^{i1x}, c_t^{i1y}, c_t^{i2x}, c_t^{i2y}, c_t^{i3x}, c_t^{i3y}, c_t^{i4x}, c_t^{i4y}, v_t^i)$ is the state of a texton and $\mathcal{E}$ is the set of all connected edges. The pair (c^{ikx}, c^{iky}) denotes the image coordinates of the kth vertex of the texton ($k = 1, 2, 3, 4$) and $v_t^i \in (0, 1)$ represents visibility of texton i at frame t. The first product term $\prod \varphi(x_t^i, x_t^j)$ in Equation (2) can be considered as a **lattice model** that models the probabilistic relation among textons, and the second product term $\prod \phi(x_t^i, z_t^i)$ is an **observation model** that evaluates the likelihood of texton states based on image data.

Lattice Model. We model the lattice structure as a pairwise MRF. An MRF is an undirected graph $(\mathcal{V}, \mathcal{E})$ where the joint probability is factored as a product of local potential functions at each node (each node corresponds to a texton), and the interactions are defined on neighborhood cliques. The most common form of MRF is a pairwise MRF in which the cliques are pair of connected nodes in the undirected graph. The potential function in our MRF is defined as follows:

$$\varphi(x_t^i, x_t^j) = e^{-\beta \cdot d_g(x_t^i, x_t^j)} \tag{3}$$

$$d_g(x_t^i, x_t^j) = (\|\mathbf{c}_m^i - \mathbf{c}_m^j\| - l_t^{ij})^2 \cdot v_t^i v_t^j \tag{4}$$

where β is a global weighting scalar that is applied to all springs. β weights the influence of the lattice model versus the observation model in the Markov network. d_g is a function that measures the geometric deformation (spring energy function). $\mathbf{c}_m^i \in \mathbb{R}^{2\times1}$ is the mean position of four vertices of the texton i. This potential function acts like a spring that adjusts the position of textons based on their mutual distance. The rest length l_t^{ij} of the spring is spatially dependent. To handle occlusion, v_t^i and v_t^j in Equation (4) are used to weigh the influence of a node by their visibility status.

The neighborhood configuration of the MRF in our lattice model is similar to the spring connection used in cloth motion simulation[3]. Figure 1 shows the connection of a node where the state of a node depends on the states of its twelve neighbors. It has been shown in cloth simulation that this kind of configuration provides a good balance between structural constraint and local deformations.

Observation Model. We define the image likelihood as follows:

$$\phi(x_t^i, z_t^i) \propto e^{-\frac{1}{v_t^i} d_a(x_t^i, z_t^i, T_t^i)} \tag{5}$$

where the appearance difference function d_a is weighted by the visibility score v^i of a texton so that visible textons contribute more in the likelihood function. $d_a = \sum_{r=1}^{2} \sum_{\mathbf{p}} \|z_t^{ir}(\mathbf{p}) - T_t^i(\mathbf{p})\|^2$ is the sum of squared differences (SSD) between a texton template T_t^i and the observed texton at frame t. $\mathbf{p}$ denotes a pixel location in the coordinate frame of the template. $z_t^{ir} = I_t(\mathbf{W}(\mathbf{p}; \tilde{\mathbf{a}}_t^{ir}))$ is an aligned texton obtained from the affine warp $\mathbf{W}$ whose parameters $\tilde{\mathbf{a}}_t^{ir}$ are computed by the Lucas-Kanade algorithm using the texton vertex coordinates

(c_t^{ikx}, c_t^{iky}) as the initial values (see appendix in [18]). Note that a quadrilateral texton is divided into two triangles and the vertex coordinates of each triangle are used to parameterize $\mathbf{a}_t^{i1}$ and $\mathbf{a}_t^{i2}$ respectively. If textons are tightly coupled, the textured region is modeled as a piecewise affine warp and the position of each texton vertex is affected by four neighboring textons. This enforces hard connected constraints among textons when computing $\tilde{\mathbf{a}}_t^{ir}$. If the textons are loosely coupled, $\tilde{\mathbf{a}}_t^{ir}$ of each texton is computed independently. This allows the observation model to handle more flexible motion, such as underwater texture, or people in a crowd.

Visibility Computation. The visibility of a texton is determined by constraints and measurements related to geometry and appearance of a texton. The constraints, which include topology, side length and area difference with neighboring textons, are used to decide if a texton is valid and can be included in the tracking process. The measurements define the visibility score v_t^i of a valid texton i at frame t:

$$v_t^i = \frac{1}{1+\rho}\left(\frac{s^i}{s^*} + \frac{\rho}{4}\sum_{k=1}^{4}\frac{|b_k^i - b_k^*|}{b_k^*}\right) \tag{6}$$

where ρ is a constant to weight the influence of area and side length variations in the visibility measurement. s^i and s^* are the area of texton i and the seed texton. b_k^i and b_k^* are the kth side length of texton i and the seed texton. A visibility map V is constructed based on the visibility scores of all textons:

$$V = \{M^i | M^i \in (0,1), i = 1 \ldots N\} \tag{7}$$

where $M^i = 1$ if $v_t^i \geq 0.5$; $M^i = 0$ if $v_t^i < 0.5$.

Belief Propagation. The spatial inference is solved by the belief propagation (BP) algorithm[16, 17]. Since the conventional BP algorithm works on discrete variables while the configuration of a lattice is described by continuous variables, we need to either discretize the state variables or apply continuous BP algorithms[19, 20]. For computational efficiency, we choose to use the discrete BP and adopt the sample-based statistics to represent the continuous state variables for each texton. Particle filtering[21, 22] is applied to update the particle set for each texton in the temporal tracking process.

3.3   Temporal Tracking

We adopt particle filtering to represent and maintain the distribution of the lattice configurations in temporal tracking. The belief distribution computed by the BP is used in importance sampling to draw new samples. The dynamic model is then applied to predict a set of states for each texton, and the discrete BP is applied to infer the most likely configuration based on these predicted states.

We use a second-order dynamic model, i.e., the state of the lattice at current frame depends on the states at previous two frames:

$$p(X_t | X_{t-1}, X_{t-2}) \propto \prod p(x_t^i | x_{t-1}^i, x_{t-2}^i) \tag{8}$$

where a constant velocity model with Gaussian noise is used for each texton:

$$p(x_t^i | x_{t-1}^i, x_{t-2}^i) = \mathcal{N}(x_t^i - 2x_{t-1}^i + x_{t-2}^i; 0, \Lambda_i) \qquad (9)$$

Λ_i is a diagonal matrix whose diagonal terms correspond to the variance of the state at different dimensions.

Our approach of combining BP and particle filter is similar to PAMPAS[20] in spirit, however, PAMPAS incorporates particle filter in the message propagation process within BP while we only use particle filter to carry the texton states between image frames. Note that Guskov et al.[10] also used the Markov network to associate color-coded quadrilaterals in an image with the quadrilaterals of the surface model. They did not use the Markov network to infer the position and the shape of the textons.

3.4   Template Update

As the appearance of textons vary during tracking process, it is necessary to update the texton template set. We use the template updating algorithm in [23] where the basic idea is to correct the drift in each frame by additionally aligning the current image with the template at the first frame. After aligning the current image with the previous frame, the computed warping parameters are used as the initial values in the additional alignment process. If the warping parameters obtained from the second image alignment process is close to the first one, the template is updated; otherwise, the template remains unchanged.

4   Results

4.1   Tracking Dynamic NRTs Without Occlusion

We tested our tracking algorithm on several dynamic NRTs under different types of motions[1] (Figure 5). We also compared our results against the robust optical flow algorithm as it is a general purpose tracking algorithm[24]. Although there are more sophisticated tracking algorithms, they are usually designed for certain types of problems (section 2). Due to similar appearance of NRT textons, the optical flow tracking algorithm was distracted by neighboring textons. We also tested our algorithm on a pattern viewed through disturbed water (Figure 5(b)(e)). The appearance of textons vary rapidly in the video because of surface refraction and motion blur. Despite these difficulties, our algorithm is able to track these highly dynamic and varied textons successfully. These two experiments demonstrate that, even without occlusion, general tracking algorithms like optical flow is not suitable to track a dynamic NRT in a video effectively.

The textons of the underwater texture are modeled as a loosely coupled MRF allowing flexible motion of textons. Figure 5(c)(f) show another example of tracking loosely coupled textons. In this example, a texton is defined as a local patch around the head region of a person. The marching motion presents a relatively large global motion and small local deformation of individual textons compared to the motion of tightly coupled textons. Also, the appearance of textons varies

---

[1] All video results can be seen in *http://www.cs.cmu.edu/~wclin/dnrtPAMI/dnrt.html*.

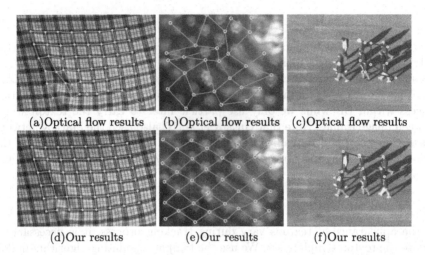

(a)Optical flow results   (b)Optical flow results   (c)Optical flow results

(d)Our results   (e)Our results   (f)Our results

Fig. 5. Comparison of dynamic NRT tracking results without occlusion (robust optical flow[24] vs. ours). (a)(d) is a dynamic NRT on slowly varying cloth. (b)(e) is a pattern seen through disturbed water; there are serious motion blur and reflection highlights in the video. (c)(f) is a crowd motion exhibiting NRT property.

more due to shadows. The underwater texture and crowd marching examples show that our algorithm is able to handle large illumination changes, rapid geometric deformation, and intensity variations in the tracking process.

4.2 Tracking Dynamic NRTs with Occlusion

Occlusion is one of the major challenges in dynamic texture tracking. Textons may leave/enter the scene, or be occluded by other objects or other textons on a folded surface. Figure 6 shows our tracking result of a folding fabric pattern under self and external occlusions. The lattice, visible textons, and occluded textons are shown in red, yellow, and cyan colors respectively. The bottom row in Figure 6 shows visibility maps of textons where black regions correspond to occluded textons and visible textons are geometrically aligned. One can observe that a few textons are occluded in the middle and two occluded by a finger in the bottom-right region in Figure 6(b). When the texton is at the boundary of a lattice, the BP inference result for the texton is less reliable since it receives messages from fewer neighboring nodes. This is the reason why there are some tracking errors in the cyan lattice at boundary, e.g, top-middle in Figure 6(c).

The results of dynamic NRT tracking can be used in many other applications, e.g., video editing, cloth motion capture, and fashion design preview (changing cloth texture). Figure 7 demonstrates a superimposing application as a result of the NRT tracking. For more tracking and video editing results, and comparisons to other tracking algorithms, please see [18].

Although our algorithm can successfully track textons through occlusion, there is another interesting research problem: can we infer the positions of textons when they are occluded? One way to solve this problem is to modify the

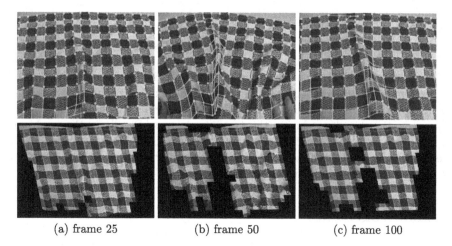

| (a) frame 25 | (b) frame 50 | (c) frame 100 |

Fig. 6. Tracking lattices (top row) and visibility map (bottom row) of a folding fabric pattern. The visible lattice, occluded lattice, visible textons, and occluded textons are shown in red, cyan, yellow, and cyan color. One can observe that there are self-occlusions due to folding in (b)(c) and external occlusion by a finger in (b).

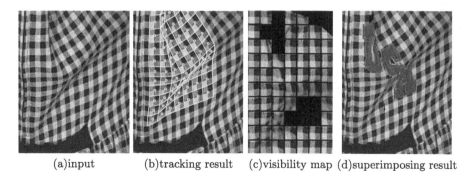

(a)input   (b)tracking result   (c)visibility map (d)superimposing result

Fig. 7. Tracking and superimposition results of a fabric pattern under occlusion

MRF model such that it can represent a folded topology under occlusion. We would like to explore this problem in the future.

5   Conclusion

We propose a lattice-based dynamic NRT tracking algorithm which combines a lattice structure model to represent the topological constraint of a dynamic NRT and a registration-based image observation model to handle the geometry and appearance variations of individual textons. We demonstrate the effectiveness of our algorithm on tracking dynamic NRTs under rapid movements, folding motion or illumination changes through different mediums. There are several remaining future research issues. First, given the captured lattice structure of an NRT on a 3D surface, a shape-from-texture algorithm may be applied to obtain the 3D geometry of the textured surface. Results from this will further expand graphics applications of our tracking algorithm. Secondly, we would like to investigate whether it is necessary to use a varying topology formalization for extremely deformed regular textures. For example, the topological structure for a crowd motion may vary drastically. It may or may not be beneficial to allow adaptive topology during the tracking process. Finally, a thorough and more comprehensive evaluation of various tracking algorithms on dynamic NRT tracking is needed to enhance and solidify our understanding of both the state of the art tracking algorithms and the dynamic NRT itself.

Acknowledgement

We thank the reviewers for their constructive comments; Robert T. Collins for providing the crowd motion video and proofreading this paper; Jing Xiao, Jiayong Zhang, Chieh-Chih Wang and Sanjiv Kumar for their suggestions on our tracking algorithm; Jasmine Collins for being the subject in the dress video. This work was supported in part by an NSF grant IIS-0099597.

References

1. Liu, Y., Lin, W.C., Hays, J.: Near-regular texture analysis and manipulation. In: ACM SIGGRAPH. (2004) 368–376
2. Liu, Y., Tsin, Y., Lin, W.C.: The promise and perils of near-regular texture. International Journal of Computer Vision 62(1-2) (2005) 145–159
3. House, D.H., Breen, D.E., eds.: Cloth Modeling and Animation. A.K. Peters, Ltd., Natick, Massachusetts (2000)
4. Cootes, T.F., Edwards, G.J., Taylor, C.J.: Active appearance models. In: ECCV. (1998) 484–498
5. Matthews, I., Baker, S.: Active appearance models revisited. International Journal of Computer Vision 60(2) (2004) 135 – 164
6. Sclaroff, S., Isidoro, J.: Active blobs. In: ICCV. (1998) 1146–1153
7. Guskov, I.: Multiscale inverse compositional alignment for subdivision surface maps. In: ECCV (1). (2004) 133–145
8. Pilet, J., Lepetit, V., Fua, P.: Real-time non-rigid surface detection. In: CVPR. (2005) 822–828
9. Scholz, V., Stich, T., Keckeisen, M., Wacker, M., Magnor, M.: Garment motion capture using color-coded patterns. In: Eurographics. (2005) 439–448
10. Guskov, I., Klibanov, S., Bryant, B.: Trackable surfaces. In: ACM Symposium on Computer Animation. (2003) 251–257
11. Pritchard, D., Heidrich, W.: Cloth motion capture. In: Eurographics. (2003)
12. Guskov, I.: Efficient tracking of regular patterns on non-rigid geometry. In: Proceedings of ICPR. (2002)
13. Khan, Z., Balch, T., Dellaert, F.: An mcmc-based particle filter for tracking multiple interacting targets. In: ECCV. (2004) 279–290

14. Yu, T., Wu, Y.: Decentralized multiple target tracking using netted collaborative autonomous trackers. In: CVPR. (2005) 939–946
15. Sudderth, E.B., Mandel, M.I., Freeman, W.T., Willsky, A.S.: Distributed occlusion reasoning for tracking with nonparametric belief propagation. In: Neural Information Processing Systems. (2004) 1369–1376
16. Yedidia, J., Freeman, W., Weiss, Y.: Understanding belief propagation and its generalizations. In: International Joint Conference on Artificial Intelligence. (2001)
17. Freeman, W.T., Pasztor, E.C., Carmichael, O.T.: Learning low-level vision. Int. J. Comput. Vision **40**(1) (2000) 25–47
18. Lin, W.C.: A lattice-based mrf model for dynamic near-regular texture tracking and manipulation. Technical Report CMU-RI-TR-05-58, Ph.D. Thesis, Robotics Institute, Carnegie Mellon University (2005)
19. Sudderth, E., Ihler, A., Freeman, W., Willsky, A.: Nonparametric belief propagation. In: CVPR. (2003) 605–612
20. Isard, M.: Pampas: real-valued graphical models for computer vision. In: CVPR. (2003) 613–620
21. Isard, M., Blake, A.: Condensation – conditional density propagation for visual tracking. Int. J. Comput. Vision **29**(1) (1998) 5–28
22. Doucet, A., Freitas, N.D., Gordon, N.: Sequential Monte Carlo Methods in Practice. Springer-Verlag (2001)
23. Matthews, I., Ishikawa, T., Baker, S.: The template update problem. IEEE Transactions on Pattern Analysis and Machine Intelligence **26**(6) (2004) 810 – 815
24. Black, M.J., Anandan, P.: The robust estimation of multiple motions: Parametric and piecewise-smooth flow fields. Computer Vision and Image Understanding **63**(1) (1996) 75–104

Simultaneous Object Pose and Velocity Computation Using a Single View from a Rolling Shutter Camera

Omar Ait-Aider, Nicolas Andreff, Jean Marc Lavest, and Philippe Martinet

Université Blaise Pascal Clermont Ferrand,
LASMEA UMR 6602 CNRS
Omar.AIT-AIDER@univ-bpclermont.fr
http://www.lasmea.fr

Abstract. An original concept for computing instantaneous 3D pose and 3D velocity of fast moving objects using a single view is proposed, implemented and validated. It takes advantage of the image deformations induced by rolling shutter in CMOS image sensors. First of all, after analysing the rolling shutter phenomenon, we introduce an original model of the image formation when using such a camera, based on a general model of moving rigid sets of 3D points. Using 2D-3D point correspondences, we derive two complementary methods, compensating for the rolling shutter deformations to deliver an accurate 3D pose and exploiting them to also estimate the full 3D velocity. The first solution is a general one based on non-linear optimization and bundle adjustment, usable for any object, while the second one is a closed-form linear solution valid for planar objects. The resulting algorithms enable us to transform a CMOS low cost and low power camera into an innovative and powerful velocity sensor. Finally, experimental results with real data confirm the relevance and accuracy of the approach.

1 Introduction

In many fields such as robotics, automatic inspection, road traffic, or metrology, it is necessary to capture clear images of objects undergoing high velocity motion without any distortion, blur nor smear. To achieve this task, there is a need to image sensors which allow very short exposure time of all the matrix pixels simultaneously. This functionality requires a particular electronic design that is not included in all camera devices. Full Frame CCD sensors, without storage memory areas, require mechanical obturator or stroboscopic light source, introducing more complexity in the vision system. Frame Transfer CCD sensors may not reach the desired frame rate or may be costly because of additional sillicium in storage areas [9].

Standard CMOS Rolling Shutter sensors are considered as low cost and low power sensors. They are becoming more frequently used in cameras. They enable adequate exposure time without reducing frame rate thanks to overlapping exposure and readout. Their drawback is that they distort images of moving

A. Leonardis, H. Bischof, and A. Pinz (Eds.): ECCV 2006, Part II, LNCS 3952, pp. 56–68, 2006.

Fig. 1. An example of distortion of a rotating ventilator observed with a Rolling Shutter camera: static object (right image) and moving object (left image)

objects because the pixels are not all exposed simultaneously but row by row with a time delay defined by the sensor technology (figure 1). This distortion may represent a major obstacle in tasks such as localization, reconstruction or default detection (the system may see an ellipse where in fact there is a circular hole). Therefore, CMOS Rolling Shutter cameras could offer a good compromise between cost and frame rate performances if the problem of deformations is taken into account.

2   Related Works and Contributions

This work, is related to our previous one presented in [1], which focused on the development of a method which maintains accuracy in pose recovery and structure from motion algorithms without sacrificing low cost and power characteristics of the sensor. This was achieved by integrating, in the perspective projection model, kinematic and technological parameters which are both causes of image deformations. The resulting algorithm, not only enables accurate pose recovery, but also provides the instantaneous angular and translational velocity of observed moving objects. Rolling shutter effects which are considered as drawbacks are transformed into an advantage ! This approach may be considered as an alternative to methods which uses image sequences to estimate the kinematic between views since it reduces the amount of data and the computational cost (one image is processed rather than several ones). In a parallel work by Meingast [7] (published after the submission of this paper), the projection in rolling shutter cameras is modelled in the case of fronto-parallel motion obtaining equations which are similar to those of Crossed-Slits cameras [13]. To our knowledge, there is no work in the vision community literature on taking into account effects of rolling shutter in pose recovery algorithms nor on computing velocity parameters using a single view. Indeed, all pose recovery methods ([6], [8], [2], [3], [10]) make the assumption that all image sensor pixels are exposed simultaneously. The work done by Wilburn et al. [11] concerned the correction of image deformation due to rolling shutter by constructing a single image using several images from a dense camera array. Using the knowledge of the time delay due to rolling shutter and the chronograms of release of the cameras, one complete image is constructed by combining lines exposed at the same instant in each image from the different cameras.

Two main contributions are presented in this paper. First, the perspective projection model of rolling shutter cameras presented in [1] is improved by removing the assumption of small motion during image acquisition. This makes the model more accurate for very fast moving objects. A novel non-linear algorithm for pose and velocity computation is then described. It generalizes the bundle adjustment method to the case of moving points. Indeed, it is based on non-linear least-square optimization of an error function defined in image metric and expressed with respect to both pose and velocity parameters (rather than to only pose parameters in classical approaches). Second, a linear algorithm for pose and instantaneous velocity computation is developed in the particular case of planar objects. This linear solution provides an initial estimate of the pose and velocity parameters and serves to initialize the non-linear algorithm.

Section 3 of this paper describes the process of image acquisition using a CMOS Rolling Shutter imager. In section 4, a general geometric model for the perspective projection of 3D point on a solid moving object is presented. Image coordinates of the point projections are expressed with respect to object pose and velocity parameters and to the time delay due to image scanning. Section 5 deals with the problem of computing pose and velocity parameters of a moving object, imaged by a Rolling Shutter camera, using point correspondences. Finally, experiments with real data are presented and analyzed in section 6.

3   What is Rolling Shutter ?

In digital cameras, an image is captured by converting the light from an object into an electronic signal at the photosensitive area (photodiode) of a solid state CCD or CMOS image sensor. The amount of signal generated by the image sensor depends on the amount of light that falls on the imager, in terms of both intensity and duration. Therefore, an on-chip electronic shutter is required to control exposure. The pixels are allowed to accumulate charge during the integration time. With global shutter image sensors, the entire imager is reset before integration. The accumulated charge in each pixel is simultaneously transferred to storage area. Since all the pixels are reset at the same time and integrate over the same interval there is no motion artifacts in the resulting image. With a CMOS image sensor with rolling shutter, the rows of pixels in the image are reset in sequence starting at the top and proceeding row by row to the bottom. The readout process proceeds in exactly the same fashion and the same speed with a time delay after the reset (exposure time). The benefit of rolling shutter mode is that exposure and readout are overlapping, enabling full frame exposures without reducing the frame rate. Each line in the image has the same amount of integration, however the start and end time of integration is shifted in time as the image is scanned (rolled) out of the sensor array as shown in Fig.2. In this case, if the object is moving during the integration time, some artifacts may appear. The faster the object moves the larger is the distortion.

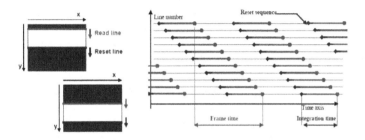

Fig. 2. Reset and reading chronograms in rolling shutter sensor (SILICON IMAGING documentation)

4   Projecting a Point with Rolling Shutter Camera

Let us consider a classical camera with a pinhole projection model defined by its intrinsic parameter matrix [10]

$$K = \begin{bmatrix} \alpha_u & 0 & u_0 \\ 0 & \alpha_v & v_0 \\ 0 & 0 & 1 \end{bmatrix}$$

Let $P = [X, Y, Z]^{\mathrm{T}}$ be a 3D point defined in the object frame. Let R and T be the rotation matrix and the translation vector between the object frame and the camera frame. Let $m = [u, v]^{\mathrm{T}}$ be the perspective projection of P on the image. Noting $\tilde{m} = [m^{\mathrm{T}}, 1]^{\mathrm{T}}$ and $\tilde{P} = [P^{\mathrm{T}}, 1]^{\mathrm{T}}$, the relationship between P and m is:

$$s\tilde{m} = K \begin{bmatrix} R & T \end{bmatrix} \tilde{P} \tag{1}$$

where s is an arbitrary scale factor. Note that the lens distortion parameters which do not appear here are obtained by calibration [5] and are taken into account by correcting image data before using them in the algorithm.

Assume now that an object of known geometry, modelled by a set of n points $P_i = [X_i, Y_i, Z_i]^{\mathrm{T}}$, undergoing a motion with instantaneous angular velocity Ω around an instantaneous axis of unit vector $a = [a_x, a_y, a_z]^{\mathrm{T}}$, and instantaneous linear velocity $V = [V_x, V_y, V_z]^{\mathrm{T}}$, is snapped with a rolling shutter camera at an instant t_0. In fact, t_0 corresponds to the instant when the top line of the sensor is exposed to light. Thus, the light from the point P_i will be collected with a delay τ_i proportional to the image line number on which P_i is projected. As illustrated in figure 3, τ_i is the time delay necessary to expose all the lines above the line which collects the light from P_i. Therefore, to obtain the projection $m_i = [u_i, v_i]^{\mathrm{T}}$ of P_i, the pose parameters of the object must be corrected in equation 1 by integrating the motion during the time delay τ_i. Since all the lines have the same exposure and integration time, we have $\tau_i = \tau v_i$ where τ is the time delay between two successive image line exposures. Thus $\tau = \frac{fp}{v_{max}}$ where fp is the frame period and v_{max} is the image height. Assuming that τ_i

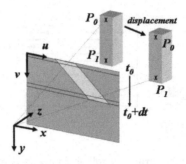

Fig. 3. Perspective projection of a moving 3D object: due to the time delay, points P_0 and P_1 are not projected from the same object pose

is short enough to consider uniform (but not necessarily small) motion during this interval, the object rotation during this interval is obtained thanks to the Rodrigues formula:

$$\delta R_i = aa^T \left(1 - \cos\left(\tau v_i \Omega\right)\right) + I \cos\left(\tau v_i \Omega\right) + \hat{a} \sin\left(\tau v_i \Omega\right)$$

where I is the 3×3 identity matrix and $\hat{a}$ the antisymetric matrix of a. The translation during the same interval, expressed in the static camera frame, is:

$$\delta T_i = \tau v_i V$$

Thus, equation 1 can be rewritten as follows:

$$s\tilde{m}_i = K \left[\delta R_i R \quad T + \delta T_i\right] \tilde{P}_i \tag{2}$$

where R and T represent now the instantaneous object pose at t_0. Equation 2 is the expression of the projection of a 3D point from a moving solid object using a rolling shutter camera with respect to object pose, object velocity and the parameter τ. One can note that it contains the unknown v_i in its two sides. This is due to the fact that coordinates of the projected point on the image depend on both the kinematics of the object and the imager sensor scanning velocity.

5   Computing the Instantaneous Pose and Velocity of a Moving Object

In this section, we assume that a set of rigidly linked 3D points P_i on a moving object are matched with their respective projections m_i measured on an image taken with a calibrated rolling shutter camera. We want to use this list of 3D-2D correspondences to compute the instantaneous pose and velocity of the object at t_0.

5.1   Non-linear Method for 3D Objects

In the general case, the scale factor of equation 2 can be removed as follows:

$$
\begin{aligned}
u_i &= \alpha_u \frac{R_i^{(1)} P_i + T_i^{(x)}}{R_i^{(3)} P_i + T_i^{(z)}} + u_0 \overset{\Delta}{=} \xi_i^{(u)} (R, T, \Omega, a, V) \\
v_i &= \alpha_v \frac{R_i^{(2)} P_i + T_i^{(y)}}{R_i^{(3)} P_i + T_i^{(z)}} + v_0 \overset{\Delta}{=} \xi_i^{(v)} (R, T, \Omega, a, V)
\end{aligned}
\tag{3}
$$

where $T_i^{(x,y,z)}$ are the components of $T_i = T + \delta T_i$ and $R_i^{(j)}$ is the jth row of $R_i = \delta R_i R$. Subsiding the right term from the left term and substituting u_i and v_i by image measurements, equation 3 can be seen as an error function with respect to pose and velocity (and possibly τ) parameters:

$$
\begin{aligned}
u_i - \xi_i^{(u)} (R, T, \Omega, a, V) &= \epsilon_i^{(u)} \\
v_i - \xi_i^{(v)} (R, T, \Omega, a, V) &= \epsilon_i^{(v)}
\end{aligned}
$$

We want to find (R, T, Ω, a, V) that minimize the following error function:

$$
\epsilon = \sum_{i=1}^{n} \left[u_i - \xi_i^{(u)} (R, T, \Omega, a, V) \right]^2 + \left[v_i - \xi_i^{(v)} (R, T, \Omega, a, V) \right]^2
\tag{4}
$$

This problem with 12 unknowns can be solved using a non-linear least square optimization if at least 6 correspondences are available. This can be seen as a bundle adjustment with a calibrated camera. Note that, in our algorithm, the rotation matrix R is expressed by a unit quaternion representation $q(R)$. Thus, an additional equation, which forces the norm of $q(R)$ to 1, is added. It is obvious that this non-linear algorithm requires an initial guess to converge towards an accurate solution.

5.2   Linear Method for Planar Objects

In this section, a linear solution which may yield an initial guess of the pose and velocity parameters that can initialize the non-linear algorithm is developed. Assuming that τ_i is short enough to consider small and uniform motion during this interval, equation 1 can be rewritten, as in [7], as follows:

$$
s\tilde{m}_i = K \left[\left(I + \tau v_i \hat{\Omega} \right) R \quad T + \tau v_i V \right] \tilde{p}_i
\tag{5}
$$

where $\hat{\Omega}$ is the antisymetric matrix associated to $\Omega = \left[\Omega^{(x)}, \Omega^{(y)}, \Omega^{(z)} \right]^T$. When points p_i are all coplanar, the projection equation 1 becomes a projective homography. By choosing an adequate object frame, all points can be written $p_i = [X_i, Y_i, 0]^T$. Noting $\tilde{p}_i = [X_i, Y_i, 1]^T$, the classical projection equation is ([12]):

$$
s\tilde{m}_i = H\tilde{p}_i
\tag{6}
$$

where $H = K [r_1 \quad r_2 \quad T]$ with r_j the jth column of R. As for the 3D object case, the velocity parameters are integrated in the projection equation as follows:

$$
s\tilde{m}_i = H\tilde{p}_i + \tau v_i D\tilde{p}_i
\tag{7}
$$

where $D = K [\omega_1 \ \omega_2 \ V]$ with ω_j the jth column of $\omega = \hat{\Omega} R$. From equation 7 one can derive a cross product which must be null:

$$\tilde{m}_i \times (H\tilde{p}_i + \tau v_i D\tilde{p}_i) = 0$$

which yields the following equation:

$$Ax = 0 \qquad (8)$$

where

$$A = \begin{bmatrix} \tilde{p}_i^T & 0^T & -u_i\tilde{p}_i^T & \tau v_i\tilde{p}_i^T & \tau v_i 0^T & -\tau v_i u_i \tilde{p}_i^T \\ 0^T & \tilde{p}_i^T & -v_i\tilde{p}_i^T & \tau v_i 0^T & \tau v_i\tilde{p}_i^T & -\tau v_i^2 \tilde{p}_i^T \end{bmatrix}$$

is a $18 \times 2n$ matrix and $x = \begin{bmatrix} h_1^T h_2^T h_3^T d_1^T d_2^T d_3^T \end{bmatrix}^T$ is the unknown vector with h_j, d_j being the jth columns of respectively H and D. Equation 8 can be solved for x using singular value decomposition (SVD) as explained in [4].

Once x is computed, the pose parameters are derived, following [12], as follows:

$$r_1 = \lambda_h K^{-1} h_1, \quad r_2 = \lambda_h K^{-1} h_2, \quad r_3 = r_1 \times r_2, \quad T = \lambda_h K^{-1} h_3 \qquad (9)$$

where $\lambda_h = \frac{1}{\|K^{-1}h_1\|}$.

The translational velocity vector is obtained by:

$$V = \lambda K^{-1} d_3 \qquad (10)$$

and angular velocity parameters are obtained by first computing columns 1 and 2 of matrix ω:

$$\omega_1 = \lambda_d K^{-1} d_1, \qquad \omega_2 = \lambda_d K^{-1} d_2 \qquad (11)$$

where $\lambda_d = \frac{1}{\|K^{-1}d_1\|}$, and then extracting Ω as follows:

$$\Omega^{(x)} = \frac{\omega_{12}R_{12} - \omega_{22}R_{11}}{R_{32}R_{11} - R_{31}R_{12}}, \quad \Omega^{(y)} = \frac{\omega_{11}R_{22} - \omega_{21}R_{21}}{R_{31}R_{22} - R_{32}R_{21}}, \quad \Omega^{(z)} = \frac{\omega_{11}R_{32} - \omega_{21}R_{31}}{R_{31}R_{22} - R_{32}R_{21}} \qquad (12)$$

6   Experiments

The aim of this experimental evaluation is first to illustrate our pose recovery algorithm accuracy in comparison with classical algorithms under the same acquisition conditions, and second, to show its performances as a velocity sensor. The algorithm was tested on real image data. A reference 3D object with white spots was used. Sequences of the moving object at high velocity were captured with a Silicon Imaging CMOS Rolling Shutter camera SI1280M-CL, calibrated using the method described in [5]. Acquisition was done with a 1280×1024 resolution and at a rate of 30 frames per second so that $\tau = 7.15 \times 10^{-5}$ s. Image point coordinates were accurately obtained by a sub-pixel accuracy estimation of the white spot centers and corrected according to the lens distortion parameters. Correspondences with model points were established with a supervised method. The pose and velocity parameters were computed for each image using first our

Fig. 4. Image samples of pure translational motion

Table 1. RMS re-projection error (pixel)

Image number	Linear algorithm		Classical algorithm		Non linear algorithm	
	RMS-u	RMS-v	RMS-u	RMS-v	RMS-u	RMS-v
1	9.30	16.00	0.14	0.12	0.15	0.13
2	14.08	17.95	1.71	1.99	0.10	0.09
3	5.24	8.06	3.95	4.18	0.11	0.09
4	11.33	14.21	7.09	7.31	0.09	0.07
5	9.25	11.02	5.56	6.73	0.13	0.12
6	12.26	13.04	1.87	3.02	0.18	0.11
7	9.85	11.56	0.25	0.12	0.25	0.17

algorithm, and compared with results obtained using the classical pose recovery algorithm described in [5]. In the latter, an initial guess is first computed by the algorithm of Dementhon [2] and then the pose parameters are accurately estimated using a bundle adjustment technique.

Figure 4 shows image samples from a sequence where the reference object was moved following a straight rail, forcing its motion to be a pure translation. In the first and last images of the sequence, the object was static. Pose parameters corresponding to these two static views were computed accurately using the classical algorithm. They serve as ground-truth values to validate our algorithm when velocity is null. The reference object trajectory was then assumed to be the 3D straight line relating the two extremities. Table 1 shows the RMS pixel re-projection error obtained using the pose computed with the classical algorithm and a classical projection model from the one hand-side, and the pose computed with our algorithms and the rolling shutter projection model from the other hand-side. Column 2 shows results obtained with the linear algorithm using only nine coplanar points of the pattern. Note that these results are obtained using the minimum number of correspondences required from the linear algorithm and can thus be improved. Anyhow, even under these conditions, the method remains accurate enough to correctly initialize the non-linear algorithm. Results in columns 3 and 4 show errors obtained using respectively a classical algorithm and our non-linear algorithm. One can see that errors obtained with static object views are similar. However, as the velocity increases, the error obtained with the classical algorithm becomes too important while the error obtained with our algorithm remains small.

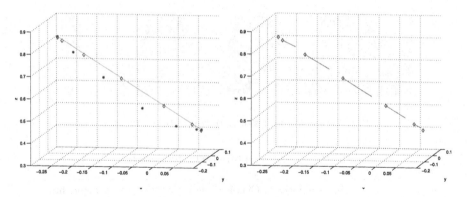

Fig. 5. Pose and velocity results: reconstructed trajectory (left image), translational velocity vectors (right image)

Table 2. Distances from computed poses to reference trajectory (cm)

Image number	1	2	3	4	5	6	7
Classical algorithm	0.00	0.19	0.15	1.38	3.00	4.54	0.00
Our algorithm	0.28	0.34	0.26	0.32	0.32	0.11	0.10

Table 3. Angular deviation of computed poses from reference orientation (deg.)

Image number	1	2	3	4	5	6	7
Dementhon's algorithm	0.00	2.05	4.52	6.93	6.69	3.39	0.30
our algorithm	0.17	0.13	0.17	0.34	1.09	0.91	0.40

Let us now analyze pose recovery results shown in figure 5. The left-hand side of this figure shows 3D translational pose parameters obtained by our non-linear algorithm and by the classical algorithm (respectively represented by square and *-symbols). Results show that the two algorithms give appreciably the same results with static object views (first and last measurements). When the velocity increases, a drift due to the distortions appears in the classical algorithm results while our algorithm remains accurate (the 3D straight line is accurately reconstructed by pose samples) as it is illustrated on Table 2 where are represented distances between computed poses with each algorithm and the reference trajectory. Table 3 presents computed rotational pose parameters. Results show the deviation of computed rotational pose parameters from the reference orientation. Since the motion was a pure translation, orientation is expected to remain constant. As one can see, a drift appears on classical algorithm results while our algorithm results show a very small deviation due only to noise on data.

Another result analysis concerns the velocity parameters. Figure 5 shows that the translational velocity vector is clearly parallel to the translational axis (up to noise influence). Table 4 represents magnitude of computed velocity vectors

Table 4. Computed translational velocity magnitude in comparison with measured velocity values (m/s)

Image number	1	2	3	4	5	6	7
Measured values	0.00	1.22	2.02	2.32	1.55	0.49	0.00
Computed values	0.06	1.10	1.92	2.23	1.54	0.50	0.02

Table 5. Computed rotational velocities (rad/s)

Image number	1	2	3	4	5	6	7
our algorithm	0.04	0.07	0.05	0.01	0.15	0.11	0.12

in comparison with measured values. These reference values were obtained by dividing the distance covered between each two successive images by the frame period. This gives estimates of the translational velocity mean value during each frame period. Results show that the algorithm recovers correctly acceleration, deceleration and static phases. Table 5 represents computed rotational velocity parameters. As expected, the velocity parameter values are small and only due to noise.

In the second experiment, the algorithm was tested on coupled rotational and translational motions. The previously described reference object was mounted on a rotating mechanism. Its circular trajectory was first reconstructed from a set of static images. This reference circle belongs to a plan whose measured normal vector is $N = [0.05, 0.01, -0.98]^{\mathrm{T}}$. Thus, N represents the reference rotation axis. An image sequence of the moving object was then captured. Figure 6 shows samples of images taken during the rotation, where rolling shutter effects appear clearly. The left part of figure 7 represents the trajectory reconstructed with a classical algorithm (*-symbol) and with our algorithm (square symbol). As for the pure translation, results show that the circular trajectory was correctly reconstructed by the poses computed with our algorithm, while a drift is observed on the results of the classical algorithm as the object accelerates. The right part of the figure shows that translational velocity vectors were correctly oriented (tangent to the circle). Moreover, the manifold of instantaneous rotation axis vectors was also correctly oriented. Indeed, the mean value of the angles between

Fig. 6. Image samples of coupled rotational and translational motions

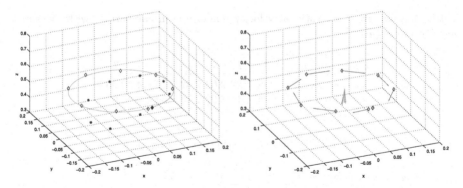

Fig. 7. Pose and velocity results for coupled rotational and translational motion: reconstructed trajectory (left image), rotational and translational velocities (right image)

Table 6. Computed and measured rotational velocity magnitudes (rad/s)

Image number	1	2	3	4	5	6	7	8	9	10
Measured values	0.00	1.50	9.00	11.20	10.50	10.20	10.10	10.00	10.00	7.50
Computed values	0.06	1.20	8.55	10.38	10.32	10.30	9.80	9.90	9.73	8.01

the computed rotation axis and N is 0.50 degrees. Results in table 6 shows a comparison of the computed rotational velocity magnitudes and the values estimated from each two successive images.

7   Conclusion and Perspectives

An original method for computing simultaneously the pose and instantaneous velocity (both translational and rotational) of rigid objects was presented. It profits from an inherent defect of rolling shutter CMOS cameras consisting in exposing one after the other the rows of the image, yielding optical distortions due to high object velocity. Consequently, a novel model of the perspective projection of a moving 3D point onto a rolling shutter camera image was introduced. From this model, an error function equivalent to collinearity equations in camera calibration was defined in the case of both planar and non-planar objects. In the planar case, minimizing the error function takes the form of a linear system, while in the non-planar case it is obtained through bundle adjustment techniques and non-linear optimization. The approach was validated on real data showing its relevance and feasibility. Hence, the proposed method in the non planar case is not only as accurate as similar classical algorithms in the case of static objects, but also preserves the accuracy of pose estimation when the object is moving. However, in the planar case, the experimental results were only accurate enough to initialize the non-planar method but these results were obtained with the minimal number of points.

In addition to pose estimation, the proposed method gives the instantaneous velocity using a single view. Thus, it avoids the use of finite differences between successive images (and the associated constant velocity assumption) to estimate a 3D object velocity. Hence, carefully taking into account rolling shutter turns a low cost imager into a powerful pose and velocity sensor. Indeed, such an original tool can be useful for many research areas. For instance, instantaneous velocity information may be used as evolution models in motion tracking to predict the state of observed moving patterns. It may also have applications in robotics, either in visual servoing or dynamic identification. However, in the latter case, accuracy needs to be quantified by independent means on accurate ground-truth values within an evaluation framework, such as laser interferometry or accurate high-speed mechanisms, before the proposed method can serve as a metrological tool.

From a more theoretical point of view, several issues open. First, the proposed method uses a rolling shutter camera model based on instantaneous row exposure, but it should be easily extendable to more general models where each pixel has a different exposure time. One could also imagine that an uncalibrated version of this method could be derived for applications where Euclidean information is not necessary (virtual/augmented reality or qualitative motion reconstruction, for instance). Finally, another point of interest could be the calibration of the whole system (lens distortion + intrinsic parameters + rolling shutter time) in a single procedure.

References

[1] O. Ait-Aider, N. Andreff, J. M. Lavest, and P. Martinet. Exploiting rolling shutter distortions for simultaneous object pose and velocity computation using a single view. In *Proc. IEEE International Conference on Computer Vision Systems*, New York, USA, January 2006.

[2] D. Dementhon and L.S. Davis. Model-based object pose in 25 lines of code. *International Journal of Computer Vision*, 15(1/2):123–141, June 1995.

[3] M. Dhome, M. Richetin, J. T. Lapreste, and G. Rives. Determination of the attitude of 3-d objects from a single perspective view. *IEEE Transactions on Pattern Analysis and Machine Intelligence*, 11(12):1265–1278, December 1989.

[4] R. Hartley and A. Zisserman. *Multiple View Geometry in Computer Vision*. Cambridge University Press, 2000.

[5] JM. Lavest, M. Viala, and M. Dhome. Do we really need an accurate calibration pattern to achieve a reliable camera calibration. In *Proceedings of ECCV98*, pages 158–174, Freiburg, Germany, June 1998.

[6] D. G. Lowe. Fitting parameterized three-dimensional models to image. *IEEE Transactions on Pattern Analysis and Machine Intelligence*, 13(5):441–450, May 1991.

[7] M. Meingast, C. Geyer, and S. Sastry. Geometric models of rolling-shutter cameras. In *Proc. of the 6th Workshop on Omnidirectional Vision, Camera Networks and Non-Classical Cameras*, Beijing, China, October 2005.

[8] T. Q. Phong, R. Horaud, and P. D. Tao. Object pose from 2-d to 3-d point and line correspondences. *International Journal of Computer Vision*, pages 225–243, 1995.

[9] A. J. P. Theuwissen. *Solid-state imaging with chargecoupled devices*. Kluwer Academic Publishers, 1995.

[10] R. Y. Tsai. An efficient and accurate camera calibration technique for 3d machine vision. In *Proc. IEEE Conference on Computer Vision and Pattern Recognition*, pages 364–374, Miami Beach, 1986.

[11] B. Wilburn, N. Joshi, V. Vaish, M. Levoy, and M. Horowitz. High-speed videography using a dense camera array. In *IEEE Society Conference on Pattern Recognition (CVPR'04)*, 2004.

[12] Z. Zhang. A flexible new technique for camera calibration. *IEEE Transactions on Pattern Analysis and Machine Intelligence*, 22(11):1330–1334, 2000.

[13] A. Zomet, D. Feldman, S. Peleg, and D. Weinshall. Mosaicing new views: The crossed-slits projection. *IEEE Transactions on Pattern Analysis and Machine Intelligence*, 25(6):741–754, 2003.

A Theory of Multiple Orientation Estimation

Matthias Mühlich and Til Aach

RWTH Aachen University, 52056 Aachen, Germany
{matthias.muehlich, til.aach}@lfb.rwth-aachen.de

Abstract. Estimation of local orientations in multivariate signals (including optical flow estimation as special case of orientation in space-time-volumes) is an important problem in image processing and computer vision. Modelling a signal using only a *single* orientation is often too restrictive, since occlusions and transparency happen frequently, thus necessitating the modelling and analysis of *multiple orientations*.

In this paper, we therefore develop a unifying mathematical model for multiple orientations: beyond describing an arbitrary number of orientations in multivariate vector-valued image data such as color image sequences, it allows the unified treatment of *transparently* and *occludingly* superimposed oriented structures. Based on this model, we derive novel estimation schemes for an arbitrary number of superimposed orientations in bivariate images as well as for double orientations in signals of arbitrary signal dimensionality. The estimated orientations themselves, but also features like the number of local orientations or the angles between multiple orientations (which are invariant under rotation) can be used for various inspection, tracking and segmentation problems. We evaluate the performance of our framework on both synthetic and real data.

1 Introduction: (Single) Orientation Estimation

Local orientations are an important low level feature for analyzing and understanding multivariate data. The basis for the concept of orientations is the important observation that signal gradients usually vary much slower than the signal itself. However, fast variations of gradients *do* appear in signals, for instance at corners in image data. In this paper, we want to promote the perspective that limitations of the orientation concept can be overcome by considering multiple signal orientations, thus making the concept of orientations even more fundamental for signal analysis. But first, let us review single orientation estimation.

1.1 The Structure Tensor

Let $x \in \mathbb{R}^N$ be a vector in N-dimensional space. Then a function of x, e.g. $s(x)$, defines a multivariate[1] signal. Such a signal is called locally *oriented* in some region Ω if it is constant along parallel lines, i.e.

---

[1] The signal s is scalar-valued and therefore *one-dimensional*. But it depends on a multidimensional vector and is therefore correctly called a *multivariate* (here: N-variate) signal. *Multidimensional* signals also exist in the orientation estimation context, for instance color images (which are three-dimensional and bivariate).

A. Leonardis, H. Bischof, and A. Pinz (Eds.): ECCV 2006, Part II, LNCS 3952, pp. 69–82, 2006.
© Springer-Verlag Berlin Heidelberg 2006

$$s(\boldsymbol{x} + \lambda\boldsymbol{u}) = s(\boldsymbol{x}) \qquad \text{for all } \lambda \in \mathbb{R} \text{ and } \boldsymbol{x}, \boldsymbol{x} + \lambda\boldsymbol{u} \in \Omega \qquad (1)$$

with some unit vector $\boldsymbol{u}$ denoting the *orientation direction*.

A given signal is locally constant with respect to some unit vector $\boldsymbol{u}$, if its directional derivative $\frac{\partial s}{\partial \boldsymbol{u}} = \langle \boldsymbol{g}, \boldsymbol{u} \rangle$, i.e. the scalar product between signal gradient $\boldsymbol{g}$ and $\boldsymbol{u}$, is zero for all gradients computed in some local neighborhood Ω. The gradients span a subspace in which the signal is *not* oriented and consequently, the orthogonal complement of this subspace is the sought orientation (which is uniquely determined if we can find $N - 1$ linearly independent gradients).

The introduction given so far is one out of several possible approaches leading to the so-called *structure-tensor* approach for orientation estimation which can be found in pioneering work of Förstner [1], Bigün et al [2] and others. For bivariate image data ($N = 2$; generalization to arbitrary N is straightforward), we first compute the discrete derivative of the signal with respect to x and y using convolution with filters f_x and f_y: $s_x = f_x * s$ and $s_y = f_y * s$. With the image gradient $\boldsymbol{g} = (s_x, s_y)^T$, we now define the (standard) structure tensor $\mathbf{S}^{(1)}$ as local integration over the outer product of the gradient:

$$\mathbf{S}^{(1)} = f' * (\boldsymbol{g}\boldsymbol{g}^T) \qquad (2)$$

where f' is some averaging filter. (Widely used choices for f_x, f_y, and f' are (directional derivative of) Gaussian filters.) If (1) is only valid for a single orientation in general N-variate signals, then the structure tensor $\mathbf{S}^{(1)}$ has one zero eigenvalue and the corresponding eigenvector is the sought orientation. For noisy data or model violations, the eigenvector corresponding to the smallest eigenvalue defines the orientation in which the signal is "most constant".

1.2   Related Approaches

The structure tensor $\mathbf{S}^{(1)}$ is not the only possibility to analyse single-oriented structures. As pointed out in [3], higher order directional derivatives also vanish in the orientation direction:

$$\frac{\partial s}{\partial \boldsymbol{u}} = 0 \quad \text{and} \quad \frac{\partial^2 s}{\partial \boldsymbol{u}^2} = 0 \quad \text{and} \quad \frac{\partial^3 s}{\partial \boldsymbol{u}^3} = 0 \quad \text{and} \quad \cdots \qquad (3)$$

which allows to design a wide class of approaches based on combinations of different order derivatives. This freedom can be used for filter design. For instance, the book of Granlund and Knutsson [4] gives a slightly different definition of the *orientation* concept: the *invariance requirement* states that an entity which characterizes orientation must not depend on the signal variations orthogonal to the sought orientation. This defines a much stronger concept of orientation than the one defined in (1). For instance in bivariate signals (i.e. images), it forces us to design an orientation estimator such that it makes no distinction between two especially important types of oriented 1D structures: "lines" (variation on two sides; also called "ridges") and "edges" (variation only on one side). A detector that reacts uniformly on these two types of structures is called *phase invariant* and can be realized with *quadrature filters* [4] and a bandpass prefilter.

If, on the contrary, we are interested in detecting line structures only (and not edges), the second order directional derivative defines a popular filter; this can be traced back to [5]. A recent PAMI paper [6] also discusses line-specific and edge-specific orientation estimation in the context of steerable filters.

Two generalizations of the structure tensor to phase-invariant feature detectors are the *2D energy tensor* defined by Felsberg and Granlund in [7] and the *boundary tensor* proposed by Köthe in [8]. The connections between energy tensor and boundary tensor are analyzed recently by both authors in a joint paper [9]. All these approaches are based on higher (up to fourth) order derivatives.

Summarizing this section, we emphasize that the standard structure tensor approach can be extended with combinations of higher order derivatives in order to obtain advantageous properties. Odd order filters can be optimized for edge detection, even order filters for lines, and mixed order filters for phase invariant behaviour.

2   Modelling and Estimation of Multiple Orientations

Higher order derivatives in the context of orientation estimation also appear in a different line of research: the analysis of *multiple* orientations. In spite of characterizing many important low level image features like lines or edges, the underlying single orientation signal model is much too restrictive for many real signals. For instance, the presence of two oriented textures in a region Ω calls for an extended mathematical model. This observation led to the study of *double*-oriented signals (we will denote the multiplicity of orientations by M, so double orientations estimation means $M = 2$).

For image sequences, double orientation estimation means the study of two independent optical flows; this is the area where double orientation estimation appeared first in the beginning of the 90s in pioneering work of Shizawa/Mase [10, 11] (additive superposition model, grey value image sequences), followed by Shizawa/Iso [12] (additive superposition, grey value images, connection to steerable filters). More recent results can be found in [13, 14] (additive model, images; multispectral signals in the second reference; first theoretical steps towards higher multiplicity of signals beyond double orientations) and [15] (occluding model, multispectral images). However, present day algorithms are still limited to the estimation of double orientations ($M = 2$) in image or volume data ($N \leq 3$). Summarizing the previous work, we emphasize that *model* (additive or occluding), *signal dimensionality* (grey value or multispectral), *N-variate signals* (bivariate images, volumes, $N > 3$), and *multiplicity M* (double orientations or $M > 2$) define four 'orthogonal' directions for extensions of the early multiple orientations estimation work. First steps in all directions have been made, but the unifying theory is still missing. Most importantly, no experiments for triple or more orientations ($M \geq 3$) can be found anywhere in literature.

2.1   Transparent and Occluding Orientations

Two different ways of combining two or more oriented signals s_i (with $i = 1, \ldots, M$) to form a new signal s can be found in literature. The *occluding orientations model* (OOM) and the *transparent orientations model* (TOM):

Multiple orientation models:

$$(\text{OOM:}) \ \ s(\boldsymbol{x}) = s_i(\boldsymbol{x}) \ \forall \boldsymbol{x} \in \Omega_i \qquad (\text{TOM:}) \ \ s(\boldsymbol{x}) = \sum_{i=1}^{M} \alpha_i \, s_i(\boldsymbol{x}) \, . \tag{4}$$

The first model states that we take the first oriented signal if the point $\boldsymbol{x}$ is in some region Ω_1 and so on (obviously, all regions must be distinct and add up to the whole analysis region Ω). For instance, this model is applicable with $M = 2$ if the region Ω_1 corresponds to some object which occludes another object (Ω_2: background), provided that both objects can be modelled reasonably well as single-oriented structures.

The second model, TOM, assumes that all basic signals are present in the whole signal and we observe a superposition of them, weighted with some constants α_i.[2] Computing directional derivatives, we obtain the constraints:

Multiple orientation constraints, derivative forms:

$$(\text{OOM:}) \ \ \prod_{i=1}^{M} \frac{\partial s}{\partial \boldsymbol{u}_i} = 0 \qquad (\text{TOM:}) \ \ \frac{\partial^M s}{\partial \boldsymbol{u}_1 \cdots \partial \boldsymbol{u}_M} = 0 \, . \tag{5}$$

The directional derivative is defined as

$$\langle \boldsymbol{g}, \boldsymbol{u}_i \rangle = \frac{\partial s}{\partial \boldsymbol{u}_i} = \langle \boldsymbol{\nabla} s, \boldsymbol{u}_i \rangle = \sum_{j=1}^{N} \frac{\partial s}{\partial x_j} (\boldsymbol{u}_i)_j \tag{6}$$

and inserting in the left hand side of (5) yields

$$\prod_{i=1}^{M} \left(\sum_{j=1}^{N} \frac{\partial s}{\partial x_j} (\boldsymbol{u}_i)_j \right) = \sum_{k_1, \ldots, k_M = 1}^{N} (\mathcal{O})_{k_1 \cdots k_M} (\mathcal{U})_{k_1 \cdots k_M} = \langle \mathcal{O}, \mathcal{U} \rangle = 0 \tag{7}$$

where we have rewritten a product of M factors (which are sums consisting of N summands each) as a large sum of N^M summands and then as scalar product of two tensors (i.e. sum over all element-by-element products). The whole dependency on the sought orientations is encapsulated in the tensor

$$\mathcal{U} = \boldsymbol{u}_1 \otimes \cdots \otimes \boldsymbol{u}_N \tag{8}$$

---

[2] It is also possible to define the weights α_i as functions of $\boldsymbol{x}$ (instead of constants). Then, the OOM is a subset of the (generalized) TOM. Therefore, the TOM-approach can also be used for estimation under the OOM, though at the expense of needing higher order derivatives.

where "$\otimes$" denotes the tensor product operator. We now can state the multiple orientation constraints for both models. We first obtain the

---

Multiple occluding orientations constraint:

$$\langle \mathcal{O}, \mathcal{U} \rangle = 0 \quad \text{with} \quad (\mathcal{O})_{k_1 \cdots k_M} = \prod_{i=1}^{M} \frac{\partial s}{\partial x_{k_i}} \, . \tag{9}$$

Each point in Ω yields one *data tensor* $\mathcal{O}$ and from all these tensors, we have to estimate the sought orientation tensor $\mathcal{U}$ which is orthogonal (i.e. has scalar product zero) to the given data tensors. Both $\mathcal{O}$ and $\mathcal{U}$ are $N \times \cdots \times N$ tensors (all indices k_i with $i = 1, \ldots, M$ run from 1 to N). For instance, in image sequences (trivariate data, $N = 3$), $\mathcal{O}$ contains all possible products of M first order derivates w.r.t. x, y and t coordinates. Analogously, we find the

---

Multiple transparent orientations constraint:

$$\langle \mathcal{T}, \mathcal{U} \rangle = 0 \quad \text{with} \quad (\mathcal{T})_{k_1 \cdots k_M} = \frac{\partial^M s}{\partial x_{k_1} \cdots \partial x_{k_M}} \, . \tag{10}$$

At the end of this subsection, we want to stress the structural similarity of both models: the tensors constructed from signal derivatives are different (product of first derivatives in $\mathcal{O}$ versus higher order derivatives in $\mathcal{T}$), but once we have constructed the data tensor, the computation of the sought orientations (the estimation and decomposition of the orientation tensor $\mathcal{U}$) is *exactly the same.*

2.2 Symmetry Properties of the Data Tensors

The commutativity in the definitions of (9) and (10) is the key to the understanding of multiple orientations. The data tensors are invariant against any arbitrary permutation of indices and therefore have some very pronounced symmetry properties. For $M = 2$, the data tensors $\mathcal{O}$ and $\mathcal{T}$ are symmetric $N \times N$ matrices, but for higher M, we cannot rely on concepts from matrix algebra anymore. We therefore define the *space of fully symmetric M-tensors*[3] as

$$\mathbb{R}^{N \times \cdots \times N}_{\oplus} = \left\{ \mathcal{T} \in \mathbb{R}^{N \times \cdots \times N} \middle| (\mathcal{T})_{i_1 \cdots i_M} = (\mathcal{T})_{P(i_1 \cdots i_M)} \right\} \tag{11}$$

with $P(i_1 \cdots i_M)$ denoting any arbitrary permutation of the indices $i_1 \cdots i_M$.

Whereas the data tensors are fully symmetric, the orientation tensor $\mathcal{U} = u_1 \otimes \cdots \otimes u_M$ is clearly not. But the symmetry of the left operand in some scalar product (like $\langle \mathcal{T}, \mathcal{U} \rangle$) always means that the value of the scalar product does not change if the same symmetry transformations are applied to the second operand (here: $\mathcal{U}$). Hence, if $\langle \mathcal{T}, \mathcal{U} \rangle = 0$, then $\langle \mathcal{T}, \mathcal{U}' \rangle = 0$ with $\mathcal{U}'$ denoting any

---

[3] *Fully* symmetric in order to allow the term symmetric also for invariance against *special* permutations only, for instance the exchange of indices 1 and 2.

arbitrary permutation of the order of orientations in the tensor product $\mathcal{U}$.[4] As a consequence, the original tensor $\mathcal{U}$ *cannot* be recovered uniquely and any linear combination of permuted tensors solves the problem.

However, it *is* possible to describe a set of M orientations with a unique order-M tensor. The key is symmetrization: among all possible orientation tensors $\mathcal{U}$ which are orthogonal to $\mathcal{T}$ (i.e. $\langle \mathcal{T}, \mathcal{U} \rangle = 0$), there is only a single fully symmetric one (up to a non-zero scale factor): the sum over all possible permutations with *equal* weights. This means that we have to estimate the orientation tensor subject to $\mathcal{U} \in \mathbb{R}_{\oplus}^{N \times \cdots \times N}$ in order to obtain a unique solution.

All tensor scalar products can be converted to standard scalar products by stacking the tensor elements to form a long vector. But now, the symmetry properties of both operands call for a slightly modified version of vectorization. Our fully symmetric tensors have

$$k = \binom{N + M - 1}{M} \tag{12}$$

different elements ($\equiv$ degrees of freedom, DOF). Therefore, the space $\mathbb{R}_{\oplus}^{N \times \cdots \times N}$ can be mapped to $\mathbb{R}^k$. We now define

Definition 1. *Let $\mathcal{A} \in \mathbb{R}_{\oplus}^{N \times \cdots \times N}$ denote a fully symmetric tensor of order M. Then we define the mapping* VecSymm $(\cdot) : \mathbb{R}_{\oplus}^{N \times \cdots \times N} \to \mathbb{R}^k$ *with k defined in (12) as stacking all independent elements under each other in some arbitrary but fixed order. Furthermore, we define* VecSymmN $(\cdot) : \mathbb{R}_{\oplus}^{N \times \cdots \times N} \to \mathbb{N}^k$ *as counting the number of appearances (index permutations) of each element.*

Note that the VecSymmN $(\cdot)$ operation only depends on the dimensionality of the argument, not on the entries. Thus, every element of $\mathbb{R}_{\oplus}^{N \times \cdots \times N}$ produces the same VecSymmN $(\cdot)$ result. Applying these definitions to (9) and (10) now allows to generalize the single orientation constraint $\langle g, u \rangle = 0$ (gradient orthogonal to sought orientation) to $\langle \tilde{g}, \tilde{u} \rangle = 0$ with *mixed orientations gradient* vector

(OOM:) $\tilde{g} = $ VecSymm $(\mathcal{O})$ resp.   (TOM:) $\tilde{g} = $ VecSymm $(\mathcal{T})$ (13)

and *mixed orientation parameters* (MOP) vector

$$\tilde{u} = \text{VecSymmN}\,(\mathcal{U}) \cdot \text{VecSymm}\,(\mathcal{U}) \tag{14}$$

with "." indicating element-by-element multiplication. The vectors $\tilde{g}$ are the multiple orientations equivalent of the gradients. In analogy to single orientation estimation, we can therefore define the double [triple, M-] orientation structure tensor $\mathbf{S}^{(M)}$ as spatial integration (i.e. convolution with averaging filter f') over the outer product of $\tilde{g}$ with itself

$$\mathbf{S}^{(M)} = f' * (\tilde{g}\tilde{g}^T) \tag{15}$$

---

[4] Geometric interpretation: we can only estimate a *set* of M orientations and cannot identify them as "first", "second", "M-th" orientation; they are interchangeable.

and the eigenvector of $\mathbf{S}^{(M)}$ corresponding to the smallest eigenvalue will then yield the MOP vector for M orientations. But unfortunately, we cannot claim that this already solves the multiple orientation estimation problem because

a) the MOP vector has clearly too many DOF: k is a polynomial with leading term N^M, whereas M unit vectors only have $M(N-1)$ DOF, and
b) no general way exists in literature how to decompose it into its underlying orientations,[5]

i.e. what we have solved by now is just an intermediate step towards the sought set of orientation vectors.

2.3 Vector-Valued Signals

Based on early work by Di Zenzo [16] and Förstner [17], who first studied gradients of multi-band images, it is possible to derive multiple orientations structure tensors also for vector-valued signals $s(x) \in \mathbb{R}^P$ (for instance color images). Orientation estimation is also possible in such P-dimensional data, but notation gets much more complex. We therefore deferred discussion of multi-dimensional signals to this point where the generalized gradients $\tilde{g}$ have become available.

In principle, for every derivative, we now have to choose between P signal bands. In the transparent model, each component of $\tilde{g}$ is a single M-th order derivative; hence for general P, it gets vector-valued and for the structure tensor, we have to perform an additional contraction over this index, turning the outer product $\tilde{g}\tilde{g}^T$ into a matrix of scalar products.[6] For instance, multi-dimensional TOM orientation estimation for $N = 2$ and $M = 2$ means

$$\mathbf{S}^{(2)} = f' * \begin{pmatrix} \langle s_{xx}, s_{xx} \rangle & \langle s_{xx}, s_{xy} \rangle & \langle s_{xx}, s_{yy} \rangle \\ \langle s_{xx}, s_{xy} \rangle & \langle s_{xy}, s_{xy} \rangle & \langle s_{xy}, s_{yy} \rangle \\ \langle s_{xx}, s_{yy} \rangle & \langle s_{xy}, s_{yy} \rangle & \langle s_{yy}, s_{yy} \rangle \end{pmatrix} . \tag{16}$$

Under the occlusion model (M first-order derivatives), every element of the mixed orientations gradient becomes a $P \times \cdots \times P$ tensor (M factors) and computing the structure tensor means contraction over all M signal band indices. Fortunately, all elements are outer products which turns the structure tensor elements from products of $2M$ scalar values (for $P = 1$) to M scalar products of two P-vectors. Considering $N = 2$ and $M = 2$ for arbitrary P again yields $\tilde{g} = (s_x \otimes s_x, \frac{1}{2}s_x \otimes s_y + \frac{1}{2}s_y \otimes s_x, s_y \otimes s_y)^T$ (symbolic notation!) and then

$$\mathbf{S}^{(2)} = f' * \begin{pmatrix} \langle s_x, s_x \rangle^2 & \langle s_x, s_x \rangle \langle s_x, s_y \rangle & \langle s_x, s_y \rangle^2 \\ \langle s_x, s_x \rangle \langle s_x, s_y \rangle & \frac{1}{2}\langle s_x, s_x \rangle \langle s_y, s_y \rangle + \frac{1}{2}\langle s_x, s_y \rangle^2 & \langle s_x, s_y \rangle \langle s_y, s_y \rangle \\ \langle s_x, s_y \rangle^2 & \langle s_x, s_y \rangle \langle s_y, s_y \rangle & \langle s_y, s_y \rangle^2 \end{pmatrix}$$
$$\tag{17}$$

---

[5] In principle, the MOP vector itself (i.e. without decomposition into underlying orientations) could be used for applications like texture classification or tracking. However, the distance between two vectors in an highly overparameterized space is clearly suboptimal without previous projection onto the space of "valid MOP vectors".

[6] As summation and convolution commute, we can alternatively sum the P structure tensors computed for each individual signal band.

(this equation was also derived in [15]). We can thus finally compute structure tensors for an arbitrary number M of orientations, either occludingly or transparently superposed, in arbitrary P-dimensional and N-variate signals.

3   Solving the Decomposition Problem

Once an estimate $\hat{\tilde{u}}$ for the MOP vector is computed, we first reverse (14) by dividing each component by the corresponding number of permutations. Then the mapping itself can be reversed, thus producing an estimate $\hat{\mathcal{U}}$ which is a fully symmetric tensor, i.e. an element of $\mathbb{R}_{\oplus}^{N \times \cdots \times N}$. However, this tensor is in general not an element of

$$\mathbb{R}_{\circledast}^{N \times \cdots \times N} = \left\{ \sum_{P(i_1 \cdots i_M)} u_{i_1} \otimes \cdots \otimes u_{i_M} \middle| u_{i_1}, \ldots, u_{i_M} \in \mathbb{R}^N \setminus \{0\} \right\}, \qquad (18)$$

the space of *symmetrized* outer products, which we will call the space of *minimal fully symmetric tensors* from now on. Therefore, our estimate does not represent a valid set of M orientations in general. Going back to vector space, we see that the space of *valid MOP vectors* is a subset of $\mathbb{R}^k$, and only in tensor space, we have the means to define both spaces properly: any estimated tensor is a fully symmetric tensor (i.e. an element of $\mathbb{R}_{\oplus}^{N \times \cdots \times N}$), but valid tensors have to be restricted to the subspace $\mathbb{R}_{\circledast}^{N \times \cdots \times N}$. For single orientation estimation, this novel perspective on (multiple) orientation estimation coincides with the known definitions (order-1 tensors are vectors), but in general, only a tensor approach is suited to handle the symmetry constraints properly.

3.1   Multiple Orientation Estimation for Images

For bivariate images (i.e. $N = 2$), we find that $k = \binom{2+M-1}{M} = \binom{M+1}{M} = M+1$. Subtracting 1 for undefined scale, we obtain M which is the same number as $M(N-1)$ (DOF for M unit vectors in N-dimensional space) for $N = 2$. Therefore, the problem of overdetermined MOP vectors does not appear in images. This means that we have to qualify the last sentence of the previous paragraph: for images (and only for images!), the MOP vector is in fact a minimal description of the sought parameters. In images, derivatives are only possible with respect to two coordinates, say x and y. For instance, $M = 3$ yields

$$(\tilde{u})_1 = (u_1)_x (u_2)_x (u_3)_x$$
$$(\tilde{u})_2 = (u_1)_x (u_2)_x (u_3)_y + (u_1)_x (u_2)_y (u_3)_x + (u_1)_y (u_2)_x (u_3)_x$$
$$(\tilde{u})_3 = (u_1)_x (u_2)_y (u_3)_y + (u_1)_y (u_2)_x (u_3)_y + (u_1)_y (u_2)_y (u_3)_x$$
$$(\tilde{u})_4 = (u_1)_y (u_2)_y (u_3)_y \, ;$$

generalization to arbitrary M is straightforward. Every orientation vector consists of two unknowns $(u_i)_x$ and $(u_i)_y$ with the constraint $((u_i)_x)^2 + ((u_i)_y)^2 = 1$ (it must be a unit vector). However, this problem can be reformulated as an unconstrained problem easily: If $(\tilde{u})_1 = 0$, then at least one of the sought orientations is $(0, 1)^T$. Without loss of generality, we therefore can define $(u_M)_x = 0$ and $(u_M)_y = 1$, thus reducing the degree of the problem by 1. Otherwise, we divide by $(\tilde{u})_1$ and obtain the equation system

$$p_1 = x_1 + x_2 + x_3$$
$$p_2 = x_1 x_2 + x_1 x_3 + x_2 x_3$$
$$p_3 = x_1 x_2 x_3$$

with given values $p_i := \frac{(\tilde{u})_{i+1}}{(\tilde{u})_1}$ and the new unknowns $x_i := \frac{(u_i)_y}{(u_i)_x}$. The set of M values for x_i (which can be interpreted as slope of the orientation vectors) are easily found as roots of the polynomial

$$\sum_{i=0}^{M} (-1)^i (\tilde{u})_{i+1} x^{M-i} = 0 . \tag{19}$$

By combining the vertical orientation vectors with the normalized version of all $(1, x_i)^T$ vectors, we successfully solved the multiple orientations estimation problem for images.

3.2 Double Orientation Estimation in Multivariate Signals

For double orientation estimation, all tensors can be interpreted as matrices. Matrix algebra offers a convenient interpretation of the difference between fully symmetric tensors $(\mathbb{R}_{\oplus}^{N \times N})$ and its subset $\mathbb{R}_{\circledast}^{N \times N}$. While the first space is the space of symmetric $N \times N$ matrices, the latter space is the space of matrices formed by $u_1 \otimes u_2 + u_2 \otimes u_1$, i.e. the space of symmetric *rank-2* matrices.

This allows to define a very simple strategy for double-orientation estimation in general N-variate signals. We estimate the MOP vector $\tilde{u}$ and map it to the space of fully symmetric tensors (here: symmetric matrices), taking care not to forget the division by the permutation count, see (14). Let U denote the result of this operation; we now have to find the two unit vectors u_1 and u_2 which fulfill

$$U = c(u_1 \otimes u_2 + u_2 \otimes u_1) \tag{20}$$

for some scaling factor c. From

$$U u_1 = c(c' \, u_1 + u_2) \quad \text{and} \quad U u_2 = c(u_1 + c' \, u_2) \tag{21}$$

(with $c' = \langle u_1, u_2 \rangle$ denoting the cosine of the angle between u_1 and u_2) follows

$$U(u_1 + u_2) = c(c' + 1)(u_1 + u_2) \quad \text{and} \quad U(u_1 - u_2) = c(c' - 1)(u_1 - u_2) , \tag{22}$$

i.e. $u_1 - u_2$ and $u_1 + u_2$ are eigenvectors of U. Being a rank-2 matrix, U only has two non-zero eigenvalues and because $|\langle u_1, u_2 \rangle| < 1$ for $u_1 \neq u_2$, one of them is positive and one is negative. Let λ_+, λ_- denote the eigenvalues and $x_+,$

x_- the corresponding eigenvectors of U ($+$ for positive eigenvalue, $-$ for negative eigenvalue). Then the sought orientations can be found by normalizing

$$u_1 = \sqrt{\lambda_+}\, x_+ + \sqrt{-\lambda_-}\, x_- \quad \text{and} \quad u_2 = \sqrt{\lambda_+}\, x_+ - \sqrt{-\lambda_-}\, x_- . \qquad (23)$$

Given some noisy estimate for U, we can apply exactly the same strategy, now silently ignoring all intermediate eigenvalues which are close to zero (instead of being exactly zero); this yields the closest minimal fully symmetric matrix in terms of the Frobenius norm. Our scheme closely resembles to a method proposed by Shizawa and Mase for trivariate signals ($N = 3$) in [10]. The difference to our scheme is that U was corrected to the space of 3×3-matrices having rank 2 by subtracting λ_2 times the identity matrix with λ_2 denoting the (only) intermediate eigenvalue. In contrast to our scheme, this method cannot be generalized to $N > 3$ because it only works for a single intermediate eigenvalue.

Summarizing this section, we have presented multiple orientation estimation schemes for (a) $N = 2$ and arbitrary M and (b) $M = 2$ and arbitrary N. Again we stress that the decomposition schemes can be applied for both models (occluded and transparent) and for either grey value or multispectral data.

4   Experiments

We tested our algorithms on synthetic and real data. Synthetic data allow a thorough examination of the performance of an algorithm with known ground truth (under some assumed model), while testing with real data gives evidence that this modelling is accurate (at least for specific situations). Both types complement one another.

For multiple orientation estimation, the amount of parameters which can be modified is huge: the number M of superposed signals, the basic signals themselves, their orientations, their respective weight functions in the combination process, the filters used for computing the discrete derivatives, the filter used for spatial integration of the structure tensors, and the level and type of added noise. In our opinion, a thorough examination and testing of an algorithm is only possible with synthetic data and a graphical user interface (GUI) which allows easy modification of the individual input parameters and immediate feedback on the consequences it has for the estimate. Fig. 1 shows our GUI tool which we used to "explore the parameter space". It is enclosed on the electronic version of the proceedings and it is also available for download at www.lfb.rwth-aachen.de.

We found that orientation estimation under the models discussed above behaves rather robust under added noise. Figs. 2 and 3 show two examples for the combination of two transparent resp. three occluding orientations, both for added Gaussian noise with SNR of 6 dB. Thick lines: true orientations; darker thin lines: estimated orientations.

For our next experiment, we used the image of a house (fig. 4) and tested the ratio s between smallest and second-smallest eigenvalue of $S^{(M)}$ against some predefined thresholds. This allows a hierarchical testing of orientedness: if the texture (norm of image gradient) is high enough, then set $M = 1$ and

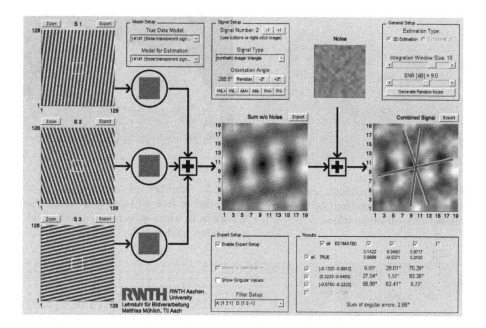

Fig. 1. The GUI which we use for experimentation with synthetic data

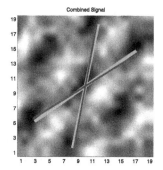

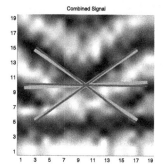

Fig. 2. Estimation of 2 transparent orientations (SNR = 6 dB)

Fig. 3. Estimation of 3 occluding orientations (SNR = 6 dB)

1. compute structure tensor $\mathbf{S}^{(M)}$ and significance value s
2. if s is lower than some threshold c_M, then compute orientation vectors for M orientations model
3. otherwise increase M by one and go to first step (provided that M is smaller or equal than some maximum value $M_{\max}$).

Applying this scheme with $M_{\max} = 3$, we obtain a segmentation of the image into areas of 1, 2, or 3 orientations, plus two classes for "not enough texture" (i.e. image more or less constant) and "not oriented" (which is a reasonable

Fig. 4. An image of a house. Different textures can be characterized by a different number of local orientations.

Fig. 5. Number of orientations (0–3) encoded in four different gray levels. The regions in white were rejected by our orientation model.

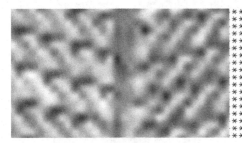

Fig. 6. Image (left) and estimated orientations (right) for each pixel at the part of the image where the two roof parts meet. We can see that the rooftiles are modelled well with *three* local orientations, and the two textures / roofs lead to two different sets of orientation estimates.

interpretation for bivariate data not fulfilling our model with $M \leq 3$). Fig. 5 shows the segmentation result which is based *only* on the number of found orientations. Also note that the image content (a house) is clearly visible in an image with only 5 different values; this demonstrates the importance of (multiple) local orientations as low level images (resp. texture) features.

For each of the regions labelled as single-, double- or triple-oriented, we also obtain the corresponding orientation vectors. Fig. 6 shows the part of the image where the two roof parts meet and it is clearly visible that the three estimated orientations do not vary much within the same roof, but are considerably different in both halves of the image (the 'stars' indicating the three orientations roughly look mirrored), thus allowing further segmentations within the regions having the same number of local orientations.

Another important application for the low level image feature "local orientation(s)" is the definition of invariance properties. For instance, the angle between two orientations defines a measure which is invariant to rotation. Therefore, the

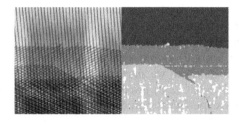

Fig. 7. Left: An x-ray image of metal gratings in a rubber product. Right: number of local orientations for each pixel.

Fig. 8. Left: enlarged part of fig. 7. Right: number of local orientations again; the defect is easily visible.

theory of multiple orientation estimation is also important for the search of corresponding regions.

A third set of experiments was carried out on x-ray images within an industrial inspection application. Fig. 7 shows an x-ray image of metal gratings in a rubber product. The superposition of such gratings gives rise to single-, double- or triple-oriented areas. This means that the theory presented in our paper can be used to detect the number of gratings (i.e. the number of orientations) and their respective orientations vectors.

More specifically, it also allows to detect defects where a metal wire is not aligned properly within the grating or extends beyond the edge. Fig. 8 shows an enlarged part of fig. 7 where such a defect is visible as model violation and therefore increase of orientation number. In the segmentation image, the defect is clearly visible as a blob of triple-oriented and non-oriented textures.

5   Summary and Conclusions

In this paper, we presented a theory for modelling textures composed from multiple dominant orientations, thus extending the well-known structure tensor framework to a unified mathematical model for M orientations in P-dimensional and N-variate signals $s(x)$. Generalization of the signal gradient to multiple directional derivatives leads to tensor-valued entities, and depending on the assumed signal model, this generalization can be done either under the occluding orientations model (OOM) or under the transparent orientations model (TOM). (One can also imagine mixed or intermediate forms which could be a topic for future research.) After the discussion of the two ways for generating data tensors, we have identified a suitable mathematical representation for a set of M orientations, namely the space of *minimal fully symmetric tensors* $\mathbb{R}_{\circledast}^{N \times \cdots \times N}$. We emphasize that this tensor representation is superior to other approaches relying on vectorization. The mixed orientation parameters (MOP) vector – which we derived for general M, N and P – can be a highly overparameterized representation of orientations. Based on this better mathematical understanding of multiple orientation estimation, we presented algorithms for multiple orientation estimation in images (the only case where the MOP vector is *not* overparameterized) and for double orientation estimation in general N-variate data. Both algorithms are applicable also to vector-valued data, for instance color images.

In the experimental part, we successfully applied multiple orientation estimation (in contrast to previous papers: beyond double orientations) to both synthetic and real data. Especially for image data, we showed that estimation of superimposed orientations (here: with $M = 0, \ldots, 3$) provides new and highly useful low level image features which appear perfectly suited for various inspection, tracking or segmentation problems.

References

1. Förstner, W.: A feature based corresponding algorithm for image matching. Intl. Arch. of Photogrammetry and Remote Sensing **26** (1986) 150–166
2. Bigün, J., Granlund, G.H.: Optimal orientation detection of linear symmetry. In: Proc. ICCV87, London, UK (1987) 433–438
3. Mester, R.: The generalization, optimization and information-theoretic justification of filter-based and autocovariance based motion estimation. In: IEEE International Conference on Image Processing, Barcelona, Spain (2003)
4. Granlund, G., Knutsson, H.: Signal Processing for Computer Vision. Kluwer (1995)
5. Eberly, D., Gardner, R., Morse, B., Pizer, S., Scharlach, C.: Ridges for image analysis. Technical Report TR93-055, Dep. of Computer Science, Univ. of North Carolina, Chapel Hill, NC, USA (1993)
6. Jacob, M., Unser, M.: Design of steerable filters for feature detection using canny-like criteria. IEEE Trans. PAMI **26** (2004) 1007–1019
7. Felsberg, M., Granlund, G.: POI detection using channel clustering and the 2d energy tensor. In: Proc. DAGM04, Springer Verlag: LNCS 3175 (2004) 103–110
8. Köthe, U.: Integrated edge and junction detection with the boundary tensor. In: Proc. ICCV03. Volume 1., Nice, France (2003) 424–431
9. Köthe, U., Felsberg, M.: Riesz-transforms versus derivatives: On the relationship between the boundary tensor and the energy tensor. In: Proc. Scale Space and PDE Methods in Computer Vision, Springer Verlag: LNCS 3459 (2005) 179–191
10. Shizawa, M., Mase, K.: Simultaneous multiple optical flow estimation. In: Proc. Int. Conf. Pattern Recognition. (1990) 274–278
11. Shizawa, M., Mase, K.: A unified computational theory for motion transparency and motion boundaries based on eigenenergy analysis. In: Proc. CVPR 1991.(1991) 289–295
12. Shizawa, M., Iso, T.: Direct representation and detecting of multi-scale, multi-orientation fields using local differentiation filters. In: Proc. CVPR 1993. (1993) 508–514
13. Aach, T., Stuke, I., Mota, C., Barth, E.: Estimation of multiple local orientations in image signals. In: Proc. ICASSP04, Montreal, Canada (2004) 553–556
14. Mota, C., Aach, T., Stuke, I., Barth, E.: Estimation of multiple orientations in multi-dimensional signals. In: Proc. ICIP04, Singapore (2004) 2665–2668
15. Mota, C., Stuke, I., Aach, T., Barth, E.: Estimation of multiple orientations at corners and junctions. In: Proc. DAGM04, Tübingen, Germany, Springer Verlag: LNCS 3175 (2004) 163–170
16. Di Zenzo, S.: A note on the gradient of a multi-image. Computer Vision, Graphics, and Image Processing **33** (1986) 116–125
17. Förstner, W., Gülch, E.: A fast operator for detection and precise location of distinct points, corners and centres of circular patterns. In: Proc. ISPRS Intercomm. Workshop. (1987) 281–305

Resolution-Aware Fitting of Active Appearance Models to Low Resolution Images

Göksel Dedeoğlu, Simon Baker, and Takeo Kanade

The Robotics Institute, Carnegie Mellon University
{dedeoglu, simonb, tk}@cs.cmu.edu

Abstract. Active Appearance Models (AAM) are compact representations of the shape and appearance of objects. Fitting AAMs to images is a difficult, non-linear optimization task. Traditional approaches
minimize the L2 norm error between the model instance and the input
image warped onto the model coordinate frame. While this works well
for high resolution data, the fitting accuracy degrades quickly at lower
resolutions. In this paper, we show that a careful design of the fitting
criterion can overcome many of the low resolution challenges. In our
resolution-aware formulation (RAF), we explicitly account for the finite
size sensing elements of digital cameras, and *simultaneously* model the
processes of object appearance variation, geometric deformation, and image formation. As such, our Gauss-Newton gradient descent algorithm
not only synthesizes model instances as a function of estimated parameters, but also simulates the formation of low resolution images in a digital camera. We compare the RAF algorithm against a state-of-the-art
tracker across a variety of resolution and model complexity levels. Experimental results show that RAF considerably improves the estimation
accuracy of both shape and appearance parameters when fitting to low
resolution data.

1 Introduction

Image analysis at low resolution has its challenges. Due to camera blur, objects
appear fuzzy, lose their boundaries, and start looking alike. This degradation
makes detection, localization, and classification tasks increasingly more difficult,
if not impractical.

In this paper, we focus on the tracking performance of Active Appearance
Models (AAM) [5, 7] in low resolution regimes. Fitting AAMs is a non-trivial
optimization task [10]. Traditional approaches minimize the L2 norm error between the model instance and the input image warped onto the model coordinate
frame [5, 7, 10]. While this formulation works well for high resolution data, its
accuracy degrades quickly at lower resolutions.

Any representation, model, and/or algorithm will perform poorly under conditions they are not built for, and the fitting of AAMs is no exception. In this
paper, we diagnose why the traditional model fitting degrades, and propose a
remedy. We show that a careful redesign of the AAM fitting criterion can indeed
overcome accuracy degradation at low resolution.

A. Leonardis, H. Bischof, and A. Pinz (Eds.): ECCV 2006, Part II, LNCS 3952, pp. 83–97, 2006.

2 Background

2.1 Active Appearance Models

An AAM [5, 7] consists of two models, namely the *shape* and *appearance* of an object. Each of these is a linear, Principal Components model learned from training data. The shape of an AAM is defined by a set of landmark locations

$$\mathbf{s} = (x_1, y_1, x_2, y_2, \ldots, x_v, y_v)^{\mathrm{T}}. \tag{1}$$

The shape model, parametrized with $\mathbf{p} = (p_1, p_2, \ldots, p_n)$, expresses any shape as a linear combination of basis shapes added onto a base shape:

$$\mathbf{s}(\mathbf{p}) = \mathbf{s}_0 + \sum_{i=1}^{n} p_i \mathbf{s}_i. \tag{2}$$

An AAM is defined in the coordinate system of the object being modeled. To express object instances in arbitrary poses, a global transform is needed. Following [10], we define four special shape bases to account for similarity transforms (scale, rotation, and two translations), and compose them with the shape model. We denote the combined geometric deformation by $\mathbf{W}(\mathbf{x}; \mathbf{p})$, where $\mathbf{x}$ is a model point coordinate being mapped onto an image coordinate.

The appearance model consists of the mean and basis images. These images are shape-normalized, *i.e.*, they are defined within the base shape $\mathbf{s}_0$. The appearance model is linear, and parametrized with $\boldsymbol{\lambda} = (\lambda_1, \lambda_2, \ldots, \lambda_m)$ as

$$A(\mathbf{x}; \boldsymbol{\lambda}) = A_0(\mathbf{x}) + \sum_{i=1}^{m} \lambda_i A_i(\mathbf{x}) \qquad \forall\, \mathbf{x} \in \mathbf{s}_0, \tag{3}$$

where $\mathbf{x}$ is a pixel coordinate in $\mathbf{s}_0$. The appearance basis images are usually defined at the same resolution as the training images.

In this paper, we consider the simpler case of *independent* AAMs [10], where the statistical dependence between the shape and appearance is ignored. While such couplings have been exploited in prior work, their advantages remain orthogonal to our discussion.

2.2 Traditional Fitting Formulation

Given a set of AAM parameters, the linear generative equations (2) and (3) can uniquely synthesize an object instance. Image analysis deals with the inverse of this process. It aims to recover those AAM parameters which *best* explain a given image. For this end, one needs to define a similarity metric to quantify what constitutes a good match, and a *fitting* algorithm for computing the parameter values which optimize the similarity metric. The choice of this fitting criterion is the main subject of this paper.

In the original AAM work by Cootes et al. [5, 6, 7], as well as its computationally efficient reformulation by Matthews and Baker [10], the fitting criterion was the sum of squared intensity differences between the synthesized model template and the *warped input image I*:

$$\sum_{\mathbf{x} \in s_0} \left[I\big(\mathbf{W}(\mathbf{x}; \mathbf{p})\big) - A(\mathbf{x}; \boldsymbol{\lambda}) \right]^2. \tag{4}$$

Note that the summation above is defined over $\mathbf{x}$, pixel coordinates in the shape-normalized template image. Since this objective function is highly nonlinear in its parameters, iterative gradient-descent methods were used to find its minimum: At each iteration, updates $\Delta\mathbf{p}$ and $\Delta\boldsymbol{\lambda}$ were computed and added to (or composed with) current estimates of $\mathbf{p}$ and $\boldsymbol{\lambda}$, respectively. Cootes et al. [5, 6, 7] assumed a constant, linear relationship between the error image and the additive updates. They learned this mapping through regression on perturbation-based training data. Matthews and Baker [10] explored linearizing the objective function just as in the Lucas-Kanade [2] registration algorithm, and achieved computational savings by switching the roles of the template and input images [9] in computing the warp update $\Delta\mathbf{p}$.

2.3   The Unsuspected Culprit in Low Resolution Problems

Any search method for optimizing the criterion (4) would suffer from a large number of local minima. In some cases, the solution might even be ambiguous. To make matters worse, these difficulties are only exacerbated when the available data is noisy and low in resolution, such as in surveillance imagery.

Let $\mathbf{u}$ denote the pixel coordinates of a low resolution observation I. As visualized in Fig. 1, the fitting criterion (4) prescribes *first warping and interpolating* the image I, and *then* comparing it against the synthesized template. Recall that the summation in (4) is defined over the pixels of the template. The latter is

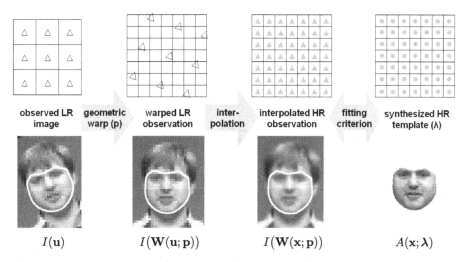

| observed LR image | geometric warp (p) | warped LR observation | inter-polation | interpolated HR observation | fitting criterion | synthesized HR template (λ) |

$$I(\mathbf{u}) \qquad\qquad I(\mathbf{W}(\mathbf{u}; \mathbf{p})) \qquad\qquad I(\mathbf{W}(\mathbf{x}; \mathbf{p})) \qquad\qquad A(\mathbf{x}; \boldsymbol{\lambda})$$

Fig. 1. Graphical representation of the traditional fitting criterion of (4). From left to right, observed images get warped, interpolated, and finally compared against the synthesized model instance. When the input image is low in resolution, significant interpolation is needed to warp it onto the model coordinate frame.

normalized to shape $\mathbf{s}_0$ at the AAM's native resolution, and remains fixed in size. Consequently, when objects appear small in comparison to the AAM, they need to be enlarged through interpolation.

This reliance on interpolation used in the traditional formulation turns out to be its *Achilles' heel* in low resolution regimes. The fitting *criterion* itself becomes increasingly suboptimal (in accuracy) with higher scaling factors. This is an artifact of formulation. Using the same gradient-descent algorithm and low resolution data, but minimizing a more carefully designed fitting criterion, we will show that we can overcome low resolution challenges.

3   Resolution-Aware Fitting (RAF)

3.1   Formulation

We propose an alternative to the fitting criterion (4). In order to better account for low resolution data, our formulation takes a generative point of view and incorporates the image formation model of a typical CCD camera [1]. We feed the AAM and its current parameters into a camera model, and compare the outcome against the observed low resolution image. Mathematically, the proposed fitting criterion is

$$\sum_{\mathbf{u}\in I}\left[I(\mathbf{u}) - B\big(\mathbf{u}; A(\mathbf{W}(\mathbf{p}); \boldsymbol{\lambda})\big)\right]^2,\tag{5}$$

where the summation is now over pixel coordinates $\mathbf{u}$ of the observed image I. The operator B simulates a low resolution image of the object, believed to be what the camera would have captured under current AAM parameters. This

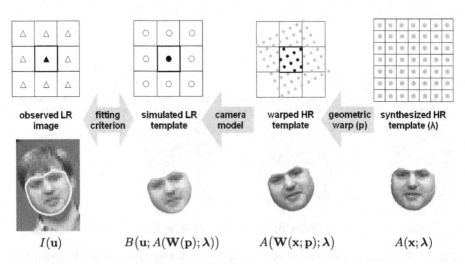

| observed LR image | fitting criterion | simulated LR template | camera model | warped HR template | geometric warp (p) | synthesized HR template (λ) |

$I(\mathbf{u})$ \qquad $B\big(\mathbf{u}; A(\mathbf{W}(\mathbf{p}); \boldsymbol{\lambda})\big)$ \qquad $A\big(\mathbf{W}(\mathbf{x}; \mathbf{p}); \boldsymbol{\lambda}\big)$ \qquad $A(\mathbf{x}; \boldsymbol{\lambda})$

Fig. 2. The Resolution-Aware Fitting (RAF) algorithm simulates the formation of low resolution images in a digital camera. In contrast to the traditional formulation (Fig. 1), the fitting criterion is defined between observed and simulated image pixels.

formulation can accommodate arbitrary camera models and point spread functions. In this paper, we use the rectangular PSF

$$B\big(\mathbf{u}; A(\mathbf{W}(\mathbf{p}); \boldsymbol{\lambda})\big) = \frac{1}{area(\mathbf{u})} \int_{\mathbf{u}' \in bin(\mathbf{u})} A\big(\mathbf{W}^{-1}(\mathbf{u}'; \mathbf{p}); \boldsymbol{\lambda}\big) d\mathbf{u}',$$

where the continuous integral is defined over $bin(\mathbf{u})$, the sensing area of the discrete pixel $\mathbf{u}$. As illustrated in Fig. 2, the blur operator itself is independent of AAM parameters. It simply averages out those template pixel intensities which map into a low resolution pixel's sensing area under the current warp $\mathbf{p}$. To express the integral above in the shape-normalized coordinate frame $\mathbf{s}_0$, we observe that $\mathbf{u}' = \mathbf{W}(\mathbf{x}; \mathbf{p})$, and consequently, $d\mathbf{u}' = |J(\mathbf{W}(\mathbf{p}))| d\mathbf{x}$,

$$B\big(\mathbf{u}; A(\mathbf{W}(\mathbf{p}); \boldsymbol{\lambda})\big) = \frac{1}{area(\mathbf{u})} \int_{\substack{\mathbf{x} \in s_0 \text{ s.t.} \\ \mathbf{W}(\mathbf{x}; \mathbf{p}) \in bin(\mathbf{u})}} A(\mathbf{x}; \boldsymbol{\lambda}) |J(\mathbf{W}(\mathbf{p}))| d\mathbf{x}.$$

In practice, we implement this integration as a discrete, Jacobian-weigthed sum over template pixels,

$$B\big(\mathbf{u}; A(\mathbf{W}(\mathbf{p}); \boldsymbol{\lambda})\big) = \frac{1}{area(\mathbf{u})} \sum_{\substack{\mathbf{x} \in s_0 \text{ s.t.} \\ \mathbf{u} - \left[\begin{smallmatrix} .5 \\ .5 \end{smallmatrix}\right] < \mathbf{W}(\mathbf{x}; \mathbf{p}) < \mathbf{u} + \left[\begin{smallmatrix} .5 \\ .5 \end{smallmatrix}\right]}} A(\mathbf{x}; \boldsymbol{\lambda}) |J(\mathbf{W}(\mathbf{p}))|. \qquad (6)$$

Observe that our formulation avoids interpolating low resolution data, and models the object appearance, geometric deformation, and the image formation processes simultaneously.

3.2   RAF Algorithm

We now present a Gauss-Newton gradient-descent scheme for the minimization of the fitting criterion (5) with respect to $\mathbf{p}$ and $\boldsymbol{\lambda}$. Until convergence, updates $\Delta\mathbf{p}$ and $\Delta\boldsymbol{\lambda}$ will be iteratively computed and added to the current estimates. The derivation below closely follows that of the *simultaneous* algorithm in [8]. Expressing A as a sum of the mean and linearly weighted basis images, the fitting criterion is

$$\sum_{\mathbf{u} \in I} \left[I(\mathbf{u}) - B\Big(\mathbf{u}; A_0(\mathbf{W}(\mathbf{p})) + \sum_{i=1}^{m} \lambda_i A_i(\mathbf{W}(\mathbf{p}))\Big) \right]^2.$$

Consider the Taylor expansion

$$\sum_{\mathbf{u} \in I} \left[I(\mathbf{u}) - B\Big(\mathbf{u}; A_0(\mathbf{W}(\mathbf{p}+\Delta\mathbf{p})) + \sum_{i=1}^{m} (\lambda_i+\Delta\lambda_i) A_i(\mathbf{W}(\mathbf{p}+\Delta\mathbf{p}))\Big) \right]^2.$$

Ignoring its second-order terms, the fitting criterion is approximately

$$\sum_{\mathbf{u}\in I}\left[I(\mathbf{u})-B\left(\mathbf{u};A_0(\mathbf{W}(\mathbf{p}))+\nabla A_0\frac{\partial \mathbf{W}}{\partial \mathbf{p}}\Delta\mathbf{p}+\sum_{i=1}^{m}(\lambda_i+\Delta\lambda_i)\left(A_i(\mathbf{W}(\mathbf{p}))+\nabla A_i\frac{\partial \mathbf{W}}{\partial \mathbf{p}}\Delta\mathbf{p}\right)\right)\right]^2.$$

For notational conciseness, denote $n + m$ steepest-descent images as

$$\mathbf{SD}_{sim}=\left[\left(\nabla A_0+\sum_{i=1}^{m}\lambda_i\nabla A_i\right)\frac{\partial \mathbf{W}}{\partial p_1},...,\left(\nabla A_0+\sum_{i=1}^{m}\lambda_i\nabla A_i\right)\frac{\partial \mathbf{W}}{\partial p_n},A_1(\mathbf{W}(\mathbf{p})),...,A_m(\mathbf{W}(\mathbf{p}))\right].$$

We can now compactly rewrite the fitting criterion as

$$\sum_{\mathbf{u}\in I}\left[I(\mathbf{u})-B\left(\mathbf{u};A_0(\mathbf{W}(\mathbf{p}))+\sum_{i=1}^{m}\lambda_i A_i(\mathbf{W}(\mathbf{p}))-\mathbf{SD}_{sim}\begin{pmatrix}\Delta\mathbf{p}\\\Delta\lambda\end{pmatrix}\right)\right]^2.$$

Observing that B is a linear operator, the objective function to be minimized is

$$\sum_{\mathbf{u}\in I}\left[I(\mathbf{u})-B\left(\mathbf{u};A_0(\mathbf{W}(\mathbf{p}))\right)+\sum_{i=1}^{m}\lambda_i B\left(\mathbf{u};A_i(\mathbf{W}(\mathbf{p}))\right)-B(\mathbf{u};\mathbf{SD}_{sim})\begin{pmatrix}\Delta\mathbf{p}\\\Delta\lambda\end{pmatrix}\right]^2,$$

whose minimum is given by

$$\begin{pmatrix}\Delta\mathbf{p}\\\Delta\lambda\end{pmatrix}=-H_{sim}^{-1}\sum_{\mathbf{u}\in I}B(\mathbf{u};\mathbf{SD}_{sim}^{\mathrm{T}})\left[I(\mathbf{u})-B\left(\mathbf{u};A_0(\mathbf{W}(\mathbf{p}))\right)+\sum_{i=1}^{m}\lambda_i B\left(\mathbf{u};A_i(\mathbf{W}(\mathbf{p}))\right)\right],$$

where H_{sim} is the Hessian with appearance variation:

$$H_{sim}=\sum_{\mathbf{u}\in I}B(\mathbf{u};\mathbf{SD}_{sim}^{\mathrm{T}})B(\mathbf{u};\mathbf{SD}_{sim}).$$

4   Quantifying the Benefits of RAF

We compared the RAF formulation (5) to the traditional formulation in (4). In particular, we compared the algorithm detailed in Section 3.2 with the simultaneous, inverse-compositional algorithm described in [11], which we refer to as AAMR-SIM. This represents a fair ground for comparison, since Matthews & Baker [10] "project out" the appearance variation. We artificially downscaled a variety of input test sequences by a range of scaling factors, and measured each algorithm's accuracy at lower input resolutions.

Independently of the resolution of a given test sequence, we initialized all algorithms with fitting results at the highest resolution. This allowed us to discard initialization quality as a confounding factor when comparing performances across resolution levels. While manual initialization is reasonable at higher resolutions, it becomes increasingly sub-optimal in lower resolutions, jeopardizing the fairness of comparisons across scales. Once in tracking mode, the fitting of each frame was initialized with the parameters of the preceding frame.

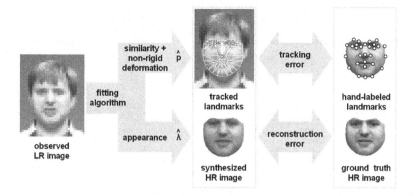

Fig. 3. We define two metrics to compare the fitting accuracy of algorithms. The average landmark tracking error combines the estimation accuracy of the similarity and non-rigid shape parameters. The reconstruction error quantifies how well the underlying high-resolution face could be inferred based only on low resolution data.

4.1 Metrics of Fit Quality

The most appropriate metric of an AAM's fit quality depends on the application at hand. For example, in an object tracking scenario, only the global pose (*i.e.*, the similarity transform parameters) may be of interest. For lip-reading, non-rigid deformations of a speaker's lips, encoded by a facial AAM's shape coefficients, may carry all the information. If the application requires synthesizing realistic face images, accurate appearance parameter estimates may be of importance.

In the lack of a specific application, we defined two metrics, illustrated in Fig. 3, to compare the fitting accuracy of the RAF and AAMR-SIM algorithms. The *tracking error* is the position error of landmarks (such as the corner of nostrils), averaged over the face: this is a combined effect of both similarity transform (scale, rotation, and translation) and non-rigid deformation parameters, as encoded by the estimate $\hat{p}$. The *reconstruction error*, on the other hand, is computed by comparing the synthesized model instance, parametrized by $\hat{\lambda}$, against the ground truth image. In addition, we report estimation errors for the coefficients of the top four principal shape and appearance modes.

For all test sequences included in this paper, only the landmark coordinates were available as hand-labeled, ground truth data. To infer the ground truth values for the similarity, non-rigid shape and appearance variables, we ran the AAMR-SIM tracker at the original resolution of the videos, and verified its convergence (each landmark's tracking error smaller than 1 high-resolution pixel). The resulting parameter estimates were then regarded as "ground truth" values.

4.2 Examples

Before presenting extensive quantitative results, some examples of our error metrics and their temporal behavior would be in order. In reporting Euclidian

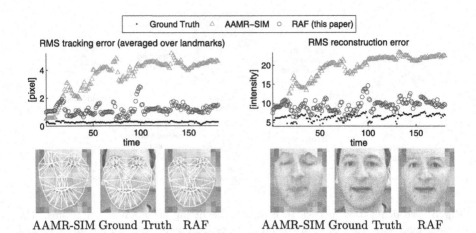

Fig. 4. The landmark tracking (upper left) and reconstruction (upper right) error metrics are plotted as a function of time for a 10-fold resolution degraded tracking experiment. Included images (bottom, captured at frame no. 102) display the mesh fits as well as synthesized model images (lower right). We overlay the latter onto pixel-replicated low resolution inputs (lower left) to demonstrate how well the underlying high-resolution image could be inferred.

distance metrics (as in translation parameters or landmark tracking error), we scale-normalize the estimates so that their numerical values are in high-resolution pixel units. Similarly, we normalize each shape and appearance coefficient according to its mode's variance, and report them in units of their standard deviation.

Fig. 4 plots error trajectories of a low resolution tracking experiment, where the subject's speaking and eye blinking were the major sources of motion. The input sequence was 10 times lower in resolution than the AAM. The error metrics indicate that RAF tracked the face consistently better than AAMR-SIM. To provide further evidence, Fig. 5 shows temporal trajectories of selected variables. Those estimated by AAMR-SIM do not follow the ground truth values, and remain mostly constant. In contrast, RAF can track the non-rigid deformations and appearance changes, amounting to a more accurate recovery of the facial expressions. We included this experiment and others in the supplemental video[1].

4.3   Test Set Statistics

It would be impractical to include time trajectories for all our experiments. In the following, we simply include the temporal mean and standard deviation of the Root Mean Squared (RMS) errors of selected variables. Note that lost trackers can easily corrupt these statistics with outliers. To prevent this, we required both trackers to produce valid results (*i.e.*, not have lost track of the face) for a fitting instance to be included in the comparison. This was achieved by visually inspecting all experiments and verifying that faces were tracked reasonably well.

---

[1] Demonstrations available at http://www.cs.cmu.edu/~dedeoglu/eccv06

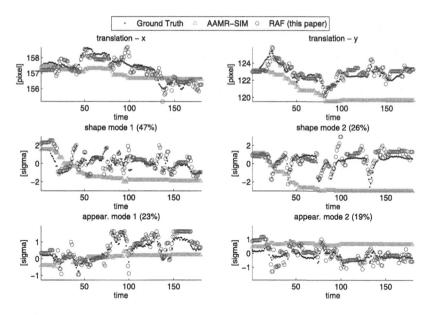

Fig. 5. Selected temporal trajectories are shown for a 10-fold resolution degraded face tracking experiment. As the supplemental video material shows, the main source of motion were the subject's speaking and eye blinking. See Fig. 4 for one example frame of this sequence. The estimates of AAMR-SIM do not follow the ground truth, and remain mostly constant. In contrast, RAF remains close to ground truth in all trajectories, indicating that it is able to extract the underlying facial expressions correctly.

Recall that each tracking experiment was initialized with the highest resolution fitting results. At lower input resolutions, such an optimistic initialization would cause the fitting performance to be overestimated at the beginning. To avoid this effect, we discarded the results of the first 20 frames of each sequence.

Fig. 6 compares the AAMR-SIM and RAF algorithms for fitting a single-person AAM. In the upper-left corner, we first provide a brief summary of experimental conditions. This AAM was built using 31 training images, and was tested on a set of 180. These were 8-bit grayscale images, and the AAM's native resolution was 100x104 pixels. We retained 95% of the total variation, yielding 11 shape and 23 appearance principal components.

The plots in Fig. 6 present extensive quantitative comparisons between the fitting algorithms. They are organized to show RMS error metrics as a function of downscaling factor. Observe how AAMR-SIM and RAF perform equally well at downsampling factor 2. This case corresponds to a minor degradation in resolution, but the fact that both algorithms perform similarly confirms the correctness of our derivations as well as implementations. Starting from downsampling factor 4, RAF brings substantial accuracy improvements across all metrics and variables of interest.

The performance of a model-based method ultimately depends on the quality of the available model. In order to investigate how the AAM fitting accuracy

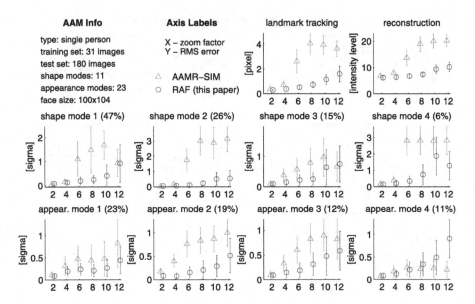

Fig. 6. Quantitative comparison between the AAMR-SIM and RAF algorithms for fitting the single-person AAM to a 180 frame-long sequence. Both algorithms perform well at half-resolution, validating the derivation and implementation of RAF. The latter brings substantial improvements across all metrics for downscaling factors 4 and higher. The principal modes are displayed in order of % energy (*i.e.*, variation) they capture.

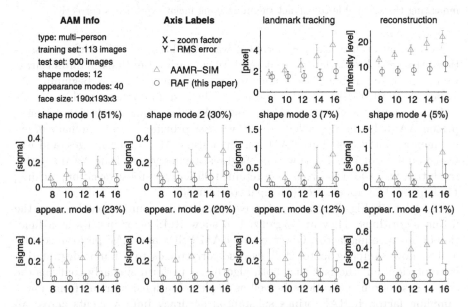

Fig. 7. Quantitative comparison between the AAMR-SIM and RAF algorithms for fitting the multi-person (5 subjects) AAM. Each reported mean and standard deviation is calculated over 900 frames, comprising 180 frames for each of 5 subjects. RAF improves the tracking, reconstruction, non-rigid shape, and appearance estimates considerably.

varies with model complexity, we also ran our experiments on a multi-person AAM, which we built using data from 5 subjects. Details of this AAM are provided in the upper-left corner of Fig. 7, organized in the same fashion as Fig. 6. The multi-person appearance model has almost twice the number of principal modes compared to the single-person case, indicating a richer sub-space being modeled. Again, RAF is observed to be consistently superior to AAMR-SIM in accuracy with regard to both tracking and reconstruction.

5   Qualitative Results

As a complementary method of comparison between the AAMR-SIM and RAF algorithms, we include a selection of synthesized model instances. For this end, we first pixel-replicated the original low resolution inputs, and then overlaid high-resolution reconstructions where the trackers thought the faces were. Many such reconstructions are included in the supplemental video.

Fig. 8 shows every second frame of a subsequence of the single-person AAM tracking experiment. Observe that RAF correctly extracts the eye blink and mouth opening, whereas AAMR-SIM does not. Fig. 9 offers a visual alternative for assessing how the trackers degrade with increased downscaling: it displays the single-person AAM results for frame no. 102 across various scales. While RAF can consistently recover the open eyes and mouth, AAMR-SIM's estimates degrade quickly: starting from downsampling factor 6, the eyes and mouth are first estimated to be half-open, and then totally closed. Similarly, Fig. 10 displays

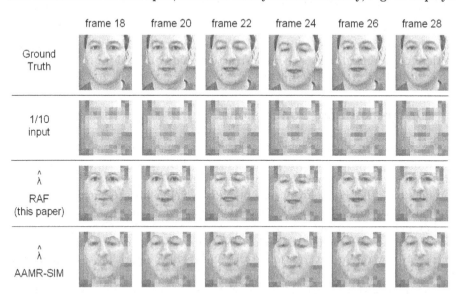

Fig. 8. Exemplar subsequence of high-resolution reconstructions, obtained by fitting the single-person AAM. Observe how RAF correctly extracts the eye blink and mouth opening, whereas AAMR-SIM does not. See complete videos at http://www.cs.cmu.edu/~dedeoglu/eccv06

Ground Truth   1/2   1/4   1/6   1/8   1/10   1/12

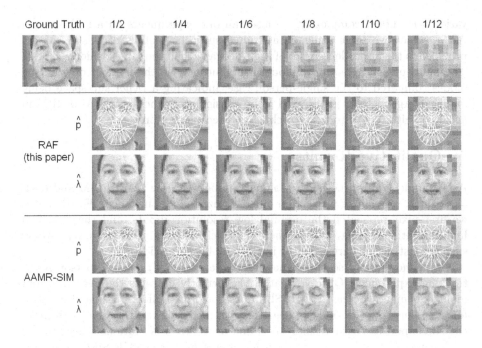

Fig. 9. We compared the AAMR-SIM and RAF algorithms over a range of scales. Increasingly lower resolution versions of input frame no. 102 are shown in the top row. While AAMR-SIM degrades quickly, RAF maintains a reasonable estimate of the face.

snapshots of different test subjects, all tracked using the multi-person AAM. For both AAMs, we find the visual reconstruction quality of RAF to be consistently superior to that of AAMR-SIM.

6   Discussion and Conclusions

In low resolution scenarios, there is significant scaling between the AAM and input images. In such cases, traditional fitting algorithms [5, 10] interpolate the observations when computing the fitting criterion. The essential novelty of our formulation is that it employs a camera model which mimics the image formation in digital cameras, and thereby avoids interpolation.

Throughout this paper, we focused on *accuracy* measures. Other factors such as robustness and computational efficiency may be as important. Indeed, in extremely low resolutions, we found the AAMR-SIM algorithm to be more robust than RAF. Given the smoothing effect of (bilinear) interpolation, this does not seem surprising. While RAF struggles among the many parameter settings which yield almost the same low resolution images, AAMR-SIM commits to an interpolated high-resolution observation, and pursues the fit.

We only fit nominal-resolution AAMs, independently of how much lower in resolution the observations were. This allowed us to reconstruct faces in

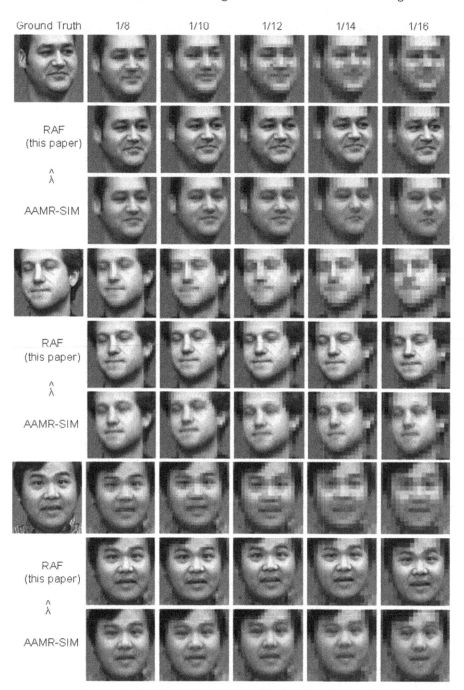

Fig. 10. Selected test frames are shown to visually compare the algorithms for fitting the multi-person AAM. The quantitative improvement in appearance estimates (Fig. 7) has visible effects. Mesh displays are omitted due to a lack of significant difference.

high-resolution. A related idea is to construct a scale-space pyramid of AAMs, and to model multiple resolutions in parallel. Due to blur, higher-level (*i.e.*, lower-resolution) AAMs would have more compact appearance models, and would therefore be easier to fit. Though this may seem to be an alternative to our approach, comparison *across models* is outside the scope of this paper. In comparing between fitting formulations across a range of resolution degradations, we used exactly the same AAMs. Our goal was to make a given fitting problem *more accurate*, rather than *finding an easier* fitting problem.

The fact that the summation in RAF's criterion is defined over observed image pixels has important consequences. Recall that the traditional fitting formulation had conveniently defined the summation over the model template pixels. Since the latter do not change as a function of the input, computational savings become possible: For instance, Matthews and Baker's [10] tracker considers the Taylor expansion for the warp parameters over the template, and pre-compute all associated Jacobians and Hessians. One area for future work is to incorporate such savings into the RAF formulation.

Our discussion remains orthogonal to practical search heuristics such as multiresolution, hierarchical and progressive [3, 4] methods. We can still exploit the advantages of these: for instance, a pyramid style algorithm would increase the robustness of RAF, complementing its accuracy at the bottom level.

In a more compherensive report [12], we argue that image-based warp estimation is an asymmetric problem: in the presence of relative scaling, the warp direction ought to be chosen such that the higher resolution image gets preblurred and warped onto the lower resolution one. As such, the AAM-based face tracking presented in this paper is an application of this general principle.

Acknowledgments. We are grateful to Iain Matthews for kindly providing the AAM Toolbox and sharing his expertise at various stages of implementation. We would also like to thank Jonas August and other members of the CMU miscreading group for discussions. The research described in this paper was supported in part by U.S. Department of Defense contract N41756-03-C4024.

References

1. D.F. Barbe: Charge-Coupled Devices. Springer-Verlag, 1980.
2. B.D. Lucas and T. Kanade: An Iterative Image Registration Technique with an Application to Stereo Vision. *Proc. of the 7th Int. Joint Conference on Artificial Intelligence*, April, 1981, pp. 674-679.
3. P. Anandan: A Computational Framework and an Algorithm for the Measurement of Visual Motion. *International Journal of Computer Vision*, Vol. 2, No. 3, Jan., 1989, pp. 283-310.
4. J. R. Bergen, P. Anandan, K. J. Hanna, and R. Hingorani: Hierarchical Model-Based Motion Estimation. *Proc. of the European Conference on Computer Vision*, May, 1992, pp. 237-252.
5. T.F. Cootes, G.J. Edwards, and C.J. Taylor: Active Appearance Models. *Proc. of the European Conference on Computer Vision*, Vol. 2, 1998, pp. 484-498.

6. G.J. Edwards, C.J. Taylor, and T.F. Cootes: Interpreting Face Images Using Active Appearance Models. *Proc. of Int. Conf. on Automatic Face and Gesture Recognition*, June, 1998, pp. 300-305.
7. T.F. Cootes, G.J. Edwards, and C.J. Taylor: Active Appearance Models. *IEEE Transactions on Pattern Analysis and Machine Intelligence*, Vol. 23, No. 6, June, 2001, pp. 681-685.
8. S. Baker, R. Gross, and I. Matthews: Lucas-Kanade 20 Years On: A Unifying Framework: Part 3. *Robotics Institute Technical Report CMU-RI-TR-03-35*, Carnegie Mellon University, November 2003.
9. S. Baker and I. Matthews: Lucas-Kanade 20 Years On: A Unifying Framework. *Int. Journal of Computer Vision*, Vol. 56, No. 3, March, 2004, pp. 221-255.
10. I. Matthews and S. Baker: Active Appearance Models Revisited. *International Journal of Computer Vision*, Vol. 60, No. 2, November, 2004, pp. 135-164.
11. R. Gross, I. Matthews, and S. Baker: Generic vs. Person Specific Active Appearance Models. *Image and Vision Computing*, Vol. 23, No. 11, Nov. 2005, pp. 1080-1093.
12. G. Dedeoglu, T. Kanade, and S. Baker: The Asymmetry of Image Registration and its Application to Face Tracking. *Robotics Institute Technical Report CMU-RI-TR-06-06, Carnegie Mellon University*, February, 2006.

High Accuracy Optical Flow Serves 3-D Pose Tracking: Exploiting Contour and Flow Based Constraints[*]

Thomas Brox[1], Bodo Rosenhahn[2], Daniel Cremers[1], and Hans-Peter Seidel[2]

[1] CVPR Group, Department of Computer Science, University of Bonn,
Römerstr. 164, 53113 Bonn, Germany
{brox, dcremers}@cs.uni-bonn.de
[2] Max Planck Center for Visual Computing and Communication,
D-66123 Saarbrücken, Germany
rosenhahn@mpi-sb.mpg.de

Abstract. Tracking the 3-D pose of an object needs correspondences between 2-D features in the image and their 3-D counterparts in the object model. A large variety of such features has been suggested in the literature. All of them have drawbacks in one situation or the other since their extraction in the image and/or the matching is prone to errors. In this paper, we propose to use two complementary types of features for pose tracking, such that one type makes up for the shortcomings of the other. Aside from the object contour, which is matched to a free-form object surface, we suggest to employ the optic flow in order to compute additional point correspondences. Optic flow estimation is a mature research field with sophisticated algorithms available. Using here a high quality method ensures a reliable matching. In our experiments we demonstrate the performance of our method and in particular the improvements due to the optic flow.

1 Introduction

To determine the 3-D pose of objects in a scene is an important task in computer vision. In this paper, we focus on the task of pose tracking, i.e., we assume the pose of the object is approximately known at the first frame of an image sequence. For not loosing this pose information over time, we seek to capture the exact 3-D object motion from one frame to the next, given an a-priori 3-D object model. The estimated motion thereby has to fit the 3-D model to some 2-D image data in the new frame. We assume rigid objects, though the concept can also be extended to more general objects modelled as kinematic chains [3, 10, 1]. So our goal is to determine 6 motion parameters, 3 for the object's rotation and 3 for its translation in space.

For estimating these parameters, one has to match 3-D features of the object model to their 2-D counterparts in the image. There are many possibilities which features to match, ranging from line matching [8] and block matching [27], up to local descriptors like SIFT [16] and free-form contour matching [23]. All of these features have their specific shortcomings. Either they are not appropriate for general objects, like lines, or they are difficult to match, consequently producing false matches that disturb the pose

---

[*] We gratefully acknowledge funding by the German Research Foundation (DFG) and the Max Planck Center for Visual Computing and Communication.

A. Leonardis, H. Bischof, and A. Pinz (Eds.): ECCV 2006, Part II, LNCS 3952, pp. 98–111, 2006.

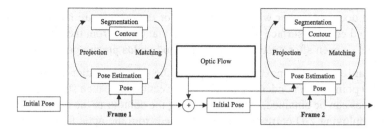

Fig. 1. Illustration of the pose tracking system. Given an initial pose, segmentation and contour based pose estimation are iterated to successively improve the extracted contour and the pose. Between frames, the optic flow helps to improve the initial pose. Furthermore, it supplements additional point correspondences for pose estimation.

estimation. The appropriateness of a feature for matching depends on the situation. In case of textured objects with many distinctive blobs, block matching and SIFT work pretty well. However, such methods may fail to match homogeneous objects with few distinctive features. Further on, block matching is only suited for translational motion and has well known problems in scenes with, e.g., rotating objects. In such cases, contour matching may work much better, as the contour is adaptive to the object's shape. However, the silhouette of very smooth and convex objects does not carry much information, and further point matches from inside the object region can be necessary to ensure unique solutions. Moreover, contour extraction and matching are susceptible to local optima.

To overcome these limitations of individual features, we propose to combine two complementary types of features. On one hand, we match the object contour extracted from the image to the object surface. This method works well for all rigid objects if two requirements are satisfied: 1) the silhouette contains enough information to provide a unique pose estimate, 2) the motion of the object from one image to the next is small enough to ensure that the contour extraction and matching do not run into a local optimum.

Additionally to the correspondences from the silhouette, we propose to add matches obtained from the optic flow, i.e., correspondences of 2-D points in successive images. If the pose in the first image is known, which is the case for pose tracking, the optic flow allows for constructing 2D-3D correspondences in the second image. Since the optic flow based features provide correspondences for points from the *interior* of the object region, they are complementary to the silhouette features and may provide uniqueness of solutions precisely in cases where the silhouettes are not sufficiently descriptive. This aims at the first shortcoming of contour based matching. To address the second shortcoming, we employ the high-end optic flow estimation method introduced in [4], which can deal with rather large displacements. With the flow based pose estimation predicting the pose in the next image, we enable a contour matching that avoids local minima and can handle much larger motion.

In experiments, we verified that the integration of these two complementary features yields a very general pose tracking approach that can deal with all kinds of rigid objects, large object motions, background clutter, light changes, noise, textured and non-textured objects, as well as partial occlusions. The information from multiple cameras can be used and it does not matter whether the object or the camera are moving. Moreover, the interlaced contour-surface matching ensures that errors from the optic flow do not accumulate, so even after many frames the method yields precise pose estimates.

Paper organization. The next section explains the pose estimation method assuming that 2D-3D point correspondences are given. In Section 3 we then show how such correspondences can be obtained, once by matching the contour to the object surface, and once by employing 2-D correspondences obtained from the optic flow. In our experiments we demonstrate the generality of the method and show in particular the improvements due to the optic flow. Section 5 finally provides a brief summary.

Related work. There exists a wide variety of pose estimation algorithms differing by the used object or image features, the camera geometry, single or multi-view geometry, and numerical estimation procedures. For an overview see [11, 22]. The first point based techniques were studied in the 80's and 90's, and pioneering work was done by Lowe [15] and Grimson [12]. A projective formulation of Lowe's work can be found in [2]. The use of 3-D Plücker lines was investigated in [25]. Point matching by means of the optic flow has been investigated, e.g., in [14] and [3], where optic flow correspondences are used in a point-based approach with a scaled orthographic camera model. In [9] the linearized optic flow constraint is integrated into a deformable model for estimating the object motion. Block matching approaches are related to optic flow based methods, though the matching is often restricted to a few interest points. Combinations of optic flow or block matching with edge maps has been presented in [17, 26]. Recently, more enhanced local descriptors have been suggested to deal with the shortcomings of block matching. A performance evaluation can be found in [18].

2 Pose Estimation

This section describes the core algorithm for point based 2D-3D pose estimation. We assume a set of corresponding points (X_i, x_i), with 4-D (homogeneous) model points X_i and 3-D (homogeneous) image points x_i. Each image point is reconstructed to a Plücker line $L_i = (n_i, m_i)$, with a unit direction n_i, and moment m_i [19]. The 3-D rigid motion we estimate is represented in exponential form

$$M = \exp(\theta\hat{\xi}) = \exp\begin{pmatrix} \hat{\omega} & v \\ 0_{3\times 1} & 0 \end{pmatrix} \tag{1}$$

where $\theta\hat{\xi}$ is the matrix representation of a twist $\xi = (\omega_1, \omega_2, \omega_3, v_1, v_2, v_3) \in se(3) = \{(v, \hat{\omega})|v \in \mathbb{R}^3, \hat{\omega} \in so(3)\}$, with $so(3) = \{\hat{\omega} \in \mathbb{R}^{3\times 3}|\hat{\omega} = -\hat{\omega}^T\}$. In fact, M is an element of the one-parametric Lie group $SE(3)$, known as the group of direct affine isometries. A main result of Lie theory is, that to each Lie group there exists a Lie algebra, which can be found in its tangential space, by derivation and evaluation at its origin; see [19] for more details. The corresponding Lie algebra to $SE(3)$ is denoted as $se(3)$. A twist contains six parameters and can be scaled to $\theta\xi$ with a unit vector ω. The parameter $\theta \in \mathbb{R}$ corresponds to the motion velocity (i.e., the rotation velocity and pitch). Variation of θ corresponds to a screw motion around an axis in space. To reconstruct a group action $M \in SE(3)$ from a given twist, the exponential function $\exp(\theta\hat{\xi}) = M \in SE(3)$ must be computed. It can be calculated efficiently by using the Rodriguez formula [19]. For pose estimation we combine the reconstructed Plücker lines with the screw representation for rigid motions and apply a gradient descent method: incidence of the transformed 3-D point X_i with the 3-D ray $L_i = (n_i, m_i)$ can be expressed as

$$(\exp(\theta\hat{\xi})X_i)_{3\times1} \times n_i - m_i = 0. \tag{2}$$

Indeed, X_i is a homogeneous 4-D vector, and after multiplication with the 4×4 matrix $\exp(\theta\hat{\xi})$ we neglect the homogeneous component (which is 1) to evaluate the cross product with n_i. Note that this constraint equation expresses the perpendicular error vector between the Plücker line and the 3-D point. The aim is to minimize this spatial error. To this end, we linearize the equation by using $\exp(\theta\hat{\xi}) = \sum_{k=0}^{\infty} \frac{(\theta\hat{\xi})^k}{k!} \approx I + \theta\hat{\xi}$, with I as identity matrix. This results in

$$((I + \theta\hat{\xi})X_i)_{3\times1} \times n_i - m_i = 0 \tag{3}$$

which can be rearranged into an equation of the form

$$A\xi = b. \tag{4}$$

Collecting a set of such equations (each is of rank two) leads to an over-determined linear system of equations in ξ. From the twist ξ one can reconstruct the group action M^1. It is then applied to X_i which results in $X_i^1 = MX_i$ as the result after the first iteration. The pose estimation is now repeated until the motion converges. For n iterations we get $M = M^n \dots M^1$ as pose of X_i to x_i. Usually 3-5 iterations are sufficient for an accurate pose.

In this setting, the extension to multiple views is straightforward: we assume N images which are calibrated with respect to the same world coordinate system and are triggered. For each camera the system matrices $A_1 \dots A_N$ and solution vectors $b_1 \dots b_N$ are generated. The equations are now bundled in one system $A = (A_1, \dots, A_N)^T$ and $b = (b_1, \dots, b_N)^T$. Since they are generated for the same unknowns ξ, they can be solved simultaneously, i.e., the spatial errors of all involved cameras are minimized.

In conclusion, given the projection matrices of the cameras and a set of 2D-3D correspondences, pose estimation comes down to solve an overdetermined linear system of equations, which takes typically 4ms for 200 point correspondences. The remaining problem of pose estimation is hence how to compute reliable point correspondences, i.e., how to match features visible in the image to features of the object model.

3   Feature Matching

The following two sections are concerned with the computation of contour based and optic flow based point correspondences. For both the contour extraction [7, 6] and the optic flow estimation [4], rather sophisticated methods are employed. We focus on describing only the models of these techniques and how they affect the pose estimation. Implementation details, such as numerical schemes, can be found in the above-mentioned papers and the references therein.

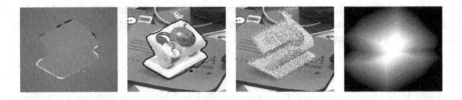

Fig. 2. Illustration of contour representations by means of level set functions. **From Left to Right:** (a) Level set function Φ. (b) Contour represented by the zero-level line of Φ. (c) Object projected to the image, given the current pose. (d) Shape prior Φ_0 derived from the object silhouette.

3.1   Contour-Surface Matching

Contour extraction. The computation of contour based correspondences is according to our prior work in [5]. It builds upon contour extraction by means of region based level set segmentation [7, 21]. In such methods, one provides an initial contour and evolves this contour for that it becomes optimal with regard to some energy model. This energy functional reads in our case:

$$E(\Phi) = -\underbrace{\int_\Omega \left(H(\Phi(x))\log p_1(F(x)) + (1 - H(\Phi(x)))\log p_2(F(x)\right)dx}_{\text{Region Statistics}}$$

$$+ \nu \underbrace{\int_\Omega |\nabla H(\Phi(x))|\, dx}_{\text{Contour Smoothness}} + \lambda \underbrace{\int_\Omega (\Phi(x) - \Phi_0(x))^2\, dx}_{\text{Shape}} \quad \rightarrow \min. \tag{5}$$

Hereby the level set function Φ represents the contour by its zero-level line [20, 7]; see Fig. 2a,b for an illustration. $H(\Phi)$ is the Heaviside function simply indicating whether a point is within the object or the background region, and $\nu = 0.6$ and $\lambda = 0.03$ are weighting parameters.

Let us take a closer look at the meaning of the three terms in the functional. The first term maximizes the a-posteriori probability of a point to belong to the assigned region. In other words: points are assigned to the region where they fit best. For a point to fit well to a region, its value must fit well to the probability density function of this region. The probability densities of the object and the background region, p_1 and p_2, are modelled as local Gaussian densities. They can be estimated given a preliminary contour and are successively updated when the contour evolves. In order to deal with textured regions, we perform the statistical modelling in the texture feature space F proposed in [6]. In case of color images it is of dimension $M = 7$. For keeping the region model manageable, the different channels are supposed to be independent, so p_1 and p_2 can be approximated by $p_i = \prod_{j=1}^{M} p_{ij}$, where p_{ij} denotes the probability density estimated in region i and channel j. Due to this statistical modelling of the regions, the contour extraction can deal with textures and is very robust under noise or other disturbances as long as one can still distinguish the regions in at least one of the image or texture channels.

The second term in (5) applies a length constraint to the contour, which effectively smoothes the contour. The amount of smoothing is determined by ν.

The last term finally takes information provided by the object model into account. The level set function Φ_0 represents the model silhouette given the current pose estimate; see Fig. 2c,d for illustration. Minimizing the distance between Φ and Φ_0 draws the contour towards the projected model, ruling out solutions that are far from its shape. Hence, pose estimation and contour extraction are coupled by this shape term: as soon as an improved pose estimate is obtained, one can compute an update of the contour and thus successively improves both the contour and the pose estimate. Each such iteration takes around 4 seconds on a 400×300 image.

Due to the sophisticated statistical region model and the integration of the object's shape, the contour can be extracted in quite general situations including background clutter, texture, and noise. However, the quality depends on a good guess of the object's pose that is involved in a) providing an initialization of Φ and b) in keeping Φ close to Φ_0.

Contour matching. Once a contour has been extracted from the image, one has to match points from this contour to 3-D points on the object surface. This is done by an iterated closest point procedure [28]. First one determines those points from the surface model that are part of the object silhouette, resulting in the 3-D object rim contour. The projection of each of these points is then matched to the closest point of the extracted contour. In this way, one obtains a 2D-3D point correspondence for each 3-D mesh point that is part of the silhouette [22, 24]. After pose estimation, a new rim contour is computed and the process is iterated until the pose converges.

These correspondences are often erroneous when the estimated pose is far from the correct pose, yet the errors tend to zero as the estimated pose gets close to the true pose. Iterating pose estimation and matching, one hopes that the estimated pose converges to the correct pose. However, the contour matching is obviously susceptible to local optima. To alleviate this problem, we use a sampling method with different (neighboring) start poses and use the resulting pose with minimum error. Depending on the number of samples, this can considerably increase the computation time, and the contour based pose tracking still stays restricted to relatively small object motions.

3.2 Optic Flow

Facing the shortcomings of contour based pose tracking, we propose the supplement of optic flow, which improves the pose tracking in two ways. Firstly, it provides additional correspondences, which makes pose estimation more robust and can resolve equivocal situations. Secondly, the object motion estimated by means of the optic flow correspondences provides a better initial guess of the pose and thus allows the tracking method to capture also large object motions.

Optic flow is defined as the 2-D vector field $\mathbf{w} := (u, v, 1)$ that matches a point in one image to the shifted point in the other image. In other words, optic flow estimation provides correspondences between the points of two images. During the past 30 years numerous techniques for optic flow estimation have emerged. Differential methods, and in particular variational methods based on the early approach of Horn and Schunck [13], are among the best performing techniques. Variational techniques combine a constancy assumption, e.g. the assumption that the gray value of a point stays constant during motion, with a smoothness assumption. Both assumptions are integrated in an energy functional that is sought to be minimized. Thanks to the smoothness constraint, which distributes information from textured areas to close-by non-textured areas, the resulting flow field is dense, i.e., there is an optic flow estimate available for each pixel in the image.

We employ the technique from [4], which is the currently most accurate optic flow estimation method available. Let $\mathbf{x} := (x, y, t)$. Then given two images $I(x, y, t)$ and $I(x, y, t + 1)$, the technique is described by the energy minimization problem

$$E(u, v) = \underbrace{\int_{\Omega} \Psi \left((I(\mathbf{x} + \mathbf{w}) - I(\mathbf{x}))^2 + \gamma (\nabla I(\mathbf{x} + \mathbf{w}) - \nabla I(\mathbf{x}))^2 \right) \, dx dy}_{\text{Data term}}$$

$$\underbrace{+\alpha \int_{\Omega} \Psi(|\nabla u|^2 + |\nabla v|^2) \, dx dy}_{\text{Smoothness term}} \quad \rightarrow \quad \min \tag{6}$$

where $\alpha = 50$ and $\gamma = 2$ are tuning parameters and $\Psi(s^2) = \sqrt{s^2 + 0.001^2}$ is a robust function which allows for outliers in both the data and the smoothness term. The data term is based on the assumption that the gray value and the gradient of a point remain constant when the point is shifted by $\mathbf{w}$. The smoothness constraint additionally requires the resulting flow field to be piecewise smooth. This optic flow estimation method has several positive properties that are important for our pose tracking task:

1. Due to non-linearized constancy assumptions, the method can deal with larger displacements than most other techniques. This ensures a good matching quality even when the object changes its pose rather rapidly.
2. It provides dense and smooth flow fields with subpixel accuracy.
3. The method is robust with respect to noise as shown in [4].
4. Thanks to the gradient constancy assumption, it is fairly robust with regard to illumination changes that appear in most real-world image sequences, e.g., due to artificial light source flickering or an automatic aperture adaptation of the camera.

Deriving 2D-3D correspondences from the optic flow. With the optic flow computed between two frames, one can establish 2D-3D point correspondences. The visible 3-D object points from the previous frame (where the pose is known) are projected to the image plane. They are then shifted according to the optic flow to their new position in the current frame. Thus, for each visible 3-D point from the last frame, one gets a correspondence to a 2-D point in the new frame.

The resulting correspondence set is used twice: firstly, it is exploited for predicting the object pose in the new frame, i.e., for getting a better pose initialization. Secondly, it is joined with the correspondence set stemming from the contour matching thus stabilizing the contour based pose estimation.

As the optic flow can also provide correspondences for points away from the rim contour of the surface, the number of correspondences is significantly larger than for the contour based matching. We therefore weight the equations (4) stemming from flow based correspondences by a factor 0.1. In this way, both correspondence sets influence the solution in an equal manner.

4   Experiments

In order to confirm the theoretical generality and robustness of the pose tracking method, it has been tested in a number of experiments using three different object models and four different image sequences.

Fig. 3 depicts an experiment where a tea box has been moved considerably between two frames. The motion is so large that the computed optic flow vectors contain errors as can be seen from the pose prediction in Fig. 3b. However, thanks to the additional contour based correspondences, the final pose result is good. Obversely, the pose estimation also fails, if only the contour based correspondences are used. This demonstrates the effective coupling of the two different ways to obtain point correspondences.

Fig. 4 depicts the coupled iteration process between contour extraction and pose estimation. As the contour evolves towards the object boundary, also the pose result improves. In return, the projected pose prohibits the contour to run away from the object in order to capture, e.g., the shadow of the tea box. Note that the setting of this experiment with a textured object, shadows, and moving background clutter rules out most alternative segmentation methods.

In the experiment depicted in Fig. 5, we tracked the pose of a quite homogeneous puncher in front of a cluttered background while the camera was moving. The camera

Fig. 3. The optic flow helps to capture the large motion of a tea box. **From Left to Right: (a)** Object pose at frame 1. **(b)** Object motion due to the estimated optic flow between frame 1 and frame 2. Gray: pose from frame 1. Black: pose prediction for frame 2. **(c)** Estimated pose at frame 2 using the optic flow and the evolving contour. **(d)** Estimated pose without the use of optic flow.

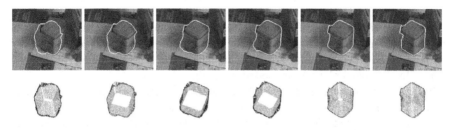

Fig. 4. Evolution of the contour and pose in Fig. 3. **From Left to Right.** Contour and pose are bad at the beginning since the optic flow estimate was erroneous, yet the contour evolves towards the object making the object pose to follow. Thereby, the shape term in the contour evolution ensures that the contour does not drift away capturing the shadow on the right.

Fig. 5. Four successive frames from a sequence with the camera moving and Gaussian noise with standard deviation 60 added (242 frames, 8fps). **Top:** Extracted contour. **Center:** Object motion due to the optic flow. Gray: pose from previous frame. Black: pose prediction at current frame. **Bottom:** Estimated pose using contour and optic flow constraints.

was moved rapidly, thus the displacements between the frames are rather large and there is a motion blur in some images. Additionally, we added severe noise to the sequence. The results reveal that both the contour extraction and the optic flow estimation method can deal with these high amounts of noise. The pose prediction due to the optic flow is very good, despite the noise and the large displacements. Due to the homogeneous object surface and the noise, methods that are based on local descriptors are likely to fail in this situation.

In Fig. 6, we disturbed the puncher by adding some stickers to its surface. Since the contour extraction can deal with textured regions, also the modified puncher can be tracked accurately. One can clearly see the motion blur due to the fast camera motion. Fig. 7 shows what happens, if only flow based correspondences are used, whereas the contour based matches are neglected. Since the flow based constraints rely on the correct pose in the previous frame, errors accumulate in the course of time. This effect is avoided by the contour based correspondences.

In Fig. 8, we show the tracking result in a stereo sequence. The used tea pot model is more complex than the objects shown before. In particular, the background region is no longer connected. Here the advantage of the level set based contour representation to be able to deal with such kinds of topologies comes into play. One can see that the handle of the pot, which is quite important for a good pose estimate, is captured in three out of the four depicted images. Thanks to the integration of information from the two cameras, this works even though the hand partially occludes the handle. At

Fig. 6. Puncher disturbed by some stickers (244 frames, 8fps). **Top row:** Frames 80, 95, 100, 110, and 120. Some images show a considerable blur due to motion or the auto-focus of the camera. In others there are reflections on the puncher. **Bottom row:** Pose results at these frames.

Fig. 7. Accumulation of errors when only flow based correspondences are used. **From Left to Right:** Pose results at frames 2, 5, 10, and 20. **Rightmost:** Pose result at frame 242 if contour *and* flow based correspondences are employed.

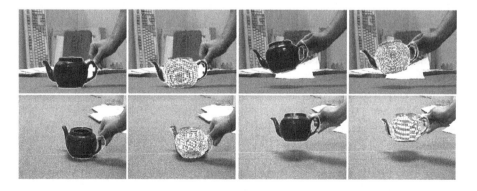

Fig. 8. Stereo sequence with partial occlusions (131 frames, 8 fps). **Top Row:** Left camera. **Bottom Row:** Right camera. **From Left to Right:** Contour at image 59. Pose at image 59. Contour at image 104. Pose at image 104.

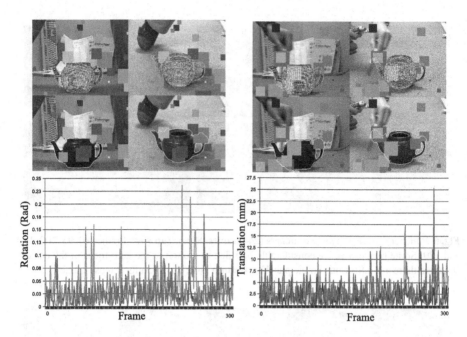

Fig. 9. Quantitative error in a static stereo scene with illumination changes and partial occlusions. The sequence has been disturbed by rectangles of random size, position, and color. **Top:** Two frames from the sequence. The right one shows the worst pose estimate according to the diagram below. **Bottom:** Rotational (left) and translational (right) errors along the three spatial axes in radians and millimeters, respectively.

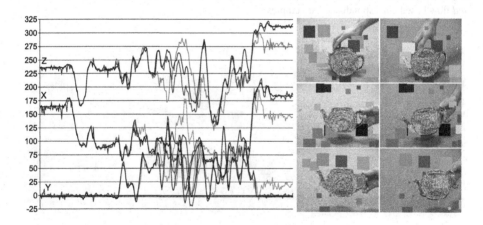

Fig. 10. Quantitative error analysis in a dynamic stereo scene disturbed by rectangles of random size, position, and color. Horizontal axis: frame number. Vertical axis: translation results (in the three spatial dimensions) **blue:** with optic flow; **gray:** without optic flow; **black:** with the undisturbed sequence. **Right:** Three stereo frames from the sequence.

this point, the optic flow providing good initializations is also very important, since the inner contour at the handle may get lost if the initialization is too far away from the correct pose.

Fig. 9 depicts a sequence where object and camera are static to allow a quantitative error measurement. The parameter settings were the same as in Fig. 8, so the object was allowed to move. The sequence has further been disturbed with rectangles of random size, position, and color which leads to occlusions of the object.

The two diagrams show the translational and angular errors along the three axes, respectively. Despite the change of the lighting conditions and partial occlusions, the error has a standard deviation of less than 7mm and 5 degrees.

Finally, Fig. 10 shows another dynamic sequence. At the beginning, the tea pot is rotated on the floor, then it is grabbed and moved around. Again the sequence has been disturbed with rectangles of random size, position, and color leading to occlusions of the object. The diagram in Fig. 10 quantifies the outcome. It shows the tracking curves for the disturbed sequence, with and without using optic flow (blue and gray, respectively) and the successful tracking of the undisturbed sequence (black) that can be regarded as some kind of ground truth. The optic flow clearly stabilizes the tracking.

The total computation time depends on the number of iterations necessary for the method to converge. For the last (and hardest) experiment we ran a setup that required approximately 2 minutes per frame on a 2.4GHz Opteron Linux machine.

5   Summary

We have suggested a pose tracking method that combines two conceptionally different matching strategies: contour matching and optic flow. Providing both qualitative and quantitative results, we have demonstrated the generality of this combination: it does not matter whether the object or the camera is moving, the method can deal with textured and homogeneous objects, as well as clutter, blurring, or noise artifacts.

In particular, we have shown that the integration of both constraints outperforms approaches that exploit only one or the other constraint. The multiresolution scheme for the optic flow estimator provides accurate contour matching even in case of larger inter-frame motion, where contour based schemes fail. The interlaced contour matching, on the other hand, prevents the accumulation of tracking errors, which is characteristic for purely optic flow based tracking systems.

References

1. A. Agarwal and B. Triggs. Tracking articulated motion using a mixture of autoregressive models. In T. Pajdla and J. Matas, editors, *Proc. 8th European Conference on Computer Vision*, volume 3023 of *LNCS*, pages 54–65. Springer, May 2004.
2. H. Araújo, R. L. Carceroni, and C. M. Brown. A fully projective formulation to improve the accuracy of Lowe's pose-estimation algorithm. *Computer Vision and Image Understanding*, 70(2):227–238, May 1998.
3. C. Bregler, J. Malik, and K. Pullen. Twist based acquisition and tracking of animal and human kinematics. *International Journal of Computer Vision*, 56(3):179–194, 2004.

4. T. Brox, A. Bruhn, N. Papenberg, and J. Weickert. High accuracy optical flow estimation based on a theory for warping. In T. Pajdla and J. Matas, editors, *Proc. 8th European Conference on Computer Vision*, volume 3024 of *LNCS*, pages 25–36. Springer, May 2004.

5. T. Brox, B. Rosenhahn, and J. Weickert. Three-dimensional shape knowledge for joint image segmentation and pose estimation. In W. Kropatsch, R. Sablatnig, and A. Hanbury, editors, *Pattern Recognition*, volume 3663 of *LNCS*, pages 109–116. Springer, Aug. 2005.

6. T. Brox and J. Weickert. A TV flow based local scale measure for texture discrimination. In T. Pajdla and J. Matas, editors, *Proc. 8th European Conference on Computer Vision*, volume 3022 of *LNCS*, pages 578–590. Springer, May 2004.

7. T. Chan and L. Vese. Active contours without edges. *IEEE Transactions on Image Processing*, 10(2):266–277, Feb. 2001.

8. P. David, D. DeMenthon, R. Duraiswami, and H. Samet. Simultaneous pose and correspondence determination using line features. In *Proc. 2003 IEEE Computer Society Conference on Computer Vision and Pattern Recognition*, volume 2, pages 424–431, 2003.

9. D. DeCarlo and D. Metaxas. Optical flow constraints on deformable models with applications to face tracking. *International Journal of Computer Vision*, 38(2):99–127, July 2000.

10. P. Fua, R. Plänkers, and D. Thalmann. Tracking and modeling people in video sequences. *Computer Vision and Image Understanding*, 81(3):285–302, Mar. 2001.

11. J. Goddard. Pose and motion estimation from vision using dual quaternion-based extended Kalman filtering. Technical report, University of Tennessee, Knoxville, 1997.

12. W. E. L. Grimson. *Object Recognition by Computer*. The MIT Press, Cambridge, MA, 1990.

13. B. Horn and B. Schunck. Determining optical flow. *Artificial Intelligence*, 17:185–203, 1981.

14. R. Koch. Dynamic 3D scene analysis through synthesis feedback control. *IEEE Transactions on Pattern Analysis and Machine Intelligence*, 15(6):556–568, 1993.

15. D. Lowe. Solving for the parameters of object models from image descriptions. In *Proc. ARPA Image Understanding Workshop*, pages 121–127, 1980.

16. D. Lowe. Distinctive image features from scale-invariant keypoints. *International Journal of Computer Vision*, 60(2):91–110, 2004.

17. E. Marchand, P. Bouthemy, and F. Chaumette. A 2D-3D model-based approach to real-time visual tracking. *Image and Vision Computing*, 19(13):941–955, Nov. 2001.

18. K. Mikolajczyk and C. Schmid. A performance evaluation of local descriptors. *IEEE Transactions on Pattern Analysis and Machine Intelligence*, 27(10):1615–1630, 2005.

19. R. Murray, Z. Li, and S. Sastry. *Mathematical Introduction to Robotic Manipulation*. CRC Press, Boca Raton, FL, 1994.

20. S. Osher and J. A. Sethian. Fronts propagating with curvature-dependent speed: Algorithms based on Hamilton–Jacobi formulations. *Journal of Computational Physics*, 79:12–49, 1988.

21. N. Paragios and R. Deriche. Geodesic active regions: A new paradigm to deal with frame partition problems in computer vision. *Journal of Visual Communication and Image Representation*, 13(1/2):249–268, 2002.

22. B. Rosenhahn. Pose estimation revisited. Technical Report TR-0308, Institute of Computer Science, University of Kiel, Germany, Oct. 2003.

23. B. Rosenhahn, C. Perwass, and G. Sommer. Pose estimation of free-form contours. *International Journal of Computer Vision*, 62(3):267–289, 2005.

24. B. Rosenhahn and G. Sommer. Pose estimation of free-form objects. In T. Pajdla and J. Matas, editors, *Proc. 8th European Conference on Computer Vision*, volume 3021 of *LNCS*, pages 414–427. Springer, May 2004.

25. F. Shevlin. Analysis of orientation problems using Plücker lines. In *International Conference on Pattern Recognition (ICPR)*, volume 1, pages 685–689, Brisbane, 1998.

26. L. Vacchetti, V. Lepetit, and P. Fua. Combining edge and texture information for real-time accurate 3D camera tracking. In *3rd International Symposium on Mixed and Augmented Reality*, pages 48–57, 2004.
27. L. Vacchetti, V. Lepetit, and P. Fua. Stable real-time 3D tracking using online and offline information. *IEEE Transactions on Pattern Analysis and Machine Intelligence*, 26(10): 1391–1391, 2004.
28. Z. Zang. Iterative point matching for registration of free-form curves and surfaces. *International Journal of Computer Vision*, 13(2):119–152, 1999.

Enhancing the Point Feature Tracker by Adaptive Modelling of the Feature Support*

Siniša Šegvić[1], Anthony Remazeilles[2], and François Chaumette[1]

[1] IRISA/INRIA Rennes, Campus de Beaulieu, 35042 Rennes cedex, France
[2] IRISA/INSA Rennes, Campus de Beaulieu, 35042 Rennes cedex, France
{sinisa.segvic, anthony.remazeilles, francois.chaumette}@irisa.fr

Abstract. We consider the problem of tracking a given set of point features over large sequences of image frames. A classic procedure for monitoring the tracking quality consists in requiring that the current features nicely warp towards their reference appearances. The procedure recommends focusing on features projected from planar 3D patches (planar features), by enforcing a conservative threshold on the residual of the difference between the warped current feature and the reference. However, in some important contexts, there are many features for which the planarity assumption is only partially satisfied, while the true planar features are not so abundant. This is especially true when the motion of the camera is mainly translational and parallel to the optical axis (such as when driving a car along straight sections of the road), which induces a permanent increase of the apparent feature size. Tracking features containing occluding boundaries then becomes an interesting goal, for which we propose a multi-scale monitoring solution striving to maximize the lifetime of the feature, while also detecting the tracking failures. The devised technique infers the parts of the reference which are not projected from the same 3D surface as the patch which has been consistently tracked until the present moment. The experiments on real sequences taken from cars driving through urban environments show that the technique is effective in increasing the average feature lifetimes, especially in sequences with occlusions and large photometric variations.

1 Introduction

Tracking point features in a sequence of image frames is an important low-level problem of early computer vision. The quality of the recovered trajectories directly affects the performance of attractive higher level tasks such as structure from motion [1], visual odometry [2], concurrent mapping and localization [3], and visual servoing [4]. However, the priorities of the desired tracking behaviour may differ between the particular contexts, since the former two involve larger numbers of "nameless" features, while the latter ones usually focus on fewer but more important landmarks. Thus, achieving the longest possible contact with

---

* The presented work has been performed within the french national project Predit Mobivip, and within the project Robea Bodega. The authors would also like to acknowledge Prof. Axel Pinz for a helpful discussion on this subject.

A. Leonardis, H. Bischof, and A. Pinz (Eds.): ECCV 2006, Part II, LNCS 3952, pp. 112–124, 2006.

each of the tracked features, being the focus of this paper, is highly desired in the latter tasks, even though the former ones can operate with considerably shorter feature lifetimes. The two main approaches for conceiving a point feature tracker are iterative first-order differential approximation [5, 6], and exhaustive matching [2, 7]. In both approaches, a straightforward implementation based on integrating inter-frame motion is a viable solution only for short-term operation, due to the incontrollable growth of the accumulated drift. It is therefore necessary either to adapt the higher-level task to work only with short feature tracks [2], if applicable, or to devise a monitoring approach which would try to correct the drift by aligning the current appearance of the feature with a previously stored template image or *reference*. The desired alignment is usually performed by minimizing the norm of the *error image*, which is obtained by subtracting the current feature from the reference [8]. Shi and Tomasi [5] have addressed the monitoring over linear deformations of the planar surface, which have been described with a 2D affine transform, under reasonable assumptions of the feature position with respect to the camera. An extension of their work has been proposed by Jin et al. [6] who devised a scheme which additionally compensated for affine photometric deformations of the grey level value in the image.

An important issue in monitored long-term tracking is being able to recognize when a match with the reference can not be confidently established any more, so that the tracking of the feature can be discontinued in order to prevent errors at the higher levels. Previously, this has been accomplished by using criteria based on the RMS (root-mean-square) residual of the error image [5], and normalized cross-correlation score combined with the ratio between the two areas [6]. However, the richer deformation models pose a bigger danger of allowing a warp producing an incorrect match with a low residual [9]. This danger can be mitigated by enlarging the size of a feature window: larger windows provide a better security that a good match score is not due to a chance. On the other hand, large features are more likely to include a 3D surface discontinuity, which usually makes a correct warp towards past appearances impossible. The odds for straddling a discontinuity are especially high if we consider the tracking of features that are initially distant. For a usual horizontal field of view of $30°$ and a resolution of 320×160 pixels, a 15×15 pixels region corresponds to a perpendicular planar patch of over $1 \times 1\,\text{m}$ at a distance of $50\,\text{m}$. In such a scenario, characteristic for an observer situated in a car moving along a straight road, there may indeed be too few planar features for the needs of a higher task.

A technique is proposed for alleviating the problems with features which are only partly projected from a distinctive quasi-planar 3D surface, while keeping the good behaviour for the true planar features. The well behaved portion of a feature window is termed as *feature support*, while its robust and adaptive detection is the main objective of the paper. The technique is related to robust estimation of the warp parameters [10, 11], but is more suitable for detecting correct feature supports which often contain statistical outliers. Here we do not consider *updating* the reference [12, 13, 11] despite its potential for increasing the tracking flexibility, since it offers less precision while requiring more processing power. The related research also includes the cumulative similarity transform [14] which is suitable only for tracking homogeneous regions, and the probabilistic filtering of the feature position [15, 13, 11], which has been used for handling temporary total occlusions.

The paper is organized as follows: the theoretical background is briefly summarized in Sect. 2. Sect. 3 describes the two complementary procedures to infer the feature support. Experimental results are described and discussed in Sect. 4, while Sect. 5 contains a short conclusion and the directions for future work.

2   Theoretical Background

2.1   General Differential Tracker with Warp Correction

Let the feature in the current frame is given by $I(\mathbf{x})$, its appearance after a warp with parameters $\mathbf{p}$ by $I_W(\mathbf{x}, \mathbf{p})$, and the corresponding reference by $I_R(\mathbf{x})$. Then the tracking consists in finding $\hat{\mathbf{p}}$ which minimizes the error image norm, or equivalently, the error over the feature window:

$$\hat{\mathbf{p}} = \arg\min_{\mathbf{p}} \sum_{\mathbf{x}} \|I_W(\mathbf{x}, \mathbf{p}) - I_R(\mathbf{x})\| . \tag{1}$$

The minimization is performed in a Gauss-Newton style, by employing a first-order Taylor expansion of the warped feature around the previous approximation of $\hat{\mathbf{p}}$. This can be expressed in different ways [8], and here we present a "forward-additive" formulation with which the best accuracy has been obtained. The current feature warped with a sum of the previous parameter vector $\mathbf{p}$ and an unknown additive improvement $\Delta\mathbf{p}$ is therefore approximated as:

$$I_W(\mathbf{x}, \mathbf{p} + \Delta\mathbf{p}) \approx I_W(\mathbf{x}, \mathbf{p}) + \frac{\partial I_W}{\partial \mathbf{p}} \cdot \Delta\mathbf{p} . \tag{2}$$

The scalar residual norm appearing in (1) can now be represented as:

$$R(\Delta\mathbf{p}) = \sum_{\mathbf{x}} \|I_W(\mathbf{x}, \mathbf{p} + \Delta\mathbf{p}) - I_R(\mathbf{x})\|$$

$$\approx \sum_{\mathbf{x}} \|I_W(\mathbf{x}, \mathbf{p}) + \frac{\partial I_W}{\partial \mathbf{p}} \cdot \Delta\mathbf{p} - I_R(\mathbf{x})\| . \tag{3}$$

For clarity, we omit the arguments, denote the previous error image as e, and introduce $\mathbf{g}$ as the transposed warped feature gradient over the warp parameters:

$$R(\Delta\mathbf{p}) \approx \sum_{\mathbf{x}} \|e + \mathbf{g}^\top \Delta\mathbf{p}\| . \tag{4}$$

The requirement (1) can be enforced by finding a $\Delta\hat{\mathbf{p}}$ for which the gradient of the residual vanishes. In case of the L2 norm, this is easy to perform:

$$\frac{\partial R(\Delta\hat{\mathbf{p}})}{\partial \Delta\hat{\mathbf{p}}} \approx \sum_{\mathbf{x}} 2 \cdot (e + \mathbf{g}^\top \Delta\hat{\mathbf{p}}) \cdot \mathbf{g}^\top = \mathbf{0}^\top . \tag{5}$$

After transposing both ends of (5), we arrive at the final expression for an iteration in the context of a general warp (note that e is a scalar function):

$$\sum_{\mathbf{x}} (\mathbf{g}e + \mathbf{g}\mathbf{g}^\top \Delta \hat{\mathbf{p}}) = \mathbf{0} \ . \tag{6}$$

Thus, in each iteration, the additive improvement is calculated by solving a linear system of equations. The procedure stops when the norm of the improvement $\|\Delta \hat{\mathbf{p}}\|$ falls below a threshold, or when the new feature position falls outside the image bounds, or when the determinant $|\mathbf{g}\mathbf{g}^\top|$ becomes too small.

2.2   Tracker with Isotropic Scaling and Contrast Compensation

In order to mitigate the danger that a physically unrelated image patch might be well transformed towards the reference, a trade-off between the modelling power and the tracking security should be carefully chosen. For our application, a good balance is obtained by a 5-dimensional warp consisting of a 2-dimensional translational offset $(\mathbf{d})$, an isotropic scaling parameter (m), and the two parameters of the affine contrast compensation model (λ, δ) [6]. It is convenient to express the warp in terms of geometric and photometric components as $\mathbf{p} = (\mathbf{q}, \mathbf{r})$, where $\mathbf{q} = (m, \mathbf{d})$, and $\mathbf{r} = (\lambda, \delta)$. The warped feature is then obtained as:

$$I_W(\mathbf{x}, \mathbf{p}) = \lambda \cdot I(m * \mathbf{x} + \mathbf{d}) + \delta = U(I(T(\mathbf{x}, \mathbf{q})), \mathbf{r}) \ . \tag{7}$$

In order to use the general formulation from 2.1, an expression for $\frac{\partial I_W}{\partial \mathbf{p}} = [\frac{\partial U}{\partial \mathbf{q}} \frac{\partial U}{\partial \mathbf{r}}]$ must be derived using the chain rule. The second term is simpler to obtain:

$$\frac{\partial U}{\partial \mathbf{r}}(I(T(\mathbf{x}, \mathbf{q})), \mathbf{r}) = \begin{bmatrix} I_T & 1 \end{bmatrix} \ , \tag{8}$$

where I_T is the current feature warped with T: $I_T = I(T(\mathbf{x}, \mathbf{q}))$. The derivation of the first term is a little bit more involved:

$$\frac{\partial U}{\partial \mathbf{q}}(I(T(\mathbf{x}, \mathbf{q})), \mathbf{r}) = \frac{\partial U}{\partial I}(I(T(\mathbf{x}, \mathbf{q})), \mathbf{r}) \cdot \frac{\partial I}{\partial T}(T(\mathbf{x}, \mathbf{q})) \cdot \frac{\partial T}{\partial \mathbf{q}}(\mathbf{x}, \mathbf{q})$$

$$= \lambda \cdot I_T^x \cdot \begin{bmatrix} x_1 & 1 & 0 \\ x_2 & 0 & 1 \end{bmatrix} = \lambda \begin{bmatrix} I_T^x \mathbf{x} & I_T^{x1} & I_T^{x2} \end{bmatrix} \ , \tag{9}$$

where I_T^x is the gradient in the feature warped by T: $I_T^x = \frac{\partial I}{\partial T}(T(\mathbf{x}, \mathbf{q}))$. The combined result, (9) and (8), can be plugged into (6), with $\mathbf{g}$ given by:

$$\mathbf{g}^\top = \begin{bmatrix} I_T^x \mathbf{x} & I_T^{x1} & I_T^{x2} & I_T & 1 \end{bmatrix} \ . \tag{10}$$

2.3   The Running Average Gaussian Estimation

The proposed tracking approach relies on estimating the gray scale value distribution for each single pixel within the feature window. This can be achieved by a space-efficient approximation of the running average, which has been extensively used in the field of the background subtraction. For each feature pixel x, the current estimate of a distinct normal distribution is updated as follows [16]:

$$\mu_{x,t} = (1 - \alpha) \cdot \mu_{x,t-1} + \alpha \cdot x_t$$
$$\sigma_{x,t}^2 = (1 - \alpha) \cdot \sigma_{x,t-1}^2 + \alpha \cdot (x_t - \mu_{x,t})^2 . \tag{11}$$

The parameter $\alpha \in \langle 0, 1 \rangle$ represents the learning rate, or alternatively, how many previous frames are taken into account for the estimate. Although there are no guarantees that a certain pixel is normally distributed (indeed, the pixels which are interesting in our context may have arbitrary distributions, depending on the scene), the estimates do offer an insight into the pixel mean and variability.

3   The Feature Support Concept

3.1   Assumptions and Basic Notions

The high level application context assumes robot navigation in urban environment, controlled by techniques in which a long term contact with the features from a given set is highly desired. The considerations are therefore focused on tracking over a significant forward motion, as illustrated in Fig. 1. The features which are visible throughout the whole sequence are located quite far from the initial observer location, so that they experience considerable changes of scale and photometry. The 3D surfaces projecting into initial feature windows are quite large (due to the distance), so that many features cross a discontinuity. In fact, since parts of the scenery behind the car (to the left from #28 and to the right from #39) were out of the field of view in some frames of the sequence, #20 is the only feature in Fig. 1(a), for which the final appearance does not substantially deviate from the affine transformation model. The proposed concept strives to enlarge the application field of a differential tracker with warp correction onto the features for which the initial windows are only partly projected from a plane. The resulting convergence of the feature support provides a valuable shape information allowing the non-rectangular features to be introduced in

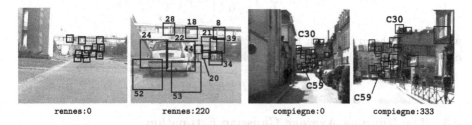

rennes:0   rennes:220   compiegne:0   compiegne:333

Fig. 1. Illustration of the tracking task: central portions of the first and the last frames of the sequences **rennes** and **compiegne**, with the designated windows of the tracked features

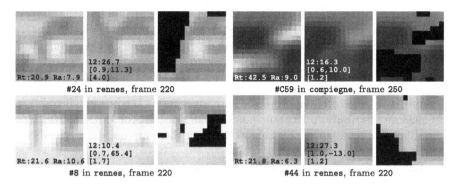

Fig. 2. The enlarged triples of the reference, the warped current feature and the feature support (non-masked areas) for the four features from Fig. 1. The numbers in the reference images indicate the RMS residuals for the whole feature window (Rt), and for the feature support only (Ra). The numbers in the warped features indicate the smaller eigenvalue of the second-order moment matrix (l_2), the photometric warp (λ, δ) and the isotropic scaling (m).

(6), and in the calculation of the monitoring residual. To illustrate the proposed objectives, the obtained supports for several features from sequences **rennes** and **compiegne** are shown in Fig. 2. The need for feature support arises most often when the feature is on a foreground structure occluding the background, either because the feature is at the boundary (**#24**, **#C59**), or the structure has holes (**#8**). The concept can also be helpful if the feature is situated on a background structure which is at times occluded by the foreground (**#44**), and when there are complex surface radiance variations which can not be counterbalanced by a feature-wide contrast compensation model (**#C59**). The relation between the obtained residuals (Ra≪Rt, see Fig. 2) illustrates the effectiveness of the technique.

3.2   The Volatile Feature Support Due to a Robust Rejection Rule

In the first investigated approach, the pixels not belonging to the feature support are identified as outliers within the distribution of the squared grey level value within the current error image $\{e_i^2\}$. The outliers are detected following a robust X84 rejection rule, which has also been used to reject the entire features (not the individual pixels), based on the magnitude of their RMS residual [17]. The rule uses the median as an estimator for the distribution location, while the scale of the distribution is estimated by the median absolute deviation (MAD):

$$C_{e^2} = \text{med}\{e_i^2\}$$
$$\text{MAD}_{e^2} = \text{med}\{|e_i^2 - C_{e^2}|\} . \tag{12}$$

Due to a further noise suppression, much better results are obtained when *temporally smoothed* values are used within (12). This can be achieved by substituting the error image pixels e_i with a difference between the mean value of the warped feature pixel estimated by (11), and the corresponding reference pixel.

The pixels of the feature support can finally be identified by testing for:

$$(|e_i^2 - C_{e^2}|) < \max(\text{th}_{\min}, k \cdot \text{MAD}_{e^2}) . \tag{13}$$

The choice of $k = 5$ is often appropriate here, since $5 \cdot \text{MAD}$ corresponds to $3.5 \cdot \sigma$ in a Gaussian distribution. Experiments have shown that the threshold $\text{th}_{\min}$ is required for suppressing the bad behaviour when there are no real outliers.

3.3   The Persistent Feature Support Due to Temporal Consistency

Experiments have shown that the previous approach for inferring the feature support is surprisingly effective in increasing the tolerance to the occasional outliers. However, that approach assumes that all the inlier error image pixels come from the same distribution, which is rarely the case. Good features usually have pixels originating from different materials which are likely to generate different error distributions. Thus, the obtained instances of the feature support usually do not resemble the part of the window projected from a continuous surface.

The second approach makes a more explicit check for the temporally consistent feature pixels, by analyzing the standard deviation estimated by (11). During the motion of the observer, the pixels belonging to a different continuous surface than the one which is consistently tracked, will refer to different points of the scene. In the case of natural scenes which are rich in texture, this will be reflected by occasional spikes in the standard deviation. These spikes can be detected by a threshold on the standard deviation σ^{th}, while the corresponding pixels can be persistently excluded from the feature support. An inverse process (adding a pixel to the feature support if it is consistently similar to the reference) could be employed for recovering after temporary occlusions. This has not been performed in our experiments, since for the most frequent foreground features it implies relinquishing the valuable information about the feature shape, which is not always attainable (e.g. when the background is homogenous).

A critical notion in both approaches is controlling the learning rate of the Gaussian estimates in (11). A fixed value would not be acceptable, since it would imply obtaining different results for different dynamics of the same motion. Perhaps the best solution would be to modulate α_0 by a perceived translational displacement with respect to the structure on which the feature resides. However, this would bring a serious increase of the implementation complexity, due to the coupling of the tracker with pose estimation. A simpler solution is therefore proposed, in which the modulating factor is computed from the interframe change of geometric warp parameters $\mathbf{d}$ and m:

$$\alpha = \alpha_0 \cdot \rho(|\Delta m| \cdot w_x + |\Delta d_x|, |\Delta m| \cdot w_y + |\Delta d_y|) , \tag{14}$$

where ρ is a 2D metric, and (w_x, w_y) are the feature window dimensions. If the camera motion is strictly translational and the feature occludes the background at infinity, the proposed solution gives each background fraction a fair amount in the distribution of a feature pixel. The behaviour would be less satisfactory for a chiefly rotational motion and for occlusions of distant features, but these cases do not occur in many realistic situations, as confirmed by experiments.

3.4 Multiscale Considerations

Due to the expected increase in the feature scale, it is suitable to initialize the tracking by the features at the smallest feasible scale. In order to ensure a good behaviour for large features (e.g. the feature #24 in Fig. 2 is more than 4 times larger than the reference), the tracking is performed at the level of the image pyramid which most closely resembles the previous scale of the feature. This is achieved by a simple scaling of the parameters of the geometrical warp before and after the tracking procedure for each individual feature. However, due to discretization issues, this sometimes causes artificial spikes in the parameters of the pixel Gaussians. The mean estimates for the feature pixels are therefore reinitialized to the corresponding actual values at each change of the pyramid level, in order to avoid the degradation of the feature support.

4   Experimental Results

The performed experiments were directed towards three different goals. The first goal was to investigate whether a threshold on the feature RMS residual can be at least partially substituted by other, hopefully more discriminative indicators of bad tracking. The second goal was to obtain a qualitative insight into the benefits of the proposed technique, by analyzing its sensitivity to the change of feature monitoring parameters. The final goal was an objective assessment of the influence of the technique to the measured lifetime of the tracked features.

The provided experimental results were obtained exclusively by the persistent support described in 3.3. The volatile approach described in 3.2 was not evaluated due to the ad-hoc threshold in (13), which undermines the capability to find a right ballance between the feature longevity and the tracking security. The recovered support is used for restricting the area of the feature window both in the tracking equations (6), as well as in the sum for calculating the error image norm (1). In order to be able to deal with large scale changes, a 3-level image pyramid is employed, obtained by successive smoothing and 1:2 subsampling. The switch of the pyramid level occurs whenever the feature window at the current resolution becomes greater than 1.8 times the size of the reference. The initial feature windows are 15×15 pixels wide, while the feature support modelling parameters are: $\alpha_0 = 0.005$, $\sigma^{th} = 12$. The source code used for performing the experiments is based on a public implementation of the KLT feature tracker [5] (see http://www.ces.clemson.edu/~stb/klt/) .

4.1 Criteria for Evaluating the Warp Correction Quality

Knowing when to abandon the tracking is a very important quality of a point tracker. In the previous work [5, 6], this was achieved chiefly by relying on the

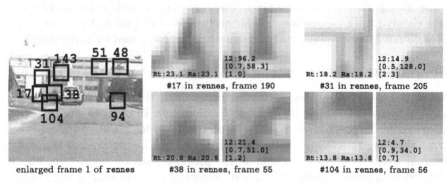

Fig. 3. The position of some features from **rennes** which will be discussed in the further text (left), and the four problematic ones (right). The abrupt magnification change test detects #17 and #31, but not #38. The gradient test detects "dissolved" features such as #104. See Fig. 2 for annotations.

RMS residual. However, the discriminative power of that criterion in real scenes with complex photometric variations leaves to desire, since for a given threshold, there are often both correctly rejected and incorrectly tracked features. For illustration, similar non-masked residuals (Rt) are obtained for the good features in Fig. 2, and for the problematic ones in Fig. 3 (#17, #31, #38, #104). The two most difficult situations for a point tracker are (i) when a foreground structure occludes the feature, which then tends to "jump" onto the foreground, and (ii) when the feature is on a face which is nearly parallel to the motion, when the warp may approach singularity. In both cases, the tracker may diverge from a consistent local minimum, but fortunately, this often can be detected by observing some common divergence symptoms. The latter scenario can be detected by testing for a "blanc wall" condition within the warped feature, by setting a threshold on the smaller eigenvalue of the second-order moment matrix [9]. Naturally, in the proposed context, the test is only performed for the pixels of the feature support. This test is very effective in avoiding tracking errors in low gradient areas, where a bad match often produces a small residual (see #104 in Fig. 3). Despite the efficacy in pruning the bad features, the test is a candidate for refinement because some features can be well tracked in spite of the low gradient (#48, #51 and #94 in Fig. 3).

Although the foreground structure and the background feature may be quite similar, as for features #17 (the car occludes the fence), #38 (the car occludes the bush), and #31 (the car occludes the building) in Fig. 3, the transfer is seldom smooth. This can be detected by an abrupt change of the recovered warp parameters. In particular, a threshold of 10% on the interframe relative magnification change[1] detects many of such situations, while seldom reporting false alarms.

---

[1] This is also true for other affine degrees of freedom: anisotropic scaling, skew, rotation. These parameters are not allowed since they actually decrease the tracking quality, by providing a way for the tracker to "escape" towards wrong local minima.

Nevertheless, the transfer of the feature #38 (see Fig. 3) involves only a 6% interframe relative magnification change. The proposed technique deals successfully with this situation since the feature support decreases with the occlusion, and the tracking is abandoned when a threshold of 40% is reached. However, as explained in 3.3, this would not work for a very distant feature, since the modulation factor for α would have been zero. Thus, unfortunately, the residuum threshold can not be completely avoided in the current implementation.

4.2 Sensitivity to Threshold Parameters

The choice of the threshold parameters used to detect the bad tracking is a trade-off between the security and the multiplicity of the tracked features. For the case of the RMS residual threshold, this is illustrated in Table 1. The results

Table 1. Count of features tracked until the end of **rennes**, for different thresholds on RMS residual r. For the discussion on feature #38, see 4.1 and Fig. 3.

	$r = 10$	$r = 15$	$r = 20$	$r = 25$
without feature support	1	3	8	12+#38
with feature support	3	11	13	13

suggest that the feature support offers better tracking results, even with a stricter residuum threshold. For example, the basic tracker with $r = 25$ produces a 18% magnification error for #8, while #18 is discontinued due to the abrupt magnification change. Both features are well tracked using the proposed technique, while the development of their supports is shown in Fig. 4.

Similar considerations hold for the threshold on the condition of the second-order moment matrix. If this threshold is released, two more features survive to the last frame in the basic tracker (#94, #143), only one of which is well

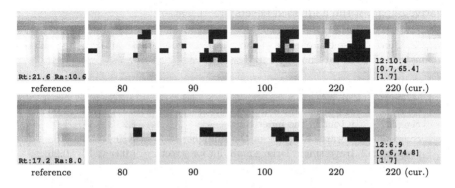

Fig. 4. The development of the support for the two features #8 (up) and #18 (down) from **rennes**, which are not correctly tracked when the feature support is not used. See Fig. 2 for annotations.

tracked. However, when feature support is used, additional two features are tracked without errors (#48, #51, all in Fig. 3).

4.3 Quantitative Experiments

The effects of the proposed technique are quantitatively evaluated on several real sequences taken from cars moving in urban environments. In the experiments, we test whether the proposed technique can provide longer feature lifetimes even with a more restrictive residuum threshold. We consider eight sequences which are briefly described in Table 2, while a more detailed presentation is available at `http://www.irisa.fr/lagadic/demo-cv-tracking-eng.html`. Each sequence from the table has been acquired during about one minute of mainly translational movement of the vehicle on which the camera was mounted. For each sequence, the tracking procedure was invoked with and without the feature support enabled, for different combinations of the RMS residual threshold. The relation between the two sets of obtained lifetimes (l_{FS}^i) and (l_{noFS}^i), has been analysed exclusively for features in which the tracking was discontinued due to the one of the criteria described in 4.1. In particular, we do not consider the features discontinued after a contact with the image border, which introduces a bias towards shorter-living features. Two different measures of average feature lifetime were used:

1. geometric average of individual lifetime ratios: $M_g = \sqrt[n]{\prod_i l_{FS}^i / l_{noFS}^i}$
2. ratio of the total feature lifetime: $M_a = (\sum_i l_{FS}^i)/(\sum_i l_{noFS}^i)$

The latter measure is judged as better since it reduces the bias towards short-living features. The obtained results are summarized in Table 2, and they show that the proposed technique favourably influences the feature lifetimes. Besides the occlusions and large photometric variations, the technique also allows to deal with structural changes, affecting the roof silhouettes (see #C30 in Fig. 1), and moderate affine deformations occurring on the pavement signalization. Conversely, the results for `compiegne2` and `compiegne3` suggest that there is no negative impact if the addressed effects are absent.

Table 2. Quantitative comparison of the total feature lifetime ratio M_a, for different combinations of RMS thresholds $R_{FS} : R_{noFS}$

sequence	description	15:15	20:20	15:20
rennes	approaching a building with holes	1.32	1.14	1.06
rennes2	a tour in the inner court	1.23	1.11	1.01
compiegne	towards a square in the sunlight	1.20	1.23	1.03
compiegne2	traversing a large square into a street	1.09	1.10	0.96
compiegne3	a very narrow street	1.05	1.07	0.93
compiegne4	a street bordered by buildings and trees	1.17	1.18	0.98
antibes1	some trees on the left and far away	1.09	1.13	0.99
antibes2	a narrow downhill winding street	1.07	1.07	1.02

5 Conclusions and the Future Work

A technique for increasing the feature lifetimes in extended real sequences acquired during a mainly translational forward motion of the observer has been presented. The technique addresses "almost good" features, for which the deformations during the tracking can not be completely explained by linear transforms, due to occlusions, photometric variations or small structural developments. The experiments suggest that the technique favourably affects the tracking quality, on both accounts of the correct tracking and the correct rejection.

The future work will be concentrated on applying the technique in the field of the autonomous robot navigation. There we would like to explore the potential of using all geometric warp parameters recovered by the tracking procedure $(\mathbf{d}, m)$. Further improvements might be obtained by devising more sophisticated ways to regulate the modulation speed α for estimating the distribution parameters of the warped feature pixels. An eventual faster convergence would allow the monitoring procedure to rely more heavily on the size and the shape of the feature support, and consequently further improve the chances for early detection of ill-conditioned situations, and confident tracking during extended time intervals.

References

1. Faugeras, O.D., Maybank, S.: Motion from point matches: multiplicity of solutions. Int. J. Comput. Vis. **4** (1990) 225–246
2. Nistér, D., Naroditsky, O., Bergen, J.: Visual odometry. In: Proc. of CVPR, Washington, DC, USA, IEEE (2004) 652–659
3. Davison, A.: Real-time simultaneous localisation and mapping with a single camera. In: Proc. of ICCV, Nice, France (2003) 1403–1410
4. Malis, E., Chaumette, F., Boudet, S.: 2 1/2 D visual servoing. IEEE Trans. RA **15** (1999) 234–246
5. Shi, J., Tomasi, C.: Good features to track. In: Proc. of CVPR. (1994) 593–600
6. Jin, H., Favaro, P., Soatto, S.: Real-time feature tracking and outlier rejection with changes in illumination. In: Proc. of ICCV. Volume 1. (2001) 684–689
7. Ma, Y., Soatto, S., Košecká, J., Sastry, S.: An Invitation to 3-D Vision: From Images to Geometric Models. Springer-Verlag, New York, USA (2004)
8. Baker, S., Matthews, I.: Lucas-Kanade 20 years on: A unifying framework. Int. J. Comput. Vis. **56** (2004) 221–255
9. Kenney, C., Manjunath, B., Zuliani, M., Hewer, G., van Nevel, A.: A condition number for point matching with application to registration and postregistration error estimation. IEEE Trans. PAMI **25** (2003) 1437–1454
10. Odobez, J.M., Bouthemy, P.: Robust multiresolution estimation of parametric motion models. J. Vis. Commun. Image R. **6** (1995) 348–365
11. Arnaud, E., Mémin, E., Cernuschi-Frias, B.: Conditional filters for image sequence based tracking - application to point tracking. IEEE Trans. IP **14** (2005) 63–79
12. Matthews, I., Ishikawa, T., Baker, S.: The template update problem. In: Proc. of British Machine Vision Conference. (2003)

13. Nguyen, H.T., Smeulders, A.W.M.: Fast occluded object tracking by a robust appearance filter. IEEE Trans. PAMI **26** (2004) 1099–1104
14. Darrell, T., Covell, M.: Correspondence with cumulative similarity transforms. IEEE Trans. PAMI **23** (2001) 222–227
15. Loutas, E., Diamantaras, K., Pitas, I.: Occlusion resistant object tracking. In: Proc. of ICIP. (2001) II: 65–68
16. Stauffer, C., Grimson, W.: Adaptive background mixture models for real-time tracking. In: Proc. of CVPR, IEEE (1999) II: 246–252
17. Fusiello, A., Trucco, E., Tommasini, T., Roberto, V.: Improving feature tracking with robust statistics. Pattern Anal. Appl. **2** (1999) 312–320

Tracking Objects Across Cameras by Incrementally Learning Inter-camera Colour Calibration and Patterns of Activity

Andrew Gilbert and Richard Bowden

CVSSP, University of Surrey, Guildford,
GU2 7XH, England
{a.gilbert, r.bowden}@surrey.ac.uk

Abstract. This paper presents a scalable solution to the problem of tracking objects across spatially separated, uncalibrated, non-overlapping cameras. Unlike other approaches this technique uses an incremental learning method, to model both the colour variations and posterior probability distributions of spatio-temporal links between cameras. These operate in parallel and are then used with an appearance model of the object to track across spatially separated cameras. The approach requires no pre-calibration or batch preprocessing, is completely unsupervised, and becomes more accurate over time as evidence is accumulated.

1 Introduction

The aim of this paper is to automatically track objects between cameras (inter camera). This is often termed object "handover", where one camera transfers a tracked object or person to another camera. To do this we need to learn about the relationships between the cameras, without colour, or spatial pre-calibration. In summary, an ideal tracking system could be described as one that, upon initialisation is able to work immediately, as more data becomes available will improve performance, and is adaptable to changes in the camera's environment.

To achieve this the system needs to be able to learn both the spatial and colour relationships between non-overlapping cameras. This allows the system to determine if a newly detected object has previously been tracked on another camera, or is a new object. The approach learns these spatial and colour relationships, though unlike previous work it does not require pre-calibration or explicit training periods. Incremental learning of the object's colour variation and movement, allows the accuracy of tracking to increase over time without supervised input.

The paper firstly gives a brief background of inter camera tracking and calibration. With section 3 describing the intra camera tracking and its use in creating the inter camera links is described in section 4. Sections 5 and 6 explain the spatial block subdivision to improve the representation of links and how the links and an object appearance model is used to track inter camera. Incremental camera colour calibration is explained in section 7, with experiments and results that combine both approaches presented in Section 8.

A. Leonardis, H. Bischof, and A. Pinz (Eds.): ECCV 2006, Part II, LNCS 3952, pp. 125–136, 2006.

2   Background

Early tracking algorithms [1][2] required both camera calibration and overlapping fields of view (FOV). These are needed to compute the handover of tracked objects between cameras. Additionally Chang [3] required a 3D model of the environment using epipolar geometry, to allow for the registration of objects across the different overlapping cameras. The requirement that cameras have an overlapping FOV is impractical due to the large number of cameras required and the physical constraints upon their placement.

Kettnaker and Zabih [4] presented a Bayesian solution to track people across cameras with non-overlapping FOVs. However the system required calibration, with the user providing a set of transition probabilities and their expected duration *a priori*. This means that the environment and the way people move within it must be known. In most surveillance situations this is unrealistic.

Probabilistic or statistical methods have seen some of the greatest focus to solve inter camera tracking. They all use the underlying principle that through accumulating evidence of movement patterns over time it is likely that common activities will be discovered. Huang and Russel [5] presented a probabilistic approach to tracking cars on a highway, modelling the colour appearance and transition times as gaussian distributions. This approach is very application specific, using only two calibrated cameras with vehicles moving in one direction in a single lane. Javed, *et al* [6] present a more general system by learning the camera topology and path probabilities of objects using Parzen windows. This is a supervised learning technique where transition probabilities are learnt during training using a small number of manually labeled trajectories. Dick and Brooks [7] use a stochastic transition matrix to describe patterns of motion both intra and inter camera. For both systems the correspondence between cameras has to be supplied as training data *a priori*. The system required an offline training period where a marker is carried around the environment. This would be infeasible for large systems and can not adapt to cameras being removed or added ad hoc without recalibration.

KaewTraKulPong and Bowden [8] or Ellis *et al* [9] do not require *a priori* correspondences to be explicitly stated, instead they use the observed motion over time to establish reappearance periods. Ellis learns the links between cameras, using a large number of observed objects to form reappearance period histograms between the cameras. Bowden instead uses appearance matching to build up fuzzy histograms of the reappearance period between cameras. This allows a spatio-temporal reappearance period to be modelled. In both cases batch processing was performed on the data which limits their application.

Colour is often used in the matching process. Black *et al* [10] use a non-uniform quantisation of the HSI colour space to improve illumination invariance, while retaining colour detail. KaewTraKulPong and Bowden [11] uses a Consensus-Colour Conversion of Munsell colour space (CCCM) as proposed by Sturges et al [12]. This is a coarse quantisation based on human perception and provides consistent colour representation inter-camera. Most multi camera surveillance systems assume a common camera colour response. However, even cameras of the same type will exhibit differences which can cause significant colour errors. Pre-calibration of the cameras is normally performed with respect to a single known object, such as the 24 main colour GretagMacbeth [13] ColorCheckerTM chart used by Ilie and Welch [14]. Porikli [15] proposes a distance metric and model function to evaluate the inter camera colour response. It is based on a correlation matrix computed from three 1-D quantised RGB colour histograms and a model function obtained from the minimum cost path traced within the correlation matrix. Joshi [16] similarly proposes a RGB to RGB transform between images. By using a 3x3 matrix, inter channel effects can be modelled between the red, green, and blue components.

3   Object Tracking and Description

The test environment consists of 4 non-overlapping colour cameras in an office building, with the layout shown in Figure 1. The area between cameras contains doors and corners removing smooth motion inter camera. The video feeds are multiplexed together to form a time synchronized single video, fed into a P4 windows PC in real time. To detect objects the static background colour distribution is modelled [11] in a similar fashion to that originally presented by Stauffer and Grimson [17]. A gaussian mixture model on a per-pixel basis is used to form the foreground vs background pixel segmentation, learnt using an online approximation to expectation maximisation. Shadows are identified and removed by relaxing a models constraint on intensity but not chromaticity, and the foreground object is formed using connected component analysis on the resulting binary segmentation. Objects are linked temporally with a Kalman filter to provide movement trajectories within each camera, illustrated in Figure 1.

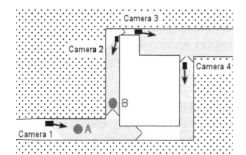 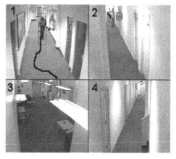

Fig. 1. (Left)The top down layout of the camera system, (Right) The tracking environment used

3.1   Colour Similarity

Once the foreground objects have been identified, an object descriptor is formed for inter camera correlation. The colour histogram is used to describe the objects appearance as it is spatially invariant and through quantisation, some invariance to illumination can be achieved. Several colour spaces and quantisation levels were investigated including the HSI (8x8x4) approach proposed by Black *et al* [10], the Consensus-Colour Conversion of Munsell colour space (CCCM) [12] and differing levels of conventional RGB quantisation. Without calibrating camera colour responses, CCCM produced marginally superior results and was selected for initial object correlation, for further details see [18]. CCCM works by breaking RGB colour into 11 basic colours. Each basic colour represents perceptual colour category established through a physiological study of how human's categorise colour. This coarse quantisation provides a consistent colour representation inter-camera prior to quantisation. With calibration, quantised RGB performs best as will be seen in Section 7.

4   Building the Temporal Links Between Cameras

To learn the spatial links between cameras, we make use of the key assumption that, given time, objects (such as people) will follow similar routes inter camera and that the repetition of the routes will form marked and consistent trends in the overall data. These temporal links inter camera can be used to link camera regions together, producing a probabilistic distribution of an objects movement between cameras.

Linking all regions to all others is feasible in small scale experimental systems. However, as the number of cameras increase, the number of possible links required to model the posterior increases exponentially. With each camera in a system of 20 cameras having 3 entry or exit regions, a total of 3540 links would be required to ensure that all possibilities are covered. As links increase, the amount of data required to learn these relationships also increases and the approach becomes infeasible. However, most of the links between regions are invalid as they correspond to impossible routes. Thus to use the available resources effectively a method is required to distinguish between valid and invalid links. Most solutions to this problem require either batch processing to identify entry/exit points or hand labeling of the links between regions (impractical in large systems). Both of these approaches are unable to adjust to changes in the environment or camera position. This section proposes a method that is initially coarsely defined but then refines itself over time to improve accuracy as more data becomes available. It has the ability to adjust to any changes that might occur in the environment without a complete system restart.

4.1   Region Links

The system starts by identifying links at the basic camera-to-camera level, discarding unused or invalid links. Valid links can then be subdivided to provide a higher level of detail. The tracking algorithm automatically tracks objects within the camera's FOV and forms a colour appearance model for the object or person. The colour histogram $B = (b_1, b_2....b_n)$ is the median histogram recorded

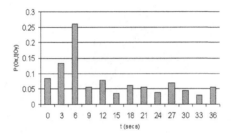

Fig. 2. An example of a probability distribution showing a distinct link between two regions

for an object over its entire trajectory within a single camera. All new objects that are detected are compared to previous objects within a set time window, T. The colour similarity is calculated and combined together, to form a discrete probability distribution over time based on this reappearance period T. Thus the frequency f of a bin ϕ is calculated as:

$$f_\phi = \sum_{\forall i} \sum_{\forall j} \begin{cases} H_{ij} & (t_i^{end} - t_j^{start}) < \phi \\ 0 & otherwise \end{cases} \quad \forall \phi < T \tag{1}$$

where t_i^{start} and t_i^{end} are the entry and exit times of object i respectively, T is the maximum allowable reappearance period. H_{ij} is the histogram intersection of objects i and j given by $H_{ij} = \sum_{k=1}^{11} min(B_{ik}, B_{jk})$. Frequencies are only calculated for an object i that disappears from region y followed by a reappearance in region x ($f^{x|y}$). Normalising the total area by $\sum_i^T f_{\phi=0}^{x|y}$, an estimate to the conditional transition probability $P(O_{x,t}|O_y)$ is obtained. An example of $P(O_{x,t}|O_y)$ is shown in Figure 2 where $O_{x,t}$ is object x at time t. The distinct peak at 6 seconds indicates a link between the two regions.

5   Incremental Block Subdivision and Recombination

This section explains how the system identifies valid links and therefore when to subdivide the connected blocks. Eventually, adjacent neighbouring blocks can be recombined to form larger blocks if found to have similar distributions.

The system is based on a rectangular subdivision. Initially, at the top level, the system starts with one block for each of the four cameras. This allows tracking to start immediately with links initially uniformly distributed. The twelve links (ignoring self transitions) between the blocks are learnt over time using the method described in the previous section. After sufficient evidence has been accumulated, determined by the degree of histogram population, the noise floor level is measured for each link. This could be determined with statistical methods such as the average and standard deviation, however, through experimentation, double the Median of all the values of the probability distribution was found to provide consistent results. If the maximum peak of the distribution is

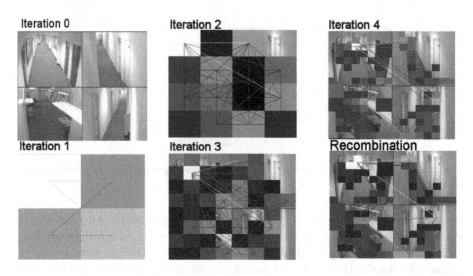

Fig. 3. The iterative process of splitting the blocks on the video sequence

found to exceed the noise floor level, this indicates a possible correlation between the two blocks (eg Figure 2).

If a link is found between two blocks, they are both subdivided to each create four new equal sized blocks. The previous data is then reused and incorporated with future evidence to form links in the newly subdivided blocks. It is likely that many of the blocks will not form coherent links, and if a link has no data in it, it is removed to minimise the number of links maintained. Figure 3 shows how the blocks are removed and subdivided over time. Table 1 shows the number of links maintained and dropped at each iteration, along with the amount of data used. It can be seen that with each iteration, the number of possible links increases dramatically, whereas the number of valid links maintained by the system are considerably less. The policy of removing unused and invalid regions improves system scalability.

As the process proceeds the blocks start to form the entry and exit points of the cameras, Figure 3 (interation 4) shows the result after 4 subdivisions. The lighter blocks have a higher importance determined by the number of samples each link contains. As the number of iterations increase, the size of the

Table 1. Table of number of links maintained and dropped in each split

Iteration	Amount of Data	Total Possible Blocks	Total Possible Links	Number of Blocks maintained	Total Possible Links	Initial links	Dropped links	Links maintained
1	1000	4	12	4	12	12	0	12
2	5000	16	240	16	240	240	45	195
3	10000	64	4032	60	2540	1631	688	943
4	10000	256	65280	191	36290	36134	34440	1694

linked blocks decrease and thus reduce the number of samples detected in each block. Low numbers of samples result in unreliable distributions. To counter this, blocks which are found to have similar distributions to neighbouring blocks are combined together to increase the overall number of samples within that block (as illustrated in the right image in Figure 3(recombination)). This reduces the number of blocks and therefore links maintained, and increases the accuracy of those links. Should new evidence be identified in previously discarded blocks, eg if a door is suddenly opened, the affected blocks can be recombined to the previous level of subdivision.

6   Calculating Posterior Appearance Distributions

This section describes how the weighted links between blocks can be used to weight the observation likelihood of tracked people. Over time the posterior becomes more accurate as the iterative block splitting process (described previously) takes place. Given an object which disappears in region y we can model its reappearance probability over time as;

$$P(O_t|O_y) = \sum_{\forall x} w_x P(O_{x,t}|O_y) \tag{2}$$

where the weight w_x at time t is given as

$$w_x = \frac{\sum_{i=0}^{T} f_\phi^{x|y}}{\sum_{\forall y} \sum_{i=0}^{T} f_\phi^{x|y}} \tag{3}$$

This probability is then used to weight the observation likelihood obtained through colour similarity to obtain a posterior probability of a match, across spatially separated cameras. Tracking objects is then achieved by maximising the posterior probability within a set time window.

7   Modelling Colour Variations

The CCCM colour quantisation descriptor used in the previous section, assumes a similar colour response between cameras. However this is seldom the case. Indeed the cameras of Figure 1 show marked difference in colour response even to the human eye. Therefore, a colour calibration of these cameras is proposed that can be learnt incrementally as with the distribution previously discussed.

The system uses the initial CCCM colour descriptor to form posterior distributions, in parallel to forming the colour transformation matrices between cameras. Novelly, the tracked people are automatically used as the calibration objects, and a transformation matrix is formed incrementally to model the colour changes between cameras. However, the people used are not identical sizes, therefore a point to point transformation is unavailable. We therefore use the colour descriptor matched between regions in different cameras to provide the calibration. Equation 4 shows the transformation matrix between image I and the transformed image T using 2 bin RGB quantisation in this simple example.

$$[I_{r_1}\ I_{r_2}\ I_{g_1}\ I_{g_2}\ I_{b_1}\ I_{b_2}] * \begin{bmatrix} t_{r_1r_1} & t_{r_1r_2} & t_{r_1g_1} & t_{r_1g_2} & t_{r_1b_1} & t_{r_1b_2} \\ t_{r_2r_1} & t_{r_2r_2} & t_{r_2g_1} & t_{r_2g_2} & t_{r_2b_1} & t_{r_2b_2} \\ t_{g_1r_1} & t_{g_1r_2} & t_{g_1g_1} & t_{g_1g_2} & t_{g_1b_1} & t_{g_1b_2} \\ t_{g_2r_1} & t_{g_2r_2} & t_{g_2g_1} & t_{g_2g_2} & t_{g_2b_1} & t_{g_2b_2} \\ t_{b_1r_1} & t_{b_1r_2} & t_{b_1g_1} & t_{b_1g_2} & t_{b_1b_1} & t_{b_1b_2} \\ t_{b_2r_1} & t_{b_2r_2} & t_{b_2g_1} & t_{b_2g_2} & t_{b_2b_1} & t_{b_2b_2} \end{bmatrix} \simeq [T_{r_1}\ T_{r_2}\ T_{g_1}\ T_{g_2}\ T_{b_1}\ T_{b_2}]$$

$$(4)$$

t_{xy} is the term that specifies how much the input from colour channel x contributes to the output of colour channel y. Transformation matrices are formed between the four cameras. Six transformations along with their inverses provide the twelve transformations required to transform objects between the four cameras. As camera calibration is refined the illumination changes that affected the success of the original correlation methods investigated in [18] and section 3, are reduced. This allows other less coarse quantisation (such as RGB) to be used with improved performance as will be shown.

The six transformation matrices for the four cameras are initialised as identity matrices assuming a uniform prior of colour variation between camera. When a person is tracked inter camera and is identified as the same object, the difference between the two colour descriptors, is modelled by the transform matrix t from Equation 4. The matrix t is calculated by computing the transformation that maps the person's descriptor from the previous camera I to the person's current descriptor T. This transformation is computed via SVD. The matrix t is then averaged with the appropriate camera transformation matrix, and repeated with other tracked people to gradually build a colour transformation between cameras. This method will introduce small errors, however it is in keeping with the incremental theme of the paper. Allowing the system to continually update and adapt to the colour changes between cameras as more data becomes available.

To form the transform matrices a number of different quantisations were examined. A 3x3 matrix of the median colour of a person, was found to be too coarse, losing too much colour information. The 11 bin CCCM quantisation used to create the posterior distributions is an arbitrary labeling, not metric and therefore cannot be represented by a linear transformation. However it is more accurate than RGB without calibration. With calibration RGB performs better. A number of RGB quantisations were investigated with varying accuracy, however a parzen window gives a stable accuracy of 77% over a range of quantisation levels.

8   Results

The final system starts uncalibrated with uniform priors for all distributions and identity matrices for colour transforms. It uses no supervised learning of its environment, instead automatically adding information as it becomes available. This

Table 2. Table of results of using CCCM colour similarity alone, colour calibration alone, posterior distribution weighting of CCCM similarity and a combination of all three. With an increasing number of refinements of the blocks.

Block split	Total Data Used	Accuracy:		
		Posterior Distrib Weights	4 bin RGB Colour Calib alone	Combined weight + colour model
CCCM Colour only	0	55%	42%	55%
1	500	60%	55%	68%
2	1000	63%	60%	69%
3	5000	68%	60%	76%
4	10000	73%	67%	78%

section demonstrates the performance of the incrementally constructed spatio-temporal weights, the inter camera colour calibration and the result of combining both approaches. The data used consisted of 10,000 objects tracked over a period of 72 hours of continuous operation. Evaluation was performed using an unseen ground-truthed 20 minute sequence with 300 instances of people tracked for more than 1 second.

Initially, the experiment has no *a priori* information of the environment, using only the CCCM colour similarity between objects to correlate inter camera. The posterior probability of the object match is gained by multiplying the colour similarity by the reappearance probability (3). At each refinement the accuracy increases as indicated in Table 2. After 5 days and 10,000 tracked objects each camera has been split 4 times resulting in a possible 64 regions per camera. At this point accuracy has increased from the base 55% of colour similarity alone to 73%. Equally our incremental learning scheme for colour calibration can be applied. Again as additional objects are added into the colour transformation matrices the accuracy of colour similarity for RGB increases from 42% to 67%.

Obviously it would be beneficial to combine both of these methods to further increase performance. The first level of block refinement and reappearance period estimation is constructed and the posterior appearance of objects used for colour calibration. This provides a boost in performance as apposed to using colour similarity alone. Once a colour transformation is available, a transformed RGB

Table 3. Looking at iterations of the colour calibration to further improve accuracy

Iteration	Total Data Used	Accuracy:		
		Posterior Distrib Weights	4 bin RGB Colour Calib alone	Combined weight + colour model
Inital results from block splitting	10,000	73%	67%	78%
1	10,000	73%	69%	80%
2	10,000	73%	70%	81%
3	10,000	73%	70%	81%

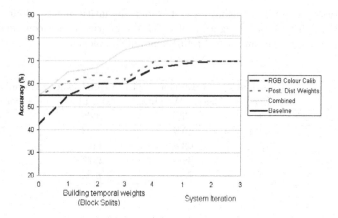

Fig. 4. Comparing the accuracies of; the baseline colour CCCM similarity, colour calibration alone, posterior distributions weights alone (space) and the combination of spatio-temporal weighted colour calibration over a number of program iterations

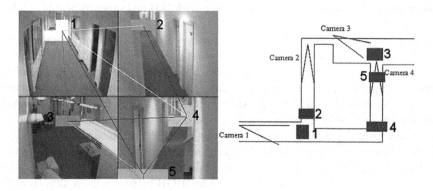

Fig. 5. Both the main entry and exit points and a top down layout of the camera system environment with these blocks marked

colour descriptor can be used in learning the second level of block refinement. This process can be repeated where colour calibration can further increase the accuracy of block refinement and vice versa. This is indicated in Table 2 where using this interative scheme raises detection performance from 55% to 78%.

Of course this process can be continued until performance converges to a stable level. Table 3 shows a further 3 iterations without additional data or block refinement providing a final accuracy of 81% which is a significant improvement upon colour similarity alone. This is the stable point for this system without more data being added.

The graph in Figure 4, shows how the accuracy increases both over block splits (shown in Table 2), and program iterations (shown in Table 3). The greatest overall increase in accuracy is in the combination of both posterior distribution weights and colour calibration of the cameras. The increase in accuracy allows the system to fulfill the three ideals stated in the introduction, of working immediately, improving performance as more data is accumulated, and can adapt to changes in its environment.

The main entry/exit blocks and links after 4 iterations are shown in Figure 5, along with a spatial map of the blocks.

9   Conclusions

We have described an approach to automatically derive the main entry and exit areas in a camera probabilistically using incremental learning, while simultaneously the colour variation inter camera is learnt to accommodate inter-camera colour variations. Together these techniques allow people to be tracked between spatially separated uncalibrated cameras with up to 81% accuracy, importantly using no *a priori* information in a completely unsupervised fashion. This is a considerable improvement over the baseline colour similarity alone of 55%. The spatio-temporal structure of the surveillance system can be used to weight the observation likelihood extracted through the incrementally calibrated colour similarity. The incremental colour calibration and posterior distribution weighting are both completely automatic, unsupervised and able to adapt to changes in the environment. The incremental technique ensures that the system works immediately but will become more accurate over time as additional data is acquired.

Acknowledgements

This work is supported by an EPSRC/Imaging Faraday partnership industrial CASE award sponsored by Overview Ltd.

References

1. Cai, Q., Agrarian, J.: "Tracking Human Motion using Multiple Cameras". Proc. International Conference on Pattern Recognition (1996) 67–72
2. Kelly, P., Katkere, A., Kuramura, D., Moezzi, S., Chatterjee, S.: "An Architecture for Multiple Perspective Interactive Video". Proc. of the 3rd ACE International Conference on Multimedia (1995) 201–212
3. Chang, T., Gong, S.: "Bayesian Modality Fusion for Tracking Multiple People with a Multi-Camera System". Proc. European Workshop on Advanced Video-based Surveillance Systems (2001)
4. Kettnaker, V., Zabih, R.: "Bayesian Multi-Camera Surveillance". Proc. IEEE Computer Vision and Pattern Recognition (1999) 253–259
5. Huang, T., Russell, S.: "Object Identification in a Bayesian Context". Proc. International Joint Conference on Artificial Intelligence (IJCAI-97), Nagoya, Japan (1997) 1276–1283
6. Javed, O., Rasheed, Z., Shafique, K., Shah, M.: "Tracking Across Multiple Cameras with Disjoint Views". Proc. IEEE International Conference on Computer Vision (2003) 952–957

7. Dick, A., Brooks, M.: "A Stochastic Approach to Tracking Objects Across Multiple Cameras". Australian Conference on Artificial Intelligence (2004) 160–170
8. KaewTrakulPong, P., Bowden, R.: "A Real-time Adaptive Visual Surveillance System for Tracking Low Resolution Colour Targets in Dynamically Changing Scenes". Journal of Image and Vision Computing. Vol 21, Issue 10, Elsevier Science Ltd (2003) 913–929
9. Ellis, T., Makris, D., Black, J.: "Learning a Multi-Camera Topology". Joint IEEE Workshop on Visual Surveillance and Performance Evaluation of Tracking and Surveillance (VS-PETS) (2003) 165–171
10. Black, J., Ellis, T., Makris, D.: "Wide Area Surveillance with a Multi-Camera Network". Proc. IDSS-04 Intelligent Distributed Surveillance Systems (2003) 21–25
11. KaewTrakulPong, P., Bowden, R.: "Towards Automated Wide Area Visual Surveillance: Tracking Objects Between Spatially Separated, Uncalibrated Views". In Proc. Vision, Image and Signal Processing, Vol 152, issue 02 (2005) 213–224
12. Sturges, J., Whitfield, T.: "Locating Basic Colour in the Munsell Space". Color Research and Application, 20(6):364-376 (1995)
13. : Gretagmacbeth Color Management Solutions. (www.gretagmacbeth.com)
14. Ilie, A., Welch, G.: "Ensuring Color Consistency across Multiple Cameras". Techincal Report TR05-011 (2005)
15. Porikli, F.: "Inter-Camera Color Calibration by Cross-Correlation Model Function". IEEE International Conference on Image Processing (ICIP),Vol. 2, (2003) 133–136
16. Joshi, N.: "Color Calibrator for Arrays of Inexpensive Image Sensors". MS Thesis, Stanford University Department of Computer Science, (2004)
17. Stauffer, C., Grimson, W.: "Learning Patterns of Activity using Real-time Tracking". PAMI, 22(8) (2000) 747–757
18. Bowden, R., Gilbert, A., KaewTraKulPong, P.: "Tracking Objects Across Uncalibrated Arbitrary Topology Camera Networks, in Intelligent Distributed Video Surveillance Systems". S.A Velastin and P Remagnino Eds. Chapt 6, IEE, London, to be published (2005)

Monocular Tracking of 3D Human Motion with a Coordinated Mixture of Factor Analyzers

Rui Li[1], Ming-Hsuan Yang[2], Stan Sclaroff[1], and Tai-Peng Tian[1]

[1] Boston University, Boston, MA 02215, USA
{lir, sclaroff, tian}@cs.bu.edu
[2] Honda Research Institute, Mountain View, CA 94041, USA
myang@honda-ri.com

Abstract. Filtering based algorithms have become popular in tracking human body pose. Such algorithms can suffer the curse of dimensionality due to the high dimensionality of the pose state space; therefore, efforts have been dedicated to either smart sampling or reducing the dimensionality of the original pose state space. In this paper, a novel formulation that employs a dimensionality reduced state space for multi-hypothesis tracking is proposed. During off-line training, a mixture of factor analyzers is learned. Each factor analyzer can be thought of as a "local dimensionality reducer" that locally approximates the pose manifold. Global coordination between local factor analyzers is achieved by learning a set of linear mixture functions that enforces agreement between local factor analyzers. The formulation allows easy bidirectional mapping between the original body pose space and the low-dimensional space. During on-line tracking, the clusters of factor analyzers are utilized in a multiple hypothesis tracking algorithm. Experiments demonstrate that the proposed algorithm tracks 3D body pose efficiently and accurately , even when self-occlusion, motion blur and large limb movements occur. Quantitative comparisons show that the formulation produces more accurate 3D pose estimates over time than those that can be obtained via a number of previously-proposed particle filtering based tracking algorithms.

1 Introduction

Tracking articulated human motion is of interest in numerous applications: video surveillance, gesture analysis, human computer interfaces, computer animation, etc. Various tracking algorithms have been proposed that require neither special clothing nor markers on the human body. A number of algorithms track body motion in the image plane (2D), thereby avoiding the need for complex 3D models or camera calibration information. While these methods are usually efficient, only 2D joint locations and angles can be inferred. As a result, the 2D methods have difficulty in handling occlusions and they are inutile for applications where accurate 3D information is required. To better understand human motion, 3D tracking algorithms resort to detailed 3D articulated models which require significantly more degrees of freedom. Consequently, algorithms that are able to handle high-dimensional, non-linear data efficiently and effectively are essential to the success of 3D human tracking algorithms.

A. Leonardis, H. Bischof, and A. Pinz (Eds.): ECCV 2006, Part II, LNCS 3952, pp. 137–150, 2006.
© Springer-Verlag Berlin Heidelberg 2006

In this paper, we propose an efficient and accurate algorithm for tracking 3D articulated human motion given monocular video sequences. We exploit the physical constraints of human motion by learning a low-dimensional latent model from high-dimensional motion capture data. A probabilistic algorithm is employed to perform non-linear dimensionality reduction and clustering concurrently within a global coordinate system. The projected data forms clusters within the globally coordinated low-dimensional space; this makes it possible to derive an efficient multiple hypothesis tracking algorithm based on the distribution modes. By tracking in low-dimensional space, we avoid the sample impoverishment problem [1] and retain the simplicity of the multiple hypothesis tracking algorithm at the same time. Given clusters formed in the latent space, temporal smoothness is only enforced within each cluster. In experiments with real video, the system reliably tracks body motion during self-occlusions and in the presence of motion blur. The system can accurately track large movements of the human limbs in adjacent time steps by propagating each cluster's information over time in the multiple hypothesis tracking algorithm. A quantitative comparison shows that the formulation produces more accurate 3D pose estimates than those obtained via a number of previously-proposed particle filtering based tracking algorithms.

2   Related Work

In this section, we first outline recent progress in particle filtering based tracking algorithms. We then give a quick review of dimensionality reduction algorithms, followed by a discussion of algorithms that solve the tracking problem in the dimensionality reduced space.

2.1   Particle Filtering

Particle filtering methods have been applied widely in tracking applications. Unfortunately, the number of particles needed to sufficiently approximate the state posterior distribution can explode when the state vector is high dimensional. Various approaches have been proposed to alleviate this problem. One common approach is to reposition the particles according to some importance function [2] to ensure a high survival rate [3]. For example, particles can be resampled using weighted resampling [3] or repositioned using deterministic search [4, 5] to localize the set of particles around significant maxima of the importance function. Other methods employ a coarse to fine search on the weighting function, e.g., the annealed particle filter [6] or layered sampling [7]. If the particle dynamics can be factored into independent components, then partitioned sampling [3] can be used to improve the performance of the particle filter.

2.2   Non-linear Dimensionality Reduction Algorithms

Dimensionality reduction algorithms are popular techniques to discover compact representations of high-dimensional data. As a classic dimensionality reduction algorithm, Principal Component Analysis (PCA) is inadequate to handle the non-linear behavior inherent to our problem domain. Locally Linear Embedding (LLE) [8], Isomap [9] and Laplacian Eigenmaps [10] are some representative non-linear dimensionality reduction algorithms – but unfortunately, these techniques are typically not invertible. Inverse mapping of particles (proposals) back to the original human pose space is needed in order to reweight the particles given the image measurements. A number of existing dimensionality reduction methods provide inverse mappings, such as Charting [11], Locally Linear Coordination (LLC) [12] and the Gaussian Process Latent Variable Model (GPLVM) [13]. In principle, any dimensionality reduction technique that provides an inverse mapping will be applicable. LLC is chosen in our algorithm because it is a probabilistic algorithm that performs non-linear dimensionality reduction and clustering concurrently within a global coordinate system. The projected data forms clusters within the globally coordinated low-dimensional space; this makes it possible to derive an efficient multiple hypothesis tracking algorithm based on distribution modes.

2.3   Human Motion Tracking

There is a broad range of work related to human motion tracking. See [14] for a recent survey as our focus is on the subclass of stochastic tracking algorithms.

Following the seminal work of [15], the CONDENSATION algorithm has been adapted for human motion tracking [4, 6]. Multiple Hypothesis Tracking [16] tracks modes in a simpler piece-wise Gaussian distribution. In [17], exemplars are incorporated into the CONDENSATION algorithm. A more specific motion model and accurate background modelling using learning are used in [18, 19].

Recently, researchers have proposed the use of dimensionality reduction techniques on the state space to reduce the size of the body pose state vector. This is justified by the insight that the space of possible human motions is intrinsically low-dimensional [20, 21, 22]. Particle filtering with the reduced state space will be faster because significantly fewer particles are required to adequetely approximate the state space posterior distribution. Recent works [23, 24, 25] are most closely related to our proposed algorithm for tracking human in a dimensionality-reduced space. In [23], two different regression algorithms are used for the forward mapping (dimensionality reduction) and inverse mapping. The representatives used in the regression are chosen in an heuristic manner [23]. In [25], GPLVM and a second order Markov model are used for tracking applications. The learned GPLVM model is used to provide model prior. Tracking is then done by minimizing a cost of 2D image matching, with the negative log-likelihood of the model prior as the regularization term. Both [23] and [25] advocate the use of gradient descent optimization techniques; hence, the low-dimensional space learned has to be smooth. An alternative approach [24] employs the GPLVM in a modified particle filtering algorithm where samples are drawn from the low-dimensional latent space. The GPLVM model in this case is used as a good non-linear dimensionality reduction algorithm. The smoothness enforced in the low-dimensional space by the learning algorithms in these three papers works well for tracking small limb movements, but may fail when large limb movements occur over time. In the case of using gradient descent optimization techniques, good initialization is required for the success of such techniques.

As will be shown in the rest of this paper, Locally Linear Coordination (LLC) leads to a principled way of solving the embedding and inverse mapping problems. Instead of enforcing smoothness everywhere in the latent space, this algorithm preserves the clustering behavior of similar high-dimensional data points and separates different clusters in the global coordinate system. The model learned from the LLC is then used in the algorithm for multiple hypothesis tracking of 3D human body motion.

3   Formulation

There are two main components in the proposed tracking algorithm as shown in Fig. 1. The first component is an off-line algorithm that learns a bidirectional mapping function between the low-dimensional space and the original pose space. The second component is an on-line algorithm for articulated human pose tracking that makes use of a modified multiple hypothesis tracking algorithm; the modes of this multiple hypothesis tracker are propagated over time in the embedded space.

3.1   Learning the Global Coordination Model

Roweis *et. al.* [26] proposed a model which performs a global coordination of local coordinate systems in a mixture of factor analyzers (MFA). Each factor analyzer (FA) can also be regarded as a local dimensionality reducer. The assumption is that both the high-dimensional data $\mathbf{y}$ and its global coordinate $\mathbf{g}$ are generated from the same set of latent variables s and $\mathbf{z}_s$, where each discrete hidden variable s refers to the s-th FA and each continuous hidden variable $\mathbf{z}_s$ represents the low-dimensional local coordinates in the s-th FA.

In the MFA model, data generated from s-th FA with prior probability $P(s)$, and the distribution of $\mathbf{z}_s$ are Gaussian: $\mathbf{z}_s|s \sim \mathcal{N}(0, \mathbf{I})$, where $\mathbf{I}$ is the identity

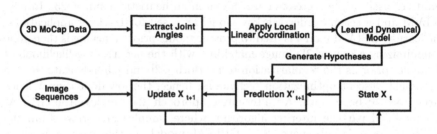

Fig. 1. Overview of our algorithm

matrix. Given s and $\mathbf{z}_s$, $\mathbf{y}$ and the global coordinate $\mathbf{g}$ are generated by the following linear equations:

$$\mathbf{y} = \mathbf{T}_{L_s}\mathbf{z}_s + \boldsymbol{\mu}_s + \mathbf{u}_s,$$
$$\mathbf{g} = \mathbf{T}_{G_s}\mathbf{z}_s + \boldsymbol{\kappa}_s + \mathbf{v}_s, \tag{1}$$

where $\mathbf{T}_{L_s}$ and $\mathbf{T}_{G_s}$ are the transformation matrices, $\boldsymbol{\mu}_s$ and $\boldsymbol{\kappa}_s$ are uniform translations between the coordinate systems, $\mathbf{u}_s \sim \mathcal{N}(0, \Lambda_{u_s})$ and $\mathbf{v}_s \sim \mathcal{N}(0, \Lambda_{v_s})$ are independent zero mean Gaussian noise terms. The following probability distributions can be derived from Eq. 1, 1:

$$\mathbf{y}|s, \mathbf{z}_s \sim \mathcal{N}(\mathbf{T}_{L_s}\mathbf{z}_s + \boldsymbol{\mu}_s, \Lambda_{\mathbf{u}_s})$$
$$\mathbf{g}|s, \mathbf{z}_s \sim \mathcal{N}(\mathbf{T}_{G_s}\mathbf{z}_s + \boldsymbol{\kappa}_s, \Lambda_{\mathbf{v}_s}). \tag{2}$$

With $\mathbf{z}_s$ being integrated out, we have

$$\mathbf{y}|s \sim \mathcal{N}(\boldsymbol{\mu}_s, \Lambda_{\mathbf{u}_s} + \mathbf{T}_{L_s}\mathbf{T}_{L_s}^T)$$
$$\mathbf{g}|s \sim \mathcal{N}(\boldsymbol{\kappa}_s, \Lambda_{\mathbf{v}_s} + \mathbf{T}_{G_s}\mathbf{T}_{G_s}^T). \tag{3}$$

The inference of global coordinate $\mathbf{g}$ conditioned on a data point $\mathbf{y}_n$ can be rewritten as

$$p(\mathbf{g}|\mathbf{y}_n) = \sum_s p(\mathbf{g}|\mathbf{y}_n, s)p(s|\mathbf{y}_n), \tag{4}$$

where

$$p(\mathbf{g}|\mathbf{y}_n, s) = \int p(\mathbf{g}|s, \mathbf{z}_s)p(\mathbf{z}_s|s, \mathbf{y}_n)d\mathbf{z}_s. \tag{5}$$

Given Eq. 1, both $p(\mathbf{g}|s, \mathbf{z}_s)$ and $p(\mathbf{z}_s|s, \mathbf{y}_n)$ are Gaussian distributions, $p(\mathbf{g}|\mathbf{y}_n, s)$ also follows a Gaussian distribution. Since $p(s|\mathbf{y}_n) \propto p(\mathbf{y}_n|s)p(s)$ can be computed and viewed as a weight, $p(\mathbf{g}|\mathbf{y}_n)$ is essentially a mixture of Gaussians. Though the mappings from $\{s, \mathbf{z}_s\}$ to $\mathbf{y}$ and $\mathbf{g}$ are linear, the mappings between them are not. An EM algorithm is proposed in [26] to learn this global coordination by maximizing the likelihood of the data, with an additional variational penalty term to encourage consistency of internal coordinates of each factor analyzer. This algorithm requires a user given trade-off parameter between modeling data and having consistent local coordinate systems. This algorithm suffers from the same problems of standard EM approaches, i.e., inefficiency and local minima.

Teh and Roweis came up with an efficient two stage model learning algorithm in [12]. By leveraging on the mixture of local models to collapse large groups of points together, their proposed algorithm works only with the groups rather than individual data points in the global coordination. In the two-stage model learning process, first the MFA between $\mathbf{y}$ and $(s, \mathbf{z}_s)$ is learned as proposed in [27]. Given the learned MFA model with S factor analyzers, $\mathbf{z}_{ns}$ is the expected local coordinate in the s-th FA for each data point $\mathbf{y}_n$. Let r_{ns} denote the likelihood, $p(\mathbf{y}_n|s)$. From Eqs. 1 and 2, $\mathbf{g}_n$, the expected global coordinate of $\mathbf{y}_n$ is defined as:

$$\mathbf{g}_n = \sum_s r_{ns}(\mathbf{T}_{G_s}\mathbf{z}_{n_s} + \boldsymbol{\kappa}_s) = \mathbf{L}\mathbf{u}_n, \tag{6}$$

where
$$\mathbf{L} = [\mathbf{T}_{G_1}, \kappa_1, \mathbf{T}_{G_2}, \kappa_2 \ldots, \mathbf{T}_{G_S}, \kappa_S]$$
and
$$\mathbf{u}_n^T = [r_{n_1}\mathbf{z}_{n_1}^T, r_{n_1}, r_{n_2}\mathbf{z}_{n_2}^T, r_{n_2}, \ldots, r_{n_S}\mathbf{z}_{n_S}^T, r_{n_S}].$$

Let $\mathbf{G} = [\mathbf{g}_1, \mathbf{g}_2, \ldots, \mathbf{g}_N]^T$ be the global coordinates of the whole data set (the rows of $\mathbf{G}$ corresponding to the coordinated data points) and $\mathbf{U} = [\mathbf{u}_1, \mathbf{u}_2, \ldots, \mathbf{u}_N]^T$, we then have a compact representation $\mathbf{G} = \mathbf{UL}$. We want to estimate $\mathbf{L}$. To determine $\mathbf{L}$, we need to minimize a cost function that incorporates the topological constraints that govern $\mathbf{g}_n$. The cost function used here is based on LLE [8]. For each data point $\mathbf{y}_n$, we denote its nearest neighbors as $\mathbf{y}_m$ ($m \in N_n$) and minimize the following:

$$\xi(\mathbf{Y}, \mathbf{W}) = \sum_n \left\| \mathbf{y}_n - \sum_{m \in N_n} w_{nm}\mathbf{y}_m \right\|^2$$
$$= Tr(\mathbf{Y}^T(\mathbf{I} - \mathbf{W}^T)(\mathbf{I} - \mathbf{W})\mathbf{Y}), \tag{7}$$

with respect to $\mathbf{W}$ and subject to the constraint $\sum_{m \in N_n} w_{nm} = 1$. Here the set of training data points is $\mathbf{Y} = [\mathbf{y}_1, \mathbf{y}_2, \ldots, \mathbf{y}_N]^T$ where each row of $\mathbf{Y}$ corresponds to a training data point. The weights w_{nm} are unique and can be obtained via constrained least squares. These weights represent the locally linear relationships between $\mathbf{y}_n$ and its neighbors. In a similar fashion, we can define the following cost function:

$$\xi(\mathbf{G}, \mathbf{W}) = \sum_n \left\| \mathbf{g}_n - \sum_{m \in N_n} \mathbf{g}_m \right\|^2$$
$$= Tr(\mathbf{G}^T(\mathbf{I} - \mathbf{W}^T)(\mathbf{I} - \mathbf{W})\mathbf{G})$$
$$= Tr(\mathbf{L}^T\mathbf{A}\mathbf{L}), \tag{8}$$

where $A = \mathbf{U}(\mathbf{I} - \mathbf{W}^T)(\mathbf{I} - \mathbf{W})\mathbf{U}^T$. To ensure $\mathbf{G}$ is invariant to translations, rotations and scaling, the following constraints are defined,

$$\frac{1}{N}\sum_n \mathbf{g}_n = 0 \tag{9}$$

and

$$\frac{1}{N}\sum_n \mathbf{g}_n\mathbf{g}_n^T = \frac{1}{N}\mathbf{G}^T\mathbf{G} = \mathbf{L}^T\mathbf{B}\mathbf{L} = \mathbf{I}, \tag{10}$$

where $\mathbf{I}$ is the identity matrix and $\mathbf{B} = \frac{1}{N}\mathbf{U}^T\mathbf{U}$. Both the cost function Eq. 8 and the constraints Eq. 10 are quadratic and the optimal $\mathbf{L}$ is determined by solving a generalized eigenvalue problem [12]. Let $d \ll D$ be the dimensionality of the underlying manifold that $\mathbf{y}$ is generated from. The 2nd to $(d+1)^{th}$ smallest generalized vectors solved from $\mathbf{Av} = \lambda\mathbf{Bv}$ form the columns of $\mathbf{L}$. The whole process is summarized in Fig. 2.

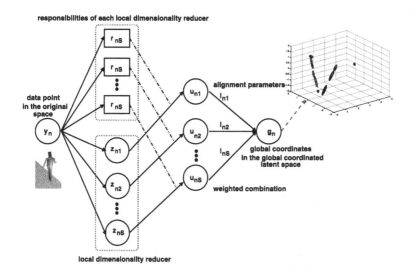

Fig. 2. The two stage learning process of [12]

3.2   Learning the Joint Angle Configurations

In our application for using LLC to learn the dimensionality reduced space, each training data **y** is a column vector that consists of joint angles computed from motion capture data. We adopt the same 3D cylindrical model used in [18]; we ignore the global translation. The dimension of **y** is 28 and 1900 frames from a motion capture sequence with a person walking are used for training. **Y** is used to represent the collection of training data $\mathbf{y}_n$, $n = 1, \ldots N$ and $N = 1900$. In the LLC learning, the dimension for variables **z** in each MFA is 3 and the number of mixtures $S = 10$. In the global coordination stage, the dimension of the latent space variable **g** is 3 (these parameters were determined empirically). The learning algorithm is summarized in Algorithm 1. Clusters are obtained through the two stage learning process described above. Each cluster is modeled as a Gaussian distribution in the latent space with its own mean vector and covariance matrix as shown in Fig. 3. This cluster-based representation leads to a straightforward algorithm for multiple hypothesis tracking, as described in Section 3.3.

Algorithm 1. Learning the globally coordinated space of human motion

---

Compute local linear reconstruction weights w_{nm} based on Eq. 7 using **Y**
Train a mixture of local dimensionality reducers.
    Apply this mixture to training human motion poses **Y**.
    Obtain a local representation $\mathbf{z}_{ns}$ and responsibility r_{ns} for each submodel s and each data point $\mathbf{y}_n$.
Form the matrix **U** and compute **A** and **B** from Eq. 8, Eq. 9 and Eq. 10.
Solve the generalized eigenvalue problem $\mathbf{Av} = \lambda \mathbf{Bv}$ and form **L** as described in Section 3.1.
Return $\mathbf{G} = \mathbf{UL}$ and **L**.

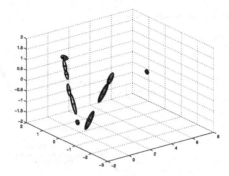

Fig. 3. The learned globally coordinated latent space. Each ellipsoid represents a cluster in the latent space, where mean is the centroid and covariances are the axes of the ellipsoids.

3.3   3D Articulated Human Tracking

In the application to 3D articulated human tracking, at each time instance, the tracker state vector is represented by $\mathcal{X}_t = (\mathbf{P}_t, \mathbf{g}_t)$. $\mathbf{P}_t$ is the 3D location of the pelvis (which is the root of the kinematic chain of the 3D human model) and $\mathbf{g}_t$ is the point in latent space. Once tracker state has been initialized, the basic idea of a filtering based tracking algorithm is to maintain a time-evolving probability distribution over the tracker state. Let $\mathbf{Z}_t$ denote the aggregation of past image observations (i.e. $\mathbf{Z}_t = \{\mathbf{z}_1, \mathbf{z}_2, \ldots, \mathbf{z}_t\}$). Assuming $\mathbf{z}_t$ is independent of $\mathbf{Z}_{t-1}$ given $\mathcal{X}_t$, we have the following standard equation:

$$p(\mathcal{X}_t | \mathbf{Z}_t) \propto p(\mathbf{z}_t | \mathcal{X}_t) p(\mathcal{X}_t | \mathbf{Z}_{t-1}) \qquad (11)$$

Here we use a multiple hypothesis tracker (MHT) together with the learned LLC model for the tracking task. As LLC provides clusters in the latent space as a step in the global coordination, it is natural to make use of the centers of the clusters as the initial modes in the MHT ($p(\mathbf{g}|\mathbf{z}_s, s)$ follows a Gaussian distribution). Given that in each cluster, the points in the latent space represent the poses that are similar to each other in the original space, we can apply a much simpler dynamical model in the prediction step of the filtering algorithm. The modified MHT is summarized in Algorithm 2. To compute the likelihood for the current prediction and the input video frame, first the silhouette of the current video frame is extracted through background subtraction. The predicted model is then projected onto the image and the chamfer matching cost between the projected model and the image silhouettes is considered to be proportional to the negative log-likelihood. We use the same model proposed by [28], which consists of a group of cylinders. The MHT algorithm proposed here differs from the algorithm proposed in [16] in the use of the latent space to generate proposals in a principled way. This is in contrast with [16], where the modes were selected empirically and the distributions were assumed to be piecewise Gaussian. While in the proposed algorithm, the output from the off-line learning algorithm

Algorithm 2. A Modified Multiple Hypothesis Tracker
___
for each time instance t **do**
  Prediction:
  generate the prior density $p(\mathcal{X}_t|\mathbf{Z}_{t-1})$ by passing through the modes of $p(\mathcal{X}_t|\mathbf{Z}_{t-1}$
  through a simple constant velocity predictor.

  Likelihood computation:
  1. Create the initial hypothesis seeds by sampling the distribution of $p(\mathcal{X}_t|\mathbf{Z}_{t-1})$.
     Note the samples of **g** are drawn around the modes of **G** in the latent space
     based on the covariance matrix of each cluster in the latent space.
  2. Obtain the modes (local maxima) of the likelihood function $p(\mathbf{z}_t|\mathcal{X}_t)$ by computing the matching cost of the samples.
  3. Measure the local statistics associated with each likelihood mode.

  Posterior density computation:
  The posterior density $p(\mathcal{X}_t|\mathbf{Z}_t)$ is updated through Eq. 11.
end for
___

(LLC) forms clusters (each cluster is described by a Gaussian distribution in latent space), the samples generated from the latent space are indeed drawn from a piecewise Gaussian distribution. The choice of modes to propagate over time becomes straightforward given the statistics of the clusters in the latent space.

4   Experiments

The proposed algorithm has been tested in tracking walking humans. The data set and calibration information were obtained from [28]. The video data set shows a person walking, as captured simultaneously from four different viewpoints. Sigal *et. al.* have used the multiple view information for 3D tracking [28]. We only need monocular sequences, and so we use each of the four videos as an individual test sequence for our algorithm. Our proposed tracker is able to track reliably over 400 frames for all four test sequences (there are 596 frames in each sequence).

We conducted a quantitative comparison of our method (where 10 modes are used) against (1) simple particle filtering, (2) annealed particle filtering [6], and (3) the tracking algorithm proposed by [24] where the GPLVM was used for nonlinear dimensionality reduction. We used 2000 particles for the simple particle filtering algorithm and 200 particles for our implementation of [24]. Ten layers and 100 particles for each layer are used in the annealed particle filtering algorithm, following the setup of [6]. The frame rate for both our proposed method and the method of [24] on a 1.6GHz machine with 512MB RAM was approximately one minute per frame, while the annealed particle filtering algorithm took two minutes per frame. The frame rate of the simple particle filtering was about four minutes per frame due to the large number of particles. In both our proposed algorithm and [24], the global translation was modeled separately by simple linear dynamics learned from motion capture data.

Fig. 4 shows the accuracy of the four different tracking algorithms. As proposed in [28], the error is measured as the absolute distance in millimeters between the true and estimated marker positions on the body limbs. 15 markers are chosen which correspond roughly to the locations of the joints and "ends" of the limbs. As can be seen in the graph of Fig. 4, our proposed method is consistently more accurate and the simple particle filtering algorithm does much worse than all other methods. Smart sampling, or a dimensionality reduction method can greatly improve the performance of particle filtering based tracking. Based on the performance reported in [28] (up to 50 frames), our proposed algorithm is able to track reliably over a longer time on monocular video sequences (all 400 frames, for all four sequences).

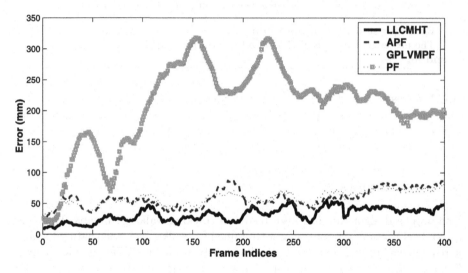

Fig. 4. Estimation Error

Figs. 5 and 6 show example tracking results and the corresponding 3D poses. The results of particle filtering are not shown here due to the large error. With a learned prior model, both the proposed algorithm and particle filtering with GPLVM are able to track reliably when self-occlusion or motion blur occurred. In contrast, annealed particle filtering usually loses track of some body limbs. At frame 183 in Fig. 5, particle filtering with GPLVM loses track of the subject's left arm. The strength of the GPLVM (global smoothness) in this case may be its weakness. As GPLVM ensures temporal smoothness, it may learn a over-smoothed density function and consequently fail to capture large pose change over time. This over-smoothing effect is also demonstrated in the tracking result of frame 70 in Fig. 6, where the left leg movement was underestimated. In contrast, our method propagates modes over time. At each time step, the samples are generated from each mode separately and temporal smoothness is only enforced on samples drawn from the same cluster; hence, our proposed algorithm is able to capture large movements accurately.

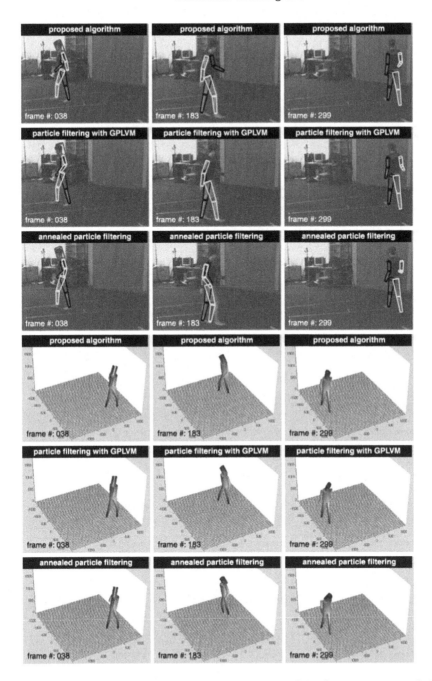

Fig. 5. Selected frames of the tracking results from one of the four sequences and the corresponding 3D poses. The proposed algorithm was able to track the pose reliably while the other two failed to track the movement of the limbs, e.g., forearm (frame 38 and 299) and legs (frame 183). See http://cs-people.bu.edu/lir/tracking for videos.

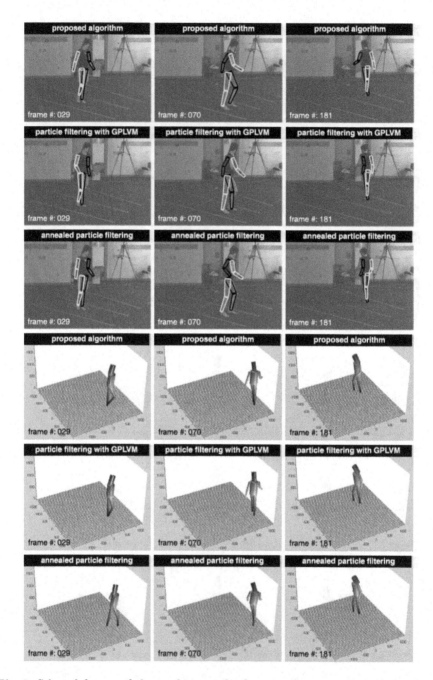

Fig. 6. Selected frames of the tracking results from another sequence and the corresponding 3D poses. The proposed algorithm was able to track the pose reliably while the other two failed to track the movement of the certain limbs, this is similar to what has been observed in Fig.5. See http://cs-people.bu.edu/lir/tracking for videos.

5   Conclusions and Future Work

We have proposed a algorithm for tracking 3D body poses. The proposed algorithm is able to track long sequences of video robustly. The experiments demonstrate that our tracker performs much better than the recent tracking algorithms proposed by [6] and [24]. It is also shown that our tracker is capable of handling self-occlusions, motion blur and large movement over time. The tracking algorithm is tested on sequences that contain similar motion with respect to the training data set. Currently we only learned the model of human walking. Essentially, with the proposed learning algorithm, multiple motions can be clustered in the globally coordinated system; hence, more complicated tracking tasks can be accomplished using the same tracking algorithm when more data becomes available. Another promising direction is to recognize activities during tracking by analyzing the mode jumping in the latent space. It is likely that motions from the same category will form clusters together in the latent space, so whenever a mode jumping occurs, there is likely a change of activity.

Acknowledgments

This work was conducted while the first author was an intern at Honda Research Institute in 2005. Work at Boston University was supported in part through NSF grants IIS-0308213, IIS-0208876, EIA-0202067 and ONR grant N00014-03-1-0108. The authors thank A. Balan, M. Black and L. Sigal at Brown University for providing the motion capture data set and code for performance comparison.

References

1. King, O., Forsyth, D.A.: How does CONDENSATION behave with a finite number of samples? In: Proc. European Conf. on Computer Vision (ECCV). (2000) 695–709
2. Isard, M., Blake, A.: ICondensation : Unifying low-level and high-level tracking in a stochastic framework. In: Proc. European Conf. on Computer Vision (ECCV). (1998) 893–908
3. MacCormick, J., Blake, A.: A probabilistic exclusion principle for tracking multiple objects. In: Proc. IEEE International Conf. on Computer Vision (ICCV). (1999) 572–578
4. Sminchisescu, C., Triggs, B.: Covariance scaled sampling for monocular 3D body tracking. In: Proc. IEEE Conf. on Computer Vision and Pattern Recognition (CVPR). (2001) 447–454
5. Sullivan, J., Rittscher, J.: Guiding random particles by deterministic search. In: Proc. IEEE International Conf. on Computer Vision (ICCV). (2001) 323–330
6. Deutscher, J., Blake, A., Reid, I.: Articulated body motion capture by annealed particle filtering. In: Proc. IEEE Conf. on Computer Vision and Pattern Recognition (CVPR). (2000) 126–133
7. Sullivan, J., Blake, A., Isard, M., MacCormick, J.: Bayesian object localization in images. International Journal of Computer Vision (IJCV) 44 (2001) 111–135

8. Roweis, R., Saul, L.: Nonlinear dimensionality reduction by locally linear embedding. Science **290** (2000) 2323–2326
9. Tenenbaum, J., Silva, V., Langford, J.: A global geometric framework for nonlinear dimensionality reduction. Science **290** (2000) 2319–2323
10. Belkin, M., Niyogi, P.: Laplacian eigenmaps and spectral techniques for embedding and clustering. In: Advances in Neural Information Processing Systems (NIPS). (2001) 585–591
11. Brand, M.: Charting a manifold. In: Advances in Neural Information Processing Systems (NIPS). (2002) 961–968
12. Teh, W.Y., Roweis, S.: Automatic alignment of local representations. In: Advances in Neural Information Processing Systems (NIPS). (2002) 841–848
13. Lawrence, N.D.: Gaussian process models for visualization of high dimensional data. In: Advances in Neural Information Processing Systems (NIPS). (2003)
14. Wang, L., Hu, W.M., Tan, T.N.: Recent development in human motion analysis. Pattern Recognition **36** (2003) 585–601
15. Isard, M., Blake, A.: CONDENSATION : conditional density propagation for visual tracking. International Journal of Computer Vision (IJCV) **29** (1998) 5–28
16. Cham, T.J., Rehg, J.M.: A multiple hypothesis approach to figure tracking. In: Proc. IEEE Conf. on Computer Vision and Pattern Recognition (CVPR). (1999) 239–245
17. Toyama, K., Blake, A.: Probabilistic tracking in a metric space. In: Proc. IEEE International Conf. on Computer Vision (ICCV). (2001) 5057
18. Sidenbladh, H., Black, M.J., Fleet, D.J.: Stochastic tracking of 3D human figures using 2D image motion. In: Proc. European Conf. on Computer Vision (ECCV). (2000) 702–718
19. Sidenbladh, H., Black, M.J.: Learning image statistics for Bayesian tracking. In: Proc. IEEE International Conf. on Computer Vision (ICCV). (2001) 709–716
20. Elgammal, A., Lee, C.S.: Inferring 3D body pose from silhouettes using activity manifold learning. In: Proc. IEEE Conf. on Computer Vision and Pattern Recognition (CVPR). (2004) 681–688
21. Grochow, K., Martin, S.L., Hertzmann, A., Popovic, Z.: Style-based inverse kinematics. In: ACM Computer Graphics (SIGGRAPH). (2004) 522–531
22. Safonova, A., Hodgins, J.K., Pollard, N.S.: Synthesizing physically realistic human motion in low dimensional, behavior-specific spaces. In: ACM Computer Graphics (SIGGRAPH). (2004) 514 – 521
23. Sminchisescu, C., Jepson, A.: Generative modelling for continuous non-linearly embedded visual inference. In: Proc. IEEE International Conf. on Machine Learning (ICML). (2004) 140–147
24. Tian, T.P., Li, R., Sclaroff, S.: Tracking human body pose on a learned smooth space. Technical Report 2005-029, Boston University (2005)
25. Urtasun, R., Fleet, D.J., Hertzmann, A., Fua, P.: Priors for people tracking from small training sets. In: Proc. IEEE International Conf. on Computer Vision (ICCV). (2005) 403–410
26. Roweis, R., Saul, L., Hinton, G.E.: Global coordination of local linear models. Advances in Neural Information Processing Systems (NIPS) (2001) 889–896
27. Ghahramani, Z., Hinton, G.E.: The EM algorithm for mixtures of factor analyzers. Technical Report CRG-TR-96-1, University of Toronto (1996)
28. Sigal, L., Bhatia, S., Roth, S., Black, M.J., Isard, M.: Tracking loose-limbed people. In: Proc. IEEE Conf. on Computer Vision and Pattern Recognition (CVPR). (2004) 421–428

Balanced Exploration and Exploitation Model Search for Efficient Epipolar Geometry Estimation

Liran Goshen[1] and Ilan Shimshoni[2]

[1] Faculty of Industrial Engineering & Management, Technion,
Haifa 32000, Israel
[2] Department of Management Information Systems, Haifa University,
Haifa 31905, Israel

Abstract. The estimation of the epipolar geometry is especially difficult where the putative correspondences include a low percentage of inlier correspondences and/or a large subset of the inliers is consistent with a degenerate configuration of the epipolar geometry that is totally incorrect. This work presents the Balanced Exploration and Exploitation Model Search (BEEM) algorithm that works very well especially for these difficult scenes.

The BEEM algorithm handles the above two difficult cases in a unified manner. The algorithm includes the following main features: (1) Balanced use of three search techniques: global random exploration, local exploration near the current best solution and local exploitation to improve the quality of the model. (2) Exploits available prior information to accelerate the search process. (3) Uses the best found model to guide the search process, escape from degenerate models and to define an efficient stopping criterion. (4) Presents a simple and efficient method to estimate the epipolar geometry from two SIFT correspondences. (5) Uses the locality-sensitive hashing (LSH) approximate nearest neighbor algorithm for fast putative correspondences generation.

The resulting algorithm when tested on real images with or without degenerate configurations gives quality estimations and achieves significant speedups compared to the state of the art algorithms!

1 Introduction

The estimation of the epipolar geometry is an important task in computer vision. The RANdom SAmple Consensus algorithm (RANSAC) [1] has been widely used in computer vision in particular for recovering the epipolar geometry.

The estimation of the epipolar geometry is especially difficult in two cases. The first difficult situation is when the putative correspondences include a low percentage of inliers. In such a situation, the number of required iterations is usually high. A popular stopping criterion in a RANSAC like algorithm is

$$I = \log(1-p)/\log(1-\alpha^s) \approx \log(1-p)/\alpha^s, \tag{1}$$

A. Leonardis, H. Bischof, and A. Pinz (Eds.): ECCV 2006, Part II, LNCS 3952, pp. 151–164, 2006.

where s is the size of the random sample, I is the number of iterations, α is the inlier rate, and p is the required probability [1, 2]. For example, for $\alpha = 0.15$ the number of needed iterations for $s = 7$ and $s = 2$ are $I = 2,695,296$ and $I = 202$ respectively, for $p = 0.99$.

Several approaches have been suggested to speed-up the RANSAC algorithm. In [3] the random sampling was replaced by guided sampling. The guidance of the sampling is based on the correlation score of the correspondences. PROSAC [4] exploits the linear ordering defined on the set of correspondences by the similarity function used in establishing putative correspondences. PROSAC samples are drawn from progressively larger sets of top-ranked correspondences. LO-RANSAC [5] exploits the fact that the model hypothesis from an uncontaminated minimal sample is often sufficiently near the optimal solution and a local optimization step is applied to selected models. In our previous work [6] the algorithm generates a set of weak motion models (WMMs) and generates an outlier correspondence sample. Using these the probability that each correspondence is an inlier is estimated and enable to guide the sampling. In [7, 8] it was suggested to use three affine region to region matches to estimate the epipolar geometry in each RANSAC sample. Under this framework s in Eq. (1) is changed from seven to three, reducing considerably the number of iterations.

The second difficult situation is when a large subset of inliers is consistent with a degenerate epipolar geometry. This situation often occurs when the scene includes a degeneracy or close to degenerate configurations. In this case standard epipolar geometry estimation algorithms often return an epipolar geometry with a high number of inliers that is however totally incorrect. The estimation of the fundamental matrix in such situations has been addressed before. In [9] a RANSAC-based algorithm for robust estimation of epipolar geometry in the possible presence of dominant scene plane was presented. The algorithm detects samples in which at least five correspondences are consistent with an homography. This homography is then used to estimate the epipolar geometry by the plane and parallax algorithm.

Consider the following two examples. Figure 1(a) shows the flowerpot image scene in which the inlier rate is low and it includes a dominant degenerate configuration. In this scene 17% out of 252 putative correspondences are inliers and 70% of the inliers lie in a small part of the scene which yields a degenerate configuration. A computation of the fundamental matrix based on only inliers from this small space results in a very unstable fundamental matrix. On this scene RANSAC often fails to find the correct fundamental matrix. Figure 1(a) shows a typical result of RANSAC. A dot represents inliers from the degenerate configuration, a circle represents inliers not belonging to the degenerate configuration and the × represents an outlier that RANSAC detected as inlier. In this example RANSAC succeeded to find all the inliers that belong to the degenerate configuration but failed to find any inliers outside it. This is demonstrated in Figure 1(b), which shows the square root of the symmetric epipolar distance of the inlier from the fundamental matrix. The distances of the inliers outside the degenerate configuration are large. Although, a large number of inliers were found, the precision of the resulting fundamental matrix is very low. The number of iterations for this scene according to Eq. (1) for $p = 0.99$ is over one million. Figure 1(c) shows another example in which the inlier rate is 16.5% out of 310 putative correspondences and it includes a dominant plane degenerate configuration. In this scene 78% of the inliers lie near the plane. Figure 1(c) shows a typical result of the RANSAC which succeed to find part of the inliers that lie near the plane and failed to find any inliers not close to the plane. As a result, the fundamental matrix is totally incorrect as can be seen in Figure 1(d). The number of iterations for this scene according to Eq. (1) is again over one million.

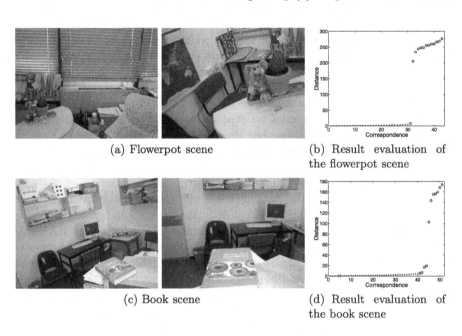

(a) Flowerpot scene

(b) Result evaluation of the flowerpot scene

(c) Book scene

(d) Result evaluation of the book scene

Fig. 1. Image scenes and quality evaluation

In this paper we propose a novel algorithm for robust estimation of epipolar geometry. The algorithm handles the above two difficult cases in a unified manner. The algorithm can handle not only planar degeneracy, but scenes that include a variety of degeneracies or close to degenerate configurations.

The balanced exploration and exploitation model search (BEEM) algorithm includes a balanced use of three search techniques: global random exploration, local exploration near the current best solution and local exploitation to improve the quality of the model. Moreover, it exploits available prior information, the distance ratio of the closest to second-closest neighbors of a keypoint, to accelerate the search process. Also, it uses the best found model to guide the search process, escape from degenerate models and define an efficient stopping criterion. This is done by indirectly updating the probability that a correspondence is an inlier and by a smart sampling strategy. In addition, a simple and efficient method to estimate the epipolar geometry from two SIFT correspondences is presented. The matching is sped up using the LSH [10] approximate nearest neighbor algorithm. The generation of the SIFT features can be sped up using the approximation described in [11].

The resulting algorithm when tested on real images with or without degenerate configurations gives quality estimations and achieves significant speedups, especially in scenes that include the aforementioned difficult situations.

2   Exploration and Exploitation

Any efficient search algorithm must use two general techniques to find the global maximum: exploration to investigate new and unknown areas in the search space and exploitation to make use of knowledge found at points previously visited to help find better points. These two requirements are contradictory, and a good search algorithm must strike a balance between them. A purely random search is good at exploration, but does no exploitation, while a purely hill climbing method is good at exploitation, but does little exploration. Combinations of these two strategies can be quite effective, but it is difficult to know where the best balance lies.

Robust estimation of the fundamental matrix can be thought of a search process. The search is for the parameters of the fundamental matrix and the set of inliers. Therefore, algorithms that estimate the epipolar geometry can be analyzed according to the way they combine the above techniques. The RANSAC algorithm [1] samples in each iteration a minimal subset of points and computes from it a model. This random process is actually an indirect global exploration of the parameter space. In the PbM algorithm [12, 13] each exploration iteration is followed by a standard exploitation step. A hill climbing procedure over the parameter space is performed using a local search algorithm. The LO-RANSAC algorithm [5] makes an exploitation step only when a new good model is found in an exploration iteration. The exploitation step is performed by choosing the random sample only from the set of suspected inliers, the model's support set. In cases that there exists a degenerate configuration the exploitation step tends to enlarge the support set but it includes only inliers belonging to the degeneracy.

One disadvantage of the above methods is that they do not have a step similar to the local exploration step that exists in methods like simulated annealing, i.e. even if they find a relatively good model that includes a large number of inliers, they do not use this information after the exploitation step. Once the exploitation step is over, they return to random sampling hoping to find by chance a better model. We suggest to add an intermediate technique that uses the previous best solution and explores its neighborhood looking for a better solution whose support set is larger and includes most of the support set of the previous best solution. To achieve this we need to generate a sample of inliers which includes beside members of the support set other correspondences. Once we have a "good" previous solution it can be assumed that the vast majority of its support set are inliers. Therefore, when choosing a subset for the RANSAC step, we choose most of the subset from the support set and the rest from points that are outside the support set. When such a subset consists only of inliers the support set of the resulting model tends to break out from the confines of the set of inliers belonging to degeneracy yielding a more correct solution.

When incorporating a local exploration step into the algorithm several questions have to be addressed. First, local exploration is only effective when the best previous support set includes nearly only inliers. So, it is essential to be able to recognize such sets. Second, depending on the quality of the set a balance between the application of global exploration, local exploration and exploitation has to be struck. Finally, how to incorporate available prior information about the quality of each putative correspondence into the general scheme.

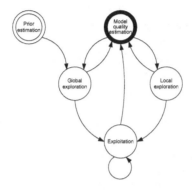

Fig. 2. State diagram of the balanced exploration and exploitation model search (BEEM) algorithm

The BEEM algorithm includes all the above components. Its state diagram is presented in Figure 2. The algorithm includes the following states:

- **Prior estimation.** Use prior available information to estimate the probability that a correspondence is an inlier. This probability is used to guide the sampling in the other states.
- **Global exploration.** Sample a minimal subset of correspondences and instantiate the model from the subset. If the size of the support set of the formed model is larger than all the models that were formed in this state goto the *exploitation* state, otherwise goto to the *model quality estimation* state.
- **Model quality estimation.** Estimate the quality of the best model found until now based on the size of its support set and the number of iterations that the algorithm has performed until now. Use this quality estimate to choose probabilistically the next state, *global exploration* or *local exploration*.
- **Local exploration.** Sample a subset of correspondences from the support set of the best model and sample a subset of correspondences from the rest of the correspondences. Instantiate the model from the union of the two subsets. If the size of its support set is larger than all the models that were

previously formed in this state goto the *exploitation* state, otherwise goto to the *model quality estimation* state.

- **Exploitation.** Iteratively try to improve the last formed model.

The various components of the algorithm are described in the following sections.

3   Using Prior Information of the Match

The best candidate match for each SIFT keypoint from the first image is found by identifying keypoints in the second image whose descriptor is closest to it in a Euclidian distance sense. Some features from the first image will not have any correct match in the second image. Therefore, it is useful to have the ability to discard them. A global threshold on the distance to the closest feature does not perform well, as some descriptors are much more discriminative than others. A more effective measure as suggested by [14] is obtained by comparing the distance of the closest neighbor to that of the second-closest neighbor. This measure performs well because for correct matches the closest neighbor is significantly closer than the closest incorrect match. For false matches, there will likely be a number of other false matches within similar distances due to the high dimensionality of the feature space. We can think of the second-closest match as providing an estimate of density of the false matches within this region of the feature space and at the same time identifying specific instances of feature ambiguity.

Let r_i be the distance ratio of the closest to the second-closest neighbors of the ith keypoint of the first image. Figure 3(a) shows the value of this measure for real image data for inliers and outliers. In [14] it was suggested to reject all matches in which the distance ratio is greater than $r_{tresh} = 0.8$. The probabilistic meaning of this is that each correspondence whose score is below this threshold is sampled uniformly. PROSAC exploits this ratio even more and its samples are drawn from progressively larger sets from the set of correspondences ordered by

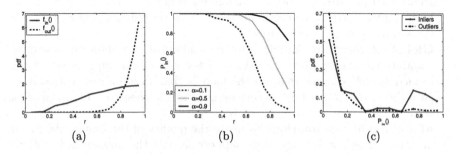

(a)   (b)   (c)

Fig. 3. (a) The empirical distributions of the distance ratio, r, for inlier and outliers were generated based on twenty image pairs. (b) The probability that a correspondence is an inlier as a function of r for several values of the inlier rate, α. (c) The distributions of the estimated probability $P_{in}()$ of the inliers and the outliers, for the book scene image pair.

this ratio. This improves the performance of the algorithm. In this work we make an additional step by giving an empirical probabilistic meaning to this ratio.

The distance ratio can be thought of as a random variable and is modeled as a mixture model:

$$f_r(r_i) = f_{in}(r_i)\alpha + f_{out}(r_i)(1 - \alpha),$$

where $f_{in}(r_i) = f(r_i|p_i \leftrightarrow p_i' \ inlier)$, $f_{out}(r_i) = f(r_i|p_i \leftrightarrow p_i' \ outlier)$, and α is the mixing parameter which is the probability that any selected correspondence is an inlier. The probability, $P_{in}(i)$, that correspondence $p_i \leftrightarrow p_i'$ is an inlier can be calculated using Bayes' rule:

$$P_{in}(i) = \frac{f_{in}(r_i)\alpha}{f_{in}(r_i)\alpha + f_{out}(r_i)(1 - \alpha)}. \qquad (2)$$

We estimate this probability in a non-parametric manner. We generate two samples from real images:

- S_{in}, a sample of $\tilde{N}_{in}$ inlier ratio distances.
- S_{out}, a sample of $\tilde{N}_{out}$ outlier ratio distances.

We estimates $f_{in}()$ and $f_{out}()$ using a kernel density estimator over S_{in} and S_{out} respectively.

We estimate α for a given image pair using curve fitting of the empirical cumulative distribution function (cdf) of S_{in}, S_{out} and the set of ratios of the putative correspondences. Once α has been estimated $P_{in}()$ can be estimated for all putative correspondences using Eq. (2). Figure 3(b) shows the probability $P_{in}()$ for several values of α. Figure 3(c) shows the distributions of the estimated $P_{in}()$ of the inliers and the outliers, for the book scene image pair. As can be seen in the graph, a large portion of the correspondences that got high probabilities are indeed inliers. In this example the inlier rate is 16.5% and the estimated α is 15.7% which is quite accurate.

4 Epipolar Geometry from Two SIFT Correspondences

In [7, 8] it was suggested to use three affine region to region matches to estimate the epipolar geometry in each RANSAC sample. The novelty here is to use the SIFT descriptor in the computation in a similar manner. The SIFT descriptor is a very powerful descriptor for image matching. This descriptor is invariant to the similarity transformation. The ability to generate epipolar geometry from two SIFT correspondences instead of seven point correspondences is expected to reduce significantly the run-time according to Eq. (1). We suggest a simple method to estimate the epipolar geometry from two SIFT correspondences. Each SIFT keypoint is characterized by its location $p = (x, y)$, orientation θ of the dominant gradient and its scale s. We generate for each SIFT keypoint a set of four points $((x, y), (x + ls\cos(\theta), y + ls\sin(\theta), (x + ls\cos(\theta + \frac{2\pi}{3}), y + ls\sin(\theta + \frac{2\pi}{3}), (x + ls\cos(\theta + \frac{4\pi}{3}), y + ls\sin(\theta + \frac{4\pi}{3}))$. We set $l = \frac{7}{8}\frac{w}{2}$, where w is the width of the descriptor window. Thus, the three additional points lie within the descriptor window. A set of two SIFT correspondences gives a set of eight point correspondences. These can be used to estimate the fundamental matrix using the linear normalized eight-point algorithm [15]. A SIFT correspondence is consistent with the hypothesized epipolar geometry only when all coincident four point correspondences, $(p_{s1}, p_{s2}, p_{s3}, p_{s4}) \leftrightarrow (p'_{s1}, p'_{s2}, p'_{s3}, p'_{s4})$, are consistent. The location of the first point in the set is quite accurate, whereas, the location of the last three points are less accurate because they are approximated from the SIFT characteristics. We use the error thresholds d for the first point in the set and $d\sqrt{s's}$ for the other three, where s and s' are the scale SIFT parameters of the keypoints of the first and the second SIFT descriptors respectively and d is a threshold parameter.

One may wonder how accurate is the estimation of the fundamental matrix using the 2-SIFT method. The 2-SIFT method generates four point correspondences from each SIFT keypoint. These four points are usually quite close to each other and the last three points are estimated less accurately. Therefore, a fundamental matrix which is based on such point correspondences is expected to be less accurate. To check the severity of this problem, the estimation quality of the 2-SIFT method, 7-point algorithm, normalized 8-point algorithm with 8 and 9 point correspondences were checked. Two types of real scenes without any dominant degenerate configurations were checked: a scene moving sideways and a scene moving forward. For each scene the inlier SIFT correspondences were found. For each algorithm in each scene $10,000$ samples were taken from the inlier correspondences. For each sample a fundamental matrix was calculated and the number of correspondences consistent with the model was checked. Figure 4 shows the results. The results of the 2-SIFT method are less accurate than the 7-point algorithm and the 9-point algorithm as expected. However, it usually recovers enough supporting inliers to initialize the fundamental matrix estimation process. Clearly, the use of the exploitation step after the 2-SIFT method is very important. To improve the estimation quality, we checked one more method, the 2-SIFT without singularity constraint (2-SIFT-NSC) method. In this method the singularity constraint of the fundamental matrix is not enforced. The result is usually an illegal model, but in the sample step of the algorithm it is not necessary to work with legal models, because the main purpose of the sample

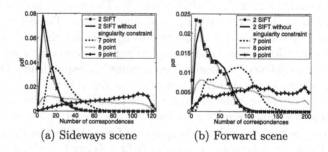

(a) Sideways scene   (b) Forward scene

Fig. 4. Algorithm evaluation

step is to detect large amounts of supporting inliers. The results of the 2-SIFT-NSC method which are also shown in Figure 4 outperform the 2-SIFT method. The reason for this is that the singularity constraint enforcement applied in the 8-point algorithm is not optimal since all the entries of the fundamental matrix do not have equal importance. Note also that the 2-SIFT-NSC method requires less computational cost, because it does not enforce the singularity constraint. For the above reasons we use the 2-SIFT-NSC method in our algorithm.

5   Best Found Model Quality Estimation

In the model quality estimation state the algorithm estimates the quality of the best found model as an inlier model, i.e. a model that nearly all the members of its support set are inliers. When an inlier model is detected it can help accelerate the search process using the local exploration state, whereas using an outlier model in that state is useless. In such situations we want to cause the BEEM algorithm to perform global exploration. To achieve this we have to estimate the probability that the model is supported by outliers that are by chance consistent with it. Let $P_{om}(i)$ be the probability that at most i outliers support an outlier model. Let $N_{best} = \max\{N_i\}_{i=1}^I$ be the maximal size of the support set after I iterations achieved by model M_{best}, where N_i is the size of the support set of the ith iteration. Using the above definitions, the probability, P_q, that M_{best} is not an outlier model is estimated. This is equivalent to the probability that in all of the I iterations the support set of size N_{best} could not be achieved by an outlier model. Thus,

$$P_q = \forall_{i=1}^I Prob(N_i < N_{best}) = \prod_{i=1}^I Prob(N_i < N_{best}) = (P_{om}(N_{best} - 1))^I.$$

The BEEM algorithm uses the probability P_q as an estimate to the quality of the best found model. We estimate $P_{om}()$ using several unrelated image pairs in a non-parametric manner. We ran the algorithm for the above image pairs and

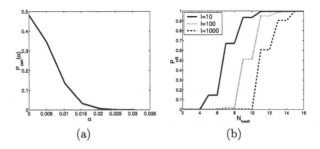

(a)   (b)

Fig. 5. (a) The cdf $P_{om}()$ as function of the inlier rate, α. (b) The probability P_q as function of N_{best} for $I = 10$, $I = 100$ and $I = 1000$ where the number of putative correspondences is set to 400.

recorded the size of the support sets of the outlier models. Figure 5(a) shows the cdf $P_{om}()$ as a function of the inlier rate, α. Figure 5(b) shows the probability P_q as function of N_{best} for $I = 10$, $I = 100$ and $I = 1000$, where the number of putative correspondences is set to 400. Note that when the number of iterations increases the "belief" of the algorithm in small subsets decreases. As a result, the algorithm tends to do more global exploration.

6   The Algorithm

Up to this point, we have described the principles of the BEEM algorithm. Now, we will combine them all together, yielding the complete epipolar geometry estimation algorithm. The algorithm is summarized in Algorithm 1. The details of the algorithm are as follows:

Fundamental matrix generation. The generation of the fundamental matrix given a subset S of SIFT correspondences is done as follows: if $2 \leq |S| < 7$ then we use the normalized eight-point algorithm, where each SIFT correspondence provides four point correspondences, as described in Section 4. If $|S| = 7$ then we use the seven-point algorithm with seven points, one from each SIFT

Algorithm 1. The BEEM algorithm.

1: **Prior estimation.**
   Estimates α and $P_{in}()$ of the set C of putative correspondences.
2: **Global exploration.**
   a) Sample according to $P_{in}()$ a subset of two SIFT correspondences from C.
   b) Instantiate the fundamental matrix F.
   c) If the support set S of F is the best found in this state then goto *Exploitation* else goto *Model quality estimation*.
3: **Exploitation.**
   a) Execute local optimization with inner RANSAC over S until I_l repetitions without improvement.
   b) If found model with largest support until now keep its support set in S_{best}.
4: **Model quality estimation.**
   a) Estimate P_q.
   b) If the *stoping criterion* is satisfied terminate.
   c) Choose with probability P_q to goto *Local exploration* else goto *Global exploration*.
5: **Local exploration.**
   a) Sample according to $P_{in}()$ a subset of SIFT correspondences from S_{best}.
   b) If $P_q < 1$ then sample according to $P_{in}()$ a single SIFT from $C \setminus S_{best}$. else choose the next SIFT correspondence from $C \setminus S_{best}$.
   c) Instantiate the fundamental matrix F.
   d) If the support set S of F is the largest found in this state then goto *Exploitation* else goto *Model quality estimation*.

---

correspondence. If $|S| > 7$ then we use the standard normalized eight-point algorithm with $|S|$ keypoints provided from the SIFT correspondences.

Exploitation. This state is very similar to the local optimization method described in [5] with a small improvement. In this state a new sampling procedure is executed. Samples are selected only from the support set S of the previous state. New models are verified against the whole set of putative correspondences. The size of the sample is set to $\min(S/2, N_F)$, where N_F is set to 14. For each fundamental matrix generated from a sample, all the correspondences in its support set are used to compute a new model using the linear algorithm. This process is repeated until no improvement is achieved. The modification we made to the original LO-RANSAC is that whenever a larger support set is found the exploitation process restarts again with it. The algorithm exits this state to the model quality estimation state after ten iterations without improvement.

Local exploration. The parameter space close to the best model found so far is searched in this state by choosing a sample of size $\min\left(|S_{best}|/2, N_F - 1\right)$ SIFT correspondences from S_{best} and a single SIFT correspondence from $C \setminus S_{best}$. The fundamental matrix is instantiated from the union of the above subset and the single SIFT correspondence, where the single SIFT correspondence always contributes four point correspondences. This way, the algorithm has a better chance to escape from degenerate configurations.

Once P_q is equal to one, the sampling strategy for correspondences from $C \setminus S_{best}$ changes. Each time a new maximum is found, i.e. S_{best} was updated, the correspondences in $C \setminus S_{best}$ are sorted in decreasing order according to $P_{in}()$. In each iteration a single SIFT correspondence is chosen from $C \setminus S_{best}$ according to the sorting order.

Stopping criterion. The BEEM algorithm terminates if in the last $|C| - |S_{best}|$ exploration samples the subset S_{best} was not updated and if P_q is equal to one in these samples. This criterion ensures with high confidence that nearly all the inliers will be detected. This suggested stopping criterion usually terminates much earlier than in the standard approach, because once the algorithm finds a model with an adequate number of inliers, P_q is estimated as one and the algorithm enters the final local exploration iterations. Because the correspondences in $C \setminus S_{best}$ are sorted in decreasing order according to $P_{in}()$, the rest of the inliers are rapidly found. Once S_{best} ceases to change $|C| - |S_{best}|$ iterations are performed. In the experiments that we have performed, the number of iterations until an adequate number of inliers are found is usually very small, thanks to the various components of the BEEM algorithm. As a result, the total number of iterations of the BEEM algorithm is in practice slightly higher than the number of outliers in the putative correspondence set. This number is much lower than the bound given by Eq. (1).

7   Experiments

The proposed algorithm was tested on many image pairs of indoor and outdoor scenes several of which are presented here. The cases that are presented
here are difficult cases in which the inlier rate is low and include a dominant
degeneracy.

For each image we applied the SIFT method to detect the keypoints. The
descriptors of the first image were then stored in an LSH data structure and the
descriptors of the second image were used for querying the data structure to find
their approximate nearest neighbors to generate putative correspondences. We
used the adapted version of the LSH [16] with data driven partitions. The LSH
algorithm is simple for implementation and efficient. For example, the running
time for the generation of the putative correspondences of the book scene was
reduced from 25.6 seconds using a simple linear search to 0.45 seconds using the
LSH algorithm on a Pentium 4 CPU 1.70GHz computer.

For illustration reasons, we divided the set of putative correspondences into
three sets: outliers, inliers belonging to the degenerate configuration and the rest
of the inliers of which most of them have to be part of the support set in order to
generate an accurate fundamental matrix. The images of the scenes are shown
in Figures 1 and 6. Their details are given in Table 1.

For each scene six algorithms were tested: the BEEM algorithm, LO-RANSAC
using samples of two SIFT correspondences to generate fundamental matrixes
(2SIFT LO-RANSAC), RANSAC using samples of two SIFT correspondences
(2SIFT RANSAC), LO-RANSAC using samples of seven point correspondences
where the samples were sampled according to the probability $P_{in}(i)$ (7pt

(a) Board scene   (b) Car scene

Fig. 6. Image scenes

Table 1. The characteristics of the tested scenes. For each scene the table gives the
type of degeneracy, number of correspondences, inlier rate, BEEM estimation of the
inlier rate, the number of outliers, the number of inliers, the number of inliers belonging
to the degeneracy, and the number of inliers not belonging to the degeneracy.

Scene	Degeneracy	N	α	$\hat{\alpha}$	Out.	In.	Deg. In.	Non-Deg. In.
Flowerpot	Small region	252	0.17	0.25	210	42	30	12
Book	Plane	310	0.17	0.16	260	50	44	6
Board	Plane	276	0.27	0.25	201	75	57	18
Cars	Several small regions	272	0.17	0.11	225	47	35	12

Table 2. Experiment results

Algorithm	Success	Iterations	In.	N.Deg.	Success	Iterations	In.	N.Deg.
	Flowerpot scene				Book scene			
BEEM	100%	(5.0) 213	40.6	11.2	95%	(6.3) 279	44.1	5.6
2SIFT LO-RANSAC	30%	356	29.8	3.6	5%	660	27.2	0.6
2SIFT RANSAC	0%	880	16.9	0	0%	2,449	11.2	0.2
7pt P-LO-RANSAC	65%	10,000	34.6	7.9	30%	10,000	35.1	1.8
7pt LO-RANSAC	15%	10,000	27.2	2.4	0%	10,000	19.9	0.2
7pt RANSAC	0%	10,000	19.5	1.2	0%	10,000	16.5	0.5
	Board scene				Car scene			
BEEM	90%	(1.7) 207	72.4	15.6	100%	(2.5) 230	44.8	10.9
2SIFT LO-RANSAC	5%	90	57.8	1.9	30%	533	31.3	5.7
2SIFT RANSAC	0%	1,964	31.9	1.0	0%	1,236	14.8	1.0
7pt P-LO-RANSAC	15%	10,000	61.3	4.9	70%	10,000	39.2	8.2
7pt LO-RANSAC	5%	10,000	57.9	2.1	25%	10,000	27.25	3.9
7pt RANSAC	0%	10,000	53.6	1.1	0%	10,000	18.05	2.3

P-LO-RANSAC), LO-RANSAC using samples of seven point correspondences (7pt LO-RANSAC), and RANSAC using samples of seven point correspondences (7pt RANSAC). The termination criterion for RANSAC and LO-RANSAC was based on Eq. (1), for $p = 0.99$. In cases where the number of iterations exceeded ten thousand the algorithm also terminated. Each algorithm has been applied to each image pair twenty times. For each algorithm the following statistics are presented: the success rate defined as the percentage of the experiments in which at least 75% of the inliers were found and at least 50% of the inliers outside the degenerate configuration were found, the number of iterations until the termination of the algorithm, the number of inliers found, and the number of inliers outside the degenerate configuration found. For the BEEM algorithm, in the iteration column the number of global exploration iterations is also given denoted in parentheses.

The results clearly show that the BEEM algorithm outperforms the other algorithms in the way that it deals with degeneracies, detecting almost always most of the inliers outside of the degenerate configuration. The quality of the results as represented by the overall number of detected inliers is also much higher. Finally, the number of iterations until termination of the algorithm is much lower than for the other algorithms. Finally, the number of global exploration iteration of the BEEM algorithm is very low as a result of the use of the prior information and the 2-SIFT method. As mentioned in the previous section, the number of iterations of the BEEM algorithm is in practice slightly higher than the number of outliers in the putative correspondence set. This number is much lower than the number of iterations of the other algorithms. The results of the other algorithms demonstrate the contribution of each component of the BEEM algorithm to the quality of the detection.

References

1. Fischler, M., Bolles, R.: Random sample consensus: A paradigm for model fitting with applications to image analysis and automated cartography. Comm. of the ACM **24** (1981) 381–395
2. Torr, P.: Motion segmentation and outlier detection. In: PhD thesis, Dept. of Engineering Science, University of Oxford. (1995)
3. Tordoff, B., Murray, D.: Guided sampling and consensus for motion estimation. In: European Conference on Computer Vision. (2002) I: 82–96
4. Chum, O., Matas, J.: Matching with PROSAC: Progressive sample consensus. In: CVPR. (2005) I: 220–226
5. Chum, O., Matas, J., Kittler, J.: Locally optimized RANSAC. In: German Pattern Recognition Symposium. (2003) 236–243
6. Goshen, L., Shimshoni, I.: Guided sampling via weak motion models and outlier sample generation for epipolar geometry estimation. In: CVPR. (2005) I: 1105–1112
7. Schaffalitzky, F., Zisserman, A.: Multi-view matching for unordered image sets, or "how do i organize my holiday snaps?". In: ECCV. (2002) I: 414–431
8. Chum, O., Matas, J., Obdrzalek, S.: Enhancing RANSAC by generalized model optimization. In: ACCV. (2004) II: 812–817
9. Chum, O., Werner, T., Matas, J.: Two-view geometry estimation unaffected by a dominant plane. In: CVPR. (2005) I: 772–779
10. Gionis, A., Indyk, P., Motwai, R.: Similarity search in high dimensions via hashing. In: ICVL. (1999) 518–529
11. Grabner, M., Grabner, H., Bischof, H.: Fast approximated sift. In: Asian Conference on Computer Vision. (2006) 918–927
12. Chen, H., Meer, P.: Robust regression with projection based m-estimators. In: International Conference on Computer Vision. (2003) 878–885
13. Rozenfeld, S., Shimshoni, I.: The modified pbM-estimator method and a runtime analysis technique for the ransac family. In: CVPR. (2005) I: 1113–1120
14. Lowe, D.: Distinctive image features from scale-invariant keypoints. IJCV **60** (2004) 91–110
15. Hartley, R.: In defense of the eight-point algorithm. IEEE Trans. Patt. Anal. Mach. Intell. **19** (1997) 580–593
16. Georgescu, B., Shimshoni, I., Meer, P.: Mean shift based clustering in high dimensions: A texture classification example. In: ICCV. (2003) 456–463

Shape-from-Silhouette with Two Mirrors and an Uncalibrated Camera

Keith Forbes[1], Fred Nicolls[1], Gerhard de Jager[1], and Anthon Voigt[2]

[1] Department of Electrical Engineering,
University of Cape Town, South Africa
{kforbes, nicolls, gdj}@dip.ee.uct.ac.za
[2] Automation and Informatics Research, De Beers Group Services,
Johannesburg, South Africa
Anthon.Voigt@debeersgroup.com

Abstract. Two planar mirrors are positioned to show five views of an object, and snapshots are captured from different viewpoints. We present closed form solutions for calculating the focal length, principal point, mirror and camera poses directly from the silhouette outlines of the object and its reflections. In the noisy case, these equations are used to form initial parameter estimates that are refined using iterative minimisation. The self-calibration allows the visual cones from each silhouette to be specified in a common reference frame so that the visual hull can be constructed. The proposed setup provides a simple method for creating 3D multimedia content that does not rely on specialised equipment. Experimental results demonstrate the reconstruction of a toy horse and a locust from real images. Synthetic images are used to quantify the sensitivity of the self-calibration to quantisation noise. In terms of the silhouette calibration ratio, degradation in silhouette quality has a greater effect on silhouette set consistency than computed calibration parameters.

1 Introduction

Shape-from-silhouette is a popular technique for creating 3D models of real world objects; silhouettes can often easily be extracted from images in a controlled environment. If camera pose and internal parameters are known, then the *visual hull* [7] can be computed by intersecting the visual cones corresponding to silhouettes captured from multiple viewpoints. The visual hull is often a good approximation to the 3D shape of the object and is useful for tasks such as 3D multimedia content creation.

We propose a simple setup for capturing images of an object from multiple well-distributed viewpoints. Two mirrors are used to create five views of an object: a view directly onto the object, two reflections, and two reflections of reflections (see Fig. 1). Two or more images of the object and its reflections are captured from different camera positions (without altering the internal parameters) to obtain a well-distributed set of silhouettes. Since the method requires only readily available equipment (two bathroom-style mirrors and a digital camera) it provides the non-specialist user with a simple, low-cost means for creating 3D multimedia content from real objects. The user provides segmented images as input, and our software provides a visual hull model of the

A. Leonardis, H. Bischof, and A. Pinz (Eds.): ECCV 2006, Part II, LNCS 3952, pp. 165–178, 2006.

Fig. 1. Two images of a double mirror setup positioned so that five views of the object can be seen. Note that the camera has moved between shots, but the mirrors and object have not moved.

object. Other methods [10, 8] typically require specialist equipment such as turntables, calibration objects, or multi-camera setups.

We provide closed form solutions for the focal length, principal point, and pose associated with each silhouette view. These values are computed directly from the silhouette outlines: no calibration markers or point correspondences are required. First, each five-view image is considered separately. Four epipoles are computed from the silhouette outlines. Each image constrains the principal point to lie on a line. The intersection of these lines yields the camera's principal point. The positions of the epipoles provide constraints that allow the focal length of the camera to be computed. The mirror normals are a function of the focal length, principal point, and positions of the epipoles. Once the mirror normals are known, the orientation associated with each silhouette view is computed with respect to the camera. Next, the positional component is computed using the epipolar tangency constraint.

In some cases, five-view visual hulls provide a reasonable representation of the 3D shape of the object. However, the visual hull model can be improved by merging multiple five-view silhouette sets of the same rigid object into a single large silhouette set. We show how multiple five-view silhouette sets can be specified in a common reference frame using closed form solutions. This allows visual hulls to be computed from an arbitrary number of well-distributed views of an object.

A refined solution is obtained by treating the closed form solutions as initial estimates and then adjusting parameters to minimise the sum-of-square distances between epipolar tangencies and corresponding projected epipolar tangents. The various parameters are decoupled so that iterative refinement is applied at several steps using small numbers of parameters at each step, thus limiting the dimensionality of the search space.

The paper is organised as follows. Section 2 provides a brief overview of related work. In Section 3 we demonstrate how a silhouette image of an object and its reflection can be used to compute the epipole from the silhouette outlines; this result will be used in computing the calibration parameters. Section 4 describes the geometry of the double mirror setup that is used to capture multiple views of an object. Section 5 presents closed form solutions for calculating focal length, principal point, mirror normals and positions from the silhouette outlines observed in images captured using our setup. In Section 6 we show how a nonlinear iterative minimisation can be used to refine the solution given by the closed form solutions in the presence of noise. Experimental results using real and synthetic data are presented in Section 7. Section 8 summarises the paper.

2   Related Work

The computer vision literature describes various approaches for capturing silhouettes of an object from multiple viewpoints so that the visual hull can be computed. Several approaches use the silhouettes themselves to estimate camera parameters.

Wong and Cipolla [13] describe a system that is calibrated from silhouette views using the constraint of circular motion. Once an initial visual hull model is constructed from an approximately circular motion sequence, additional views from arbitrary viewpoints can be added to refine the model. The user must manually provide an approximate initial pose for each additional view which is then refined using an iterative optimisation. Their method of minimising the sum-of-square reprojection errors corresponding to all outer epipolar tangents is used in our work to provide a refined solution.

Sinha et al. [12] make use of outer epipolar tangents to calibrate a network of cameras using silhouettes. Random sampling is used to identify consistent corresponding epipolar tangencies to use for computing initial parameter estimates.

Okatani and Deguchi [11] use a camera with a gyro sensor so that the orientation component associated with each silhouette view is known. An iterative optimisation method is then used to estimate the positional component from the silhouettes by enforcing the epipolar tangency constraint.

Bottino and Laurentini [1] provide methods for determining viewpoints from silhouettes for the case of orthographic viewing directions parallel to the same plane. This type of situation applies to observing a vehicle on a planar surface, for instance.

Many works describe the use of mirrors for generating multiple views of a scene. For example, Gluckman and Nayar [5] discuss the geometry and calibration of a two mirror system using point correspondences. Hu et al. [6] describe a setup similar to ours, however they use constraints imposed by both the silhouette outlines and point correspondences for calibration.

In earlier work [4], we describe a similar method to the one we describe in this paper. However, the previous work assumes an orthographic projection model and requires a dense search of parameter space to determine initial estimates. In this paper, we improve on the method by providing closed form solutions for the initial parameter estimates using a perspective camera model. Moriya et al. [9] describe a related idea. Epipoles are computed from the silhouette outlines of three shadows of a solid cast onto a plane, and are shown to be collinear.

3   Epipoles from Bitangent Lines

This section deals with the case in which a camera views an object and its reflection. We show how the epipole corresponding to the virtual camera (the reflection of the real camera) can be computed directly from the silhouette outlines of the real object and the virtual object in the image captured by the real camera. This result will be used to calculate the positions of epipoles for the double mirror setup.

Fig. 2 shows an example of a camera observing a real object and its reflection in a mirror. The virtual camera is also shown. Consider a plane Π_1 that passes through the camera centres C_R and C_V and touches the real object at the point P_{R1}. By symmetry,

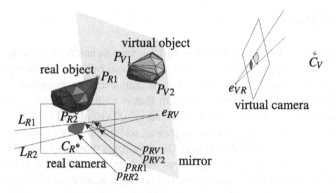

Fig. 2. A camera viewing an object and its reflection. The epipole e_{RV} corresponding to the virtual camera can be computed from the silhouette bitangent lines L_{R1} and L_{R2}.

Π_1 will touch the virtual object at the point P_{V1} which is the reflection of P_{R1}. Since Π_1 is tangent to both objects and contains the camera centres C_R and C_V, P_{R1} and P_{V1} are *frontier points* [3]. They project onto the silhouette outlines on the real image at points p_{RR1} and p_{RV1}. The points p_{RR1}, p_{RV1} and the epipole e_{RV} (the projection of C_R into the real image) are therefore collinear, since they lie in both Π_1 and the real image plane. The bitangent line L_{R1} passing through these three points can be computed directly from the silhouette outlines: it is simply the line that is tangent to both silhouettes. Another bitangent line L_{R2} passes through the epipole and touches the silhouettes on the opposite side to L_{R1}. These tangency points lie on a plane Π_2 that is tangent to the opposite side of the object and passes through both camera centres. Provided that the object does not intersect the line passing through both camera centres, there will be two outer epipolar tangent lines L_{R1} and L_{R2} that touch the silhouettes on either side.

The position of the epipole e_{RV} can therefore be computed by determining L_{R1} and L_{R2} from the silhouette outlines; it is located at the intersection of L_{R1} and L_{R2}. Note that the epipole is computed without requiring knowledge of the camera pose and without requiring any point correspondences.

We also note that by symmetry, the real camera's silhouette view of the virtual object is a mirror image of the virtual camera's silhouette view of the real object. The silhouette view observed by a reflection of a camera is therefore known if the camera's view of the reflection of the object is known.

4 Double Mirror Setup

Fig. 3 shows a double mirror setup that is used to capture five silhouette views of an object in a single image. The camera is centred at C_R and observes a real object O_R. The camera also captures the image of four virtual objects O_{V1}, O_{V2}, O_{V12}, and O_{V21}. Object O_{V1} is the reflection of O_R in Mirror 1; O_{V2} is the reflection of O_R in Mirror 2; O_{V12} is the reflection of O_{V1} in Mirror 2; and O_{V21} is the reflection of O_{V2} in Mirror 1.

Our method requires six virtual cameras to be considered. The virtual cameras are reflections of the real camera C_R. The virtual cameras C_{V1}, C_{V2}, C_{V12}, and C_{V21} are

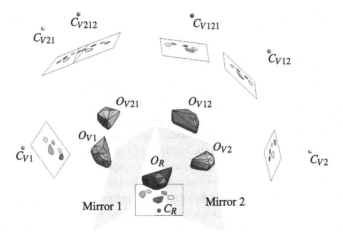

Fig. 3. Mirror setup showing one real and four virtual objects, and one real and six virtual cameras

required, as their silhouette views of the real object are the same as the silhouettes observed by the real camera (or reflections thereof). Since we have access to the silhouettes from the real camera, we can determine the silhouettes observed by the four virtual cameras. Each of the five cameras' silhouette views of the real object can be used to compute the five-view visual hull of the object.

The virtual cameras C_{V121} (the reflection of C_{V12} in Mirror 1), and C_{V212} (the reflection of C_{V21} in Mirror 2) are to be considered too, since it turns out that their epipoles can be computed directly from the five silhouettes observed by the real camera. These epipoles, together with the epipoles from the virtual cameras C_{V1} and C_{V2} can then be used to calculate the focal length of the camera.

5 Analytical Solution

This section presents a method to calculate the focal length and principal point of the camera and the poses of the virtual cameras relative to the pose of the real camera for the five camera views in an image. Next, a method for determining camera motion between snapshots is presented. This allows all silhouettes from all images to be specified in a common reference frame. Closed form solutions in which the required parameters are determined from the silhouette outlines alone are provided. Silhouette outlines are represented by polygons, and pixels are assumed to be square.

First, we show how lines that are tangent to pairs of silhouettes can be used to calculate the positions of four epipoles corresponding to four virtual cameras. The principal point is constrained by the epipoles to a line in each image; the intersection of the lines is the principal point. Next, we show how the focal length is a function of the relative positions of the four epipoles. Once the focal length is known, we show that mirror and camera orientation is easily determined from the positions of two epipoles. The positional component of the poses is computed using the epipolar tangency constraint.

Finally, we show how the camera poses between shots are constrained by the constant positions of the mirrors with respect to the object.

5.1 Four Epipoles from Five Silhouettes

Here, we show how the epipoles are computed from pairs of silhouettes using the result explained in Section 3: the epipole corresponding to a camera's reflection can be computed from the camera's silhouette image of an object and its reflection by finding the intersection of the two outer bitangent lines. Fig. 4 shows how the epipoles e_{V1}, e_{V2}, e_{V121}, and e_{V212} are computed from the outlines of the five silhouettes observed by the real camera. The distances a, b, and c between the epipoles will be used for computing the focal length. The outline γ_{RR} corresponds to the object O_R, and γ_{RV1} corresponds to O_{V1} which is the reflection of O_R in Mirror 1. The intersection of the pair of lines that are tangent to both γ_{RR} and γ_{RV1} is therefore the epipole e_{V1}, since C_{V1} is the reflection of C_R in Mirror 1. The pair of lines that are tangent to both γ_{RV2} and γ_{RV12} also meet at e_{V1}, since O_{V12} is the reflection of O_{V2} in Mirror 1. Similarly, the pairs of lines that are tangent to both γ_{RR} and γ_{RV2}, and to γ_{RV1} and γ_{RV21} meet at e_{V2}.

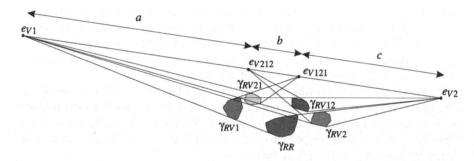

Fig. 4. Computing epipoles e_{V1}, e_{V2}, e_{V121}, and e_{V212} from the silhouette outlines in an image

Consider C_R observing O_{V1}. Object O_{V21} is related to O_{V1} through three reflections. Object O_{V1} must be reflected by Mirror 1 (to get O_R) and then Mirror 2 (to get O_{V2}) and then again by Mirror 1 to get O_{V21}. The effect of these three reflections can be considered to be a single reflection. Applying the triple reflection to C_R gives C_{V121}. The pair of lines that are tangent to both γ_{RV1} and γ_{RV21} therefore meet at e_{V121}. This is again because a camera (C_R) is observing silhouettes of an object (O_{V1}) and its reflection (O_{V12}), so the projection of the camera's reflection (C_{V121}) can be computed from the silhouette bitangent lines. Similarly, the pair of lines that are tangent to both γ_{RV2} and γ_{RV12} meet at e_{V212}.

Note that the epipoles e_{V1}, e_{V2}, e_{V121}, and e_{V212} are collinear, since they all lie in both the image plane of the real camera and in the plane Π_C in which all camera centres lie.

5.2 Focal Length and Principal Point from Epipoles

We now show how the focal length is computed from the positions of the four epipoles. This will be done by considering the positions of the camera centres in the plane Π_C.

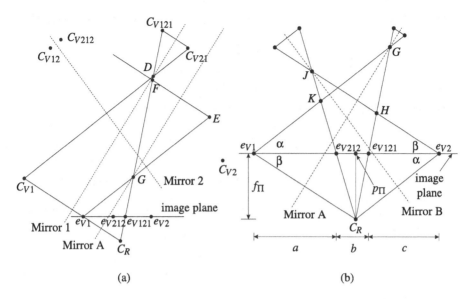

(a)   (b)

Fig. 5. Diagrams showing (a) the intersections of Mirror 1, Mirror A and Mirror 2 with Π_C along with the positions of the cameras and epipoles, all of which lie in Π_C, and (b) computing f_π and p_π from the four epipoles e_{V1}, e_{V2}, e_{V121}, and e_{V212}

First we introduce two new mirrors, Mirrors A and B, that do not correspond to physical mirrors in the scene. This approach makes the problem of calculating the focal length tractable. Mirror A has the same orientation as Mirror 1, but is positioned so that it passes midway between e_{V1} and C_R (see Fig. 5a in which the positions of points in Π_C are shown). The point e_{V1} is therefore the reflection of C_R in Mirror A. Point E is the reflection of e_{V1} in Mirror 2, and F is the reflection of E in Mirror A. Note that F lies on the ray passing through e_{V121} and C_R. Also note that F will stay on this line if the position (but not the orientation) of Mirror 2 changes. This is because triangles $\triangle C_R C_{V1} D$ and $\triangle C_R e_{V1} G$ are similar.

Fig. 5b shows the positions of the epipoles and C_R in Π_C. The distances a, b, and c between the epipoles (as shown in the figure) are used to compute the distance f_Π between C_R and the image plane in the plane Π_C. The distance f_Π is then used to calculate the focal length. The figure also shows Mirror B which has the same orientation as Mirror 2, and is positioned midway between C_R and e_{V2}. The line joining e_{V2} to its reflection in Mirror B meets Mirror B at point J which projects onto e_{V212}.

The triangle $\triangle H e_{V2} C_R$ is similar to $\triangle C_R e_{V1} G$, the line segment from e_{V121} to e_{V2} is of length c, and the line segment from e_{V1} to e_{V121} is of length $a + b$. This indicates that the ratio of the sides of $\triangle H e_{V2} C_R$ to $\triangle C_R e_{V1} G$ is $c : (a + b)$. This means that $d(e_{V1}, G) = d(C_R, e_{V2})(a + b)/c$.

Similarly, the triangle $\triangle K e_{V1} C_R$ is similar to $\triangle C_R e_{V2} J$, the line segment from e_{V1} to e_{V212} is of length a, and the line segment from e_{V212} to e_{V2} is of length $b + c$. This indicates that the ratio of the sides of $\triangle K e_{V1} C_R$ to $\triangle C_R e_{V2} J$ is $a : (b + c)$. Therefore $d(e_{V2}, J) = d(C_R, e_{V1})(b + c)/a$.

This allows us to write $d(C_R, e_{V1})$ in terms of $d(C_R, e_{V2})$, since $\triangle C_R e_{V2} J$ is similar to $\triangle C_R e_{V1} G$:

$$d(C_R, e_{V1}) = \frac{\sqrt{c\,(c+b)\,a\,(a+b)}}{c\,(c+b)} d(C_R, e_{V2}). \tag{1}$$

We now know the sides of $\triangle C_R e_{V1} G$ up to a scale factor.
The angle $\angle C_R e_{V1} G = \alpha + \beta$ can be computed using the cosine rule:

$$\cos(\alpha + \beta) = 1/2 \frac{\sqrt{c\,(c+b)\,a\,(a+b)}}{(c+b)\,(a+b)}. \tag{2}$$

The cosine rule can be used to determine the sides of $\triangle e_{V1} C_R e_{V2}$. (The angle $\angle e_{V1} C_R e_{V2} = 180° - \alpha - \beta$.)

We can now (with the help of the Matlab Symbolic Toolbox for simplification) state f_Π in terms of a, b, and c:

$$f_\Pi = 1/2 \frac{\sqrt{3ac + 4ab + 4cb + 4b^2}\,(a+b+c)\sqrt{a}\sqrt{c}}{a^2 + ab + c^2 + cb + ac}. \tag{3}$$

The point closest to C_R on the line containing the epipoles, is

$$\mathbf{p}_\Pi = \mathbf{e}_{V1} + 1/2 \frac{(2a + 2b + c)\,a\,(a+b+c)}{a^2 + ab + c^2 + cb + ac} \frac{\mathbf{e}_{V2} - \mathbf{e}_{V1}}{\|\mathbf{e}_{V2} - \mathbf{e}_{V1}\|}. \tag{4}$$

The line passing through $\mathbf{p}_\Pi$ and perpendicular to the line containing the epipoles passes through the principal point p_0. The principal point can therefore be computed as the intersection of two such lines from two images of the scene. (If the principal point is assumed to lie at that the image centre, then a single snapshot could be used.)

The focal length (the distance from C_R to the image plane) can now be calculated from $\mathbf{p}_\Pi$, the principal point p_0 and f_Π.

5.3   View Orientations

Once the focal length of the camera has been calculated, the view orientation can be computed relatively easily. The mirror normal directions $\mathbf{m}_1$ and $\mathbf{m}_2$ are computed from the focal length, the principal point p_0 and the epipoles e_{V1} and e_{V2}:

$$\mathbf{m}_1 = - \begin{bmatrix} \mathbf{e}_{V1} - \mathbf{p}_0 \\ f \end{bmatrix}, \quad \mathbf{m}_2 = - \begin{bmatrix} \mathbf{e}_{V2} - \mathbf{p}_0 \\ f \end{bmatrix}. \tag{5}$$

A 3×3 matrix R that represents a reflection by a mirror with unit normal $\hat{\mathbf{m}} = [m_x, m_y, m_z]^T$ is used to calculate view orientation:

$$R = \begin{pmatrix} -m_x^2 + m_y^2 + m_z^2 & -2m_x m_y & -2m_x m_z \\ -2m_x m_y & m_x^2 - m_y^2 + m_z^2 & -2m_y m_z \\ -2m_x m_z & -2m_y m_z & m_x^2 + m_y^2 - m_z^2 \end{pmatrix}. \tag{6}$$

5.4   View Positions

The point C_{V1} is constrained to lie on the line passing through e_{V1} and C_R. Similarly, the point C_{V2} is constrained to lie on the line passing through e_{V2} and C_R. Since absolute scale cannot be inferred from the image (if the scene were scaled, the image would not change), we fix C_{V1} at unit distance from C_R. The only positional unknown across the entire setup is now the position of C_{V2} on the line passing through e_{V2} and C_R.

To solve for w, the distance from C_R to C_{V2}, the epipolar tangency constraint is used: a tangent to a silhouette that passes through the epipole must be tangent to the corresponding point in its projection onto the image plane of the opposite view. The relationship between the views of C_{V1} and C_{V2} is used to enforce this constraint.

The poses of the cameras C_{V1} and C_{V2} are specified by 4×4 rigid transform matrices from the reference frame of the real camera:

$$M = \begin{pmatrix} R & \mathbf{t} \\ \mathbf{0}^T & 1 \end{pmatrix}, \tag{7}$$

where the translational component $\mathbf{t}$ is given by $\mathbf{t} = 2(m_x p_x + m_y p_y + m_z p_z)(m_x, m_y, m_z)^T$ and $(p_x, p_y, p_z)^T$ is a point on the mirror.

The matrix $M_1 M_2^{-1}$ represents the rigid transform from the reference frame of C_{V2} to that of C_{V1}.

The point p_{V2} is one of two outer epipolar tangencies formed by lines passing through e_{V2V1} (the projection of C_{V1} onto the image plane of camera C_{V2}) and tangent to the silhouette observed by the camera C_{V2}.

The point p_{V1V2} is the projection of p_{V2} into camera C_{V1}. It must correspond to p_{V1}, one of two outer epipolar tangencies formed by lines passing through e_{V1V2} (the projection of C_{V2} onto the image plane of camera C_{V1}).

The epipolar tangency constraint is expressed as

$$(\mathbf{p}_{V1V2} \times \mathbf{e}_{V1V2}) \cdot \mathbf{p}_{V1} = 0, \tag{8}$$

where $\mathbf{p}_{V1V2}$, $\mathbf{e}_{V1V2}$, and $\mathbf{p}_{V1}$ are represented by homogeneous coordinates. In other words, the line passing through $\mathbf{p}_{V1V2}$ and $\mathbf{e}_{V1V2}$ must also pass through $\mathbf{p}_{V1}$.

Equation 8 can be specified in terms of p_{V1}, p_{V2}, the computed orientation and camera internal parameters, and w. The Matlab Symbolic Toolbox was used to determine a solution for w (the equation is too large to reproduce here). Unfortunately, we do not know the values of either p_{V1} or p_{V2}, since the epipoles from which they may be computed are functions of the unknown w.

The values of p_{V1} and p_{V2} can be determined by exhaustive search, by finding the polygon vertex pair that fulfils the epipolar tangency constraint. Instead, we remove the need for an exhaustive search by using a parallel projection approximation to determine approximate correspondences. The tangencies are selected as the support points for outer tangent pairs that are parallel to the projected viewing direction. Unless the camera is very close to the object, this method selects either the same vertices, or vertices very close to the true tangencies under a perspective projection.

5.5   Combining Five-View Silhouette Sets

The calibration procedure described above allows five silhouette views from one image to be specified in a common reference frame. The pose and internal parameters of the four virtual cameras and one real camera are known. The silhouettes observed by these cameras are also known: the silhouettes observed by the virtual cameras are those observed by the real camera of the corresponding virtual object.

The next step is to specify the silhouette sets from two or more images in a common reference frame. This is easily achieved, since the mirror poses are known with respect to the real camera for each image. The five-view silhouette sets are aligned by aligning the mirrors across sets. There are two additional degrees of freedom that the mirrors do not constrain: a translation along the join of the mirrors, and an overall scale factor. These are approximated using the epipolar tangency constraint and a parallel projection model (as for computing w): each five-view silhouette set is scaled and translated along the mirror join so that outer epipolar tangents coincide with the projected tangents from silhouettes in the other silhouette set. Each silhouette pair between different sets gives an estimate of translation and scale. The average result over all pairings is used.

6   The Refined Self-calibration Procedure

The method described in Section 5 provides a means for computing all calibration parameters. However, better results are obtained if parameter estimates are refined at several steps. This is done by adjusting the parameters to minimise the sum-of-of square distances between epipolar tangencies and corresponding projected tangents using the Levenberg-Marquardt method. The geometry of the problem naturally allows for parameters to be decoupled from one another, allowing minimisation to be applied to small numbers of parameters at a time.

The first step of the procedure is to determine which silhouettes correspond to which camera views for each of the five silhouettes in the image. This is done by ordering the five silhouettes along the convex hull of the five silhouettes, and then considering the five possible arrangements. The four epipoles e_{V1}, e_{V2}, e_{V121}, and e_{V212} are computed for each of the five possible arrangements. The lowest sum-of-square distances between silhouette tangents passing through the epipoles and tangents on the corresponding silhouettes is used to select the correct arrangement.

In the presence of noise, the tangent line intersections used to calculate the four epipoles will, in general, produce epipoles that are not collinear. The epipoles e_{V1} and e_{V2} each lie at the intersection of four tangent lines. In the presence of noise, four tangent lines will not intersect at a point. For a refined estimate, the positions of the four epipoles are parameterised using only six degrees of freedom, so that the epipoles are constrained to be collinear. The sum-of-square distances from tangency points to the corresponding tangent lines generated by the opposite silhouette is minimised. The tangent lines pass through the appropriate epipole and touch the silhouette. To form a starting point for the minimisation, the tangent line intersections are computed, and the points closest to an orthogonal regression line through the intersection points are used.

Focal length and principal point values are then computed for each image, averaged, and adjusted to minimise reprojection error. The unknown positional component is computed next for each image. Parameters are then adjusted by minimising reprojection error using all possible silhouette pairings between silhouettes within each set.

Finally, the five view sets are merged into a single large set as described in Section 5.5. A final minimisation adjusts all parameters simultaneously to minimise the sum-of-square distances across all silhouette pairings.

7   Experimental Results

Experiments were performed using real data to obtain qualitative results, and synthetic data to quantify the calibration performance degradation in the presence of noise.

7.1   Real Image Data

The proposed method was tested using a toy horse. Two 2592 × 1944 images captured from two viewpoints are shown in Fig. 1. The five silhouettes in each image were determined using an intensity threshold.

The resultant visual hull model is shown the third column of Fig. 6. The figure also shows visual hull models created using only the five silhouettes from each of the images. This demonstrates the improvement in the quality of the model obtained by merging the silhouette sets. Note that both five-view visual hulls have regions of extra volume that are not present in the ten-view visual hull.

The angle between the mirrors was computed to be 73.1 degrees. The focal length was computed to be 2754 pixels and the principal point located at (1306, 981). This compares with values of 2875 and (1297, 958) computed using a checkerboard calibration method (see www.vision.caltech.edu/bouguetj). Note, however, that a direct comparison of individual parameters does not necessarily provide a good indication of the quality of the calibration parameters. The calibration parameters should provide an accurate mapping from 2D image points to 3D rays *in the volume of interest*. The interplay between the different parameters can result in different parameter

Fig. 6. Two views of the visual hull of the horse formed from the silhouettes in image 1 (*first column*), the silhouettes in image 2 (*second column*), and all ten silhouettes (*third column*)

Fig. 7. Two input images and resultant visual hull model of a toy locust

sets varying to some degree in magnitude, yet still providing a good mapping in the volume of interest. A difference in principal point location can largely be compensated for by a difference in translation parameters, for instance. A more meaningful measure of calibration parameter quality using the *silhouette calibration ratio* is described in Section 7.2.

Fig. 7 shows another example: a visual hull model of a toy locust.

7.2   Synthetic Image Data

Synthetic images were used to investigate the sensitivity of the method to noise. To ensure realistic parameter values were considered, the synthetic images were based on the real images of the toy horse. Exact polygonal projections of the ten-view polyhedral visual hull of the horse were generated using the output provided by the real images. This provides an exactly consistent set of silhouettes.

Quantisation noise was introduced by rendering the polygonal silhouettes, firstly at the original image resolution, and then at successively lower resolutions. Visual hulls

Fig. 8. Visual hull models created at 2, 8, and 15 times reduction of the original resolution (*left to right*), with iterative refinement (*top row*), and without iterative refinement (*bottom row*)

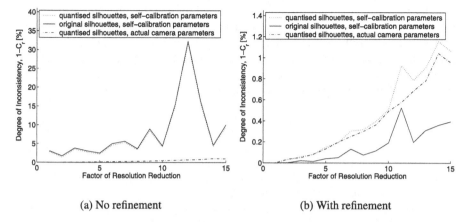

(a) No refinement   (b) With refinement

Fig. 9. Plots of image resolution versus silhouette inconsistency measured using the silhouette calibration ratio for self-calibration (a) without, and (b) with refinement

computed with and without iterative refinement are shown in Fig. 8 for three resolution levels. Note that without refinement, the computed calibration parameters cause the common volume of the visual cones to reduce substantially as the noise is increased.

Boyer [2] introduced the silhouette calibration ratio C_r as a measure of the combined quality of silhouettes and camera parameters. His reasoning is as follows. Ideally, some point on any viewing ray in a silhouette must intersect all $n-1$ other visual cones of an n-view silhouette set. The ratio of the actual maximum number of intersections for points on the ray to $n-1$ is a measure of consistency; C_r is the mean value for all rays from all silhouettes. We use $1-C_r$ as a measure of inconsistency.

Fig. 9 shows plots of $1-C_r$ versus the degree of resolution reduction. Results are also shown with the computed camera parameters and exact silhouettes, as well as quantised silhouettes and exact camera parameters. The plots show that without refinement, the poor accuracy of the camera parameters is a greater contributor to inconsistency than the quantisation of the silhouettes alone. However, for the refined camera parameters, the quantised silhouettes and exact camera parameters are more inconsistent than the exact silhouettes and the computed camera parameters, demonstrating the accuracy of the refined calibration method.

8 Summary

We have presented a method for creating 3D models from real world objects for the non-specialist. The method requires only readily-available equipment: two off-the-shelf planar mirrors, and a digital camera. Once provided with the software, the non-specialist user will easily be able to create 3D multimedia content from real objects.

By positioning the mirrors so that five views of the object can be seen, and capturing two or more images of the scene, we have shown how the internal parameters and poses associated with each silhouette can be computed from the silhouette outlines alone.

In the noisy case, closed form solutions are used for initial parameter estimates that are refined by Levenberg-Marquardt minimisation of sum-of-square reprojection error.

Experimental results demonstrating the quality of models created using real images have been presented. Synthetic images have been used to demonstrate the computed camera parameters have less of an effect on quality as measured by the silhouette calibration ratio than the noisy silhouettes from which they are computed.

References

1. A. Bottino and A. Laurentini. Introducing a new problem: Shape-from-silhouette when the relative positions of the viewpoints is unknown. *IEEE Transactions on Pattern Analysis and Machine Intelligence*, 25(11), November 2003.
2. Edmond Boyer. Camera calibration using silhouettes. Technical Report 5559, INRIA, 2005.
3. Roberto Cipolla and Peter Giblin. *Visual Motion of Curves and Surfaces*. Cambridge University Press, 2000.
4. K. Forbes, A. Voigt, and N. Bodika. Visual hulls from single uncalibrated snapshots using two planar mirrors. In *Proc. 15th South African Workshop on Pattern Recognition*, 2004.
5. J.M. Gluckman and S.K. Nayar. Planar catadioptric stereo: Geometry and calibration. In *Proc. IEEE Conference on Computer Vision and Pattern Recognition*, 1999.
6. B. Hu, C.M. Brown, and R.C. Nelson. Multiple-view 3-D reconstruction using a mirror. Technical Report TR863, Computer Science Dept., U. Rochester, May 2005.
7. Aldo Laurentini. The visual hull concept for silhouette-based image understanding. *IEEE Transactions on Pattern Analysis and Machine Intelligence*, 16(2):150–162, 1994.
8. W. Matusik, C. Buehler, and L. McMillan. Polyhedral visual hulls for real-time rendering. In *Proceedings of Twelfth Eurographics Workshop on Rendering*, 2001.
9. T. Moriya, F. Beniyama, K. Matsumoto, T. Minakawa, K. Utsugi, and H. Takeda. Properties of three shadows on a plane. In *Proceedings of the 12th International Conference in Central Europe on Computer Graphics, Visualization and Computer Vision*, 2004.
10. A. Mülayim, U. Yilmaz, and V. Atalay. Silhouette-based 3D model reconstruction from multiple images. *IEEE Transactions on Systems, Man and Cybernetics*, 33(4), 2003.
11. T. Okatani and K. Deguchi. Recovering camera motion from image sequence based on registration of silhouette cones. In *IAPR Workshop on Machine Vision Applications*, 2000.
12. S. Sinha, M. Pollefeys, and L. McMillan. Camera network calibration from dynamic silhouettes. In *Proc. IEEE Conference on Computer Vision and Pattern Recognition*, 2004.
13. K.-Y. K. Wong and R. Cipolla. Reconstruction of sculpture from its profiles with unknown camera positions. *IEEE Transactions on Image Processing*, 13(3):381–389, 2004.

Robust and Efficient Photo-Consistency Estimation for Volumetric 3D Reconstruction

Alexander Hornung and Leif Kobbelt

Computer Graphics Group, RWTH Aachen University
{hornung, kobbelt}@cs.rwth-aachen.de

Abstract. Estimating photo-consistency is one of the most important ingredients for any 3D stereo reconstruction technique that is based on a volumetric scene representation. This paper presents a new, illumination invariant photo-consistency measure for high quality, volumetric 3D reconstruction from calibrated images. In contrast to current standard methods such as normalized cross-correlation it supports unconstrained camera setups and non-planar surface approximations. We show how this measure can be embedded into a highly efficient, completely hardware accelerated volumetric reconstruction pipeline by exploiting current graphics processors. We provide examples of high quality reconstructions with computation times of only a few seconds to minutes, even for large numbers of cameras and high volumetric resolutions.

1 Introduction

Volumetric multi-view stereo reconstruction, originally introduced by Seitz et al. [1, 2], has recently been shown to produce 3D models from photographs or video sequences with fairly high quality [3, 4]. The basic principle in volumetric reconstruction is to find a classification for all elements (*voxels*) within a discretized volume whether they belong to the surface of the 3D object or not.

Probably the most central aspect of all these techniques is the estimation of the so called *photo-consistency* of a given voxel. The fundamental idea is that only voxels intersected by the object's surface have a consistent appearance in the input images, while other voxels project to incompatible image patches (Fig. 1). Currently there are two major approaches to this problem, either focusing on efficient computability or quality of the reconstruction.

Originally photo-consistency was measured based on the color variance of a voxel [1], assuming perfectly Lambertian and well textured surfaces under constant illumination conditions. Despite these restrictions this method is still widely used [5, 6] because of its computational efficiency and the often acceptable quality, e.g., for time-critical applications such as new view synthesis [7]. Since then the original approach has been improved in several ways. Bonet et al. [8] suggested extensions considering transparency. Zýka and Sára [9] present a statistical method for reliable outlier rejection. A probabilistic framework for space carving was presented by Broadhurst et al. [10]. Histogram-based color consistency tests were introduced by Stevens et al. [11], and Yang et al. [12] addressed the problems of textureless regions and specular highlights.

A. Leonardis, H. Bischof, and A. Pinz (Eds.): ECCV 2006, Part II, LNCS 3952, pp. 179–190, 2006.

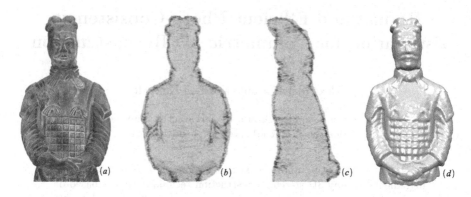

Fig. 1. An example for our improved photo-consistency measure for 3D reconstruction from images (a). Cuts through the computed consistency volume from a front and a side view for the warrior model are shown in (b) and (c) respectively. Darker colors indicate higher consistency values. The clear maximum at the actual surface location allows for reconstructed 3D models of high quality (d).

In recent work focusing on the quality of the reconstructed 3D model, photo-consistency is commonly evaluated based on more sophisticated consistency measures such as sum-of-squared-differences (SSD) or normalized cross-correlation (NCC) [13] of image patches instead of color variances. This greatly reduces ambiguous color configurations and accounts for changes in illumination because of the involved normalization step. Esteban et al. [3] present a technique based on deformable models, while Vogiatzis et al. [4] use global graph-cut optimization to find an optimal surface within a discretized volume that satisfies photo-consistency as well as smoothness constraints. Both methods achieve a very high quality of the reconstructed models. However both papers point out several open issues of NCC-based consistency estimation such as the question whether to use planar model- or image-aligned surface patches. In both cases projective warping can introduce a considerable matching error already for medium-baseline and non epipolar-aligned images. Our work resolves these restrictions based on a new, color normalized supersampling approach and specifically supports these recent optimization-based reconstruction techniques [3, 4].

A further important aspect besides the quality of a photo-consistency measure is its efficiency. Computation times up to several hours are common even in recent NCC-based work [3, 4] due to the much higher computational complexity. Although this could be considered acceptable with respect to the very high quality of the reconstructions, it is often still time-consuming to find optimal parameter settings in practice. Szeliski [14] addressed performance using adaptively refined grids. Partially hardware accelerated implementations of space carving were presented by Prock et al. [15] and Sainz et al. [16]. Solutions for hardware accelerated visual hulls and improved voxel visibility estimation have been discussed in [7, 17, 18]. Li et al. [7] presented a first completely hardware-based solution, Yang et al. [19] described a hardware-based SSD estimation for real-time stereo. However, these works either have conceptual limitations in their applicability to recent optimization based approaches, or they have restrictions concerning the accuracy of the results or the complexity of the input data.

To resolve the above mentioned restrictions this paper presents a new implementation of the complete volumetric reconstruction pipeline. Most importantly, this includes a new approach to compute the photo-consistency of a voxel. Our consistency measure combines the advantages of the two above mentioned approaches, resulting in an illumination invariant, computationally efficient photo-consistency estimation for high quality 3D reconstruction. It improves robustness by resolving the problem of matching between surface samples even for completely unconstrained camera configurations, and is not restricted to planar surface approximations. We show how this consistency measure as well as all the other important stages of the volumetric reconstruction pipeline, namely visual hull and visibility determination, can be implemented in a highly efficient way by exploiting current graphics hardware, without any restrictions concerning the volumetric resolution, the number of images, nor the computational accuracy.

2   Photo-Consistency Estimation

Assuming fully calibrated, foreground segmented input images I_j of an object the general volumetric reconstruction pipeline consists of the following steps:

For each voxel v within a discretized volume one first has to determine whether it is contained in the visual hull of the object or if it lies in irrelevant parts of the volume. Voxels projecting to the background in one of the images I_j can be instantly marked as unoccupied space and skipped by further computations. We present an efficient background rejection test to estimate the object's visual hull in Sect. 3.1.

As emphasized by Vogiatzis et al. [4] the next important step is to use an initial geometry proxy such as the visual hull to determine whether a voxel v is visible in an input image I_j, or if it is occluded by other voxels. For basic visibility information one can compute approximate normals for each v by estimating tangent planes at the visual hull boundary and propagating the resulting normal directions inwards through the remaining volume. However, one additionally has to account for occlusions caused by other voxels. We present an efficient solution for this problem in Sect. 3.2.

After these initial steps we know in which images I_j a voxel v is visible. There exist two major approaches for the actual photo-consistency estimation which we will briefly introduce here to motivate our modified consistency measure.

Generally the photo-consistency $\phi(v)$ of a voxel is computed by comparing image patches P_j resulting from projecting v into images $I_j, j \in \{0, \ldots, N-1\}$ where v is visible according to the above mentioned visibility estimation. The original space carving approach [2] computes the color of a voxel v in image I_j as the average color c_j of all pixels $p_j^i \in P_j$, and computes $\phi(v)$ by applying a transfer function f to the color variance:

$$c_j = \frac{1}{|P_j|}\sum_i I_j(p_j^i), \quad \bar{c} = \frac{1}{N}\sum_j c_j, \quad \phi(v) = f\left(\frac{1}{N}\sum_j (c_j - \bar{c})^2\right). \quad (1)$$

This variance-based photo-consistency measure supports efficient computation and unconstrained camera setups. However, it is quite sensitive in practice to non-Lambertian, weakly textured surfaces, and varying illumination.

A more sophisticated approach used in recent work [3, 4] is to compare the intensity functions resulting from projecting v to images I_j and I_k by (normalized) cross-correlation (NCC). Suppose we approximate the unknown surface s intersecting voxel v by a planar surface patch (Fig. 2 a). The respective intensity functions can be compared by placing m object space samples p^0 to p^{m-1} on this patch, and evaluating their respective image space projections p_j^i and p_k^i, $0 \le i < m$ in images I_j and I_k. Since s is unknown one generally computes an approximate solution by doing a pixel-wise comparison of simple, image-aligned patches P_j and P_k instead:

$$\mathbf{c}_j = (I_j(p_j^0) - c_j, \dots, I_j(p_j^{m-1}) - c_j)^T, \quad \hat{\mathbf{c}}_j = \frac{\mathbf{c}_j}{\|\mathbf{c}_j\|}, \quad \phi(v) = f\left(\hat{\mathbf{c}}_j^T \cdot \hat{\mathbf{c}}_k\right), \quad (2)$$

with $p_j^i \in P_j$, $m = |P_j|$, c_j as defined in (1), and f being a transfer function applied to the NCC of P_j and P_k. This method strongly reduces potential color ambiguities and accounts for changes in illumination due to the involved normalization step. But despite these advantages there remains a number of open issues with this approach.

While the NCC is computed for pairs of image patches only, one has to combine results for more than two images to compute the actual photo-consistency ϕ. Vogiatzis et al. [4] propose to compute the average NCC for all image pairs, while Esteban et al. [3] compute the NCC with a single reference image. But more importantly one of the main problems of the above approach is the fact that pixels p_j^i and p_k^i in the images I_j and I_k respectively might not correspond to the same surface sample in object space. Hence image-aligned patches provide acceptable results only for medium baseline, epipolar-aligned images while setups with arbitrary camera configurations are difficult to handle. On the other hand as mentioned by Esteban et al. [3] more sophisticated planar model-aligned patches provide valid results only if the approximation is already quite close to the true object surface (Fig. 2 a).

2.1 Voxel Supersampling

To overcome the aforementioned problems we propose a new approach to create consistent *object* space samples p^i such that the matching error does not depend on the quality of the current surface approximation or view alignment but only on the volumetric resolution of the voxel grid.

Photo-consistency can be considered as a function $\phi(x, y, z)$ defined in continuous 3-space where the scene to be reconstructed is embedded. This function vanishes for points (x, y, z) lying exactly on the surface s, has small values in its immediate vicinity, and has larger positive values (which however do not

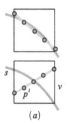 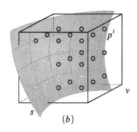 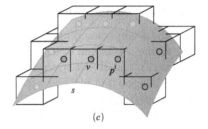

(a)   (b)   (c)

Fig. 2. For previous patch based methods the sampling error strongly depends on the approximation quality of the planar geometry proxy to the surface s (a). Our photo-consistency estimation is based on spatially supersampling a voxel v (b). The samples p^i are weighted equally since the exact position and orientation of s cannot be predicted at sub-voxel accuracy. At higher resolutions our approach allows us to use non-planar surface approximations at v (c) for the photo-consistency estimation.

necessarily increase for larger distances) everywhere else. If we do not have any reliable information about the exact location of the surface s within a given voxel, the best consistency indicator that we can check is to simply integrate the function $\phi(x, y, z)$ over the whole interior of the voxel. The value of this integral is expected to be relatively small in those voxels that are intersected by the surface. Obviously the integration of ϕ has to be done numerically, i.e., by supersampling the considered voxel at sub-voxel resolution (Fig. 2 b).

Within each voxel v we therefore uniformly distribute m equally weighted samples p^i in object-space and compute the colors for each of these samples separately by projecting them into the respective input images. This approach effectively eliminates the matching problem between the different images and samples even for completely unconstrained camera positions. To preserve the illumination invariance of the NCC-based approach we apply a similar color normalization step $\mathbf{c}_j^i \rightarrow \hat{\mathbf{c}}_j^i$ as in (2) to the colors of all 3D samples p^0 to p^{m-1} in a particular image I_j.

Instead of a pairwise correlation estimation which can either be biased by the reference camera [3] or which introduces an $O(n^2)$ complexity to evaluate all pairs [4] for each sample p^i, we compute a weighted variance of the normalized colors $\hat{\mathbf{c}}_j^i$ over all images. This allows us to take a weighted contribution of all images into account simultaneously, with the possibility to respect effects such as blurring at grazing viewing angles. We weigh the contribution of each image I_j to a voxel v using a Gaussian weight w_j (with $\sum_j w_j = 1$) of the angle between the approximate voxel normal and the voxel-to-camera direction in 3D space.

The final photo-consistency is simply computed as the sum of normalized color variances per sample:

$$\phi(v) = \frac{1}{m} \sum_i \phi(p^i), \quad \phi(p^i) = \mathrm{VAR}_j(w_j \hat{\mathbf{c}}_j^i) = \sum_j w_j(\hat{\mathbf{c}}_j^i)^2 - \left(\sum_j w_j \hat{\mathbf{c}}_j^i \right)^2. \quad (3)$$

If we want to consider the full three channel color space instead of just one intensity channel, the number of input images n simply increases to $3n$.

2.2   Surface Sampling

The above supersampling approach provides a robust consistency measure as long as the projection of a voxel covers at least a few pixels in the input images. However, if the object space voxels are too small relative to the pixel resolution of the images this method tends to become unstable due to alias errors, e.g., when applying bilinear interpolation of color values (Fig. 5 c). Hence we have to enlarge the integration domain in this case by adding neighboring voxels. If we have additional information about which neighboring voxels are probably intersected by the surface, e.g., in an iterative optimization setting, we are in fact able to use non-planar geometry proxies for the consistency estimation.

Once an initial surface approximation is available it is straightforward to compute the k-nearest neighbor voxels which are intersected by the surface. E.g., for a technique such as [4] we can easily compute a signed distance field from the current surface within the remaining volume. Then the corresponding k-nearest neighbors for each voxel are found among its neighbors lying on the same level set.

Instead of supersampling a single voxel v we can now create samples p^i for each of the m closest neighbor voxels (Fig. 2 c) and simply compute the photo-consistency as described in Sect. 2.1. While this is conceptually similar to the patch-based NCC, we can exploit a non-planar surface approximation in contrast to planar patches using NCC. Again, the matching problem is implicitly avoided. This approach results in smooth surface reconstructions even at high volumetric resolutions relative to the resolution of the input images (Fig. 5).

3   Efficient GPU-Based Implementation

In comparison to the most simple form of NCC-based approaches our method introduces additional computational overhead since we have to compute the projections of each of the object space samples p^i instead of only the voxel center. In this section we will show how to compensate this overhead by exploiting the capabilities of programmable commodity graphics hardware.

The main benefit of using GPUs as general purpose processors is their inherent parallel processing capability. As we will show, our presented photo-consistency measure as well as further important steps during volumetric reconstruction can be effectively parallelized, resulting in significantly reduced processing times by using current GPU-features [20] such as vertex and fragment shader, floating point support, and efficient multi-resolution texture processing.

The underlying idea when transferring an arbitrary algorithm to the GPU is to exploit the possibility to execute a custom program for each generated vertex and fragment independently and in parallel instead of using the standard 3D rendering pipeline. Because of the floating point support of recent GPUs even quite complex input data can be processed by encoding it in the color channels of one or more textures. By simply drawing a screen-sized quad we generate $w \times h$ fragments on which a custom algorithm is executed. This means we effectively run this algorithm on the texture encoded input data $w \times h$-times in one single rendering pass. The output data of the algorithm can then be accessed by reading it from the color channels of the framebuffer. The following sections present our implementation of a fully hardware accelerated reconstruction pipeline. Our OpenGL-based shader implementations are available on our webpage *http://www.rwth-graphics.de*.

In the following we assume that the volumetric scene representation is based on an adaptively refined grid (adaptive octree), and that we have pre-computed a multi-resolution pyramid of each input image [13]. Although the following algorithms explicitly address the multi-resolution capabilities of modern GPUs, they can be easily simplified to single resolution versions.

3.1   Visual Hull Estimation

For efficient voxel rejection based on segmented images we use a floating point texture T_p to encode the 3D position p for each voxel v in the (r,g,b)-channels of a single texture element (texel). Furthermore we initialize a texture T_b with a *false*-entry for each v as a boolean background mask. To avoid the complex estimation of a voxel's projected area P_j we load a texture mipmap T_I for each image I_j to the GPU and perform a single multi-resolution texture lookup in T_I such that $|P_j| \approx 1$. Projection matrices and the voxel size are transferred as environment parameters.

As described above we can execute a custom fragment program for each voxel v by drawing a screen-sized quad such that each v is represented by a single fragment f. The 3D position of each v is retrieved by a texture lookup $p := T_p(f)$. Then the projected position p_j and footprint size s_j of v in I_j are computed and a texture lookup $b_j := T_I(p_j, s_j)$ is used to check whether v is projected to the background in I_j. The results for all images are accumulated by updating the boolean background mask $T_b(f) := b_j \vee T_b(f)$ which is finally evaluated on the CPU. Since combined reading and writing to a texture is not supported on current GPUs the accumulation step is implemented using OpenGL framebuffer objects and two textures as alternating rendering targets [20].

The amount of voxels which can be encoded into a texture is limited by the maximum available texture size. Thus we run this algorithm repeatedly until all voxels are processed. For n images, v voxels, and a texture size of $w \times h$, this algorithm needs v/wh iterations with n image uploads for each pass.

3.2   Visibility Estimation

The next important step is the voxel visibility estimation based on the visual hull boundary V. The following approach is inspired by the ideas of GPU-based splat rendering by Botsch et al. [21] and uses techniques similar to their splat-based shadow-mapping, resulting in reduced processing times by several orders of magnitude in comparison to a standard approach such as ray-casting (Table 1).

The difficulty lies in choosing a proper occlusion surface for computing the visibility of voxels $v \in V$, since the thickness of V is more than one voxel. How-

Fig. 3. For the visibility estimation of a voxel v in image I_j we first store the depth values of all backfacing voxels v_b in a depth map T_d (a). The visibility of each v can then be evaluated by a depth comparison of v and the corresponding entry in T_d (b).

ever this problem can be effectively solved using only the backfacing boundary of V. After computing the visual hull and normals as described in Sect. 2 we set the OpenGL projection matrix to the corresponding projection matrix of I_j and render all backfacing $v \in V$ as splats (circular discs in object space) into the depth buffer T_d. The splat radius is set in correspondence to the voxel size. The result is a dense depth map (Fig. 3 a) of all outer boundary voxels on the backside of surface s as seen from image I_j. Then the visibility for all v in I_j can be computed efficiently by a simple depth comparison.

Similar to Sect. 3.1 a fragment program loads for each fragment f the corresponding voxel position $p := T_p(f)$. The depth d of p in eye-space can then be compared to the depth value d_V of the front-most boundary voxel projecting to the same image position using a simple texture lookup in T_d (Fig. 3 b). Then v is visible iff $d < d_V$. The number of necessary iterations is identical to Sect. 3.1.

3.3 Photo-Consistency Estimation

The GPU-based photo-consistency estimation is slightly more involved than the previous steps because of the supersampling and color normalization. Assume we create m samples p^i per voxel v (Fig. 2). We encode the data of each sample in a separate texel such that a single voxel v is represented by a sequence of m texels (Fig. 4). In addition to the 3D positions p^i we also store the normal directions in another texture T_n to compute individual camera weights w_j. Auxiliary attributes such as the range of texture coordinates for each v are stored in T_a. The visibility computed in Sect. 3.2 is stored in an occlusion texture T_o. Finally, the image I_j, the corresponding projection matrix, and the voxel size are transferred to the GPU as a texture mipmap T_I and additional environment parameters. Similar to Sect. 3.1 color integration is avoided by a lookup in the corresponding mipmap level of T_I such that $|P_j| \approx 1$. The accumulated color values for solving (3) are stored in a texture T_{accum}. A fragment f is generated for every sample p^i of each voxel. Then, for all images I_j and fragments f, we run the following algorithm:

1. Projection pass:
   (a) Compute sample color $\mathbf{c}_j^i := T_I(p_j^i, s_j^i)$
   (b) Compute camera weight w_j based on T_n and T_o
   (c) Store color and weight $T_c(f) := (\mathbf{c}_j^i, w_j)$

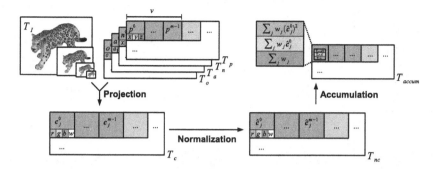

Fig. 4. Our hardware accelerated photo-consistency estimation is based on a three step rendering process. Using texture-encoded input data, we first compute projected color values for each sample p^i. These colors are then normalized and finally accumulated for the final consistency estimation.

2. Normalization pass:
   (a) Loop over all samples $c_j^k, 0 \le k < m$ (using T_a) and normalize $c_j^i \rightarrow \hat{c}_j^i$
   (b) Store normalized color and weight $T_{nc}(f) := (\hat{c}_j^i, w_j)$
3. Accumulation pass:
   (a) Get $(\hat{c}_j^i, w_j) := T_{nc}(f)$
   (b) Add $w_j \left(\hat{c}_j^i\right)^2$, $w_j \hat{c}_j^i$, and w_j to the accumulation buffer T_{accum}

Since we have three color channels per $\hat{c}_j^i$ we accumulate the $3 + 3 + 1$ values computed in step 3b in two output buffers using multiple render targets [20]. The evaluation of these buffers and the summation over samples i in (3) is done in software since a GPU implementation would generate redundant summations for all fragments f corresponding to the samples of a single voxel. For n images, v voxels, m samples per voxel, and a texture size of $w \times h$, this algorithm needs vm/wh passes with n image uploads for each pass.

4   Results

The following section presents our evaluation of the presented method in terms of quality and efficiency. Our reference system for performance evaluation is a Linux-based Intel Pentium 4 with 3.2 GHz, 2 GB of main memory, and a NVIDIA GeFore 6800. We captured video sequences of the Warrior- (Fig. 1) and Leo-model (Fig. 5) with an uncalibrated turn-table setup and an image resolution of 1024×768. The Bahkauv-statue (Fig. 5) was captured using a hand-held video camera with an image resolution of 720×576. We pre-processed the video streams using standard structure-from-motion and segmentation techniques. All models were reconstructed by an iterative multi-resolution implementation of [4] consisting of our proposed volumetric reconstruction pipeline and a graph-cut based surface extraction at a volumetric resolution of 512^3.

The number of samples for each voxel was set to $m = 3^3$ for all experiments, approximately corresponding to a 5×5 image patch for NCC-based techniques.

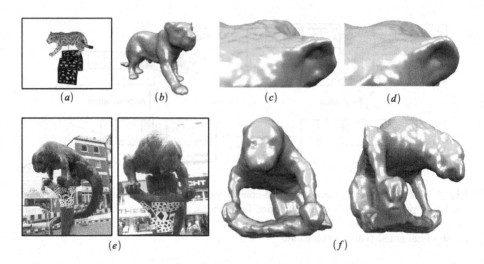

Fig. 5. Image (a) shows one of the original 46 input images of the Leo-model. The 3D model (b) was obtained using a graph-cut based technique [4]. Small oscillations and artifacts can occur for supersampled voxels projecting to less than a few pixels (c). Our surface sampling using neighboring voxels significantly improves the results (d). The approximate image size of the Leo-head is 140^2 pixels. The 30 images used for the reconstruction of the Bahkauv-statue (e) were captured using a hand-held video camera. We are able to reconstruct a quite detailed model (f) despite the specular surface and other illumination artifacts.

For lower values of about 2^3 samples particularly difficult areas such as the quite deep concavities of the Warrior's arms or small features such as the ears of the Leo model could not be properly reconstructed. For higher resolutions we did not observe a significant improvement of the reconstruction quality. However, our proposed surface sampling approach which includes neighboring voxels as discussed in Sect. 2.2 significantly improves reconstruction results for high voxel resolutions, so that one can achieve highly detailed, smooth reconstructions (Fig. 5) without the use of high resolution cameras. In our experiments we applied the surface sampling approach for volumetric resolutions, where a single voxel projects to less than 5^2 pixels. The reconstruction of the Bahkauv shows that a reconstruction is possible even under difficult lighting conditions with non-Lambertian, weakly textured surfaces.

Table 1 shows the performance of our GPU-based implementation in comparison to our CPU-based reference implementation. Although there is a certain overhead associated with loading images and voxel data to the GPU we achieve acceleration factors of 3 to 85. Using our multiresolution implementation of [4] the overall reconstruction time for all presented models was less than 10 minutes. Please note that computation times reported in related work [4,3] range from about 40 minutes to several hours for comparable target resolutions and hardware. Our input data and results are available at *http://www.rwth-graphics.de*.

Table 1. Comparison of computed voxels per second for our hardware-based method and our software implementation (in parentheses) for different input complexities.

Images	Voxels v	Visual hull v/s	Visibility v/s	Consistency v/s	Total time
26	2M	19.4M (1.6M)	3.7M (55K)	350K (109K)	2.7m (24m)
26	4M	33.8M (1.7M)	4.6M (55K)	375K (122K)	5.1m (46m)
51	4M	42.0M (1.7M)	4.7M (56K)	423K (139K)	8.8m (87m)
126	4M	49.4M (1.8M)	4.7M (56K)	450K (139K)	20m (215m)
126	16M	50.2M (1.8M)	4.8M (56K)	450K (140K)	82m (858m)

5   Conclusion and Future Work

In this work we presented a new and efficient approach to compute the photo-consistency of voxels for volumetric 3D stereo reconstruction. Our method resolves several restrictions of previous methods such as the matching of surface patches, biased consistency estimation, and the necessity of epipolar-aligned images, while preserving important features such as illumination invariance. We showed furthermore how this consistency test as well as other important reconstruction steps can be efficiently implemented using commodity graphics hardware, leading to a fully hardware accelerated, high quality reconstruction pipeline for volumetric stereo.

As future work, we plan to incorporate methods to improve the handling of non-Lambertian surfaces. Although the Bahkauv-statue could be reconstructed with acceptable quality, we think that photo-consistency measures should explicitly model specularities and other surface properties [3, 12] for improved results.

Finally we could not yet exploit the full potential of our hardware implementation, since we observed a strong performance breakdown for texture sizes larger than 2048^2. This is probably related to the fact that some of the more recent OpenGL features still have open issues. Since the data transfer to and from the GPU is the main bottleneck of our method, we expect an approximately 4 times higher performance for texture sizes of 4096^2 because of the reduced number of iterations (and hence image uploads) for each algorithm.

Acknowledgements

We would like to acknowledge the helpful discussions with Mario Botsch, Martin Habbecke, and Volker Schönefeld.

References

1. Seitz, S.M., Dyer, C.R.: Photorealistic scene reconstruction by voxel coloring. In: CVPR. (1997) 1067–1073
2. Kutulakos, K.N., Seitz, S.M.: A theory of shape by space carving. International Journal of Computer Vision **38** (2000) 199–218

3. Esteban, C.H.: Stereo and Silhouette Fusion for 3D Object Modeling from Uncalibrated Images Under Circular Motion. PhD thesis, Ecole Nationale Supérieure des Télécommunications (2004)

4. Vogiatzis, G., Torr, P., Cipolla, R.: Multi-view stereo via volumetric graph-cuts. In: CVPR. (2005) 391–398

5. Sinha, S., Pollefeys, M.: Multi-view reconstruction using photo-consistency and exact silhouette constraints: A maximum-flow formulation. In: ICCV. (2005)

6. Slabaugh, G.G., Schafer, R.W., Hans, M.C.: Image-based photo hulls for fast and photo-realistic new view synthesis. Real-Time Imaging 9 (2003) 347–360

7. Li, M., Magnor, M., Seidel, H.P.: Hardware-accelerated rendering of photo hulls. Computer Graphics Forum 23 (2004) 635–642

8. Bonet, J.S.D., Viola, P.A.: Roxels: Responsibility weighted 3D volume reconstruction. In: ICCV. (1999) 418–425

9. Zýka, V., Sára, R.: Polynocular image set consistency for local model verification. In: Workshop of the Austrian Association for Pattern Recognition. (2000) 81–88

10. Broadhurst, A., Drummond, T., Cipolla, R.: A probabilistic framework for space carving. In: ICCV. (2001) 388–393

11. Stevens, M.R., Culbertson, W.B., Malzbender, T.: A histogram-based color consistency test for voxel coloring. In: ICPR. (2002) 118–121

12. Yang, R., Pollefeys, M., Welch, G.: Dealing with textureless regions and specular highlight: A progressive space carving scheme using a novel photo-consistency measure. In: ICCV. (2003) 576–584

13. Gonzalez, R.C., Woods, R.E.: Digital Image Processing. Prentice Hall (2002)

14. Szeliski, R.: Rapid octree construction from image sequences. Computer Vision, Graphics and Image Processing: Image Understanding 58 (1993) 23–32

15. Prock, A.C., Dyer, C.R.: Towards real-time voxel coloring. In: Image Understanding Workshop. (1998) 315–321

16. Sainz, M., Bagherzadeh, N., Susin, A.: Hardware accelerated voxel carving. In: SIACG. (2002) 289–297

17. Culbertson, W.B., Malzbender, T., Slabaugh, G.G.: Generalized voxel coloring. In: Workshop on Vision Algorithms. (1999) 100–115

18. Eisert, P., Steinbach, E., Girod, B.: Multi-hypothesis, volumetric reconstruction of 3-d objects from multiple calibrated camera views. In: ICASSP. (1999) 3509–3512

19. Yang, R., Pollefeys, M.: Multi-resolution real-time stereo on commodity graphics hardware. In: CVPR. (2003) 211–217

20. OpenGL extension registry. ⟨http://www.opengl.org/⟩

21. Botsch, M., Hornung, A., Zwicker, M., Kobbelt, L.: High-quality surface splatting on today's GPUs. In: Eurographics Symp. on Point-Based Graphics. (2005) 17–24

An Affine Invariant of Parallelograms and Its Application to Camera Calibration and 3D Reconstruction

F.C. Wu, F.Q. Duan, and Z.Y. Hu

National Laboratory of Pattern Recognition,
Institute of Automation, Chinese Academy of Sciences,
P.O. Box 2728, Beijing 100080, P.R. China
{fcwu, fqduan, huzy}@nlpr.ia.ac.cn

Abstract. In this work, a new affine invariant of parallelograms is introduced, and the explicit constraint equations between the intrinsic matrix
of a camera and the similar invariants of a parallelogram or a parallelepiped are established using this affine invariant. Camera calibration
and 3D reconstruction from parallelograms are systematically studied
based on these constraints. The proposed theoretical results and algorithms have wide applicability as parallelograms and parallelepipeds are
not rare in man-made scenes. Experimental results on synthetic and real
images validate the proposed approaches.

1 Introduction

Camera calibration is a necessary step to extract metric information from 2D
images. The camera calibration can be classified as: (1). Calibrated object based
approaches, such as calibration based on 3D object [1], [2], [3], 2D planar object
[4], [5], and 1D line segment [6]. (2). Self-calibration, such as calibration based on
Kurppa's equations [7], [8], [9], the absolute conic and the absolute quadric [10],
[11], [12], [13]. (3). Scene's structure information or camera's motion information
based calibration, such as calibration based on parallelism [14], [16], orthogonality [15], [16], and pure rotation of camera [17]. In the paper, our attention is
focused on parallelism based camera calibration.

We find a new affine invariant of parallelograms, which is one of our main
contributions in the paper. Although the affine invariant is very simple in mathematics, the projections of parallelograms and parallelepipeds, as well as the
explicit constraint equations between the intrinsic matrix of a camera and the
similar invariants of a parallelogram or parallelepiped are easily obtained by
this affine invariant. Based on these results, we can obtain the following conclusions: From the projections of a parallelogram across n views, 2(n-1) quadratic
constraint equations on the camera intrinsic parameters can be obtained. In
particular, from the projections of a rectangle or diamond across n views, n linear constraint equations and (n-1) quadratic constraint equations are obtained;
From the projections of m coplanar parallelograms across n views, there exist
at most 2n independent quadratic constraints on the intrinsic parameters of

A. Leonardis, H. Bischof, and A. Pinz (Eds.): ECCV 2006, Part II, LNCS 3952, pp. 191–204, 2006.

cameras. In particular, if there are two parallelograms with the same similar parameters or with the same side-lengths in the scene, then 2n linear constraints can be obtained; From the projections of m non-coplanar parallelograms across n views, the intrinsic parameters and the motion parameters of cameras, the similar invariants of parallelograms, and the global Euclidean reconstruction of parallelograms can be linearly computed using some prior knowledge on the cameras or on the parallelograms.

For camera calibration based on a single parallelogram, to our best knowledge, the quadratic constraint equations obtained in the paper seem to be original, and do not appear in other places. For rectangle and diamond, the usually used constraints in the literature are the linear constrains, which come from orthogonality, the quadratic constraints given in the paper are of new discovery. For non-coplanar parallelograms based camera calibration and Euclidean reconstruction, our calibration method is similar to the classical self-calibration, only difference is that in our method, the use of the prior knowledge of the parallelograms makes the number of required images decrease.

M. Wilczkowiak, P. Sturm and E. Boyer reported their works on parallelepipeds in [16]. They use the factorization-based approach to compute the intrinsic parameters and the motion parameters of cameras, the similar invariants of parallelepipeds, and the global Euclidean reconstruction of parallelepipeds. In our work, the case of parallelepipeds can be integrated into the parallelogram-based framework as a special case of multiple non-coplanar parallelograms. As the factorization-based approach, our method can also compute camera motion parameters and Euclidean reconstruction of the parallelepipeds simultaneously.

In the paper, a 3D point is denoted by $\mathbf{X} = [x, y, z]^\tau$, and a 2D point is denoted by $\mathbf{m} = [u, v, 1]^\tau$. The camera is of the pinhole model, then under the camera coordinate system, a 3D point $\mathbf{X}$ is projected to its image point $\mathbf{m}$ by $\alpha\mathbf{m} = K\mathbf{X}$, where α is the projection depth of 3D point $\mathbf{X}$, K the camera intrinsic matrix.

The paper is organized as follows. In Section 2, the invariants of parallelograms are introduced, and the projections of parallelograms or parallelepipeds, as well as the explicit constraint equations between the intrinsic matrix of a camera and the similar invariants of a parallelogram or a parallelepiped are shown. Camera calibration and 3D reconstruction are elaborated in Section 3. Experiments are reported in Section 4. Conclusions are given at the end of this paper.

2   Invariants and Projections of Parallelograms

2.1   Invariants of Parallelograms

Let $\{\mathbf{X}_i : i = 1, 2, 3, 4\}$ be the four vertices of a parallelogram, and we always assume $\overrightarrow{\mathbf{X}_1\mathbf{X}_2} = \overrightarrow{\mathbf{X}_3\mathbf{X}_4}$ in the paper. Then, the parameters,

$$t = \frac{\|\mathbf{X}_3 - \mathbf{X}_1\|}{\|\mathbf{X}_2 - \mathbf{X}_1\|}, \quad \cos\theta = \frac{(\mathbf{X}_3 - \mathbf{X}_1)^\tau(\mathbf{X}_2 - \mathbf{X}_1)}{\|\mathbf{X}_3 - \mathbf{X}_1\| \cdot \|\mathbf{X}_2 - \mathbf{X}_1\|}, \tag{1}$$

are the similar invariants since similarity transformation preserves the length ratio of two line segments and the angle of two lines. The parameters $\{t, \theta\}$ in fact determine the shape of a parallelogram.

Definition 2.1. *Given a parallelogram* $\{\mathbf{X}_i : i = 1, 2, 3, 4\}$, *the matrix:*

$$\eta = \begin{bmatrix} 1 & t\cos\theta \\ t\cos\theta & t^2 \end{bmatrix} \tag{2}$$

is called the similar parameter matrix of this parallelogram.

Next, we introduce an affine invariant of parallelograms, which is crucial in the paper. From $\overrightarrow{\mathbf{X}_1\mathbf{X}_2} = \overrightarrow{\mathbf{X}_3\mathbf{X}_4}$, we have $\mathbf{X}_4 - \mathbf{X}_3 = \mathbf{X}_2 - \mathbf{X}_1$, and thus,

$$\mathbf{X}_4 = \mathbf{X}_2 - \mathbf{X}_1 + \mathbf{X}_3 = [\mathbf{X}_1, \mathbf{X}_2, \mathbf{X}_3][-1, 1, 1]^\tau.$$

Let $\mathbf{X} = [\mathbf{X}_1, \mathbf{X}_2, \mathbf{X}_3]$, then

$$\mathbf{X}^{-1}\mathbf{X}_4 = [-1, 1, 1]^\tau. \tag{3}$$

Because an affine transformation preserves the parallelism and the length ratio of two parallel segments, the equation (3) is an affine invariant of parallelograms.

2.2 Projections of Parallelograms

From the affine invariant (3), we can easily obtain the projection of parallelograms and the explicit constraint equations between the camera intrinsic parameters and the similar invariants of a parallelogram.

Proposition 2.1. *Suppose* $\{\mathbf{m}_i\}$ *are image of a parallelogram* $\{\mathbf{X}_i\}$, *and let*

$$[q_1, q_2, q_3]^\tau = [-\mathbf{m}_1, \mathbf{m}_2, \mathbf{m}_3]^{-1}\mathbf{m}_4, L = [q_2\mathbf{m}_2 - q_1\mathbf{m}_1, q_3\mathbf{m}_3 - q_1\mathbf{m}_1]. \tag{4}$$

Then we have:
1. Under the camera coordinate system,

$$\mathbf{X}_i = \alpha_4 q_i K^{-1}\mathbf{m}_i, i = 1, 2, 3, 4^1 \tag{5}$$

2. The intrinsic parameters of the camera and the similar invariants of the parallelogram satisfy:

$$(||\mathbf{X}_2 - \mathbf{X}_1||^2/\alpha_4^2)\eta = L^\tau \varpi L. \tag{6}$$

Where α_4 *is the projection depth of point* $\mathbf{X}_4$; $\varpi = K^{-\tau}K^{-1}$ *is IAC* .

Proof. Under the camera coordinate system, we have

$$\mathbf{X}_i = \alpha_i K^{-1}\mathbf{m}_i, i = 1, 2, 3, 4. \tag{7}$$

---
[1] In the paper, we always assume $q_4 = 1$.

Thus, $X = [X_1, X_2, X_3] = K^{-1}[m_1, m_2, m_3]diag[\alpha_1, \alpha_2, \alpha_3]$. Hence, we obtain $X^{-1} = diag[1/\alpha_1, 1/\alpha_2, 1/\alpha_3][m_1, m_2, m_3]^{-1}K$, and

$$
\begin{aligned}
X^{-1}X_4 &= diag[1/\alpha_1, 1/\alpha_2, 1/\alpha_3][m_1, m_2, m_3]^{-1}K(\alpha_4 K^{-1}m_4) \\
&= diag[\alpha_4/\alpha_1, \alpha_4/\alpha_2, \alpha_4/\alpha_3][m_1, m_2, m_3]^{-1}m_4 \\
&= [-\alpha_4 q_1/\alpha_1, \alpha_4 q_2/\alpha_2, \alpha_4 q_3/\alpha_3]^\tau
\end{aligned}
$$

By the affine invariant (3), we have $\alpha_i = \alpha_4 q_i, i = 1, 2, 3$. Substituting them into the equation (7), we obtain the equation (5).

We have $X_j - X_1 = \alpha_4 K^{-1}(q_j m_j - q_1 m_1)$ by the equation (5), and thus,

$$
\|X_2 - X_1\|^2 \eta = \begin{bmatrix} (X_2 - X_1)^\tau (X_2 - X_1) & (X_2 - X_1)^\tau (X_3 - X_1) \\ (X_2 - X_1)^\tau (X_3 - X_1) & (X_3 - X_1)^\tau (X_3 - X_1) \end{bmatrix} = \alpha_4^2 L^\tau \varpi L.
$$

Hence, the equation (6) holds.

Remark 2.1. Since $X_4 - X_3 = X_2 - X_1$ and $X_4 - X_2 = X_3 - X_1$, from the equations (5), we can obtain $q_2 m_2 - q_1 m_1 = q_4 m_4 - q_3 m_3 \overset{\Delta}{=} v_1$, $q_3 m_3 - q_1 m_1 = q_4 m_4 - q_2 m_2 \overset{\Delta}{=} v_2$. It is not difficult to see that $v_1 (v_2)$ is a homogeneous coordinate of the vanishing point of the parallel sides $X_1 X_2 // X_3 X_4$ ($X_1 X_3 // X_2 X_4$). This is because $v_1^\tau (m_1 \times m_2) = v_1^\tau (m_3 \times m_4) = 0$, $v_2^\tau (m_1 \times m_3) = v_2^\tau (m_2 \times m_4) = 0$.

If the camera intrinsic parameters are known, we have following corollaries:

Corollary 2.1. *From the image of a parallelogram, we can recover its shape, i.e., we can determine its similar invariants.*

Corollary 2.2. *If the length of one side of a parallelogram is known, from its image we can determine the length of the other side and the distances from the parallelogram vertices to the camera center.*

Remark 2.2. In the classical PnP problem [18], in order to compute the distances between control points and the camera center from images of the control points, it is necessary to know the distances between each pair of control points. From the corollary 2.1 and 2.2, we can obtain an interesting result: If the four control points are vertices of a parallelogram, we only need to know the distance between a pair of control points for computing the distances between these control points and the camera center.

2.3 Projections of Parallelepipeds

Let $\{X_1, ..., X_8\}$ be 8 vertices of a parallelepiped, and we always assume $\overrightarrow{X_1 X_2} = \overrightarrow{X_3 X_4} = \overrightarrow{X_5 X_6} = \overrightarrow{X_7 X_8}$. Then, the parameters

$$
t_1 = \frac{\|X_3 - X_1\|}{\|X_2 - X_1\|}, \quad t_2 = \frac{\|X_5 - X_1\|}{\|X_2 - X_1\|}, \quad \cos\theta = \frac{(X_3 - X_1)^\tau (X_2 - X_1)}{\|X_3 - X_1\| \cdot \|X_2 - X_1\|},
$$

$$
\cos\phi = \frac{(X_5 - X_1)^\tau (X_2 - X_1)}{\|X_5 - X_1\| \cdot \|X_2 - X_1\|}, \quad \cos\varphi = \frac{(X_5 - X_1)^\tau (X_3 - X_1)}{\|X_5 - X_1\| \cdot \|X_3 - X_1\|},
$$

are the similar invariants of parallelepipeds, and they determine the shape of a parallelepiped.

Definition 2.2. *Given a parallelepiped*$\{\mathbf{X}_i\}$*, the matrix:*

$$\mu = \begin{bmatrix} 1 & t_1\cos\theta & t_2\cos\phi \\ t_1\cos\theta & t_1^2 & t_1t_2\cos\varphi \\ t_2\cos\phi & t_1t_2\cos\varphi & t_2^2 \end{bmatrix} \tag{8}$$

is called the similar parameter matrix of this parallelepiped.

Suppose $\{\mathbf{m}_i\}$ are the image of parallelepiped $\{\mathbf{X}_i\}$, and let

$$[q_1, q_2, q_3]^\tau = [-\mathbf{m}_1, \mathbf{m}_2, \mathbf{m}_3]^{-1}\mathbf{m}_4, \quad [q_5, q_6, \tilde{q}_3]^\tau = [-\mathbf{m}_5, \mathbf{m}_6, \mathbf{m}_3]^{-1}\mathbf{m}_4.$$

By proposition 2.1, we have $\alpha_4q_3K^{-1}\mathbf{m}_3 = \mathbf{X}_3 = \alpha_4\tilde{q}_3K^{-1}\mathbf{m}_3$, and thus, $q_3 = \tilde{q}_3$. Hence,

$$[q_1, q_2, q_3, q_5, q_6]^\tau = (A^\tau A)^{-1}A^\tau \begin{bmatrix} \mathbf{m}_4 \\ \mathbf{m}_4 \end{bmatrix}, \tag{9}$$

where $A = \begin{bmatrix} -\mathbf{m}_1 & \mathbf{m}_2 & \mathbf{m}_3 & 0 & 0 \\ 0 & 0 & \mathbf{m}_3 & -\mathbf{m}_5 & \mathbf{m}_6 \end{bmatrix}$. We can prove the following proposition.

Proposition 2.2. *Let* $M = [q_2\mathbf{m}_2 - q_1\mathbf{m}_1, \ q_3\mathbf{m}_3 - q_1\mathbf{m}_1, q_5\mathbf{m}_5 - q_1\mathbf{m}_1]$. *Then, we have:*

1. The coordinates of vertex $\mathbf{X}_i$ *under the camera coordinate system can be expressed as:*

$$\mathbf{X}_i = \alpha_4q_iK^{-1}\mathbf{m}_i, i = 1, 2...6. \tag{10}$$

2. The intrinsic parameters of the camera and the similar invariants of the parallelepiped satisfy:

$$(\|\mathbf{X}_2 - \mathbf{X}_1\|^2/\alpha_4^2)\mu = M^\tau \varpi M. \tag{11}$$

Remark 2.3. The matrix M can be computed directly from the image of a parallelepiped, which does not depend on the similar invariants. The equation (11) establishes a duality between the intrinsic parameters of a camera and the similar invariants of a parallelepiped. The result is also obtained in [16] using a different method, but they do not show the explicit expression of matrix M.

3 Calibration and 3D Reconstruction

In this section, we only discuss the camera calibration and 3D reconstruction based on parallelograms. The parallelepipeds based calibration and 3D reconstruction are similar to those on non-coplanar parallelograms. Here we omit the calibration and 3D reconstruction based on parallelepipeds due to space limit.

3.1 m Coplanar Parallelograms in n Views

Proposition 3.1. *Given the* n *images*$\{\mathbf{m}_{ki}^{(j)} : i = 1, 2, 3, 4; j = 1, 2...n\}$ *of* m *coplanar parallelograms* $\{\mathbf{X}_{ki}\}$, k=1, 2...m, *let*

$$[q_{k1}^{(j)}, q_{k2}^{(j)}, q_{k3}^{(j)}]^{\tau} = [-\mathbf{m}_{k1}^{(j)}, \mathbf{m}_{k2}^{(j)}, \mathbf{m}_{k3}^{(j)}]^{-1}\mathbf{m}_{k4}^{(j)},$$

$$L_{kj} = [q_{k2}^{(j)}\mathbf{m}_{k2}^{(j)} - q_{k1}^{(j)}\mathbf{m}_{k1}^{(j)}, q_{k3}^{(j)}\mathbf{m}_{k3}^{(j)} - q_{k1}^{(j)}\mathbf{m}_{k1}^{(j)}].$$

Then, we have 2m(n-1) quadratic constraint equations on the cameras' intrinsic parameters:

$$\frac{(L_{kj}^{\tau}\varpi_j L_{kj})_{11}}{(L_{kj}^{\tau}\varpi_j L_{kj})_{22}} = \frac{(L_{k1}^{\tau}\varpi_1 L_{k1})_{11}}{(L_{k1}^{\tau}\varpi_1 L_{k1})_{22}}, \quad \frac{(L_{kj}^{\tau}\varpi_j L_{kj})_{12}}{(L_{kj}^{\tau}\varpi_j L_{kj})_{22}} = \frac{(L_{k1}^{\tau}\varpi_1 L_{k1})_{12}}{(L_{k1}^{\tau}\varpi_1 L_{k1})_{22}}. \tag{12}$$

Where $\varpi_j = \mathbf{K}_j^{-\tau}\mathbf{K}_j^{-1}$ is the jth camera's IAC.

Proof. By proposition 2.1, we have

$$\|\mathbf{X}_{k2}^{(j)} - \mathbf{X}_{k1}^{(j)}\|^2 \eta_k = \alpha_{k4}^{(j)} L_{kj}^{\tau}\varpi_j L_{kj}, \ j = 1, 2...n; k = 1, 2...m, \tag{13}$$

where

$$\mathbf{X}_{ki}^{(j)} = \alpha_{k4}^{(j)} q_{ki}^{(j)} \mathbf{K}_j^{-1}\mathbf{m}_{ki}^{(j)}, \ i = 1, 2, 3, 4 \tag{14}$$

are the coordinates of the kth parallelogram's vertices under the jth camera coordinate system. From $\|\mathbf{X}_{k2}^{(j)} - \mathbf{X}_{k1}^{(j)}\| = \|\mathbf{X}_{k2} - \mathbf{X}_{k1}\|$, $j = 1, 2...n$, we have

$$\alpha_{k4}^{(j)} L_{kj}^{\tau}\varpi_j \ L_{kj} = \alpha_{k4}^{(1)} L_{k1}^{\tau}\varpi_1 L_{k1}, \ j = 2, 3...n; k = 1, 2...m.$$

By eliminating the scale factors in the above equations, we can obtain 2m(n-1) quadratic constraint equations (12).

Among the 2m(n-1) quadratic constraint equations, there exist at most 2n independent constraints. Because the n images of a metric plane (i.e., the projections of circular points on the plane can be computed) can only provide 2n independent constraints for the IACs, ϖ_j, the number of independent constraints cannot exceed 2n in the case of m coplanar parallelograms.

Corollary 3.1. *If $\{\mathbf{X}_{ki}\}$ is a rectangle, the 2nd constraint equations in (12) become n linear constraint equations:*

$$(L_{kj}^{\tau}\varpi_j \ L_{kj})_{12} = 0, \ j = 1, 2...n \tag{15}$$

which are from the orthogonality.

Corollary 3.2. *If $\{\mathbf{X}_{ki}\}$ is a diamond, the 1st constraint equations in (12) become n linear constraint equations:*

$$(L_{kj}^{\tau}\varpi_j \ L_{kj})_{11} = (L_{kj}^{\tau}\varpi_j \ L_{kj})_{22}, \ j = 1, 2...n \tag{16}$$

which are from the diamond's similar invariant, $t_k = 1$.

Remark 3.1. By the orthogonality of diamond's two diagonals, we also can obtain a linear constraint equation from each image. However, we can prove that such linear constraint equations are equivalent to the equations (16). For rectangle and diamond, the usually used constraints in the literature are the linear constrains. To our knowledge, the quadratic constraints are of new discovery.

For coplanar parallelograms, the following propositions are interesting.

Proposition 3.2. *If two parallelograms have the same similar invariants, then from their n images we can obtain 2n linear constraint equations on the intrinsic parameters of the cameras:*

$$\tilde{L}_{2j}^{\tau} \varpi_j \tilde{L}_{2j} = s\tilde{L}_{1j}^{\tau} \varpi_j \tilde{L}_{1j}, \; j = 1, 2...n, \tag{17}$$

where,

$$\tilde{L}_{kj} = [\tilde{q}_{k2}^{(j)} \mathbf{m}_{k2}^{(j)} - \tilde{q}_{k1}^{(j)} \mathbf{m}_{k1}^{(j)}, \tilde{q}_{k3}^{(j)} \mathbf{m}_{k3}^{(j)} - \tilde{q}_{k1}^{(j)} \mathbf{m}_{k1}^{(j)}], \tag{18}$$

$$\tilde{q}_{ki}^{j} = \frac{\det[q_{11}^{(j)} \mathbf{m}_{11}^{(j)}, q_{12}^{(j)} \mathbf{m}_{12}^{(j)}, q_{13}^{(j)} \mathbf{m}_{13}^{(j)}]}{\det[q_{k1}^{(j)} \mathbf{m}_{k1}^{(j)}, q_{12}^{(j)} \mathbf{m}_{12}^{(j)} - q_{11}^{(j)} \mathbf{m}_{11}^{(j)}, q_{13}^{(j)} \mathbf{m}_{13}^{(j)} - q_{11}^{(j)} \mathbf{m}_{11}^{(j)}]} q_{ki}^{j}, \tag{19}$$

$$s = \frac{\|(\tilde{q}_{23}^{(j)} \mathbf{m}_{23}^{(j)} - \tilde{q}_{21}^{(j)} \mathbf{m}_{21}^{(j)}) \times (\tilde{q}_{22}^{(j)} \mathbf{m}_{22}^{(j)} - \tilde{q}_{21}^{(j)} \mathbf{m}_{21}^{(j)})\|}{\|(\tilde{q}_{13}^{(j)} \mathbf{m}_{13}^{(j)} - \tilde{q}_{11}^{(j)} \mathbf{m}_{11}^{(j)}) \times (\tilde{q}_{12}^{(j)} \mathbf{m}_{12}^{(j)} - \tilde{q}_{11}^{(j)} \mathbf{m}_{11}^{(j)})\|}. \tag{20}$$

Remark 3.2. In the above proposition, there should exist a 2D rotation between the two similar parallelograms. Otherwise, the proposition does not hold. In addition, this proposition can be generalized to the case of two similar figures with four point correspondences, i.e., if two coplanar figures with four point correspondences are similar, then from their n images we can obtain 2n linear constraint equations on the intrinsic parameters of the cameras.

Proposition 3.3. *If two parallelograms have the same side-lengths, then from their n images we can obtain 2n linear constraint equations on the intrinsic parameters of the cameras:*

$$(\tilde{L}_{2j}^{\tau} \varpi_j \tilde{L}_{2j})_{11} = (\tilde{L}_{1j}^{\tau} \varpi_j \tilde{L}_{1j})_{11}, \; (\tilde{L}_{2j}^{\tau} \varpi_j \tilde{L}_{2j})_{22} = (\tilde{L}_{1j}^{\tau} \varpi_j \tilde{L}_{1j})_{22}, \; j = 1, ...n. \tag{21}$$

3.2   m Non-coplanar Parallelograms in n Views

In this section, we mainly show a linear method in the case of multiple noncoplanar parallelograms in multiple views to compute the intrinsic parameters and the motion parameters of cameras, the similar parameters of parallelograms, and global Euclidean reconstruction of parallelograms using some prior knowledge on the cameras or on the parallelograms.

Suppose there are m parallelograms $\{\mathbf{X}_{ki}\}$, k=1, 2...m, in a scene, and among them there exist at least two non-coplanar parallelograms. Given the n images $\{\mathbf{m}_{ki}^{(j)}\}$ of the parallelograms, and let

$$[q_{k1}^{(j)}, q_{k2}^{(j)}, q_{k3}^{(j)}]^{\tau} = [-\mathbf{m}_{k1}^{(j)}, \mathbf{m}_{k2}^{(j)}, \mathbf{m}_{k3}^{(j)}]^{-1} \mathbf{m}_{k4}^{(j)},$$

$$L_{kj} = [q_{k2}^{(j)} \mathbf{m}_{k2}^{(j)} - q_{k1}^{(j)} \mathbf{m}_{k1}^{(j)}, q_{k3}^{(j)} \mathbf{m}_{k3}^{(j)} - q_{k1}^{(j)} \mathbf{m}_{k1}^{(j)}].$$

Table 1. Linear constraints on ϖ_1 from prior information of camera

Prior information of camera	Linear constraints on ϖ_1
zero skew	$(H_{1j}^{-\tau}\varpi_1 H_{1j}^{-1})_{12} = 0$
principal point at origin	$(H_{1j}^{-\tau}\varpi_1 H_{1j}^{-1})_{13} = (H_{1j}^{-\tau}\varpi_1 H_{1j}^{-1})_{23} = 0$
known aspect ratio $\tau = f_v/f_u$	$\tau^2(H_{1j}^{-\tau}\varpi_1 H_{1j}^{-1})_{22} - (H_{1j}^{-\tau}\varpi_1 H_{1j}^{-1})_{11} = 0$

Table 2. Linear constraints on ϖ_1 from prior information of parallelogram

Prior information of parallelogram	Linear constraints on ϖ_1
$\theta_k = \pi/2$	$(L_{k1}^T\varpi_1 L_{k1})_{12} = 0$
$t_{k1} = 1$	$(L_{k1}^T\varpi_1 L_{k1})_{11} = (L_{k1}^T\varpi_1 L_{k1})_{22}$
two coplanar parallelograms with the same similar invariants	constraint equations (17)
two coplanar parallelograms with the same side-lengths	constraint equations (21)

By proposition 2.1, the coordinates of the kth parallelogram's vertices under the jth camera coordinate system are:

$$X_{ki}^{(j)} = \alpha_{k4}^{(j)} q_{ki}^{(j)} K_j^{-1} m_{ki}^{(j)} : i = 1, 2, 3, 4. \tag{22}$$

By remark 2.1, the image points,$v_{k1}^{(j)} = q_{k2}^{(j)} m_{k2}^{(j)} - q_{k1}^{(j)} m_{k1}^{(j)}$ and $v_{k2}^{(j)} = q_{k3}^{(j)} m_{k3}^{(j)} - q_{k1}^{(j)} m_{k1}^{(j)}$, are the vanishing points of the two pair of parallel sides of the kth parallelogram in the jth image plane. We can linearly determine the infinite homography H_{1j} between the 1st view and the jth view from the vanishing point correspondences,$\{v_{k1}^{(1)} \leftrightarrow v_{k1}^{(j)}, v_{k2}^{(1)} \leftrightarrow v_{k2}^{(j)}, k = 1, 2...m\}$. Hence, we can obtain the 5n-5 constraint equations on the IACs:

$$\omega_j = s_j H_{1j}^{-\tau}\varpi_1 H_{1j}^{-1}, j = 2, 3...n, \tag{23}$$

where s_j is an unknown scale factor. On the other hand, by proposition 2.2, we have the constraints on (η_k, ϖ_j):

$$\eta_k = t_{kj} L_{kj}^T \varpi_j L_{kj}, j = 1, 2...n; k = 1, 2...m, \tag{24}$$

where t_{kj} is an unknown scale factor.

Note that all the constraints (23) and (24) are nonlinear. However, using some prior knowledge on the cameras, from the constraints (23) we can obtain linear constrains on ϖ_1 (see Tab.1); using some prior knowledge on the parallelograms, from the constraints (24) we can also obtain linear constrains on ϖ_1 (see Tab.2).

Intrinsic parameters and similar invariants. From the above discussions, we can see that using some prior knowledge on the cameras or/and on the parallelograms, from a few images of the parallelograms we can linearly determine

ϖ_1 up to a scale factor. Once ϖ_1 is obtained, ϖ_j can be obtained up to a scale factor by the equations (23), and thus η_k can also be determined up to a scale factor by the equations (24).

After ϖ_j and η_k are determined up to scale factors, we can compute the intrinsic parameter matrix K_j from ϖ_j, e.g., using Choleskey decomposition; and setting $(\eta_k)_{11} = 1$, we obtain the similar invariants $\{t_k, \theta_k\}$.

3D reconstruction and motion recovery. Let $[R_j, t_j]$ be the motion from the 1st view to the jth view. By the equation (22), we have

$$\alpha_{k4}^{(j)} q_{ki}^{(j)} K_j^{-1} m_{ki}^{(j)} = \alpha_{k4}^{(1)} q_{ki}^{(1)} R_j K_1^{-1} m_{ki}^{(1)} + t_j, \ i = 1,2,3,4; \ k = 1,2...m, \quad (25)$$

$$R_j K_1^{-1}(q_{ki}^{(1)} m_{ki}^{(1)} - q_{k1}^{(1)} m_{k1}^{(1)}) = (\alpha_{k4}^{(j)}/\alpha_{k4}^{(1)}) K_j^{-1}(q_{ki}^{(j)} m_{ki}^{(j)} - q_{k1}^{(j)} m_{k1}^{(j)}), \\ i = 2,3,4; \ k = 1,2...m. \quad (26)$$

and thus, we can obtain $(\alpha_{k4}^{(j)}/\alpha_{k4}^{(1)})^2 w_{ki}^{(j)} = w_{ki}^{(1)}$, where:

$$w_{ki}^{(j)} = (q_{ki}^{(j)} m_{ki}^{(j)} - q_{k1}^{(j)} m_{k1}^{(j)})^\tau \varpi_j (q_{ki}^{(j)} m_{ki}^{(j)} - q_{k1}^{(j)} m_{k1}^{(j)}).$$

Then,

$$\alpha_{k4}^{(j)}/\alpha_{k4}^{(1)} = \sqrt{(1/3)\sum_{i=2}^{4}(w_{ki}^{(1)}/w_{ki}^{(j)})} \triangleq \beta_{kj} \ k = 1,2...m, \quad (27)$$

Substituting (27) into (26), we have

$$R_j K_1^{-1}(q_{ki}^{(1)} m_{ki}^{(1)} - q_{k1}^{(1)} m_{k1}^{(1)}) = \beta_{kj} K_j^{-1}(q_{ki}^{(j)} m_{ki}^{(j)} - q_{k1}^{(j)} m_{k1}^{(j)}), \\ i = 2,3,4; \ k = 1,2...m. \quad (28)$$

Let

$$B_{kj} = [q_{k2}^{(1)} m_{k2}^{(1)} - q_{k1}^{(1)} m_{k1}^{(1)}, q_{k3}^{(1)} m_{k3}^{(1)} - q_{k1}^{(1)} m_{k1}^{(1)}, q_{k4}^{(1)} m_{k4}^{(1)} - q_{k1}^{(1)} m_{k1}^{(1)}], \quad (29)$$

$$C_{kj} = [q_{k2}^{(j)} m_{k2}^{(j)} - q_{k1}^{(j)} m_{k1}^{(j)}, q_{k3}^{(j)} m_{k3}^{(j)} - q_{k1}^{(j)} m_{k1}^{(j)}, q_{k4}^{(j)} m_{k4}^{(j)} - q_{k1}^{(j)} m_{k1}^{(j)}]. \quad (30)$$

Then, the equations (28) can be written as the matrix form:

$$R_j K_1^{-1}[B_{1j}, B_{2j}, ..., B_{mj}] = K_j^{-1}[\beta_{1j} C_{1j}, \beta_{2j} C_{2j}, ..., \beta_{mj} C_{mj}].$$

Because there exist non-coplanar parallelograms, $rank[B_{1j}, B_{2j}, ..., B_{mj}] = 3$, and thus we have

$$R_j = K_j^{-1} \underbrace{[\beta_{1j} C_{1j}, \beta_{2j} C_{2j}, ..., \beta_{mj} C_{mj}][B_{1j}, B_{2j}, ..., B_{mj}]^+}_{D_j} K_1. \quad (31)$$

Substituting (27) and (31) into (25), we can obtain the constraints on $(\alpha_{k4}^{(1)}, t_j)$:

$$(q_{ki}^{(1)} D_j m_{ki}^{(1)} - \beta_{kj} q_{ki}^{(j)} m_{ki}^{(j)})\alpha_{k4}^{(1)} + K_j t_j = 0. \quad (32)$$

Let

$$E_{kj} = \begin{bmatrix} q_{k1}^{(1)} D_j m_{k1}^{(1)} - \beta_{kj} q_{k1}^{(j)} m_{k1}^{(j)} \\ \vdots \\ q_{k4}^{(1)} D_j m_{k4}^{(1)} - \beta_{kj} q_{k4}^{(j)} m_{k4}^{(j)} \end{bmatrix}, k = 1, 2...m; j = 2, 3...n, \qquad (33)$$

$E_j = diag[E_{1j}, E_{2j}, ..., E_{mj}], C = \underbrace{[I_3, I_3, ..., I_3]^T}_{12m} (I_3$ is the unit matrix of order 3).

Then, the equations (32) can be written as the matrix form:

$$\underbrace{\begin{bmatrix} E_2 \ CK_2 \\ \vdots \quad \ddots \\ E_n \qquad\qquad CK_n \end{bmatrix}}_{E} \begin{bmatrix} \alpha \\ \tau \end{bmatrix} = 0, \qquad (34)$$

where $\alpha = [\alpha_{14}^{(1)}, \alpha_{24}^{(1)}, ..., \alpha_{m4}^{(1)}]^T, \tau = [t_2^\tau, t_3^\tau, ..., t_n^\tau]^T$. Hence, the least squares solution of the equations (32) is the unit right singular vector corresponding to the smallest singular value of E, and denoted as

$$\tilde{\alpha} = \left[\tilde{\alpha}_{14}^{(1)}, \tilde{\alpha}_{24}^{(1)}, ..., \tilde{\alpha}_{m4}^{(1)}\right]^T, \tilde{\tau} = \left[\tilde{t}_2^\tau, \tilde{t}_3^\tau, ..., \tilde{t}_n^\tau\right]^T. \qquad (35)$$

By the equations (22), the coordinates of the parallelograms' vertices under the 1st camera coordinate system can be expression as

$$X_{ki}^{(1)} = \alpha_{k4}^{(1)} q_{ki}^{(1)} K_1^{-1} m_{ki}^{(1)}, i = 1, 2, 3, 4; k = 1, 2...m.$$

Substituting $\alpha_{k4}^{(1)} = \tilde{\alpha}_{k4}^{(1)}$ into the above equations, we can obtain an Euclidean reconstruction of the parallelograms under the 1st camera coordinate system:

$$X_{ki}^{(1)} = \tilde{\alpha}_{k4}^{(1)} q_{ki}^{(1)} K_1^{-1} m_{ki}^{(1)}, i = 1, 2, 3, 4; k = 1, 2, ..., m. \qquad (36)$$

4   Experimental Results

4.1   Synthetic Data

The case of parallelograms. This experiment is to study the performance of the calibration using parallelograms. We only report the calibration from one image. The used prior information on the camera was zero skew and known principal point. The camera's setting is $(f_u, f_v, s, u_0, v_0) = (1000, 900, 0, 512, 512)$. The image resolution is of 1024×1024 pixels. The parallelograms were generated as follows: At first, a parallelepiped was generated, then, we randomly generated two parallelograms with the same similar invariants on one plane and two parallelograms with the same side-lengths on the other plane. As [16], the parallelepiped orientation varies from that shown in Fig.1 left (both of the two planes are parallel to x axes of the camera) to that of Fig.1 right (a degenerate configuration, both of the two planes are parallel to the optical axes).

Fig. 1. Parallelepiped orientations in the case of parallelograms

The continuous rotation between the two positions is parameterized by an angle ranging from $0°$ (Fig.1 left) to $90°$ (Fig.1 right). In order to provide more statistically meaningful results, we performed 100 trials. In each trial, Gaussian noise of standard deviation 1 pixel was added to each vertex image of the parallelograms. Calibration was considered to be failed if the estimated matrix ω was not positive definite.

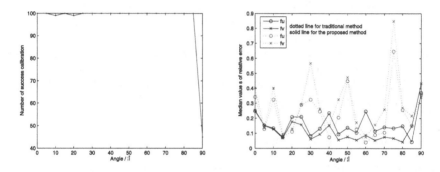

Fig. 2. Calibration results with the change of the relative camera-parallelepiped rotation angle. Left: the number of successful calibration; Right: the relative error of the estimation of f_u and f_v.

The calibration method described here is compared with the traditional method. The traditional method uses the 16 vertices of the parallelograms to estimate the projection matrix, and determines intrinsic parameter by QR-decomposition of the 3×3 sub-matrix of the projection matrix. Fig.2 shows the number of successful calibrations of the proposed method and the relative error of the estimated intrinsic parameters for both the parallelogram-based approach and the tradition approach, where the value at each pose is the mean of 100 independent trials (computed using only results of trails with valid calibration for the proposed method). It can be seen from Fig.2 that the parallelogram-based method is superior to the traditional method in general cases.

The case of parallelepipeds. This experiment is to study the performance of the calibration, camera motion estimation and reconstruction using parallelepipeds. We only report the case of one parallelepiped in two views. The two cameras' settings are $(f_u, f_v, s, u_0, v_0) = (1000, 900, 0, 512, 512)$ and

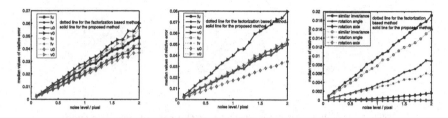

Fig. 3. Results for case of parallelepipeds (dotted line: factorization-based method, solid line: our method). left: the first camera parameters. middle: the second camera parameters. left: camera motion parameters and similar invariants.

(900, 800, 0, 512, 512) respectively. The image resolution is of 1024 × 1024 pixels. The test data were generated by a random rigid transformation of a canonical cube. We performed 1000 tests. In each test, Gaussian noise was added to each image point of the parallelepiped vertices. The used prior information was: the parallelepiped has three right angles and the cameras have zero skew.

Our proposed method is compared to M.Wilczkowiak's factorization-based method. Fig.3 shows the relative error of the estimated parameters for both methods, where the value at each noise level is the mean of 1000 independent tests. From the figure, we can see that the two approaches perform comparably and the factorization-based method is slightly better.

4.2 Results on Real Scenes

Calibration object. Fig.4(up)shows the original image and the calibration parallelograms. The two coplanar parallelograms are similar, and the other two coplanar parallelograms are of same side-lengths. The image size is 2048 × 1536. The used prior information is zero skew and known principal point. The camera parameters obtained by the traditional method and the proposed method are (3723, 3715.7, 7.9, 1003.4, 759.4) and (3720.8, 3739.9, 0, 1024, 768) respectively. The estimated parameters are used for our 3D reconstruction process for comparing the calibration results of the two methods. The similar invariants of the parallelograms estimated from the two methods are shown in Tab.3. The estimated angle of the two calibration planes is 88.99° and 89.38° for the traditional method and proposed method respectively. From the comparison of the estimated similar invariants and the estimated angle, we can see the result is

Table 3. The comparison of the similar invariants $(t, \cos\theta)$

parallelograms	The 1th		The 2th		The 3th		The 4th	
real value	1	0	1	0	1.491	0.447	1.491	0.447
traditional method	1.01	0.004	0.982	0.019	1.501	0.442	1.497	0.472
proposed method	1.006	0.001	0.984	0.015	1.491	0.447	1.506	0.467

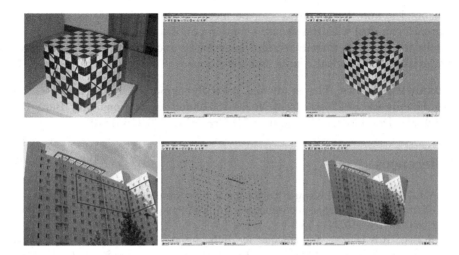

Fig. 4. Left: the original image, middle: the 3D points, right: texture mapping result from a different view

slightly better for the proposed method. Fig.4(up) shows the reconstructed 3D points by our method and the texture mapping result from a different viewpoint.

Outdoor scene. The image and the calibration parallelepiped are shown in Fig.4(low). The image size is 1024×768. The used prior information is: the parallelepiped has right angles; the camera has zero skew and unit aspect ratio. The intrinsic parameters obtained by our proposed method and by M.Wilczkowiak's method are (1354.6, 1354.6, 0, 586.3, 382) and (1359.5, 1359.5, 0, 588.5, 380) respectively. The similar invariants obtained by the two methods are $(t_1, t_2) =$ (2.6285, 1.1403) $(t_1/t_2 = 2.305)$ and (2.6303, 1.1421) $(t_1/t_2 = 2.303)$ respectively. The real value of t_1/t_2 is 2.5. We can see the similar invariants obtained by the two methods are very close to the real value. Fig.4(low)shows the reconstructed 3D points by our method and the texture mapping result from a different viewpoint, where the estimated angle of the two calibration planes was $89.986°$. By the comparison of the similar invariants and the camera parameters, we can see the results are very close for the two approaches.

5   Conclusion

In this paper, a new affine invariant of parallelogram is introduced, by which the projections of the parallelogram and parallelepiped, and the explicit constraint equations between the camera's intrinsic matrix and the similar invariants of a parallelogram or a parallelepiped are obtained. From these constraints, we presented an approach for camera calibration, motion estimation, and 3D reconstruction from a few uncalibrated images based on some geometric constraints on the scene. Commonly available constraints, such as parallelism, coplanarity, right angles, and length ratios, can be nicely modeled via parallelogram. The approach can deal with the scene to contain parallelograms and parallelepipeds simultaneously. Experimental results on synthetic and real images also validated the presented theoretical results and algorithms.

Acknowledgments. This study was partially supported by the National Science Foundation of China Grant No.60575019 and the National Key Basic Research and Development Program (973) Grant No. 2004CB318107.

References

1. Y.I.Abdel-Aziz, H.M.Karara: Direct linear transformation from comparator coordinates into object space coordinates. In: ASP Symposimy on Colse-Range Photogrammetry. (1971) 1–18
2. R.Tsai, R.K.Lenz: A technique for fully automous and efficient 3d robotics hand/eye calibration. IEEE Trans. Robotics and Automation **5** (1989) 345–358
3. R.Tsai: An efficient and accurate camera calibration technique for 3d machine vision. In: Proc. CVPR. (1986) 364–374
4. Zhang, Z.: Flexible camera calibration by viewing a plane from unknown orientations. In: Proc.ICCV. (1999) 666–673
5. Sturm, P., S.J.Maybank: On plane-based camera calibration: A general algorithm, singularities, applications. In: Proc. CVPR. (1999) 432–437
6. Zhang, Z.: Camera calibration with one-dimensional objects. In: Proc. ECCV. (2002) 161–174
7. J.Maybank, S., O.D.Faugeras: A theory of self-calibration of a moving camera. IJCV **8** (1992) 123–152
8. R.I.Hartley: Estimation of relative camera positions for uncalibrated cameras. In: Proc. ECCV. (1992) 579–587
9. R.I.Hartley: An algorithm for self calibration from several views. In: Proc. CVPR. (1994) 908–912
10. M.Pollefeys, Gool, L., Osterlinck, A.: The modulus constraint: a new constraint for self-calibration. In: Proc. ICPR. (1996) 31–42
11. M.Pollefeys, Gool, L.: A stratified approach to metric self-calibration. In: Proc. CVPR. (1997) 407–412
12. R.I.Hartley, Agapite, L., E.Hayman, I.Reid: Camera calibration and search for infinity. In: Proc. ICCV. (1999) 510–517
13. B.Triggs: Auto-calibration and the absolute quadric. In: Proc. CVPR. (1997) 609–614
14. B.Caprile, V.Torre: Using vanishing points for camera calibration. IJCV. **4** (1990) 127–140
15. C.Chen, C.Yu, Y.Hung: New calibration-free approach for augmented reality based on parameterized cuboid structure. In: Proc. ICCV. (1999) 30–37
16. M.Wilczkowiak, P.Sturm, Boyer, E.: Using geometric constraints through parallelepipeds for calbration and 3d modeling. IEEE-T PAMI. **27** (2005) 194–207
17. Hartely, R.: Self-calibration of stationary cameras. IJCV **22** (1997) 5–23
18. W.J.Wolfe, Mathis, D.: The perspective view of three points. IEEE-T PAMI. **13** (1991) 66–73

Nonrigid Shape and Motion from Multiple Perspective Views

René Vidal[1,2] and Daniel Abretske[2]

[1] Center for Imaging Science, Department of BME, Johns Hopkins University
[2] Department of Computer Science, Johns Hopkins University

Abstract. We consider the problem of nonrigid shape and motion recovery from point correspondences in multiple perspective views. It is well known that the constraints among multiple views of a rigid shape are multilinear on the image points and can be reduced to bilinear (epipolar) and trilinear constraints among two and three views, respectively. In this paper, we generalize this classic result by showing that the constraints among multiple views of a nonrigid shape consisting of K shape bases can be reduced to multilinear constraints among $K + \lceil (K + 1)/2 \rceil, \cdots, 2K + 1$ views. We then present a closed form solution to the reconstruction of a nonrigid shape consisting of two shape bases. We show that point correspondences in five views are related by a nonrigid quintifocal tensor, from which one can linearly compute nonrigid shape and motion. We also demonstrate the existence of intrinsic ambiguities in the reconstruction of camera translation, shape coefficients and shape bases. Examples show the effectiveness of our method on nonrigid scenes with significant perspective effects.

1 Introduction

The past few decades have witnessed significant advances on the reconstruction of *static scenes* observed by a moving camera under the assumption that the scene is *Lambertian*, *rigid* and *static*. The Lambertian assumption is crucial to the problems of tracking, optical flow and correspondences, because the intensity of a point is independent of the view point. Given optical flow or point correspondences, the assumption of a rigidly moving camera observing a static world enables us to both recover the camera motion as well as reconstruct the rigid shape of the scene.

Recently, there have been attempts to relax each one of these assumptions. For example, the generalized constant brightness constraint allows one to compute optical flow for non Lambertian scenes. Likewise, the multibody fundamental matrix [11] allows one to reconstruct *dynamic scenes* consisting of multiple rigid motions. As for the third assumption, there have been two main approaches to dealing with *nonrigid scenes*. In direct approaches [5, 12], a static camera observes a nonrigid scene whose temporal evolution exhibits certain stationarity, e.g., water, foliage, steam, etc. These scenes are called *dynamic textures*, and have been successfully modeled as the output of a time invariant linear dynamical system. In feature-based methods [2, 3, 4, 9, 10, 13], a rigidly moving *affine* camera observes a nonrigid shape that deforms as a linear combination of rigid shapes with time varying coefficients. This assumption allows one to recover nonrigid shape and motion using extensions of the classical rigid factorization algorithm

A. Leonardis, H. Bischof, and A. Pinz (Eds.): ECCV 2006, Part II, LNCS 3952, pp. 205–218, 2006.

[8]. For instance, [4] uses multiple matrix factorizations to enforce orthonormality constraints on camera rotations. [2] uses a non-linear optimization method called flexible
factorization. [10] uses a trilinear optimization algorithm that alternates the computation of shape bases, shape coefficients, and camera rotations. Unfortunately, all these
methods fail to reconstruct the correct shape and motion, because rotation constraints
are not sufficient to guarantee a unique solution. [13] not only provides a complete
characterization of the space of ambiguous solutions, but also proposes a closed form
solution by enforcing additional *shape constraints* on the shape bases.

A key assumption of these approaches is that the projection model is *affine*. Although one can use nonlinear optimization to extend affine methods to the perspective
case, e.g., [1], it is well known that iterative schemes applied to multilinear problems
are very sensitive to initialization. The objective of this paper is to understand the algebraic constraints among multiple views of a nonrigid shape and to develop algebraic
methods for nonrigid shape reconstruction that can be used for initializing optimization-
based schemes. To the best of our knowledge, there is no prior work addressing these
issues.

In this paper, we look at the problem of nonrigid shape and motion recovery from
multiple *perspective views*. We first study the geometry of the problem, particularly the
nature of the constraints among shape, motion and point correspondences. We show
that the constraints among multiple views of a nonrigid scene can be derived from a
rank constraint on the so-called *nonrigid multiple view matrix*. In the case of K shape
bases, we prove that these algebraic constraints can be reduced to multilinear constraints
among $K + \lceil (K + 1)/2 \rceil, \cdots, 2K + 1$ views of the image points,[1] thus ruling out the
existence of epipolar or trilinear geometry for nonrigid scenes. We then show how to
exploit these multilinear constraints for reconstructing a nonrigid shape consisting of
$K = 2$ rigid shapes. We demonstrate the existence of a *nonrigid quintifocal tensor*,
which can be linearly estimated from the given point correspondences. We exploit algebraic properties of this tensor to compute nonrigid fundamental matrices among pairs of
views. This leads to a linear algorithm for computing camera rotation and point depths.
We also discuss the existence of intrinsic ambiguities in the reconstruction of camera
translations, shape bases and shape coefficients. We then present examples showing the
effectiveness of our method on nonrigid scenes with significant perspective effects.

2   Nonrigid Multiple View Geometry

Consider a nonrigid shape consisting of K shape bases, i.e. each 3-D point $\boldsymbol{X}_f$ at frame
f is a linear combination of K rigid shapes $\{B_k \in \mathbb{R}^3\}_{k=1}^K$

$$\boldsymbol{X}_f = \sum_{k=1}^{K}(c_{fk}B_k), \tag{1}$$

where $\{c_{fk}\}$ are the *shape coefficients*. Assume now that this nonrigid shape is observed
by a moving perspective camera whose pose in the fth frame is given by (R_f, T_f)

---

[1] Classical multilinear constraints in structure from motion show up as the special case $K = 1$.

$\in SE(3)$. Therefore, the projection $x_f \in \mathbb{P}^2$ of X_f is related to its depth λ_f, the camera motion (R_f, T_f), the shape bases $\{B_k\}$ and the shape coefficients $\{c_{fk}\}$ by the equation

$$\lambda_f x_f = R_f \sum_{k=1}^{K} (c_{fk} B_k) + T_f. \tag{2}$$

In this section, we show that one can algebraically eliminate depth and shape bases from the above equations, and derive algebraic constraints relating image points $\{x_f\}$, camera motion $\{R_f, T_f\}$ and shape coefficients $\{c_{fk}\}$ only. Furthermore, we show that the constraints among multiple views of a nonrigid shape can be reduced to multilinear constraints among $K + \lceil (K+1)/2 \rceil, \cdots, 2K+1$ views.

2.1 One Shape Basis

For the sake of simplicity, we first review the well-known results in the case of one rigid shape. We refer the reader to [7] for further details. Note that if $K = 1$ we do not need to consider shape coefficients, hence we can assume without loss of generality that $c_{f1} = 1$ and $X = B_1$. Also, we assume without loss of generality that $(R_1, T_1) = (I, 0)$. Combining these observations with (2) we obtain $\lambda_1 x_1 = B_1$ and $\lambda_f x_f = \lambda_1 R_f x_1 + T_f$ for $f = 2, 3, \ldots, F$. We can eliminate λ_f from this equation by multiplying by $\widehat{x_f}$ on both sides, where $\widehat{x} \in so(3)$ is the skew-symmetric matrix generating the cross product by x. This multiplication yields $\lambda_1 \widehat{x_f} R_f x_1 + \widehat{x_f} T_f = 0$. Since this equation holds for all $f = 2, 3, \ldots, F$, we can write the motion equations for all frames in terms of a single linear equation

$$M_1 \begin{bmatrix} \lambda_1 \\ 1 \end{bmatrix} = \begin{bmatrix} \widehat{x_2} R_2 x_1 & \widehat{x_2} T_2 \\ \vdots & \vdots \\ \widehat{x_F} R_F x_1 & \widehat{x_F} T_F \end{bmatrix} \begin{bmatrix} \lambda_1 \\ 1 \end{bmatrix} = 0. \tag{3}$$

The matrix $M_1 \in \mathbb{R}^{3(F-1) \times 2}$ is called the *multiple view matrix* [7].

From (3), note that the vector $\begin{bmatrix} \lambda_1 \\ 1 \end{bmatrix}$ lives in the right null space of M_1, hence

$$\text{rank}(M_1) \leq 1. \tag{4}$$

The implication of this result is that the determinant of any 2×2 sub-matrix of M_1 is equal to zero. By simply counting the ways we can choose two rows from M_1, it becomes immediately obvious that we can only select rows in such a way as to depend on either two or three views: Two view constraints are obtained by considering two rows from the same block of three frames, e.g., rows 1 and 2, while three view constraints are obtained by considering two rows from two different blocks of three frames, e.g., rows 1 and 4. Two view constraints can be reduced to the well-known epipolar constraint as shown in [7], while three view constraints are the well-known trilinear constraints [6]. This shows that the constraints among multiple views of a rigid scene are multilinear and algebraically dependent on the constraints among two and three views.

2.2 Multiple Shape Bases

Consider now a nonrigid shape consisting of K shape bases. Note that there is an ambiguity in the definition of the shape bases and coefficients, because for any invertible $L \in \mathbb{R}^{K \times K}$ one can choose a new set of shape bases $[B_1 \ B_2 \cdots B_K] \to [B_1 \ B_2 \cdots B_K]L$ and coefficients $\begin{bmatrix} c_{f1} \\ \vdots \\ c_{fK} \end{bmatrix} \to L^{-1} \begin{bmatrix} c_{f1} \\ \vdots \\ c_{fK} \end{bmatrix}$ that yield the same point in 3D space X_f.

[13] proposes to resolve this ambiguity by enforcing the following *basis constrains*

$$c_{kk} = 1, k = 1, \ldots, K \quad c_{jk} = 0, j \neq k = 1, \ldots, K. \tag{5}$$

Combining the basis constraints with the motion equations in (2) for $f = 1 \ldots K$ leads to $\lambda_k x_k = R_k B_k + T_k$ for $k = 1, \ldots, K$, hence we can solve for the shape bases as $B_k = R_k^\top (\lambda_k x_k - T_k)$. After choosing the reference frame so that $(R_1, T_1) = (I, 0)$, we can express the motion equations for frames $f = K + 1, \ldots, F$ as

$$\lambda_f x_f = \lambda_1 c_{f1} R_f x_1 + R_f \sum_{k=2}^{K} c_{fk} R_k^\top (\lambda_k x_k - T_k) + T_f. \tag{6}$$

We now proceed as before using the cross product with x_f to eliminate the depths $\{\lambda_f\}$ for $f = K + 1, \ldots, F$. The final result is a matrix equation of the following form

$$M_K \lambda_K \doteq \begin{bmatrix} \widehat{x_{K+1}} Q_{K+1} x_1 & \widehat{x_{K+1}} S_{K+1}^2 x_2 & \cdots & \widehat{x_{K+1}} S_{K+1}^K x_K & \widehat{x_{k+1}} V_{k+1} \\ \vdots & \vdots & & \vdots & \vdots \\ \widehat{x_F} Q_F x_1 & \widehat{x_F} S_F^2 x_2 & \cdots & \widehat{x_F} S_F^K x_K & \widehat{x_F} V_F \end{bmatrix} \begin{bmatrix} \lambda_1 \\ \vdots \\ \lambda_K \\ 1 \end{bmatrix} = 0, \tag{7}$$

where

$$Q_f = c_{f1} R_f, \ S_f^k = c_{fk} R_f R_k^\top, \ V_f = T_f - \sum_{k=2}^{K} c_{fk} R_f R_k^\top T_k.$$

The *nonrigid multiple view matrix* $M_K \in \mathbb{R}^{3(F-K) \times (K+1)}$ has the vector of depths λ_K in the first K frames in its right null space, hence it satisfies the rank constraint

$$\text{rank}(M_K) \leq K. \tag{8}$$

Therefore, we can eliminate the vector of depths in the first K frames, λ_K, by enforcing that the determinant of each $(K + 1) \times (K + 1)$ sub-matrix of M_K be zero. Since each block of three rows of M_K provides only two linearly independent equations, in choosing $K + 1$ rows we need at least $\lceil \frac{K+1}{2} \rceil$ blocks. Therefore, the determinant involving the minimum number of views contains $K + \lceil \frac{K+1}{2} \rceil$ views. Note that this is much smaller than the minimum number of affine views, which is $(3K^2 + 3K)/2$ [13]. On the other hand, if we choose one row per block, then the determinants involve $K + (K + 1) = 2K + 1$ views. We have shown the following.

Theorem 1 (Algebraic dependency of multiple view constraints for K shape bases). *Consider a moving camera observing a nonrigid shape consisting of K shape bases. The equations relating camera motion, shape bases, shape coefficients and image points can be reduced to a set of algebraic constraints that do not depend on the shape bases and involve only $K + \lceil \frac{K+1}{2} \rceil, \ldots, 2K + 1$ views at a time.*

Corollary 1. *The constraints among multiple views of a rigid shape ($K = 1$) can be reduced to constraints among two and three views.*

The next step is to understand whether the multiple view constraints are multilinear on the image points, as in the rigid case. To this end, note first that image points in one of the first K frames appear in only one column of M_K at a time, hence multiple view constraints are necessarily *linear* in each one of the first K views. However, the constraints on a point in the remaining $F - K$ frames can be either linear or quadratic, depending on whether we choose one or two rows per block, respectively. This can be seen by considering how one might choose rows from M_K when forming the determinant of a $(K+1) \times (K+1)$ submatrix. One can choose either one or two rows corresponding to each frame. If a single row is chosen from a frame then the constraints must be linear in points from that frame since that point only appears in a single row of the submatrix. However, when two rows are chosen from a single frame, it may still be possible that the resulting constraint remains linear and does not become quadratic on the point from that frame. The following theorem shows that this is indeed the case.

Theorem 2 (Multilinear constraints for K shape bases). *The algebraic constraints among multiple views of a nonrigid shape consisting of K shape bases can be reduced to a set of multilinear constraints on $K + \lceil \frac{K+1}{2} \rceil, \ldots, 2K + 1$ views of the image points. The coefficients of these multilinear constraints depend on the camera motion and the shape coefficients, but not on the shape bases.*

In what follows, we prove the theorem in the particular cases $K = 2$ and $K = 3$, to then extend the proof to arbitrary K.

Multilinear constraints for two shape bases. We already know that in this case the algebraic constraints among multiple views can be reduced to those among four and five views. Moreover, we have already shown that the constraints among five views are multilinear in the point correspondences, because all minors of M_2 involve one row per view. We are left with proving that the constraints among four views are also multilinear.

Without loss of generality, consider views 1 through 4, and choose two rows of M_2 from the 3rd view and one from the 4th view. As choosing these three rows is equivalent to choosing three lines ℓ_{31}, ℓ_{32} and ℓ_4 such that $\ell_{31}^\top x_3 = \ell_{32}^\top x_3 = \ell_4^\top x_4 = 0$, the algebraic constraint among these four views can be written as

$$\Delta_2(x_1, x_2, x_3, x_4) = \det \left(\begin{bmatrix} \ell_{31}^\top Q_3 x_1 & \ell_{31}^\top S_3 x_2 & \ell_{31}^\top V_3 \\ \ell_{32}^\top Q_3 x_1 & \ell_{32}^\top S_3 x_2 & \ell_{32}^\top V_3 \\ \ell_4^\top Q_4 x_1 & \ell_4^\top S_4 x_2 & \ell_4^\top V_4 \end{bmatrix} \right). \tag{9}$$

Before proceeding further, we need the following technical lemma, whose proof follows by direct calculation.

Lemma 1. *Let* $x = (x_1, x_2, 1)^\top$, $\ell_1 = (1, 0, -x_1)^\top$ *and* $\ell_2 = (0, 1, -x_2)^\top$. *Then for all* $a, b \in \mathbb{R}^3$ *we have that*

$$\det\left(\begin{bmatrix} \ell_1^\top a & \ell_1^\top b \\ \ell_2^\top a & \ell_2^\top b \end{bmatrix}\right) = b^\top \widehat{x} a. \tag{10}$$

After expanding Δ_2 along the bottom row of the matrix in (9) and applying Lemma 1 three times, we see that Δ_2 is in fact equal to

$$\Delta_2 = \ell_4^\top Q_4 x_1 (V_3^\top \widehat{x_3} S_3 x_2) - \ell_4^\top S_4 x_2 (V_3^\top \widehat{x_3} Q_3 x_1) + \ell_4^\top V_4((S_3 x_2)^\top \widehat{x_3} Q_3 x_1), \tag{11}$$

which is multilinear in (x_1, x_2, x_3, ℓ_4), hence in (x_1, x_2, x_3, x_4), as claimed.

Multilinear constraints for three shape bases. In this case, the multiple view matrix M_3 has four columns, hence one can form constraints on 5, 6 or 7 views. The case of 7 views is obviously multilinear, as one chooses a single row from each frame (4,5,6,7).

In the case of 6 views one must choose two rows from one frame and two more rows from two other frames. Without loss of generality consider choosing two rows from the 4th frame, a row from the 5th frame and a row from the 6th frame. This is equivalent to choosing lines $\ell_{41}, \ell_{42}, \ell_5$ and ℓ_6 such that $\ell_{41}^\top x_4 = \ell_{42}^\top x_4 = \ell_5^\top x_5 = \ell_6^\top x_6 = 0$. Such a choice leads to the following determinant

$$\Delta_3(x_1, x_2, x_3, x_4, x_4, x_6) = \det\left(\begin{bmatrix} \ell_{41}^\top Q_4 x_1 & \ell_{41}^\top S_4^2 x_2 & \ell_{41}^\top S_4^3 x_3 & \ell_{41}^\top V_4 \\ \ell_{42}^\top Q_4 x_1 & \ell_{42}^\top S_4^2 x_2 & \ell_{42}^\top S_4^3 x_3 & \ell_{42}^\top V_4 \\ \ell_5^\top Q_5 x_1 & \ell_5^\top S_5^2 x_2 & \ell_5^\top S_5^3 x_3 & \ell_5^\top V_5 \\ \ell_6^\top Q_6 x_1 & \ell_6^\top S_6^2 x_2 & \ell_6^\top S_6^3 x_3 & \ell_6^\top V_6 \end{bmatrix}\right). \tag{12}$$

We know that Δ_3 is linear in each of x_1, x_2, x_3, x_5 and x_6. The question is whether Δ_3 is also linear in x_4. Let $x_4 = (x_4, y_4, 1)^\top$, $\ell_{41} = (1, 0, -x_4)^\top$ and $\ell_{42} = (0, 1, -y_4)^\top$. If we expand Δ_3 along the last row of the matrix in (12), we obtain

$$\Delta_3 = (\ell_6^\top Q_6 x_1) \Delta_{21}(x_2, x_3, x_4, x_5) - (\ell_6^\top S_6^2 x_2) \Delta_{22}(x_1, x_3, x_4, x_5) + \\ (\ell_6^\top S_6^3 x_2) \Delta_{23}(x_1, x_2, x_4, x_5) - (\ell_6^\top V_6) \Delta_{24}(x_1, x_2, x_3, x_4, x_5), \tag{13}$$

where each Δ_{2i} is of the same form as the determinant seen in equation (9), thus multilinear in its entries. Therefore, Δ_3 is also multilinear in $(x_1, x_2, x_3, x_4, x_5, x_6)$.

In the case of 5 views, without loss of generality choose two rows from the 4th frame and two rows from the 5th frame, and let $x_i = (x_i, y_i, 1)^\top$, $\ell_{i1} = (1, 0, -x_i)^\top$ and $\ell_{i2} = (0, 1, -y_i)^\top$. Such a choice gives the following determinant

$$\tilde{\Delta}_3(x_1, x_2, x_3, x_4, x_5) = \det\left(\begin{bmatrix} \ell_{41}^\top Q_4 x_1 & \ell_{41}^\top S_4^2 x_2 & \ell_{41}^\top S_4^3 x_3 & \ell_{41}^\top V_4 \\ \ell_{42}^\top Q_4 x_1 & \ell_{42}^\top S_4^2 x_2 & \ell_{42}^\top S_4^3 x_3 & \ell_{42}^\top V_4 \\ \ell_{51}^\top Q_5 x_1 & \ell_{51}^\top S_5^2 x_2 & \ell_{51}^\top S_5^3 x_3 & \ell_{51}^\top V_5 \\ \ell_{52}^\top Q_5 x_1 & \ell_{52}^\top S_5^2 x_2 & \ell_{52}^\top S_5^3 x_3 & \ell_{52}^\top V_5 \end{bmatrix}\right). \tag{14}$$

After expanding $\tilde{\Delta}_3$ along the first column of the matrix, we obtain

$$\tilde{\Delta}_3 = \ell_{41}^\top c \Delta_{25}(x_2, x_3, \ell_{42}, x_5) - \ell_{42}^\top c \Delta_{25}(x_2, x_3, \ell_{41}, x_5) \\ + \ell_{51}^\top d \Delta_{26}(x_2, x_3, x_4, \ell_{52}) - \ell_{52}^\top d \Delta_{26}(x_2, x_3, x_4, \ell_{51}) \tag{15}$$

where $c = Q_4 x_1$, $d = Q_5 x_1$, and $\Delta_{25}(\cdot, \cdot, \cdot, \cdot)$ and $\Delta_{26}(\cdot, \cdot, \cdot, \cdot)$ are determinants of 3 by 3 matrices that depend linearly on each of the quantities in the parentheses by direct application of Lemma 1. Since Lemma 1 also implies that $(\boldsymbol{\ell}_{f1}^\top \boldsymbol{y})(\boldsymbol{\ell}_{f2}) - (\boldsymbol{\ell}_{f2}^\top \boldsymbol{y})(\boldsymbol{\ell}_{f1}) = \widehat{\boldsymbol{y}} x_f$, the expression for $\tilde{\Delta}_3$ reduces to

$$\tilde{\Delta}_3 = \Delta_{25}(x_2, x_3, \boldsymbol{\ell}_{41}^\top c \boldsymbol{\ell}_{42} - \boldsymbol{\ell}_{42}^\top c \boldsymbol{\ell}_{41}, x_5) + \Delta_{26}(x_2, x_3, x_4, \boldsymbol{\ell}_{51}^\top d \boldsymbol{\ell}_{52} - \boldsymbol{\ell}_{52}^\top d \boldsymbol{\ell}_{51})$$
$$= \Delta_3(x_2, x_3, \widehat{c} x_4, x_5) + \tilde{\Delta}_3(x_2, x_3, x_4, \widehat{d} x_5),$$

which is in fact linear in x_4 and x_5 as claimed.

Multilinear constraints for multiple shape bases. In the case of K shape bases, the constraints among multiple views are simply minors of the multiple view matrix M_K. Each minor is formed by choosing $K + 1$ rows from M_K. Without loss of generality, assume we choose two rows from each one of the first m blocks, and one row from each one of the next $K + 1 - 2m$ blocks. We obtain the following determinant

$$\Delta_K = \det \begin{pmatrix} \begin{bmatrix} \boldsymbol{\ell}_{K+1,1}^\top Q_{K+1} x_1 & \cdots & \boldsymbol{\ell}_{K+1,1}^\top S_{K+1}^K x_K & \boldsymbol{\ell}_{K+1,1}^\top V_{K+1} \\ \boldsymbol{\ell}_{K+1,2}^\top Q_{K+1} x_1 & \cdots & \boldsymbol{\ell}_{K+1,2}^\top S_{K+1}^K x_K & \boldsymbol{\ell}_{K+1,2}^\top V_{K+1} \\ \vdots & & \vdots & \vdots \\ \boldsymbol{\ell}_{K+m,1}^\top Q_{K+m} x_1 & \cdots & \boldsymbol{\ell}_{K+m,1}^\top S_{K+m}^K x_K & \boldsymbol{\ell}_{K+m,1}^\top V_{K+m} \\ \boldsymbol{\ell}_{K+m,2}^\top Q_{K+m} x_1 & \cdots & \boldsymbol{\ell}_{K+m,2}^\top S_{K+m}^K x_K & \boldsymbol{\ell}_{K+m,2}^\top V_{K+m} \\ \hline \boldsymbol{\ell}_{K+m+1}^\top Q_{K+m+1} x_1 & \cdots & \boldsymbol{\ell}_{K+m+1}^\top S_{K+m+1}^K x_K & \boldsymbol{\ell}_{K+m+1}^\top V_{K+m+1} \\ \vdots & & \vdots & \vdots \\ \boldsymbol{\ell}_{2K-m+1}^\top Q_{2K-m+1} x_1 & \cdots & \boldsymbol{\ell}_{2K-m+1}^\top S_{2K-m+1}^K x_K & \boldsymbol{\ell}_{2K-m+1}^\top V_{2K-m+1} \end{bmatrix} \end{pmatrix} \tag{16}$$

It is clear that Δ_K is linear in each x_i with $i \leq K$, because each image point appears only in one column of the matrix in (16). Similarly, it is clear that Δ_K is linear in each x_i with $i > K + m$, because each image point appears in only one row of the matrix in (16). The fact that Δ_K is also linear in each x_i with $K + 1 \leq i \leq K + m$ follows by repeated application of the following lemma since the upper portion of the matrix in (16) is of the exact form called for by the lemma.

Lemma 2. *Let* $a_{ij} \in \mathbb{R}^3$, $x_i = (x_i, y_i, 1)^\top$, $\boldsymbol{\ell}_{i1} = (1, 0, -x_i)^\top$ *and* $\boldsymbol{\ell}_{i2} = (0, 1, -y_i)^\top$. *Then, for* k *even,* $\Delta_k = \det(M_k)$ *is linear in each* x_i, *where*

$$M_k = \begin{bmatrix} \boldsymbol{\ell}_{11}^\top a_{11} & \cdots & \boldsymbol{\ell}_{11}^\top a_{1k} \\ \boldsymbol{\ell}_{12}^\top a_{11} & \cdots & \boldsymbol{\ell}_{12}^\top a_{1k} \\ \vdots & \cdots & \vdots \\ \boldsymbol{\ell}_{\frac{k}{2}1}^\top a_{\frac{k}{2}1} & \cdots & \boldsymbol{\ell}_{\frac{k}{2}k}^\top a_{\frac{k}{2}k} \\ \boldsymbol{\ell}_{\frac{k}{2}2}^\top a_{\frac{k}{2}1} & \cdots & \boldsymbol{\ell}_{\frac{k}{2}2}^\top a_{\frac{k}{2}k} \end{bmatrix} \in \mathbb{R}^{k \times k}. \tag{17}$$

Proof. The proof proceeds by strong induction. The example of three shape bases and five views proves the case of $k = 2$. Now assume that this holds for up to $k = n - 2$.

We will proceed to show that it holds for $k = n$. Consider $\mathcal{M}_n$ and consider the result of expanding $\det(\mathcal{M}_n)$ along the first column of $\mathcal{M}_n$. Without loss of generality we may consider just minors associated with the last two entries of this column. If the result holds for these minors then it must hold for all other minors since $\mathcal{M}_n$ is composed of similar 2 by k blocks. These minors have the form

$$\ell_{n2}^\top a_{n1} \Delta_{n-1}(\ell_{n1}, \ell_{(n-1)1}, \ell_{(n-1)2}, ..., \ell_{11}, \ell_{12}) - \ell_{n1}^\top a_{n1} \Delta_{n-1}(\ell_{n2}, \ell_{(n-1)1}, \ell_{(n-1)2}, ..., \ell_{11}, \ell_{12})$$
$$= \Delta_{n-1}(\boldsymbol{x}_n \widehat{\boldsymbol{a}_{n1}}, \ell_{(n-1)1}, \ell_{(n-1)2}, \ldots, \ell_{11}, \ell_{12}),$$

where the last equality follows from Lemma 1. By direct calculation it can be seen that

$$\Delta_{n-1}(\boldsymbol{x}_n \widehat{\boldsymbol{a}_{n1}}, \ell_{(n-1)1}, \ell_{(n-1)2}, ..., \ell_{11}, \ell_{12}) = \sum_{j=2}^{n} a_{n1}^\top \widehat{\boldsymbol{x}_n} a_{nj} \Delta_{n-2}(\ell_{(n-1)1}, \ell_{(n-1)2}, ..., \ell_{11}, \ell_{12}).$$

By the induction hypothesis Δ_{n-2} is multilinear, hence $\det(M_n)$ is multilinear as claimed.   ∎

3   Reconstruction of Two Shape Bases

Given that the constraints among multiple views of a nonrigid shape are multilinear, the next question is how to exploit such constraints in order to recover camera motion and nonrigid shape. In this section, we show how to do so in the case of a nonrigid shape consisting of two shape bases seen in five views. First, we demonstrate that the quintilinear constraints can be expressed in terms of a single tensor, which can be linearly estimated from the given point correspondences. Next, we study properties of this tensor that, surprisingly, demonstrate the existence of geometric entities analogous to epipolar lines and fundamental matrices for nonrigid motions. We exploit such properties in order to linearly solve for camera motion. Finally, we demonstrate the existence of ambiguities in the reconstruction of camera translation, shape coefficients and shape bases. These ambiguities are intrinsic to the nonrigid shape and motion problem, in the sense that they show up in the case of affine cameras as well. Surprisingly, they have not received wide attention in the literature, being only briefly discussed in [1].

3.1   The Nonrigid Quintifocal Tensor

From the previous section, we know that in the case of 5 views, the multilinear constraints are determinants of 3×3 sub-matrices of the multiple view matrix $M_2 \in \mathbb{R}^{9 \times 3}$. Furthermore, in the case of quintilinear constraints, each sub-matrix is formed by choosing three rows from each one of the three blocks of M_2. Therefore, we can write a single quintilinear constraint for a point-point-line-line-line correspondence as

$$\mathcal{T}(\boldsymbol{x}_1, \boldsymbol{x}_2, \ell_3, \ell_4, \ell_5) = \det \left(\begin{bmatrix} \ell_3^\top Q_3 \boldsymbol{x}_1 & \ell_3^\top S_3 \boldsymbol{x}_2 & \ell_3^\top V_3 \\ \ell_4^\top Q_4 \boldsymbol{x}_1 & \ell_4^\top S_4 \boldsymbol{x}_2 & \ell_4^\top V_4 \\ \ell_5^\top Q_5 \boldsymbol{x}_1 & \ell_5^\top S_5 \boldsymbol{x}_2 & \ell_5^\top V_5 \end{bmatrix} \right) = 0. \qquad (18)$$

By expanding this determinant as a polynomial in x_1, x_2, ℓ_3, ℓ_4, ℓ_5, we may write the quintilinear constraint as

$$\sum_{ijkmn=1}^{3} T_{ijkmn} x_{1i} x_{2j} \ell_{3k} \ell_{4m} \ell_{5n} = 0, \tag{19}$$

where T_{ijkmn} are the coefficients of the polynomial. We define the *nonrigid quintifocal tensor* $T \in \mathbb{R}^{3 \times 3 \times 3 \times 3 \times 3}$ as the collection of all these coefficients.

Note that each point correspondence provides $2^3 = 8$ linear equations in the 242 unknowns in T, because we can choose two lines ℓ_f for each x_f for $f = 3, 4, 5$. Therefore, in order to determine T linearly, we need at least 31 point correspondences.

Notation. For ease of notation, we will drop the summation and subscripts in multi-linear expressions such as $\sum T_{ijkmn} x_{1i} x_{2j} l_{3k} l_{4m} l_{5n}$ and write them as $x_1 x_2 \ell_3 \ell_4 \ell_5 T$. We will also write the matrix whose (ij)th entry is $\sum_{kmn} T_{ijkmn} l_{3k} l_{4m} l_{5n}$ as $\ell_3 \ell_4 \ell_5 T$ (or whichever indices are being considered), and the vector whose ith entry is given by $\sum_{jkmn} T_{ijkmn} x_{2j} l_{3k} l_{4m} l_{5n}$ as $x_2 \ell_3 \ell_4 \ell_5 T$ (similarly for other indices).

3.2 Recovering Camera Motion Via Nonrigid Epipolar Geometry

In this subsection, we present some algebraic and geometric properties of the quintifocal tensor T. We show that even though epipolar geometry is not defined for nonrigid shapes, there still exist algebraic entities that play the analogous role of geometric entities such as epipolar lines and essential matrices, which are only defined for a single rigid shape. These properties lead to a linear algorithm for recovering nonrigid epipolar lines, nonrigid essential matrices, and camera rotations from the quintifocal tensor.

At the core of the proposed method, we find a set of rank constraints on slices of T, as stated in the following lemma.

Lemma 3 (Rank constraints on slices of the quintifocal tensor). *Let T be a nonrigid quintifocal tensor. Then, $rank(x_1 x_2 \ell_i T) \leq 2$ for $i = 3, 4, 5$, and $rank(\ell_3 \ell_4 \ell_5 T) \leq 2$.*

Proof. It follows by direct calculation that $x_1 x_2 \ell_3 \ell_4 \ell_5 T = \ell_4^\top \mathcal{M} \ell_5$, where

$$\mathcal{M} = Q_4 x_1 (V_5^\top (\ell_3^\top S_3 x_2) - x_2^\top S_5^\top (\ell_3^\top V_3)) - S_4 x_2 (V_5^\top (\ell_3^\top Q_3 x_1) - x_1^\top Q_5^\top (\ell_3^\top V_3))$$
$$+ V_4 (x_2^\top S_5^\top (\ell_3^\top Q_3 x_1) - x_1^\top Q_5^\top (\ell_3^\top S_3 x_2)).$$

Taking ℓ_5 as $(V_5^\top (\ell_3^\top S_3 x_2) - x_2^\top S_5^\top (\ell_3^\top V_3)) \times (V_5^\top (\ell_3^\top Q_3 x_1) - x_1^\top Q_5^\top (\ell_3^\top V_3))$ gives the right null space of $\mathcal{M} = x_1 x_2 \ell_3 T$. One may compute the left and right null spaces of $x_1 x_2 \ell_4 T$, $x_1 x_2 \ell_5 T$ and $\ell_3 \ell_4 \ell_5 T$ in an analogous fashion. ∎

It follows from Lemma 3 that $x_1 x_2 \ell_3 T$ is of the form

$$x_1 x_2 \ell_3 T = a(x_1) b(x_2)^\top + c(x_2) d(x_1)^\top + e f(x_1, x_2)^\top, \tag{20}$$

where $f(x_1, x_2)$ must be a linear combination of $b(x_2)$ and $d(x_1)$ so that $x_1 x_2 \ell_3 T$ be rank 2. This implies that the null space of $x_1 x_2 \ell_3 T$ is of the form $b(x_2) \times d(x_1)$.

As the choice of x_1 and x_2 is arbitrary, we may fix x_2 and compute the null space of $x_1 x_2 \ell_3 \mathcal{T}$ for two different values of x_1, say x_{11} and x_{12}. Taking the cross product of the two null space vectors gives the following linear combinations of V_5 and $S_5 x_2$:

$$(b(x_2) \times d(x_{11})) \times (b(x_2) \times d(x_{12})) \sim b(x_2) \sim (\ell_3^\top S_3 x_2) V_5 - (\ell_3^\top V_3) S_5 x_2. \quad (21)$$

By repeating the above procedure for another choice of ℓ_3, we obtain a second linear combination of V_5 and $S_5 x_2$. The cross product of these two linear combinations is $\widehat{V_5} S_5 x_2$, which is the *nonrigid epipolar line* of x_2 in the 5th view according to the *nonrigid fundamental matrix* $\widehat{V_5} S_5$ relating the 2nd and 5th views. This leads to the following algorithm for recovering the camera rotations and the V vectors:

1. Choose x_1, x_2 and ℓ_3 and compute the right null space a_1 of $x_1 x_2 \ell_3 \mathcal{T}$. Repeat for another choice of x_1 to obtain a_2. Set $b_1 = a_1 \times a_2$. The vector b_1 is now proportional to $V_5^\top (\ell_3^\top S_3 x_2) - x_2^\top S_5^\top (\ell_3^\top V_3)$.
2. Repeat step 1 for a new choice of ℓ_3 to get b_2. Set $c = b_1 \times b_2 \sim \widehat{V_5} S_5 x_2$.
3. Repeat steps 1 and 2 for multiple choices of x_2 and linearly solve for the fundamental matrix $\widehat{V_5} S_5$ from $c \times \widehat{V_5} S_5 x_2 = 0$. Subsequently solve for V_5 and S_5 using a modified version of the 8-point algorithm that enforces $\lambda_f > 0$ for $f = 1, 2, \ldots, 5$.[2]
4. Recover Q_5 using steps 1-3, but allowing x_2 to vary instead of x_1.
5. Recover S_4, Q_4 and V_4 from the left null space of $x_1 x_2 \ell_3 \mathcal{T}$ in an analogous way.
6. Recover Q_3, S_3 and V_3 from the left null space of $x_1 x_2 \ell_5 \mathcal{T}$ in an analogous way.

3.3 Recovering Shape Coefficients and Depths Via Factorization

Once we have the rotations and the V vectors we can return to our original system of equations (6) and solve for the shape coefficients and depths. To this end, let x_{fp} be the image of point $p = 1, \ldots, P$ in frame $f = 1, \ldots, 5$ and let λ_{fp} be its depth. Also, let γ_f be the unknown scale up to which V_f is recovered. From (7) we have that

$$\left[\widehat{x_{fp}} R_f x_{1p} \quad \widehat{x_{fp}} R_f R_2^\top x_{2p} \quad \widehat{x_{fp}} V_f \right] \begin{bmatrix} c_{f1} \lambda_{1p} \\ c_{f2} \lambda_{2p} \\ \gamma_f \end{bmatrix} = 0, \quad f = 3, 4, 5. \quad (22)$$

We can solve these linear system for all $f = 3, 4, 5$ and $p = 1, \ldots, P$ and build $3 \times P$ matrices W_1 and W_2 whose (f, p) entries are given by

$$W_1(f, p) = \frac{c_{f1} \lambda_{1p}}{\gamma_f} \quad \text{and} \quad W_2(f, p) = \frac{c_{f2} \lambda_{2p}}{\gamma_f}, \quad (23)$$

---

[2] Given $\widehat{V_5} S_5$, the 8-point algorithm for rigid scenes gives 4 solutions for (S_5, V_5). The correct solution must satisfy $\lambda_2, \lambda_5 > 0$, which can be easily checked, because there are closed form formulae for λ_2 and λ_5 given (S_5, V_5) and (x_2, x_5). In the nonrigid case, however, (x_2, x_5) are *not* images of the same point in 3D space, hence one cannot obtain closed form formulae for the depths. In fact, from the equation $\lambda_f x_f = \lambda_1 c_{1f} R_f x_1 + \lambda_2 c_{2f} R_f R_2^\top x_2 + V_f$, we see that one can only solve for $c_{1f} \lambda_1$, $c_{2f} \lambda_2$, λ_3, λ_4 and λ_5. In order to check if $\lambda_1, \lambda_2 > 0$, we make the additional assumption that $c_{if} > 0$, and look for the pair (S_5, V_5) that results in the maximum number of positive depths. The assumption that $c_{if} > 0$ corresponds to rearranging the frames so that the 1st and 2nd frame form a convex basis for the 3rd, 4th and 5th frames.

respectively. Notice that both W_1 and W_2 are rank-1 matrices, hence we can obtain the depths $\{\lambda_{1p}\}$ and $\{\lambda_{2p}\}$, each one up to a different scale factor, from the SVD of W_1 and W_2, respectively. Similarly, we can obtain the vector $(c_{f1}, c_{f2})^\top$ up to a scale factor γ_f, also from the SVD of W_1 and W_2.

3.4 Refining Shape Coefficients and Depths Via an Iterative Approach

The previous section detailed an algorithm for recovering the depths and shape coefficients using only factorization. However, factorization algorithms can and often do perform poorly in the presence of noise. To that end, we suggest the following iterative method (initialized by the previous factorization approach). First notice that if one knew the λ_{fp}'s or the c_{fi}'s in (22), then it should be possible to recover the others. In fact, by knowing the depths we can build a matrix $G \in \mathbb{R}^{3P \times 3}$ whose rows have the form

$$G_p = \begin{bmatrix} \lambda_{1p}\widehat{x_{fp}}R_f x_{1p} & \lambda_{2p}\widehat{x_{fp}}R_f R_2^\top x_{2p} & \widehat{x_{fp}}V_f \end{bmatrix} \in \mathbb{R}^{3 \times 3}.$$

Similarly if we knew the coefficients, we could build a matrix $H \in \mathbb{R}^{3F \times 3}$ with rows

$$H_f = \begin{bmatrix} c_{f1}\widehat{x_{fp}}R_f x_{1p} & c_{f2}\widehat{x_{fp}}R_f R_2^\top x_{2p} & \widehat{x_{fp}}V_f \end{bmatrix} \in \mathbb{R}^{3 \times 3}.$$

The null space of G or H gives the shape coefficients or the depths, respectively, in the first two frames. Thus one can iterate between these two steps until convergence. While this iterative method will give a correct estimate of the depths, we would like to point out that it does not give accurate coefficients due to the existence of intrinsic ambiguities which we discuss in the following section.

3.5 Ambiguities in Nonrigid Reconstruction

In this section, we discuss various ambiguities in nonrigid motion and shape recovery from multiple perspective views and relate them to those discussed in previous works such as [1]. It is important to understand that these ambiguities are not specific to our algorithm, but rather intrinsic to the problem of nonrigid shape and motion recovery under the assumption that a nonrigid shape is a linear combination of shape basis.

Scale ambiguity. It was very briefly discussed in [1] that there exists a scale ambiguity between the bases. However, the implications of this scale ambiguity or the primary cause of its existence were not discussed in any detail. We now refer the reader back to (23) and point out that when recovering the λ_1's and λ_2's, each quantity is being estimated independently from the other. Therefore, we can only recover the coefficients and the depths up to an unknown scale factor for each of the five frames. In the case of K shape bases, one may eliminate $K + 1$ of these scales (assuming a maximal number of frames are used) by imposing the constraint that the coefficients sum to one. To a degree this is a physically meaningful constraint which simply enforces that the shapes in the scene be barycentric combinations of the shape bases. As a simple example one can consider the case of rigid motion. Rigid motion can be thought of as a scene with a single shape bases and in this case the shape coefficients must be one. Unfortunately, we can only eliminate the scales of the frames after the Kth frame in this manner so we are left with K extra scale factors. The problem is that it is impossible to determine the relative scale of one basis to another. Due to this inherent ambiguity, it is actually impossible to recover the correct shape coefficients and thus the shape bases. Therefore, our experimental results have focused upon the recovery of rotations, V vectors and the depths of the first two frames. For ground truth comparison, however, the true V vectors cannot be determined without knowing both the coefficients and the rotation and translation of the second frame. Therefore, in our real world examples, we focus solely on camera rotations.

Translational ambiguity. Note also that there is an ambiguity in the simultaneous reconstruction of the translations T_f and bases B_k, because $B'_{kp} = B_{kp} + B$, for $p = 1, \ldots, P$, and $T'_f = T_f - R_f B \sum_{k=1}^{K} c_{kf}$ are also valid solutions for all $B \in \mathbb{R}^3$.

4   Experimental Results

To evaluate our algorithm effectiveness, we tested it on random synthetic experiments, a structured synthetic experiment similar to the two bases case in [13], and on a real world video sequence. As per the preceding analysis of ambiguities, we focus on the recovered rotations for the structured synthetic data and the real world experiments.

Random synthetic data. We randomly generated bases, coefficients, rotations and translations for an image of size 1000 by 1000. We run the iterative algorithm with 135 iterations. The error in rotation is calculated as $\cos^{-1}((\text{trace}(R\hat{R}^\top) - 1)/2)$, and the error in depth as the angle between true and estimated vector of all depths. Fig. 1 shows the mean errors averaged over 400 trials, except for a small percentage of outliers.[3]

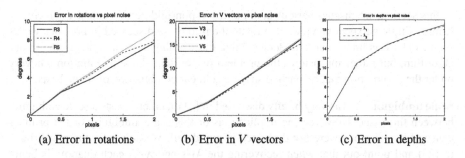

(a) Error in rotations   (b) Error in V vectors   (c) Error in depths

Fig. 1. Mean error in depths, rotations, and V vectors after outlier removal

There are two primary sources of error: the noisy estimation of the tensor and the scale check of the eight point algorithm. If one uses the correct tensor, even with noisy data, the recovered estimates of rotation and the V vectors are virtually error free. The

---

[3] Due to the ambiguities in reconstruction, the algorithm gives large errors in a small percentage of trials. A trial was considered to be an outlier when the depth or rotation error was greater that 20 degrees or when the error in the V vectors was greater than 25 degrees.

Table 1. Rotation errors for a structured synthetic scene

	R_3 perspective error	R_4 perspective error	R_5 perspective error
Xiao's approach	6.41°	4.43°	4.62°
Our approach	0.00°	0.00°	0.00°

primary cause of outliers would seem to be the scale check of the eight point algorithm. This scale check can in some cases fail to choose the correct solution. When this happens we generally see errors becoming quite close to 90 degrees.

Structured synthetic data. In this experiment we positioned 31 points in the following manner: 7 points were positioned on the corners of a unit cube at the origin, the remaining 24 points were divided into three groups of 8 points and then placed evenly along each of the coordinate axes. The 7 points were held fixed while the points along the axes translated in a positive direction along the axes and were perturbed by a small random amount in the respective off-axes directions. The camera was initially positioned to be at (20,20,20) facing the origin. The camera was then allowed to pan around the origin, and translate towards and away from the origin as the structure of the scene deformed. The data was projected in a perspective manner. We compared our algorithm to the one proposed in [13]. The mean errors over 400 trials are displayed in Table 1.

Real world experiments. The sequence shown in Fig. 2 was used to test our algorithm. 32 points were chosen by hand to generate the tensor estimates and another 8 static scene points were chosen in each frame to generate an 8-point algorithm estimate of the rotations, which was then used as our ground truth. The 1st and 5th images were taken as the reference, rather than the 1st and 2nd, hence rotations errors were measured for the 2nd, 3rd and 4th frame, relative to the 1st. The respective errors were 0.16°, 5.94° and 2.55°, which is expected, as frames 3 and 4 were the noisiest frames in the sequence.

(a) Frame 1   (b) Frame 2   (c) Frame 3   (d) Frame 4   (e) Frame 5

Fig. 2. Real world test sequence

5 Summary and Conclusions

We have presented a geometric approach to nonrigid shape and motion recovery from multiple *perspective views*. We demonstrated that the constraints among multiple views of a nonrigid scene are multilinear, and proposed an algorithm for the reconstruction of two shape bases in five perspective views. We also examined the existence of intrinsic ambiguities in the reconstruction of nonrigid scenes.

Acknowledgements. This work has been supported by Hopkins WSE startup funds, and by grants NSF CAREER IIS-0447739 and ONR N000140510836.

References

1. H. Aanaes and F. Kahl. Estimation of deformable structure and motion. In *ECCV Workshop on Vision and Modelling of Dynamic Scenes*, 2002.
2. M. Brand. Morphable 3D models from video. In *IEEE Conf. on Computer Vision & Pattern Recognition*, pages 456–463, 2001.
3. Matthew Brand and Rahul Bhotika. Flexible flow for 3D nonrigid tracking and shape recovery. In *IEEE Conf. on Computer Vision & Pattern Recognition*, pages 315–322, 2001.
4. C. Bregler, A. Hertzmann, and H. Biermann. Recovering non-rigid 3D shape from image streams. In *IEEE Conf. on Computer Vision & Pattern Recognition*, pages 2690–2696, 2000.
5. G. Doretto, A. Chiuso, Y. Wu, and S. Soatto. Dynamic textures. *International Journal of Computer Vision*, 51(2):91–109, 2003.
6. R. Hartley and A. Zisserman. *Multiple View Geometry in Computer Vision*. Cambridge, 2000.
7. Y. Ma, Kun Huang, R. Vidal, J. Košecká, and S. Sastry. Rank conditions on the multiple view matrix. *International Journal of Computer Vision*, 59(2):115–137, 2004.
8. C. Tomasi and T. Kanade. Shape and motion from image streams under orthography. *International Journal of Computer Vision*, 9(2):137–154, 1992.
9. L. Torresani and C. Bregler. Space-time tracking. In *European Conference on Computer Vision*, pages 801 – 812, 2002.
10. L. Torresani, D. Yang, E. Alexander, and C. Bregler. Tracking and modeling non-rigid objects with rank constraints. In *IEEE Conf. on Computer Vision and Pattern Recognition*, pages 493–500, 2001.
11. R. Vidal, Y. Ma, S. Soatto, and S. Sastry. Two-view multibody structure from motion. *International Journal of Computer Vision*, 2006.
12. R. Vidal and A. Ravichandran. Optical flow estimation and segmentation of multiple moving dynamic textures. In *IEEE Conf. on Computer Vision & Pattern Recognition*, pages 516–521, 2005.
13. Jing Xiao, Jin-Xiang Chai, and Takeo Kanade. A closed-form solution to non-rigid shape and motion recovery. In *European Conference on Computer Vision*, pages 573–587, 2004.

3D Surface Reconstruction Using Graph Cuts with Surface Constraints*

Son Tran and Larry Davis

Dept. of Computer Science, University of Maryland,
College Park, MD 20742, USA
{sontran, lsd}@cs.umd.edu

Abstract. We describe a graph cut algorithm to recover the 3D object surface using both silhouette and foreground color information. The graph cut algorithm is used for optimization on a color consistency field. Constraints are added to improve its performance. These constraints are a set of predetermined locations that the true surface of the object is likely to pass through. They are used to preserve protrusions and to pursue concavities respectively in the first and the second phase of the algorithm. We also introduce a method for dealing with silhouette uncertainties arising from background subtraction on real data. We test the approach on synthetic data with different numbers of views (8, 16, 32, 64) and on a real image set containing 30 views of a toy squirrel.

1 Introduction

We consider the problem of reconstructing the 3D surface of an object from a set of images taken from calibrated viewpoints. The information exploited includes the object's silhouettes and its foreground color or texture. 3D shape recovery using silhouettes constitutes a major line of research in computer vision, the shape-from-silhouette approach. In methods employing silhouettes only (see e.g. [1]), voxels in a volume are carved away until their projected images are consistent with the set of silhouettes. The resulting object is the visual hull. In general, the visual hull can be represented in other forms such as bounding edges ([2]), and can be reconstructed in a number of different ways. The main drawback of visual hulls is that they are unable to capture concavities on the object surface ([3]).

A 3D surface can also be reconstructed using color or texture consistency between different views. Stereo techniques find the best pixel matching between pairs of views and construct disparity maps which represent (partial) shapes. Combining from multiple stereo maps has been studied, but is quite complicated ([4]). Space carving ([5]) and recent surface evolution methods (e.g. [6], [7]) use a more general consistency check among multiple views.

The combination of both silhouettes and foreground color to reconstruct an object's surface has been studied in a number of recent papers ([7], [8], [9]).

---

* This work is supported by the NSF grant IIS-0325715 entitled ITR: New Technology for the Capture, Analysis and Visualization of Human Movement.

A. Leonardis, H. Bischof, and A. Pinz (Eds.): ECCV 2006, Part II, LNCS 3952, pp. 219–231, 2006.

Our work is motivated by [8] and [10] where the graph cut algorithm serves as the underlying 3D discrete optimization tool. The near global optimality properties of the graph cut algorithm are discussed in [11]. As noted in [8] and in other works however, the graph cut algorithm usually prefers shorter cuts, which leads to protrusive parts of the object surface being cut off. We overcome this limitation with a two-phase procedure. In the first phase (phase I), protrusions are protected during the optimization by forcing the solution to pass close to a set of predetermined surface points called "constraint points". In the second phase (phase II), concavities on the object surface are aggressively pursued. Silhouette uncertainties, which are important in practice but have been ignored in previous research ([8], [9], ...) are also taken into account.

1.1 Related Works

The application of reliable surface points to constrain the reconstruction of a surface appears in a number of recent papers ([2], [7], [9], ...). Isidoro et al ([7]) refine the shape and texture map with an EM-like procedure; the evolution of the shape at each iteration is anchored around a set of locations called frontier points. Cheung et al ([2]) use another set of points called color surface points to align multiple visual hulls constructed at different times to obtain a closer approximation to the object's true surface. Usually, these points have no special patterns on the surface. In some cases, however, they might lie on continuous curves such as the rims in [9], where each (smooth and closed) rim is a contour generator. The mesh of rims can be used to partition the surface into local patches. Surface estimation is then performed individually for each patch, with some interaction to ensure certain properties such as smoothness.

The identification of these surface points is typically based on the silhouettes and color/photo consistency. A frontier point in [7] is the point with lowest texture back-projection error among those on the evolving surface that project onto a single silhouette point. Frontier points are recomputed at each iteration. The rims in [9] are built with a rim mesh algorithm. In order for the mesh to exist, certain assumptions have to be made, the most limiting one being no self-occlusion. In [2], the colored surface points are searched for along bounding edges which collectively represent the surface of the object.

Surface reconstruction methods that use color or texture such as [2], [8], [7], [9] and most stereo algorithms involve optimization. The original space carving algorithm ([5]) used a simple greedy algorithm. Other examples of local methods include stochastic search ([7]) and, recently, surface evolution using level sets or PDEs (e.g. [6]). Local techniques are often sensitive to initialization and local minimum. Here, we use the 3D graph cut algorithm which is more global in scope ([11]). It was applied in [3] to solve the occupancy problem and in [10] for 3D image segmentation. The work described in [7] has similar motivation to ours: developing a constrained graph cut solution to object surface recovery. Their constraints are based on the rim mesh mentioned above. Multiple interconnected sub-graphs are built, with one for each rim mesh face. Our constraint points are not required to form rims and we use only one graph; our formulation is most similar to [8], which is the departure point for our research. Section 2 describes the basic steps of the formulation from [8].

2 Volumetric Graph Cuts

Following [8], we first construct the visual hull V from the set of N image silhouettes, denoted $\{Sil_i\}$. V is used as the initial approximation to the object shape. A photo consistency field for all voxels $v \in V$ is constructed and used as the graph on which a graph cut optimization is performed. Visibility for a voxel $v \in V$, $Vis(v)$, is approximated with the visibility of the closest voxel to v on the surface S_{out} of V. The consistency score for v, $\rho(v)$ is the weighted normalized cross correlation (NCC) between the pairs of local image patches that v projects to in the different views:

$$\rho(v) = \sum_{C_i, C_j \in Vis(v)} w(pos(C_i, C_j))NCC(p(C_i, v), p(C_j, v)) \qquad (1)$$

where $w(pos(C_i, C_j)$ is a weight depending on the relative position of the two camera centers C_i and C_j (small when the difference between the viewing angles of the i-th and j-th cameras is large and vice versa); $p(C_i, v)$ is the local image patch around the image of v in the i-th image I_i .

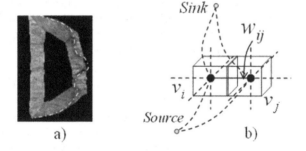

a)   b)

Fig. 1. a) a slice of the photo consistency field, yellow line denotes the true surface. b) Nodes and edges in the graph G.

If the surface, S_{out}, of the visual hull, V, is not far from the actual surface S^*, then with consistency computed this way, voxels that lie on S^* would have smallest ρ values (Figure 1.a). Therefore, finding S^* can be formulated as an energy minimization problem, where the energy is defined as

$$E(S) = \iint_S \rho(x)dA \qquad (2)$$

A graph cut algorithm can be used to solve this problem in a manner similar to [12] and [10]. Each voxel is a node in the graph, G, with a 6-neighbor system for edges. The weight for the edge between voxel (node) v_i and v_j is defined as

$w(v_i, v_j) = 4/3\pi h^2(\rho(v_i) + \rho(v_j))/2$ (Figure 1.b), where h is the voxel size. S_{out} and S_{in} — the surface inside V at a distance d from S_{out} — form an enclosing volume in which S^* is assumed to lie. Similar to [12] and [9], every voxel $v \in S_{in}(S_{out})$ is connected to the $Sink$ ($Source$) node through an edge with very high weight. With the graph G constructed this way, the graph cut algorithm is then applied to find S^*.

3   Graph Cut with Surface Point Constraints

As mentioned in [8], the above procedure suffers from the limitation that the graph cut algorithm prefers shorter cuts. This produces inaccurate surfaces at protrusions, which are often cut off ([8]). We address this problem by constraining the solution cut to pass through certain surface points. First we show how to identify those points. Next, we show how to enforce the solution cut to pass through or close to them. Finally, methods for dealing with silhouette uncertainty are included.

3.1   Constraint on Surface Points

Assume, to begin with, that the set of silhouettes has absolute locational certainty. Every ray (C_i, p_i^j) from a camera center C_i through a point p_i^j on the silhouette Sil_i has to touch the object surface at at least one point P ([2], [9]) (Figure 2.a). In [2], the authors search for P along this ray. We, additionally, take into account the discretization of the silhouette and make the search region not a single ray (C_i, p_i^j) but a surface patch $s \subset S_{out}$ where $s = \{v \mid v \in S_{out}$ and v *projects to* p_i^j *through* $C_i\}$. Since every voxel on S_{out} has to project onto some point on some silhouette $\{Sil_i\}$, the union of all s is S_{out}. Therefore, S_{out} is completely accounted for when we search for all P's. In [7], the authors also use the projection from object space to silhouettes to find the search regions for their set of constraint points. However, these regions, and therefore the resulting constraint points, lie on an evolving surface and have to be recomputed at each step of their iterative procedure. Here, the determination of P is done only once and is based on S_{out}, the surface of the original visual hull.

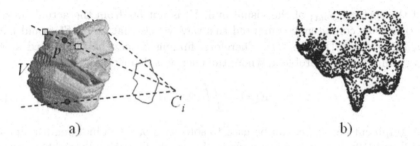

Fig. 2. a) Rays touch V's surface at p, b) Example of the set of constraint points, **P**

Let $\mathbf{P}$ denotes the set of all such P's. To identify the location of each $P \in \mathbf{P}$ within its corresponding search region, we use color or texture information from the image foreground. Ideally, the images of such voxels should have zero consistency score ρ or zero color variance. Practically, they are voxels whose projections have the lowest ρ within a search region. Figure 2.b shows an example of the constraint points, $\mathbf{P}$, for the synthetic face that is used in the experiments in section 5. Note that their distribution is quite general and they do not obviously form rims. This creates difficulties for approaches that assume exact silhouette information such as [9] and [13] . By marking which sub-regions of S_{out} are produced by which camera, $\mathbf{P}$ can be constructed in time linear in the number of voxels in S_{out}.

If the average number of points on a silhouette is n_s, then the number of points in $\mathbf{P}$ is $N.n_s$. Many of them lie on protrusive parts of the object surface. In general, $\mathbf{P}$ provides a large set of constraints for the graph cut optimization.

3.2 Graph Cut with Surface Constraint Points

Given the set of surface constraint voxels, $\mathbf{P}$, we want to construct a cut that passes through every voxel $p \in \mathbf{P}$. Unfortunately, it is difficult to introduce such constraints directly into the 3D graph cut algorithm. Instead, we adopt an indirect approach by blocking the solution surface from cutting a continuous region that connects p and S_{in}. Figure 3.a illustrates the blocking region: it is a curve $bl(p)$ from the surface point $p \in \mathbf{P}$ to S_{in}. More generally, a blocking region can be represented as a blurred volume around the blocking curves using a Gaussian blurring function. We next describe how to construct $bl(p)$.

Let $D(S)$ and $\nabla D(S)$ denote the 3D distance transform of a surface S and the gradient of the distance transform, respectively. For each $p \in \mathbf{P}$, the corresponding curve $bl(p)$ is constructed using $\nabla D(S_{out})$ and $\nabla D(S_{in})$ as follows. First, starting from p, we move along $\nabla D(S_{out})$ for a small distance l. Second, we follow $-\nabla D(S_{in})$ until S_{in} is met. Points are added into $bl(p)$ as we move. To avoid redundancy, if a point is met that has been added to some previously constructed $bl(p')$, we stop collecting points for $bl(p)$. This procedure is carried out for all points in $\mathbf{P}$.

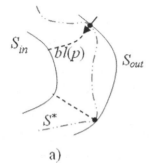

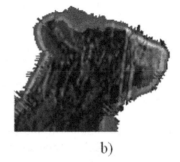

a)   b)

Fig. 3. a) Blocking regions (curves). b) Locational uncertainties (gray areas) of the contour extracted from a difference image.

$D(S_{out})$ can be considered as an implicit shape representation with the zero-level set being S_{out}; so, the normal of S_{out} at a surface point p is the gradient of $D(S_{out})$, i.e. $\nabla D(S_{out})$, evaluated at that point. Therefore, in the first step, we initially move in the direction of the normal of S_{out} at p. Given that p is assumed to be on the true surface, S^*, by moving this way, we will reduce the chance of erroneously "crossing" S^*. After a small distance l, we could have continued to move along $\nabla D(S_{out})$. However, we switch to moving along $-\nabla D(S_{in})$ for the following reasons. First, if we have a group of constraint points that are close together, then their respective $bl(p)$'s built by using $\nabla D(S_{out})$ will usually meet and collapse into a single curve well before S_{in} is reached. Such a merge is not desirable when the graph cut weight from a voxel v in $bl(p)$ to the $Sink$ node is not set to infinity, but to some other smaller value. (This is necessary for dealing with noise and discretization ambiguities - see below). Second, there are places where the above gradient fields vanish, and we must either abandon constructing the current $bl(p)$ or need several bookkeeping steps such as making small random jumps to take care of this issue. Of the two gradient fields, $\nabla D(S_{in})$ is more homogenous and this happens less frequently to it.

This procedure constructs the set of all blocking curves **BL** through which the solution cut should not pass. This constraint might be incorporated into the graph cut algorithm by setting the weights of the edges from each voxel in **BL** to the $Sink$ node to be infinity. However, the set **P** (and hence **BL**) often contains false positives, so this strategy can lead to significant errors. Therefore, instead, for every voxel $v \in$ **BL**, we set $w(v, Sink) = 4/3\pi h^2$, where h is the voxel size. This is the maximum weight for the edges between any two neighboring voxels in V. This uniform weight setting works well provided that the silhouette set is accurate, as shown in experiments on synthetic data in section 5.

Incorporating silhouette uncertainties. When dealing with real image sequences, errors in background subtraction and from the morphological operations typically employed to find silhouettes introduce artifacts ([3]). So, there is always uncertainty in silhouette extraction. We would, of course, like our silhouette to be as accurate as possible. But we still need to measure the local positional uncertainty of the silhouette and incorporate this uncertainty into the surface estimation algorithm. We extract silhouettes in the following way. First a background image, I_{bgr}, is subtracted from the image I, with $\triangle I = |I - I_{bgr}|$. Then, a small threshold $\theta_I = 2\sigma_{noise}$ is applied to $\triangle I$ to get the largest connected component BW_{obj}, which is assumed to contain the object's true silhouette. Next, along the boundary of BW_{obj}, we find the set P_{fix} - a set of high confidence silhouette points - where $P_{fix} = \{p \mid \triangle I > \Theta_I\}$ and Θ_I is a large threshold. Finally, an active contour method is applied to $\triangle I$ with points in P_{fix} being part of the contour and fixed. So, we first identify boundary sections with high likelihood of being on the silhouette and recover the rest of the silhouette with an active contour. The associated uncertainties for points on contours are measured with a quadratic function as described below.

The uncertainties on the location of the silhouette affect the process of finding **P**. To account for them, we need to determine the probability that a point in **P** is really on S^*. It is estimated with a combination of cues from silhouette and photometric consistency, i.e.

$$\Pr(p \in \mathbf{P}) \sim \Pr(PhotoConsistency(p), a \in Sil_i) \qquad (3)$$

where p projects to the point a on the silhouette Sil_i through the camera center C_i. Assuming that photo consistency and silhouette uncertainty are independent, we have

$$\Pr(p \in \mathbf{P}) \sim \Pr(PhotoConsistency(p))\Pr(a \in Sil_i) \qquad (4)$$
$$\sim \rho(p)\Pr(a \in Sil_i) \qquad (5)$$

where, similar to [3], $\Pr(a \in Sil_i)$ is a truncated linear function of $|\triangle I(a)|^2$. (Figure 3.b illustrates uncertainty measure along the contour extracted from a difference image).

The search region, $s \subset S_{out}$, for a constraint voxel p described in section 3.1 is now extended to a sub-volume around s with a thickness proportionate to $\Pr(a \in Sil_i)$. Note that the extension is also outwards in addition to inwards. To determine the color consistency value for the searched points that are outside V which haven't been computed so far, we dilate V with a small disk (e.g. a disk of 5×5 pixels) and proceed with the ρ computation described in section 2. Instead of applying uniform weight to the edges connecting voxels in **BL** to the *Sink* node, we now weight these edges for $p \in \mathbf{P}$ and for voxels that are in the associated $bl(p)$ using $\Pr(p \in \mathbf{P})$.

4   A Second Phase to Handle Concavities

As discussed in section 3.1, the set of surface constraint points, **P**, provides a large set of constraints on surface recovery which tend to best capture protrusive parts of the object's surface. So, the surface reconstructed by the first stage of recovery (phase I) is generally accurate over such areas. This is supported by the experiments described in section 5. On the other hand, it is well known that the silhouette does not contain information about concave regions of the surface ([3]). In addition, the graph cut algorithm, which prefers shorter cuts, will not follow a concavity well unless we "aggressively" pursue it.

We propose the procedure in figure 4 as a second phase to correct the estimation of the surface over concave regions.

We first (step 1) divide all of the voxels on the surface S_I into three groups. The first group, $\mathbf{P}_{surf}$, has small ρ (or high photo consistency); the second group, $\mathbf{P}_{outside}$, consists of voxels with high ρ ; and the last group consists of the remaining voxels. Percentile(S, θ) returns the ρ value which is the θ-th percentile of the ρ score for S_I. The parameters θ_1 and θ_2 determine the size of each group. In general, their appropriate values depend on the properties of the surface under consideration. Although as we observed, the final result is not very sensitive to these parameters. For the experiments in section 5, θ_1 and θ_2 are set to 0.7 and 0.95 respectively.

Let S_I be the surface constructed by the algorithm in phase I.

Step 1. From S_I, extract two sets of points $\mathbf{P}_{surf}$ and $\mathbf{P}_{outside}$,

$$\mathbf{P}_{surf} = \{v \mid v \in S_I \text{ and } \rho(v) < \text{Percentile}(S_I, \theta_1)\} \tag{6}$$

$$\mathbf{P}_{outside} = \{v \mid v \in S_I \text{ and } \rho(v) > \text{Percentile}(S_I, \theta_2)\} \tag{7}$$

Step 2. Using the procedure in section 3.2 to find $\mathbf{BL}_{inside} = \cup_{v \in \mathbf{P}_{surf}} bl(v)$.
Set the weight $w(v, Sink)$ for all $v \in \mathbf{BL}_{inside}$ using the previous method.

Step 3. Get $\mathbf{BL}_{outside} = \cup_{v \in \mathbf{P}_{outside}} bl(v)$ with the procedure in section 3.2
For all $v \in \mathbf{BL}_{outside}$ and $v \notin \mathbf{BL}_{inside}$

$$w(v, Source) = c.\Pr(v \text{ is outside } S^*) = c. \int_{d(v)}^{\infty} \exp(-p^2/\sigma_{surf}^2)dp \tag{8}$$

where c is a normalizing constant, $d(v)$ is the distance from v to S_{out}.
The weights for all remaining voxels are set using photo consistency scores as
before.

Step 4. Perform the graph cut algorithm to extract the final surface, S_{II}.

Fig. 4. The steps of the second phase

Since all voxels in $\mathbf{P}_{surf}$ lie on S_I and have high photo consistency (small ρ),
we assume that they belong to or are very close to the true surface S^*. Therefore,
in step 2, we connect them and all the voxels in their associated $\mathbf{BL}_{inside}$ to the
Sink node. Essentially, we treat $\mathbf{P}_{surf}$ in a similar way to the set of constraint
points, $\mathbf{P}$, in phase I.

On the other hand, the voxels in $\mathbf{P}_{outside}$ have low photo consistency (high
ρ), so in step 3 we connect them to the *Source* node. By doing so, we effectively
assume that these voxels are outside the true surface S^* (and hence do not belong
to the object's occupancy volume). The reasons we do this are as follows. Any
such voxel is unlikely to lie on the actual surface S^*, so is either inside or outside
of it. If such a voxel were inside the true surface S^*, then the surface region
on S^* that "covers" it would either be protrusive (case 1 - fig. 5) or concave
(case 2 - fig. 5). If this region were protrusive (case 1), then it would likely have
been captured by the constraint points, P, so would have been included in S_I
by phase I. If that region were concave (case 2), then the phase I graph cut
algorithm would have included the region in S_I, instead of $\mathbf{P}_{outside}$, because it
would have incurred a smaller cutting cost. This is because voxels that lie on
that region would have low ρ, while the voxels in $\mathbf{P}_{outside}$ have high ρ and form
even more concave (or "longer") surface regions. Therefore, voxels in $\mathbf{P}_{outside}$
are assumed to be outside of S^* (case 3 - fig. 5), the only remaining possibility.

Moreover, the region of S^* that lies "under" $\mathbf{P}_{outside}$ is assumed to be concave.
Therefore, to better recover it, we bias the solution cut inwards by treating the
blocking curves $\mathbf{BL}_{outside}$ differently. Voxels on these curves are assumed to be
outside S^* with a probability distribution that decreases as the distance of these

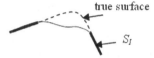  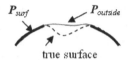

Case 1, unlikely since there will be constraint points if the true surface is protrusive.

Case 2, impossible since true surface is "shorter" and would has been assigned to S_I

Case 3, the possible case, where true surface is inside S_I

Fig. 5. Possible displacements of S_I and S^*. The solid curve represents S_I with bold segments for $\mathbf{P}_{surf}$ and thin segments for $\mathbf{P}_{outside}$. Of these cases, only case 3 is likely.

voxels from S_{out} increases (note that we use S_{out} instead of S_I). We model the probability of the surface location as a Gaussian distribution $N(S_m, \sigma^2_{surf})$, where S_m is a "mean surface" midway between S_{out} and S_{in}. The variance σ^2_{surf} is set to be $(1/4d)^2$ for the experiments in section 5, where d is the distance from S_{in} to S_{out}. This leads to approximating the probability that a voxel v is outside of S^* with the cumulative distribution of $N(S_m, \sigma^2_{surf})$, and so the weight from voxels in $\mathbf{BL}_{outside}$ to the *Source* node is computed using (8) in step 3.

5   Experimental Results

We demonstrate the performance of our approach on both synthetic and real data (640×480 images). Volumetric discretization are $256 \times 256 \times 256$ for all

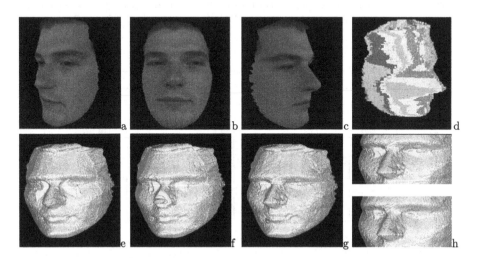

Fig. 6. Synthetic face reconstruction: a-c) Three of the images collected; d) visual hull V; e-f) using basic step, $\lambda = .3$ and .1; g) using constraint points P after phase I; h) after phase II (bottom) as compared to after phase I (top)

experiments. The synthetic experiment is with a textured head (figure 6.a-c). Note that the nose is quite protrusive and the eye areas are concave. For the results in figure 6, twenty images and the associated calibration information were constructed. Figure 6.d shows the visual hull V obtained from the silhouettes. Each colored patch of the surface S_{out} is "carved" by some camera. Patches from any single camera may not be connected and so are rims ([9]). Moreover, if self-occlusion occurs, some patches may not contain any true surface points at all. Figure 6.e and 6.f show the result of using the basic algorithm from [8] described in section 3.1 with different ballooning factors, λ, to overcome the preference of the algorithm to shorter cuts. As can be seen, if λ is too high (0.3), the protrusive parts (the nose) are preserved, but the concave regions (the eyes) suffer. Lowering λ (0.1) helps to recover concave areas but at the price of losing protrusive parts. Figure 6.g shows the result of phase I when constraint points are used. Protrusive parts are well preserved now. However, the concave regions still are still not accurately recovered: the eye areas are nearly flat. Figure 6.h compares the results of phase I (the top part) and phase II (the bottom part), where the eye areas are now improved.

In the second experiment, we measure the reconstruction errors of the synthetic face when different numbers of views are used (8, 16, 32, and 64). In generating images, the viewing direction of the camera is always towards the center of the face. For every set of views, the camera is placed in positions that are arbitrary, but distributed roughly even in front of the face. For the basic algorithm, λ is set to 0.15 to get a balance between the recovery of protrusions and concavities. Since the ground truth for the face is given as a cloud of points, G_0, we use the 3D distance transform to measure the recovery error E. Specifically, for a surface S, $E(S, G_0) = (D(S, G_0) + D(G_0, S))/(|S| + |G_0|)$, where $D(S, G_0)$ is the sum of distances from all points in S to G_0. $E(S, G_0)$ is thus the average distance between points in S and G_0 (in voxel units). Figure 7 shows the

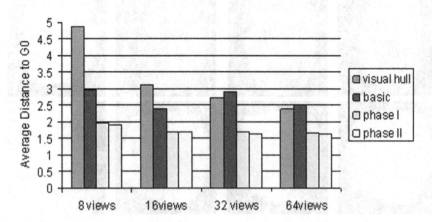

Fig. 7. Recovery errors for different set of views. For each group, from left to right, values are respectively for visual hull, basic algorithm and our phase I, II results. (A unit along the y-axis corresponds to the size of a voxel).

reconstruction errors. The visual hull V produces quite a large error with 8 views but is noticeably better as the number of views increases. For the basic algorithm, with $\lambda = 0.15$, some protrusions are cut off. Note that since the cutting off effects can have unpredictable consequences, the reconstruction error can increase as the number of views increases (although not significantly). Adding more views in this case turns out to be "helping" the nose of the face to be more cut off. As a result, the visual hull may produce better results for larger number of views. Our methods behave consistently and produce better performance. Our result with 8 views, although with no discernible improvement for more than 16 views, is better than the visual hull with 64 views. The error of our method compared to the basic algorithm, is reduced roughly 33%. Note that in term of average error distance, phase II is not much better than phase I. This is because the focus of phase II is only on small (concave) portions left by phase I ($\theta_2 = 0.95$, section 4).

In the third experiment, 30 real images of a colored plastic squirrel were collected. We imaged the object under natural lighting conditions with a cluttered background, and moved the camera around the object. Due to self-shadowing and the arrangement of the light sources, the object is well lit on one side and poorly lit on the other side (see figures 8.a and 8.b for examples). The color information from the poorly lit side is noisy and tends to saturate to black. These 30 images are divided roughly even for both sides. The object's actual size is about $300 \times 150 \times 300$ mm^3 (width-length-height); this is also the size of the discretized volume used. Camera calibration was done using a publicly available tool box with the principal point's uncertainty from $1.4 - 1.7$ pixels. Silhouette extraction is performed using the method described in section 3.2. The silhouettes can be 1 to 5 pixels off from the "true" silhouettes. Figure 8.c show the visual hull constructed from them. Assuming that these silhouettes are exact leads to undesirable consequences. Figure 8.d shows the result of the basic algorithm. Even when we add the set of constraint points, our algorithm (phase I) still produces bad results: a number of incorrect bumps and dents on the surface. Figure 8.e, top row, zooms in on some of them (the image are smoothen for better visualization). Adding silhouette uncertainties (bottom row) produce much improved results. To allow for comparison with the basic algorithm, the dilated visual hull discussed at the end of section 3.2 is also used for it.

For the well lit side of the object, figure 8.f shows the result of the basic algorithm and figure 8.g shows the result of our methods (phase I). Figure 8.h compares the two results on several places: the top row is for the basic algorithm and the bottom row is for ours. The phase I and phase II give nearly the same result. In other words, phase II has little effects on this well-illuminated side.

For poorly lit side of the object, figure 8.k shows the result of the basic algorithm, figure 8.l is for phase I and figure 8.m is for phase II. Note the difference between the two legs and along the tail.

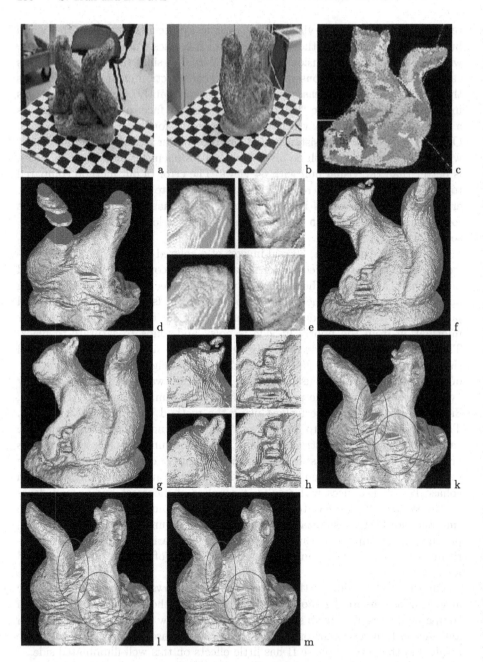

Fig. 8. Reconstruction of the squirrel object. a-b) two of the images collected; c) the visual hull V; d-e) the result of the basic algorithm and our phase I when silhouettes are assumed exact (see text). Well lit area results: f) the basic algorithm; g) our phase I algorithm; h) some detailed comparison between the basic algorithm (top row) and the final result of phase I (bottom row). Poorly lit area results: k) the basic, l) phase I and m) phase II algorithms. Note the differences inside the red circles.

References

1. Szeliski, R.: Rapid octree construction from image sequences. CVGIP: Image Understanding **57** (1993) 23–32
2. Cheung, G.K.M., Baker, S., Kanade, T.: Visual hull alignment and refinement across time: A 3d reconstruction algorithm combining shape-from-silhouette with stereo. In: Proc. IEEE Conf. Computer Vision and Pattern Recognition (CVPR-2003). (2003) 375–382
3. Snow, D., Viola, P., Zabih, R.: Exact voxel occupancy with graph cuts. In: Proc. IEEE Conf. Computer Vision and Pattern Recognition (CVPR-2000). (2000) 345–352
4. Paris, S., Sillion, F., Long, L.: A surface reconstruction method using global graph cut optimization. In: Proc. Asian Conf. Computer Vision (ACCV-2004). (2004)
5. K. Kutulakos, K., Seitz, S.: A theory of shape by space carving. In: Proc. IEEE Int'l Conf. Computer Vision (ICCV-1999). (1999) 307–314
6. Solem, J., Kahl, F., Heyden, A.: Visibility constrained surface evolution. In: Proc. IEEE Conf. Computer Vision and Pattern Recognition (CVPR-2005). (2005) 892–900
7. Isidoro, J., Sclaroff, S.: Stochastic refinement of the visual hull to satisfy photo-metric and silhouette consistency constraints. In: Proc. IEEE Int'l Conf. Computer Vision (ICCV-2003). (2003) 1335–1342
8. Vogiatzis, G., Torr, P., Cippola, R.: Multi-view stereo via volumetric graph-cuts. In: Proc. IEEE Conf. Computer Vision and Pattern Recognition (CVPR-2005). (2005) 391–399
9. Sinha, S.N., Pollefeys, M.: Multi-view reconstruction using photo-consistency and exact silhouette constraints: A maximum-flow formulation. In: Proc. IEEE Int'l Conf. Computer Vision (ICCV-2005). (2005) I:349–356
10. Boykov, Y., Kolmogorov, V.: Computing geodesics and minimal surfaces via graph cuts. In: Proc. IEEE Int'l Conf. Computer Vision (ICCV-2003). (2003) 26–33
11. Boykov, Y., Veksler, O., Zabih, R.: Fast approximate energy minimization via graph cuts. IEEE Trans. Pattern Anal. and Machine Intell. **23** (2001) 1222–1239
12. Boykov, Y., Jolly, M.P.: Interactive graph cuts for optimal boundary and region segmentation of objects in n-d images. In: Proc. IEEE Int'l Conf. Computer Vision (ICCV-2001). (2001) 105–112
13. Esteban, C.H., Schmitt, F.: Silhouette and stereo fusion for 3d object modeling. In: Proc. 4th Int'l Conf. on 3D Digital Imaging and Modeling (3DIM 2003). (2003) 46–53

Trace Quotient Problems Revisited

Shuicheng Yan[1] and Xiaoou Tang[1,2]

[1] Department of Information Engineering,
The Chinese University of Hong Kong, Hong Kong
[2] Microsoft Research Asia, Beijing, China

Abstract. The formulation of *trace quotient* is shared by many computer vision problems; however, it was conventionally approximated by an essentially different formulation of *quotient trace*, which can be solved with the generalized eigenvalue decomposition approach. In this paper, we present a direct solution to the former formulation. First, considering that the feasible solutions are constrained on a Grassmann manifold, we present a necessary condition for the optimal solution of the trace quotient problem, which then naturally elicits an iterative procedure for pursuing the optimal solution. The proposed algorithm, referred to as Optimal Projection Pursuing (OPP), has the following characteristics: 1) OPP directly optimizes the trace quotient, and is theoretically optimal; 2) OPP does not suffer from the solution uncertainty issue existing in the quotient trace formulation that the objective function value is invariant under any non-singular linear transformation, and OPP is invariant only under orthogonal transformations, which does not affect final distance measurement; and 3) OPP reveals the underlying equivalence between the trace quotient problem and the corresponding trace difference problem. Extensive experiments on face recognition validate the superiority of OPP over the solution of the corresponding quotient trace problem in both objective function value and classification capability.

1 Introduction

In recent decades, a large family of algorithms [19]—supervised or unsupervised; stemming from statistical or geometry theory — has been proposed to provide different solutions to the problem of dimensionality reduction [2][4][12][15][16][19]. Many of them, such as Linear Discriminant Analysis (LDA) [1] and Locality Preserving Projection (LPP) [6], eventually come down to the trace quotient problem [17][20] as follows

$$W^* = arg \max_{W^\mathrm{T} CW=I} \frac{Tr(W^\mathrm{T} AW)}{Tr(W^\mathrm{T} BW)} . \tag{1}$$

Here A, B, and C are all symmetric positive semidefinite; $Tr(\cdot)$ denotes the trace of a matrix; I is an identity matrix and W is the pursued transformation matrix for dimensionality reduction. Commonly, the null space of matrix C lies within the null space of both A and B, that is, $null(C) \in null(A) \bigcap null(B)$. Due to the lack of a direct efficient

A. Leonardis, H. Bischof, and A. Pinz (Eds.): ECCV 2006, Part II, LNCS 3952, pp. 232–244, 2006.
© Springer-Verlag Berlin Heidelberg 2006

solution for Eq. (1), the quotient trace problem $Tr((W^{T}BW)^{-1}(W^{T}AW))$ is often discussed instead and the generalized eigenvalue decomposition (GEVD) [20] approach is applied for a direct closed-form solution.

If W is a vector, it is theoretically guaranteed that the optimal solution of (1) is the eigenvector corresponding to the largest eigenvalue of GEVD by using the Lagrange Multiplier method. GEVD can provide an optimal solution to the quotient trace problem, yet it is not necessarily optimal for the trace quotient problem when W is in the form of a matrix. Moreover, the solution from GEVD is unstable when matrix B is singular; and Principal Component Analysis (PCA) [14] is often used beforehand to avoid the singularity issue. However, it is often observed that the algorithmic performance is extremely sensitive to the retained dimension of PCA. All these motivate us to pursue an efficient and theoretically sound procedure to solve the trace quotient problem.

More specifically, our contributions are as follows. First, we prove that GEVD cannot provide an optimal solution to the trace quotient problem. Then, we present a necessary condition for the optimal solution of the trace quotient problem by taking into account the fact that the feasible solutions are constrained to lie on a Grassmann manifold. Finally, by following the necessary condition, an efficient procedure is proposed to pursue the optimal solution of the trace quotient problem. As a product, the necessary condition indicates the underlying equivalence between the trace quotient problem and the corresponding trace difference problem.

The rest of the paper is organized as follows. In section 2, we introduce the trace quotient problem and the corresponding quotient trace problem, and then discuss the infeasibility of the GEVD method in solving the trace quotient problem. In Section 3, a necessary condition for the optimal solution of the trace quotient problem is presented, which naturally elicits an iterative procedure to pursue the optimal solution. Extensive experiments on face recognition are demonstrated in Section 4 to show the superiority of our proposed algorithm over GEVD. Finally, in Section 5, we conclude the paper and provide discussions of future work.

2   Trace Quotient Problem

Denote the sample set as matrix $X = [x_1, x_2, \cdots, x_N]$, $x_i \in \mathbb{R}^m$ is an m-dimensional vector. For supervised learning tasks, the class label of the sample x_i is assumed to be $c_i \in \{1, 2, \cdots, N_c\}$ and n_c denotes the sample number of the c-th class.

2.1   Trace Quotient Problem vs. Quotient Trace Problem

A large family of algorithms for subspace learning [6] ends with solving a trace quotient problem as in (1). Among them, the most popular ones are the Linear Discriminant Analysis (LDA) [17] algorithm and its kernel extension. LDA searches for the most discriminative directions that maximize the quotient of the inter-class scatter and the intra-class scatter

$$W^* = arg \max_{W^TW=I} \frac{Tr(W^TS_bW)}{Tr(W^TS_wW)}$$

(2)

$$S_b = \sum_{c=1}^{N_c} n_c(m_c - m)(m_c - m)^T, S_w = \sum_{i=1}^{N}(x_i - m_{c_i})(x_i - m_{c_i})^T$$

Here m_c is the mean of the samples belonging to the c-th class and m is the mean of all samples; $W \in \mathbb{R}^{m \times k}$ is the pursued transformation matrix for dimensionality reduction. The objective function of (2) has explicit semantics for both numerator and denominator and they characterize the scatters measured by the Euclidean distances in the low dimensional feature space

$$Tr(W^TS_bW) = \sum_{c=1}^{N_c} n_c \| W^Tm_c - W^Tm \|^2, \quad Tr(W^TS_wW) = \sum_{i=1}^{N} \| W^Tx_i - W^Tm_{c_i} \|^2.$$

(3)

A direct way to extend a linear algorithm to a nonlinear case is to utilize the kernel trick [5][9][18]. The intuition of the kernel trick is to map the data from the original input space to a higher dimensional Hilbert space as $\phi : x \to \mathcal{F}$ and then the linear algorithm is performed in this new feature space. It can be well applied to the algorithms that only need to compute the inner products of the data pairs $k(x, y) = \phi(x) \cdot \phi(y)$. For LDA, provided that $W = [\phi(x_1), \phi(x_2), ..., \phi(x_N)]M$, where $M \in \mathbb{R}^{N \times k}$ and $K \in \mathbb{R}^{N \times N}$ is the kernel Gram matrix with $K_{ij} = k(x_i, x_j)$, we have

$$M^* = arg \max_{M^TKM=I} \frac{Tr(M^TKS_bKM)}{Tr(M^TKS_wKM)}.$$

(4)

Obviously, LDA and its kernel extension both follow the formulation of trace quotient as in (1); generally, there is no closed-form solution for (2) and (4) when $k > 1$.

Instead of directly solving the trace quotient problem, many researchers study another formulation, called the quotient trace problem here, to pursue the most discriminative features as follows

$$W^* = arg \max_{W} Tr((W^TBW)^{-1}(W^TAW)).$$

(5)

Notice that commonly there is no constraint on matrix W in the quotient trace problem and it is solved by the generalized eigenvalue decomposition (GEVD) method

$$Aw_i = \lambda_i Bw_i, \quad i = 1, ..., k.$$

(6)

Here w_i is the eigenvector corresponding to the i-th largest eigenvalue λ_i. Despite extensive study of the quotient trace problem, it suffers the following disadvantages: 1) it is invariant under any nonsingular linear transformation, which results in the uncertainty of the Euclidean metric on the derived low dimensional feature space; and 2) unlike the trace quotient problem, there does not exist explicit semantics for the objective function of quotient trace problem. Therefore, compared with the quotient trace formulation, the trace quotient formulation is more reasonable; and in the following, we study the problem of how to directly solve the trace quotient problem.

2.2   Is Generalized Eigenvalue Decomposition Approach Feasible?

Based on the constraint on the transformation matrix and the *Lagrange Multiplier* method, the trace quotient problem (1) is equivalent to maximizing

$$F(W,\lambda) = Tr(W^{\mathrm{T}}AW) - \lambda\,(Tr(W^{\mathrm{T}}BW) - c)\,. \qquad (7)$$

Here, c is a constant and λ is the Lagrange Multiplier. When W is a vector, *i.e.* $k = 1$, the problem (1) is simplified to maximizing $F(W,\lambda) = W^{\mathrm{T}}AW - \lambda\,(W^{\mathrm{T}}BW - c)$. It is easy to prove that the optimal solution is the eigenvector corresponding to the largest eigenvalue calculated from the generalized eigenvalue decomposition method as in (6). Yet, when W is a matrix, *i.e.* $k > 1$, the problem is much more complex, and intuitively it was believed that the leading eigenvectors from GEVD were more valuable in discriminating power than the later ones, since the individual trace quotient, namely eigenvalue, from the leading eigenvector is larger than those from later ones. However, no theoretical proof was ever presented to justify using GEVD for solving the trace quotient problem. Here, we show that GEVD is infeasible for the following reasons. For simplicity, we discuss the LDA formulation with the constraint $W^{\mathrm{T}}W = I$.

Orthogonality: The derived eigenvectors from GEVD are not necessarily orthogonal. Let the Singular Value Decomposition of the final projection matrix W be

$$W = U\Lambda V^{\mathrm{T}}\,. \qquad (8)$$

The right orthogonal matrix V is free for the trace quotient, thus the derived solution is equal to $U\Lambda$ in the sense of rotation invariance. In this point, GEVD does not find a set of unit projection directions, but weighted ones. The left column vector of U maybe is more biased when the original feature is transformed to the low dimensional space, which conflicts with the unitary constraint.

Theoretical Guarantee: There is no theoretical proof to guarantee that the derived projection matrix can optimally maximize the trace quotient. Actually, the projection vector from GEVD is evaluated in an individual manner and the collaborative trace quotient will be easily biased by the projection direction with larger values of $(w^{\mathrm{T}}Bw, w^{\mathrm{T}}Aw)$. For example, for projection directions w_1, w_2, w_3, if their trace values are as follows (*e.g.* A=diag{10.0, 100.0, 2.0} and B=diag{1.0, 20.0, 1.0})

	w_1	w_2	w_3
$w^{\mathrm{T}}Aw$	10.0	100.0	2.0
$w^{\mathrm{T}}Bw$	1.0	20.0	1.0

then the combination of w_1 and w_3 (with trace quotient 6) is better than that of w_1 and w_2 (with trace quotient 5.24) although the single trace quotient from w_2 is larger than that from w_3. Thus, *it is not true that the eigenvector corresponding to the larger eigenvalue of GEVD is always superior to that from a smaller one in the trace quotient problem.*

Necessary Condition: It was commonly believed that the optimal solution of (1) should satisfy

$$\partial F(W,\lambda)/\partial W = 0. \tag{9}$$

Yet, the solution may not exist at all if directly setting the gradient as zero,

$$\partial F(W,\lambda)/\partial W = 2(A-\lambda B)W = 0. \tag{10}$$

It means W is the null subspace of the weighted difference of matrix B and A, *i.e.* $A-\lambda B$. In the LDA formulation, when $m < N - N_c$, matrix B is of full rank, and for most λ, $A - \lambda B$ is also of full rank; consequently there does not exist matrix $W \in \mathbb{R}^{m \times k}$ with independent columns that satisfies (7). As we will analyze later, the fundamental reason that GEVD fails to find the optimal solution is that it does not consider that the feasible solution of (1) is constrained to lie on a lower dimensional Grassmann manifold (or a transformed one when matrix C is not equal to I), not the whole matrix space, and the derivative should also be constrained to lie on the Grassmann manifold, instead of the matrix space.

All the above analyses show that the GEVD cannot provide an optimal solution for the trace quotient problem. In the following, we will present our solution to this problem.

3 Optimal Solution to Trace Quotient Problem

For the trace quotient problem (1), let the Singular Value Decomposition of matrix C be

$$C = U_c \Lambda_c U_c^{\mathrm{T}}, \; U_c \in \mathbb{R}^{m \times n}, \quad n \geq k. \tag{11}$$

Here Λ_c only contains positive diagonal elements, and denote $Q = \Lambda_c^{1/2} U_c^{\mathrm{T}} W$. As we have the assumption that $null(C) \in null(A) \bigcap null(B)$, we can constrain the matrix W in the space spanned by the column vectors of U_c and we have $W = U_c \Lambda_c^{-1/2} Q$, then

$$Q^* = arg \max_{Q^{\mathrm{T}}Q=I} \frac{Tr(Q^{\mathrm{T}}\Lambda_c^{-1/2}U_c^{\mathrm{T}}AU_c\Lambda_c^{-1/2}Q)}{Tr(Q^{\mathrm{T}}\Lambda_c^{-1/2}U_c^{\mathrm{T}}BU_c\Lambda_c^{-1/2}Q)}. \tag{12}$$

It is still a trace quotient problem, yet with the unitary and orthogonal constraints; hence in the following, we only discuss the trace quotient problem with the unitary and orthogonal constraints.

3.1 Necessary Condition for Optimal Solution

When the solution of the trace quotient problem is constrained to be columnly orthogonal and unitary, the solution space is not the whole matrix space any more, instead, mathematically, all the feasible solutions constitute a Grassmann manifold [3]. Before describing the procedure to solve the trace quotient problem, we introduce the concepts of the Grassmann manifold and its tangent space.

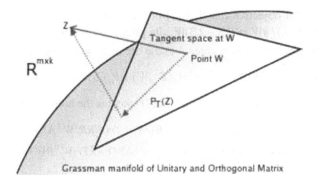

Fig. 1. The illustration of the relationship between the original matrix space, Grassmann manifold, and the projection to the tangent space. Note that it is unnecessary for gradient vector Z to be zero, instead, only its projection to the horizontal space of the tangent space is required to be zero for the trace quotient problem.

Grassmann Manifold [3]: All feasible matrices $W \in \mathbb{R}^{m \times k}$ with unit and orthogonal column vectors, *i.e.* $W^TW = I$, constitute a continuous curved hyper-surface in the original matrix space, namely a Grassmann manifold, as shown in Figure 1. Commonly, a Grassmann manifold is associated with an objective function $F(W)$, such as the objective function in (7), yielding $F(WR) = F(W)$ for any orthogonal matrix $R \in \mathbb{R}^{k \times k}$.

If for two columnly orthogonal matrices W_1 and W_2 , there exists an orthogonal matrix R so that $W_1 = W_2R$, then we call W_1 and W_2 homogeneous, denoted as $W_1 \sim W_2$. Thus, on the Grassmann manifold, the objective function $F(W)$ is invariant to all matrices that are homogeneous.

Projection on the Tangent Space [3]: As a curved hyper-surface, the movement of any point on the manifold always follows a direction in the tangent space as shown in Figure 1. All matrices M in the tangent space at point W satisfy

$$W^TM + M^TW = 0 . \tag{13}$$

And for any matrix Z, its projection on the tangent space is defined as

$$P_T(Z) = \tfrac{1}{2}W(W^TZ - Z^TW) + (I - WW^T)Z . \tag{14}$$

Considering the homogeneity condition, not all variations in tangent space will result in a change of the objective function. The tangent space is decomposed into the direct sum of a vertical space and a horizontal space, where only the directions in the horizontal space actually contribute to the change of the objective function. It is proved [3] that the projection of any vector Z on the horizontal space at W is

$$P_H(Z) = (I - WW^T)Z . \tag{15}$$

For the equivalent objective function (7) of the trace quotient problem, the gradient vector $Z = \partial F(W, \lambda)/\partial W = 2(A - \lambda B)W$. Its projection on the tangent space directly lies within the horizontal space, since A and B are both symmetric and

$$P_T(Z) = W(W^T(A - \lambda B)W - W^T(A^T - \lambda B^T)W) + P_H(Z) = 0 + P_H(Z) = P_H(Z). \quad (16)$$

Also, it is easy to prove that the function (7) satisfies the homogeneity condition

$$F(WR, \lambda) = Tr(R^T W^T A WR) - \lambda Tr(R^T W^T BWR) = Tr(WRR^T W^T A) - \lambda Tr(WRR^T W^T B)$$

$$= Tr(WW^T A) - \lambda Tr(WW^T B) = Tr(W^T AW) - \lambda Tr(W^T BW) = F(W, \lambda)$$

$$(17)$$

The second and fourth steps are derived from the fact that, for any two matrices $M_1 \in \mathbb{R}^{m \times k}$, $M_2 \in \mathbb{R}^{k \times m}$, we have $Tr(M_1 M_2) = Tr(M_2 M_1)$.

As the solution space is constrained on a Grassmann manifold, the necessary condition for the optimality of the projection matrix is that the projection on the horizontal space at point W of the gradient vector $\partial F(W, \lambda)/\partial W = 2(A - \lambda B)W$ is zero, *i.e.*

$$(I - WW^T)(AW - \lambda BW) = 0. \quad (18)$$

Then, the column vectors of the matrix $AW - \lambda BW$ all lie in the space spanned by the column vectors of W, and there exists a matrix $P \in \mathbb{R}^{k \times k}$ satisfying

$$AW - \lambda BW = WP. \quad (19)$$

By multiplying W^T on the left side of (19), we have

$$W^T AW - \lambda W^T BW = W^T WP = P. \quad (20)$$

Therefore, P is a symmetric matrix. Let its singular value decomposition be

$$P = U_p \Lambda_p U_p^T. \quad (21)$$

Then, there exists a homogeneous solution $W_p = WU_p$ satisfying

$$(A - \lambda B)W_p = W_p \Lambda_p. \quad (22)$$

It means that the projection vectors are the eigenvectors of a weighted difference matrix; consequently, we have the following claim.

Theorem. (Necessary condition for the optimal solution) For the trace quotient problem, there exists an optimal solution whose column vectors are the eigenvectors of the corresponding weighted trace difference problem, *i.e.* $(A - \lambda B)W_p = W_p \Lambda_p$.

The above theorem reveals a very interesting point that the trace quotient problem is equal to a properly weighted trace difference problem in objective function. However, these two problems are still different in some aspects. First, for the weighted trace difference problem, such as the work in MMC [8] for discriminant analysis, the solution is directly the leading eigenvectors, while in the trace quotient problem the optimal projection does not always consist of the leading eigenvectors. Secondly, there is no criterion to guide selection of the weight in the trace difference problem; while in the trace quotient problem the weight can be determined by maximizing the trace quotient, which directly motivates our following procedure to pursue the optimal solution of the trace quotient problem.

3.2 Procedure to Optimal Projection Pursuing

From (22), the optimal solution can be directly determined by Lagrange Multiplier λ ; thus we can rewrite the optimal transformation matrix corresponding to λ as $W(\lambda)$. Then, the objective function in (1) is changed to a function only related to λ ,

$$G(\lambda) = \frac{Tr(W(\lambda)^{\mathrm{T}} A W(\lambda))}{Tr(W(\lambda)^{\mathrm{T}} B W(\lambda))} . \tag{23}$$

The objective function is nonlinear and it is intractable to directly compute the gradient. However, the experiments show that the objective function is of a single peak, and some plots of the trace quotient distribution with respect to the Lagrange Multiplier λ are plotted in Figure 2. The observations encourage us apply multi-scale search to pursue the optimal weight. The details are listed in procedure-1.

Note that in procedure-1, for each Lagrange Multiplier λ , the column vectors of the optimal projection matrix $W(\lambda)$ are not exactly the leading eigenvectors corresponding to the largest eigenvalues of (22). Thus we utilize a backward elimination method to search for the optimal solution for a given weight parameter, *i.e.* the eigenvector is omitted, if the remaining ones lead to the largest trace quotient, in each step until reduced to the desired feature dimension.

Procedure to pursue optimal solution of trace quotient problem

---

1. Set parameter range: Set a proper parameter range $[a^0, b^0]$ for parameter search. In this work, a^0 is set as 0, and b^0 is experientially set as the quotient of the largest eigenvalue of A and the smallest positive eigenvalue of B, which makes most eigenvalues of (22) negative.

2. Multi-scale search: For $t = 1, 2, \ldots, T_{\max}$, Do

    a) Segment $[a^{t-1}, b^{t-1}]$ into L parts by $\lambda_i^t = a^{t-1} + (i-1)(b^{t-1} - a^{t-1})/(L-1)$, $i=1,..,L$.

    b) Compute the optimal $W(\lambda_i^t)$ and the corresponding trace quotient Tr_i^t .

    c) From the left side, if $\lambda_{i_a}^t$ is the first point satisfying $Tr_{i_a}^t < Tr_{i_a+1}^t$ and $Tr_{i_a+1}^t \geq Tr_{i_a+2}^t$, then set $a^t = \lambda_{i_a}^t$; from the right side, if $\lambda_{i_b}^t$ is the first point satisfying $Tr_{i_b}^t < Tr_{i_b-1}^t$ and $Tr_{i_b-1}^t \geq Tr_{i_b-2}^t$, then set $b^t = \lambda_{i_b}^t$.

    d) If $b^t - a^t < \varepsilon (= 0.1$ in this work), then exit.

3. Output the final optimal solution from (22) by setting $\lambda = (Tr_{i_a}^t + Tr_{i_b}^t)/2$.

Procedure-1. Optimal Solution Pursuing of Trace Quotient Problem

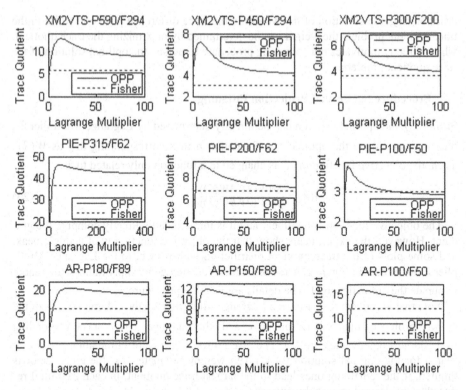

Fig. 2. The trace quotient vs. the Lagrange Multiplier (λ) in the databases XM2VTS, PIE and AR. Note that we plot the trace quotient of PCA+LDA (plotted as *Fisher* in the legends) as a line as its trace quotient value is fixed and free to the Lagrange Multiplier. We can find that the maximum trace quotient of OPP is consistently larger than that from PCA+LDA; while the trace quotient comparison between PCA+LDA and MMC (namely $\lambda = 1$) is not so clear, neither one is consistently better than the other one.

4 Experiments

In this section, three benchmark face databases, XM2VTS [10], CMU PIE [13] and AR [11] are used to evaluate the effectiveness of the proposed procedure to solve the trace quotient problem. The objective function of Linear Discriminant Analysis (2) is applied owing to its popularity; and the new procedure, referred to as OPP (**O**ptimal **P**rojection **P**ursuing), is compared with the popular PCA+LDA [1] and MMC [8], *i.e.* OPP with $\lambda = 1$. In all the experiments, the nearest neighbor method is used as a classifier for final classification based on the Euclidian distance. The trace quotient distributions with respect to the Lagrange Multiplier on the three databases are plotted in Figure 2. The results show that the derived optimal trace quotient from OPP is consistently larger than that from GEVD. In all the experiments, the parameter L in the procedure to pursue the optimal solution of the trace quotient problem is set to 8 and generally we need about three iterations to converge.

XM2VTS Database [10]: The XM2VTS database contains 295 persons and each person has four frontal images taken in four sessions. All the images are aligned by fixing the locations of two eyes and normalized in size of 64*64 pixels. In our experiments, we use 295*3 images from the first three sessions for model training; the first session is used as a gallery set and the probe set is composed of the 295 images from the fourth session. Three sets of experiments are conducted to compare the performances of OPP, PCA+LDA and MMC. In each experiment, we use different combinations of Principal Component Analysis (PCA) [7][14] dimension ($N - N_c$, moderate and small number) and final dimension, denoted as Pm/Fn in all experiments. Note that actually OPP and MMC need no PCA step, so for a fair comparison with PCA+LDA, PCA is conducted before both OPP and MMC. Table 1 shows the recognition accuracies of the three algorithms. The comparison results show that OPP outperforms MMC and PCA+LDA in all cases.

Table 1. Recognition rates (%) of PCA+LDA, MMC and OPP on XM2VTS database

	P590/F294	P450/F294	P300/F200
PCA+LDA	79.0	75.3	84.4
MMC	83.7	83.4	82.0
OPP	94.2	88.8	88.8

CMU PIE Database [13]: The CMU PIE (Pose, Illumination and Expression) database contains more than 40,000 facial images of 68 persons. In our experiment, five near frontal poses (C27, C05, C29, C09 and C07) and illuminations indexed as 08, 10, 11 and 13 are used. 63 persons are used for data incompleteness. Thus, each person has twenty images and all the images are aligned by fixing the locations of two eyes and normalizing to size 64*64 pixels. The data set is randomly partitioned into the gallery and probe sets. Six images of each person are randomly selected for training and also used for the gallery set, and the remaining fourteen images are used for testing. We also conduct three experiments on the PIE database. Table 2 lists the comparison results and it again shows that OPP is consistently superior to the other two algorithms.

Table 2. Recognition rates (%) of PCA+LDA, MMC and OPP on PIE database

	P315/F62	P200/F62	P100/F50
PCA+LDA	88.9	88.0	87.6
MMC	88.1	87.8	85.0
OPP	92.1	94.1	91.6

AR Database [11]: The AR face database contains over 4,000 frontal face images of 126 people. We use 90 persons with three images from the first session and another three images from the second session. All the images are aligned by fixing the locations of two eyes and normalizing in size to 72*64 pixels. The data set is randomly partitioned into gallery and probe sets. Three images of each person are randomly selected

Table 3. Recognition rates (%) of PCA+LDA, MMC and OPP on AR database

	P180/F89	P150/F89	P100/F50
PCA+LDA	94.1	90.7	95.2
MMC	78.9	78.5	76.3
OPP	98.2	95.9	96.7

Table 4. Recognition rates (%) of KDA, kernel MMC and OPP on three databases

	XM2VTXS	CMU PIE	AR
KDA	92.2	87.8	94.4
KMMC	86.4	88.3	81.5
KOPP	97.0	93.1	98.5

for training and as the gallery set; and the remaining three images are used for testing. The experimental details are listed in Table 3. The results show that MMC does not obtain satisfactory performance and OPP is the best.

We also apply the OPP algorithm to optimize the objective function of Kernel Discriminant Analysis, compared with the traditional method as reported in [18]. The Gaussian kernel is applied and the final feature dimension is set to $N_c - 1$ in all the experiments. Table 4 lists all the experimental results on the three databases. From the results, we can see that the solution from OPP is much better than the other two algorithms in classification capability.

From the above experimental results, we can have some interesting observations:

1.   The quotient value derived from OPP is much larger than that from PCA+LDA and MMC; meanwhile, the comparison between PCA+LDA and MMC is unclear, neither one is consistently superior to the other one.
2.   In all the experiments, the recognition rate of OPP is consistently superior to that of PCA+LDA and MMC in all the cases. Similar to the trace quotient value, the performances of PCA+LDA and MMC are comparable.
3.   All the results show that the trace quotient criterion is more suitable than the quotient trace criterion for feature extraction owing to its explicit semantics of the numerator and denominator.
4.   Recently, many other formulations of matrices A and B in the trace quotient problem were proposed [19]; the advantage of the OPP solution can be easily generalized to these new algorithms.

5   Conclusions

In this paper, we studied the problem of directly solving the trace quotient problem. First, we derived a necessary condition for the optimal solution based on the fact that the feasible solution is constrained to lie on a Grassmann manifold and the final solution is rotation invariant. Then, we presented a procedure to pursue the optimal solution based on the necessary condition. An interesting point is that the necessary condition reveals the underlying equivalence between the trace quotient problem and the corresponding trace difference problem, which provides theoretical guidance on how to select the optimal weight for the trace difference problem. Moreover, the study of how to pursue a solution on the Grassmann manifold is general, and can be easily extended to optimize general objective functions with solutions constrained on the Grassmann manifold.

Acknowledgement

Here, we would like to thank Chunjing Xu for the valuable discussion and the help to draw the figure 1; also we would like to thank Dong Xu for the help of the experiment section. This work is supported by a joint grant from HKSAR Research Grant Council and Natural Sciences Foundation of China (RGC N_CUHK409/03).

References

[1] P. Belhumeur, J. Hespanha and D. Kriegman. "Eigenfaces vs. Fisherfaces: Recognition Using Class Specific Linear Projection", IEEE Trans. Pattern Analysis and Machine Intelligence, vol. 19, No. 7, 1997, pp. 711-720.

[2] M. Belkin and P. Niyogi. "Laplacian Eigenmaps and Spectral Techniques for Embedding and Clustering", Advances in Neural Information Processing System 15, Vancouver, British Columbia, Canada, 2001.

[3] A. Edelman, T. A. Arias and S. T. Simth. "The Geometry of Algorithms with Orthogonality Constraints," SIAM J. Matrix Anal. Appl. Vol. 20, No. 2, pp.303-353.

[4] K. Fukunaga, Statistical Pattern Recognition, Academic Press, 1990.

[5] D. Hand. "Kernel Discriminant Analysis". Research Studies Press, Chichester, 1982

[6] X. He, S. Yan, Y. Hu, P. Niyogi, and H. Zhang. "Face Recognition using Laplacianfaces", IEEE Transactions on Pattern Analysis and Machine Intelligence, Vol. 27, No. 3, Mar. 2005.

[7] I. Joliffe. "Principal Component Analysis". Springer-Verlag, New York, 1986.

[8] H. Li, T. Jiang, K. Zhang. "Efficient and Robust Feature Extraction by Maximum Margin Criterion", Advances in Neural Information Processing Systems 16, 2004.

[9] J. Lu, K. N. Plataniotis and N. Venetsanopoulos, "Face Recognition Using Kernel Direct Discriminant Analysis Algorithms", IEEE Trans. On Neural Networks, Aug. 2002.

[10] J. Luettin and G. Maitre. "Evaluation Protocol for the Extended M2VTS Database (XM2VTS)," DMI for Perceptual Artificial Intelligence, 1998.

[11] A. Martinez and R. Benavente. "The AR Face Database", http://rvl1.ecn.purdue.edu/~aleix/aleix_faceDB.html, 2003.

[12] A. Shashua and A. Levin. "Linear Image Coding for Regression and Classification using the Tensor-rank Principle", IEEE Conf. on Computer Vision and Pattern Recognition (CVPR), Dec. 2001, Hawaii.

[13] T. Sim, S. Baker, and M. Bsat. "The CMU Pose, Illumination, and Expression (PIE) Database", Proceedings of the IEEE International Conference on Automatic Face and Gesture Recognition, May, 2002.

[14] M. Turk and A. Pentland. "Face Recognition Using Eigenfaces", IEEE Conference on Computer Vision and Pattern Recognition, Maui, Hawaii, 1991.

[15] M. Vasilescu and D. Terzopoulos, "Multilinear Subspace Analysis for Image Ensembles",
      Proc. Computer Vision and Pattern Recognition Conf. (CVPR '03), Vol.2, June, 2003,
      93-99.
[16] X. Wang and X. Tang. "A unified framework for subspace face recognition," IEEE Trans.
      Pattern Analysis and Machine Intelligence, vol. 26, No. 9, 2004, pp. 1222 – 1228.
[17] W. Wilks. "Mathematical Statistics", Wiley, New York, 1963.
[18] M. Yang, "Kernel Eigenfaces vs. Kernel Fisherfaces: Face Recognition Using Kernel
      Methods", in Proc. of the 5th Int. Conf. on Automatic Face and Gesture Recognition,
      Washington D. C., May 2002.
[19] S. Yan, D. Xu, B. Zhang and H. Zhang. "Graph Embedding: A General Framework for
      Dimensionality Reduction", Proc. Computer Vision and Pattern Recognition Conf. 2005.
[20] J. Ye, R. Janardan, C. Park, and H. Park. "An optimization criterion for generalized dis-
      criminant analysis on undersampled problems", IEEE Transactions on Pattern Analysis
      and Machine Intelligence, V. 26, pp. 982-994, 2004.

Learning Nonlinear Manifolds from Time Series

Ruei-Sung Lin[1,*], Che-Bin Liu[1,**], Ming-Hsuan Yang[2],
Narendra Ahuja[1], and Stephen Levinson[1]

[1] University of Illinois at Urbana-Champaign, Urbana, IL 61801, USA
[2] Honda Research Institute, Mountain View, CA 94041, USA

Abstract. There has been growing interest in developing nonlinear dimension-ality reduction algorithms for vision applications. Although progress has been made in recent years, conventional nonlinear dimensionality reduction algorithms have been designed to deal with stationary, or independent and identically dis-tributed data. In this paper, we present a novel method that learns nonlinear mapping from time series data to their intrinsic coordinates on the underlying manifold. Our work extends the recent advances in learning nonlinear manifolds within a global coordinate system to account for temporal correlation inherent in sequential data. We formulate the problem with a dynamic Bayesian network and propose an approximate algorithm to tackle the learning and inference problems. Numerous experiments demonstrate the proposed method is able to learn nonlin-ear manifolds from time series data, and as a result of exploiting the temporal correlation, achieve superior results.

1 Introduction

Dimensionality reduction algorithms has been successful applied to vision problems for decades. Yet many tasks can be better approached with nonlinear methods, and re-cently there has been growing interests in developing nonlinear dimensionality reduc-tion (NLDR) algorithms for vision applications. Nonlinear dimensionality reduction aims at representing high dimensional data with low dimensional intrinsic parameters. For data assumed to be distributed along a low dimensional nonlinear manifold, solving NLDR is equivalent to recovering their intrinsic coordinates. There exist two main ap-proaches that transform data to their intrinsic parameters within a global coordinate sys-tem. Embedding methods such as Isomap [1] and LLE [2] find the intrinsic coordinates on the manifold from a set of samples. However, one limitation is that these algorithms discover the underlying embeddings rather than mapping functions from observed data. An alternative approach is to find a nonlinear mapping between the data and their intrin-sic coordinates, either with a combination of local linear models [3][4][5], or a single nonlinear function [6][7][8].

All the abovementioned methods assume that the observed data samples are station-ary or independent, identically (i.i.d.) distributed. However, numerous real world ap-plications, e.g., object tracking and motion synthesis, entail analyzing continuous data sequences where strong temporal correlation inherent in samples should be taken into

---

* Current affiliation: Motorola Labs, Schaumburg, IL 60196.
** Current affiliation: Epson Research & Development Inc., Palo Alto, CA 94304.

A. Leonardis, H. Bischof, and A. Pinz (Eds.): ECCV 2006, Part II, LNCS 3952, pp. 245–256, 2006.
© Springer-Verlag Berlin Heidelberg 2006

consideration. Consequently, it is essential to extend a conventional NLDR algorithm to account for temporal dependence in the data, thereby discovering sample dynamics along the manifold.

Few attempts have been made to tackle the NLDR problems for time series. Examples include [9] that extends the standard generative topographic mapping to handle sequential data within the hidden Markov model framework, [10] that modifies the Isomap algorithm with heuristics to find the underlying embedding from data sequences, and [8] which applies a semi-supervised regression model to learn nonlinear mapping from temporal data. Nevertheless, these algorithms are mainly concerned with learning the nonlinear embedding or mapping functions. Less effort is made to model the dynamic process of the intrinsic coordinates on the manifold.

In this paper, we address both nonlinear dimensionality reduction with bidirectional projection and the dynamics of time series data within a single statistical framework. We propose a model that learns the nonlinear mapping from time series that is capable of performing dynamic inference. Building on the work on the global coordination model [3] which provides a generative approach for the nonlinear mapping with a mixture of factor analyzers, we extend this graphical model to a dynamic Bayesian network (DBN) by adding links among the intrinsic coordinates to account for temporal dependency. Although the exact inference of this model is intractable, we exploit unique properties of nonlinear mapping within the global coordination model and propose an efficient approximate algorithm. We show that by applying this approximate algorithm, this DBN becomes a generalized Kalman filter for nonlinear manifold where model parameters are constantly adjusted.

We take a variational learning approach to estimate model parameters. Given initial values of the parameters, we use our approximate inference algorithm to estimate the statistics of latent variables. Then based on these statistics, we update the model parameters in the DBN. With this iterative process, the learning algorithm converges to a local optimum. For concreteness, we demonstrate the merits of this DBN with applications such as object tracking and video synthesis in which it is essential to model the sample dynamics on the underlying manifold.

The rest of this paper is organized as follows. We first briefly review the global coordination model [3] in Section 2. Next, we present an extension of this model to a DBN in which temporal correlation is taken into consideration in Section 3. Based on this DBN, we propose an approximate inference method and a learning algorithm for model parameters. Experimental results on synthetic and real world applications are presented in Section 4. We conclude this paper with discussions on the proposed model and future work in Section 5.

2   Global Coordination of Local Linear Models

The global coordination model is an extension of mixture of factor analyzers in which latent variables are aligned in a global coordinate system. Denote $y \in \mathcal{R}^D$ the observed data, s the index of the selected linear model, and $z_s \in \mathcal{R}^d$ the latent variables in the s-th local linear model. The joint probability of these parameters is:

$$P(y, z_s, s) = P(y|z_s, s)P(z_s|s)P(s) \tag{1}$$

in which $P(s)$ is the prior probability of local model s, $P(z_s|s)$ is a zero mean univariate Gaussian, i.e., $P(z_s|s) = \mathcal{N}(0, I_d)$, and $P(y|z_s, s)$ is defined by a factor analyzer:

$$P(y|z_s, s) = \frac{1}{\sqrt{(2\pi)^D |\Psi_s|}} \exp(-\frac{1}{2}(y - \Lambda_s z_s - \mu_s)^T \Psi_s^{-1}(y - \Lambda_s z_s - \mu_s)) \quad (2)$$

Since the latent variable z_s is defined within the local coordinate system of s-th local model, the global coordination algorithm transforms z_s to the corresponding intrinsic parameter within a global coordinate system. Let g denote the global coordinate of data y that is generated from s-th local linear model with z_s, the transformation is defined by

$$g(s, z_s) = A_s z_s + \kappa_s, \quad P(g|s, z_s) = \delta(g - A_s z_s - \kappa_s) \quad (3)$$

where A_s is a full ranked matrix to ensure a bidirectional mapping, and κ_s is an offset. Given this model, the mapping from y to g is described by:

$$P(g|y) = \sum_s P(g|y, s)P(s|y) \quad (4)$$

where

$$P(g|y, s) = \int P(g|s, z_s)P(z_s|s, y)dz_s \quad (5)$$

and the mapping from g to y is defined as:

$$P(y|g) = \sum_s P(y|g, s)P(s|g). \quad (6)$$

Although $P(g|y)$ and $P(y|g)$ are in the form of mixture of Gaussians, the distributions of $P(g|y)$ and $P(y|g)$ are expected to be unimodal since ideally the mapping between g and y should be one to one. For example given two mixture components s_i and s_j, the posterior distributions for global coordinates of a data point computed by (6) should be as identical as possible since g is the global coordinate of y. That is, $P(g|y, s_i)$ should be close to $P(g|y, s_j)$ as possible, i.e., $P(g|y, s_i) \approx P(g|y, s_j)$. This unimodal constraint is imposed in learning the global coordination of local linear models by Roweis et al. [3], and we take a similar approach. For mappings between y and g, $E[P(g|y)]$ and $E[P(y|g)]$ are used in this work.

Learning the global coordination model is equivalent to estimating parameters $\{(\Lambda_s, \mu_s, A_s, \kappa_s)\}$ from a set of observed data. This is an ill-posed problem since global coordinates of the data set are unknown. A few methods have been recently been proposed to address this issue. Wang et. al. [5] apply Isomap [1] to obtain global coordinates of the data, and learn the model parameters by solving a regression problem. Roweis et. al. [3] present an algorithm in which a regularization term is introduced to enforce the alignment constraints, and model parameters are estimated using variational algorithms. Nevertheless, both approaches have limitations as the method in [5] requires a good Isomap embedding, and the algorithm in [3] might have serious local minimal problems. In addition, both methods assume observations are i.i.d. samples without taking the temporal dependence into consideration.

3 Dynamic Global Coordination Model

To account for the temporal relationship among data samples, we incorporate the global coordination method into a dynamic model. Now observations $\{y_t\}$ are a temporal sequence generated from a Markovian process $\{g_t\}$ and the mapping from g_t to y_t is based on (6). The resulting dynamic Bayesian network is depicted in Figure 1.

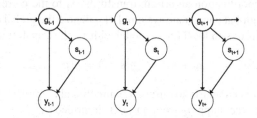

Fig. 1. Our dynamic Bayesian networks that is based on the temporal dependency among the global coordinates

3.1 Inference

We now provide the inference algorithms for the model. Although the DBN shown in Figure 1 is structurally complex, it becomes a simple state-space model if we marginalize out s_t at each time step.

$$P(g_t|y_{1:t}) \propto \sum_{s_t} P(y_t|g_t, s_t)P(s_t|g_t) \int P(g_t|g_{t-1})P(g_{t-1}|y_{1:t-1})dg_{t-1}$$

$$= P(y_t|g_t) \int P(g_t|g_{t-1})P(g_{t-1}|y_{1:t-1})dg_{t-1} \tag{7}$$

Note that $P(y_t|g_t)$ is composed of a mixture of Gaussians. If we compute (7) directly for exact inference, the number of mixtures in the posterior distribution will grow exponentially as the time index increases, thereby making the problem intractable. As discussed earlier, the ideal mapping between y and g at any time instance should be one to one. For efficient inference, we apply the first order Generalized Pseudo Bayesian (GPB) algorithm [11] to approximate $P(y_t|g_t)$, which can be shown to be the best single Gaussian approximation in the KL sense.

In this work, we compute $P(y_t|g_t)$ with Bayes rule

$$P(y_t|g_t) = \frac{P(g_t|y_t)P(y_t)}{P(g_t)} \tag{8}$$

and neglect the effect of $P(g_t)$ for the reason that will be explained in the next section. That is, we approximate $P(y_t|g_t)$ using the joint probability $P(y_t, g_t)$. Since $P(y_t)$ is a constant with known y_t, we carry out GPB approximation using $P(g_t|y_t)$.

Let (μ_t, Σ_t) denote the mean and the covariance matrix of the Gaussian that we use to approximate $P(g_t|y_t)$, and likewise $P(g_t|y_t, s_t) \sim \mathcal{N}(\mu_t^s, \Sigma_t^s)$. From (4), (μ_t, Σ_t) can be estimated by minimizing the weighted KL-distance:

$$(\mu_t, \Sigma_t) = \arg\min_{\mu,\Sigma} \sum_s P(s_t|y_t) KL(\mathcal{N}(\mu_t^s, \Sigma_t^s)||\mathcal{N}(\mu, \Sigma)). \tag{9}$$

and the analytic solution is

$$\mu_t = \sum_s P(s_t|y_t)\mu_t^s, \quad \Sigma_t = \sum_s P(s_t|y_t)\left(\Sigma_t^s + (\mu_t - \mu_t^s)(\mu_t - \mu_t^s)^T\right). \tag{10}$$

In our work, the dynamic model is set to be $P(g_t|g_{t-1}) = \mathcal{N}(Cg_{t-1}, \hat{Q})$ where C is the system matrix. Since $P(y_t|g_t)$ and $P(g_t|g_{t-1})$ are now both Gaussians, as a result the posterior distribution $P(g_t|y_{1:t})$ in (7) is also a Gaussian.

Let $P(g_t|y_{1:t}) \sim \mathcal{N}(g_t^t, \Sigma_t^t)$ and $P(g_t|y_{1:t-1}) \sim \mathcal{N}(g_t^{t-1}, \Sigma_t^{t-1})$. It can be shown that in our dynamic Bayesian network,

$$g_t^{t-1} = Cg_{t-1}^{t-1}, \quad \Sigma_t^{t-1} = C\Sigma_t^{t-1}C^T + \hat{Q}, \tag{11}$$

and

$$\Sigma_t^t = \left((\Sigma_t^{t-1})^{-1} + \Sigma_t^{-1}\right)^{-1} \tag{12}$$

$$g_t^t = \Sigma_t^t\left((\Sigma_t^{t-1})^{-1}g_t^{t-1} + \Sigma_t^{-1}\mu_t\right) \tag{13}$$

Likewise, it follows that for the cases of smoothing and lag-one smoothing with our model:

$$\mu_t^T = \mu_t^t + J_t(\mu_{t+1}^T - \mu_{t+1}^t) \tag{14}$$

$$\Sigma_t^T = \Sigma_t^t + J_t\left(\Sigma_{t+1}^T - \Sigma_{t+1}^t\right)J_t^T \tag{15}$$

$$J_t = \Sigma_t^t C^T [\Sigma_{t+1}^t]^{-1} \tag{16}$$

$$\Sigma_{t,t-1}^T = \Sigma_t J_{t-1}^T + J_t\left(\Sigma_{t+1,t}^T - C\Sigma_t^t\right)J_{t-1}^T \tag{17}$$

where $\Sigma_{t,t-1}^T = E\left[(g_t - \mu_t^T)(g_{t-1} - \mu_{t-1}^T)^T|y_{1:T}\right]$.

It should be emphasized that although our filtering and smoothing procedures are similar to the ones used in standard Kalman filter, our model is a generalized filter. While Kalman filter performs dynamic inferences on a linear manifold, our model extends this framework and performs dynamic inference on a nonlinear manifold. Therefore, unlike a standard Kalman filter which uses a fixed Gaussian for the measurement function $P(y_t|g_t)$, in our model μ_t and Σ_t are adaptively updated according to y_t to account for the nonlinearity on the manifold as in shown in (10).

3.2 Learning

We take a variational approach to learn the model parameters. Let $\theta = \{(\Lambda_s, \mu_s, A_s, \kappa_s, \Psi_s), C, \hat{Q}\}$ denote the set of model parameters. Using Jensen's inequality,

$$\log P(y_{1:T}|\theta) \geq \Phi = \sum_{s_{1:T}} \int Q(g_{1:T}, s_{1:T}|\theta) \log\left(\frac{P(y_{1:T}, g_{1:T}, s_{1:T}|\theta)}{Q(g_{1:T}, s_{1:T}|\theta)}\right) dg_{1:T} \tag{18}$$

We first define a proper function Q and then learn the model parameters using an EM algorithm. Starting with the initial value $\theta^{(0)}$, in the E-step we maximize Φ with respect to $Q(g_{1:T}, s_{1:T}|\theta^{(0)})$. In the M-step we fix Q and update the model parameters θ to maximize Φ. This iterative procedure continues until it reaches convergence.

In this work, we factorize $Q(g_{1:T}, s_{1:T}|\theta)$ into two components:

$$Q(g_{1:T}, s_{1:T}|\theta) = Q(s_{1:T}|\theta)Q(g_{1:T}|\theta) \tag{19}$$

For $Q(g_{1:T}|\theta)$, we want it to be close to $P(g_{1:T}|y_{1:T}, \theta)$ as possible. Let $\tilde{P}(g_{1:T}|y_{1:T}, \theta)$ denote the approximation of $P(g_{1:T}|y_{1:T}, \theta)$ computed by our inference algorithm discussed in Section 3.1, and set $Q(g_{1:T}|\theta) = \tilde{P}(g_{1:T}|y_{1:T}, \theta)$. For $Q(s_{1:T}|\theta)$, we further factorize it to $Q(s_{1:T}|\theta) = \prod_{t=1}^{T} Q(s_t|\theta)$, and define $Q(s_t|\theta) = q_{s,t}$ where $q_{s,t}$ is a scalar.

It follows that,

$$\begin{aligned}
\Phi = &\sum_{t=1}^{T}\sum_{s=1}^{S} q_{s,t} \int \tilde{P}(g_t|y_{1:T}, \theta) \log P(y_t, g_t, s_t|\theta) dg_t \\
&+ \sum_{t=2}^{T} \int \tilde{P}(g_t, g_{t-1}|y_{1:T}, \theta) \log P(g_t|g_{t-1}) dg_t dg_{t-1} \\
&- \sum_{t=1}^{T}\sum_{s=1}^{S} q_{s,t} \log q_{s,t} - \int \tilde{P}(g_{1:T}|y_{1:T}, \theta) \log \tilde{P}(g_{1:T}|y_{1:T}, \theta) dg_{1:T}
\end{aligned} \tag{20}$$

Notice that in the E-step we do not compute $\tilde{P}(g_{1:T}|y_{1:T}, \theta)$, but rather $\tilde{P}(g_t|y_{1:T}, \theta)$ and $\tilde{P}(g_t, g_{t-1}|y_{1:T}, \theta)$ for all t. With known $\tilde{P}(g_t|y_{1:T}, \theta)$, the dynamic model is factorized into T global coordination models at each time instance, and $q_{s,t}$ is:

$$q_{s,t} = \frac{\exp(-\mathcal{E}_{s,t})}{\sum_s \exp(-\mathcal{E}_{s,t})}, \quad \mathcal{E}_{s,t} = \int \tilde{P}(g_t|y_{1:T}, \theta) \log P(y_t, g_t, s_t|\theta) dg_t \tag{21}$$

In the M-step with known $\tilde{P}(g_t|y_{1:T}, \theta)$ and $q_{s,t}$, the model parameters are updated as follows. Let $q_s = \sum_t q_{s,t}$,

$$P(s) = q_s / \sum_s q_s \tag{22}$$

$$\kappa_s = q_s^{-1} \sum_t q_{s,t} \mu_t^T \tag{23}$$

$$\mu_s = q_s^{-1} \sum_t q_{s,t} y_t \tag{24}$$

Also denote $y_{s,t} = y_t - \mu_s$, $g_{s,t} = \mu_t^T - \kappa_s$, $M_s = \sum_t q_{s,t} y_{s,t} g_{s,t}^T$ and $N_s = \sum_t q_{s,t}[\Sigma_t^T + g_{s,t} g_{s,t}^T]$, we obtain the remaining model parameters in θ:

$$\Lambda_s = M_s N_s^{-1} A_s \tag{25}$$

$$[\Psi_s]_i = q_s^{-1} \sum_t q_{s,t} \left\{ [y_{s,t} - \Lambda_s A_s^{-1} g_{s,t}]_i^2 + [\Lambda_s A_s^{-1} \Sigma_t^T A_s^{-T} \Lambda_s^T]_i \right\} \tag{26}$$

$$A_s^{-1} = (I + \Lambda_s^T \Psi_s^{-1} \Lambda_s)^{-1} \{ A_s^T q_s + \Lambda_s^T \Psi_s^{-1} M_s \} N_s^{-1} \tag{27}$$

As for the dynamic model, denote $D_{t,t-1} = \Sigma_{t,t-1}^T + (\mu_t^T)(\mu_{t-1}^T)^T$ and $D_t^T = \Sigma_t^T + (\mu_t^T)(\mu_t^T)^T$:

$$C_{new} = \left[\sum_{t=2}^{T} D_{t,t-1}^T \right] \left[\sum_{t=2}^{T} D_{t-1}^T \right]^{-1} \tag{28}$$

$$\hat{Q}_{new} = \frac{1}{T-1} \sum_{t=2}^{T} (D_t^T - C_{new} D_{t,t-1}) \tag{29}$$

These equations bear similarities to the work by Roweis et al. [3], but at its core they are rather different by design. In our model, the estimation of g_t is conditioned on the whole observation sequence $y_{1:T}$, i.e., $\tilde{P}(g_t|y_{1:T}, \theta)$, whereas in [3] the estimation of g_t is conditioned on a single, i.i.d. sample y_t. That is, our model is developed within a dynamic context in which temporal correlation is taken into consideration.

Note that in our algorithm, when factorizing $P(y_{1:T}, g_{1:T}, s_{1:T})$,

$$P(y_{1:T}, g_{1:T}, s_{1:T}) = P(g_1) \prod_{t=2}^{T} P(g_t|g_{t-1}) \prod_{t=1}^{T} P(y_t|s_t, g_t) P(s_t|g_t) \tag{30}$$

we use joint probability $P(s_t, g_t)$ instead of $P(s_t|g_t)$. Neglecting $P(g_t)$ here makes the model consistent with our inference procedure described in the previous section. As a matter of fact, $P(g_t)$ has little effect on computing $\log \left(P(y_{1:T}, g_{1:T}, s_{1:T}|) / \tilde{P}(g_{1:T} | y_{1:T}) \right)$ since $P(g_t)$ in $P(y_{1:T}, g_{1:T}, s_{1:T})$ and $\tilde{P}(g_{1:T}|y_{1:T})$ can be canceled out.

4   Experiments

We apply the proposed algorithm to learn nonlinear manifolds and sample dynamics from time series for a few applications. Comparative studies are carried out to show the merits of the proposed method that takes temporal dependence into design, thereby better recovering the underlying manifold from time series data. More experimental results are available on our web site (http://www.ifp.uiuc.edu/~rlin1/dgcm.html).

4.1   Synthetic Data

We first test our algorithm with a synthetic data set generated from a 2D manifold and embedded in a 3D space as shown in Figure 2. The data points are generated by a 2D random walk, similar to the data set tested in [8], in a rectangle area $[0, 5] \times [-3, 3]$, and then embedded in 3D by a mapping function $f(x, y) = (x, |y|, \sin(\pi y)(y^2 + 1)^{-2} + 0.3y)$. Notice that this data set is challenging as it is difficult to estimate the neighborhood structure around the neck where the manifold is folded.

The second and third columns of Figure 2 show the results using the method by Roweis et al [3] and our algorithm. Notice that without taking the temporal information into consideration, the random walk path on the 2D manifold cannot be recovered correctly and thereby the 3D lifted points near the neck region are tangled together.

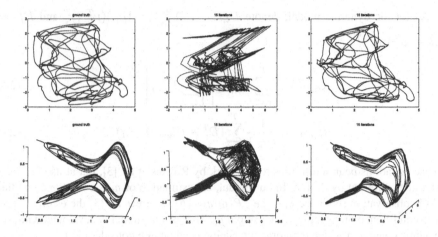

Fig. 2. Synthetic data: (left column) ground truth data points generated from a random walk path in 2D and its embedding in 3D space. (middle column) recovered 2D manifold and its 3D lifting using the method by Roweis et al. after 15 iterations [3]. (right column) recovered 2D manifold and its 3D lifting using parameters after 15 iterations.

Compared to the ground truth on the first column, our method recovers the 2D manifold better than the unsupervised nonlinear manifold learning algorithm without taking temporal dependence into consideration. In contrast to the semi-supervised method presented in [8], our algorithm is able to discover the underlying 2D manifold from 3D time series as the temporal correlation is exploited in estimating local neighborhood structures without any supervision.

4.2   Object Tracking

We apply the proposed dynamic model to an object tracking problem based on appearance. Images of an object appearance are known to be embedded on a nonlinear manifold, and a sequence of observations is expected to form a smooth trajectory on the manifold. Exploiting this strong temporal dependency, we can better track an object by exploring the trajectory of the mapped global coordinates on the appearance manifold from observed images. The graphical model for object tracking is shown in Figure 3 where x_t is the video frame at time t, location parameters l_t specifies the location of the tracked object in x_t, and g_t is the global coordinates of the object's appearance in x_t.

The state vector includes the location parameters and the global coordinates of the observed image, thereby making it ineffective to employ a simple particle filter for tracking. However, we can factorize the posterior as:

$$P(l_t, g_t | y_{1:t}) = P(g_t | x_{1:t}, l_t) P(l_t | x_{1:t}) \tag{31}$$

Using our inference algorithm (Section 3.1), $P(g_t | x_{1:t}, l_t)$ is approximated as an Gaussian distribution. Therefore, our tracker can sample particles only on l_t and model $P(g_t | x_{1:t}, l_t)$ using an analytical distribution. That is, our tracker can use Rao-Blackwellized particle filter (RBPF) [12] for efficient tracking.

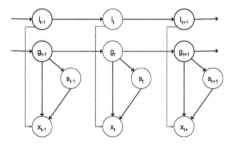

Fig. 3. Extension of our dynamic global coordination model for object tracking. Based on this model, we apply Rao-Blackwellized particle filter for efficient tracking.

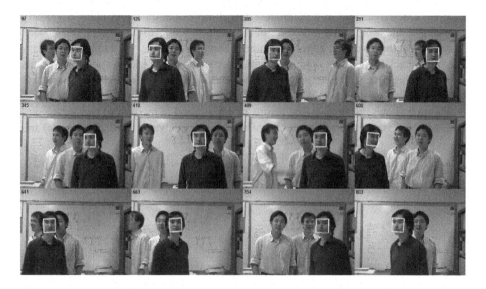

Fig. 4. Tracking results (left to right on each row): a target with large pose variation and moving in close proximity of similar faces. Our algorithm is able to track the target person in different pose, without confusing with other people.

We test our model on a face tracking experiment which undergoes large pose variations. In our tracking video, there are other faces around the target object. We first test the video using a baseline tracker that tracks location parameters l_t only, and use a mixture of factor analyzers as the measurement function. The result shows that this tracker might track the wrong target when the two faces are close. On the other hand, our tracker is able to track the target well even though several similar objects appear in close proximity because we exploit the temporal dependency in the appearance images of the target (i.e., global coordinates). Figure 4 shows the tracking results using the proposed method. More detail on incorporating a RBPF into our dynamic model and experimental results are available on our web page.

4.3   Video Synthesis

We demonstrate merits of the proposed algorithm on a video synthesis problem. The image sequences are taken from a database of textured motion [13] where most videos have 170 by 115 pixel resolution and contain 120 to 150 frames. Such problem has been referred to a dynamic texture problem where scene appearance is modeled in a linear subspace [14]. However, scene appearance is usually complex and rarely linear. In addition, for a short video, thus a sparse data set, temporal correlations between image frames offer additional information to robustly learn its underlying low-dimensional manifold.

In our experiment, we learn the nonlinear manifold of scene appearance using our proposed algorithm by setting the system matrix C in our dynamic model to be an identity matrix, i.e., $P(g_t|g_{t-1}) = \mathcal{N}(g_{t-1}, \hat{Q})$. For each sequence, we model the underlying scene dynamics as a continuous low-dimensional trajectory along a globally coordinated manifold using a mixture of 20-dimensional factor analyzers. From each learned trajectory, we then generate synthesized videos by drawing samples and mapping them back to the image space. Note that care needs to be taken in sampling points along the learned trajectory to prevent drifts. Otherwise the synthesized images may not look realistic.

Figure 5 shows the synthesized results of our method (a mixture of two factor analyzers for river sequence and a mixture of three factor analyzers for flag sequence) and

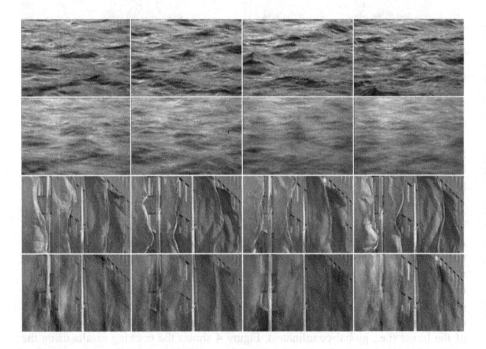

Fig. 5. Synthesized results by our method (first and third rows) and the dynamic texture algorithm (second and fourth rows). Clearly the images synthesized by our method are significantly crisper than the ones generated by the dynamic texture algorithm.

the dynamic texture approach [14]. More videos and details of our sampling algorithm can be found on our web page.

Clearly the images synthesized by our method (first and third rows) are significantly crisper than the ones generated by the dynamic texture algorithm (second and fourth rows). The results are not surprising as complex scene dynamics inherent in videos can be better modeled on a globally coordinated nonlinear manifold rather than a linear dynamic system (LDS). Although the closed-loop LDS approach [15] improves results by [14], it also models scene appearance in a linear subspace and therefore cannot synthesize high-quality videos of complex scenes such as our flag example.

5 Concluding Remarks

Numerous vision problems entail analyzing time series where the underlying nonlinear manifold as well as strong temporal correlation among the data should be learned and exploited. In this paper, we extend the global coordination model within a dynamic context to learn the nonlinear manifolds and the dynamics inherent in time series data. Positing this problem within a Bayesian framework, we present an approximate algorithm for efficient inference and parameter learning. The proposed algorithm finds numerous applications from which the merits are demonstrated. Our future work includes finding better initialization methods in learning model parameters, and applying the proposed algorithm to other problem domains.

Acknowledgments

We thank David Forsyth and the anonymous reviewers for their valuable comments. The support of the Office of Naval Research under grant N00014-03-1-0107 is gratefully acknowledged.

References

1. Tenenbaum, J.B., de Silva, V., Langford, J.C.: A global geometric framework for nonlinear dimensionality reduction. Science **290** (2000) 2319–2323
2. Roweis, S., Saul, L.: Nonlinear dimensionality reduction by locally linear embedding. Science **290** (2000) 2323–2326
3. Roweis, S., Saul, L., Hinton, G.E.: Global coordination of local linear models. In: Advances in Neural Information Processing Systems. Volume 14. (2001) 889–896
4. Brand, M.: Charting a manifold. In: Advances in Neural Information Processing Systems. Volume 15. (2002) 961–968
5. Wang, Q., Xu, G., Ai, H.: Learning object intrinsic structure for robust visual tracking. In: Proceedings of IEEE Conference on Computer Vision and Pattern Recognition. Volume 2. (2003) 227–234
6. Elgammal, A., Lee, C.S.: Inferring 3d body pose from silhouettes using activity manifold learning. In: Proceedings of IEEE Conference on Computer Vision and Pattern Recognition. Volume 2. (2004) 681–688
7. Urtasun, R., Fleet, D.J., Hertzmann, A., Fua, P.: Priors for people tracking from small training sets. In: Proceedings of IEEE International Conference on Computer Vision. (2005) 403–410

8. Rahimi, A., Recht, B., Darrell, T.: Learning appearance manifolds from video. In: Proceedings of IEEE Conference on Computer Vision and Pattern Recognition. Volume 1. (2005) 868–875
9. Bishop, C.M., Hinton, G.E., Strachan, I.G.: GTM through time. In: Proceedings of IEE Fifth International Conference on Artificial Neural Networks. (1997) 11–116
10. Jenkins, O.C., Mataric, M.: A spatio-temporal extension to Isomap nonlinear dimension reduction. In: Proceedings of International Conference on Machine Learning. (2004 441–448
11. Bar-Shalom, Y., Li, X.: Estimation and Tracking: Principles, Techniques, and Software. Artech House (1993)
12. Khan, Z., Balch, T., Dellaert, F.: A Rao-Blackwellized particle filter for eigentracking. In: Proceedings of IEEE Conference on Computer Vision and Pattern Recognition. Volume 2. (2004) 980–986
13. Szummer, M.: MIT temporal texture database. (ftp://whitechapel.media.mit.edu/pub/szummer/temporal-texture/)
14. Soatto, S., Doretto, G., Wu, Y.: Dynamic textures. In: Proceedings of IEEE International Conference on Computer Vision. Volume 2. (2001) 439–446
15. Yuan, L., Wen, F., Liu, C., Shum, H.Y.: Synthesizing dynamic texture with closed-loop linear dynamic system. In: Proceedings of European Conference on Computer Vision. Volume 2. (2004) 603–616

Accelerated Convergence Using Dynamic Mean Shift

Kai Zhang[1], Jamesk T. Kwok[1], and Ming Tang[2]

[1] Department of Computer Science,
The Hong Kong University of Science and Technology,
Clear Water Bay, Kowloon, Hong Kong
{twinsen, jamesk}@cs.ust.hk
[2] National Laboratory of Pattern Recognition,
Institute of Automation, Chinese Academy of Sciences,
Beijing 100080, China
tangm@nlpr.ia.ac.cn

Abstract. Mean shift is an iterative mode-seeking algorithm widely used in pattern recognition and computer vision. However, its convergence is sometimes too slow to be practical. In this paper, we improve the convergence speed of mean shift by dynamically updating the sample set during the iterations, and the resultant procedure is called *dynamic mean shift* (DMS). When the data is locally Gaussian, it can be shown that both the standard and dynamic mean shift algorithms converge to the same optimal solution. However, while standard mean shift only has linear convergence, the dynamic mean shift algorithm has superlinear convergence. Experiments on color image segmentation show that dynamic mean shift produces comparable results as the standard mean shift algorithm, but can significantly reduce the number of iterations for convergence and takes much less time.

1 Introduction

Mean shift is a nonparametric, iterative mode-seeking algorithm widely used in pattern recognition and computer vision. It was originally derived by Fukunaga and Hostetler [1] for nonparametric density gradient estimation, and was later generalized by Cheng [2]. Recent years have witnessed many successful applications of mean shift in areas such as classification [3, 4], image segmentation [5, 6], object tracking [7] and video processing [8].

In a general setting [2], there are two data sets involved in mean shift, namely, the sample (or data) set $\mathcal{S}$, and the "cluster centers" set $\mathcal{T}$. In the standard mean shift algorithm [2], $\mathcal{T}$ evolves iteratively by moving towards the mean, as $\mathcal{T} \leftarrow \mathbf{mean}(\mathcal{T})$. Here, $\mathbf{mean}(\mathcal{T}) = \{\mathbf{mean}(\mathbf{x}) : \mathbf{x} \in \mathcal{T}\}$,

$$\mathbf{mean}(\mathbf{x}) = \frac{\sum_{s \in \mathcal{S}} K(\mathbf{s} - \mathbf{x}) w(\mathbf{s}) \mathbf{s}}{\sum_{s \in \mathcal{S}} K(\mathbf{s} - \mathbf{x}) w(\mathbf{s})},$$

K is the kernel and w is the weight function. The algorithm terminates when a fixed point $\mathbf{mean}(\mathcal{T}) = \mathcal{T}$ is reached.

A. Leonardis, H. Bischof, and A. Pinz (Eds.): ECCV 2006, Part II, LNCS 3952, pp. 257–268, 2006.

However, the mean shift algorithm often converges too slowly to be practical on large-scale applications [9]. Works on improving its convergence are relatively few. Recently, Fashing and Tomasi [10] showed that mean shift is closely related to optimization methods, particularly Newton's method and bound optimization. They conjectured that information on the shape of the kernel K can be used to tighten the bound for faster convergence. However, the difficulty is in finding a bound which is computationally easy to maximize [10]. On a more practical side, Yang et al. [9] proposed an improved mean shift algorithm based on quasi-Newton methods. This leads to faster convergence. However, approximating the Hessian matrix and determining the search direction in each iteration become more computationally expensive. Consequently, while the complexity of the standard mean shift algorithm is only linear in the data dimensionality, that of Yang et al.'s method rises to cubic.

In this paper, we improve the convergence speed of the mean shift algorithm by dynamically updating the sample set S, depending on its behavior in the iterations. In particular, we focus on the case where S is updated iteratively based on the set of cluster centers T computed in the previous step. This modified procedure will be called *dynamic* mean shift (DMS), as opposed to the traditional, *static* mean shift (SMS) algorithm. We will prove that, under certain conditions, this procedure gradually shrinks the data set, and converges asymptotically to the same density maximum as SMS, but with a higher convergence rate (to be more specific, superlinear convergence instead of linear convergence). Besides, the DMS algorithm is also very efficient in that its computational complexity is only linear in the data dimensionality.

The rest of this paper is organized as follows. Section 2 gives a brief review on the traditional mean shift algorithm. Section 3 then describes the dynamic mean shift algorithm. A detailed discussion on its faster convergence properties will be presented in Section 4. Experimental results on color image segmentation are presented in Section 5, and the last section gives some concluding remarks.

2   Standard Mean Shift Algorithm

Let $S = \{\mathbf{x}_1, \mathbf{x}_2, \ldots, \mathbf{x}_n\}$ be a set of samples in the d-dimensional space $\mathbb{R}^d$. Using kernel k, the kernel density estimator at $\mathbf{x}$ is given by [3]

$$\hat{f}_K(\mathbf{x}) = \frac{1}{n} \sum_{i=1}^{n} |\mathbf{H}_i|^{-\frac{1}{2}} K(\mathbf{x} - \mathbf{x}_i; \mathbf{H}_i),$$

where $\mathbf{H}_i$ is a symmetric, positive definite $d \times d$ bandwidth matrix associated with $\mathbf{x}_i$. Instead of referring to kernel K, it is often convenient to use its *profile* $k : [0, \infty) \to \mathbb{R}$ defined by $K(\mathbf{x}; \mathbf{H}) = k(\mathbf{x}'\mathbf{H}^{-1}\mathbf{x})$. To emphasize its dependence on $\mathbf{H}$, we also sometimes write $k(\mathbf{x}'\mathbf{H}^{-1}\mathbf{x})$ as $k_{\mathbf{H}}(\mathbf{x})$.

The *mean shift vector* is defined as [1, 2]

$$\mathbf{m}(\mathbf{x}) \equiv \mathbf{H}_{\mathbf{x}} \cdot \frac{\sum_{i=1}^{n} \mathbf{H}_i^{-1}\mathbf{x}_i |\mathbf{H}_i|^{-\frac{1}{2}} k'_{\mathbf{H}_i}(\mathbf{x} - \mathbf{x}_i)}{\sum_{i=1}^{n} |\mathbf{H}_i|^{-\frac{1}{2}} k'_{\mathbf{H}_i}(\mathbf{x} - \mathbf{x}_i)} - \mathbf{x}, \tag{1}$$

where $\mathbf{H}_{\mathbf{x}}^{-1} \equiv \frac{\sum_{i=1}^{n} \mathbf{H}_{i}^{-1}|\mathbf{H}_{i}|^{-\frac{1}{2}} k'_{\mathbf{H}_{i}}(\mathbf{x}-\mathbf{x}_{i})}{\sum_{i=1}^{n} |\mathbf{H}_{i}|^{-\frac{1}{2}} k'_{\mathbf{H}_{i}}(\mathbf{x}-\mathbf{x}_{i})}$. It can be shown that [3]:

$$\mathbf{m}(\mathbf{x}) = \frac{c}{2}\mathbf{H}_{\mathbf{x}}\frac{\hat{\nabla}f_{K}(\mathbf{x})}{\hat{f}_{G}(\mathbf{x})}, \qquad (2)$$

where $\hat{f}_{G}(\mathbf{x})$ is the density estimator using kernel $G(\mathbf{x}; \mathbf{H}_{i}) = -ck'(\mathbf{x}'\mathbf{H}_{i}^{-1}\mathbf{x})$, and c is a normalization constant such that G integrates to one. Equation (2) shows that the mean shift vector $\mathbf{m}(\mathbf{x})$ points towards the direction of maximum increase of the density. Therefore, if we initialize the cluster center set $T^{(t)} = \{\mathbf{y}_{1}^{(t)}, \mathbf{y}_{2}^{(t)}, \cdots, \mathbf{y}_{n}^{(t)}\}$ as the original sample set S, i.e., $T^{(0)} = S$, then the iteration

$$\mathbf{y}^{(t+1)} = \mathbf{y}^{(t)} + \mathbf{m}(\mathbf{y}^{(t)}), \quad t = 0, 1, 2, \ldots$$

can be used to locate the local maxima of the estimated density of S.

In this paper, we are particularly interested in the case where the data set follows the normal distribution $\mathcal{N}(\boldsymbol{\mu}, \boldsymbol{\Sigma})$, with mean $\boldsymbol{\mu}$ and covariance matrix $\boldsymbol{\Sigma}$. This is an assumption commonly used in the theoretical analysis of the mean shift algorithm (e.g., [3]), and is expected to hold at least locally. As will be shown in the sequel, this allows us to obtain the convergence rates explicitly for both the standard and dynamic versions of the mean shift algorithm.

Suppose the use of the Gaussian kernel with fixed bandwidth $\mathbf{H}$ in the mean shift algorithm. Under the normality assumption of the data distribution, the estimated density $\hat{f}_{K}$ will also be a Gaussian asymptotically, with mean $\boldsymbol{\mu}$ and covariance $\boldsymbol{\Sigma} + \mathbf{H}$ [11]. Plug this into (2), then the mean shift vector $\mathbf{m}(\mathbf{x})$ at $\mathbf{x}$ becomes (note that when K is Gaussian, we have $c = 2$ and $K = G$ in (2) [3])

$$\mathbf{m}(\mathbf{x}) = \mathbf{H}\frac{\hat{\nabla}f_{G}(\mathbf{x})}{\hat{f}_{G}(\mathbf{x})} = -\mathbf{H}(\mathbf{H} + \boldsymbol{\Sigma})^{-1}(\mathbf{x} - \boldsymbol{\mu}). \qquad (3)$$

3   The Dynamic Mean Shift Algorithm

In the standard mean shift algorithm, the data set S is fixed and only the cluster center set T is updated. Each point in T will keep moving based on the mean shift vector (1) at each step until it reaches a local maximum, and then another point in T will be processed. In contrast, the dynamic mean shift algorithm updates both S and T. In each DMS iteration, after moving all the points in T along their mean shift vectors for one step, we then use the shifted cluster center set T' to replace the data set S for the next iteration. More formally, denote the sample set and the cluster center set at the tth iteration by $S^{(t)} = \{\mathbf{x}_{1}^{(t)}, \mathbf{x}_{2}^{(t)}, \ldots, \mathbf{x}_{n}^{(t)}\}$ and $T^{(t)} = \{\mathbf{y}_{1}^{(t)}, \mathbf{y}_{2}^{(t)}, \ldots, \mathbf{y}_{n}^{(t)}\}$ respectively. They are first initialized as $T^{(0)} = S^{(0)} = S$, the original set of samples. At the tth iteration, we have

$$\mathbf{y}_{i}^{(t+1)} = \frac{\sum_{\mathbf{x}_{i}^{(t)} \in S^{(t)}} K\left(\mathbf{x}_{i}^{(t)} - \mathbf{y}_{i}^{(t)}\right)\mathbf{x}_{i}^{(t)}}{\sum_{\mathbf{x}_{i}^{(t)} \in S^{(t)}} K\left(\mathbf{x}_{i}^{(t)} - \mathbf{y}_{i}^{(t)}\right)}, \quad i = 1, 2, \ldots, n.$$

The shifted cluster center set $T^{(t+1)} = \{\mathbf{y}_1^{(t+1)}, \mathbf{y}_2^{(t+1)}, \ldots, \mathbf{y}_n^{(t+1)}\}$ then replaces the sample set at the next iteration,

$$S^{(t+1)} = T^{(t+1)},$$

and the whole process is repeated until a fixed state $S^{(t+1)} = S^{(t)}$, or equivalently, $T^{(t+1)} = T^{(t)}$, is reached.

In the following Sections, we study some properties of this dynamic mean shift algorithm. As mentioned in Section 1, a key advantage of this dynamic version over the standard one is its faster convergence. Hence, we will postpone and dedicate its detailed discussion to Section 4.

3.1   Gradual Shrinking of the Samples

As mentioned in Section 1, we assume that the samples follow a d-dimensional normal distribution, i.e., $S = S^{(0)} \sim \mathcal{N}(\boldsymbol{\mu}, \boldsymbol{\Sigma})$ with mean $\boldsymbol{\mu} \in \mathbb{R}^d$ and covariance matrix $\boldsymbol{\Sigma} \in \mathbb{R}^{d \times d}$. Recall that this assumption holds at least in the local neighborhood of each sample in S. Moreover, we assume the use of a Gaussian kernel with fixed bandwidth $\mathbf{H}$ (which is positive definite). Besides, the identity matrix will be denoted $\mathbf{I}$, vector/matrix transpose denoted by the superscript $'$, and the determinant of a matrix $\mathbf{A}$ by $|\mathbf{A}|$.

Proposition 1. *Assume that the sample set $S^{(t)} = \{\mathbf{x}_i^{(t)}\}$ at the tth iteration follows $\mathcal{N}(\boldsymbol{\mu}, \boldsymbol{\Sigma}^{(t)})$. After one dynamic mean shift iteration, the updated sample set $S^{(t+1)} = \{\mathbf{x}_i^{(t+1)}\}$ still follows a normal distribution $\mathcal{N}(\boldsymbol{\mu}, \mathbf{P}^{(t)} \boldsymbol{\Sigma}^{(t)} (\mathbf{P}^{(t)})')$, where*

$$\mathbf{P}^{(t)} = \mathbf{I} - \mathbf{H}(\mathbf{H} + \boldsymbol{\Sigma}^{(t)})^{-1}. \tag{4}$$

Proof. After one iteration, sample $\mathbf{x}_i^{(t)}$ will be moved, according to (3), to

$$\mathbf{x}_i^{(t+1)} = \mathbf{x}_i^{(t)} + \mathbf{m}(\mathbf{x}_i^{(t)}) = \left(\mathbf{I} - \mathbf{H}(\mathbf{H} + \boldsymbol{\Sigma}^{(t)})^{-1}\right)\mathbf{x}_i^{(t)} + \mathbf{H}(\mathbf{H} + \boldsymbol{\Sigma}^{(t)})^{-1}\boldsymbol{\mu}$$

$$= \mathbf{P}^{(t)}\mathbf{x}_i^{(t)} + \mathbf{C}^{(t)}, \tag{5}$$

where $\mathbf{P}^{(t)} = \mathbf{I} - \mathbf{H}(\mathbf{H} + \boldsymbol{\Sigma}^{(t)})^{-1}$, and $\mathbf{C}^{(t)} = \mathbf{H}(\mathbf{H} + \boldsymbol{\Sigma}^{(t)})^{-1}\boldsymbol{\mu}$. Hence, $S^{(t)}$ and $S^{(t+1)}$ are related by a linear transform. Since $S^{(t)}$ follows $\mathcal{N}(\boldsymbol{\mu}, \boldsymbol{\Sigma}^{(t)})$, $S^{(t+1)}$ also follows a normal distribution with mean $\mathbf{P}^{(t)}\boldsymbol{\mu} + \mathbf{C}^{(t)} = (\mathbf{I} - \mathbf{H}(\mathbf{H} + \boldsymbol{\Sigma}^{(t)})^{-1})\boldsymbol{\mu} + \mathbf{H}(\mathbf{H} + \boldsymbol{\Sigma}^{(t)})^{-1}\boldsymbol{\mu} = \boldsymbol{\mu}$ and variance $\mathbf{P}^{(t)}\boldsymbol{\Sigma}^{(t)}(\mathbf{P}^{(t)})'$. $\square$

Remark: In other words, after one dynamic mean shift iteration, the sample mean will remain unchanged while the covariance is updated to

$$\boldsymbol{\Sigma}^{(t+1)} = \mathbf{P}^{(t)} \boldsymbol{\Sigma}^{(t)} (\mathbf{P}^{(t)})'. \tag{6}$$

Moreover, as the original data set S is assumed to be a Gaussian, all the $S^{(t)}$'s will also remain as Gaussians.

Before a detailed study on how the covariance $\boldsymbol{\Sigma}^{(t)}$ of the sample set $S^{(t)}$ evolves in the DMS iterations, we first introduce two useful lemmas.

Lemma 1. *Given two symmetric, positive semi-definite matrices* $\mathbf{A}$ *and* $\mathbf{B}$, *all the eigenvalues of* $\mathbf{C} = \mathbf{AB}$ *are non-negative.*

Proof. Let the eigen-decompositions of $\mathbf{A}$ and $\mathbf{B}$ be $\mathbf{A} = \mathbf{Q}_1 \Lambda_1 \mathbf{Q}_1'$, $\mathbf{B} = \mathbf{Q}_2 \Lambda_2 \mathbf{Q}_2'$, where the columns of $\mathbf{Q}_1$ and $\mathbf{Q}_2$ contain the eigenvectors of $\mathbf{A}$ and $\mathbf{B}$, respectively, and the diagonal matrices Λ_1 and Λ_2 contain their corresponding eigenvalues. Let $\mathbf{Q} = \mathbf{Q}_1' \mathbf{Q}_2$ (which is orthonormal) and $\mathbf{M} = \mathbf{Q}_1' \mathbf{C} \mathbf{Q}_1$, then $\mathbf{M} = \mathbf{Q}_1' \mathbf{Q}_1 \Lambda_1 \mathbf{Q}_1' \mathbf{Q}_2 \Lambda_2 \mathbf{Q}_2' \mathbf{Q}_1 = \Lambda_1 \mathbf{N}$, where $\mathbf{N} = \mathbf{Q} \Lambda_2 \mathbf{Q}'$ is positive semi-definite. Let λ be an eigenvalue of $\mathbf{M}$, i.e., $\mathbf{M} v = \lambda v$. Note that $\mathbf{M}$ and $\overline{\mathbf{N}} \equiv \Lambda_1^{1/2} \mathbf{N} \Lambda_1^{1/2}$ share the same eigenvalues as $\mathbf{M} v = \lambda v \Rightarrow \Lambda_1 \mathbf{N} v = \lambda v \Rightarrow (\Lambda_1^{1/2} \mathbf{N} \Lambda_1^{1/2})(\Lambda_1^{-1/2} v) = \lambda (\Lambda_1^{-1/2} v)$, and $\mathbf{M}$ also has the same eigenvalues with $\mathbf{C}$, therefore $\mathbf{C}$ must have the same eigenvalues with $\overline{\mathbf{N}}$. Moreover, $v' \overline{\mathbf{N}} v = v' \Lambda_1^{1/2} \mathbf{N} \Lambda_1^{1/2} v = (\Lambda_1^{1/2} v)' \mathbf{N} (\Lambda_1^{1/2} v) \geq 0$ for all v's as $\mathbf{N}$ is positive semi-definite. Therefore, $\overline{\mathbf{N}}$ is positive semi-definite, and all its eigenvalues will be non-negative. So all the eigenvalues of $\mathbf{C}$ must be non-negative, too. $\square$

Lemma 2. *For the* $\mathbf{P}^{(t)}$ *defined in (4),* $|\mathbf{P}^{(t)}| < 1$ *for all t.*

Proof. From (4),

$$\mathbf{P}^{(t)} = \mathbf{I} - \left((\mathbf{H} + \boldsymbol{\Sigma}^{(t)})\mathbf{H}^{-1}\right)^{-1} = \mathbf{I} - \left(\mathbf{I} + \boldsymbol{\Sigma}^{(t)}\mathbf{H}^{-1}\right)^{-1}. \qquad (7)$$

Let the eigen-decomposition of $\boldsymbol{\Sigma}^{(t)} \mathbf{H}^{-1}$ be

$$\boldsymbol{\Sigma}^{(t)} \mathbf{H}^{-1} = \mathbf{U}^{(t)} \boldsymbol{\Lambda}^{(t)} (\mathbf{U}^{(t)})^{-1}, \qquad (8)$$

where the columns of $\mathbf{U}^{(t)}$ contain the eigenvectors of $\boldsymbol{\Sigma}^{(t)} \mathbf{H}^{-1}$, and $\boldsymbol{\Lambda}^{(t)} = \mathrm{diag}(\lambda_1, \lambda_2, \ldots, \lambda_d)$ contains its eigenvalues. Then $\mathbf{P}^{(t)}$ can be decomposed as (after some simplifications)

$$\mathbf{P}^{(t)} = \mathbf{I} - (\mathbf{I} + \boldsymbol{\Sigma}^{(t)} \mathbf{H}^{-1})^{-1} = \mathbf{U}^{(t)} \left(\mathbf{I} - (\mathbf{I} + \boldsymbol{\Lambda}^{(t)})^{-1}\right) (\mathbf{U}^{(t)})^{-1},$$

and its determinant can be written as

$$|\mathbf{P}^{(t)}| = |\mathbf{I} - (\mathbf{I} + \boldsymbol{\Lambda}^{(t)})^{-1}| = \left| \mathrm{diag}\left(\frac{\lambda_1}{1 + \lambda_1}, \frac{\lambda_2}{1 + \lambda_2}, \cdots, \frac{\lambda_d}{1 + \lambda_d}\right) \right| \qquad (9)$$

Note that both $\boldsymbol{\Sigma}^{(t)}$ and $\mathbf{H}$ (and hence $\mathbf{H}^{-1}$) are symmetric, positive semi-definite. Therefore, using Lemma 1, the eigenvalues of $\boldsymbol{\Sigma}^{(t)} \mathbf{H}^{-1}$ must all be non-negative, i.e., $\lambda_i \geq 0$. Hence, except for the meaningless case where all λ_i's are zero, we always have $|\mathbf{P}^{(t)}| < 1$ according to (9). $\square$

Proposition 2. $|\boldsymbol{\Sigma}^{(t)}|$ *decreases with t, and* $\lim_{t \to \infty} |\boldsymbol{\Sigma}^{(t)}| = \lim_{t \to \infty} |\mathbf{P}^{(t)}| = 0$.

Proof. From (6), $|\boldsymbol{\Sigma}^{(t)}| = |\boldsymbol{\Sigma}^{(t-1)}| \cdot |\mathbf{P}^{(t-1)}|^2$. Since $|\mathbf{P}^{(t)}| < 1$ by Lemma 2, $|\boldsymbol{\Sigma}^{(t)}|$ will decrease with t. Suppose $|\mathbf{P}^{(\tau)}| = \max_{0 \leq \tau \leq t-1} |\mathbf{P}^{(t)}|$. Note that $|\mathbf{P}^{(t)}| < 1$ for all $t \geq 0$, therefore $|\mathbf{P}^{(\tau)}| < 1$. So we have

$$|\boldsymbol{\Sigma}^{(t)}| = |\boldsymbol{\Sigma}^{(0)}| \cdot \prod_{j=0}^{t-1} |\mathbf{P}^{(j)}|^2 < |\boldsymbol{\Sigma}^{(0)}| \cdot \prod_{j=0}^{t-1} |\mathbf{P}^{(\tau)}|^2 = |\boldsymbol{\Sigma}^{(0)}| \cdot |\mathbf{P}^{(\tau)}|^{2t} \to 0,$$

as $t \to \infty$. Using (8), we have $|\boldsymbol{\Lambda}^{(t)}| = |\boldsymbol{\Sigma}^{(t)}\mathbf{H}^{-1}| = |\boldsymbol{\Sigma}^{(t)}|/|\mathbf{H}|$. Therefore,

$$\lim_{t \to \infty} |\boldsymbol{\Lambda}^{(t)}| = \lim_{t \to \infty} |\boldsymbol{\Sigma}^{(t)}\mathbf{H}^{-1}| = 0, \tag{10}$$

and all the eigenvalues (λ_is) of $\boldsymbol{\Sigma}\mathbf{H}^{-1}$ will also approach zero. Substituting this into (9), we then have $\lim_{t \to \infty} |\mathbf{P}^{(t)}| = 0$. $\qquad\square$

Remark: Note that $|\boldsymbol{\Sigma}^{(t)}|$ can be used as a measure of the spread of the sample set $\mathcal{S}^{(t)}$ at the tth iteration. Hence, Proposition 2 implies that $\mathcal{S}^{(t)}$ gradually shrinks, and the amount of shrinkage is determined by $|\mathbf{P}^{(t)}|$.

Due to the data shrinkage, a fixed-bandwidth kernel will cover more and more samples in $\mathcal{S}^{(t)}$ as the algorithm proceeds. In other words, using a fixed bandwidth here achieves the same effect as using a variable bandwidth in the standard mean shift algorithm on the original sample set $\mathcal{S}$. Note that the use of variable bandwidth is often superior to the fixed bandwidth case [5].

On the other hand, as the amount of data shrinkage can differ significantly along different directions, this can lead to both very small and very large variance components. This can be problematic if the local covariance matrix of $\mathcal{S}^{(t)}$ is chosen as the bandwidth, as its inverse may be badly scaled. To avoid this numerical problem, one can simply replace the very small eigenvalues of the local covariance matrix by some small number.

3.2   Stopping Rule

The data shrinking behavior discussed in Section 3.1 also allows the design of more efficient stopping rules. As the samples $\mathbf{x}_i^{(t)}$'s move closer and closer towards the density peaks, so once a group of samples have converged inside a small window, they will converge to one point in the following iterations. From the clustering point of view, we will then have enough information to decide their class labels (as these samples must belong to the same class), and so the iterations for these samples can be stopped early. By removing these converged clusters, computations involved in the dynamic mean shift algorithm can be reduced. In comparison, the stopping criterion in standard mean shift is often based on the step length. Since samples usually move very slowly near the density peaks in the standard mean shift algorithm [6], our stopping rule can be much more effective.

3.3   Time Complexity

The complexities of both the standard and dynamic mean shift algorithms are $O(dsN^2)$, where d is the data dimensionality, s is the number of iterations required for convergence, and N is the number of samples. As will be shown in Section 4.2, DMS has superlinear convergence while SMS only has linear convergence. Hence, the number of iterations (s) required by DMS is typically much smaller than that by SMS. Moreover, the stopping rule discussed in Section 3.2 allows samples to be thrown away early near the end of the DMS iteration process. Thus, the number of samples (n) "actively" involved in the remaining computations gradually decreases, which further reduces the time complexity of the DMS algorithm.

One may be concerned that DMS has to move all the samples in order to update the data distribution, and this could be less efficient than the mean shift algorithm that only moves a group of selected samples [12]. Indeed, the dynamic updating of the sample distribution in DMS can be realized as well by only moving a small set of "representative" samples. By decomposing the data set into disjoint, spatially local subsets $Z_1, Z_2, \ldots, Z_m$, one can model the density at each local subset Z_i by a single Gaussian $\frac{n_i}{n}\mathcal{N}(\boldsymbol{\mu}_i, h^2\mathbf{I})$, where n_i and $\boldsymbol{\mu}_i$ are the size and mean of subset Z_i respectively, and h is the bandwidth of the kernel used in the density estimator [13]. The whole density distribution can then be modeled as a combination of these Gaussians $\frac{n_1}{n}\mathcal{N}(\boldsymbol{\mu}_1, h^2\mathbf{I}), \frac{n_2}{n}\mathcal{N}(\boldsymbol{\mu}_2, h^2\mathbf{I}), \ldots, \frac{n_m}{n}\mathcal{N}(\boldsymbol{\mu}_m, h^2\mathbf{I})$. In this variant of the DMS, we only have to shift the representatives $\boldsymbol{\mu}_i$'s, whose movement leads to the update of the corresponding Gaussians $\mathcal{N}_i$s, and hence the whole density function.

4   Convergence Properties of Dynamic Mean Shift

In Section 4.1, we will first show that both the original and dynamic mean shift algorithms converge asymptotically to the same optimal solution, when the data is locally Gaussian. We will then show in Section 4.2 that the dynamic mean shift algorithm has superlinear (and thus faster) convergence while the standard version only has linear convergence.

4.1   Asymptotic Convergence of Dynamic Mean Shift

In the following, we assume, as in Section 3.1, that the samples follow the d-dimensional normal distribution $\mathcal{N}(\boldsymbol{\mu}, \boldsymbol{\Sigma})$. This holds at least in the local neighborhood of each sample in $\mathcal{S}$. We then have the following property:

Proposition 3. *The dynamic mean shift procedure converges asymptotically to the mean $\boldsymbol{\mu}$.*

Proof. Using (3) and (7), we have

$$\mathbf{m}(\mathbf{x}^{(t)}) = -\mathbf{H}(\mathbf{H} + \boldsymbol{\Sigma}^{(t)})^{-1}(\mathbf{x}^{(t)} - \boldsymbol{\mu}^{(t)}) = -(\mathbf{I} + \boldsymbol{\Sigma}^{(t)}\mathbf{H}^{-1})^{-1}(\mathbf{x}^{(t)} - \boldsymbol{\mu}^{(t)}).$$

Moreover, from (10) in Proposition 2, we have $\lim_{t \to \infty} |\boldsymbol{\Sigma}^{(t)}\mathbf{H}^{-1}| = 0$. Therefore $\lim_{t \to \infty} \mathbf{m}(\mathbf{x}^{(t)}) = -(\mathbf{x}^{(t)} - \boldsymbol{\mu})$. Since $\boldsymbol{\mu}^{(t)} = \boldsymbol{\mu}$ by Proposition 1, one mean shift iteration will ultimately move all $\mathbf{x}^{(t)}$'s to $\mathbf{x}^{(t)} + \mathbf{m}(\mathbf{x}^{(t)}) = \boldsymbol{\mu}$, the mean of the original Gaussian. □

Remark: It is well-known that standard mean shift will find the mode of the underlying density, which is $\boldsymbol{\mu}$ in this case. Thus, both standard and dynamic mean shift converge to the same optimal solution asymptotically.

4.2 Convergence Rates

In this Section, we will show that DMS converges faster than the standard mean shift algorithm. But first, we will provide additional insight on the convergence of standard mean shift by the following 1-D example. Suppose that the data set is the 1-D Gaussian $\mathcal{N}(\mu, \sigma^2)$, the bandwidth of the Gaussian kernel is h^2, and that the iteration starts from $x^{(0)}$. Using (3), $m(x^{(0)}) = -\rho(x^{(0)} - \mu)$ where $\rho = \frac{h^2}{h^2 + \sigma^2}$. Then $x^{(0)}$ will be shifted to $x^{(1)} = x^{(0)} + m(x^{(0)}) = x^{(0)} - \rho(x^{(0)} - \mu)$. At the next iteration, the mean shift vector becomes $m(x^{(1)}) = -\rho(x^{(1)} - \mu) = -\rho(1 - \rho)(x^{(0)} - \mu)$, and $x^{(1)}$ is shifted to $x^{(2)} = x^{(1)} + m(x^{(1)})$, and so on. It is easy to show by induction that the mean shift vector is of the form $m^{(t)} = m(x^{(t)}) = -\rho(1 - \rho)^t (x^{(0)} - \mu)$. Note that $\{|m^{(t)}|\}_{t=1,2,\dots}$ is a geometric sequence that decreases monotonically, indicating slower and slower convergence. This is illustrated in Figure 1, where we set $\mu = 0$, $\sigma = 1$, $h = 0.1$, and $x^{(0)} = 3$. As can be seen, the step length indeed decreases monotonically. The corresponding step lengths for the dynamic mean shift algorithm are also shown in Figure 1. Note that not only is its step length usually much larger than that for standard mean shift, but it actually increases at the first few iterations.

In the following, we compare the convergence rates of DMS and SMS. In the optimization literature, convergence can be measured by how rapidly the iterates $\mathbf{z}^{(t)}$ converge in a neighborhood of the (local) optimum $\mathbf{z}^*$. If the error $\mathbf{e}^{(t)} = \mathbf{z}^{(t)} - \mathbf{z}^*$ behaves according to $\|\mathbf{e}^{(t+1)}\|_2 / \|\mathbf{e}^{(t)}\|_2^p \to c$, where $c > 0$ and $\|\cdot\|_2$ denotes the (vector) two-norm, then the *order of convergence* is defined to be pth order [14]. In particular, if $p = 1$, we have *first order* or *linear convergence*. Note that linear convergence can be equivalently defined as $\|\mathbf{e}^{(t+1)}\|_2 / \|\mathbf{e}^{(t)}\|_2 \leq c$. Faster convergence can be obtained if the local rate constant c tends to zero, i.e., $\|\mathbf{e}^{(t+1)}\|_2 / \|\mathbf{e}^{(t)}\|_2 \to 0$. This is also known as *superlinear convergence*.

As in previous sections, we will again focus on the case when the samples are normally distributed as $\mathcal{N}(\mu, \Sigma)$. Recall that Section 4.1 has shown that both DMS and SMS converge to the mean μ, and hence the optimum $\mathbf{z}^* = \mu$ here.

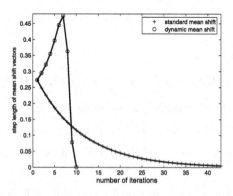

Fig. 1. Step lengths taken by DMS and SMS on a 1-D data set. Note that DMS converges in only 10 iterations.

Theorem 1. *SMS converges linearly, while DMS converges superlinearly.*

Proof. At the tth iteration, both DMS and SMS shift the current $\mathbf{x}^{(t)}$ to $\mathbf{x}^{(t+1)} = \mathbf{x}^{(t)} + \mathbf{m}(\mathbf{x}^{(t)})$. Using (3), we have

$$\mathbf{x}^{(t+1)} - \mathbf{x}^* = (\mathbf{x}^{(t)} - \boldsymbol{\mu}) - \mathbf{H}(\mathbf{H} + \boldsymbol{\Sigma})^{-1}(\mathbf{x}^{(t)} - \boldsymbol{\mu}) = \mathbf{P}^{(t)}(\mathbf{x}^{(t)} - \boldsymbol{\mu}),$$

with $\mathbf{P}^{(t)}$ defined in (4). Hence,

$$\frac{\|\mathbf{x}^{(t+1)} - \boldsymbol{\mu}\|_2}{\|\mathbf{x}^{(t)} - \boldsymbol{\mu}\|_2} = \frac{\|\mathbf{P}^{(t)}(\mathbf{x}^{(t)} - \boldsymbol{\mu})\|_2}{\|\mathbf{x}^{(t)} - \boldsymbol{\mu}\|_2} \leq \|\mathbf{P}^{(t)}\|_2,$$

by definition of the matrix two-norm[1] of $\mathbf{P}^{(t)}$ [15]. In SMS, the sample set $\mathcal{S}$ keeps unchanged. Therefore $\mathbf{P}^{(t)}$'s are all fixed at $\mathbf{P} = \mathbf{I} - \mathbf{H}(\mathbf{H} + \boldsymbol{\Sigma})^{-1}$, implying linear convergence for SMS. For DMS, we have $\lim_{t \to \infty} |\mathbf{P}^{(t)}| \to 0$ by Proposition 2, so all its eigenvalues will approach 0. Since $\|\mathbf{P}^{(t)}\|_2$ is the maximum singular value of $\mathbf{P}^{(t)}$, therefore $\|\mathbf{P}^{(t)}\|_2 \to 0$, i.e., DMS converges superlinearly. □

Here, we give an illustration on the numbers of iterations required for convergence in SMS and DMS. The data set follows the 1-D Gaussian $\mathcal{N}(0,1)$, and the bandwidth is chosen as $h = 0.5$. Figure 2(a) shows the number of iterations $N(x)$ when starting at different initial positions x's. As can be seen, DMS requires much fewer iterations than the standard mean shift algorithm. Moreover, since we know that the data set follows a normal distribution, we can also compute the average number of iterations by integrating $N(x)$ w.r.t. the (normal) density $G(x)$. Figure 2(b) plots the density-weighted number of iterations $N(x)G(x)$. The average number of iterations required by DMS is calculated to be roughly 70% less than that for SMS.

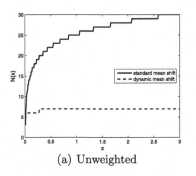
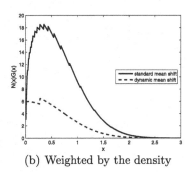

(a) Unweighted   (b) Weighted by the density

Fig. 2. Number of iterations required for convergence when starting the standard / dynamic mean shift algorithm at different positions

We now investigate the effect of the bandwidth on the number of iterations required for convergence. Again, we use the same 1-D data set that follows

---

[1] The matrix two-norm of a matrix $\mathbf{A}$ is defined as $\|\mathbf{A}\|_2 = \max_{\mathbf{x} \neq 0}\left\{\frac{\|\mathbf{A}\mathbf{x}\|_2}{\|\mathbf{x}\|_2}\right\}$. It is also equal to the maximum singular value of $\mathbf{A}$.

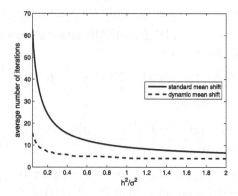

Fig. 3. The average number of iterations for convergence at various values of h^2/σ^2

$\mathcal{N}(0,1)$. As can be seen from Figure 3, DMS needs much fewer iterations than SMS when h^2/σ^2 varies from 0.1 to 2. In practice, h^2/σ^2 should be reasonably small, or else serious misclassifications may occur near the class boundaries.

5   Image Segmentation Experiments

In this Section, we compare the performance of dynamic and standard mean shift algorithms for color image segmentation. The segments are obtained by

Fig. 4. Segmentation results using SMS and DMS algorithms. Top: Original images; Middle: SMS segmentation results; Bottom: DMS segmentation results.

Table 1. Total wall time (in seconds) and the average number of iterations on the various image segmentation tasks

| | | SMS | | DMS | |
image	size	time	# iterations	time	# iterations
plane	321×481	2.62	15.79	1.84	11.86
eagle	321×481	10.03	21.78	4.77	10.79
house	192×255	12.65	20.40	6.43	10.84

clustering in the RGB feature space. The sample size, which is equal to the number of pixels in the image, can be very large (in the order of 100,000). Hence, instead of using/moving all the samples in the mean shift iterations, we only use a set of "representative" samples. As discussed in Section 3.3, the whole data set is first divided into m local subsets, each of them is modeled by a Gaussian $\gamma_i \mathcal{N}(\mathbf{u}_i, h_i^2 \mathbf{I})$. This step can be performed efficiently. Moreover, the number of clusters, m, is much smaller than the sample size. Only these m cluster means, each weighted by the γ_i, are used in the DMS and SMS algorithms. In the experiment, we use the Gaussian kernel with bandwidth $h^2\mathbf{I}$ ($h = 12$). All codes are written in VC++ and run on a 2.26GHz Pentium-III PC.

Figure 4 shows the segmentation results, and Table 1 shows the total wall time (from finding the local cluster representatives to mean shift clustering) and the number of iterations (averaged over all the cluster representatives). One can see that DMS obtains comparable segmentation results as SMS, but converges in much fewer iterations and takes much less time.

6   Conclusions

In this paper, we extend the mean shift algorithm by dynamically updating the set of samples during the iterations. This has the interesting property of gradually shrinking the sample set, and allows a fixed bandwidth procedure to achieve the same effect as variable bandwidth mean shift. More importantly, it allows faster convergence both in theory and practice. When the data is locally Gaussian, it is shown that dynamic mean shift converges to the same optimal solution as the standard version, but while standard mean shift can only converge linearly, the dynamic mean shift algorithm converges superlinearly. Experiments on color image segmentation show that dynamic mean shift produces comparable results as the standard mean shift approach, but the number of iterations and the elapsed time are both reduced by half.

Acknowledgement

This research has been partially supported by the Research Grants Council of the Hong Kong Special Administrative Region. Ming Tang is partially supported by NSFC (Grant No. 60318003 and 60572057).

268 K. Zhang, J.T. Kwok, and M. Tang

References

1. Fukunaga, K., Hostetler, L.: The estimation of the gradient of a density function, with applications in pattern recognition. IEEE Transactions on Information Theory **21** (1975) 32–40
2. Cheng, Y.: Mean shift, mode seeking, and clustering. IEEE Transactions on Pattern Analysis and Machine Intelligence **17** (1995) 790–799
3. Comaniciu, D.: An algorithm for data-driven bandwidth selection. IEEE Transactions on Pattern Analysis and Machine Intelligence **25** (2003) 281–288
4. Georgescu, B., Shimshoni, I., Meer, P.: Mean shift based clustering in high dimensions: A texture classification example. In: Proceedings of the International Conference on Computer Vision. (2003) 456–463
5. Comaniciu, D., Meer, P.: The variable bandwidth mean shift and data driven scale selection. In: Proc. ICCV. (2001) 438–445
6. Comaniciu, D., Meer, P.: Mean shift: A robust approach towards feature space analysis. IEEE Transactions on Pattern Analysis and Machine Intelligence **24** (2002) 603–619
7. Zivkovic, Z., Kröse, B.: An EM-like algorithm for color-histogram-based object tracking. In: Proceedings of the International Conference on Computer Vision and Pattern Recognition. Volume 1. (2004) 798–803
8. DeMenthon, D., Doermann, D.: Video retrieval using spatio-temporal descriptors pages. In: Proceedings of the Eleventh ACM International Conference on Multimedia. (2003) 508 – 517
9. Yang, C., Duraiswami, R., DeMenthon, D., Davis, L.: Mean-shift analysis using quasi-Newton methods. Proceedings of the International Conference on Image Processing **3** (2003) 447 – 450
10. Fashing, M., Tomasi, C.: Mean shift is a bound optimization. IEEE Transactions on Pattern Analysis and Machine Intelligence **27** (2005) 471–474
11. Stoker, T.: Smoothing bias in density derivative estimation. Journal of the American Statistical Association **88** (1993) 855–863
12. Comaniciu, D., Meer, P.: Distribution free decomposition of multivariate data. Pattern Analysis and Applications **2** (1999) 22–30
13. Zhang, K., Tang, M., Kwok, J.T.: Applying neighborhood consistency for fast clustering and kernel density estimation. In: Proceedings of the International Conference on Computer Vision and Pattern Recognition. (2005) 1001 – 1007
14. Fletcher, R.: Practical Methods of Optimization. Wiley, New York (1987)
15. Noble, B., Daniel, J.: Applied Linear Algebra. 3rd edn. Prentice-Hall, Englewood Cliffs, NJ (1988)

Efficient Belief Propagation with Learned Higher-Order Markov Random Fields

Xiangyang Lan[1,*], Stefan Roth[2,*], Daniel Huttenlocher[1], and Michael J. Black[2]

[1] Computer Science Department, Cornell University, Ithaca, NY, USA
{xylan, dph}@cs.cornell.edu
[2] Department of Computer Science, Brown University, Providence, RI, USA
{roth, black}@cs.brown.edu

Abstract. Belief propagation (BP) has become widely used for low-level vision problems and various inference techniques have been proposed for loopy graphs. These methods typically rely on ad hoc spatial priors such as the Potts model. In this paper we investigate the use of learned models of image structure, and demonstrate the improvements obtained over previous ad hoc models for the image denoising problem. In particular, we show how both pairwise and higher-order Markov random fields with learned clique potentials capture rich image structures that better represent the properties of natural images. These models are learned using the recently proposed Fields-of-Experts framework. For such models, however, traditional BP is computationally expensive. Consequently we propose some approximation methods that make BP with learned potentials practical. In the case of pairwise models we propose a novel approximation of robust potentials using a finite family of quadratics. In the case of higher order MRFs, with 2×2 cliques, we use an adaptive state space to handle the increased complexity. Extensive experiments demonstrate the power of learned models, the benefits of higher-order MRFs and the practicality of BP for these problems with the use of simple principled approximations.

1 Introduction

There are two current threads of research that are modernizing Markov random fields (MRFs) for machine vision. The first involves new algorithms based on belief propagation (BP) and graph cuts for performing approximate probabilistic (e. g., maximum *a posteriori*) inference on MRFs [1, 2, 3, 4, 5, 6]. These methods have extended the usefulness of MRFs by making inference tractable, but have often relied on ad hoc or hand-tuned models of spatial image structure with a limited spatial neighborhood structure (e. g., pairwise models). Such approaches have lacked the representational power needed to capture the rich statistics of natural scenes. The second line of research involves improving the expressive power of MRFs with higher-order models that are learned from data [7, 8, 9]. These approaches better capture the rich statistics of the natural world and

---

* The first two authors contributed equally to this work, authorship order was determined randomly.

A. Leonardis, H. Bischof, and A. Pinz (Eds.): ECCV 2006, Part II, LNCS 3952, pp. 269–282, 2006.
© Springer-Verlag Berlin Heidelberg 2006

provide a principled way of learning the model. Our goal is to combine these two lines of research to provide efficient algorithms for inference with rich, higher-order MRFs.

To that end we develop a series of principled approximations to the learned MRF models and to belief propagation. Throughout the paper we develop and test our solutions in the context of image denoising to illustrate the power of learned MRFs and the applicability of BP to these models. In particular, we exploit the recently proposed Field-of-Experts (FoE) model for learning MRFs from example data [9]. We start with the case of pairwise MRFs, where previous work on efficient inference schemes has relied on ad hoc potentials such as the Potts model [1] or the truncated quadratic [4]. While the FoE models exploit robust potentials that better match the image statistics, these potentials do not readily admit efficient inference. We develop an approximation method that, for a pairwise MRF, represents such robust potentials as a finite family of quadratics. With such a representation, the distance transform method of [4] can be employed for efficient inference. We apply the method to image denoising and find that the resulting algorithm is several times faster than regular BP, achieves a lower energy state, and is considerably more accurate than the ad hoc model proposed in [4]. We also note that in loopy graphs such as this, convergence of BP depends on the message passing scheme employed. We show that a randomized scheme helps achieve a lower energy state than synchronous updates.

It is often observed that maximum *a posteriori* (MAP) estimates using MRF models produce piecewise constant results. This is true in the case of pairwise cliques where the potential function is robust (i. e., it downweights outliers). Such results are due to the representational weakness of pairwise models, which are too local to capture the richness of natural image statistics. To alleviate these effects we use the FoE framework to learn higher-order models of images; in particular we learn an MRF with 2×2 cliques. While such a model produces much more natural results that are no longer piecewise constant, inference becomes much harder. Applying standard BP to MRFs with 2×2 cliques requires $\mathcal{O}(N^4)$ operations to compute each message, where N is the number of labels for each pixel. In case of image denoising, $N = 256$ making traditional BP algorithms impractical. Consequently we propose an approximate BP algorithm that uses an adaptive state space to reduce the number of states for each pixel, as well as a further state quantization that speeds up the message computations. Despite this approximation, the learned higher-order model outperforms learned pairwise MRF models, both visually and quantitatively.

In the following sections we introduce Markov random fields and loopy belief propagation along with our proposed approximations. We will review the related work in the context of our methods and their applicability. We present the results of experiments on image denoising that compare different MRF models as well as different BP methods.

2   Learning Markov Random Field Models of Images

In this paper we use two different types of Markov random fields to model the prior probability of images: pairwise MRFs and higher-order MRFs with larger, square-shaped cliques. The pairwise MRFs employed here are very similar to models that have been popular for a long time [10]; the higher-order MRFs follow the recently proposed Fields-of-Experts (FoE) approach [9]. Richer models of natural images have also been proposed on the basis of MRFs with multiple pairwise pixel interactions [11, 12]. We are not following this approach here, but a comparison of the benefits of these approaches deserves further study.

We assume that pixels in an image are represented as nodes V in a graph $G = (V, E)$. In the pairwise case, the set of edges E connects all nodes that are either horizontal or vertical neighbors. In the higher-order case, the set of edges fully connects all nodes in all possible square $m \times m$ image regions. The probability of an image $\mathbf{x}$ under such a Markov random field can be written as a product over all the maximal cliques C:

$$p(\mathbf{x}) = \frac{1}{Z} \prod_C \Psi(\mathbf{x}_C), \tag{1}$$

where $\mathbf{x}_C$ is the image region corresponding to clique C, Ψ is a positive potential function, and Z is a normalization term.

In the pairwise case, the potentials are typically defined as a function of the grayvalue difference of the two neighboring pixels. The grayvalue difference can be interpreted as a local approximation of the horizontal or vertical image gradient. The MRF model penalizes large gradients and so models the fact that images are often locally smooth. In the natural image statistics literature it has been observed that the marginal distribution of the image gradient is highly kurtotic [13]; marginal gradient histograms show substantial probability mass in the tails. This results from the fact that images occasionally show significant jumps in intensity that for example arise from object boundaries. In order to model this behavior, the pairwise MRF we use here relies on robust potentials based on Student t-distributions, which resemble the marginal statistics of the image gradient. If $x_{C,1}$ and $x_{C,2}$ are the two pixels for the pairwise clique $\mathbf{x}_C$, then we use the potential

$$\Psi_{\mathrm{pw}}(\mathbf{x}_C) = \left(1 + \frac{1}{2}\left(\frac{x_{C,1} - x_{C,2}}{\sigma}\right)^2\right)^{-\alpha}. \tag{2}$$

We will learn two separate parameter sets $(\sigma_{\mathrm{H}}, \alpha_{\mathrm{H}})$ and $(\sigma_{\mathrm{V}}, \alpha_{\mathrm{V}})$ for horizontal and vertical edges respectively, yielding a pairwise image prior $p_{\mathrm{pw}}(\mathbf{x})$.

The Fields-of-Experts framework [9] used in the higher-order MRF case models the clique potentials using a so-called Product of Experts (PoE) [14]. The idea behind the PoE is to model complex distributions as the product of several simpler expert distributions that each work on a low-dimensional subspace, in this case a linear 1D subspace. In the context of images, these linear 1D subspaces can be interpreted as linear filters $\mathbf{J}_i$ applied to the image patch $\mathbf{x}_C$.

It has been observed that, for a wide variety of linear filters, the statistics of the filter responses are highly kurtotic[13]. Consequently, following [9] we take the experts to be Student t-distributions. Assuming that we use K experts, we can write the prior probability of an image under the FoE model as

$$p_{m \times m}(\mathbf{x}) = \frac{1}{Z} \prod_C \prod_{i=1}^{K} \phi(\mathbf{J}_i^T \mathbf{x}_C; \alpha_i), \qquad (3)$$

where ϕ is an unnormalized t-distribution with parameter α_i:

$$\phi(\mathbf{J}_i^T \mathbf{x}_C; \alpha_i) = \left(1 + \frac{1}{2}(\mathbf{J}_i^T \mathbf{x}_C)^2\right)^{-\alpha_i}. \qquad (4)$$

Following [9], we trained both types of MRF models using a database of natural images [15]. In the case of the pairwise model we learn the parameters $\alpha_H, \alpha_V, \sigma_H$, and σ_V, while in the FoE case we learn the filters $\mathbf{J}_i$ as well as the expert parameters α_i. To make belief propagation inference tractable as detailed in Section 3, we restrict ourselves to 2×2 models and use 3 experts. We randomly cropped 2000 patches of 9×9 pixels out of the training database and found suitable parameters by (approximately) maximizing the likelihood of the data. The learning algorithm is based on stochastic gradient ascent, and uses the idea of contrastive divergence [16] to make it more efficient. Since the proposed pairwise MRF can be treated as special case of the FoE model, they can both be trained in essentially the same way. The learning procedure follows the description in [9], to which we refer the reader for more details.

3   Efficient Belief Propagation

Many low-level vision problems can be posed as problems of Bayesian inference, and can be described in the following common framework: Given some observed image $\mathbf{I}$, the goal is to estimate a hidden state $\mathbf{x}$ according to a posterior distribution $p(\mathbf{x} \mid \mathbf{I})$. The hidden state may, for example, correspond to a smoothed image in the case of image denoising, or to a dense disparity map in the case of stereo (where $\mathbf{I}$ in fact represents two images). Here a set of discrete labels is used to represent the state of each hidden variable. The posterior distribution of the hidden state $\mathbf{x}$ given the input image $\mathbf{I}$ is modeled as $p(\mathbf{x} \mid \mathbf{I}) = 1/Z \cdot p(\mathbf{I} \mid \mathbf{x}) \cdot p(\mathbf{x})$, where $p(\mathbf{I} \mid \mathbf{x})$ is the likelihood of the observed image given a hidden labeling and $p(\mathbf{x})$ is the prior probability over labelings. Rather than relying on ad hoc spatial priors, we use the learned priors introduced above, a pairwise prior $p_{pw}(\mathbf{x})$ and a higher-order prior $p_{2x2}(\mathbf{x})$. Because the normalization term Z is unknown and intractable to compute in general, we will sometimes refer to the energy $E(\mathbf{x}; \mathbf{I})$ of a labeling $\mathbf{x}$; that is, the unnormalized log-posterior. The energy is related to the posterior distribution through $p(\mathbf{x} \mid \mathbf{I}) = 1/Z \cdot \exp\{-E(\mathbf{x}; \mathbf{I})\}$. Note that maximizing the posterior probability is equivalent to minimizing the energy.

There are two basic ways of estimating this labeling, one of which is to compute the expectation of the posterior $p(\mathbf{x} \mid \mathbf{I})$ and the other is to compute the maximum (i. e., the MAP estimate). We consider both of these problems here, but use the former as a running example for discussing the proposed algorithms. In general finding exact solutions to these estimation problems is hard for loopy graphs, but approximation approaches based on graph cuts [1, 3, 17, 18] and loopy belief propagation [6, 18, 19] have been found to often work well in practice. The focus of this paper is the family of loopy belief propagation algorithms. In order to apply them to Bayesian inference problems, the posterior must factor into products over relatively small numbers of variables in order to be computationally feasible. In particular it is customary to require that the prior factor into a product of functions Ψ_h over small subsets of nodes C_h (cliques in the underlying hidden layer) and the likelihood factors into a product of functions Ψ_o over small subsets of nodes C_o (often individual nodes, e. g., in image denoising),

$$p(\mathbf{x}\,|\,\mathbf{I}) = \frac{1}{Z} \prod_{C_o} \Psi_o(\mathbf{x}_{C_o};\,\mathbf{I}) \prod_{C_h} \Psi_h(\mathbf{x}_{C_h}), \tag{5}$$

where $\mathbf{x}_{C_o}$ corresponds to the cliques of the likelihood and $\mathbf{x}_{C_h}$ corresponds to the cliques of the spatial prior. In the description of the message passing algorithm below, we will handle both types of cliques and potentials in a unified way, i. e., $p(\mathbf{x}\,|\,\mathbf{I}) = 1/Z \cdot \prod_C \Psi_C(\mathbf{x}_C;\,\mathbf{I})$.

Both pairwise and higher-order models can be considered in a common framework using factor graphs [19]. A factor graph is a bipartite graph with edges connecting two kinds of nodes, variable nodes and factor nodes. A variable node corresponds to an individual random variable x_i, while a factor node corresponds to a subset (clique) of random variables $\mathbf{x}_C$, whose potential function $\Psi_C(\mathbf{x}_C;\,\mathbf{I})$ is a specific term in the factorized form of the posterior distribution. Edges in the factor graph connect each factor node to those variables that are involved in its potential function. For models defined on the image grid, the x_i and the associated variable nodes can be seen as corresponding to image pixels, and the $\mathbf{x}_C$ and the associated factor nodes correspond to local neighborhoods (cliques) in the image. See Figure 3 for examples of factor graph representations for a pairwise MRF and a 2×2 MRF on an image grid. These graphical illustrations include nodes corresponding to the observed data at each pixel.

Belief propagation operates by passing messages between nodes until convergence (which is generally not guaranteed but is usually observed in practice). All message entries are usually initialized to the same value to represent an uninformative prior. We now turn to the message update rules for the sum-product BP algorithm on a factor graph [6, 19], in which case each iteration contains two types of message updates.

For the first type of message, a variable node i sends a message $n_{i \to C}(x_i)$ to a neighboring factor node C. To do so it computes the product of the messages received from its other neighboring factor nodes,

$$n_{i \to C}(x_i) = \prod_{C' \in \mathcal{N}(i) \setminus C} m_{C' \to i}(x_i), \tag{6}$$

where $\mathcal{N}(i) \setminus C$ denotes the neighboring factor nodes of i other than C.

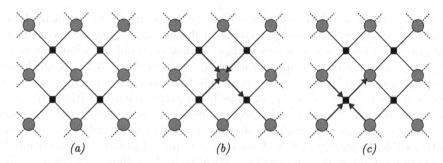

Fig. 1. *(a)* Factor graph structure of an image prior with 2 × 2 cliques. Red circles correspond to variable nodes (image pixels) and black squares correspond to factor nodes (cliques representing local neighborhood). *(b)* Message passing from a variable node to a factor node (cf. Eq. (6)). *(c)* Message passing from a factor node to a variable node (cf. Eq. (7)).

For the second type of message, a factor node C sends a message $m_{C \to i}$ to a neighboring variable node i. To do so it assembles all the messages received from its other neighboring variable nodes weighted with its associated potential function $\Psi_C(\mathbf{x}_C; \mathbf{I})$,

$$m_{C \to i}(x_i) = \sum_{\mathbf{x}_C \setminus x_i} \Psi_C(\mathbf{x}_C; \mathbf{I}) \prod_{i' \in \mathcal{N}(C) \setminus i} n_{i' \to C}(x_{i'}), \qquad (7)$$

where $\mathbf{x}_C \setminus x_i$ denotes the variables of $\mathbf{x}_C$ other than x_i. That is, $\mathbf{x}_C$ is the cross product space of a set of random variables and the summation is done over all the variables of that cross product space except x_i. Recall that $\Psi_C(\mathbf{x}_C; \mathbf{I})$ is the clique potential for clique C in Eq. (5).

We should note that in the pairwise case this factor graph approach results in the same calculations as the loopy belief propagation algorithms on a 4-connected grid that have recently been used by a number of researchers in computer vision (e.g., [4, 5, 20]).

These message updates are iterated until an equilibrium point is reached, at which point the belief of each individual variable node can be computed as

$$b_i(x_i) = \prod_{C \in \mathcal{N}(i)} m_{C \to i}(x_i). \qquad (8)$$

Taking the belief as an approximation of the marginal posterior probability, we can then estimate a state for each variable node by taking its expected value.

The sum-product technique that we have presented here approximates the marginal posterior probabilities of the variable nodes. In contrast, the max-product technique is used to approximately compute the MAP estimate. The main differences are the replacement of sums by maximizations in the message update equations, and the replacement of expectation by maximization to compute a final label for each variable node. The max-product formulation has often been used for pixel labeling problems such as stereo and image denoising, whereas the sum-product formulation may be more appropriate to interpolation problems where non-integer solutions may be desired.

The running time for either the sum-product or max-product BP algorithm on a factor graph is $\mathcal{O}(MN^k)$, where M is the number of image pixels, N is the number of possible labels for each pixel, and k is the maximum clique size. For problems like image denoising with $N = 256$ labels corresponding to image intensities, the computational cost is very large. In the next two subsections, we introduce simple but effective techniques to speed up BP algorithms for learned potentials of pairwise and 2×2 MRFs.

3.1 Pairwise MRFs

Standard belief propagation on a 4-connected grid for pairwise MRFs is in general still a computationally demanding task, because it requires $\mathcal{O}(M \cdot N^2)$ steps. It has recently been shown [4] that max-product belief propagation can be carried out more efficiently for pairwise MRFs with certain kinds of potentials by exploiting a distance transform technique. In these cases, the time complexity is linear rather than quadratic in the number of labels, i.e., $\mathcal{O}(MN)$. In particular, if the negative log of the pairwise potentials can be expressed as the lower envelope of (possibly truncated) quadratic or absolute value functions of the pairwise pixel difference then the distance transform technique can be applied.

We extend this work here by applying the distance transform technique to MRFs where the potentials have been learned from data. To that end, we exploit the fact that a large set of robust error functions can be written as the infimum over a family of quadratics as shown by Black and Rangarajan [21]. As discussed earlier, we model the pairwise potentials using Student-t distributions (see Eq. (2)). The t-distribution has the corresponding robust error function $\rho(y) = \alpha \log \left(1 + \frac{1}{2} \left(\frac{y}{\sigma}\right)^2\right)$, where y is the grayvalue difference between neighboring pixels. A derivation similar to the one in [21] reveals that this robust function can be written as $\rho(y) = \inf_z E(y, z)$ with

$$E(y, z) = \frac{y^2}{2\sigma^2} z + z - \alpha + \alpha \log \frac{\alpha}{z}, \qquad (9)$$

which is a quadratic function in y and where z is an "outlier process". Instead of writing the negative log of the potential as the infimum over all possible z values in the range $[0, \alpha]$, we approximate it as the minimum (lower envelope) over a fixed, discrete set of z values. Given a fixed number k of quadratics, we find a good approximation by a simple local optimization of the Kullback-Leibler divergence between the learned t-distribution and the probability density corresponding to the lower envelope of the quadratics. We compute the KL divergence using a discrete histogram with range $[-255, 255]$ and 10 bins per gray level. To improve numerical stability we modify the log of the z values and upper bound the z values with a simple penalty function so that $z \leq \alpha$. Figure 2

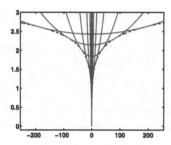 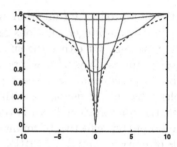

Fig. 2. Approximation of the negative log of a Student-t distribution as the lower envelope of 8 quadratics. *(left)* Full grayvalue range $[-255, 255]$. *(right)* Detail of the same approximation over the range $[-10, 10]$.

shows how the negative log of a t-distribution is approximated with 8 quadratics. In the experimental results section, we compare these approximations using 4 and 8 quadratics (using the efficient linear-time distance transform algorithm) with the actual t-distribution (using the conventional quadratic-time algorithm). For details of the distance transform method the reader is referred to [4].

3.2   Higher-Order MRFs

Our experiments show that pairwise models as just described suffer from the problem that the optimal solution is piecewise constant (see Figure 4). To overcome this problem, we have to move to using higher-order MRF priors as introduced in Section 2 and illustrated in Figure 1(a). Unfortunately, applying the factor graph belief propagation algorithm directly is infeasible for such models. For $m \times m$ maximal cliques the summation (or maximization in the max-product case) in Eq. (7) is taken over $N^{m \cdot m - 1}$ terms, which is prohibitively expensive even in the 2×2 case with $N = 256$ labels.

In order to alleviate this problem, we devised a simple, but effective adaptive state space procedure. In many applications, we can fairly reliably estimate a grayvalue range for each pixel that will contain the optimal solution as well as most of the probability mass of the belief. To determine the working range for denoising problems, we find the minimal and maximal grayvalue in a 3×3 search window around each pixel. To avoid overestimating the range in the presence of noise, we preprocess the image for the range determination step with a very small amount of Gaussian smoothing ($\sigma = 0.7$); denoising is carried out on the original image. When performing the sum-product or max-product operation for a specific pixel i within a factor node C with size 2×2 (see Eq. (7)), we discretize the label set for the other 3 member pixels into h bins over that range, and only consider those h^3 different combinations. Furthermore, we can reduce the computation time for the message updates from Eq. (6) and Eq. (7) by restricting them to the determined range. By using this adaptively quantized state space, the time complexity of BP for a 2×2 MRF model decreases to $\mathcal{O}(M \cdot N \cdot h^3)$.

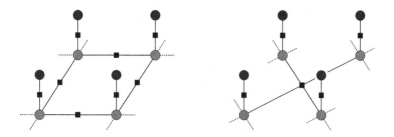

Fig. 3. Graphical model structure for image reconstruction. The round nodes represent observed (blue) and hidden (light red) variables; the square nodes are the factor nodes indicating the clique structure. *(left)* Pairwise Markov random field for image denoising. *(right)* Field-of-Experts model for denoising with 2 × 2 cliques in the prior.

4   Belief Propagation and Image Denoising

To focus on the effects of the different models and our approximations we choose an inference problem with a simple likelihood term: image denoising with known additive noise. As it is common in the denoising literature (e. g., [22]) we assume that images have been contaminated with artificial i. i. d. Gaussian noise, which also facilitates quantitative evaluation. We furthermore assume that the standard deviation σ is known; we use $\sigma = 10$ and $\sigma = 20$ here. We can thus write the likelihood of noisy image $\mathbf{I}$ given the true image $\mathbf{x}$ as

$$p(\mathbf{I} \mid \mathbf{x}) \propto \prod_{j=1}^{M} e^{-\frac{(x_j - I_j)^2}{2\sigma^2}}. \tag{10}$$

When we combine the Gaussian likelihood with the pairwise prior $p_{\mathrm{pw}}(\mathbf{x})$, the posterior distribution has the form of a pairwise Markov random field, where each observed pixel I_j is connected to a hidden, true pixel x_j, and the hidden pixels are all connected to their horizontal and vertical neighbors. When combined with the 2×2 prior, 2×2 patches of hidden variables are connected with a single factor node, while the observed pixels I_j are still connected to their hidden counterparts x_j. Figure 3 illustrates these two structures.

For quantitative evaluation we use a set of 10 images from the test set of the Berkeley segmentation dataset [15]. The images are reduced to half their original size for efficiency reasons, and only the luminance channel is used. The denoising performance is measured using the peak signal-to-noise ratio (PSNR) averaged over all 10 images (PSNR $= 20 \log_{10}(255/\sigma_e)$, where σ_e is the standard deviation of the reconstruction error), as well as a perceptually-based image similarity metric SSIM [23].

Learned pairwise models. We first compared the learned pairwise MRF to the hand-defined MRF model from [4], which uses truncated quadratic potentials. In both cases, the denoised image is computed with max-product belief propagation using 20 iterations (equivalently implemented as the min-sum algorithm).

Table 1. Average denoising performance of various inference techniques and models on 10 test images

		Model from [4]	pairwise MRF		2 × 2 MRF	
			t-dist.	8 quad.		
		max-pr.	max-pr.	max-pr.	max-pr.	sum-pr.
$\sigma = 10$	PSNR	21.98dB	30.73dB	29.56dB	**30.89dB**	30.42dB
	SSIM [23]	0.772	0.876	0.844	**0.881**	0.876
$\sigma = 20$	PSNR	20.82dB	26.66dB	25.92dB	26.85dB	**27.29dB**
	SSIM	0.630	0.754	0.711	0.755	**0.772**

On a 3GHz Xeon, one BP iteration on a 256 × 256 image takes about 30 seconds. We find that the model proposed here substantially outperforms the model from [4] using the suggested parameters, both visually and quantitatively. As detailed in Table 1, the PSNR of the learned model is better by more than 5dB. Figure 4 shows one of the 10 test images, in which we can see that the denoising results from the learned model show characteristic piecewise constant patches, whereas the results from the hand-defined model are overly smooth in many places. Even though the performance of the truncated quadratic model could potentially be increased by hand-tuning its parameters, we refrained from doing so to demonstrate how learned MRFs can lead to competitive denoising results without requiring any manual parameter tuning. Nevertheless, we should note that BP inference is several times slower in the learned MRF case.

Random message updates. Based on our observation that the beliefs would not converge in case of the learned model and synchronous message updates (even though the energy seemingly converged), we also applied asynchronous message update schemes. A fixed, checkerboard-like update scheme led to some improvement in the behavior, but we found that random message updates led to the most reliable convergence behavior. At every iteration, each message is updated with a fixed probability, otherwise the previous state is kept. Table 2 shows that random updates led to a dramatic decrease in energy, but no considerable change in PSNR. Moreover, faint checkerboard-like artifacts that were visible before disappear after applying random updates. The update probability does not seem to have any substantial effect on the results (as long as it is not 100%).

Approximate potentials. We then investigated how the approximations of the learned potentials as a lower envelope of quadratics affect the denoising results as well as the running time. We found that max-product BP with 8 quadratics is about 6 times faster in practice than when the Student-t potentials are used. The approximation with only 4 quadratics is even faster by a factor of 2. Table 2 shows that the PSNR deteriorates by about 1dB when the approximate potentials are used (both with and without random updates); nevertheless, this still considerably outperforms the hand-designed model from [4]. We also report the average energy $\bar{E}$ of the reconstructed images in all cases computed using the original model and normalized by the number of pixels. Surprisingly, the

Fig. 4. Image denoising. **Top row:** *(left)* Original image. *(middle)* Noisy image ($\sigma = 10$). *(right)* Max-product BP with model from [4]. **Middle row:** *(left)* Max-product BP with t-distribution potentials. *(middle)* Max-product BP with approximate potentials (8 quadratics). *(right)* Max-product BP with learned 2×2 model. **Bottom row:** Detail view. From left to right: Model from [4], BP with t-distribution potentials, BP with approximate potentials (8 quadratics), BP with learned 2×2 model.

Table 2. Average denoising performance on 10 images for pairwise BP algorithms with and without the use of approximate models. The update percentage denotes the probability of each message being updated during a particular iteration.

	Student-t potentials				8 quadratics		4 quadratics	
Update percentage	25%	50%	75%	100%	50%	100%	50%	100%
$\sigma = 10$ E	1.595	1.594	1.594	2.071	1.348	2.687	**1.347**	2.681
PSNR in dB	30.73	30.73	30.73	**30.74**	29.56	29.60	29.54	29.57
SSIM [23]	0.876	0.876	0.876	**0.876**	0.844	0.842	0.843	0.841
$\sigma = 20$ E	1.189	1.182	1.182	2.606	1.025	2.892	**1.024**	2.907
PSNR in dB	26.64	26.66	**26.67**	26.67	25.92	25.96	25.90	25.95
SSIM	0.753	0.754	**0.755**	0.750	0.711	0.705	0.710	0.704

reconstructions using the approximate model have a lower energy than the results from the original model. We have not identified any intuitive interpretation of this fact, except that this evidences that BP may not be able to find the global optimum due to the loopiness of the graph.

Higher-order models. Next, we applied the learned higher-order MRF model with 2×2 cliques to the denoising problem. We used the adaptive state space approach as described above, and quantized the maximization with 8 graylevels; the potential functions are not approximated in this case. One iteration takes around 16 minutes for the setup described above. Since this approximation is possible for both max-product and sum-product BP, we report results for both algorithms. Table 1 compares both algorithms to a selection of pairwise MRFs (always with 50% update probability). We can see that the higher-order model outperforms the pairwise priors by about $0.15 - 0.2$dB (with Student-t potentials), and that the sum-product algorithm seems to be more appropriate with large amounts of noise. The perceptual similarity metric exhibits the same relative performance. Visually, the results no longer exhibit any piecewise constancy. Edges are preserved using both types of models, but smoothly varying regions are preserved better using the richer, higher-order prior.

We have also compared the presented results to an implementation of a simple gradient descent inference algorithm as suggested in [9]. This algorithm attempts to locally maximize the posterior density. We found that gradient descent achieves comparable results in terms of PSNR and SSIM, in some cases performing better than BP, in others worse. For both noise levels, the average energy of the max-product BP solution is slightly higher than that of the gradient descent algorithm (possibly due to the state space adaptation).

5   Conclusions and Future Work

In this paper we have combined efficient belief propagation inference algorithms with learned MRFs in order to solve low level vision problems. In particular, we demonstrated the use of learned pairwise MRF models and 2×2 MRF models with robust potential functions that better capture the spatial properties of natural images. In image denoising applications we found that BP based on these learned models substantially outperforms BP based on previous ad hoc MRFs, and that higher-order MRFs lead to both visually and quantitatively superior results.

Naively applying standard BP inference algorithms on these learned MRF models is difficult due to the non-convex functional form of the robust potential function, as well as the exponential explosion of the number of computations for the message updates in the case of 2×2 cliques. We introduced two effective approximation techniques to address these difficulties. First, for the pairwise case we used a finite family of quadratics to approximate the negative log of the learned robust potential function. This permits the application of distance transform techniques to speed up the running time from quadratic to linear in the number of labels. This approximation technique is quite general and can apply to graphical models in many contexts. Second, in the case of higher-order models such as 2×2 MRFs, we avoid explicitly searching over the whole state space by determining a plausible small set of configurations for a clique.

We observed that for the pairwise model a random message update scheme can improve the convergence speed as well as result in a significantly lower energy than a standard synchronous message update scheme. We also found that approximating the robust pairwise potential function by a lower envelope of quadratics results in a lower energy state than directly using the robust potential. These results reinforce the need to develop a better understanding of BP in computer vision research.

Comparing the BP results to a simple gradient descent inference technique, we found that belief propagation yields competitive, but not superior results. Our hypothesis is that this may be due to the likelihood being unimodal in the denoising case for which simple inference techniques can perform well. Nevertheless, both the inference and learning techniques developed in this paper are of general use beyond the application to image denoising. In the future, we plan to apply these efficient belief propagation techniques to low-level vision applications with multi-modal likelihoods, such as stereo or optical flow, in which case belief propagation may lead to superior results. Such problems often also have a smaller labeling set, and may thus allow us to use models of even higher-order.

Acknowledgments. S.R. and M.J.B. were supported by Intel Research and NSF IIS-0535075. This support is gratefully acknowledged.

References

1. Boykov, Y., Veksler, O., Zabih, R.: Fast approximate energy minimization via graph cuts. IEEE PAMI **23**(11) (2001) 1222–1239
2. Boykov, Y., Kolmogorov, V.: An experimental comparison of min-cut/max-flow algorithms for energy minimization in vision. IEEE PAMI **26**(9) (2004) 1124–1137
3. Kolmogorov, V., Zabih, R.: Multi-camera scene reconstruction via graph cuts. In: ECCV. Volume 2352 of LNCS., Springer (2002) 82–96

4. Felzenszwalb, P.F., Huttenlocher, D.P.: Efficient belief propagation for early vision. In: CVPR. Volume 1. (2004) 261–268
5. Tappen, M.F., Russell, B.C., Freeman, W.T.: Efficient graphical models for processing images. In: CVPR. Volume 2. (2004) 673–680
6. Yedidia, J.S., Freeman, W.T., Weiss, Y.: Constructing free energy approximations and generalized belief propagation algorithms. Technical Report TR-2004-040, Mitsubishi Electric Research Laboratories, Cambridge, Massachusetts (2004)
7. Zhu, S.C., Wu, Y., Mumford, D.: Filters, random fields and maximum entropy (FRAME): Towards a unified theory for texture modeling. IJCV $27(2)$ (1998) 107–126
8. Paget, R., Longstaff, I.D.: Texture synthesis via a noncausal nonparametric multiscale Markov random field. IEEE T. Image Proc. $7(6)$ (1998) 925–931
9. Roth, S., Black, M.J.: Fields of experts: A framework for learning image priors. In: CVPR. Volume 2. (2005) 860–867
10. Geman, S., Geman, D.: Stochastic relaxation, Gibbs distributions and the Bayesian restoration of images. IEEE PAMI 6 (1984) 721–741
11. Gimel'farb, G.L.: Texture modeling by multiple pairwise pixel interactions. IEEE PAMI $18(11)$ (1996) 1110–1114
12. Zalesny, A., van Gool, L.: A compact model for viewpoint dependent texture synthesis. In: SMILE 2000 Workshop. Volume 2018 of LNCS. (2001) 124–143
13. Huang, J.: Statistics of Natural Images and Models. PhD thesis, Brown University (2000)
14. Hinton, G.E.: Products of experts. In: ICANN. Volume 1. (1999) 1–6
15. Martin, D., Fowlkes, C., Tal, D., Malik, J.: A database of human segmented natural images and its application to evaluating segmentation algorithms and measuring ecological statistics. In: ICCV. Volume 2. (2001) 416–423
16. Hinton, G.E.: Training products of experts by minimizing contrastive divergence. Neur. Comp. $14(8)$ (2002) 1771–1800
17. Agarwala, A., Dontcheva, M., Agrawala, M., Drucker, S., Colburn, A., Curless, B., Salesin, D.H., Cohen, M.: Interactive digital photomontage. ACM SIGGRAPH $23(3)$ (2004) 294–302
18. Tappen, M.F., Freeman, W.T.: Comparison of graph cuts with belief propagation for stereo, using identical MRF parameters. In: ICCV. Volume 2. (2003) 900–907
19. Kschischang, F.R., Frey, B.J., Loelinger, H.A.: Fractor graphs and the sum-product algorithm. IEEE T. Info. Th. $47(2)$ (2001) 498–519
20. Sun, J., Zhen, N.N., Shum, H.Y.: Stereo matching using belief propagation. IEEE PAMI $25(7)$ (2003) 787–800
21. Black, M.J., Rangarajan, A.: On the unification of line processes, outlier rejection, and robust statistics with applications in early vision. IJCV $19(1)$ (1996) 57–92
22. Portilla, J., Strela, V., Wainwright, M.J., Simoncelli, E.P.: Image denoising using scale mixtures of Gaussians in the wavelet domain. IEEE T. Image Proc. $12(11)$ (2003) 1338–1351
23. Wang, Z., Bovik, A.C., Sheikh, H.R., Simoncelli, E.P.: Image quality assessment: From error visibility to structural similarity. IEEE T. Image Proc. $13(4)$ (2004) 600–612

Non Linear Temporal Textures Synthesis: A Monte Carlo Approach[*]

Andrea Masiero and Alessandro Chiuso

Department of Information Engineering,
University of Padova,
Via Gradenigo, 6/b, 35100 Padova, Italy
{andrea.masiero, chiuso}@dei.unipd.it

Abstract. In this paper we consider the problem of temporal texture modeling and synthesis. A temporal texture (or dynamic texture) is seen as the output of a dynamical system driven by white noise. Experimental evidence shows that linear models such as those introduced in earlier work are sometimes inadequate to fully describe the time evolution of the dynamic scene. Extending upon recent work which is available in the literature, we tackle the synthesis using non-linear dynamical models. The non-linear model is never given explicitly but rather we describe a methodology to generate samples from the model. The method requires estimating the "state" distribution and a linear dynamical model from the original clip which are then used respectively as target distribution and proposal mechanism in a rejection sampling step. We also report extensive experimental results comparing the proposed approach with the results obtained using linear models (*Doretto et al.*) and the "closed-loop" approach presented at ECCV 2004 by *Yuan et al.*

1 Introduction

Modeling of complex scenes such as texture has been subject of intensive research in the past years. Models of physical phenomena are widely used in a number of field such as Control, Econometrics, Bioengineering and so on; in computer vision several tasks - such as synthesis, recognition, classification, segmentation - connected to video sequences are facilitated when a model is available (see for instance [3] for a specific example related to textures).

Statistical-based models appeared soon to be the useful tool to tackle the problem; this line of work was pioneered by Julesz (see [7]). After that, much work has been done (see for instance [22, 19, 21, 6] just to cite a few references) which addresses the problem of modeling and synthesis of (static) textured images.

In this work we are interested instead in the "temporal" evolution of textured images which we call temporal or dynamic textures. "Temporal" textures have been first studied in [15] while the terminology "dynamic textures" was

[*] This work has been supported in part by RECSYS project of the European Community and by the national project *New methods and algorithms for identification and adaptive control of technological systems* funded by MIUR.

A. Leonardis, H. Bischof, and A. Pinz (Eds.): ECCV 2006, Part II, LNCS 3952, pp. 283–294, 2006.

introduced in [2]; there a "dynamic textures" was defined to be a sequence of (textured) images $\{\mathbf{I}(t), t = 1, .., T\}$, indexed by time t, which can be modeled as the output of a (time-invariant) dynamical system of the form

$$\begin{cases} \mathbf{x}_{t+1} = f(\mathbf{x}_t, \mathbf{w}_t) \\ \mathbf{y}_t = h(\mathbf{x}_t, \mathbf{v}_t) \end{cases} \tag{1}$$

where $\mathbf{y}_t = \text{vec}\{\mathbf{I}(t)\}$, and $\mathbf{w}_t$, $\mathbf{v}_t$ are zero mean independent white noise processes. The vector $\mathbf{x}_t$ is the "state" process and has dimension n as small as possible.

To be precise, in [2] only identification of linear models have been discussed $(f(\mathbf{x}_t, \mathbf{w}_t) = A\mathbf{x}_t + B\mathbf{w}_t)$ and the corresponding output $I(t)$ was called a *linear dynamic texture*.

Similar (model based) approaches can also be found in [5, 15]; interesting results concerning temporal textures have been introduced [17, 18, 8]; recent developments have also been described in [14].

An extension of the methodology found in [2] which proposes to consider "closed-loop" dynamical systems has been recently presented in [20].

In this paper we shall concentrate on models of the form (1). In particular we shall see that linear-gaussian dynamical systems used in [2, 5] are often inadequate to represent and synthesize real-world sequences; this suggests that more sophisticated models are needed.

To do so we shall assume that the output map $h(\cdot, \cdot)$ is linear, i.e. $\mathbf{y}_t = C\mathbf{x}_t + \mathbf{v}_t$, as was done in [2]; under this assumption the state can be directly constructed using standard Principal Component Analysis. This is done in Section 2. Under our assumption that the model is stationary, we can assume that there exists an invariant density $\pi(x)$ for the state vector $\mathbf{x}$. Using a standard Kernel density estimator $\hat{\pi}(x)$ we verify that $\pi(x)$ departs sharply from a Gaussian density. See Section 3. The estimated density $\hat{\pi}(x)$ provides, at the same time, (i) the motivation for our study and (ii) the basic object which allows to construct a non-linear texture model.

We shall provide experimental evidence showing that the new method yields increased image quality; the estimated invariant density $\hat{\pi}(\mathbf{x})$ shall also provide a tool to measure "quality" of texture sequences synthesized using different procedures. See figures 5, 6 and the related comments in the paper.

Notation

The following notation shall be used throughout: boldface letters $\mathbf{x}$ shall denote random vectors. A discrete time random process, i.e. an indexed collection of random vectors, shall be denoted as $\{\mathbf{x}_t\}$, $t \in \mathbb{Z}$ where t is the time index. Lowercase letters shall denote the sample value of the corresponding random vector (e.g. x_t is the sample value of $\mathbf{x}_t$). Capital letters shall denote matrices; $X^\top$ denote the transpose of the matrix X, $X(i, j)$ is the element in position i, j of the matrix X. We shall use Matlab notation for row or column selections: e.g. $X(i : j, :)$ will be the matrix formed by the rows of X with indexes from i to j. $\|X\|_F$ is the Frobenius norm of X, i.e. $\|X\|_F = \sqrt{\sum_{i,j} X(i,j)^2}$.

2   Stationary Dynamical Model

Consider a sequence of images $\{I(t)\}$, $t = 1, .., T$ (the "data"); each image is represented as an $r \times c$ matrix of positive real numbers denoting (gray-scale) pixel intensity values. A straightforward extension can be done to deal with color images.

We shall think that the images $\{I(t)\}$ are samples from a stochastic process $\{\mathbf{I}(t)\}$; without loss of generality we shall assume that $\{\mathbf{I}(t)\}$ is zero mean; this can always be obtained by simple data pre-processing. Defining the vectorized images $\mathbf{y}_t = \text{vec}(\mathbf{I}(t))$, we shall consider time invariant dynamical models of the form (1) where the output equation is linear, i.e.:

$$\begin{cases} \mathbf{x}_{t+1} = f(\mathbf{x}_t, \mathbf{w}_t) \\ \mathbf{y}_t = C\mathbf{x}_t + \mathbf{v}_t \end{cases} \tag{2}$$

The state-update equation $\mathbf{x}_{t+1} = f(\mathbf{x}_t, \mathbf{w}_t)$ can also be modeled through a transition kernel $p(x_{t+1}|x_t)$ which models $\mathbf{x}_{t+1}$ conditionally on $\mathbf{x}_t$.

The dimension p of $\mathbf{y}_t$ is equal to the product $r \cdot c$. Since the output dimension is typically much larger that the number of data (images) available, i.e. $p = r \cdot c >> T$, it is necessary to perform a first dimensionality reduction step.

This step, which is borrowed from [2], is based on Principal Component Analysis and can be formalized as follows. Let us define the data matrix $Y \triangleq \begin{bmatrix} y_1 \ y_2 \ \cdots \ y_T \end{bmatrix}$ where recall that $y_i := \text{vec}\{I(i)\}$.

Using the Singular Value Decomposition (SVD hereafter) algorithm we can rewrite Y as the product of three matrices $Y = USV^\top$ where U and V are matrices with orthonormal columns, i.e. $U^\top U = I_T$, $V^\top V = I_T$ while S is diagonal $S = \text{diag}(\sigma_1, \ldots, \sigma_T), \sigma_i \geq \sigma_j$ for $i \geq j$.

Retaining the first n columns $U(:, 1 : n)$, $V(:, 1 : n)$ of the matrices U and V respectively and the upper left block $S(1 : n, 1 : n)$ of the matrix S provides the best rank n approximation[1] of the matrix Y,

$$Y \simeq U(:, 1 : n)S(1 : n, 1 : n)V(:, 1 : n)^\top;$$

in fact, as Y_n ranges in the set of rank-n $p \times T$, $\|Y - Y_n\|_F$ is minimized by letting $Y_n = U(:, 1 : n)S(1 : n, 1 : n)V(:, 1 : n)^\top$.

Now we define

$$X \triangleq S(1 : n, 1 : n)V(:, 1 : n)^\top , \quad \hat{C} \triangleq U(:, 1 : n) , \quad x_t \triangleq X(:, t), \ 1 < t < T$$

$$E \triangleq Y - \hat{C}X , \quad v_t \triangleq y_t - \hat{y}_t, \quad \hat{y}_t \triangleq \hat{C}x_t \quad 1 < t < T$$

Observe that, being U unitary, $x_t = \hat{C}^\top y_t$, $1 < t < T$.

The matrix $\hat{C} = U(:, 1 : n)$ containing the first n "singular vectors" can be seen as an estimate of the matrix C in (2); it provides an approximate basis for the image space in the sense that $\hat{y}_t = \hat{C} \cdot (\hat{C}^\top y_t)$ is an approximation of the image y_t which is expressed as a linear function of the columns of $\hat{C}$. This

---

[1] In the Frobenius norm.

basis is "data driven" in the sense that it is tailored on the data itself. This is extremely useful and results in a rather compact representation of the data, in the sense that good approximations $\hat{y}_t$ can be obtained with relatively small n.

Of course one may rise several critics to this approach; for instance the SVD does not preserve positivity of the entries of each columns of $\hat{C}$ (i.e. the columns of $\hat{C}$ are not themselves images). Furthermore the technique is linear in nature. Several extensions are possible, starting from dimensionality reduction techniques which preserve positivity based on Kullback-Leibler [9, 4] pseudo distance (or I-divergence), to non-linear versions of SVD such as Kernel CCA [12, 10]. In this paper we shall not discuss these issues which would take us far from our goal.

Instead, we now go back to model (2), and study its statistical properties. We shall assume that the time invariant model (2) admits a unique invariant density $\pi(x)$, i.e. that,

1. the state evolution preserves the density $\pi(x)$
2. for any initial state density $\pi_0(x)$, the state density $\pi_t(x)$ (at time t) of the system (2) initialized at $\pi_0(x)$ converges to $\pi(x)$ as t grows.

We shall not discuss further this assumption nor enter into the mathematical details which are out of the scope of this conference.

Having access to samples $\hat{x}_t = \hat{C}^\top y_t$ of the state process $\mathbf{x}_t$ one may try to estimate the density $\pi(x)$. Our purpose is twofold:

1. show that a linear model is, most of the times, inadequate
2. provide an algorithm to generate samples from a dynamical system of the form (2) which admits $\hat{\pi}(x)$ as invariant density.

3   Non-parametric Density Estimator

Our purpose is to find an estimator for the state invariant density $\pi(x)$. The state $\mathbf{x}_t$ lives in an n-dimensional space, where n ranges in the interval $[20, 50]$ in typical examples. Therefore we are after estimating a probability density in a high dimensional space, which is known to be a rather difficult problem; see [11]. In our setup the problem is made even more challenging by the fact that usually a rather limited number T of samples is available. Typically, even for long video sequences, T is of the order of 500.

We consider density estimators of the Kernel type:

$$\hat{\pi}(x) = \frac{1}{Tk^n} \sum_{t=1}^{T} \mathcal{K}\left(x - \hat{x}_t, \Sigma_k\right) \tag{3}$$

where $\hat{x}_t = \hat{C}^\top y_t$ is the estimated state at time t. $\mathcal{K}$ is a suitable kernel parametrized by the matrix Σ_k and the positive number k which may be seen as a "regularization" parameter which controls the "width" of the Kernel $\mathcal{K}$. A typical choice is the Gaussian kernel, where $\mathcal{K}\left(\cdot, \Sigma_k\right)$ is a gaussian density with zero mean and covariance matrix $\Sigma_k = k^2 I_n$.

For a complete discussion on kernel estimation, for the choice of Σ_k and of the kernel $\mathcal{K}$ see [13] and [11].

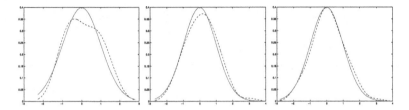

Fig. 1. Kernel estimation of a zero mean, unit variance Gaussian density with 40 (left), 80 (middle), 120 (right) samples. Solid: Gaussian density. Dotted: Kernel estimate.

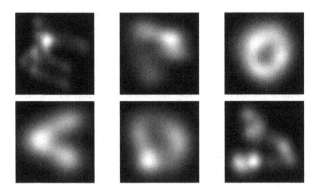

Fig. 2. Estimated joint density of the first and second component of the state in the temporal texture sequences (from left to right, top to bottom: beach, flame, river, smoke, steam, waterfall). A white zone is a high probability zone and viceversa.

In order to help the reader to gain some intuition we report in figure 1 an example of Kernel density estimators for a scalar Gaussian random variable using respectively $T = 40, 80, 120$ independent samples.

For the sake of illustration we have computed the joint probability density of the first two state components, which are also those corresponding to higher "energy". In figure 2 we show as a gray level image the value of the estimated state density corresponding to several texture sequences (bash, flame river, smoke, steam, waterfall) available in public databases[2].

It should be clear from the plots that the joint density of the first two components is rather far from being Gaussian. Therefore, a linear gaussian model such that used in [2], represent only a rough approximation of the data.

A first modification has been proposed in [1] where a linear model forced by non-gaussian noises was used. The noise densities were estimated using a version of ICA. The results presented in [1] were encouraging; several artifacts obtained by the linear Gaussian model were eliminated using the linear model with a non-gaussian noise.

---

[2] See *http://www.cc.gatech.edu/cpl/projects/graphcuttextures/* and *http:// vismod. media.mit.edu/ pub/szummer/temporal-texture/*

In this paper we take a different approach. Instead than modifying the noise density, we try to construct a transition Kernel $p(x_{t+1}|x_t)$ which, at the same time:

1. captures the dynamic behavior and
2. admits $\hat{\pi}(x)$ as an invariant density

Static Texture Synthesis

In order to demonstrate the effectiveness of our approach we first show how the invariant density estimate $\hat{\pi}(x)$ can be utilized to generate new textured images.

The invariant density $\pi(x)$ induces through the map $\mathbf{y}_t = C\mathbf{x}_t$ a density $p(y)$ in the image space. In this sense $\hat{x}_t = \hat{C}^\top y_t$ can be regarded as image features extracted through the "filters" $\hat{C}^\top$ and $\pi(x)$ is a density in the feature space.

Generating a "new" image $y = \text{vec}(I)$ can be done by: (i) sampling a "feature vector" x from $\pi(x)$ and (ii) generating the image according to $y = Cx$. Please note that we can only sample from $\hat{\pi}(x)$, the kernel estimate of $\pi(x)$; given our choice of a gaussian Kernel, $\hat{\pi}(x)$ turns out to be a mixture (with equal weights) of gaussian densities; this makes particularly easy the sampling step which simply consists in: (i) choose at random an index $j \in [1, T]$, (ii) sample from a gaussian with mean x_i and covariance matrix Σ_k.

We report in figure 3 images sampled according to this strategy compared with images from the original sequence. The three images from the original sequence are chosen somewhat arbitrarily and are only intended to visually represent three "typical" images of the sequence.

Original images

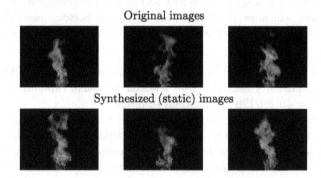

Synthesized (static) images

Fig. 3. Three examples of original images vs. (static) synthesized images in a flame sequence

4   Temporal Texture Synthesis

In the previous Section we have seen that the estimated invariant density can be used as a tool to generate new static texture images with the same spacial statistics of the original texture. However we are interested in generating sequences which preserve both the spacial and the temporal statistics.

Of course there are infinitely many dynamical models of the form (2) which admits $\hat{\pi}(x)$ as invariant density.

As an example consider the simple linear dynamical system $\mathbf{x}_{t+1} = a\mathbf{x}_t + b\mathbf{w}_t$ where $\mathbf{w}_t$ is zero mean, unit variance gaussian white noise. Assuming $|a| < 1$ there exists a unique invariant density, which is gaussian with zero mean and variance $\sigma_x^2 = b^2/(1 - a^2)$. Fixing the invariant density amounts therefore to fixing σ_x^2. For any given σ_x^2 one can choose any arbitrary a_0 so that $\|a_0\| < 1$ which, together with $b = \sqrt{(1 - a_0^2)\sigma_x^2}$ gives the desired invariant density.

The same happens in our situation; we are given (estimated) the invariant density and want to choose a transition Kernel $p(x_{t+1}|x_t)$ which: (i) has $\hat{\pi}(x)$ as invariant density and (ii) describes well the temporal behavior of the data sequence.

This appear to be a difficult task for general non linear dynamical models $f(\mathbf{x}_t, \mathbf{w}_t)$.

Since an "approximate model" is already available from "linear dynamic textures" of [2], we propose to consider the linear model

$$\begin{cases} \mathbf{x}_{t+1} = A\mathbf{x}_t + \mathbf{w}_t \\ \mathbf{y}_t = C\mathbf{x}_t + \mathbf{v}_t \end{cases} \tag{4}$$

as an "initial estimate" of the more general (nonlinear) model (2) which has to be suitable refined in order to match the estimated invariant density $\hat{\pi}(x)$.

We shall not enter into the details of how A and the noise covariance $\Sigma_w = \text{Var}(\mathbf{w}_t)$ can be estimated. We refer the reader to [2] for the details and assume that estimates $\hat{A}$, $\hat{\Sigma}_w$ have been computed.

The basic idea (very simple to be honest) is to use a *rejection sampling* technique (see [16]) to construct a dynamical model which admits $\hat{\pi}(x)$ as invariant density.

Let us denote with $p(x; m, \Sigma)$ the density of a gaussian random vector with mean m and variance Σ and define

$$Q(x) := \int \hat{\pi}(z) p(x; \hat{A}z, \hat{\Sigma}_w) \, dz$$

Note that $Q(x)$ would be the density of the state at time $t+1$ of the linear model (4) if the state density at time t was $\hat{\pi}(x)$. Note that, if $\hat{\pi}(z)$ was the invariant density associated to (4) then $Q(x)$ would be equal to $\hat{\pi}(x)$. As we have seen however this is not true; our scope is to modify the transition kernel $p(x_{t+1}; \hat{A}x_t, \hat{\Sigma}_w)$ so that $\hat{\pi}(x)$ is in fact invariant for the new kernel.

The rejection sampling technique requires that one chooses a constant c so that

$$\frac{\hat{\pi}(x)}{cQ(x)} \leq 1$$

Note that once $\pi(x)$ and $Q(x)$ are available, the constant c can be computed numerically off-line[3].

Assume that, at time s,

$$x_s \sim \hat{\pi}(x). \tag{5}$$

Repeat the following for $t \geq s$.

---

[3] For reasons of space we shall not enter into the details of this computation.

Procedure 1 [Texture generation]

1. *Sample[4] x_{t+1}^p from a gaussian density $p(x; \hat{A}x_t, \hat{\Sigma}_w)$, i.e. generate a new sample according to the linear dynamic texture model (4).*
2. *Accept the sample, i.e. set $x_{t+1} = x_{t+1}^p$ with probability*

$$\frac{\hat{\pi}(x_{t+1}^p)}{cQ(x_{t+1}^p)}$$

otherwise go back to step one and repeat until a sample is accepted

It is possible to show that, provided (5) is satisfied, the samples x_t, $t \geq s$ are all distributed according to $\hat{\pi}(x)$.

Remark 1. Note that, if $\hat{\pi}(x)$ was the invariant density of the model (4), then $Q(x) = \hat{\pi}(x)$. It follows that choosing $c = 1$, $\frac{\hat{\pi}(x)}{cQ(x)} = 1$ and in step 2 above each sample x_{t+1}^p would be accepted. This means that our procedure does not modify the transition kernel if not needed.

Speeding up the Procedure

The proposal density used in step 1 of Procedure 1 while encoding the dynamical properties captured by the linear dynamical model (4), may result in a very low synthesis speed due to the low acceptance probability in step 2 of Procedure 1.

Therefore in our simulation examples we have used a modified proposal density of the form

$$q(x|\hat{x}_t) \propto \frac{1 + (\alpha^\nu - 1)p(x; \hat{A}\hat{x}_t, \hat{\Sigma}_w)}{\alpha^\nu} \sum_{i=1}^{T} p(x; \hat{x}_t, \alpha\hat{\Sigma}_k) \quad \alpha \geq 1, \quad \nu > 1 \quad (6)$$

For large values of α (6) reduces to the linear model (4) used in step 1 of Procedure 1, while when α is "small" (6) tends to $\hat{\pi}(x)$.

Therefore for small α's, while the synthesis becomes faster since the proposal density is "close" to the invariant density, the dynamical information gets lost. In the extreme case of $\alpha = 1$ one is left with a sequence of independent samples from the invariant density $\pi(x)$.

Choice of a reasonable value of α trading speed and dynamical coherence of the sequence is outside of the scope of this paper and shall not be discussed here. The results presented in the paper are obtained using $\alpha = 3$ and $\nu = 5$. Of course Q in step 2 of Procedure 1 needs to be modified accordingly.

5   Results

We compare synthesized sequences using procedure 1 with few frames from the original sequences, see Figure 4. Unfortunately it is hard to judge the quality of the synthesized sequence from just few frames. Some movies showing the

---

[4] The superscript ^{p} stands for "proposed".

Beach Sequence: original

Beach Sequence: synthesized

Fig. 4. Three frames from a beach sequence

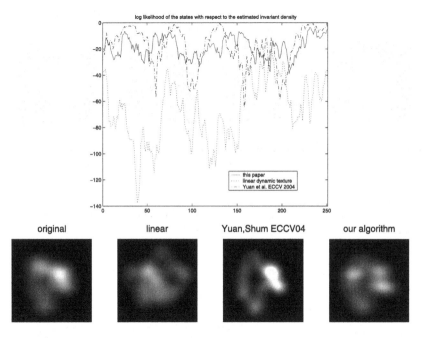

Fig. 5. Log-likelihood (top) and estimated density (bottom) of the first two components of the state (flame sequence) synthesized using the linear algorithm [2](solid line), our algorithm (dotted line) and Yuan et al. algorithm [20](dash-dotted line)

results on different texture sequences of the approach of this paper compared with linear models [2] and closed-loop LDS [20] can be obtained upon request form the authors. The visual quality of the sequence is improved with respect to linear models, but at the price of an increased computational load due to the rejection sampling step. The modified proposal described in (6) does indeed result in a faster procedures which nevertheless remains far slower that those proposed in [2, 20].

The estimated invariant density $\hat{\pi}(x)$ can also be used as a "likelihood function" to analytically measure the image quality. In figures 5 and 6 we compare the

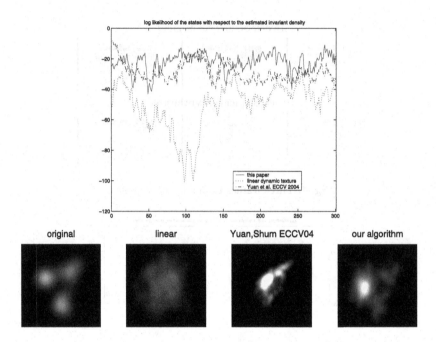

Fig. 6. Log-likelihood (top) and estimated density (bottom) of the first two components of the state (grass sequence) synthesized using the linear algorithm [2](solid line), our algorithm (dotted line) and Yuan et al. algorithm [20](dash-dotted line)

Table 1. Kullback-Leibler divergence between the state density estimated from frames of the original movie and that estimated from frames synthesized with, respectively, linear dynamic texture [2], Yuan et al. [20] and our algorithm

movie	linear dynamic texture	Yuan ECCV 2004	our algorithm
flame	0.44915	0.18414	0.099459
grass	0.68545	2.1566	0.62835
pond	0.17316	0.059503	0.12853
river	0.30051	0.079848	0.050529
smoke	2.5953	12.9136	1.0732
waterfall	1.6501	1.7689	0.9594

likelihood $\hat{\pi}(x_i)$, $i = 1, .., T$ of a sequence x_i generated using the approach of this paper with the likelihood obtained from the linear Gaussian model in [2] and the closed-loop LDS of [20][5].

In figures 5 and 6 we plot the state densities (first two components of the state) estimated from the original $(\hat{\pi}(x))$ and synthesized $(\hat{\pi}_s(x))$ sequences using

---

[5] Of course the results depend on the particular choice of the user parameters (e.g. Kernel width for our approach, past and future horizons in closed-loop LDS etc.). We have optimized the parameters choice of each method so as to obtain the best results in the particular examples we consider.

linear models [2], the algorithm of this paper and closed-loop LDS [20]. In table 1 we also report the Kullback-Leibler pseudo-distance

$$KL(\hat{\pi} \| \hat{\pi}_s) = \int \hat{\pi}(x) \log \frac{\hat{\pi}(x)}{\hat{\pi}_s(x)} \, dx \tag{7}$$

between $\hat{\pi}$ and $\hat{\pi}_s$. Keep in mind that the densities $\hat{\pi}(x)$ and $\hat{\pi}_s(x)$ are estimated from data and also the integral in (7) had to be computed numerically. For instance the poor results in the "smoke" sequence may be attributed to the fact that the original clip is very short (about 50 frames). Note also that ideally our procedure produce samples from the density $\hat{\pi}$; as the length of the simulated clip goes to infinity, $\hat{\pi}_s$ - the estimated density from the synthesized sequence - becomes closer and closer to $\hat{\pi}$ and therefore the numbers in the third column of Table 1 should tend to zero.

6   Conclusions

In this paper we have shown that linear gaussian models are often inadequate to describe real word "dynamic texture" sequences. This conclusion stems from the fact that the estimated invariant measure $\hat{\pi}(x)$ is rather far from being gaussian. We therefore proposed to tackle dynamic texture synthesis using a class of non-linear dynamical models; the method take advantage of results on linear texture modeling which are available in the literature and borrows tools from multivariate statistics (Kernel density estimators) and Monte Carlo methods (Rejection Sampling). The simulation results show a considerable improvement over linear methods of [2] and a slight improvement over closed-loop LDS of [20].

Furthermore, the estimated invariant density provides a data driven measure of the image quality as a likelihood of synthesized states.

Unfortunately the proposed method suffers several drawbacks: first of all the estimation of the invariant measure $\hat{\pi}(x)$ requires, in principle, a large amount of data which are in practice hardly available. Second the computational load is considerably increased due to the rejection sampling step.

References

1. A. Bissacco, P. Saisan, and S. Soatto, "Dynamic modeling of human gaits," in *Proc. of the IFAC Symposium on System Identification*, 2003.
2. G. Doretto, A. Chiuso, S. Soatto, and Y. Wu, "Dynamic textures," *International Journal of Computer Vision*, vol. 51, no. 2, pp. 91–109, February 2003.
3. G. Doretto, D. Cremers, P. Favaro, and S. Soatto, "Dynamic texture segmentation," in *Proceedings of the International Conference on Computer Vision*, vol. 2, Nice, France, October 2003, pp. 1236–1242.
4. L. Finesso and P. Spreij, "Approximate nonnegative matrix factorization via alternating minimization," in *Proc. of the 16th International Symposium on MTNS*, Leuven, July 2004, pp. 223–252.

5. A. Fitzgibbon, "Stochastic rigidity: Image registration for nowhere-static scenes," in *Proc. IEEE International Conf. Computer Vision (ICCV)*, vol. 1, Vancouver, Canada, 2001, pp. 662–670.

6. D. Heeger and J. Bergen, "Pyramid-based texture analysis/synthesis," in *SIGGRAPH 95 Conf. Proc.*, 1995.

7. B. Julesz, "Visual pattern discrimination," *IRE Trans. on Information Theory*, vol. 8, pp. 84–92, 1962.

8. V. Kwatra, A. Schdl, I. Essa, G. Turk, and A. Bobick, "Graphcut textures: Image and video synthesis using graph cuts," in *Proc. ACM Transactions on Graphics (SIGGRAPH 2003)*, 2003.

9. D. Lee and H. S. Seung, "Algorithms for non-negative matrix factorization," in *In Advances in Neural and Information Processing Systems 13 (T.K. Leen, T.G. Dietterich and V. Tresp Eds.).* MIT Press, 2001, pp. 556–562.

10. B. Scholkopf, A. Smola, and K.-R. Muller, "Nonlinear component analysis as a kernel eigenvalue problem," *Neural Computation*, p. 12991319, 1998.

11. D. W. Scott, *Multivariate Density Estimation, Theory, Practice, and Visualization.* John Wiley and Sons, 1992.

12. J. Shawe-Taylor and N. Cristianini, *Kernel Methods for Pattern Analysis.* Cambridge University Press, 2004.

13. B. W. Silverman, *Density estimation for Statistics and Data Analysis.* Chapman and Hall, 1986.

14. M. Sznaier, O. Camps, and C. Mazzaro, "Finite horizon model reduction of a class of neutrally stable systems with applications to texture synthesis and recognition," in *CDC 2004*, 2004.

15. M. Szummer and R. Picard, "Temporal texture modeling," in *IEEE International Conference on Image Processing (ICIP)*, vol. 3, Lausanne, Switzerland, 1996, pp. 823–826.

16. H. Tanizaki, *Nonlinear Filters: Estimation and Applications (Second Edition).* Springer-Verlag, 1996.

17. Y. Wang and S. Zhu, "A generative method for textured motion: Analysis and synthesis," in *Proc. IEEE European Conf. Computer Vision (ECCV)*, 2002, pp. 583–598.

18. ——, "Analysis and synthesis of textured motion: Particles and waves," *IEEE Trans. on Patt. Anal. and Mach. Intell.*, vol. 26, no. 10, pp. 1348–1363, 2004.

19. Y. Wu, S. Zhu, and X. Liu, "Equivalence of julesz ensembles and frame models," *Int'l Journal of Computer Vision*, vol. 38, no. 3, pp. 247–267, 2000.

20. L. Yuan, F. Wen, C. Liu, and H. Shum, "Synthsizing dynamic texture with closed-loop linear dynamic system," in *Proc. of European Conf. on Computer Vision (ECCV)*, 2004, pp. 603–616.

21. S. Zhu, X. Liu, and Y. Wu, "Exploring texture ensembles by efficient markov chain monte carlo," *IEEE Trans. on Patt. Anal. and Mach. Intell.*, vol. 22, no. 6, pp. 554–569, 2000.

22. S. Zhu, Y. Wu, and D. Mumford, "Minimax entropy principle and its application to texture modeling," *Neural Computation*, vol. 9, no. 8, 1997.

Curvature-Preserving Regularization of Multi-valued Images Using PDE's

David Tschumperlé

GREYC Image (CNRS UMR 6072), 6 Bd du Maréchal Juin, 14050 Caen Cedex, France
David.Tschumperle@greyc.ensicaen.fr

Abstract. We are interested in diffusion PDE's for smoothing multi-valued images in an anisotropic manner. By pointing out the pros and cons of existing tensor-driven regularization methods, we introduce a new constrained diffusion PDE that regularizes image data while taking curvatures of image structures into account. Our method has a direct link with a continuous formulation of the Line Integral Convolutions, allowing us to design a very fast and stable algorithm for its implementation. Besides, our smoothing scheme numerically performs with a sub-pixel accuracy and is then able to preserves very thin image structures contrary to classical PDE discretizations based on finite difference approximations. We illustrate our method with different applications on color images.

1 Introduction

Computing regularized versions of corrupted images has always been a desirable goal in the field of computer vision. It is useful, either to restore degraded images, or - more indirectly - as a pre-processing step that eases further data analysis. Since the pioneering work of Perona-Malik [21], the framework of anisotropic diffusion PDE's has particularly raised a strong interest for such a task : it has the ability to smooth data in a *nonlinear* way, allowing the preservation of significant image discontinuities. PDE's are local formulations which are well adapted to deal with degraded images containing local or semi-local data corruption sources : Gaussian noise, scratches or compression artifacts are local degradations usually encountered in digital images. Important historical steps in PDE-based image regularization have been reached with the extension of the classical heat flow to deal with anisotropic smoothing [21, 17, 25, 36], the interpretation of diffusion PDE's as gradient descents of energy functionals [2, 8, 10, 13, 24], and the link between regularization PDE's and the concept of non-linear scale spaces [1, 18, 19]. Extensions of these techniques have been more recently tackled to deal with general multi-valued images (including colors) [26, 31, 32, 37], fields of unit vectors [14, 20, 29], orthonormal matrices [11, 31], positive-definite matrices [11, 31], or image data defined on implicit surfaces [3, 9, 30]. Despite this wide range of existing formalisms, all regularization methods have something in common : they locally *smooth* the image along one or several directions of the space that are different at each image point. Typically, the principal smoothing direction is chosen to be parallel to the image contours, resulting in an *anisotropic* regularization that do not destroy edges. As a requirement, defining a correct *smoothing behavior* is one of the first aim of a good regularization algorithm, the second being the precision of the smoothing process itself :

A. Leonardis, H. Bischof, and A. Pinz (Eds.): ECCV 2006, Part II, LNCS 3952, pp. 295–307, 2006.
© Springer-Verlag Berlin Heidelberg 2006

it must respect the pre-defined smoothing geometry as much as possible. This general principle has been recently adopted in [32, 36] with the proposal of regularization PDE's designed to fit a given (user-defined) underlying local smoothing geometry, modeled as a field of diffusion tensors. Separating the smoothing geometry from the regularization itself allows to unify a lot of previously proposed equations into generic formulations, and generally provides a *local geometric interpretation* of the corresponding processes.

Here, we first propose a quick analysis of these unifying methods, then introduce a comparable tensor-driven diffusion PDE that regularizes multi-valued images *while respecting specific curvature constraints*. We show that this general formalism, which is naturally positioned between the two previous ones, has interesting smoothing properties. Moreover, it is directly related to the framework of LIC's (Line Integral Convolutions, firstly proposed by Cabral & Leedom [6]). This analogy leads to the proposal of an efficient LIC-based scheme that implements our proposed method. It allows the preservation of thin image structures, thanks to its sub-pixel accuracy and runs up to three times faster than classical explicit scheme thanks to its high stability. Results are finally illustrated with applications on color images, including denoising, inpainting and non-linear resizing.

2 Anisotropic Smoothing of Images with PDE's: A Review

2.1 Local Geometry and Diffusion Tensors

We consider a noisy multi-valued image $\mathbf{I} : \Omega \rightarrow \mathbb{R}^n$ ($n = 3$ for color images), defined on $\Omega \subset \mathbb{R}^2$. I_i denotes the particular vector channel i of $\mathbf{I}$: $\mathbf{I}_{(\mathbf{X})} = \left(I_{1(\mathbf{X})}, ..., I_{n(\mathbf{X})}\right)^T$. PDE-based regularizations act as local smoothers of $\mathbf{I}$ along defined directions depending themselves on the local configuration of the pixel intensities : one wants to smooth $\mathbf{I}$ mostly along directions of the edges if there are any. Naturally, this means we need first to retrieve the *local geometry* of $\mathbf{I}$. As pointed out in [12, 36], it may be seen as the definition of these important features at each image point $\mathbf{X} = (x, y) \in \Omega$:

- Two orthogonal directions $\theta^+_{(\mathbf{X})}$, $\theta^-_{(\mathbf{X})} \in S^1$ (unit vectors of $\mathbb{R}^2$) directed along the local maximum and minimum variations of image intensities at $\mathbf{X}$. The direction θ^- corresponds to the edge direction, when there is one.
- Two corresponding positive values $\lambda^+_{(\mathbf{X})}$, $\lambda^-_{(\mathbf{X})}$ that measure the effective variations of image intensities (local signal contrast) along $\theta^+_{(\mathbf{X})}$ and $\theta^-_{(\mathbf{X})}$ respectively.

This geometry can be retrieved by the field $\mathbf{G}$ of *structure tensors*, which is a natural tensor-valued extension of the gradient field for multi-valued images [12] :

$$\forall \mathbf{X} \in \Omega, \quad \mathbf{G}_{(\mathbf{X})} = \sum_{i=1}^{n} \nabla I_{i(\mathbf{X})} \nabla I^T_{i(\mathbf{X})} \quad \text{where} \quad \nabla I_i = \left(\frac{\partial I_i}{\partial x} \; \frac{\partial I_i}{\partial y} \right)^T \quad (1)$$

A Gaussian-smoothed version $\mathbf{G}_\sigma = \mathbf{G} * G_\sigma$ is usually computed to retrieve a more coherent geometry (the standard deviation σ being proportional to the *noise scale* [36]). Then, the spectral elements of $\mathbf{G}_{\sigma(\mathbf{X})}$ give at the same time the contrast (eigenvalues λ^-, λ^+) and the orientations (eigenvectors $\theta^- \perp \theta^+$) of the local image structures.

Once the local geometry $\mathbf{G}_\sigma$ of the image $\mathbf{I}$ has been determined, authors of [32, 36] propose to design a particular field $\mathbf{T} : \Omega \to P(2)$ of *diffusion tensors* which specifies the local smoothing geometry that *should drive the regularization process*. $\mathbf{T}$ naturally depends on the spectral elements λ^-, λ^+ and θ^-, θ^+ of $\mathbf{G}_\sigma$:

$$\forall \mathbf{X} \in \Omega, \quad \mathbf{T}_{(\mathbf{X})} = f^-_{(\lambda^+, \lambda^-)} \, \theta^- \theta^- + f^+_{(\lambda^+, \lambda^-)} \, \theta^+ \theta^{+T} \tag{2}$$

Basically, the functions $f^{+/-} : \mathbb{R}^2 \to \mathbb{R}$ set the strengths of the desired smoothing along the corresponding directions $\theta^{+/-}$. Several choices for $f^{+/-}$ are possible, depending on the considered application. For image denoising, a possible choice is (proposed in [10, 31, 32]) : $f^{+/-}_{(\lambda_+, \lambda_-)} = \frac{1}{(1+\lambda^+ + \lambda^-)^{p_\pm}}$, with $p_- < p_+$.

Intuitively, if a pixel $\mathbf{X}$ is located on an image contour ($\lambda^+_{(\mathbf{X})}$ is high) then the smoothing must be performed mostly along the contour direction $\theta^-_{(\mathbf{X})}$ with a strength inversely proportional to the local contrast. Conversely, if $\mathbf{X}$ is located on a flat region ($\lambda^+_{(\mathbf{X})}$ is low), the smoothing must be performed in all possible directions (isotropic behavior), leading then to $\mathbf{T} \simeq \mathbb{I}_d$ (identity matrix). Modeling the local smoothing geometry as a field $\mathbf{T}$ of diffusion tensors is the first stage proposed both in [32, 36]. The desired smoothing must be applied then, using a possible choice of diffusion PDE's, as detailed below. Most existing regularization PDE's [1, 2, 3, 4, 8, 10, 13, 18, 19, 21, 24, 25, 26] may be seen as particular cases of such diffusion equations with different tensor fields $\mathbf{T}$.

2.2 The Divergence-Based PDE

A corrupted multi-valued image $\mathbf{I} : \Omega \to \mathbb{R}^n$ can be anisotropically regularized "along" a diffusion tensor field $\mathbf{T} : \Omega \to P(2)$ by the following divergence PDE :

$$\forall i = 1, .., n, \quad \frac{\partial I_i}{\partial t} = \text{div}\left(\mathbf{T}\nabla I_i\right) \tag{3}$$

This tensor-driven regularization equation has been introduced in [36], and adapted for color/multi-valued images in [37]. Note that $\mathbf{T}$ is the same for all image channels I_i, ensuring that the I_i are smoothed along a *common multi-valued geometry*, contrary to an uncorrelated channel-by-channel approach. Despite its popularity, the PDE (3) *does not strictly respect the geometry* $\mathbf{T}$, since the smoothing performed is not always the one that could be expected. Particularly, consider the case of choosing $\mathbf{T}_{1(\mathbf{X})} = \left(\frac{\nabla I}{\|\nabla I\|}\right)\left(\frac{\nabla I}{\|\nabla I\|}\right)^T$ or $\mathbf{T}_{2(\mathbf{X})} = \mathbb{I}_d$ (identity matrix). For scalar images, these different fields both lead to the well known *heat flow equation* $\frac{\partial I}{\partial t} = \Delta I$ that is equivalent to the convolution of the image I by a normalized Gaussian kernel (isotropic smoothing [15]), despite the pure anisotropic form of $\mathbf{T}_{1(\mathbf{X})}$. The divergence is indeed a differential operator which makes the PDE (3) implicitly depending on the spatial variations of $\mathbf{T}$. It is actually not conceivable to easily define a pointwise smoothing behavior $\mathbf{T}$ with a divergence equation (3).

2.3 The Trace-Based PDE

In order to better respect the local smoothing geometry $\mathbf{T}$, we have proposed in [31, 32] a tensor-driven PDE, similar to (3), but based on a *trace* operator :

$$\forall i = 1, .., n, \qquad \frac{\partial I_i}{\partial t} = \text{trace}\,(\mathbf{T}\mathbf{H}_i) \tag{4}$$

$\mathbf{H}_i$ stands for the Hessian of I_i. As noticed in [31, 32], the evolution of (4) has an interesting geometric interpretation in terms of local image filtering with spatially varying short-time Gaussian kernels $G_t^{\mathbf{T}}{}_{(\mathbf{X})} = \frac{1}{4\pi t}\exp\left(-\frac{\mathbf{X}^T\,\mathbf{T}^{-1}\,\mathbf{X}}{4t}\right)$, locally oriented by the tensor $\mathbf{T}_{(\mathbf{X})}$. It particularly ensures that the smoothing is truly done along the predefined smoothing geometry $\mathbf{T}$. As $trace()$ is not a differential operator, the spatial variation of $\mathbf{T}$ does not trouble the diffusion directions here and two differently shaped tensors necessarily lead to distinct smoothing behaviors.

Unfortunately, this analysis also points out one important drawback of the trace-based formulation. On curved structures (like corners), the Gaussian behavior of the smoothing is not desirable : when the local variation of the edge orientation θ^- is high, a Gaussian filter tends to *round* corners, since an oriented Gaussian kernel is not curved itself. This classical behavior is also best known as the "mean curvature flow" effect, characterized by the equation $\frac{\partial I}{\partial t} = \frac{\partial^2 I}{\partial \theta^{-2}}$. This is illustrated on Fig.1b where (4) has been applied on a real color image and $\mathbf{T}$ has been defined as (2) (then $f^- \neq 0$). Here, the mean curvature flow effect results in blending parallel thin curved structures. To avoid this over-smoothing, one usually try to vanish $f^{+/-}$ on curved structures (corners). But the detection of such structures on noisy images is a hard task. Conversely, image under-smoothing on edges may occur when one wants to limit the diffusion too much. There is a difficult trade-off between complete noise removal and preservation of curved structures, when using trace-based PDE's (4). This kind of regularization process does not care about the *curvature* of the smoothing directions, and by extension, of the curvature of the image contours. Taking this curvature into account is a very

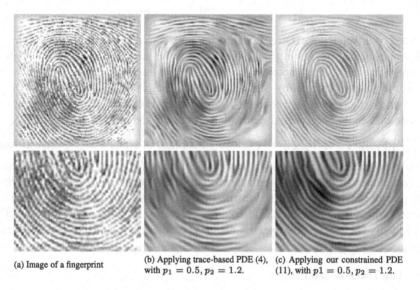

(a) Image of a fingerprint

(b) Applying trace-based PDE (4), with $p_1 = 0.5, p_2 = 1.2$.

(c) Applying our constrained PDE (11), with $p1 = 0.5, p_2 = 1.2$.

Fig. 1. Comparisons between trace PDE (4) and our proposed curvature-preserving PDE's (11)

desirable goal and has motivated the work presented in this paper. For illustration purposes, results of our proposed curvature-preserving equation is shown on Fig.1c.

3   The Framework of Curvature-Preserving PDE's

3.1   The Single Direction Case

We introduce now the general idea of curvature-preserving PDE's, focusing first on image regularization along a *vector field* $\mathbf{w} : \Omega \rightarrow \mathbb{R}^2$ instead of a tensor field $\mathbf{T}$. We consider then a local smoothing everywhere along a single varying direction $\frac{\mathbf{w}}{\|\mathbf{w}\|}$, with a strength $\|\mathbf{w}\|$. The two spatial components of $\mathbf{w}$ are denoted by $\mathbf{w}_{(\mathbf{x})} = (u_{(\mathbf{x})}\ v_{(\mathbf{x})})^T$. We define the *curvature-preserving* regularization PDE that smoothes $\mathbf{I}$ along $\mathbf{w}$ by :

$$\forall i = 1,\ldots,n, \qquad \frac{\partial I_i}{\partial t} = \text{trace}\left(\mathbf{w}\mathbf{w}^T\,\mathbf{H}_i\right) + \nabla I_i^T \mathbf{J}_\mathbf{w}\mathbf{w} \tag{5}$$

where $\mathbf{J}_\mathbf{w}$ stands for the Jacobian of $\mathbf{w}$, and $\mathbf{H}_i$ the Hessian of I_i.

Let us study more closely how (5) is related to $\mathbf{w}$. We consider the curve $\mathcal{C}^{\mathbf{X}}_{(a)}$ defining the *integral curve* of $\mathbf{w}$, starting from $\mathbf{X}$ and parameterized by $a \in \mathbb{R}$ (Fig.2a) :

$$\mathcal{C}^{\mathbf{X}}_{(0)} = \mathbf{X} \qquad \text{and} \qquad \frac{\partial \mathcal{C}^{\mathbf{X}}_{(a)}}{\partial a} = \mathbf{w}(\mathcal{C}^{\mathbf{X}}_{(a)}) \tag{6}$$

We denote by $\mathcal{F}$ the family of integral curves of $\mathbf{w}$. A second-order Taylor development of $\mathcal{C}^{\mathbf{X}}_{(a)}$ around $a = 0$ is $\mathcal{C}^{\mathbf{X}}_{(h)} = \mathcal{C}^{\mathbf{X}}_{(0)} + h\frac{\partial \mathcal{C}^{\mathbf{X}}_{(a)}}{\partial a}\big|_{a=0} + \frac{h^2}{2}\frac{\partial^2 \mathcal{C}^{\mathbf{X}}_{(a)}}{\partial a^2}\big|_{a=0} + O(h^3)$, i.e :

$$\mathcal{C}^{\mathbf{X}}_{(h)} = \mathbf{X} + h\mathbf{w}_{(\mathbf{X})} + \frac{h^2}{2}\,\mathbf{J}_{\mathbf{w}_{(\mathbf{X})}}\mathbf{w}_{(\mathbf{X})} + O(h^3)$$

with $h \rightarrow 0$, and $O(h^n) = h^n\,\epsilon_n$. Then, we can compute a second-order Taylor development of $I_i(\mathcal{C}^{\mathbf{X}}_{(a)})$ around $a = 0$, which corresponds to the variations of the image intensity near $\mathbf{X}$ when following the integral curve $\mathcal{C}^{\mathbf{X}}$:

$$I_i(\mathcal{C}^{\mathbf{X}}_{(h)}) = I_{i(\mathbf{X})} + h\nabla I_{i(\mathbf{X})}^T\left(\mathbf{w}_{(\mathbf{X})} + \frac{h}{2}\,\mathbf{J}_{\mathbf{w}_{(\mathbf{X})}}\mathbf{w}_{(\mathbf{X})}\right) + \frac{h^2}{2}\text{trace}\left(\mathbf{w}_{(\mathbf{X})}\mathbf{w}_{(\mathbf{X})}^T\mathbf{H}_i\right) + O(h^3)$$

The second derivative of the function $a \rightarrow I_i(\mathcal{C}^{\mathbf{X}}_{(a)})$ at $a = 0$ is then :

$$\frac{\partial^2 I_i(\mathcal{C}^{\mathbf{X}}_{(a)})}{\partial a^2}\Big|_{a=0} = \lim_{h\rightarrow 0}\ \frac{1}{h^2}\left[I_i(\mathcal{C}^{\mathbf{X}}_{(h)}) + I_i(\mathcal{C}^{\mathbf{X}}_{(-h)}) - 2I_i(\mathcal{C}^{\mathbf{X}}_{(0)})\right]$$

$$= \text{trace}\left(\mathbf{w}_{(\mathbf{X})}\mathbf{w}_{(\mathbf{X})}^T\mathbf{H}_{i(\mathbf{X})}\right) + \nabla I_i^T\mathbf{J}_{\mathbf{w}_{(\mathbf{X})}}\mathbf{w}_{(\mathbf{X})} \tag{7}$$

This is exactly the right term in our curvature-preserving PDE (5). Actually, (5) can be seen individually for all integral curves of $\mathcal{F}$ instead of each point $\mathbf{X} \in \Omega$: consider another point $\mathbf{Y} \in \mathcal{C}^{\mathbf{X}}$. Then, there exist $\epsilon \in \mathbb{R}$ such that $\mathbf{Y} = \mathcal{C}^{\mathbf{X}}_{(\epsilon)}$. Indeed, $\mathcal{C}^{\mathbf{X}}$ and $\mathcal{C}^{\mathbf{Y}}$ describe the same curve (6) with different parameterizations : $\forall a \in \mathbb{R},\ \ \mathcal{C}^{\mathbf{Y}}_{(a)} = \mathcal{C}^{\mathbf{X}}_{(\epsilon+a)}$.

 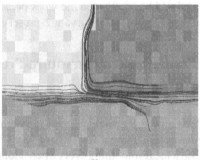

(a) Integral curve of a vector field **w**.

(b) Example of integral curves $C^{\mathbf{X}}_{(a)}$ when **w** is the lowest eigenvector of the structure tensor $\mathbf{G}_\sigma$ of a color image **I**.

Fig. 2. Integral curve $C^{\mathbf{X}}$ of vector fields $\mathbf{w} : \Omega \rightarrow \mathbb{R}^2$

As (5) is verified on **Y**, then $\frac{\partial I_i(C^{\mathbf{X}}_{(a)})}{\partial t}|_{a=\epsilon} = \frac{\partial^2 I_i(C^{\mathbf{X}}_{(a)})}{\partial a^2}|_{a=\epsilon}$. This is obviously true for $\epsilon \in \mathbb{R}$ since (5) is verified for all points **Y** lying on the integral curve $C^{\mathbf{X}}$. Then, the PDE (5) may be also written as : $\forall C \in \mathcal{F}, \quad \forall a \in \mathbb{R}, \quad \frac{\partial I_i(C_{(a)})}{\partial t} = \frac{\partial^2 I_i(C_{(a)})}{\partial a^2}$.

We recognize thus a *one-dimensional heat flow constrained on* C. This is very different from a heat-flow *oriented* by **w**, as in $\frac{\partial I_i}{\partial t} = \frac{\partial^2 I_i}{\partial \mathbf{w}^2}$ since the curvatures of integral curves of **w** are now implicitly taken into account. In particular, the velocity of our constrained equation has the interesting property to vanish when image intensities are locally constant on C, whatever the curvature of C is. In this context, defining a field **w** that is tangent everywhere to the image structures allows the preservation of these structures, even if they are curved (this concerns corners particularly, Fig.2b and Fig.1c). This is not the case with divergence (3) or trace-based PDE's (4).

The existence and unicity of the solutions of (5) are not directly approached in this article, although we show below that these solutions can be approximated by the line integral convolution technique, which is a well-posed analytical approach [6].

3.2 Curvature-Preserving PDE's and Line Integral Convolutions

Line Integral Convolutions (LIC) have been first introduced in [6] as a technique to create a textured image $\mathbf{I}^{LIC}$ that represents a vector field $\mathbf{w} : \Omega \rightarrow \mathbb{R}^2$. The idea consists in smoothing an image $\mathbf{I}^{noise}$ - containing only noise - by averaging its pixel values along the integral curves of **w**. Actually, a continuous formulation of a LIC is :

$$\forall \mathbf{X} \in \Omega, \qquad \mathbf{I}^{LIC}_{(\mathbf{X})} = \frac{1}{N} \int_{-\infty}^{+\infty} f(p) \, \mathbf{I}^{noise}(C^{\mathbf{X}}_{(p)}) \, dp \qquad (8)$$

where $f : \mathbb{R} \rightarrow \mathbb{R}$ is an even function (strictly decreasing to 0 on $\mathbb{R}^+$) and $C^{\mathbf{X}}$ is defined as the *integral curve* (6) of **w** through **X**. The normalization factor N allows the preservation of the average pixel value along $C^{\mathbf{X}}$ and is equal to $N = \int_{-\infty}^{+\infty} f(p) \, dp$. As noticed in previous section, our curvature-preserving PDE (5) can be seen as the one-dimensional heat flow $\frac{\partial I_i(C_{(a)})}{\partial t} = \frac{\partial^2 I_i(C_{(a)})}{\partial a^2}$ constrained on the integral curve $C^{\mathbf{X}} \in \mathcal{F}$.

Using the variable substitution $\mathbf{L}_{(a)} = \mathbf{I}(\mathcal{C}_{(a)}^{\mathbf{X}})$, this PDE becomes $\frac{\partial \mathbf{L}}{\partial t}(a) = \mathbf{L}_{(a)}^{''}$. The solution $\mathbf{L}^{[t]}$ at time t is known to be the convolution of $\mathbf{L}^{[t=0]}$ by a normalized Gaussian kernel G_t (see [15]) : $\mathbf{L}_{(a)}^{[t]} = \int_{-\infty}^{+\infty} \mathbf{L}_{(p)}^{[t=0]} G_{t(a-p)} \, dp$ with $G_{t(p)} = \frac{1}{\sqrt{4\pi t}} \exp\left(-\frac{p^2}{4t}\right)$. Substituting $\mathbf{L}$ with $a = 0$, and remembering that $\mathcal{C}_{(0)}^{\mathbf{X}} = \mathbf{X}$ and $G_{t(-p)} = G_{t(p)}$:

$$\forall \mathbf{X} \in \Omega, \qquad \mathbf{I}_{(\mathbf{X})}^{[t]} = \int_{-\infty}^{+\infty} \mathbf{I}^{[t=0]}(\mathcal{C}_{(p)}^{\mathbf{X}}) \, G_{t(p)} \, dp \qquad (9)$$

Thus, the equation (9) is a particular form of the continuous LIC-based formulation (8) with a Gaussian weighting function $f = G_t$. Here, the normalization factor is $N = \int_{-\infty}^{+\infty} G_{t(p)} \, dp = 1$. Intuitively, the evolution of our curvature-preserving PDE (5) may be seen as the application of local convolutions by normalized one-dimensional Gaussian kernels *along integral curves* $\mathcal{C}$ of $\mathbf{w}$, which is a possibly *curved* filtering instead of an oriented one. Applying this setting on a multi-valued image $\mathbf{I}$, with $\mathbf{w}$ being the lowest eigenvector of the structure tensor field $\mathbf{G}$ (i.e. the contour direction) allows the preservation of curved image structures. This is illustrated on Fig.2b, where few integral lines $\mathcal{C}^{\mathbf{X}}$ are shown, around a typical T-junction structure. Note how the streamlines rotate when arriving at the junction.

Note that (9) is an analytical solution of (5) when $\mathbf{w}$ *does not evolve over time*. This is generally not true when dealing with general nonlinear regularization PDE's, where the smoothing geometry is re-evaluated at each time step. We can anyway perform several iterations of our LIC scheme (9), where the vector field $\mathbf{w}$ is updated at each iteration, exactly as it is done in explicit PDE implementations, where the smoothing geometry $\mathbf{w}$ is considered as constant between two successive time steps t and $t + dt$.

3.3   Between Traces and Divergence Formulations

It is worth to notice than our curvature-preserving PDE (5) is naturally positioned between the trace and divergence formulations. We can express $\mathrm{div}\left(\mathbf{w}\mathbf{w}^T \nabla I_i\right)$ as

$$\mathrm{div}\left(\mathbf{w}\mathbf{w}^T \nabla I_i\right) = \mathrm{trace}\left(\mathbf{w}\mathbf{w}^T \mathbf{H}_i\right) + \nabla I_i^T \mathbf{J}_{\mathbf{w}} \mathbf{w} + \mathrm{div}(\mathbf{w})\nabla I_i^T \mathbf{w}$$

The first term corresponds to the trace PDE (4) (that smoothes locally $\mathbf{I}$ along $\mathbf{w}$), the two first terms correspond to our *curvature-constrained* regularization PDE (5), (that smoothes locally $\mathbf{I}$ along $\mathbf{w}$ while taking the curvature of integral curves $\mathcal{C}$ of $\mathbf{w}$ into account), and the three terms together correspond to the classical divergence PDE (3) that performs local diffusions of $\mathbf{I}$ along $\mathbf{w}$. In our point of view, the last term $\mathrm{div}(\mathbf{w})\nabla I_i^T \mathbf{w}$ is responsible for the perturbations of the effective smoothing direction (as described in section 2.2) and is not desirable for image regularization purposes. Our proposed curvature-constrained PDE (5) allows at the same time the full respect of the pre-defined smoothing directions $\mathbf{w}$, while preserving images structures which are curved along $\mathbf{w}$. Note also that we can also see our curvature-preserving PDE (5) as the corresponding divergence-based equation minus the term $\mathrm{div}(\mathbf{w})\nabla I_i^T \mathbf{w}$. Thus, where $\mathbf{w}$ is a divergence-free field, the divergence and curvature-preserving approaches are strictly equivalent.

3.4 Extension to Multi-directional Smoothing

Here, we extend our single-direction smoothing PDE (5) so that it can deal with a tensor-valued geometry $\mathbf{T} : \Omega \rightarrow P(2)$, instead of a single vector-valued geometry $\mathbf{w}$. Indeed, a diffusion tensor can describe much more complex smoothing behaviors (isotropic and anisotropic) than single directions (only anisotropic). This extension is not straightforward : curvatures and integral curves of tensor-valued fields $\mathbf{T}$ are not easily defined. Instead, we propose to locally decompose a tensor-driven smoothing process by several vector-driven smoothing processes along different orientations. We first notice that $\int_{\alpha=0}^{\pi} a_\alpha a_\alpha^T \, d\alpha = \frac{\pi}{2} \mathbb{I}_d$ with $a_\alpha = \left(\cos\alpha \ \ \sin\alpha \right)^T$. Then, any 2×2 tensor $\mathbf{T}$ may be written as : $\mathbf{T} = \frac{2}{\pi} \sqrt{\mathbf{T}} \left(\int_{\alpha=0}^{\pi} a_\alpha a_\alpha^T \, d\alpha \right) \sqrt{\mathbf{T}}$ where $\sqrt{\mathbf{T}} = \sqrt{f^+} \mathbf{u}\mathbf{u}^T + \sqrt{f^-} \mathbf{v}\mathbf{v}^T$ stands for the square root of $\mathbf{T}$. One can easily verify that $(\sqrt{\mathbf{T}})^2 = \mathbf{T}$ and $(\sqrt{\mathbf{T}})^T = \sqrt{\mathbf{T}}$. Thus, the tensor $\mathbf{T}$ may be written as :

$$\mathbf{T} = \frac{2}{\pi} \int_{\alpha=0}^{\pi} (\sqrt{\mathbf{T}}a_\alpha)(\sqrt{\mathbf{T}}a_\alpha)^T \, d\alpha \qquad (10)$$

We have split the tensor $\mathbf{T}$ into a sum of *atomic* tensors $(\sqrt{\mathbf{T}}a_\alpha)(\sqrt{\mathbf{T}}a_\alpha)^T$, each being purely anisotropic and directed only along the vector $\sqrt{\mathbf{T}}a_\alpha \in \mathbb{R}^2$. The equation (10) naturally suggests to decompose any tensor-driven regularization PDE into a sum of single direction smoothing processes, each of them respecting the overall geometry $\mathbf{T}$. For instance, if $\mathbf{T} = \mathbb{I}_d$ (identity matrix), the tensor is isotropic and $\forall \alpha \in [0, \pi]$, $\sqrt{\mathbf{T}}a_\alpha = a_\alpha$. The resulting smoothing will be then performed in all directions a_α of the plane with the same strength, while if $\mathbf{T} = \mathbf{u}\mathbf{u}^T$ (where $\mathbf{u} \in S^1$), the tensor is purely anisotropic and : $\forall \alpha \in [0, \pi]$, $\sqrt{\mathbf{T}}a_\alpha = (\mathbf{u}^T a_\alpha)\mathbf{u}$. The resulting smoothing will be then performed only along the direction $\mathbf{u}$ of the tensor $\mathbf{T}$.

Then, considering that each single direction smoothing must be done with a curvature-preserving PDE (5), we define the following constrained regularization PDE, acting on a multi-valued image $\mathbf{I}$ and driven by a tensor-valued smoothing geometry $\mathbf{T}$:

$$\frac{\partial I_i}{\partial t} = \frac{2}{\pi} \int_{\alpha=0}^{\pi} \text{trace}\left((\sqrt{\mathbf{T}}a_\alpha)(\sqrt{\mathbf{T}}a_\alpha)^T \mathbf{H}_i \right) + \nabla I_i^T \, \mathbf{J}_{\sqrt{\mathbf{T}}a_\alpha} \sqrt{\mathbf{T}}a_\alpha \, d\alpha,$$

which can be simplified as :

$$\forall i = 1, \dots, n, \qquad \frac{\partial I_i}{\partial t} = \text{trace}(\mathbf{T}\mathbf{H}_i) + \frac{2}{\pi} \nabla I_i^T \int_{\alpha=0}^{\pi} \mathbf{J}_{\sqrt{\mathbf{T}}a_\alpha} \sqrt{\mathbf{T}}a_\alpha \, d\alpha \qquad (11)$$

where $a_\alpha = \left(\cos\alpha \ \ \sin\alpha \right)^T$, and $\mathbf{J}_{\sqrt{\mathbf{T}}a_\alpha}$ stands for the Jacobian of the vector field $\Omega \rightarrow \sqrt{\mathbf{T}}a_\alpha$. A similar idea of smoothing decomposition along all orientations of the plane can be also found in [35]. As in the single direction case, (11) may be seen as a trace-based equation (4), where an extra term has been added in order to respect the curvature of all integral lines passing through the tensor-valued geometry $\mathbf{T}$.

4 Implementation and Applications

The implementation of our regularization method (11) benefits from the LIC-based interpretation of curvature-preserving PDE's presented in section 3.2. Indeed, we can explicitly discretize (11) by the Euler scheme : $\mathbf{I}^{[t+dt]} = \mathbf{I}^{[t]} + \frac{2dt}{N} \left(\sum_{k=0}^{N-1} \mathcal{R}(\sqrt{\mathbf{T}}a_\alpha) \right)$

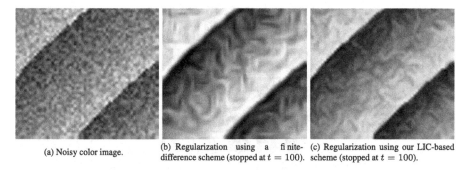

(a) Noisy color image.

(b) Regularization using a finite-difference scheme (stopped at $t = 100$).

(c) Regularization using our LIC-based scheme (stopped at $t = 100$).

Fig. 3. Comparison between traditional and LIC-based implementations of our PDE (11)

(a) Denoising of the "baboon" color image (19.3s).

(b) Watered effect suppression in a color image (11s).

(c) Suppression of JPEG compression artifacts in the "Lena" image (6.4s).

(d) Suppression of quantification artifacts in a 8bits color image (12.8s).

(e) Denoising of a digital photograph with digital noise (5.6s).

(f) Creating painting effects with over-smoothing procedures (26s).

Fig. 4. Results of color image regularization using our curvature-preserving PDE's (11)

(a) Inpainting a cage (middle) in a color image (left). Inpainted in 4m11s (right).

(b) Removing subtitles from a movie frame (11s).

(c) *Left :* Zoom of (b).   *Right :* Reconstruction of a color image where 50% of the pixel values have been suppressed (1m01s).

From left to right : First row : Original color image, bloc-resizing, bicubic resizing, PDE-based resizing.

Fig. 5. Result of our curvature-preserving PDE (11) for interpolation of color images. (More results at *http://www.greyc.ensicaen.fr/˜dtschump/greycstoration/*).

where $\alpha = k\pi/N$ (in the interval $[0, \pi]$), dt is the usual temporal discretization step and $\mathcal{R}(\mathbf{w})$ represents a discretization of the curvature-preserving PDE (5) that preserves curvatures along the single direction $\mathbf{w}$. If we write this expression as :

$\mathbf{I}^{[t+dt]} = \frac{1}{N} \left(\sum_{k=0}^{N-1} \mathbf{I}^{[t]} + 2dt \, \mathcal{R}(\sqrt{\mathbf{T}} a_\alpha) \right)$, we can express it as the averaging of different LIC's along vector fields $\sqrt{\mathbf{T}} a_\alpha$:

$$\mathbf{I}^{[t+dt]} = \frac{1}{N} \left(\sum_{k=0}^{N-1} \mathbf{I}^{[t]}_{LIC(\sqrt{\mathbf{T}} a_\alpha)} \right)$$

The only difficult part here is the LIC implementation which needs the computation of integral curves. A classical second-order Runge-Kutta integration [23] has been used with success for our implementation. On one hand, our scheme allows the preservation of thin image structures from a numerical point of view : the smoothing is performed along integral curves of $\mathbf{w}$, with a sub-pixel accuracy (see comparisons with a classical finite difference discretization, Fig.3). On the other hand, this scheme is unconditionally stable and allows to choose very large time steps dt, without visible artifacts in the obtained regularization ($dt \simeq 50$ in our experiments). As a result,the algorithm performs very fast ($\simeq \times 3$) compared to traditional diffusion PDE implementations.

Fig.4 and 5 present different application results of our curvature-preserving PDE (11), implemented by the LIC-based scheme and applied on 24bits RGB color images $\mathbf{I} : \Omega \rightarrow [0, 255]^3$. All experiments have been performed on a single-CPU PC 2.8 Ghz running Linux. Possible application range covers color image regularization (PDE is applied on the entire image), inpainting (PDE is applied only inside regions to inpaint), and non-linear resizing (similar to inpainting with a sparse mask). See [31, 32] for more precisions on how diffusion PDE's are used in these contexts. Processing time is displayed for each example. Other results, as well as the C++ source code of the proposed algorithm can be found at : http://www.greyc.ensicaen.fr/~dtschump/greycstoration/.

References

1. L. Alvarez, F. Guichard, P.L. Lions, J.M. Morel. *Axioms and fundamental equations of image processing*. Arch. for Rational Mechanics and Analysis, Vol.123, No.3, pp.199–257, 1993.
2. G. Aubert and P. Kornprobst. *Mathematical Problems in Image Processing: PDE's and the Calculus of Variations*, Applied Math. Sciences, Vol.147, Springer-Verlag, January 2002.
3. M. Bertalmio, L.T. Cheng, S. Osher, and G. Sapiro. *Variational Problems and PDE's on Implicit Surfaces*. Comput. and Visual. in Science, Vol.174, No.2, pp.759–780, 2001.
4. M. Bertalmio, G. Sapiro, V. Caselles, and C. Ballester. *Image inpainting*. ACM SIGGRAPH, Int. Conf. on Computer Graphics and Interactive Techniques, pp.417–424, 2000.
5. M.J. Black, G. Sapiro, D.H. Marimont, and D. Heeger. *Robust anisotropic diffusion*. IEEE Transaction on Image Processing, Vol.7, No.3, pp.421–432, 1998.
6. B. Cabral and L.C. Leedom. *Imaging vector fields using line integral convolution*. SIGGRAPH'93, in Computer Graphics Vol.27, pp.263–272, 1993.
7. R. Carmona and S. Zhong. *Adaptive Smoothing Respecting Feature Directions*. IEEE Transactions on Image Processing, Vol.7, No.3, pp.353–358, 1998.
8. A. Chambolle and P.L. Lions. *Image recovery via total variation minimization and related problems*. Nümerische Mathematik, Vol.76, No.2, pp.167–188, 1997.

9. T. Chan and J. Shen. *Variational restoration of non-flat image features : Models and algorithms.* SIAM Journal of Applied Mathematics, Vol.61, No.4, pp.1338–1361, 2000.

10. P. Charbonnier, L. Blanc-Féraud, G. Aubert, M. Barlaud. *Deterministic edge-preserving regularization in computed imaging.* IEEE Trans. on Image Proc., Vol.6 (2), 1997.

11. C. Chefd'hotel, D. Tschumperlé, R. Deriche, and O. Faugeras. *Regularizing Flows for Constrained Matrix-Valued Images.* Journ. of Math. Imaging and Vision, Vol.20 (2), Jan. 2004.

12. S. Di Zenzo *A note on the gradient of a multi-image.* Computer Vision, Graphics and Image Processing, Vol.33, pp.116-125, 1986.

13. R. Kimmel, R. Malladi, and N. Sochen. *Images as embedded maps and minimal surfaces: movies, color, texture, and volumetric medical images.* IJCV, Vol.39 (2), Sept. 2000.

14. R. Kimmel and N. Sochen. *Orientation diffusion or how to comb a porcupine.* Journal of Visual Communication and Image Representation, Vol.13, pp.238–248, 2002.

15. J.J. Koenderink. *The structure of images.* Biological Cybernetics, Vol.50, pp.363–370, 1984.

16. P. Kornprobst, R. Deriche, and G. Aubert. *Nonlinear operators in image restoration* IEEE Conference on Computer Vision and Pattern Recognition, pp 325-331, June 1997.

17. K. Krissian. *Multiscale Analysis : Application to Medical Imaging and 3D Vessel Detection.* Ph.D. Thesis, INRIA-Sophia Antipolis/France, 2000.

18. T. Lindeberg. *Scale-Space Theory in Computer Vision.* Kluwer Academic Publishers, 1994.

19. M. Nielsen, L. Florack, and R. Deriche. *Regularization, scale-space and edge detection filters.* Journal of Mathematical Imaging and Vision, Vol.7, No.4, pp.291–308, 1997.

20. P. Perona. *Orientation diffusions.* IEEE Trans. on Image Proc., Vol.7 (3), pp.457–467, 1998.

21. P. Perona and J. Malik. *Scale-space and edge detection using anisotropic diffusion.* IEEE Trans. on Pattern Anal. and Machine Intell., Vol.12 (7), pp.629–639, 1990.

22. T. Preusser and M. Rumpf. *Anisotropic nonlinear diffusion in flow visualization.* IEEE Visualization Conference, 1999.

23. W.H. Press, B.P. Flannery, S.A. Teukolsky, and W.T. Vetterling. *"Runge-Kutta Method"* in Numerical Recipes, Cambridge University Press, pp. 704-716, 1992.

24. L. Rudin, S. Osher, and E. Fatemi. *Nonlinear total variation based noise removal algorithms.* Physica D, Vol.60, pp.259–268, 1992.

25. G. Sapiro. *Geometric Partial Differential Equations and Image Analysis.* Cambridge University Press, 2001.

26. G. Sapiro and D.L. Ringach. *Anisotropic diffusion of multi-valued images with applications to color filtering.* IEEE Transactions on Image Processing, Vol.5, No.11, pp.1582–1585, 1996.

27. N. Sochen, R. Kimmel, and A.M. Bruckstein. *Diffusions and confusions in signal and image processing.* Journal of Mathematical Imaging and Vision, Vol.14, No.3, pp.195–209, 2001.

28. D. Stalling and H.C. Hege. *Fast and Resolution Independent Line Integral Convolution.* SIGGRAPH, 22nd Ann. Conf. on Computer Graphics, pp.249–256, 1995.

29. B. Tang, G. Sapiro, and V. Caselles. *Direction diffusion.* IEEE International Conference on Computer Vision, pp.1245, 1999.

30. B. Tang, G. Sapiro, and V. Caselles. *Diffusion of general data on non-flat manifolds via harmonic maps theory : The direction diffusion case.* IJCV, Vol.36 (2), pp.149–161, 2000.

31. D. Tschumperlé *PDE's Based Regularization of Multi-valued Images and Applications.* PhD Thesis, Université de Nice-Sophia Antipolis/France, December 2002.

32. D. Tschumperlé and R. Deriche *Vector-Valued Image Regularization with PDE's : A Common Framework for Different Applications.* IEEE Trans. on PAMI, Vol.27, No.4, April 2005.

33. D. Tschumperlé. *The CImg Library :* http://cimg.sourceforge.net. The C++ Template Image Processing Library.

34. B. Vemuri, Y. Chen, M. Rao, T. McGraw, T. Mareci, and Z. Wang. *Fiber tract mapping from diffusion tensor MRI.* IEEE Workshop on Variat. and Level Set Methods, July 2001.
35. J. Weickert. *Anisotropic Diffusion Filters for Image Processing Based Quality Control.* 7th European Conference on Mathematics in Industry, pp.355–362, 1994.
36. J. Weickert. *Anisotropic Diffusion in Image Processing.* Teubner-Verlag, Stuttgart, 1998.
37. J. Weickert. *Coherence-Enhancing Diffusion of Colour Images.* Image and Vision Computing, Vol.17, pp.199–210, 1999.
38. J. Weickert and T. Brox. *Diffusion and Regularization of Vector and Matrix-valued Images.* Inverse Problems, Image Analysis, and Medical Imaging, Vol.313 of Contemporary Mathematics, pp.251–268, 2002.

Higher Order Image Pyramids*

Joshua Gluckman

Polytechnic University,
Dept. of Computer and Information Science,
Brooklyn, New York

Abstract. The scale invariant property of an ensemble of natural images is examined which motivates a new early visual representation termed the higher order pyramid. The representation is a non-linear generalization of the Laplacian pyramid and is tuned to the type of scale invariance exhibited by natural imagery as opposed to other scale invariant images such as $1/f$ correlated noise and the step edge. The transformation of an image to a higher order pyramid is simple to compute and straightforward to invert. Because the representation is invertible it is shown that the higher order pyramid can be truncated and quantized with little loss of visual quality. Images coded in this representation have much less redundancy than the raw image pixels and decorrelating transformations such as the Laplacian pyramid. This is demonstrated by showing statistical independence between pairs of coefficients. Because the representation is tuned to the ensemble redundancies the coefficients of the higher order pyramid are more efficient at capturing the variation within the ensemble which leads too improved matching results. This is demonstrated on two recognition tasks, face recognition with illumination changes and object recognition which viewpoint changes.

1 Introduction

It has been argued for some time that the problem of early vision is to determine the most efficient method for representing images. Early formulations of this theory were given by Atteneave and Barlow who argued for redundancy reduction through the efficient coding hypothesis [2] [3]. The rational is rooted in information theory: if later visual processes are to perform probabilistic inference the input should be as statistically independent as possible The implication for early vision is that images should be coded to match the expected input, the ensemble of natural images (for examples see Fig. 1). Since, considerable advances have been made in understanding this ensemble by studying the statistics of natural images and arguably the most important feature to emerge is scale invariance (see [4] for a recent review). While multi-resolution representations such as the Laplacian, steerable, and wavelet pyramids are motivated by scale invariance they are not necessarily tuned to the type of scale invariance found in images.

In this paper we present a novel method for representing images which is motivated by the type of scale invariance found in the ensemble of natural images. This representation is a non-linear transformation based on the Laplacian

---

* This work was supported by a NSF ITR award no. IIS-0219078.

A. Leonardis, H. Bischof, and A. Pinz (Eds.): ECCV 2006, Part II, LNCS 3952, pp. 308–320, 2006.

Fig. 1. Examples of natural images from the Van Hatteren database [1]

pyramid of Burt and Adelson [5] and is referred to as the higher order image pyramid. Because the transformation is invertible it is shown that the higher order pyramid can be quantized and truncated with little loss of visual quality. Once an image is coded the bits of the higher order pyramid exhibit far less redundancy than the raw image pixels and linear transformations such as the Laplacian pyramid. This is shown by demonstrating that the mutual information between pairs of coefficients is near zero.

Tuning a representation to the ensemble redundancies implies the representation efficiently captures the variation within the ensemble. Capturing this variation leads to improvements in recognition tasks. This is demonstrated by showing improved matching using the higher order pyramid on an object recognition task with varying viewpoint and a face recognition task with varying illumination.

2   Scale Invariance

The first statistical evidence of scale invariance was found by Field who discovered a $1/f$ power law in the amplitude spectra of natural images indicating that spatial correlations are scale invariant [6]. Further evidence was found by Ruderman and by Zhu and Mumford who demonstrated that histograms of derivative filtered images are consistent across scale indicating scaling in the higher order statistics [7] [8]. Although the presence of scale invariance in images is clear, no method exists for fully taking advantage of this property. One reason for this is the lack of a simple model that suggests how to represent the type of scale invariance found in images. Next, we develop such a model.

The type of scale invariance seen in images is examined by considering the behavior of each particular image as the scale is reduced. Once particular images are considered the range of intensities is fixed, hence the moments are finite. Then scale invariance appears in the expected value of the moments of the distribution of intensity as scale is reduced which is

310   J. Gluckman

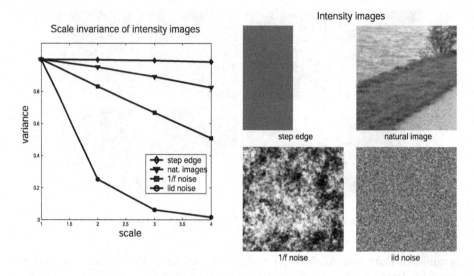

Fig. 2. The variance in intensity as a function of scale (the number of times the images are downsampled) for a pure step edge, a set of natural images, $1/f$ noise, and iid noise. The step edge, $1/f$ noise, and natural images all exhibit scale invariance indicated by a slow linear decay.

$$E\{|I(x/s)|^k\}, \tag{1}$$

where $I(x)$ is an image, s is the spatial scale, and the expectation E is taken over an ensemble of images. We assume the mean intensity is subtracted from each image so k is a central moment.

Fig. 2 shows the result of estimating (1) for $k = 2$ using 40 images selected from the van Hateren database [1]. A scale change of $I(x)$ is implemented by smoothing and downsampling. Each image is repeatedly blurred, downsampled and a variance ($k = 2$) is estimated. For each scale the variances of all 40 images are averaged. The plot shows the reduction in variance as a function of scale and compares the behavior of images to that of a pure step edge, $1/f$ noise, and iid noise. All plots are normalized to 1 at the first scale. The step edge, the images, and $1/f$ noise all exhibit scale invariance because the variance falls linearly. The same result is found for the higher moments implying

$$E\{|I(x/s)|^k\} = E\{|I(x/(2s))|^k\} + K. \tag{2}$$

The actual value of the constant K is unimportant. However, for images K lies somewhere between that of a step edge and $1/f$ noise,

$$K_{1/f} < K_{\text{images}} < K_{\text{step}}. \tag{3}$$

What differentiates images is the *rate* at which the moments decay with scale.

Multi-resolution representations such as the Laplacian pyramid are motivated by the fact that images exhibit scale invariance. These representations code

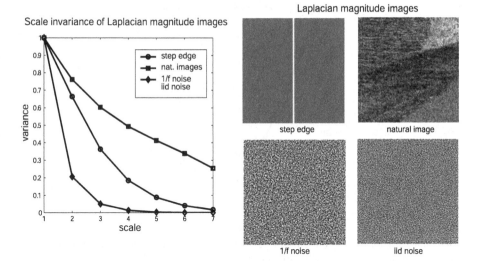

Fig. 3. The variance of the Laplacian magnitude as a function of scale for a pure step edge, a set of natural images, and $1/f$ noise. Only the natural images are scale invariant.

$$L(x/s) = I(x/s) - I(x/(2s)),$$

which is the prediction error between scales. However, such representations do not explicitly differentiate between step edges, $1/f$ noise, and natural images. To describe the type of scale invariance that images exhibit, L must be examined.

Although L, the levels of a Laplacian pyramid, are no longer scale invariant according to eq. (2) they still resemble images which suggests a hidden scale invariance. Indeed, if a new image (the Laplacian magnitude) is defined

$$I^{(2)} = \log|L| \qquad (4)$$

which is independent of the sign then scale invariance reappears. The log function is used to reduce the sensitivity of the statistics to the extreme values. The fact that redundancy exists in the magnitude is well known and has been documented by Simoncelli et al [9] [10] [11]. Here it is shown that the form of the redundancy is scale invariance. Next, the same experiment is repeated except using $I^{(2)}$ for each of the 40 natural images, the step edge, the $1/f$ noise, and the iid noise.

Fig. 3 shows the result of the experiment. Now the behavior of images is very different. The Laplacian magnitude of a step edge is a line edge and the Laplacian magnitude of $1/f$ noise is similar to iid noise neither of which have scale invariance. For natural images the Laplacian magnitude appears scale invariant. Furthermore, if we start from a lower scale and include the data from Fig. 2 the same pattern emerges as in the first experiment (see Fig. 4). Thus $I^{(2)}$ for natural images behaves like I meaning both (2) and (3) hold. Therefore, we define the following sequence

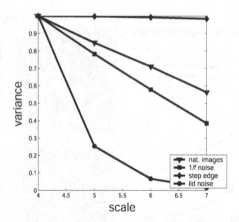

Fig. 4. The plot for the natural images from Fig. 3 is combined with the plot for the other images from Fig. 2. The rate of decay for the Laplacian magnitude of the natural images is similar to that of the intensity images.

$$I^{(1)}(x/s) = I(x/s)$$
$$I^{(n)}(x/s) = \log|I^{(n-1)}(x/s) - I^{(n-1)}(x/(2s))|,$$

and assume that if (2) and (3) are true for $I^{(n)}$ they are true for $I^{(n+1)}$. Just as the Laplacian pyramid is a representation that assumes I is scale invariant, the higher order pyramid is a representation that assumes $I^{(1)}, I^{(2)}, I^{(3)} \dots$ are scale invariant. The implication is that the higher order pyramid is tuned to the type of scale invariance of natural images and not that of other scale invariant images such as $1/f$ noise and the step edge. In the next section the construction of the higher order image pyramid is described.

3   Higher Order Pyramids

We begin with a description of the Laplacian pyramid on which higher order pyramids are based. The Laplacian pyramid is motivated by the scale invariance of $I^{(1)}$ and only codes the information at each scale that is not predicted by the lower scale. The transformation $\mathcal{L}$ constructs a Laplacian pyramid for an image I and is defined by the set,

$$\mathcal{L}(I) = \{L_1, L_2, \dots, L_s, G\}, \tag{5}$$

where $L_i = I(x/2^{i-1}) - I(x/2^i)$ are levels of the pyramid. L_1 is the finest scale, L_s is the coarsest scale and G is the lowpass residual. Using $\mathcal{L}_i$ to refer to the ith member of the set $\mathcal{L}$, it is straightforward to invert $\mathcal{L}$ by

$$I = \mathcal{L}^{-1} = \sum_{i=1}^{s+1} \mathcal{L}_i \tag{6}$$

where upsampling and convolution are implicit (for details see [5]).

A higher order pyramid is motivated by the scale invariance of $I^{(1)}, I^{(2)}, I^{(3)} \ldots$ where the prediction error is $L_i/|L_i|$ which are the sign bits. However, the sign operation introduces aliasing and is not rotationally invariant which is why scale invariance does not appear until the lower scales (see the abscissa axis of Fig. 3). Rather than coding the sign bits we code

$$C(I) = \{L_1(x)/M_1(x/2), \ldots, L_s(x)/M_s(x/2), G\} \quad (7)$$

where $M_i = |L_i|$. The operation $L_i(x)/M_i(x/2)$ is accomplished by dividing a level of the Laplacian pyramid by its magnitude after blurring, downsampling, and upsampling. Thus, C constructs a pyramid on the input image I and divides each level by a reduced resolution version of the magnitude at that level. The result is a contrast normalized Laplacian pyramid. The higher order pyramid differs from other contrast normalized image representations by explicitly representing the magnitudes as well via additional pyramids [7] [12]. The higher order pyramid is recursively defined by the set

$$\mathcal{H}^{(1)}(I) = \{C(I), \{\log M_1(x/2), \ldots, \log M_s(x/2)\}\} \quad (8)$$

$$\mathcal{H}^{(n)}(I) = \{C(I), \{\mathcal{H}^{(n-1)}(\log M_1(x/2)), \ldots, \mathcal{H}^{(n-1)}(\log M_s(x/2))\}\}. \quad (9)$$

Because this is a doubly recursive representation there are two notions of depth, s the number of times the scale is reduced when building the pyramids and n the number of times pyramids are built on the images $I^{(1)}, I^{(2)}, I^{(3)} \ldots$. We refer to n as the order of the pyramid. A first order pyramid, $\mathcal{H}^{(1)}$, is a contrast normalized Laplacian pyramid along with $I^{(2)}$ the residual magnitude images. A second order pyramid, $\mathcal{H}^{(2)}$, constructs a first order pyramid on each of the residual magnitudes and keeps the $I^{(3)}$ residuals . For higher orders this process is repeated. Fig. 5 demonstrates a higher order pyramid built up to order 3. Each time the order is increased the residual magnitudes decrease in scale by a factor of 2. It is straightforward to show that the total number of coefficients is twice the number of pixels. Hence, the representation is twice overcomplete.

$\mathcal{H}$ is a set with two elements each of which is a set. The notation $\mathcal{H}_{1,i}$ refers to the ith member of the first set and $\mathcal{H}_{2,i}$ refers to the ith member of the second set. Using this notation it is straightforward to invert the pyramid by

$$\mathcal{H}^{(n)^{-1}} = \sum_{i=1}^{s} \mathcal{H}_{1,i} \exp\left(\mathcal{H}_{2,i}^{-1}\right) + \mathcal{H}_{1,s+1}, \quad (10)$$

$$\mathcal{H}^{(1)^{-1}} = \sum_{i=1}^{s} \mathcal{H}_{1,i} \exp\left(\mathcal{H}_{2,i}\right) + \mathcal{H}_{1,s+1}, \quad (11)$$

which recursively collapses all of the pyramids and multiplies back in the magnitudes. Like the Laplacian pyramid, there is no loss of information when inverting the higher order pyramid.

For any order, the pyramid can be inverted without the residual magnitudes which we refer to as a truncated pyramid. This is done by redefining eq. 11 to

$$\mathcal{H}^{(1)^{-1}} = \sum_{i=1}^{s} \mathcal{H}_{1,i} + \mathcal{H}_{1,s+1}. \quad (12)$$

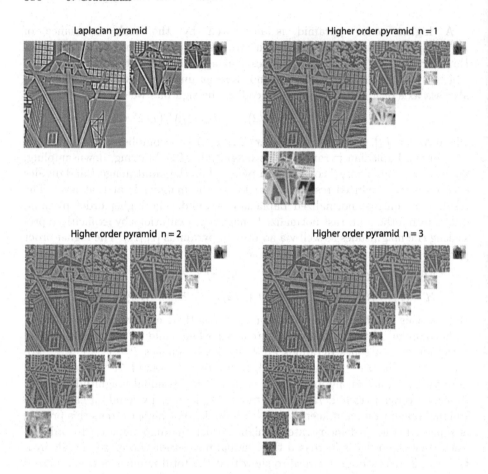

Fig. 5. A higher order pyramid is built from a Laplacian pyramid which in this example is three levels deep along with a lowpass residual. A first order pyramid, $n = 1$, is a contrast normalized pyramid with a residual magnitude shown below each level. A second order pyramid, $n = 2$, builds first order pyramids on the magnitudes that are larger than the lowpass residual. A third order pyramid repeats the process.

Although the result is a loss of information, the visual quality of the reconstructed images rapidly improves as n increases. The transformation is also stable with respect to quantization in that visual quality also rapidly improves with the size of the quantization bins. Fig. 6 demonstrates examples of reconstructed images from truncated pyramids with coefficients quantized to integer values resulting in an average entropy of 2.2 bits per coefficient.

4   Experiments

Three experiments are performed. The first is application independent and measures the degree to which pairs of coefficients are independent. The reason for

original image   second order pyramid   first order pyramid

Fig. 6. The images are examples of inverting the higher order pyramid after truncating (removing the residual magnitudes) and quantizing the coefficients. The residual magnitude becomes significantly less important as the order increases. Furthermore, the transformation is stable with respect to quantization of the coefficients.

this test is that the efficiency of a representation is reflected by the lack of redundancy or independence in the coefficients of the representation. The second and third experiments are recognition tests. A good representation should lead to improved matching. The rational is that a less redundant representation is a better space in which to perform matching in the presence of uncertainty. In our experiments two types of uncertainty are considered, face recognition with illumination changes and object recognition with viewpoint changes. In all of our experiments the Laplacian and higher order pyramids are implemented using a 7-tap binomial filter and image borders are handled via reflection.

4.1   Redundancy

To test for redundancy the joint distribution for a pair of coefficients is measured from a set of 40 natural images. For each image, statistics are gathered for all pairs of coefficients displaced by 5 pixel positions in the diagonal direction. This is done for the raw image pixels, for a level in the Laplacian pyramid, and for a level in the higher order pyramid. A distance of 5 is chosen to ensure the coefficients are not within the support of the convolution filter.

The distributions are displayed as conditional distributions in Fig. 7 where intensity represents the likelihood of y conditioned on the value of x. The Laplacian pyramid has the familiar bowtie shape documented by Simoncelli [9]. This is indicative of the fact that the magnitudes are correlated. Meanwhile the coefficients of the higher order pyramid are clearly independent because the likelihood of x is the same for all values of y. This is also reflected by the mutual information shown below each plot. Similar results are found for different spatial offsets

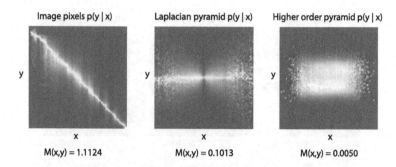

Image pixels p(y | x)   Laplacian pyramid p(y | x)   Higher order pyramid p(y | x)

M(x,y) = 1.1124   M(x,y) = 0.1013   M(x,y) = 0.0050

Fig. 7. Conditional distributions for pairs of coefficients at the same spatial offset. In the pixel domain the coefficients are correlated. In the Laplacian pyramid they are decorrelated but still dependent because the variance of y scales with x. In the higher order pyramid they are independent. Below each graph is M the measured mutual information between the coefficients for each representation.

both within and between different levels of the higher order pyramid. Independence has also been demonstrated after applying contrast normalization [12]. However because the higher order pyramid is invertible we can be sure that the independence does not arise from destroying information. It is important to note that correlations exist for neighboring pairs of coefficients within and between levels however these are not due to redundancy in natural images but arise from the convolution. Hence, they exist even for noise images.

4.2 Face Recognition with Illumination Changes

Using the Yale illumination face database and experimental setup reported in [13], we test the ability of higher order pyramids to perform face recognition in the presence of illumination changes. The database contains 10 faces each under 64 different illuminants. They are grouped into 5 subsets according to the severity of the direction of illumination. Example are shown in Fig. 8(a). Each face is cropped and downsampled to a resolution of 96 × 80 pixels. We compared the matching performance of the representations shown in Fig. 8(b). The pyramids are constructed 3 levels deep and the lowpass residual and the residual magnitude images are not used. Because the levels of the pyramids are subsampled each level is weighted by $4^{(s-1)}$ so that all levels contribute equally. Then each representation is treated as a vector of coefficients and matching is done with normalized cross correlation. One image of each persons face is used as the training image and the remaining 630 images are used as test images. For all representations log intensities are used.

The results are reported in Fig. 9 and demonstrate a clear advantage for the higher order pyramid as compared to the Laplacian pyramid and the raw image pixels. For further comparison the results from Chen et al. are also included [13]. It should be pointed out that all of the other methods with the exception ofGradient Angle use all of the images in Subset 1 and 2 for training.

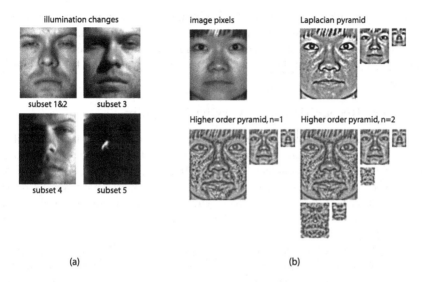

(a)   (b)

Fig. 8. (a) Examples from the Yale illumination face database. Recognition is done using normalized cross correlation with the representations in (b).

Furthermore, Subset 5, the one with the most sever illumination directions, is not used in any of the other experiments.

The Gradient Angle method learns, from a database of images, an illumination insensitive weighting of the magnitude of the gradient. Because the magnitudeis

Face recognition error rate (%) vs. Illumination				
Method	Subset 1&2	Subset 3	Subset 4	Subset 5
Eigenfaces	0	16.7	69.3	–
Linear subspace	0	1.7	12.9	–
Cones-attached	0	0.8	9.3	–
Gradient Angle	0	0.0	1.4	–
Cones-cast	0	0.0	0.0	–
Image pixels	0.6	15.0	47.9	46.3
Laplacian pyramid	0	1.7	10.0	24.2
Higher order pyramid, n=1	0	0	8.6	11.6
Higher order pyramid, n=2	0	0	0	0

Fig. 9. Face recognition error rates. The methods in **bold** are experiments we performed using normalized cross correlation and the other results are from [13]. The images are grouped into subsets according to the severity of the illuminant direction. Subset 5 is the most severe and is not included in the results reported by the other methods. Out of 630 test images the second order pyramid had no errors.

sensitive to illumination the Gradient Angle method is a form of contrast normalization thus bears a resemblance to the first order pyramid. However, the perfect performance of the second order pyramid indicates that representing the magnitude (in a less redundant space) rather than normalizing the magnitude is important.

4.3   Object Recognition with Varying Viewpoint

Using the recently available Amsterdam object database [14], we test the ability of higher order pyramids to perform recognition in the presence of viewpoint changes. This is a large database containing 1000 small objects. Each object is imaged on a rotational stage from 72 positions at 5° increments. We used the grey scale dataset at quarter resolution which was further downsampled to a resolution of 72 × 96 pixels. In addition log intensities are used. Examples of some of the objects are shown in Fig. 10.

For each object, N evenly spaced training views are used. Each test image is matched between all training views. Again we tested the performance of matching using the image pixels, the Laplacian pyramid, and the higher order pyramid where each representation is treated as a vector of weighted coefficients. The depth of the pyramids is the same as the face recognition experiment except the lowpass residual images are included this time. In the face recognition experiment the lowpass residual is too dependent on illumination. Furthermore, sum of squared distances (SSD) is used rather than normalized correlation due to the use of the lowpass images. One important difference between the object images and the face images is the background. In order to avoid the background biasing the results the mean vector is computed for the entire set of training views. This mean vector is then subtracted from each training vector and from each test vector prior to computing the SSD.

Due to the size of the database 10 trials are performed on subsets of 100 randomly selected objects. For each trial N training images are used for each of the 100 chosen objects and 5000 test images are randomly chosen from among

Fig. 10. Example of objects from the Amsterdam library of object images (ALOI)

the 7200 images of the chosen objects. Below are the recognition error rates averaged over the 10 trials for $N = 6, 8, 12$. In all cases the second order pyramid outperforms the other representations.

Object recognition error rate (%) vs. number of training views			
Representation	6 views	8 views	12 views
Image pixels	6.90	3.72	1.56
Laplacian pyramid	5.83	2.81	1.01
Higher order pyramid, n=1	4.10	2.08	0.63
Higher order pyramid, n=2	3.74	1.50	0.31

5   Discussion

The scale invariant properties of natural images leads to the higher order pyramid as an early visual representation which is simple to compute and straightforward to invert. Images coded in the space of higher order pyramids exhibit far less redundancy than the raw image pixels and decorrelating transformations such as the Laplacian pyramid. This is demonstrated by showing the independence between pairs of coefficients and improved matching in two recognition experiments. The recognition experiments are only intended to demonstrate the potential for redundancy reduction as a goal for the representation of visual patterns and the higher order pyramid as a step in this direction. The real benefit is the further processing of the higher order pyramid and the incorporation of learning techniques.

It is interesting to note that the representation is not oriented. Because a Laplacian pyramid is used to construct the higher order pyramid the basis functions are all circularly symmetric Gaussian functions albeit combined in a non-linear way. This might seem strange given the wide spread use of oriented filters such as Gabor functions and steerable derivatives throughout computer vision. In addition, oriented receptive fields are commonplace in computational models of human vision. Furthermore, it is well known that the optimal linear basis in which to represent natural images is made up of oriented basis functions [6] [15] [16]. If we assume that scale invariance as defined in this paper is a natural description of images then we must ask why use oriented basis functions. We briefly speculate on some possible answers. (1) The model proposed here does not fully capture the scale invariance of images. (2) Other statistical properties of images that are not implied by scale invariance are more important. (3) Oriented basis functions are simply the best way to represent scale invariance when restricted to a linear framework. However, in a non-linear framework they may no longer be needed.

References

1. van Hateren, J.: Independent component filters of natural images compared with simple cells. Proc. of the R. Stat. Soc. of London B **265** (1998) 359–366
2. Attneave, F.: Some informational aspects of visual perception. Psych. Rev. **61** (1954) 183–193
3. Barlow, H.: Possible principles underlying the transformaiton of senosry messages. In: Sensory Commuincation. MIT Press (1961)
4. Zhu, S.: Statistical modeling and coneptualization of visual patterns. IEEE Trans. on Pattern Analaysis and Machine Intelligence **25** (2003) 691–712
5. Burt, P., Adelson, E.: The laplacian pyramid as a compact image code. IEEE Trans. on Communications. **31** (1983) 532–540
6. Field, D.: Relations between the statistics of natural images and the response properties of cortical cells. J. of the Opt. Soc. of Am. A **4** (1987) 2379–
7. Ruderman, D.: The statistics of natural images. Network **5** (1993) 477–500
8. Zhu, S., Mumford, D.: Prior learning and gibbs reactionn-diffusion. IEEE Trans. on Pattern Analysis and Machine Intelligence **19** (1997) 1236–
9. Simoncelli, E., Adelson, E.: Noise removal via bayesian wavelet coding. In: Int'l Conf. on Image Processing. (1996) 379–382
10. Simoncelli, E., Freeman, W.: The steerable pyramid: A flexible architecture for multi-scale derivative computation. In: Int'l Conf. on Image Processing. (1995)
11. Buccigrossi, R., Simoncelli, E.: Image compression via joint statistical characterization in the wavelet domain. IEEE Trans. on Image Processing **8** (1999) 1688–
12. Schwartz, O., Simoncelli, E.: Natural signal statistics and sensory gain control. Nature Neuroscience **4** (2001) 819–825
13. Chen, H., Belhumeur, P., Jacobs, D.: In search of illumination invariants. In: Proc. of the IEEE Conf. on Computer Vision and Pattern Recognition. (2000)
14. Geusebroek, J., Burghouts, G., Smeulders, A.: The amsterdam library of object images. Int'l J. Computer Vision **61** (2005) 103–112
15. Olshausen, B., Field, D.: Emergence of simple-cell receptive field properties by learning a sparse code for natural images. Nature **381** (1996) 607–609
16. Bell, A., Sejnowski, T.: The independent components of natural scenes are edge filters. Vision Research **37** (1997) 3327–38

Image Specific Feature Similarities

Ido Omer and Michael Werman

School of Computer Science,
The Hebrew University of Jerusalem,
Jerusalem 91904, Israel
{idom, werman}@cs.huji.ac.il

Abstract. Calculating a reliable similarity measure between pixel features is essential for many computer vision and image processing applications. We propose a similarity measure (affinity) between pixel features, which depends on the feature space histogram of the image. We use the observation that clusters in the feature space histogram are typically smooth and roughly convex. Given two feature points we adjust their similarity according to the bottleneck in the histogram values on the straight line between them. We call our new similarities *Bottleneck Affinities*. These measures are computed efficiently, we demonstrate superior segmentation results compared to the use of the Euclidean metric.

1 Introduction

Calculating a similarity measure between pixels is a fundamental step in many computer vision and image processing algorithms. Many of these algorithms depend on a reliable affinity (or distance measure) between pixels for their calculations. The affinities are either measured between different pixels of the same image in case of segmentation and edge detection, or between pixels from neighbouring frames in case of optical flow calculation, motion segmentation and tracking.

In most of these applications, pixel affinity is calculated as a simple function of the Euclidean distance between the pixels' features (usually $e^{-distance^2}$) in some feature space. Common feature spaces are the one-dimensional gray scales feature space, two or three dimensional colour spaces and higher dimensional ($\sim 50D$) texture feature spaces. Different researches suggest using different feature spaces for achieving optimal results in various applications, but no particular feature space is considered optimal by the whole community (A survey of the properties of different colour spaces for image segmentation can be found in [1], while [2] provides a basic survey of different texture features). Other approaches include learning pixel affinity and feature space clustering.

Fowlkes et al. suggested a high level approach for learning pixel affinity calculations using a dataset of human segmented images as ground truth [3]. Their approach for affinity calculation uses the combination of several feature spaces and information from the image itself (edges) through a high level learning mechanism. While the approach is suitable for segmentation and similar time

A. Leonardis, H. Bischof, and A. Pinz (Eds.): ECCV 2006, Part II, LNCS 3952, pp. 321–333, 2006.

consuming applications, it is less suitable for online applications or other computationally efficient applications. Another drawback is the generalization of the method, which is not straightforward. For example, generalizing the approach to handle affinity calculations between pixels in successive frames requires massive human assistance.

A different approach for providing pixel affinity is by using feature space clustering [4]. This approach tries to exploit image specific characteristics rather than learn a general rule for the affinities calculations. Although this approach can be efficient and easy for generalization, it implies clustering of the feature space (hard or soft) which is prone to errors due to noise and other difficulties.

We claim that given two feature points, u and w, with equal Euclidean distances from a third feature point v, it stands to reason that if w and v share the same cluster, while u is located within another cluster, the affinity of w and v is larger than the affinity of u and v.

The motivation for our approach is obvious when looking at the synthetic one-dimensional feature histogram in Figure 1. Our main observation is that the histogram provides us with the additional knowledge that the feature values belong to two different Gaussian distributions. While v and w are very likely belong to the same source and should be considered similar, v and u seem to belong to two different sources and should be considered dissimilar.

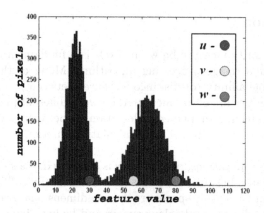

Fig. 1. (a) An example of a one-dimensional features histogram. Given the above histogram, it stands to reason to claim that a pixel having a feature value of v is similar to a pixel having a feature value of w and dissimilar to a pixel having a feature value of u although the Euclidean distance between the feature values v and w is identical to that of v and u.

This work suggests a straightforward and efficient approach to affinity calculations that exploits image specific attributes while not explicitly applying clustering of the feature space. We do so by introducing the *Bottleneck Affinities* - a simple mechanism for estimating the likelihood that two feature points belong to the same cluster in the feature space. We estimate this likelihood by analyzing the histogram values on the straight line connecting the two feature points in the feature space histogram. A sparsely populated region along this line (in the histogram domain) is considered a "bottleneck" and indicates that the two points probably belong to two different clusters. We therefore decrease their affinity measure. Similarly, a densely populated line indicates that the points belong to the same cluster and we therefore increase their affinity measure.

Our approach utilizes the typical smooth and convex structure of clusters in the *RGB* histogram of images. This structure is the result of scene properties and the (digital) image acquisition process. We discuss the structure of the clusters in the next section (section 2). Section 3 describes our algorithm and discusses implementation issues. The results are shown in section 4, while section 5 summarizes and suggests possible extensions to this work.

2 Histogram Clusters

This section discusses the physical properties that affect cluster structure in an image feature space histogram.

Figure 2 shows a simple image, containing a small number of dominant colours along with a two-dimensional projection of its RGB histogram. The difficulty in modelling the clusters in the histogram domain is evident from this example. The clusters have no particular shape, and methods like the *Gaussian Mixture Model* are not suitable for this kind of problem. The large amount of noise makes the task of clustering a difficult one even for this simple scene. Nevertheless, it is obvious that the histogram contains different clusters. For most pairs of feature points, the problem of estimating a likelihood measure for the points to belong to the same cluster seems significantly easier than the actual clustering problem. Our algorithm is aimed at utilizing this observation.

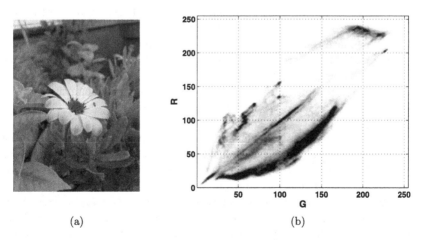

(a)   (b)

Fig. 2. (a) Sample image and (b) its RG histogram (a projection of the *RGB* histogram upon the RG axis), darker colour represents a denser histogram bin

For the sake of simplicity, this discussion refers to three-dimensional colour features (RGB values). We will address the generalization of the discussion to other feature spaces at the end of this section.

Our algorithm takes advantage of three well studied image properties. The first property is the *piecewise smooth world* assumption which has been used before in many computer vision and image processing applications such as boundary detection [5], image segmentation [6], noise reduction [7] and more. The second property is that monochromatic scene objects create nearly convex elongated clusters in the RGB histogram [8]. The third property is image blur due to the optics of the camera and the finite size of the pixel [9].

The first and second properties imply that for two feature points belonging to the same monochromatic object, all the bins along the line connecting them (in the histogram domain) are populated. Due to the third property, the same holds for textured objects as well. The justification for the last claim lies in the following fact: While locally, in the image plain, there is no difference between the blurring of edges due to texture and due to boundaries, globally - in the histogram domain there is a big difference between these phenomena. Boundaries between objects are scarce and therefore produce a small number of interpolated values. The line in the histogram between pixels from neighbouring objects is therefore scarcely populated. In textured regions the same texture components (texels) are blurred repeatedly. The line between pixels from two different texels (of the same texture) in the histogram is well populated.

Figure 3 demonstrates the difference in the histogram domain between edges due to object boundaries and edges due to texture. In the figure we show real images of a synthetic scene along with their GB histogram (a projection of their RGB histogram upon the GB plane). There are only a few pixels with interpolated values in figure (a) and the two clusters are well separated in the histogram domain (b). In figure (c) many of the pixels have interpolated values and the region between the two clusters in the histogram domain (d) is densely populated. Figure 4 shows an image along with the edge maps according to the Euclidean metric (b) and to our bottleneck distance measure (c). For visualization purposes we show the square root of the edge maps (the difference is visually prominent when looking at the squared root). Both edge maps were normalized to the range of [0..1]. Notice how in the bottleneck edge map boundaries between objects are maintained while the intensity of edges due to texture (the sculptures surface) is decreased.

Refining Our Assumption: In order for our approach to separate feature points only when they belong to different clusters in the feature space histogram, the cluster should be convex. In real life, these clusters are usually not entirely convex as can be seen if figure 2, and one could claim that our heuristic should fail. Fortunately, although not entirely convex, the clusters are usually convex in a small neighborhood in the feature space histogram and are therefore locally convex. Since most applications calculate affinity only in limited neighborhoods around pixels, our heuristic rarely fails. The justification lies in the smoothness assumption. Due to this assumption, neighboring pixels that belong to the same

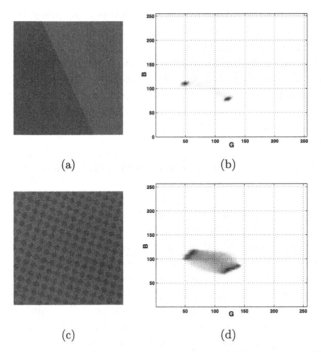

Fig. 3. (a) An image of a synthetic scene containing two objects and its GB histogram (b). (c) An image of a synthetic scene containing a texture (two *texels*) and its GB histogram (d).

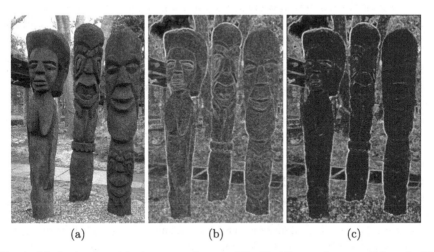

Fig. 4. (a) An image with the squared root of its Euclidean edge map (b) and of its bottleneck edge map (c) (the differences are more easily seen when looking at the squared root). The values in both maps are normalized to the range of [0..1]. Notice how the bottleneck edge map maintains edges between objects while the edge values inside the sculptures are significantly lowered.

object (or piece) have similar features (the changes are smooth within the object) and therefore reside in the same locally convex region of the cluster. Our empirical results support this claim.

Although in the entire section we referred to RGB features, we would like to point out that our main argument, smoothness due to scene and camera properties, is a fundamental property of natural images and is not related to a specific set of features. Our experimental results support this observation as we clearly show in the results section.

3   Defining and Computing the Bottleneck Affinities

We implemented a simple and efficient algorithm that utilizes our observation of the typical structure of clusters in the feature space histogram for calculating the *bottleneck affinities*. Given two feature points, our distance measure is the Euclidean distance between the points multiplied by a *Bottleneck factor (bnf)*. This factor receives a low value ($bnf < 1$) for points which our algorithm decided are likely belong to the same cluster and, a high value ($bnf > 1$) for points which our algorithm decided belong to different clusters.

Given two feature points p_1 and p_2, a feature space histogram H, and $L(p_1, p_2)$ - the straight line connecting the two feature points in the histogram domain, we calculate the bnf according to the following formula:

$$bnf(p_1, p_2) = \frac{2min(H(p_1), H(p_2))}{2min(H(L(p_1, p_2))) + min(H(p_1), H(p_2))}$$

Where $H(p)$ is the histogram value at the bin whose coordinates are given by the feature point p and $min(H(L(p_1, p_2)))$ is the minimum histogram value along the line connecting the two points in the histogram domain (excluding the value at the two end points). The term $min(H(p_1), H(p_2))$ was added to the denominator for stabilization reasons. We chose the exact criteria for calculating the bnf due to its simplicity. Our experience shows that other, similar formulas produce very similar results.

A more thorough analysis of the histogram values along the line may produce yet better results, the exact formula may depend on the sparseness/denseness of the histogram, the amount of noise and other factors, but as we show in our results section, even this simple criterion yields very good results.

We believe that the **main contribution** of this paper is in introducing a new approach to computing the affinities rather than in the specific formula suggested.

We implemented the algorithm as a C routine that is called from Matlab (mex file). Since Matlab is our development environment, our implementation is only suitable for algorithms that calculate affinities or distance measures for the original input image like *Normalized Cuts (Ncut)* [10] and other spectral clustering algorithms. The implementation is not suitable for algorithms that iteratively change pixel values like the *MeanShift* algorithm [11] since we can not efficiently update our histogram dynamically in each iteration. Nevertheless we are confident that given a dynamic implementation of the histogram (for example in C++) iterative algorithms may benefit from our affinity calculations as well.

Since high dimensional histograms are extremely sparse, our method can not be applied directly for modifying affinity calculations of texture features. Texture is usually represented as a feature vector, holding the response of the pixel's neighbourhood to a large number of filters (typically, around 50). Even using a quantization, allowing only four possible values for each coordinate we get a feature histogram with 4^{50} bins and we hardly ever get two pixels in the same bin. We address this problem by projecting the high dimensional feature vectors onto their first three principal components. Even with this drastic dimensionality reduction, using our affinity measures with the projected histogram dramatically improves the segmentation results compared with those achieved by using Euclidean affinities in the full dimensional space (using Euclidean distance in the projected subspace produced poor results).

Computationally, calculating the histogram distance between two points, p_1 and p_2, in the feature space is linear in n - the number of bins along the line connecting the points in the histogram domain. Since most of the applications calculate distances (or affinity) only in a small neighbourhood, and neighbouring pixels tend to be similar, in average, n is very small. The average computational time for computing the affinity between one pixel and the rest of the image in a 480*320 image is 2 seconds on a Pentium4 2.4Ghz computer. Constructing a Matlab sparse matrix with histogram affinity scores of 11*11 neighbourhood around each pixel in an image of the same size took an average of 200 seconds, 80 of which were spent on the actual affinity calculations. For comparison, building the same matrix with Euclidean affinity scores took around 140 seconds, 24 of which were spent on the actual affinity calculations. In addition, the actual segmentation process (given the affinity matrix) took at least twice that time ($\sim$ 7 minutes), the computational overhead due to our method is therefore nearly negligible.

When calculating affinities between texture features, our approach even proved marginally more efficient than calculating the Euclidean distance, since we work in a projected three dimensional subspace, while the Euclidean distance was calculated in a much higher dimension.

4   Results

We demonstrate the competence of our pixel affinity through the results of segmentation algorithms using both color and texture features. We chose the *Ncut* algorithm for our demonstration since it is a well known image segmentation algorithm that is easily adopted to use with various affinity measures, affinities were computed in an 11*11 neighbourhoods around each pixel. We ran the algorithm twice over the Berkeley segmentation dataset, once using Euclidean affinities and the other using our *bottleneck affinities*. We provide both the Berkeley segmentation benchmark results for both runs and a few qualitative examples.

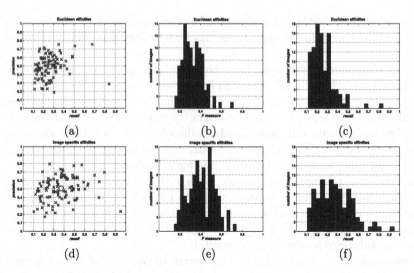

Fig. 5. Benchmark results of the *Ncut* algorithm using color features and Euclidean affinities: (a) precision/recall segmentation results (mean precision/recall in red circle), (b) F-measure histogram and (c) recall histogram. Benchmark results of the *Ncut* algorithm using color features and bottleneck affinities: (d) precision/recall segmentation results (mean precision/recall in red circle), (e) F-measure histogram and (f) recall histogram.

The Berkeley segmentation dataset contains 100 test images. All images in the dataset were manually segmented by humans and these segmentations are considered as ground truth. Berkeley's benchmark tool calculates *precision, recall* and *F-measure* (the harmonic mean of the precision and recall scores) for the automatically segmented images according to these human segmented images. Figure 5 provides benchmark results for images segmented by the *Ncut* algorithm using color (RGB) features. The results in the figure are: Precision/recall graph (a,d), the F-measure histogram (b,e) and the recall histogram (c,f). Using our affinity measure improved the F-measure from 0.33 to 0.41 - an improvement of 24%. The recall rate improved from 0.26 to 0.37 - an improvement of 42%. The improvement in precision was only marginal, from 0.49 to 0.50 - an improvement of 2%. Using *bottleneck affinities* produced better segmentation results (compared to using the Euclidean metric) for 82 out of the 100 images in the dataset. Figure 6 provides benchmark results for images segmented by the *Ncut* algorithm using texture features. The texture features used are the Leung-Malik filter bank [12] (a total of 48 filters). We also tried using the Schmidt filter bank [13] (a total of 13 filters) but received inferior results. The code for both filter banks was obtained from [14]. The results in the figure are: Precision/recall graph (a,d), the F-measure histogram (b,e) and the recall histogram (c,f). Using our affinity measure improved the F-measure from 0.2 to 0.28 - an improvement of 39%. The recall rate improved from 0.15 to 0.24 - an improvement of 56%. The precision rate has improved from 0.34 to 0.39 - an improvement of 13%. Using *bottleneck affinities* produced better segmentation results (compared to

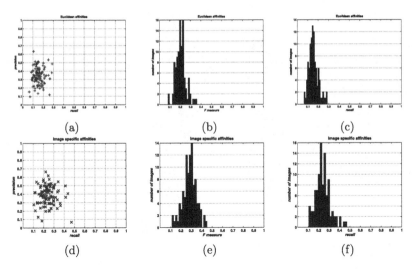

(a)   (b)   (c)

(d)   (e)   (f)

Fig. 6. Benchmark results of the *Ncut* algorithm using texture features and Euclidean affinities: (a) precision/recall segmentation results (mean precision/recall in red circle), (b) F-measure histogram and (c) recall histogram. Benchmark results of the *Ncut* algorithm using texture features and bottleneck affinities: (d) precision/recall segmentation results (mean precision/recall in red circle), (e) F-measure histogram and (f) recall histogram.

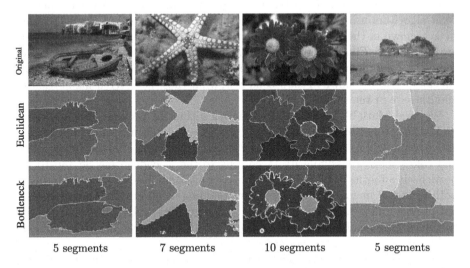

5 segments   7 segments   10 segments   5 segments

Fig. 7. Segmentation results of the *Ncut* algorithm using texture features in 15*15 neighbourhoods (each cluster is colored using its mean intensity) according to Euclidean affinities (second row) and to our bottleneck affinities (third row)

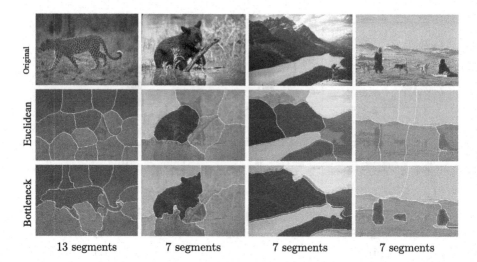

Fig. 8. Segmentation results of the *Ncut* algorithm using texture features in 15*15 neighbourhoods (each cluster is colored using its mean intensity) according to Euclidean affinities (second row) and to our bottleneck affinities (third row)

using the Euclidean metric) for 92 out of the 100 images in the dataset. It is important to mention that these results were achieved for the filter responses alone, without incorporating gray-scale information, hence they are not high.

Figure 7 provides a comparison of segmentation results achieved using the *Ncut* algorithm using RGB features. Results achieved using the Euclidean metric are shown in the second row, while those achieved using bottleneck affinities are in the third. Figure 8 provides a comparison of segmentation results achieved using the *Ncut* algorithm using texture features. Results achieved using the Euclidean metric are shown in the second row, while those achieved using bottleneck affinities are in the third.

We used Matlab's graph-partitioning algorithm for providing an additional evaluation of our *bottleneck affinities*. Graph vertices represented image pixels and edge weights were calculated as the sum of distance in the image plane and color-features dissimilarity (according to the Euclidean metric and to the bottleneck affinities). The algorithm is computationally expensive in terms of both time and memory, since it requires building a full graph. We therefore do not provide full benchmark results for that algorithm, rather we provide a few examples. The results are found in Figure 9. All the images in this experiment were segmented to up to 8 segments.

We did not compare our algorithm to the Fowlkes et. al. algorithm because the approaches are entirely different; our approach is a low level one that works on a single feature space, while Fowlkes et. al. use a high level approach that combines cues from several feature spaces and from the image plane itself. Moreover, their approach can use our algorithm as a subroutine. We also did not compare our approach to that of feature space clustering since this approach is rarely used and our past experience with it produced inferior results.

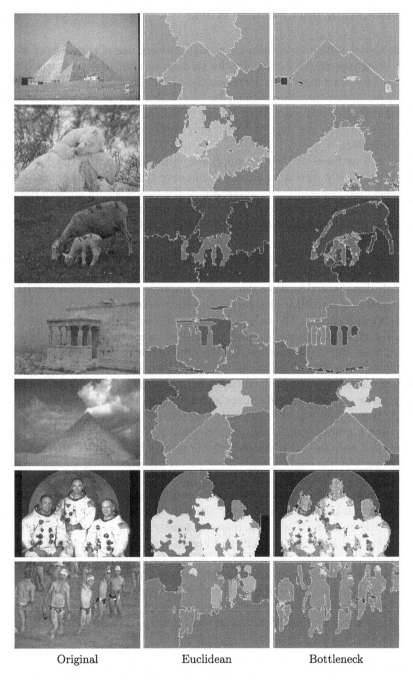

Original   Euclidean   Bottleneck

Fig. 9. Segmentation results of Matlab's average-link graph partitioning algorithm using RGB features. Results achieved using the Euclidean metric are in the second column. Results achieved using the bottleneck affinities are in the third column. All images were automatically segmented into up to 8 (not necessarily continuous) segments.

332 I. Omer and M. Werman

5 Discussion and Future Work

We introduced *bottleneck affinities*, a straightforward and efficient approach that utilizes image specific characteristics for calculating similarity measures between pixel features. Our algorithm decreases the affinity between two feature points when it estimates that they belong to two different clusters, while increasing their affinity when estimating they belong to the same cluster. We do so without explicitly clustering the data and with only weak assumptions on the structure of these clusters.

Although we have justified our approach with the claim that the data is both smooth and nearly convex in nature, we believe that for most applications the smoothness requirement is the important of the two, since for smooth data, linearity in a small neighbourhood is obtained automatically according to Taylor's theorem and most applications calculate affinity only in a small neighbourhood around pixels.

We demonstrated the advantages of our affinities compared to the Euclidean distance measure for segmentation both in a three-dimensional color space and in a high dimensional texture space. The improved segmentation results were achieved for only a small additional computational cost, compared with the use of the Euclidean metric, in the case of the three-dimensional colour features. In the case of the high-dimensional texture features our algorithm proved slightly more efficient than the Euclidean metric. We are confident that other applications that rely on pixel affinity measures will benefit from our algorithm.

Better results may be obtained through using a more thorough analysis of the feature space and allowing for more general paths between the feature points (and by this, giving up the convexity requirement). Representing the feature space using a graph, where vertices store density measurement of the neighborhood around each feature point and edges represent Euclidean distance between neighboring features enables calculating (dis)similarities using shortest path algorithms that consider both the paths's length (distance) and the density along the path in the feature space. We are currently working in this direction and already achieve better results but for the cost of a larger computational time. We currently studying how to combine the density information with the distance information and seeking for an efficient algorithm to do so. The graph representation has other advantages as well, probably the most important of which is that it enables working in an arbitrary high dimension without difficulties, which is useful for calculating affinities between texture features.

We further believe that the method may be applied to clustering and affinity measuring for different kinds of data and we intend to try it in different domains.

References

1. Cheng, H.D., Jiang, X., Sun, Y., Wang, J.: Color image segmentation: advances and prospects. Pattern Recognition **34** (2001) 2259–2281
2. Tuceryan, M., Jain, A.K.: Texture analysis. (1993) 235–276

3. Fowlkes, C., Martin, D., Malik, J.: Learning affinity functions for image segmentation: Combining patch-based and gradient-based approaches. Computer Vision and Pattern Recognition (CVPR) (2003)
4. Comaniciu, D., Meer, P.: Robust analysis of feature spaces: color image segmentation. In: CVPR '97: Proceedings of the 1997 Conference on Computer Vision and Pattern Recognition (CVPR '97), Washington, DC, USA, IEEE Computer Society (1997) 750
5. Mumford, D., Shah, J.: Boundary detection by minimizing functionals, I. In: Proc. IEEE Conf. on Computer Vision and Pattern Recognition. (1985) 22–26
6. Vese, L.A., Chan, T.F.: A multiphase level set framework for image segmentation using the mumford and shah model. International Journal of Computer Vision **50** (2002) 271–293
7. Spokoiny, V.: Estimation of a function with discontinuities via local polynomial fit with an adaptive window choice. Annals of Statistics (1998) 1356–1378
8. Gevers, T., Smeulders, A.W.M.: Color-based object recognition. Pattern Recognition **32** (1999) 453–464
9. Park, S., Schowengerdt, R.: Image sampling, reconstruction, and the effect of sample scene phasing. Applied Optics **21** (1982) 3142–3151
10. Shi, J., Malik, J.: Normalized cuts and image segmentation. IEEE Transactions on Pattern Analysis and Machine Intelligence (PAMI) (2000)
11. Comaniciu, D., Meer, P.: Mean shift analysis and applications. In: ICCV '99: Proceedings of the International Conference on Computer Vision-Volume 2, Washington, DC, USA, IEEE Computer Society (1999) 1197
12. Leung, T., Malik, J.: Representing and recognizing the visual appearance of materials using three-dimensional textons. Int. J. Comput. Vision **43** (2001) 29–44
13. Schmid, C.: Constructing models for content-based image retrieval. In: International Conference on Computer Vision & Pattern Recognition. (2001)
14. (http://www.robots.ox.ac.uk/~vgg/research/texclass/filters.html) Visual Geometry Group, University of Oxford.

Coloring Local Feature Extraction

Joost van de Weijer and Cordelia Schmid

GRAVIR-INRIA, 655 Avenue de l'Europe, Montbonnot 38330, France
{Joost.van-de-Weijer, Cordelia.Schmid}@inrialpes.fr

Abstract. Although color is commonly experienced as an indispensable quality in describing the world around us, state-of-the art *local* feature-based representations are mostly based on shape description, and ignore color information. The description of color is hampered by the large amount of variations which causes the measured color values to vary significantly. In this paper we aim to extend the description of **local** features with color information. To accomplish a wide applicability of the color descriptor, it should be robust to : 1. photometric changes commonly encountered in the real world, 2. varying image quality, from high quality images to snap-shot photo quality and compressed internet images. Based on these requirements we derive a set of color descriptors. The set of proposed descriptors are compared by extensive testing on multiple applications areas, namely, matching, retrieval and classification, and on a wide variety of image qualities. The results show that color descriptors remain reliable under photometric and geometrical changes, and with decreasing image quality. For all experiments a combination of color and shape outperforms a pure shape-based approach.

1   Introduction

There exists broad agreement that local features are an efficient tool for object representation due to their robustness with respect to occlusion and geometrical transformations [1]. A typical application based on local features starts with the detection phase, in which features are localized. If desired the patches are transformed to be invariant with respect to orientation, scale, and affine transformations (see Fig. 1). Invariant representations are subsequently extracted by a descriptor. The descriptor should robustly represent both the shape and the color of the features. A considerable amount of research has been dedicated to robust local shape descriptors. An extensive study by Mikolajczyk and Schmid [2] reported the SIFT descriptor [3] to perform best. The description of local color has received relatively little attention, and as a result most local features-based methods [3],[4],[5] use only luminance and ignore color information. The aim of this article is to enrich local feature-based methods with color information.

A lot of work has been dedicated to global color features for color object recognition. Ballard and Swain [6] described objects by their color histograms. Moreover, to obtain invariance with respect to lighting geometry the use of normalized *rgb* histograms was advocated. This method remained however variant with respect to illuminant changes. To tackle this problem Funt and Finlayson

A. Leonardis, H. Bischof, and A. Pinz (Eds.): ECCV 2006, Part II, LNCS 3952, pp. 334–348, 2006.
© Springer-Verlag Berlin Heidelberg 2006

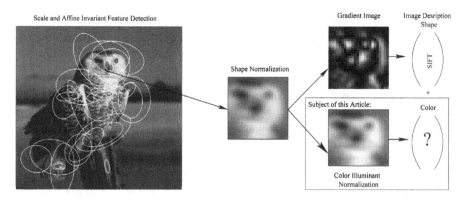

Fig. 1. Overview of a local feature-based method divided in a feature detection and a feature description phase. The aim of this article is to enrich the local feature description with color information.

[7] proposed an illuminant invariant indexing method, which was however variant with respect to lighting geometry. Finlayson et al. [8] combined the theories of [6] and [7] and proposed a indexing method which is both invariant to shading and illuminant changes. All methods remained however variant with respect to specularities. Gevers and Smeulders [9] propose invariants for specularity, in combination with illuminant and lighting geometry. The work was later extended to the derivative structure of images in [10], [11], leading to e.g. photometric invariant edge and corner detection. Furthermore, Gevers and Stokman [12] observed that instabilities, caused by the non-linear transformation to compute the photometric invariants, hamper practical use of photometric invariance theory. Based on an error analysis robust photometric invariants are proposed.

We extend local feature descriptors with color information, by concatenating a color descriptor, $\mathbf{K}$, to the shape descriptor, $\mathbf{S}$, according to

$$\mathbf{B} = \left(\hat{\mathbf{F}}, \lambda \hat{\mathbf{K}}\right) \tag{1}$$

where $\mathbf{B}$ is the combined color and shape descriptor and λ is a weighting parameter, and $\hat{\ }$ indicates that the vector is normalized. For the shape description we rely on the SIFT descriptor [3]. Since the color descriptor is to be used in combination with a shape descriptor it does not need to contain any spatial information, which leads us to use local histograms. From the analysis of the color literature, discussed above, we deduce the following criteria to which these local color histograms should adhere:

1. photometric robustness: the descriptor should be robust to photometric variations such as shadow, shading, specularities and changes of the light source.
2. geometric robustness: the descriptor should be invariant with respect to geometrical changes, such as viewpoint, zoom, and object orientation variations.
3. photometric stability: the descriptor should adequately handle the instabilities introduced by photometric invariant transformations.

4. generality: the color descriptor should be applicable to a wide variety of applications such as matching, retrieval and classification. Furthermore, it should be robust to variations in image quality, from high quality images to compressed snapshot quality images.

After discussing a physical reflectance model in section 2, we design several color feature descriptors in accordance with the four criteria, in section 3. In section 4 experimental results are given and section 5 contains concluding remarks.

Related to the research proposed in this paper is the work of Mindru et al. [13]. They propose a combined color and shape description of the local neighborhood based on color moments, which are invariant to illuminant color. Since, we aim for a color description, which will be used in combination with the SIFT shape description, we have not pursued this path. Furthermore, in [14] local moments-based descriptors were found to be relatively unstable. Matas et al. [15] describe a method which, based on the modes in the local histogram, computes invariant signatures. The method uses fixed scales, and seems hard to use as an extension to a scale invariant feature detector, where the number of modes for a single feature is often higher than the two or three discussed in [15].

2   Color Preliminaries

In this section the color theory needed for the design of the color descriptors is summerized. We assume that the scene consists of inhomogeneous materials (including e.g. papers and plastics) and we exclude homogeneous materials such as metals. Furthermore, we model the light source locally, i.e. for the extend of a single feature, as a single light source, $e(\lambda)$, where λ is the wavelength. For multiple light sources we assume that the combination can be approximated as a single light source for the local feature. In this case, the measured values, $C \in \{R, G, B\}$, of the camera with spectral sensitivities f^C, are modelled [16] by integrating over the visible spectrum ω,

$$C(\mathbf{x}) = m^b(\mathbf{x}) \int_\omega b(\lambda, \mathbf{x}) e(\lambda) f^C(\lambda) \, d\lambda + m^i(\mathbf{x}) \int_\omega i(\lambda) e(\lambda) f^C(\lambda) \, d\lambda. \quad (2)$$

The reflection of the light consist of two parts: 1. a body reflection part, which describes the light which is reflected after interaction with the surface albedo b, and 2. the interface reflection which describes the part of the light that is immediately reflected at the surface, causing specularities. We assume neutral interface reflection, meaning that the Fresnel reflectance i is independent of λ. Accordingly, we will omit i in further equations. The geometric dependence of the reflectance is described by the terms m^b and m^i which depend on the viewing angle, light source direction and surface orientation. $\mathbf{x}$ denotes the spatial coordinates, and bold face is used to indicate vectors.

Ambient or diffuse light, i.e. light coming from all directions, is not modelled by Eq. 2 [16]. Diffuse light occurs in outdoor scenes where there is next to the dominant illuminant, i.e. the sun, diffuse light coming from the sky. Similarly, it occurs in indoor situations where diffuse light is caused by reflectances from walls and ceilings. Shafer [16] models the diffuse light, a, by a third term

$$C(\mathbf{x}) = m^b(\mathbf{x}) \int_\omega b(\lambda, \mathbf{x}) e(\lambda) f^C(\lambda) d\lambda + m^i(\mathbf{x}) \int_\omega e(\lambda) f^C(\lambda) d\lambda + \int_\omega a(\lambda) f^C(\lambda) d\lambda$$

(3)

The camera sensitivities, f^C, can be approximated as delta functions, thereby simplifying the reflection function to

$$C(\mathbf{x}) = m^b(\mathbf{x}) b^C(\mathbf{x}) e^C + m^i(\mathbf{x}) e^C + a^C.$$

(4)

This function together with its derivative,

$$C_\mathbf{x}(\mathbf{x}) = m_x^b(\mathbf{x}) b^C(\mathbf{x}) e^C + m^b(\mathbf{x}) b_x^C(\mathbf{x}) e^C + m_x^i(\mathbf{x}) e^C,$$

(5)

will be used in the following sections to derive photometric invariants. Throughout the paper we will use a subscript to indicate spatial differentiation, and we use boldface to indicate vectors over the three channels, e.g. $\mathbf{C} = \{R, G, B\}$.

3   Color Feature Description

In this section we derive a set of color descriptors in accordance with the requirements put forward in section 1. Robustness with respect to photometric variation is discussed in section 3.1 and 3.2. The second criterion, geometrical robustness is handled in section 3.3. Photometric stability issues raised by criterion 3 are handled in section 3.4.

3.1   Photometric Robustness: Color Constancy

In section 2 we derived how the measured sensor values depend on both the color of the illuminant interacting with the object, and the color of the diffuse illuminant. In this section two simple algorithms [17], [18] are described for color illuminant normalization (see method overview in Fig .1).

We first consider the case for which there is no diffuse illuminant present ($a^C = 0$). The relation between two images of the same scene, $\mathbf{C}^1$ and $\mathbf{C}^2$, taken under different illuminants, is modelled by a scalar multiplication, since

$$C^2(\mathbf{x}) = \left(m^b(\mathbf{x}) b^C(\mathbf{x}) + m^i(\mathbf{x})\right) e_2^C = \lambda^C C^1(\mathbf{x})$$

(6)

where $\lambda^C = e_2^C / e_1^C$. The colors in the two scenes are hence related by a diagonal matrix $\mathbf{C}_2 = \mathbf{\Lambda}\mathbf{C}_1$. This diagonal matrix relation is well-known and is a consequence of assuming delta functions for the sensitivities of the cameras. Although the delta function assumption seems rather blunt it describes reality surprisingly well [19]. From Eq. 6 it is easily proven that, in the absence of diffuse light, invariance with respect to the illuminant can be obtained, by a normalization of each color channel:

$$C^*(\mathbf{x}) = \frac{C(\mathbf{x})}{\overline{C(\mathbf{x})}}$$

(7)

where the bar indicates a spatial average: $\bar{a} = \int_S a\,dx \big/ \int_S dx$, and S is the surface of the patch. The Grey-World hypothesis [17], assuming average reflectance in the world to be grey, leads to a similar correction for the illuminant.

Let us now consider the case where there is, next to a dominant illuminant, diffuse light present. For this case Eq. 6 does not hold, instead the images are related via $C_2 = \Lambda C_1 + a$. However, a relation similar to Eq. 7 exists between the derivatives of these images, since from Eq. 5 it follows that

$$C_x^2(\mathbf{x}) = \lambda^C C_x^1(\mathbf{x}).\tag{8}$$

Invariance with respect to the dominant illuminant, Λ, can hence be obtained by normalization of the color channels with their average derivative

$$C^*(\mathbf{x}) = \frac{C(\mathbf{x})}{|C_x(\mathbf{x})|}.\tag{9}$$

The absolute is taken to avoid division by zero. Since $C(\mathbf{x})$ is dependent on the diffuse illuminant, the resulting image, C^*, is also. However, its derivatives, C_x^*, are no longer dependent on either the dominant illuminant or the diffuse illuminant. The recently proposed Grey-Edge hypothesis [18], assuming average reflectance of differences in the world to be grey, leads to a similar correction for the illuminant.

3.2   Photometric Robustness: Color Invariance

This section will discuss the photometric invariants on which the color descriptors will be based. With color invariance we refer here to scene incidental variations such as shadows, shading and specularities. A brief overview of photometric invariants known from literature is given here (for more details see e.g. [9], [20]).

Zero-order invariants. Let us first consider the case of a matte surface ($m^i = 0$) and no diffuse lighting ($a^C = 0$). For this case normalized rgb can be considered invariant with respect to lighting geometry and viewpoint, m^b. Since,

$$r = \frac{R}{R+G+B} = \frac{m^b b^R e^R}{m^b \left(b^R e^R + b^G e^G + b^B e^B\right)}.\tag{10}$$

Similar equations hold for normalized g and b.

Furthermore, in the case of a white illuminant ($e^R = e^G = e^B = e$) and specular reflectance ($m^i \neq 0$), opponent colors [9] can be proven to be invariant with respect to specularities, m^i. Since,

$$\begin{aligned} O1 &= \tfrac{1}{\sqrt{2}}\left(R - G\right) = \tfrac{1}{\sqrt{2}}\left(m^b e\left(b^R - b^G\right) + m^i e - m^i e\right) \\ O2 &= \tfrac{1}{\sqrt{6}}\left(R + G - 2B\right) = \tfrac{1}{\sqrt{6}}\left(m^b e\left(b^R + b^G - 2b^G\right) + 2m^i e - 2m^i e\right)' \end{aligned}\tag{11}$$

are invariant for m^i. The opponent colors are still variant for lighting geometry variations. Invariance with respect to both the lighting geometry and specularities is obtained by hue,

$$hue = \arctan\left(\frac{O1}{O2}\right) = \arctan\left(\frac{\sqrt{3}\left(b^R - b^G\right)}{\left(b^R + b^G - 2b^G\right)}\right) \tag{12}$$

First-order invariants. We continue by describing two photometric invariant derivatives [20]. Again consider a matte surface ($m^i = 0$). For this case, changes caused by lighting geometry variation ($m_x^b \neq 0$) are equal to

$$C_{\mathbf{x}} = \frac{m_x^b}{m^b}C, \tag{13}$$

meaning that all lighting geometry changes of $C_{\mathbf{x}}$ occur in the direction of the object color, C. Changes in the two direction perpendicular to object color are hence invariant with respect to geometry variations. These directions are equal to the angular derivatives after a spherical coordinate transformation,

$$ang1_{\mathbf{x}} = \frac{G_{\mathbf{x}}R - RG_{\mathbf{x}}}{\sqrt{R^2 + G^2}} \ , \ ang2_{\mathbf{x}} = \frac{R_{\mathbf{x}}RB + G_{\mathbf{x}}GB - B_{\mathbf{x}}R^2 - B_{\mathbf{x}}G^2}{\sqrt{(R^2 + G^2)(R^2 + G^2 + B^2)}}. \tag{14}$$

If we subsequently consider specular reflection, the derivatives of the opponent colors,

$$O1_{\mathbf{x}} = \tfrac{1}{\sqrt{2}}\left(R_{\mathbf{x}} - G_{\mathbf{x}}\right) \ , \ O2_{\mathbf{x}} = \tfrac{1}{\sqrt{6}}\left(R_{\mathbf{x}} + G_{\mathbf{x}} - 2B_{\mathbf{x}}\right) \tag{15}$$

can be proven to be invariant with respect to specular variations, similarly as in Eq. 11. If the opponent derivative is computed after applying the illuminant normalization of Eq. 9 the opponent derivative is the only invariant insensitive to a diffuse illuminant.

A combined illuminant and geometric invariant. In [8] a method, called comprehensive color image normalization (CCIN), is proposed as a global image feature. We will here apply it as a local image feature. The method proposes an iterative use of Eq. 10 and Eq. 7, and hence is invariant for both lighting geometry and illuminant color.

3.3 Geometric Robustness: Color Angles

The third criterion requires geometrical robustness with respect to changes caused by viewpoint, zoom, and object orientation. Invariance with respect to these transformation is allready partially obtained by affine invariant feature detection, however special care should be taken when working with derivative based invariants. This problem is usually overlooked in derivative-based invariance literature [7], [10], [20]. We will clarify the problem by investigating the influence of edge-sharpness for the opponent derivative. In Fig. 2a an edge is depicted. White is increasingly added to the blue patch along the y-axis (mimicking a transformation similar to specularities). The opponent derivative, $O1_x$,

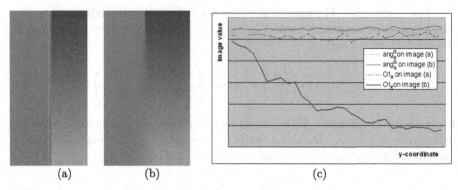

Fig. 2. (a) a red-blue edge. For the blue patch white light is added along the y-axis. (b) same as (a) but with varying smoothing along the y-axis. (c) the filter responses on the center vertical line of the images (a) and (b) of the opponent angle and the opponent derivative along the x-axis.

is invariant with respect to this phenomenon as can be seen by the constant response of the dashed black line in Fig. 2c. If we look at the opponent derivative response on the same image, but now with decreasing spatial smoothing along the y-axis, the response changes drastically. This behavior is undesired, since edge-sharpness changes occur a lot due to geometrical variation, or acquisition parameters such as zoom and focus. To overcome this problem we propose two new invariants, called color angles.

Assume that an edge can locally be modelled as a smoothed step edge

$$C\left(x\right) = \alpha^{C}\mathbf{u}\left(x\right) \otimes G^{\sigma}\left(x\right), \tag{16}$$

where α^{C} indicates the amplitude of the step edge u for the different channels C. Its derivative is equal to

$$C_{x}\left(x\right) = \alpha^{C}\tfrac{\partial}{\partial x}\left(\mathbf{u}\left(x\right) \otimes G^{\sigma}\left(x\right)\right) = \alpha^{C}\left(\left(\tfrac{\partial}{\partial x}\mathbf{u}\left(x\right)\right) \otimes G^{\sigma}\left(x\right)\right) = \alpha^{C}G^{\sigma}\left(x\right) \tag{17}$$

where we used that the derivative of a step edge is equal to the delta function $\left(\tfrac{\partial}{\partial x}\mathbf{u}\left(x\right)\right) = \delta\left(x\right)$. It is now straightforward to prove that the angles between the color channels are invariant to this smoothing and are only dependent on α^{C}, since

$$\phi = \arctan\left(\frac{R_{x}}{G_{x}}\right) = \arctan\left(\frac{\alpha^{R}}{\alpha^{G}}\right). \tag{18}$$

We can now add the geometrical invariance to the photometrical invariant derivatives derived in section 3.2. This leads to the opponent angle, $ang_{\mathbf{x}}^{O}$, and the spherical angle, $ang_{\mathbf{x}}^{S}$, with

$$ang_{\mathbf{x}}^{O} = \arctan\left(\frac{O1_{\mathbf{x}}}{O2_{\mathbf{x}}}\right) \quad, \quad ang_{\mathbf{x}}^{S} = \arctan\left(\frac{ang1_{\mathbf{x}}}{ang2_{\mathbf{x}}}\right). \tag{19}$$

Table 1. Overview of the physical events to which the photometric invariants are insensitive. Prior illuminant normalization is assumed by either Eq. 7 or Eq. 9. Invariance with respect to the diffuse lighting for the opponent angle is obtained with Eq. 9.

	lighting geometry	specularities	illuminant variations	diffuse lighting
rgb	×	-	×	-
hue	×	×	×	-
spher.ang.	×	-	×	-
opp.ang.	-	×	×	×
CCIN	×	-	×	-

In Fig. 2c the results for ang_x^O are given in red. The smoothing does not influence the response, thereby demonstrating the robustness with respect to geometrical changes of the opponent angle. Note that in [21] color angles are also mentioned. They refer however to angles of color distributions, while in this paper we study the distribution of color angles of color derivatives. In Table 1 an overview of the invariants is given. The results assume that the invariants are applied in combination with the illuminant normalization method provided in section 3.1.

3.4   Photometric Stability: Robust Local Histograms

We are now in the final stage of the construction of the descriptor. In this section we describe how the derived invariants are transformed into a robust local histogram. Photometric invariants are known to have inherent instabilities [12], which we do not want to significantly influence the final histogram. Here, we propose to adjust the weight of a color value in the histogram according to its certainty. We discuss the computation of the weight for every invariant discussed in section 3.2. For *CCIN*-method we apply the parameters as indicated in [8].

rgb-histogram. We partition the *rgb* plane in triangles of equal size. To cope with the instability for low intensities we follow [22] and consider points below a threshold intensity as being grey.

hue-histogram. The *hue* is known to be unstable around the grey axis. We follow [12] and apply an error analysis to the hue:

$$(\partial hue)^2 = \left(\frac{\partial hue}{\partial O1}\partial O1\right)^2 + \left(\frac{\partial hue}{\partial O2}\partial O2\right)^2 = \frac{1}{O1^2 + O2^2} = \frac{1}{sat^2}, \qquad (20)$$

where *sat* is the saturation (a similar results was derived for derivative of the hue in [20]). The certainty of the *hue* is hence inversely proportional to the saturation, which is what we expect. The smaller the saturation the more uncertain the *hue* estimation. We will use this relation to robustify the histogram construction, by weighting each sample by its saturation.

Opponent and spherical angle. Similarly as for the hue we apply an error analysis to the color angle equations of Eq. 19, which yield the following results

$$\partial ang_x^O = \frac{1}{\sqrt{O1_x^2 + O2_x^2}} \quad , \quad \partial ang_x^S = \frac{1}{\sqrt{ang1_x^2 + ang2_x^2}}. \tag{21}$$

Hence, we will use ∂ang_x^O as a weight for the opponent angle, and ∂ang_x^S as a weight for the spherical angle when converting them to a local color histogram. It is interesting to note that Lowe [3] intuitively arrives at the same conclusion. The orientation histogram of the SIFT descriptor is weighted with the gradient strength, which is exactly the result which would follow from an error analysis of the orientation parameter, $\theta = \arctan(f_y/f_x)$.

4   Experiments

The experiments test the color and the combined color and shape descriptor on the criteria put forward in section 1: 1. photometric robustness, 2. geometric robustness 3. photometric stability 4. generality. Although the first three criteria are tested by all experiments, the emphasis shifts: experiment 1 focusses on photometric robustness, experiment 2 demands geometrical robustness, and experiment 3 requires geometrical and photometrical robustness, and photometric stability to cope with the low quality internet images. The fourth criteria, generality, is illustrated by testing the descriptors for multiple tasks.

Experimental setup. For all the experiments we use the schema as given in Fig. 1. We use an affine invariant Harris-Laplace detector [2]. In the shape normalization step the images are reduced to 20 by 20 neighborhoods. The SIFT is computed from this shape normalized patch. For the color descriptors first color normalization is applied. Next the color descriptors, being the histograms of rgb (Eq. 10), hue (Eq. 12), $opponent\ angle$ (Eq. 19), and $spherical\ angle$ (Eq. 19), $CCIN$ [8], are computed, with the weights as proposed in section 3.4. Furthermore, $\lambda = .6$ (see Eq.1) was experimentally found to give good results, and the descriptor lengths are 128 bins for SIFT, for the one-dimensional descriptors hue, $opponent\ angle$ and $spherical\ angle$ the histogram is divided in 37 bins, for the two-dimensional descriptor rgb 121 bins are used.

4.1   Matching: Free Illumination - Controlled Geometry

To test the color descriptors with respect to photometric variations, the descriptors are compared on a matching task on three sequences (see Fig. 3). The first sequence tests the robustness with respect to color illuminant changes. It consists of a Mondrian composition captured under 11 different illuminants (the images are from the Simon Frasier data set [23]). The second sequence [2], of six images, is an outdoor scene, taken with varying exposure times. This not only provokes an intensity change but also changes the amount of diffuse light captured by the camera (as modelled in Eq. 3). The third sequence [2] contains six images and tests the descriptors with respect to geometry variations.

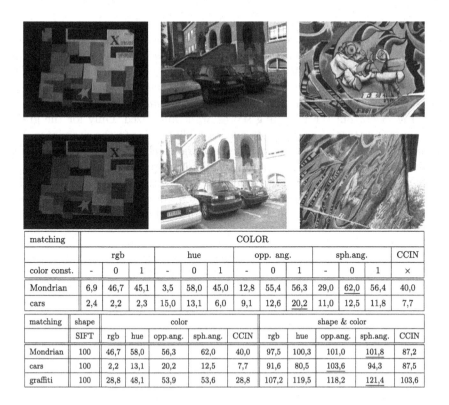

matching	COLOR											
	rgb			hue			opp. ang.			sph.ang.			CCIN
color const.	-	0	1	-	0	1	-	0	1	-	0	1	×
Mondrian	6,9	46,7	45,1	3,5	58,0	45,0	12,8	55,4	56,3	29,0	62,0	56,4	40,0
cars	2,4	2,2	2,3	15,0	13,1	6,0	9,1	12,6	20,2	11,0	12,5	11,8	7,7

matching	shape	color					shape & color				
	SIFT	rgb	hue	opp.ang.	sph.ang.	CCIN	rgb	hue	opp.ang.	sph.ang.	CCIN
Mondrian	100	46,7	58,0	56,3	62,0	40,0	97,5	100,3	101,0	101,8	87,2
cars	100	2,2	13,1	20,2	12,5	7,7	91,6	80,5	103,6	94,3	87,5
graffiti	100	28,8	48,1	53,9	53,6	28,8	107,2	119,5	118,2	121,4	103,6

Fig. 3. Top: example images, Mondrian, cars, and graffiti. Middle: relative matching scores for various color normalization methods:- = no normalization, 0 = zero-order normalization, and 1 = first-order normalization. Bottom: relative matching scores for shape, color, and shape & color.

For all sequences we compute the matching score, defined in [2] as: the ratio between the number of correct matches and the smaller number of detected regions in the pair of images. A match is the nearest neighbor in the descriptor space (using Euclidean distance). For both color and color & shape we give the matching score relative to the matching score obtained by a unique shape descriptor. Values smaller than 100 indicate a performance worse than the shape descriptor and above 100 a performance better than the shape descriptor.

We start by selecting for each of the invariants the most appropriate color illuminant normalization method. This is done by comparing the matching scores for the two sequences with illuminance changes. In Fig. 3 the matching scores of descriptors for: 1. no illuminant. 2. zero-order illuminant normalization (Eq. 7) and 3. first-order (Eq. 9) illuminant normalization are given. The necessity of color illuminant normalization becomes clear from the results on the Mondrian sequence, where a significant gain in performance is achieved. The results on the car sequence show the importance of invariance with respect to diffuse light. Due to varying exposure times the amount of diffuse light entering the camera varies.

Hence for this sequence, the opponent derivative based descriptor outperforms the others significantly, since it is the only one which is invariant with respect to diffuse light changes. *Based on these results we will, in the remainder of the experiments, apply zero-order illuminance invariance to the descriptors rgb, hue, and spherical angle, and first order illuminance invariance to the opponent angle. The CCIN explicitly uses a zero order illuminance normalization.*

In Fig. 3 bottom the matching scores are summarized. Only for the graffiti sequence a substantial gain is obtained by adding color to the descriptor. Furthermore, for the car sequence, the descriptors which are not robust to diffuse lighting fail, and the combined performance of shape and color drops below a solely shape approach. For these sequences, where the assumption of an affine transformation between the images is not broken, the shape description performs outstanding, and relatively small gains are obtained by adding color.

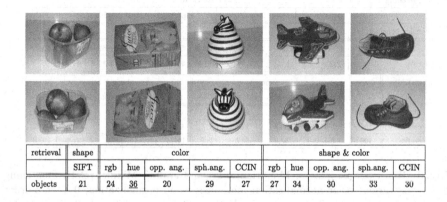

retrieval	shape	color					shape & color				
	SIFT	rgb	hue	opp. ang.	sph.ang.	CCIN	rgb	hue	opp. ang.	sph.ang.	CCIN
objects	21	24	<u>36</u>	20	29	27	27	34	30	33	30

Fig. 4. Two instantiations of five example objects from the data set, with recall scores for shape, color and color & shape

4.2   Retrieval: Controlled Illumination - Free Geometry

Robustness with respect to geometrical variations in a relatively stable photometric environment is tested with a retrieval task on a data set containing 55 objects [1], see Fig. 4. Each object is captured 5 times under varying viewpoint, and object orientations. Because retrieval based on the entire image is close to perfect on this database, we assess the usefullness to retrieval of single features. Each single features was asked to retrieve the four most probable images (there are four relevant images for each query). To measure the descriptor performance we compute the recall, defined as the number of relevant images retrieved to the total number of relevant images in the database.

In Figure 4 the average recall over all local features is given, e.g. for shape a single feature alone obtains a recall of 21 percent. On this data set a unique color description outperforms the shape description. This has two causes. Firstly, the

[1] The authors lost the origin of this data set and would appreciate any suggestions.

objects have relatively saturated colors and photometric conditions are rather stable. Secondly, the shape variations are not constrained to affine transformation as in section 4.1, thereby complicating the shape matching task. Furthermore, the domination of specular reflectances on both objects and background in combination with the spatial variation of the lighting geometry, results in the best performance for the *hue* color descriptor, which is the only descriptor robust to both lighting geometry and specularities.

4.3   Classification: Free Illumination - Free Geometry

This experiment tests the descriptors on an image classification task. Based on the descriptors in the image, a decision is made wether the image is a member of the class or not. The multi-class classification is performed on two data sets. A bird data set [4] containing 6 classes of bird species, with 100 instantiations each (see Fig. 5). The classes are divided in 50 training and 50 testing images. For the second data set we collected images from 7 soccer teams, containing 40 images per class, divided into 25 training and 15 testing images per class [2]. Although, players of other teams were allowed to appear in the images, no players being a member of the other classes in the database were allowed. Both databases consist of low-quality internet images. We use a bag-of-keypoints scheme [24]. The descriptors are clustered by a K-means algorithm which forms a set of visual words. Subsequently, each image is represented by a frequency histogram of the visual words. Based on these histograms, one-against-all classifiers are trained with a linear SVM. A test image is subsequently classified with all classifiers, and is appointed to the class for which it obtained the highest score.

In Fig. 5 the multi-class classification results for the birds data set are given. In all cases the combination of color and shape performs best. Only small gains are obtained with the zero-order invariants, *rgb*, *hue*, and *CCIN*. The derivative-based methods, the *opponent* and *spherical* angle, give considerably better results. For the soccer team data set the necessity of color information is especially apparent. Although, two of the teams have no color, and three of the teams have red as their main color, the color description performs considerably better than the solely shape-based description. The combination of color and shape further improves the results, and the 43% correct classification of shape is increased to a 73% for the combined descriptor. For these highly saturated colors, the results for the different color descriptors do not differ greatly.

The difference in performance for both the birds and the soccer teams can be explained by the different properties of the data sets. The soccer players are not only colorful, they have also undergone considerable non-affine shape transformations, reducing the performance of the SIFT descriptor. On the other hand, the non-saturated colors of the bird data set complicate the task to collect reliable color information, whereas the birds shape is relatively stable compared to the large variability encountered in the soccer team data set.

---

[2] The data set is available on http://lear.inrialpes.fr/people/vandeweijer/data

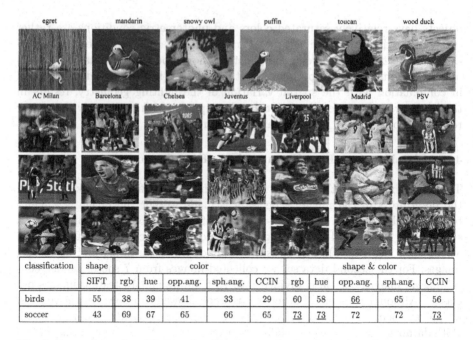

Fig. 5. Examples and multi-class classification results for the birds and soccer database

classification	shape	color					shape & color				
	SIFT	rgb	hue	opp.ang.	sph.ang.	CCIN	rgb	hue	opp.ang.	sph.ang.	CCIN
birds	55	38	39	41	33	29	60	58	_66_	65	56
soccer	43	69	67	65	66	65	_73_	_73_	72	72	_73_

5 Conclusions

In this paper, we have taken a principled approach to extend the SIFT shape descriptor with a color descriptor. Based on four criteria, namely photometric robustness, geometric robustness, photometric stability and generality, we derive a set of photometric invariant color histograms, which are used as a color descriptor. We propose a solution to dependance of derivative-based invariants to the edge-sharpness. The descriptors are tested on a matching, a retrieval, and a classification task. For the colorful objects a pure color-based approach outperforms a shape-based approach. And for all reported data the combination of shape and color outperforms a pure shape-based approach, with gains going up as much as 70 percent. Depending on the data set different color descriptors obtain the best results. However, in general we would advice to use the robust *hue* descriptor for scenes with saturated colors, such as the object data set and the soccer teams. For scenes with less saturated colors, such as the bird data set, and especially in the presence of diffuse lighting, as for the cars sequence, we would advice the color descriptor based on the *opponent angle*.

Acknowledgments

This work is supported by the Marie Curie Intra-European Fellowship Program of the Commission of the European Union.

References

1. Schmid, C., Mohr, R.: Local grayvalue invariants for image retrieval. IEEE Trans. on Pattern Analysis and Machine Intelligence **19** (1997) 530–534
2. Mikolajczyk, K., Tuytelaars, T., Schmid, C., Zisserman, A., Matas, J., Schaffalitzky, F., Kadir, T., van Gool, L.: A comparison of afine region detectors. International Journal of Computer Vision **65** (2005) 43–72
3. Lowe, D.: Distinctive image features from scale-invariant keypoints. International Journal Computer Vision **60** (2004) 91–110
4. Lazebnik, S., Schmid, C.: A maximum entropy framework for part-based texture and object recognition. In: Proc. IEEE Int'l Conf. Comp. Vision. (2005) 832–838
5. Fergus, R., Perona, P., Zisserman, A.: Object class recognition by unsupervised scale-invariant learning. In: Proceedings of the IEEE Conference on Computer Vision and Pattern Recognition. Volume 2. (2003) 264–271
6. Ballard, D.H.: Generalizing the Hough transform to detect arbitrary shapes. Pattern Recognition **12** (1981) 111–122
7. Funt, B., Finlayson, G.: Color constant color indexing. IEEE Trans. on Pattern Analysis and Machine Intelligence **17** (1995) 522–529
8. Finlayson, G.D., Schiele, B., Crowley, J.L.: Comprehensive colour image normalization. In: ECCV '98: Proceedings of the 5th European Conference on Computer Vision-Volume I, Springer-Verlag (1998) 475–490
9. Gevers, T., Smeulders, A.: Color based object recognition. Pattern Recognition **32** (1999) 453–464
10. Geusebroek, J., van den Boomgaard, R., Smeulders, A., Geerts, H.: Color invariance. IEEE Trans. Pattern Analysis Machine Intell. **23** (2001) 1338–1350
11. van de Weijer, J., Gevers, T., Geusebroek, J.: Edge and corner detection by photometric quasi-invariants. IEEE Trans. Pattern Analysis and Machine Intelligence **27** (2005) 625–630
12. Gevers, T., Stokman, H.: Robust histogram construction from color invariants for object recognition. IEEE Trans. Pattern Analysis and Machine Intelligence **26** (2004) 113–118
13. Mindru, F., Tuytelaars, T., Gool, L.V., Moons, T.: Moment invariants for recognition under changing viewpoint and illumination. Computer Vision Image Understing **94** (2004) 3–27
14. Mikolajczyk, K., Schmid, C.: A performance evaluation of local descriptors. IEEE Trans. on pattern analysis and machine intelligence **27** (2005) 1615–1630
15. Matas, J., Koubaroulis, D., Kittler, J.: Colour image retrieval and object recognition using the multimodal neighbourhood signature. In: Proc. of the European Conference on Computer Vision, London, UK, Springer-Verlag (2000) 48–64
16. Shafer, S.: Using color to seperate reflection components. COLOR research and application **10** (1985) 210–218
17. Buchsbaum, G.: A spatial processor model for object colour perception. Journal of the Franklin Institute **310** (1980)
18. van de Weijer, J., Gevers, T.: Color constancy based on the grey-edge hypothesis. In: ICIP'05, Genua, Italy (2005)
19. Finlayson, G., Drew, M., Funt, B.: Color constancy: Generalized diagonal transforms suffice. Journal of the Optical Society of America A. **11** (1994) 3011–3022
20. van de Weijer, J., Gevers, T., Smeulders, A.: Robust photometric invariant features from the color tensor. IEEE Trans. Image Processing **15** (2006) 118–127

21. Finlayson, G.D., Chatterjee, S.S., Funt, B.V.: Color angular indexing. In: ECCV 96: Proceedings of the 4th European Conference on Computer Vision-Volume II, London, UK, Springer-Verlag (1996) 16–27
22. Ohta, Y., Kanade, T., Sakai, T.: Color information for region segmentation. Computer Graphics and Image Processing **13** (1980) 222–241
23. Barnard, K., Martin, L., Funt, B., Coath, A.: A data set for colour research. Color Research and Application **27** (2002) 147–151
24. Willamowski, J., Arregui, D., Csurka, G., Dance, C.R., Fan, L.: Categorizing nine visual classes using local appearance descriptors. In: IWLAVS. (2004)

Defocus Inpainting

Paolo Favaro[1] and Enrico Grisan[2]

[1] Siemens Corporate Research,
Princeton, NJ 08540, USA
paolo.favaro@siemens.com
[2] Department of Information Engineering,
Universitá di Padova, Italy
enrico.grisan@dei.unipd.it
http://www.dei.unipd.it/enrigri

Abstract. In this paper, we propose a method to restore a single image affected by space-varying blur. The main novelty of our method is the use of recurring patterns as regularization during the restoration process. We postulate that restored patterns in the deblurred image should resemble other sharp details in the input image. To this purpose, we establish the correspondence of regions that are similar up to Gaussian blur. When two regions are in correspondence, one can perform deblurring by using the sharpest of the two as a proposal. Our solution consists of two steps: First, estimate correspondence of similar patches and their relative amount of blurring; second, restore the input image by imposing the similarity of such recurring patterns as a prior. Our approach has been successfully tested on both real and synthetic data.

1 Introduction

In many instances, images contain recurring patterns that are similar up to some transformation group. For example, the image of a tree may contain multiple instances of the same leaf at different locations, scales and orientations. In more specific applications, such as corneal imaging, one may find repeated patterns of cells or clusters of cells (see Figure 1). Due to the large aperture of the microscope, cells are not only similar up to an affine transformation, but also up to defocus. In other words, there may be cells in some locations that are blurred version of other cells. Then, one could think of restoring those cells by using the corresponding ones that are less blurred. More in general, if we are interested in restoring images belonging to a specific domain, such as corneal imaging, then one can exploit more than the lone input image. One could also use a database of corneal images to find more recurring patterns. This kind of approach is very similar in spirit to "hallucination" methods [1] which have been applied to faces with success. Our approach can be seen as an extension to these methods, which are limited to a single recurring pattern (e.g. a face) and whose position is known. In this paper, however, to keep the method focused, we consider the restoration problem in the simple case when the database is made of a single image. The extension to multiple images is straightforward.

Exemplar-based methods for inpainting [2] are also similar to our approach. As in [2], we look for *exemplars* that can be used to restore the input image. However, while

A. Leonardis, H. Bischof, and A. Pinz (Eds.): ECCV 2006, Part II, LNCS 3952, pp. 349–359, 2006.

Fig. 1. Oftentimes, images exhibit recurring patterns. For example, in natural images such patterns may be the leaves of a plant or the petals of a flower (left image). In more specific domains, such as in corneal imaging, the recurring pattern is made of cells of the cornea (right image). Notice how both the examples contain regions that are not only similar up to translation, rotation and scale, but also up to the amount of defocus.

we share the general idea of these popular methods, we do not use the same procedural methods to recover the missing information. Rather, we perform restoration by simultaneously considering all the corresponding patterns and their relative amount of defocus. This simultaneous integration allows us to automatically take into account the overlap of patterns and find the best tradeoff between them and the original input image.

In this paper, we propose a solution to the problem of deblurring a single image affected by defocus blur. Our main contribution is the formulation of a novel regularization method, which is based on the input data. As such, we relate to *image restoration* in the field of image processing [3] and *blind deconvolution* in the field of signal processing [4], which belong to the larger class of *inverse problems* [5]. Most of these problems are formulated as a linear model (either in discrete or continuous form), where the task is to infer the unknown object by *inverting* the model. The main challenge is that such inversion is *ill-posed*, as it may lead to multiple solution, or have no solution, or be such that small variations in the input data may cause large variations in the recovered unknown. The general recipe to solve ill-posed problems is to introduce *regularization* [6]. Regularization has been applied to the inverting operator [6, 7] and/or directly to the restored image. The latter approach is also known as Tikhonov regularization [6]. Our approach falls within this type of regularization methods, as we directly operate on the unknown unblurred image. Furthermore, our main strength is that we regularize the restoration of the image by using only the image itself, thus introducing texture that is familiar to the scene.

When the input image is made only of recurring patterns, our algorithm can be used to infer a depth map of the scene. This is reminiscent of shape from texture methods [8, 9], where one recovers the local orientation of an image patch. In our case, rather than using orientation, we consider the local amount of blur as a cue for shape as it has been done in *shape from defocus* [10, 11, 12, 13, 14]. Indeed, a byproduct of our algorithm is the estimation of the relative amount of blur between two similar regions, which can be directly related to depth.

In the next section, we will introduce our model of blurred images with recurring patterns. Then, we will formalize the problem of image restoration, so that it has a non-trivial and unambiguous solution (section 3). We show that despite the complexity of the model and the unknowns, the restoration problem can be solved into two steps: First, we determine the correspondences between recurring patterns and their relative amount of blur (section 4), and second, we integrate this information to restore the input image into a global optimization scheme (section 5).

2 Modeling Defocus and Recurring Patterns

In this section, we will introduce the image formation model for scenes with recurring patterns and captured by a real aperture camera. Let us start by defining the image formation model of a blurred image $I : \Omega \subset \mathbb{R}^2 \mapsto [0, \infty)$

$$I(\mathbf{y}) = \int K_\sigma(\mathbf{y}, \mathbf{x}) f(\mathbf{x}) d\mathbf{x} + n(\mathbf{y}) \quad \forall \mathbf{y} \in \Omega \tag{1}$$

where $K_\sigma : \Omega \times \mathbb{R} \times [0, \infty)$ is called the *point spread function* (PSF) [15], $f : \mathbb{R} \mapsto [0, \infty)$ is the unblurred texture of the scene and $n : \Omega \mapsto \mathbb{R}$ collects noise and distortions that are not captured by the linear term in eq. (1). The PSF K_σ depends on the amount of defocus encoded by the variable $\sigma : \Omega \mapsto [0, \infty)$, which is related to the depth of the scene $s : \Omega \mapsto [0, \infty)$ via [14]

$$\sigma(\mathbf{x}) = \frac{Dv}{2} \left| \frac{1}{v} + \frac{1}{s(\mathbf{x})} - \frac{1}{F} \right| \tag{2}$$

where D is the diameter of the lens, v the distance between the lens and the image plane and F is the focal length of the lens.

We now formalize the notion of recurrence of a pattern within a blurred image and propose a suitable representation for it. Suppose that two regions of the unblurred image $f, O \subset \Omega$ and $O' \subset \Omega$ with $O \cap O' = \emptyset$, are identical to each other. Define $T : \Omega \mapsto \Omega$ the mapping of points $\mathbf{x} \in O$ to points $\mathbf{x}' \in O'$, so that $T(\mathbf{x}) = \mathbf{x}'$. Then, we model a recurrence as

$$f(\mathbf{x}) = f(T(\mathbf{x})) \quad \forall \mathbf{x} \in O. \tag{3}$$

More in general, let us define the mapping T for all recurrences and let us call T the *correspondence map*. In other words, $T(\mathbf{x})$ tells us where to find the location of a region similar to the one around $\mathbf{x}$. When patterns are unique, then we simply have $T(\mathbf{x}) = \mathbf{x}$ $\forall \mathbf{x} \in O$, i.e. a *self-reference*. Notice that a generic correspondence map may generate *loops*. For example, there may be points $\mathbf{x} \neq \mathbf{y}$ such that $T(\mathbf{x}) = \mathbf{y}$ and $T(\mathbf{y}) = \mathbf{x}$. In our context such loops are unnecessary and undesirable. Hence, we will enforce that the correspondence map has only two types of mappings:

1. a self-reference, i.e. $T(\mathbf{x}) = \mathbf{x}$
2. a link to a self-reference, i.e. $T(T(\mathbf{x})) = T(\mathbf{x})$.

For clarity, see Figure 2.

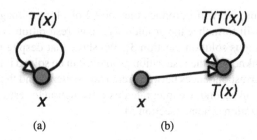

$T(x)$

$T(T(x))$

x

x

$T(x)$

(a)   (b)

Fig. 2. The two types of links admitted by the correspondence map T. On the left we have a self-reference, while on the right we show a link to a self-reference.

The correspondence map T just defined is very general and captures any type of deformation of one region to another. For instance, local affine deformations are captured by using

$$T(\mathbf{x}) = \mathbf{Ax} + \mathbf{b} \quad \forall \mathbf{x} \in O \tag{4}$$

where $\mathbf{A}$ is a 2×2 matrix and $\mathbf{b}$ a 2-dimensional vector. Later on, we will restrict the class of parametric deformations modeled by T to simple translations, i.e. such that $\mathbf{A}$ is the identity matrix in eq. (4), and we will show how to recover the translation $\mathbf{b}$ from a blurred image.

So far, the model that we have introduced can be summarized as:

$$\begin{aligned} f(\mathbf{x}) &= f(T(\mathbf{x})) \\ I(\mathbf{y}) &= \int K_\sigma(\mathbf{y}, \mathbf{x}) f(\mathbf{x}) d\mathbf{x} \end{aligned} \tag{5}$$

where we have neglected the term n for simplicity. We assume that the blurring is locally constant, and therefore it can be modeled by a shift-invariant PSF K_σ, and that the PSF is Gaussian, i.e. such that

$$K_\sigma(\mathbf{y}, \mathbf{x}) = \frac{1}{\sqrt{2\pi\sigma^2(\mathbf{y})}} \exp^{-\frac{\|\mathbf{y}-\mathbf{x}\|^2}{2\sigma^2(\mathbf{y})}}. \tag{6}$$

We will now show in the next section how to pose the problem of deblurring with recurring regions.

3   Maximizing Deblurring

Suppose that $O \subset \Omega$ is a recurring region. Then, according to eq. (5) we have that

$$I(\mathbf{y}) = \int K_\sigma(\mathbf{y}, \mathbf{x}) f(\mathbf{x}) d\mathbf{x} = \int K_\sigma(\mathbf{y}, \mathbf{x}) f(T(\mathbf{x})) d\mathbf{x}. \tag{7}$$

If now we allow the correspondence map to capture only translations, then we have $T(\mathbf{x}) = \mathbf{x} + \mathbf{b}$. By substituting the explicit expression of T in the equation above, and using the assumption that blurring is locally constant and Gaussian, it is easy to derive that

$$I(\mathbf{y}) = \int K_\sigma(\mathbf{y} + \mathbf{b}, \mathbf{x}) f(\mathbf{x}) d\mathbf{x} = \int K_{\Delta\sigma}(\mathbf{y}, \mathbf{x}) I(\mathbf{x} + \mathbf{b}) d\mathbf{x} \qquad (8)$$

where $\Delta\sigma$ is called *relative blur* and it satisfies $\Delta\sigma^2(\mathbf{y}) = \sigma^2(\mathbf{y}) - \sigma^2(\mathbf{y} + \mathbf{b})$, $\forall \mathbf{y} \in O$. Since relative blur is meaningful if and only if $\Delta\sigma(\mathbf{y}) \geq 0$, we impose that the correspondence map T maps regions to regions that are less blurred, i.e. such that $\sigma^2(\mathbf{x}) \geq \sigma^2(T(\mathbf{x}))$. Hence, by definition, regions that are self-referencing will be subject to no blurring ($\Delta\sigma = 0$).

The main advantage of eq. (8) is that it does not depend on the unblurred image f, as eq. (5), but only on the the relative blur $\Delta\sigma$ and the correspondence map T. Hence, by using eq. (8) one can decouple the problem of simultaneously estimating all the unknowns into two problems where one first recovers the relative blur and the correspondence map and then restores the unblurred image f. In this section, we will introduce the problem of recovering the first two unknowns, while we will devote section 5 to the restoration of the unblurred image f.

Now, recall eq. (8). It is easy to see that this equation is satisfied by $\Delta\sigma = 0$ and $T(\mathbf{x}) = \mathbf{x}$. This means that given a blurred image I, a correspondence map T that is always admissible is the one such that all regions are unique and hence their mapping is a self-reference. As a consequence, the relative blur will be null everywhere. Such T and $\Delta\sigma$ do not give any advantage with respect to previous methods for deblurring. To avoid this situation, we pose the problem of finding the solution with largest relative blur. Hence, to recover $\Delta\sigma$ and T we pose the following maximization problem

$$\Delta\sigma, T = \arg\max_{\Delta\sigma} \int \Delta\sigma^2(\mathbf{x}) d\mathbf{x}$$

$$\text{subject to:} \begin{cases} I(\mathbf{y}) = \int K_{\Delta\sigma}(\mathbf{y}, \mathbf{x}) I(\mathbf{x} + \mathbf{b}) d\mathbf{x} \\ T(\mathbf{x}) = \mathbf{x} & \forall \mathbf{x} | \Delta\sigma(\mathbf{x}) = 0 \\ T(\mathbf{x}) = \mathbf{x} + \mathbf{b}, \mathbf{b} \neq 0 & \forall \mathbf{x} | \Delta\sigma(\mathbf{x}) > 0 \\ T(T(\mathbf{x})) = T(\mathbf{x}) \end{cases} \qquad (9)$$

where the first constraint corresponds to eq. (8); the second one corresponds to having no relative blur between self-references; the third one corresponds to imposing the translational model whenever there is relative blur between two regions; finally, the fourth constraint imposes that T satisfies only the two types of mappings shown in Figure 2. This equation can also be interpreted as the maximization of the *amount of deblurring* that we will be able to perform in the second part of the algorithm (section 5).

4   Localization of Recurring Regions

In order to solve the problem in eq. (9), we need to recall the representation of the correspondence map T. The map T is defined jointly with the relative blur $\Delta\sigma$ as being either

$$T(\mathbf{x}) = \mathbf{x} \quad \forall \mathbf{x} | \Delta\sigma(\mathbf{x}) = 0 \qquad (10)$$

or

$$T(\mathbf{x}) = \mathbf{x} + \mathbf{b}, \mathbf{b} \neq 0 \quad \forall \mathbf{x} | \Delta\sigma(\mathbf{x}) > 0. \tag{11}$$

In other words, the relative blur defines a partition of Ω into regions where T is equal to a constant vector $\mathbf{b}$ (Figure 3). Given this representation, we propose the following approximate algorithm to solve eq. (9):

- Initialize the map T such that $T(\mathbf{x}) = \mathbf{x}$ $\forall \mathbf{x} \in \Omega$
- Quantize the relative depth into L levels
- **for each level l from L to 0**
  - **for each translation b**
    - ∗ Compute the region where all the constraints in eq. (9) are simultaneously satisfied; in particular, where eq. (8) is satisfied and where $\Delta\sigma(\mathbf{x}+\mathbf{b}) = 0$
  - Merge the new correspondences to the current map T so that the resulting map is *admissible*, i.e. such that $T(T(\mathbf{x})) = \mathbf{x}$ $\forall \mathbf{x} \in \Omega$. Indeed, although the new correspondences and the current map T are admissible on their own, when merging them there may be links with two hops. Since we start from the highest depth level and proceed to the lowest, such multiple hops are not possible and we set them to be self-references.

Once both $\Delta\sigma$ and T have been computed, we can proceed with the restoration of the unblurred image f. In the next section, we call such restoration *defocus inpainting* as we are filling in blurred regions with the corresponding sharp ones.

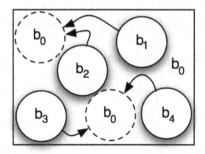

Fig. 3. A partition of the image domain Ω into regions where the relative blur is 0 ($\mathbf{b_0}$) and where it is strictly positive ($\mathbf{b_1}$, $\mathbf{b_2}$, $\mathbf{b_3}$, $\mathbf{b_4}$). Notice that multiple partitions may be in correspondence with the same region.

5 Defocus Inpainting

Image restoration is well-known to be an *ill-posed* problem [5]. To eliminate the ill-posedness, one can introduce *regularization* during the restoration process. Since we pose image restoration as an energy minimization problem, regularization can be added in the form of an additional energy term E_2, so that our solution can be found by minimizing

$$\hat{f} = \arg\min_f \int_\Omega \left(I(\mathbf{y}) - \int K_\sigma(\mathbf{y}, \mathbf{x}) f(\mathbf{x}) d\mathbf{x} \right)^2 d\mathbf{y} + \mu E_2 \tag{12}$$

where μ is a scalar that regulates the amount of regularization. Typically, the term E_2 is a prior that is introduced independently of the input image. For example, one could use a *measure of sharpness* of local patches such as the structure tensor [16].

In our approach instead, we exploit the recurrence of regions as a regularization term. We define E_2 to be

$$E_2 = \int_\Omega \left(I(\mathbf{y}) - \int K_{\Delta\sigma}(\mathbf{y}, \mathbf{z}) \int K_\sigma(\mathbf{z} + \mathbf{b}, \mathbf{x}) f(\mathbf{x}) d\mathbf{x} \right)^2 d\mathbf{y}. \qquad (13)$$

Notice that in eq. (12) one has to recover both the depth map s (encoded by the amount of blur σ) and the unblurred image f. Furthermore, such reconstruction is possible only if one knows the camera parameters. In many instances, however, such parameters are not available. In this case, we propose a method to improve the restoration of the input image I, by introducing the following constraints:

$$\begin{aligned} f(\mathbf{x}) &= I(\mathbf{x}) && \forall \mathbf{x} | T(\mathbf{x}) = \mathbf{x} \\ f(\mathbf{x}) &= f(T(\mathbf{x})) && \forall \mathbf{x} | T(\mathbf{x}) \neq \mathbf{x}. \end{aligned} \qquad (14)$$

The two equations above formalize the following procedure: if a region is self-referencing, then no restoration is performed; if a region maps to another region, since such region is sharper by construction of the correspondence map T (see section 3), then the latter one is used in place of the first one. Hence, the regularization term in this case becomes simply:

$$E_2 = \int_\Omega (f(\mathbf{x}) - I(T(\mathbf{x})))^2 d\mathbf{x} \qquad (15)$$

and the data term in eq. (12) has to be computed on the known relative blur $\Delta\sigma$ rather than σ resulting in

$$\hat{f} = \arg\min_f \int_\Omega \left(I(\mathbf{y}) - \int K_{\Delta\sigma}(\mathbf{y}, \mathbf{x}) f(\mathbf{x}) d\mathbf{x} \right)^2 d\mathbf{y} + \mu \int_\Omega (f(\mathbf{x}) - I(T(\mathbf{x})))^2 d\mathbf{x}. \qquad (16)$$

The computation of the unknown unblurred image f can then be done by performing a gradient descent on eq. (16) with the following energy gradient:

$$\nabla_f E(\mathbf{x}) = -2 \int_\Omega \left(I(\mathbf{y}) - \int K_{\Delta\sigma}(\mathbf{y}, \mathbf{x}') f(\mathbf{x}') d\mathbf{x}' \right) K_{\Delta\sigma}(\mathbf{y}, \mathbf{x}) d\mathbf{y} + 2\mu \left(f(\mathbf{x}) - I(T(\mathbf{x})) \right). \qquad (17)$$

6 Experiments

We test our algorithm on both synthetic and real data. In the case of synthetic data, we show the average performance of the method on 50 experiments with fixed shape and variable texture. In Figure 4 we show one example of the texture that has been employed in the generation of the synthetic images (a), together with the corresponding blurred image (b). In (c) we show the true depth map which can be compared to the recovered

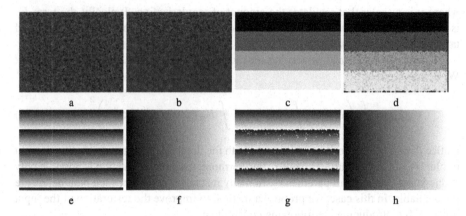

Fig. 4. One example of synthetic defocus inpainting. (a) The true unblurred image. (b) The input image. (c) The true depth map. (d) The recovered depth map. (e) and (f) the true correspondence map T where (e) corresponds to the x coordinates and (f) to the y coordinates. (g) and (h) the recovered correspondence map.

depth map in (d). In (e) and (f) we show the true correspondence map T where (e) corresponds to the x coordinates and (f) to the y coordinates; in (g) and (h) we show the recovered correspondence map. In Figure 5 we show a few snapshots of the restoration of one example (shown in Figure 4). On the leftmost image we show the given blurred image, while on the rightmost image we show the true unblurred texture.

We find that the mean restoration error is of 0.1441 with standard deviation of 0.0116, which, once compared to the error between the input image and the true unblurred image 0.3183 with standard deviation of 0.0177, shows an improvement of more that 2 times.

In the case of real experiments, we run our algorithm on images of the endothelium cell layer, that were acquired from several corneas at the Cornea Bank Berlin using an inverse phase-contrast microscope (CK 40, Olympus Co. Japan) at 100x and 200x magnification, and thus are subject to a substantial amount of defocus. The corneas were kept in hypotonic BSS for a better microscopy visualization of the endothelial

Fig. 5. Snapshots of the restoration process. For comparison, on the leftmost image we show the input image, while on the rightmost image we show the true unblurred image. In the middle we show the evolution of the gradient descent presented in section 5. Iteration time increases going from left to right.

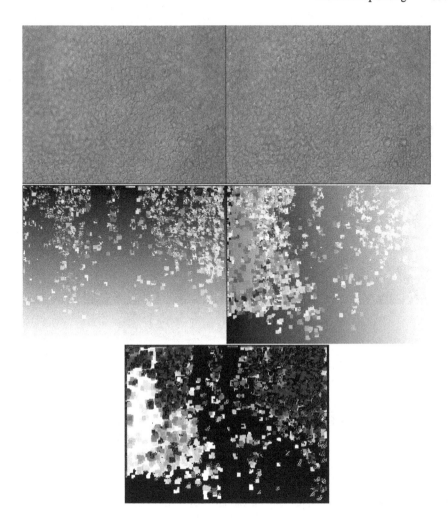

Fig. 6. (top row - left) Image of a cornea. Notice that in some portions of the image the cells are more defocused than in other locations due to the change in depth of the surface. (right) Restored image of the cornea. Notice that cells that were blurred in the original image are now restored and resemble other cells in the same image (data kindly provided by *Fondazione Banca degli Occhi di Venezia. Italy*). (second row) Visualization of the estimated correspondence map. (left) image showing the x coordinates of T. (right) image showing the y coordinates of T. Dark intensities correspond to lower values of the coordinates and vice versa for light intensities. Recall that the map $T(\mathbf{x})$ assigns a sharp patch at $T(\mathbf{x})$ to the blurred patch at $\mathbf{x}$. (bottom row) Visualization of the reconstructed blur map. Light intensities correspond to large amounts of blur, while dark intensities to low amounts of blur.

cells by osmotic stimulation of their cell membranes. In Figure 6 on the top row we show the input image (left) and the restored image (right). Notice that in the input image some location are more blurred than others due to changes in the depth of the cornea. Furthermore, notice that in the restored image most of the blurred cells are

Fig. 7. Examples of defocus inpainting on various images. (left) Input image. (right) Restored image.

restored and resemble the appearance of similar cells that are sharper. In Figure 6, second row, we show the estimated correspondence map T. For ease of visualization, the coordinates of this map are shown as two grayscale images. Notice that the algorithm detects that most sharp patches are located on the right of the input image, and that most of the blurred patches are located on the left. In Figure 6, third row, we show the estimated blur map of the scene. Notice that light intensities correspond to regions that are subject to a large amount of blur, while dark intensities correspond to regions that are subject to small amounts of blur. By visual inspection it is possible to verify that the recovered blur map correctly assigns high values to regions that are blurred in the input image.

In Figure 7 we show a number of examples where the left images are the input images, and the right images are the restored ones.

7   Conclusions

We introduced a novel paradigm for image restoration, where regularization is extracted directly from data. We exploit the assumption that the image contains recurrences of patterns that are similar up to translation and amount of defocus, and show how to model them in the context of defocused images. Then, we propose a novel solution to identify the recurring patterns, to estimate their difference in amount of blur and finally to restore the unblurred image. Our method can also be readily extended to work with multiple images, and we are currently working on handling similarity up to scale and rotations in addition to translations.

References

1. Baker, S., Kanade, T.: Limits on super-resolution and how to break them. In: IEEE Transactions on Pattern Analysis and Machine Intelligence. Volume 24. (September, 2002) 1167–83
2. Criminisi, A., Perez, P., Toyama, K.: Object removal by exemplar-based inpainting. In: CVPR03. (2003) II: 721–728
3. Katsaggelos, A.: Digital Image Restoration (Book). Springer (1991)
4. Yitzhaky, Y., Milberg, R., Yohaev, S., Kopeika, N.S.: Comparison of direct blind deconvolution methods for motion-blurred images. In: Applied Optics-IP. Volume 38. (July 1999) 4325–32
5. Bertero, M., Boccacci, P.: Introduction to inverse problems in imaging. Institute of Physics Publishing, Bristol and Philadelphia (1998)
6. Engl, H., Hanke, M., Neubauer, A.: Regularization of Inverse Problems. Kluwer Academic Publishers, Dordrecht (1996)
7. You, Y., Kaveh, M.: Blind image restoration by anisotropic diffusion. IEEE Trans. on Image Processing 8 (1999) 396–407
8. Aloimonos, Y., Swain, M.: Shape from texture. BioCyber 58 (1988) 345–360
9. Blostein, D., Ahuja, N.: Shape from texture: Integrating texture-element extraction and surface estimation. PAMI 11 (1989) 1233–1251
10. Ens, J., Lawrence, P.: An investigation of methods for determining depth from focus. IEEE Trans. Pattern Anal. Mach. Intell. 15 (1993) 97–108
11. Pentland, A.: A new sense for depth of field. IEEE Trans. Pattern Anal. Mach. Intell. 9 (1987) 523–531
12. Subbarao, M., Surya, G.: Depth from defocus: a spatial domain approach. Intl. J. of Computer Vision 13 (1994) 271–294
13. Watanabe, M., Nayar, S.: Rational filters for passive depth from defocus. Intl. J. of Comp. Vision 27 (1998) 203–225
14. Chaudhuri, S., Rajagopalan, A.: Depth from defocus: a real aperture imaging approach. Springer Verlag (1999)
15. Born, M., Wolf, E.: Principle of optics. Pergamon Press (1980)
16. Weickert, J.: Anisotropic Diffusion in Image Processing. B.G.Teubner Stuttgart (1998)

Viewpoint Induced Deformation Statistics and the Design of Viewpoint Invariant Features: Singularities and Occlusions

Andrea Vedaldi and Stefano Soatto

University of California at Los Angeles, Los Angeles – CA 90095
{vedaldi, soatto}@cs.ucla.edu

Abstract. We study the set of domain deformations induced on images of three-dimensional scenes by changes of the vantage point. We parametrize such deformations and derive empirical statistics on the parameters, that show a kurtotic behavior similar to that of natural image and range statistics. Such a behavior would suggest that most deformations are locally smooth, and therefore could be captured by simple parametric maps, such as affine ones. However, we show that deformations induced by singularities and occluding boundaries, although rare, are highly salient, thus warranting the development of dedicated descriptors. We therefore illustrate the development of viewpoint invariant descriptors for singularities, as well as for occluding boundaries. We test their performance on scenes where the current state of the art based on affine-invariant region descriptors fail to establish correspondence, highlighting the features and shortcomings of our approach.

1 Introduction

This work is concerned with the design of viewpoint-invariant discriminative local features, *i.e.* local image statistics whose dependency on viewpoint can be made arbitrarily small while maintaining non-trivial dependency on other properties of the scene, such as its shape and reflectance. This problem has been largely solved under the assumption that the scene is locally planar, Lambertian, viewed under ambient illumination and moderate changes in viewpoint. Under these conditions, local deformations can be approximated by a similarity or affine transformation, and the resulting local invariant features (see [1, 2, 3, 4, 5, 6, 7, 8] and references therein) have proven to be a powerful tool in the recognition of individual objects as well as object categories [9, 10, 11, 12, 13, 14, 15, 4, 1, 16, 17]. But *what happens when such conditions are not satisfied?*

Changes of illumination can have minor or drastic effects depending on the reflectance of the scene [18] and we will not address them here; we will continue to assume that the scene is Lambertian and viewed in ambient light, leaving illumination out of the scope of this work. Drastic changes in viewpoint could be handled by concatenations of small changes if intermediate views are available [11, 14]. However, we will not make that assumption and allow large viewpoint changes which can induce visibility artifacts such as occlusions. The local planarity assumption is violated in two cases: At singularities (e.g. ridges or corners),

A. Leonardis, H. Bischof, and A. Pinz (Eds.): ECCV 2006, Part II, LNCS 3952, pp. 360–373, 2006.

and at occluding boundaries. Here the assumption of affine deformation is violated in a neighborhood of any size, and similarity/affine invariants often (but not always) fail.[1] But *how important are singularities and occlusions? How much weight do they carry in the recognition process?* We will show that singularities and occluding boundaries are few compared to interior regular points, but they carry significant weight in that they often correspond to photometrically salient regions (as also shown indirectly by [18], Sect. 5).

Now, assuming that we agree that singular regions and occlusions are important, *can we characterize the deformations they induce on the image under changes in viewpoint? Can we exploit this knowledge to design viewpoint-invariant features for such intrinsically non-planar portions of the scene?*

As we will show, in order to design a viewpoint invariant feature for singularities and occlusions we need to attach a curvilinear (or multi-linear) local frame to the image. This is still an open area of research, which we cannot address in the limited scope of this paper. We will therefore tap onto existing techniques that allow the extraction of some discrete representation (a graph) from local analysis of the image, such as [19, 10, 12] and their variants. We will discuss their role and their limitations in generating viewpoint invariants.

1.1 State of the Art

The literature on feature extraction is too extensive to review in the limited scope of a conference paper. The reader is encouraged to consult [20] and references therein. At one end of the spectrum of work on on feature-based recognition are simple parametric deformations, e.g. affine transformations yielding a procrustean density on feature constellations (see [21] and references therein). At the opposite end are "bags of features" that retain only feature labels regardless of their mutual position (see [22, 23, 24] and references therein). Viewpoint changes induce transformations more general than affine, but far less general than an arbitrary scrambling of feature positions. Our work concentrates on the case in between, following the steps of [25, 4, 26, 27, 28].[2] More specifically, [29, 30] have proposed region descriptors for salient regions detected at or near occluding boundaries. While feature selection is traditionally addressed as a representation issue, different from the final goal of recognition, the two processes are beginning to come together [31, 32, 33]. Since viewpoint variations (under the assumptions discussed) only induce changes in the domain of the image, this work generically relates to deformable templates [34] and deformable models [35]. Our attempt to characterize the "natural deformation statistics" follows the lead of [36, 37] and others that have characterized natural image and range statistics.[3] Specific relationships with other work will be pointed out throughout the manuscript.

---

[1] Part of the art of designing a descriptor is to give it slack to absorb violations of the underlying assumptions.

[2] Even work that allows arbitrary reordering of features relies on individual features being matched across views, and therefore the affine model restricts this approach beyond its ideal generality.

[3] Including [38] that has appeared while this manuscript was under review.

1.2   Notation and Formalization of the Problem

An image is a function $I : \Lambda \to \mathbb{R}^+$; $x \mapsto I(x)$ with local domain $\Lambda \subset \mathbb{R}^2$ and range in the positive reals. Under the assumptions of Sect. 1, the value of the image at a pixel x is approximately equal to the radiance ρ of the scene at a point p on a surface $S \subset \mathbb{R}^3$, $I(x) = \rho(p)$, $p \in S$. In fixed coordinates, p projects onto $x = \pi(g_0 p)$ where $\pi : \mathbb{R}^3 \to \mathbb{P}^2$ is a canonical perspective projection and $g_0 \in SE(3)$ is the position and orientation of the camera. We say that x is the *image* of p, and p is the *pre-image* of x. These notions extend to sets; for instance, the pre-image of a ball of radius σ around x_0, $\mathcal{B}_\sigma(x_0)$, is the set $\{p \in S : \pi(g_0 p) \in \mathcal{B}_\sigma(x_0)\}$. If we consider multiple images of the same scene under changing viewpoint, we can choose one of the camera reference frames as the fixed frame, and parameterize the surface S relative to it. Then, with an abuse of notation, we can write $p = S(x)$ and we have that the generic image is given by

$$\begin{cases} I(\hat{x}) = \rho(S(x)) \\ \hat{x} = \pi(g_t S(x)) \doteq w(x), \qquad x \in \Omega. \end{cases} \tag{1}$$

Can we characterize the structure and statistics of the function $w : \Omega \subset \mathbb{R}^2 \to \mathbb{R}^2$? Can we use it to design viewpoint invariant features?

2   Natural Warping Statistics

The structure of $w : \Omega \to \mathbb{R}^2$ obviously depends on the structure of S. We distinguish between three classes of points : x_0 is an *interior regular point* (**IR**) if there exists an σ and a neighborhood $\mathcal{B}_\sigma(x_0)$ whose pre-image $S(\mathcal{B}_\sigma(x))$ is simply connected and smooth. x_0 is an *interior singular point* (**IS**) if its pre-image is a $C^1(\mathcal{B}_\sigma(x_0))$ discontinuity, *i.e.* the scene is continuous around the pre-image of x_0 but not differentiable on it. An IS point can be the image of a *wedge* (the locus of singularities is a one-dimensional submanifold of S, locally approximated by a line), or an image of a *corner* (the locus of singularities is the tip of a generalized cone). Finally, x_0 is an *occluding boundary* (**OB**) if the pre-image of any neighborhood $\mathcal{B}_\sigma(x_0)$ is not simply connected, for any choice of σ. In this case, the occluding boundary could correspond to a singularity (OBS), as is the case for polyhedra, or it could correspond to regular points on S (OBR), as is the case for the silhouette of a smooth surface . Note that viewpoint variations can change the labeling of points. For instance, an IR point can become OB and vice-versa. However, if a point is IR there will always exist a neighborhood and a set of viewpoints (depending on σ) such that the point remains IR.

2.1   Deformation Statistics Around Interior Points

The goal here is to determine the distribution of the homeomorphism $w : \Omega \subset \mathbb{R}^2 \to \mathbb{R}^2$; $x \mapsto \pi(gS(x))$ defined in (1). In order to make the notation explicit we write $\Omega \doteq x_0 + \mathcal{B}_\sigma$, with x_0 a location on the image domain and $\mathcal{B}_\sigma$ a ball of radius σ centered at the origin, discretized into N points: $\mathcal{B}_\sigma = \{x_1, \ldots, x_N\}$. Therefore,

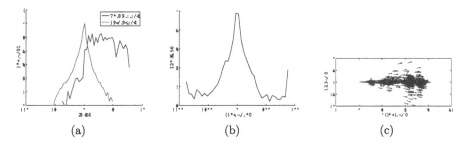

(a)   (b)   (c)

Fig. 1. *Camera motion statistics* depend heavily on the application. Ground vehicle navigation induces strongly non-Gaussian velocity distributions, as the statistics of Golem 2 driving in the DARPA Grand Challenge show (a) forward and lateral one-second displacements (b) one-second orientation variation (c) scatter plot of the vehicle relative displacement after one second (top view, restricted to fast parts of the track).

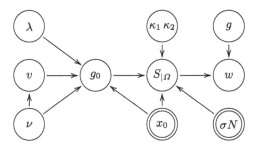

Fig. 2. *Statistical dependencies in a generative model of viewpoint warping.* Camera motion g and global shape S are rendered independent by conditioning on a local patch Ω. Local conditioning generates a dependency on x_0, σ and N, displayed as "observed" variables. The distributions $p(g_0|\lambda x_0, \nu, v)$, $p(S_{|\Omega}|g_0, \kappa_1, \kappa_2, x_0)$ and $p(w|S_{|\Omega}, g)$ encode deterministic functions resulting from simple geometrical and optical considerations (Sect. 1.2-2.1). The statistics of the other variables are determined empirically.

$\Omega \doteq \Omega(x_0, \sigma, N)$. We then call $w_i \doteq w(x_0 + x_i) - x_0 - x_i$ the displacement of the pixel $i = 1, \ldots, N$, so that we can characterize the distribution of w via the vectors $w_1, \ldots, w_N$:

$$p(w|x_0, \sigma, N) \doteq p([w_1, \ldots, w_N]|x_0, \sigma, N). \qquad (2)$$

Here x_0, σ and N are parameters of the distribution, the first indicating the position on the image plane, the second the *scale* at which the statistics are computed, the third the *sampling* of the discretization. We will now attempt to decompose the density above to elucidate its structure. The statistical dependencies are highlighted in Fig. 2.

The first step, following (1), would be to marginalize with respect to the scene S and the motion g. Done globally, this would be a tall order since g and S are not independent: One's motion within a scene depends on its shape. For instance, one typically walks on the floor while avoiding obstacles that are part of the scene S. However, since we are considering regions away from occluding boundaries, w does not depend on the entire scene S, but only on its visible portion.[4] Therefore, we condition on the pre-image of the patch Ω and only consider the *local* dependency of w on S:

$$p(w|x_0, \sigma, N) = \int p(w|g, S_{|\Omega}) dP(g, S_{|\Omega}|x_0, \sigma, N). \tag{3}$$

The advantage is that g and the local pre-image $S_{|\Omega}$ are to first approximation independent, which yields

$$p(g, S_{|\Omega}|x_0, \sigma, N) = p(g)p(S_{|\Omega}|x_0, \sigma, N).$$

Note that local conditioning introduces the dependency of $S_{|\Omega}$ from x_0, σ and N, so empirical studies must take it into consideration.

The first factor $p(g)$ is the viewer *motion* density, which is crucially dependent on the application. For human motion (or hand-held cameras), the statistics have been computed in [38]. These are rather different than those for ground vehicle navigation: Fig. 1 shows statistics of displacement and rotation of the vehicle "Golem 2" during the DARPA Grand Challenge. Rotational and translational degrees of freedom are strongly correlated due to non-holonomic constraints. At the other end of the spectrum one can imagine a *tumbling robot* where the motion density is (improper and) close to uniform $p(g) \sim \mathcal{U}(SE(3))$.

The second factor can be further decomposed by locally approximating the scene $S_{|\Omega}$ using the Darboux frame g_0, and the two principal curvatures, κ_1 and κ_2, that encode *local shape*:

$$p(S_{|\Omega}|x_0, \sigma, N) = p(\kappa_1, \kappa_2, g_0|x_0, \sigma, N) \tag{4}$$

The Darboux frame g_0 is determined by the normal ν, the principal direction v, and the position of the point $\lambda x_0 \in \mathbb{R}^3$ where x_0 is written in homogeneous coordinates and $\lambda \in \mathbb{R}^+$ is the depth along the corresponding ray.

The first observation is that the dependency of this density on x_0 is nontrivial: On the top portion of an image we usually observe the ceiling (indoor) or the sky outdoor, on the bottom we usually have a flat ground; these significantly bias the pose statistics as shown in Fig. 4. There are also dependencies on the geometry of the sensor: The shape of the pre-image of Ω for a flat sensor, or for a cylindrical or conical mirror, depends on the location x_0 on the image. These, however, are second-order effects that can be easily compensated for. Having observed these effects, we then resort to computing aggregate statistics by marginalizing over x_0. So, we are left with having to estimate the density

$$p(\kappa_1, \kappa_2, \nu, v, \lambda|\sigma, N) = p(\kappa_1, \kappa_2|\sigma, N)p(v|\nu, \sigma, N)p(\nu|\sigma, N)p(\lambda|\sigma, N) \tag{5}$$

---

[4] Strictly speaking this assumption is incorrect, as a camera motion g can turn an interior point into an occluding boundary. However, here we assume that most interior points will remain so during motion.

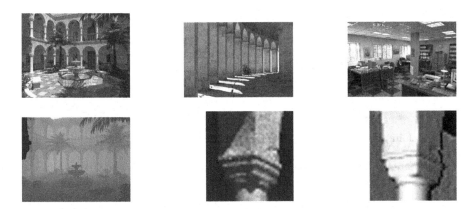

Fig. 3. A few samples from the *synthetic dataset* [39]. (Bottom-left) A range map computed from the model, with details (middle) showing fine-scale details (e.g. surface cracks) that are part of the geometry (shaded surface, right) and not just "painted" onto smooth surfaces.

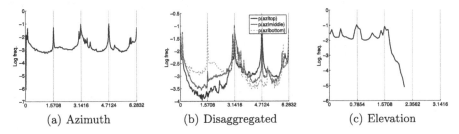

(a) Azimuth   (b) Disaggregated   (c) Elevation

Fig. 4. *Pose statistics.* (a) Histogram of the orientation of the normal vector relative to the optical axis. The peaks are due to horizontal and vertical surfaces. (b) The same statistics vary significantly if restricted to the top, middle and bottom third of the images. (c) Elevation of the normals relative to the optical axis.

which we do empirically. In order to have full control of sampling issues, we have decided to derive these statistics from simulated (ray-traced) images. While this choice presents potential dangers due to shortcuts often employed in ray-traced images, extensive sets of realistic images can be found, for which "ground truth" S is available. In our experiments we have used the datasets [39] that contains extremely detailed and realistic models (see Fig. 3).

We have observed that σ does not affect the nature of the statistics as long as $S(\Omega)$ can be approximated up to second order (recall that we are looking away from occluding boundaries). The choice of N is more delicate. Since the images are given to us at a fixed sampling rate, N and σ are naturally related. We have chosen σ corresponding to small windows of 5×5 pixels, and then implicitly chosen N by matching the scale of the mesh of S with the sampling of the image patch. We have done so by anisotropically smoothing the mesh proportionally to

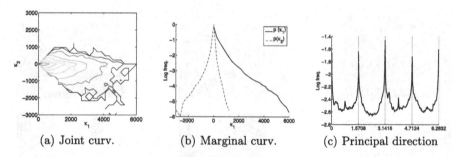

(a) Joint curv.   (b) Marginal curv.   (c) Principal direction

Fig. 5. *Shape statistics.* (a) Joint histogram of the principal curvatures κ_1, κ_2. (b) Marginal histograms. (c) Histogram of the orientation of the principal direction (projected onto the image plane).

the area of the pre-image $S(\Omega(x_0, \sigma, N))$, while preserving occluding boundaries and sharp discontinuities. Curvatures and principal directions are computed using discrete differential operators [40] on the regularized meshes. The resulting marginal and joint histograms are shown in Fig. 5. As one can expect, these statistics exhibit high kurtosis, indicating that regions of high curvature are rare. Most non-planar structures are wedges ($\kappa_2 \approx 0$) and, interestingly, saddles ($\kappa_2 < 0$), consistent with the observations of [37].

2.2   Occlusion Statistics

Empirical distributions on the frequency of occluding boundaries can be obtained directly from range images. These have already been studied in [37], and show a kurtotic behavior similar to that of curvature, indicating that occlusions are a rare event.

2.3   Saliency of Singularities and Occlusions

Although occlusions and singularities are rare events, in the sense that they represent a zero-measure subset of the scene and project onto a small subset of the image (by area), they are salient in that such geometric discontinuities often correspond to photometric discontinuities that are selected by feature detectors. For the case of occlusions, this is obvious since at occluding boundaries an arbitrarily small neighborhood contains the image of different objects. For the case of singularities, Chen et al. [18] have argued that in homogeneous materials they yield photometrically salient profiles, that they have measured empirically. To validate these results, we have tested a standard edge detector (Canny) on ray-traced images and we have examined the co-location of their responses to the curvature of the local pre-images (Fig. 6). This experiment illustrates that occlusions and singularities, although rare, are photometrically salient, and therefore *there remains the need to study feature descriptors for regions that include discontinuities.* We now move on to that problem.

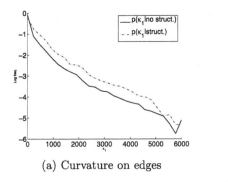
(a) Curvature on edges

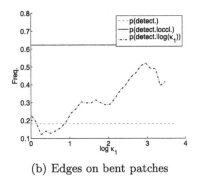
(b) Edges on bent patches

Fig. 6. *Saliency of singularities.* A Canny edge detector is implemented at a scale comparable to the scale of the patches used for the statistics (5×5 pixels). In (a) we show how the histogram of the principal curvature κ_1 varies if restricted to those patches that contain an edge (we discarded patches that contain an occluding boundary): On average, "Canny patches" have higher curvature. In (b) we sorted the patches in increasing curvature (log scale) and computed the fraction that contains an edge. We repeated this computation for all patches and the patches that contain an occluding boundary. The fraction increases significantly with the curvature and is even higher for occluding boundaries.

3   Designing Viewpoint Invariant Descriptors

The empirical evidence in the previous section suggests that image regions with discontinuities or occluding boundaries are photometrically salient, which in turn suggests that they may be distinctive and therefore useful for recognition. In this section we illustrate how to construct viewpoint invariant features for such regions. We first show how a general methodology has been used before for the case of interior-regular points and singularities, and extend it to occluding boundaries.

We will assume that we have a mechanism available to establish the origin of a local reference frame. This is the role of a *feature detector* that can pool statistics from regions of various shape and size. Detectors may localize a point on the image, or select entire regions (in case the pooled statistics are constant), which in turn can be used to establish a local frame. Around the origin we will construct a local viewpoint invariant region statistic, or *feature descriptor*.

From the image formation model (1) it is immediate to see that the equivalence class of image deformations, *i.e.* the set $\phi(I, \Omega) \doteq [I(w(x)), \ x \in \Omega \ \forall \ w]$ is a viewpoint invariant. Indeed, it is the *maximal* viewpoint invariant, in the sense that any other invariant is a function of it. Unfortunately, comparing such invariants could be difficult because it entails a search over w. Since $\phi(I, \Omega)$ is an equivalence class, any element can represent it. Therefore, one can seek a mechanism to associate a *canonical warping* $\hat{w}$ to the local image structure, as

(a) Image   (b) Sketch   (c) Frames

Fig. 7. *Local image structure as extracted in the pre-processing step.* The image in the middle shows the structures extracted by the sketch. On the right we show some of the star-like subgraphs that we manually select as candidate feature frames. The subgraphs are centered on junctions and have linear branches. Whenever no natural termination of a branch is found, a nominal value (established by looking at the maximum of a Laplacian operator centered at the junction) is used.

well as a canonical domain $\hat{\Omega}$, and use $[I(\hat{w}(x)),\ x \in \hat{\Omega}]$, or any function of it, as the invariant descriptor.[5]

3.1 Interior Regular and Singular Points

The program sketched above has been carried out successfully by many researchers for the case of affine warps: $w(x) = Ax + b$. Note that the linear terms in the local approximation can be written out, spelling explicitly the rotational and translational components of g, as $w(x) = (R + T\nu^T)x$, and the homography $(R + T\nu^T)$ can be approximated with an affine transformation $[A\ b]$. Therefore, the transformation induced by any IR point can be annihilated by an appropriate affine transformation: The scene is a plane, $S = \mathbb{R}^2$, the translational term b is fixed by a feature detector (*e.g.* Harris [42], so without loss of generality we can assume $b = 0$), and the second moment matrix, or other local intensity statistic [43], can be used to determine A. The transformation that inverts A can be interpreted as a warping of a canonical circular neighborhood $[I(\hat{w}(x)),\ x \in \mathbb{S}^1]$, or $\hat{w}$ can be though of as the transformation of a detected elliptical region Ω into a circle $\mathbb{S}^2 = \hat{w}^{-1}(\hat{\Omega})$, as in [2].

The same ideas can be easily extended to non-planar scenes [41]. In this case, the reference frame we seek to normalize using intensity statistics is not affine, but curvilinear and possibly known only up to symmetries, when the image presents regular textures or homogeneous regions [41]. The deformation induced by changes in viewpoint can be represented by a *piecewise affine transformation*, with as many components as connected elements of the singularity. For instance, an edge has 2

---

[5] Invariance is achieved through a local homeomorphic deformation of the image domain into a canonical configuration tailored to the local image structure. While fixing a homeomorphism of the image domain forces viewpoint invariance, the converse is not necessarily true; i.e. image domain deformations induced by changes of viewpoint do not cover the set of all possible homeomorphisms [41], unless the scene is planar.

affine components, a 3-D corner has 3, etc. with the tip of a cone with smooth section as a limiting case. Naturally these affine transformations are *not independent* because they have to satisfy compatibility constraints (see [41] for details).

3.2 Occluding Boundaries and Unilateral Descriptors

It is easy to show that the deformation induced by the motion of an arbitrary shape does not preserve any geometric or topological property of the silhouette [44, 45]. Indeed, given two curves, one can construct objects that, under suitable viewpoints, have the curves as silhouettes. This is not true when the object has symmetries, or when it has a particular structure, for instance a polyhedron. In the former case one can derive case-by-case invariants, which is beyond our scope here. In the latter case, occluding boundaries correspond to singularities, and we can build a *unilateral descriptor* following the lines of the previous section. We proceed with a detector in the exact same way as we did in Sect. 3.1, since a-priori we do not know whether edges in the image are due to albedo or shape. Then for each local neighborhood we construct not one, but several descriptors based on masking different sectors of the local graph, followed by rectification. Whether a given region is a singularity or an occluding boundary will only be clear at matching: If matching all N regions independently produces similarly small residuals, the singularity hypothesis is accepted, and the entire region is normalized and matched. If at least one of the N matches yields a low residual, the occlusion hypothesis is accepted, and matching is based on one sector only Figs. 8-9 illustrates few representative examples.

Once the local structure in a neighborhood of the image is extracted by a low-level feature detector, one could build a discrete representation (local graph) and compare regions by comparing their graphs. Unfortunately, such graphs are highly unstable with respect to changes of viewpoint, as failure to detect local

(a)   (b)

Fig. 8. *Background resilience.* Feature A: To achieve insensitivity to the background, we generate two unilateral SIFT descriptors, one for each side of the local frame. (a) and (b) show three patches on which the three descriptors are computed (scale is 1/6 of the radius). These features have been added to the pool of features detected by SIFT to see whether they enable correct discrimination. Of these, two do not match correctly (red lines) because they cover the background, while the other (green line) does as it covers only the foreground. Feature B: Both the bilateral and unilateral descriptors match because the background does not change substantially.

(a)   (b)

Fig. 9. *Occlusion resilience.* We generate several descriptors for each selected corner structure of Fig. 7, then add them to the pool detected by SIFT/Harris-Affine. (top) Due to visibility effects, SIFT (green) and Harris-Affine (orange) fail to match all four corners (red lines). (bottom) The unilateral descriptors that cover the foreground portion of the object are matched correctly, while the others fail. Eventually each feature is associated to its best matching descriptor (green lines). Columns (a) and (b) show the three and four descriptors extracted in the two images for the feature denoted as A (in green the matching descriptors).

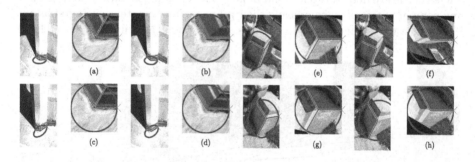

Fig. 10. *Comparing discrete structures through a generative process.* Pictures (a) and (c) show two images of the same structure re-projected by means of the normalized graph: They look similar as expected. Pictures (b) and (d) show the patches obtained when the weak structure (the central edge) is removed from the graph. Despite the graph topology changing drastically (a 3-junction becomes a corner), the re-projected patches look quite similar. Unfortunately this does not work in all cases, as depicted in pictures (e-h). Here normalization is inconsistent because the detector only considers edge-like structures.

structures results in changes of topology of the corresponding graph. Since we compare intensity statistics in a normalized frame, one could argue that if a local structure is not stable enough with respect to changes of viewpoint, that structure should not matter for matching. We illustrate this in Fig. 10 (left) where the instability in inferring local image structure is anihilated by the synthesis of the normalized patch. Indeed, since the canonical configuration is arbitrary, one can choose it to compensate for failures of the low-level feature detector.

This, however, does not always work, since missed detection changes the canonization procedure, as we illustrate in Fig. 10 (right). This is the weakest point of our method, which can be improved with mid-level processing and grouping procedures that are beyond the scope of this paper.

4   Discussion

We have derived a statistical characterization of the deformations of the image domain induced by changes of viewpoint. This shows that, while occlusions and surface singularities are rare, they are photometrically salient, which motivates their use for recognition. This prompts us to develop dedicated viewpoint invariant descriptors.

For singularities, we rely on existing methods to extract local image structure, and construct an invariant descriptor by normalizing such structure and generating a canonical radiance from it. Although the technique is general, it relies on pre-processing steps that, with the current state of the art, are problematic. Alternatively, one could use region-based segmentation approaches as a means to extract local structure ahead of computing invariant statistics. For the case of occlusions, we have developed unilateral descriptors based on masking portions of the detected regions. We have shown a few representative examples of the behavior of such descriptors for cases where existing affine invariants fail to establish correspondence. Note that we do not advocate the descriptors in Sect. 3.1-3.2 as an *alternative* to existing descriptors. They are designed to cover conditions that current descriptors are not designed for, hence be complementary. Note also that the best affine descriptors can tolerate a great deal of violation of the assumptions they are designed for, therefore many of the cases where our approach would be best suited is already covered by, say, SIFT or Harris-affine.

Considerable work remains to be done to design robust and stable low and mid-level detection schemes, but we hope that this study illustrates a general methodology that can be used to design viewpoint invariant descriptors for non-planar portions of the scene.

References

1. Lowe, D.G.: Distinctive image features from scale-invariant keypoints. IJCV **2** (2004) 91–110
2. Mikolajczyk, K., Schmid, C.: An affine invariant interest point detector. In: Proc. ECCV, Springer-Verlag (2002) 128–142

3. Schaffalitzky, F., Zisserman, A.: Viewpoint invariant texture matching and wide baseline stereo. In: Proc. ICCV. (2001)
4. Triggs, B.: Detecting keypoints with stable position, orientation, and scale under illumination changes. In: Proc. ECCV. (2004)
5. Ullman, S., Vidal-Naquet, M., Sali, E.: Visual features of intermediate complexity and their use in classification. Nature 5 (2002)
6. Kadir, T., Brady, M.: Scale saliency: A novel approach to salient feature and scale selection. In: International Conference Visual Information Engineering. (2003)
7. Lindeberg, T.: Feature detection with automatic scale selection. IJCV 30 (1998) 77–116
8. Matas, J., Chum, O., Urban, M., Pajdla, T.: Robust wide baseline stereo from maximally stable extremal regions. In: Proc. BMVC. (2002)
9. Fei-Fei, L., Fergus, R., Perona, P.: A Bayesian approach to unsupervised one-shot learning of object categories. In: Proc. ICCV. (2003)
10. Weber, M., Welling, M., Perona, P.: Unsupervised learning of models for recognition. In: Proc. ECCV. (2000)
11. Rothganger, F., Lazebnik, S., Schmid, C., Ponce, J.: 3D object modeling and recognition using affine-invariant patches and multi-view spatial constraints. In: Proc. CVPR. (2003)
12. Fergus, R., Perona, P., Zisserman, A.: Object class recognition by unsupervised scale-invariant learning. In: Proc. CVPR. (2003)
13. Sivic, J., Zisserman, A.: Video Google: A text retrieval approach to object matching in videos. In: Proc. ICCV. (2003)
14. Ferrari, V., Tuytelaars, T., Van Gool, L.: Integrating multiple model views for object recognition. In: Proc. CVPR. (2004)
15. Tuytelaars, T., Van Gool, L.: Wide baseline stereo matching based on local, affinely invariant regions. In: Proc. BMVC. (2000) 412–425
16. Dorkó, G., Schmid, C.: Object class recognition using discriminative local features. PAMI (submitted) (2004)
17. Fritz, G., Seifert, C., Paletta, L., Bischof, H.: Rapid object recognition from discriminative regions of interest. In: Proc. 19th National Conference on Artificial Intelligence. (2004) 444–449
18. Chen, H.F., Belhumeur, P.N., Jacobs, D.W.: In search of illumination invariants. In: Proc. CVPR. (2000)
19. Guo, C., Zhu, S.C., Wu, Y.N.: Towards a mathematical theory of primal sketch and sketchability. In: Proc. ICCV. (2003) 1228
20. Mikolajczyk, K., Tuytelaars, T., Schmid, C., Zisserman, A., Matas, J., Schaffalitzky, F., Kadir, T., Van Gool, L.: A comparison of affine region detectors. IJCV 1 (2004) 63–86
21. Fergus, R., Perona, P., Zisserman, A.: A sparse object category model for efficient learning and exhaustive recognition. In: Proc. CVPR. (2005)
22. Csurka, G., Dance, C.R., Dan, L., Willamowski, J., Bray, C.: Visual categorization with bags of keypoints. In: Proc. ECCV. (2004)
23. Grauman, K., Darrell, T.: Efficient image matching with distributions of local invariant features. In: Proc. CVPR. (2005)
24. Malik, J., Belongie, S., Shi, J., Leung, T.: Textons, contours and regions: Cue integration in image segmentation. In: Proc. CVPR. (1999)
25. Thureson, J., Carlsson, S.: Appearance based qualitative image description for object class recognition. In: Proc. ECCV. Volume 2. (2004)
26. Ferrari, V., Tuytelaars, T., Van Gool, L.: Simultaneous object recognition and segmentation by image exploration. In: Proc. ECCV. (2004)

27. Brown, M., Lowe, D.G.: Invariant features from interest point groups. In: Proc. BMVC. (2002)
28. Fraundorfer, F., Bischof, H.: A novel performance evaluation method of local detectors on non-planar scenes. In: Proc. CVPR. (2005)
29. Mikolajczyk, K., Zisserman, A., Schmid, C.: Shape recognition with edge-based features. In: Proc. BMVC. (2003)
30. Stein, A., Hebert, M.: Incoporating background invariance into feature-based object recognition. In: Seventh IEEE Workshop on Applications of Computer Vision (WACV). (2005)
31. Vasconcelos, N.: Feature selection by maximum marginal diversity: optimality and implications for visual recognition. In: Proc. CVPR. (2003)
32. Wold, L., Shashua, A.: Feature selection for unsupervised and supervised inference: the emergence of sparsity in a weighted-based approach. In: Proc. ICCV. (2003)
33. Levi, K., Weiss, Y.: Learning object detection from a small number of examples: the importance of good features. In: Proc. CVPR. Volume 2. (2004)
34. Grenander, U.: General Pattern Theory. Oxford University Press (1993)
35. Cootes, T.F., Taylor, C.J., Cooper, D.H., Graham, J.: Active shape models – their training and application. Comput. Vis. Image Underst. 61 (1995) 38–59
36. Huang, J., Lee, A.B., Mumford, D.: Statistics of range images. In: Proc. CVPR. (2000)
37. Yang, Z., Purves, D.: Image/source statistics of surfaces in natural scenes. Network: Comput. in Neural Syst. 14 (2003)
38. Roth, S., Black, M.J.: On the spatial statistics of optical flow. In: Proc. ICCV. (2005)
39. Piqueres, J.V.: The persistence of ignorance. http://www.ignorancia.org/ (2006)
40. Meyer, M., Desbrun, M., Schröder, P., Barr, A.H.: Discrete differential geometry for triangulated 2-manifolds. In: Proc. of VisMath. (2002)
41. Vedaldi, A., Soatto, S.: Features for recognition: Viewpoint invariance for non-planar scenes. In: Proc. ICCV. (2005)
42. Harris, C., Stephens, M.: A combined corner and edge detector. In: Proceedings of The Fourth Alvey Vision Conference. (1988) 147–151
43. Bauer, J., Bischof, H., Klaus, A., Karner, K.: Robust and fully automated image registration using invariant features. In: Proc. of Intl. Arch. of Photogram., Remote Sensing and Sptl. Inf. Sci. (2004)
44. Lazebnik, S., Sethi, A., Schmid, C., Kriegman, D.J., Ponce, J., Hebert, M.: On pencils of tangent planes and the recognition of smooth 3D shapes from silhouettes. ICJV (2002)
45. Schmid, C., Zisserman, A.: The geometry and matching of curves in multiple views. In: ECCV. (1998)

Spatio-temporal Embedding for Statistical Face Recognition from Video

Wei Liu[1], Zhifeng Li[1], and Xiaoou Tang[1,2]

[1] Department of Information Engineering,
The Chinese University of Hong Kong,
Hong Kong, China
{wliu5, zli0}@ie.cuhk.edu.hk
[2] Microsoft Research Asia, Beijing, China
xitang@microsoft.com

Abstract. This paper addresses the problem of how to learn an appropriate feature representation from video to benefit video-based face recognition. By simultaneously exploiting the spatial and temporal information, the problem is posed as learning Spatio-Temporal Embedding (STE) from raw video. STE of a video sequence is defined as its condensed version capturing the essence of space-time characteristics of the video. Relying on the co-occurrence statistics and supervised signatures provided by training videos, STE preserves the intrinsic temporal structures hidden in video volume, meanwhile encodes the discriminative cues into the spatial domain. To conduct STE, we propose two novel techniques, Bayesian keyframe learning and nonparametric discriminant embedding (NDE), for temporal and spatial learning, respectively. In terms of learned STEs, we derive a statistical formulation to the recognition problem with a probabilistic fusion model. On a large face video database containing more than 200 training and testing sequences, our approach consistently outperforms state-of-the-art methods, achieving a perfect recognition accuracy.

1 Introduction

As still image-based recognition accuracy is still too low in some practical applications comparing to other high accuracy biometric technologies, video-based face recognition has been proposed recently [15][12][6][16][7][9][13]. One major advantage of video-based techniques is that more information is available in a video sequence than in a single image. Naturally, the recognition accuracy could be improved if the abundant information can be properly exploited.

It has been demonstrated that modeling temporal dynamics is very useful to the video-based problems. Hence, recent video-based face recognition research employs them to improve recognition performance. Using the statistical coherence over time, Zhou *et al.* [16] model the joint probability distribution of identity and head motion using sequential importance sampling, which leads to a generic framework for both tracking and recognition. Liu *et al.* [9] analyze video sequences over time by HMMs, each of which learns the temporal dynamics within

A. Leonardis, H. Bischof, and A. Pinz (Eds.): ECCV 2006, Part II, LNCS 3952, pp. 374–388, 2006.

a video sequence. Comparing likelihood scores provided by the HMMs, the identity of a testing video sequence is yielded with the highest score. Because learning temporal dynamics during the recognition stage is very time-consuming, above statistical models can not suffice for the real-time requirement of automatic face recognition systems. Lee *et al.* [7] approximate a nonlinear appearance manifold which stands for one subject (person) as a collection of linear submanifolds, and encode the dynamics between them into the transition probability. The manifold learning algorithms in [7] are subject-specific and lack the discriminating power, so they do not adapt well to the face recognition scenario which is a supervised classification problem.

Opposite to face hallucination techniques [1][8][10] which try to infer the lost image content of a facial image, the video-based face recognition scenario is confronted with the abundance of consecutive frames in face videos. Hence it is crucial to efficiently exploit the spatial and temporal information.

In this paper we present a novel spatio-temporal representation for each video sequence that we call "Spatio-Temporal Embedding" (STE). The STE of a video sequence is its miniature, condensed version containing the intrinsic spatio-temporal structures inherent in the space-time video volume. Based on STEs, we develop a statistical face recognition framework from video by integrating several novel techniques including Bayesian keyframe learning for learning

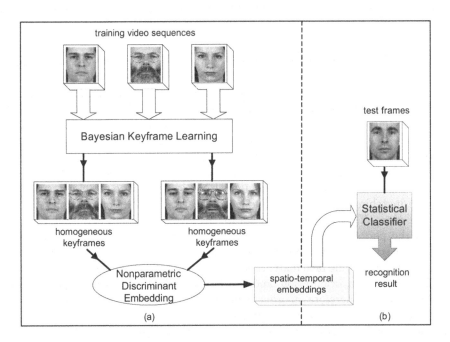

Fig. 1. The framework of our video-based face recognition approach. (a) Training stage: learn keyframes from video sequences and then arrange them into K groups of homogeneous keyframes which will be input to NDE; (b) testing stage: construct a statistical classifier in terms of learned spatio-temporal embeddings.

temporal embedding, Nonparametric Discriminant Embedding (NDE) for learning spatial embedding, and statistical classification solution. This framework takes full advantage of the effective amount of potential information in videos and at the same time overcomes the processing speed and data size problems. The detailed diagram of the proposed framework is plotted in Fig. 1.

The rest of this paper is organized as follows. In Section 2, we propose to learn temporal embedding "keyframes" which are robust to data perturbation. In Section 3, we develop NDE to further learn spatial embedding of keyframes. A statistical classifier is designed in Section 4. Experimental results on the largest standard video face database, the XM2VTS database [11], are reported in Section 5. Finally, we draw conclusion in Section 6.

2   Temporal Embedding

Recent literature proposes to extract the most representative frames called "exemplars" or "keyframes" from the raw videos. Keyframes extracted from a video sequence just span the temporal embedding of the video. However, previous approaches for extracting keyframes only consider the temporal characteristics of individual video, the extracted keyframes thus tend to differ in describing the temporal structures. In this section, we present our approach for automatically learning the homogeneous keyframes used to support discriminant analysis.

2.1   Previous Work

Krueger and Zhou [6] apply radial basis functions to select representative images as exemplars from training face videos, and this facilitates both tracking and recognition tasks. Our previous work [13] uses information in audio signals of video to locate maximum audio amplitudes of temporal segments to find the corresponding video keyframes. We [13] have demonstrated that audio-guided keyframes well represent a video sequence, and reach a satisfactory video-to-video matching level using subspace approaches.

For videos of varying frame contents, a simple matching of two video sequences frame-by-frame will not help much to video-to-video matching, since we may be matching a frame in one video with a frame of different expression in another video. This may even deteriorate the face recognition performance. The key to the performance improvement is that face frames in each sequence are in a consistent order of temporal dynamics, so that neutral face matches with neutral face and smile face matches with smile face. The consistent order implies synchronized pose, orientation, and expression variations of face images in each video sequence. Therefore, in order to make use of keyframes to boost recognition performance, keyframes across different video sequences should be extracted in a synchronized way. We call this "frame synchronization" as we will guarantee that keyframes extracted from different videos are temporally synchronized from each other.

In literature [6], the best keyframes (exemplars) are sought such that the expected distance between them and frames in the raw video sequence is minimized.

Due to the mentioned synchronization criterion for keyframe extraction, the algorithm proposed in [6] fails to generate "good" keyframes because it only works on individual video. Our work [13] succeeds in learning synchronized keyframes by utilizing audio signals in videos. Specifically, when recording video data in the XM2VTS database, each person is asked to recite two sentences "0,1,2,...,9" and "5,0,6,9,2,8,1,3,7,4" which span a video sequence of 20 seconds. Since the audio signals are in the same order over time and approximately reflect the temporal structures of videos, the audio-guided method guarantees frame synchronization. Nevertheless, in some applications, it may be difficult to get audio signals contained in videos. In addition, the method is vulnerable to data perturbation. For example, if a person reads the digit sequence "0,1,2,...,9" in a random order, skips one digit, or repeats one digit, then the audio-guided method will fail the frame synchronization and a wrong frame match may appear.

Beyond the audio limitation, we should design a novel keyframe learning approach which could comply with frame synchronization with only the image information of video data adopted.

2.2 Synchronized Frame Clustering

A prelude to learning keyframes is clustering on video frames. Previous clustering on videos only focuses on spatial (e.g. appearance) correlations and skip temporal correlations that also play an important role in clustering. For exemplars provided by XM2VTS, when one reads one particular digit, the associated frames should be mapped to the same cluster that corresponds the digit. Due to concerns of spatial and temporal continuity inherent in video data, we propose a synchronized clustering method which incrementally outputs aligned clusters across all video sequences based on K-means clustering [4].

Let $V = \{\mathbf{x}_1, \cdots, \mathbf{x}_t, \cdots, \mathbf{x}_N\}(\mathbf{x}_t \in \Re^d)$ represent a set of video frame samples belonging to the same video sequence. In this work we assume temporal coherence on the order in which data points arrive one-by-one. Let V be a stream of data, its temporal ordering specified by the corresponding subscript. For the training video set $\{V^{(i)}\}_{i=1}^M$, we cluster each one $V^{(i)}$ into K clusters $\{\mathcal{C}_k^{(i)}\}_k$ at one time, and then merge these formed clusters $\{\mathcal{C}_k^{(i)}\}_i$ into a larger one $\mathcal{C}_k = \bigcup_i \mathcal{C}_k^{(i)}$.

For clustering the sequence $V^{(i)}$, we promote the classical K-means algorithm [4] using the following spatio-temporal objective function to assign k^* to $\mathbf{x}_t^{(i)}$

$$k^* = \arg \min_{k \in \{1, \cdots, K\}} \frac{(\mathbf{x}_t^{(i)} - \bar{\mathbf{x}}_k)^T Q (\mathbf{x}_t^{(i)} - \bar{\mathbf{x}}_k)}{\lambda_1} + \frac{(t - time(\mathbf{x}_t^{(i)}, \mathcal{C}_k^{(i)}))^2}{\lambda_2}, \quad (1)$$

where $\bar{\mathbf{x}}_k$ is the average of frames in cluster $\mathcal{C}_k$; Q is an adaptive distance metric which will be updated after each sequence clustering; function $time(\mathbf{x}_t^{(i)}, \mathcal{C}_k^{(i)})$ computes the temporally nearest order in the cluster $\mathcal{C}_k^{(i)}$ for frame $\mathbf{x}_t^{(i)}$; scaling parameters λ_1, λ_2 control the trade-off between spatial and temporal similarity.

Table 1. Synchronized frame clustering algorithm

Step 1: *PCA.* To reduce the high dimensionality of images, we project the training frame ensemble $\{\mathbf{x}_t^{(i)}\}_{t,i}$ into the PCA subspace. For brevity, still use $\mathbf{x}$ to denote the frames in the PCA subspace in the following steps.

Step 2: *Initialization.* For the first video sequence $V^{(1)}$, randomly select K frames as the initial cluster center $\bar{\mathbf{x}}_1, \cdots, \bar{\mathbf{x}}_K$, then perform K-means clustering on $V^{(1)}$ by eq. (1). K small clusters $\{\mathcal{C}_k^{(1)}\}_{k=1}^K$ are obtained, with which large clusters $\{\mathcal{C}_k\}_{k=1}^K$ are generated as $\mathcal{C}_k = \mathcal{C}_k^{(1)}$ $(k = 1, \cdots, K)$. So the initial metric Q can be computed using eq. (2) in terms of initial $\{\mathcal{C}_k\}_{k=1}^K$.

Step 3: *Synchronized clustering.*
For $i = 2, \cdots, M$
    use current cluster centers $\{\bar{\mathbf{x}}_k\}_{k=1}^K$ to conduct K-means clustering on sequence $V^{(i)}$ resulting in new small clusters $\{\mathcal{C}_k^{(i)}\}_{k=1}^K$;
    update $\mathcal{C}_k \longleftarrow \mathcal{C}_k \bigcup \mathcal{C}_k^{(i)}$ $(k = 1, \cdots, K)$;
    update $\bar{\mathbf{x}}_k \longleftarrow \sum_{\mathbf{x} \in \mathcal{C}_k} \mathbf{x}/|\mathcal{C}_k|$ $(k = 1, \cdots, K)$;
    update Q with updated $\{\bar{\mathbf{x}}_k\}$ and $\{\mathcal{C}_k\}$;
End.

Outputs: Synchronized clusters $\{\mathcal{C}_k^{(i)}\}_{k=1,\cdots,K}^{i=1,\cdots,M}$ across all video sequences $\{V^{(i)}\}_{i=1}^M$.

Motivated by Relevant Component Analysis (RCA) [2] which gives a good metric with contextual information among samples explicitly encoded, a stepwise update for the metric is done absorbing the current context of clustering

$$Q \longleftarrow \left(\sum_{k=1}^K \frac{1}{|\mathcal{C}_k|} \sum_{\mathbf{x} \in \mathcal{C}_k} (\mathbf{x} - \bar{\mathbf{x}}_k)(\mathbf{x} - \bar{\mathbf{x}}_k)^T + r\mathbf{I} \right)^{-1}. \tag{2}$$

r is an regularization constant, which is often necessary when $\mathcal{C}_k$ contains a small number of frames. As long as $\{\mathcal{C}_k\}$ expand further, Q will become more accurate and reliable, even need not regularization.

To overcome the problems incurred by disordered video data, we propose a synchronized frame clustering algorithm plotted in Tab. 1. As we take centers of large clusters $\mathcal{C}_k$ as K means for clustering individual sequence, small clusters $\mathcal{C}_k^{(i)}$ across different video sequences within the same large cluster $\mathcal{C}_k$ tend to be homogeneous. What' more, historical clustering results provide the reference order for following sequence clustering. Consequently, our clustering algorithm guarantees frame synchronization and outputs synchronized and aligned clusters $\{\mathcal{C}_k^{(i)}\}_{k,i}$ across all training video sequences $\{V^{(i)}\}_i$.

2.3 Bayesian Keyframe Learning

Since the audio-guided method is sensitive to disordered video sequences, we thus propose an automatic keyframe learning method and make it robust to disordered video sequences. The learning method enables us to select not only synchronized but also distinctive keyframes spanning the temporal embeddings of videos. The intuition of this method is that excellent keyframe extraction should be pursued jointly in temporal and spatial domains.

After synchronized frame clustering, each video sequence has at most K clusters $C_k^{(i)}(k = 1, \cdots, K)$ with the consistent order. Our purpose is to select the keyframes, i.e most representative exemplars, from each particular cluster $C_k^{(i)}$ in each sequence. Given the synchronized property of clusters $C_k = \{C_k^{(i)}\}_i$, we model the co-occurrence statistics among all video frames in the constructed cluster C_k as the joint probability distribution

$$p(\mathbf{x}, C_k) \propto \exp\left(-\frac{\|\Lambda_k^{-1/2}U_k^T(\mathbf{x} - \bar{\mathbf{x}}_k)\|^2}{2}\right), \qquad (3)$$

in which the eigensystem (U_k, Λ_k) is solved by performing PCA on frames in cluster C_k, and keeping the leading eigenvectors retaining 98% of the energy.

Given each sequence $V^{(i)}(i = 1, \cdots, M)$, candidates $\mathbf{e}$ in small cluster $C_k^{(i)}$ with maximum likelihood to C_k are selected as keyframes. In practice, the frames with the m greatest conditional probabilities $p(\mathbf{e}|V^{(i)}, C_k)$ to each cluster C_k are selected as top-m keyframes. By Bayesian law, we choose the optimal exemplar $\mathbf{e}^*$ such that (the deviation parameter δ_k can be evaluated using data in C_k)

$$\begin{aligned}
\mathbf{e}^* &= \arg\max_{\mathbf{e}} \; p(\mathbf{e}|V^{(i)}, C_k) = \arg\max_{\mathbf{e}} \; p(\mathbf{e}, V^{(i)}, C_k) \\
&= \arg\max_{\mathbf{e}} \; p(V^{(i)}|\mathbf{e}, C_k)p(\mathbf{e}, C_k) = \arg\max_{\mathbf{e}} \prod_{x \in C_k^{(i)}} p(\mathbf{x}|\mathbf{e})p(\mathbf{e}, C_k) \\
&= \arg\max_{\mathbf{e}} \; \exp\left(-\sum_{x \in C_k^{(i)}} \frac{\|\mathbf{x} - \mathbf{e}\|^2}{2\delta_k^2} - \frac{\|\Lambda_k^{-1/2}U_k^T(\mathbf{e} - \bar{\mathbf{x}}_k)\|^2}{2}\right). \qquad (4)
\end{aligned}$$

Substituting all possible frames $\mathbf{e} \in C_k^{(i)}$ into eq. (4) and maximizing eq. (4), we accomplish learning the optimal K keyframes. The top-m keyframes can also be learned by adopting eq. (4) as the keyframe score. The keyframe selection strategy supported by eq. (4) is termed Bayesian keyframe learning, which effectively coordinates the co-occurrence statistics and individual representative capability of selected keyframes. So far, we have learned the temporal embedding of video sequence $V^{(i)}$, which we denote as $\mathcal{T}^{(i)}$. Its k-th component in cluster C_k is denoted as $\mathcal{T}_k^{(i)}$, and its constituent top-m keyframes are represented by $\mathbf{e}_{kj}^{(i)}(k = 1, \cdots, K, j = 1, \cdots, m)$. Within the same cluster C_k, keyframes are well synchronized and highly homogeneous.

3   Spatial Embedding

We will further learn the spatial embedding over the learned temporal embedding to achieve the final STE according to each video. This is achieved by performing a novel supervised dimensionality reduction algorithm called Nonparametric

Discriminant Embedding (NDE). We show that NDE is superior to PCA and LDA, two well-known linear dimensionality reduction algorithms. Hence, NDE endows STEs with much greater discriminating power.

3.1 Nonparametric Discriminant Embedding (NDE)

LDA is a popular feature extraction technique which aims to maximize ratio of the determinant of the between-class scatter matrix to that of the within-class scatter matrix. Assume there are c different classes, let μ_i, μ be the class mean and overall mean, and n_i the number of samples in class C_i, the within-class scatter matrix and the between-class scatter matrix are defined as

$$S_w = \frac{1}{c} \sum_{i=1}^{c} \frac{1}{n_i} \sum_{j \in C_i} (\mathbf{x}_j - \mu_i)(\mathbf{x}_j - \mu_i)^T$$

$$S_b = \frac{1}{c} \sum_{i=1}^{c} (\mu_i - \mu)(\mu_i - \mu)^T. \tag{5}$$

The LDA algorithm seeks to determine the optimal projection W which maximizes the ratio between the between-class matrix and the within-class matrix $|W^T S_b W| / |W^T S_w W|$.

Until now, numerous LDA-based methods have been proposed for face recognition [3][14]. However, an inherent problem with LDA arises from the parametric form of the between-class scatter matrix, which leads to several disadvantages. Firstly, LDA is based on the assumption that the discrimination information is equal for all classes. Therefore, it performs well under Gaussian class distributions, but not under non-Gaussian distributions. Secondly, the number of the final LDA features, f, has an upper limit of $c-1$ because the rank of the between-class matrix S_b is $c-1$ at most. It is not sufficient for complex data distribution if only $c-1$ features are used. Thirdly, due to the presence of outliers, the between class matrix S_b in LDA cannot capture the information of the boundary structure effectively, which is essential for different classes.

To overcome the above drawbacks, we propose a Nonparametric Discriminant Embedding (NDE) algorithm motivated by nonparametric discriminant analysis (NDA) [5]. The original NDA algorithm only deals with two-class pattern recognition tasks, whereas the proposed NDE algorithm is generalized to tackle multi-class pattern classification problem. The difference between NDE and LDA is in the definition of the scatter matrices. In NDE, we define the within-class and between-class scatter matrix as

$$S_w^{\mathcal{N}} = \frac{1}{c} \sum_{i=1}^{c} \frac{1}{n_i} \sum_{t=1}^{n_i} (\mathbf{x}_t^i - \mu_i(\mathbf{x}_t^i))(\mathbf{x}_t^i - \mu_i(\mathbf{x}_t^i))^T$$

$$S_b^{\mathcal{N}} = \frac{1}{c(c-1)} \sum_{i=1}^{c} \sum_{j=1, j \neq i}^{c} \sum_{t=1}^{n_i} \lambda(i,j,t)(\mathbf{x}_t^i - \mu_j(\mathbf{x}_t^i))(\mathbf{x}_t^i - \mu_j(\mathbf{x}_t^i))^T, \tag{6}$$

where $\mathbf{x}_t^i$ denotes the t-th sample of class i, and $\mu_j(\mathbf{x}_t^i)$ is the mean of local z-NNs, defined as $\mu_j(\mathbf{x}_t^i) = \sum_{p=1}^{z} \mathbf{n}_p^j(\mathbf{x}_t^i)/z$ where $\mathbf{n}_p^j(\mathbf{x}_t^i)$ is the pth nearest neighbor from class j to sample $\mathbf{x}_t^i$, and $\lambda(i, j, t)$ is a weighting function which is defined as

$$\lambda(i, j, t) = \frac{\min\left\{d^\beta(\mathbf{x}_t^i, \mathbf{n}_z^i(\mathbf{x}_t^i)), d^\beta(\mathbf{x}_t^i, \mathbf{n}_z^j(\mathbf{x}_t^i))\right\}}{d^\beta(\mathbf{x}_t^i, \mathbf{n}_z^i(\mathbf{x}_t^i)) + d^\beta(\mathbf{x}_t^i, \mathbf{n}_z^j(\mathbf{x}_t^i))}, \tag{7}$$

where β is a control parameter that can be empirically chosen between zero and infinity, and $d(\mathbf{v}_1, \mathbf{v}_2)$ is the Euclidean distance between two vectors $\mathbf{v}_1$ and $\mathbf{v}_2$. The weighting function is used to place more emphasis on the boundary information.

The NDE algorithm seeks to determine the optimal projection $\mathrm{W}_{opt} \in \Re^{d \times f}$, which maximizes the ratio between the generalized between-class matrix and within-class matrix

$$\mathrm{W}_{opt} = [\mathbf{w}_1, \mathbf{w}_2, \cdots, \mathbf{w}_f] = arg \max_{\mathrm{W}} \frac{|\mathrm{W}^T \mathrm{S}_b^{\mathcal{N}} \mathrm{W}|}{|\mathrm{W}^T \mathrm{S}_w^{\mathcal{N}} \mathrm{W}|}. \tag{8}$$

The NDE projection contains eigenvectors of the matrix $\left(\mathrm{S}_w^{\mathcal{N}}\right)^{-1} \mathrm{S}_b^{\mathcal{N}}$. From eq. (6) we have a few observations: (1) If we select $z = n_i$ and set all the weighting functions to unit value, $\mu_j(\mathbf{x}_t^i)$ will become μ_j. It means the NDE is indeed a generalized version of LDA. (2) As opposed to the conventional LDA algorithms which usually can only extract c-1 discriminative features at most, the NDE algorithm does not suffer from such limitation. The number $f(< d)$ of extracted discriminative features can be specified as desired. (3) The NDE algorithm is more effective in capturing the information of the boundary structure for different classes in contrast to the conventional LDA algorithms.

We illustrate the power of NDE with a toy problem where 3D data points are sampled from two half-spheres. The data points with 2 labels are shown in Fig. 2. Since the problem is binary classification, PCA, LDA and NDE all reduce the dimensions of raw data to 2 dimensions. Note that the LDA embedding is intrinsically in 1 dimension, for the comparative purpose we add the second dimension with the same coordinates to the intrinsic one. From the embedding results shown in Fig. 3 - Fig. 5, we can clearly observe that the PCA and LDA embeddings of two classes of points partially overlap with each other, while points from different classes are well separated with each other in the embedding results provided by NDE (Fig. 5). This demonstrated that NDE can find a better subspace than LDA or PCA in the case of abundant training data. Better results can be achieved by nonlinear methods, but most of these nonlinear methods only work on training data. NDE can be generalized outside the training points to the entire input space.

3.2   Multiple NDE

Due to the fact that NDE has an advantage over LDA when encountering with abundant training data, we will apply NDE to handle the video-based face recognition scenario which is just the classification problem with many samples. In details, we conduct multiple NDE to extract discriminative features for training

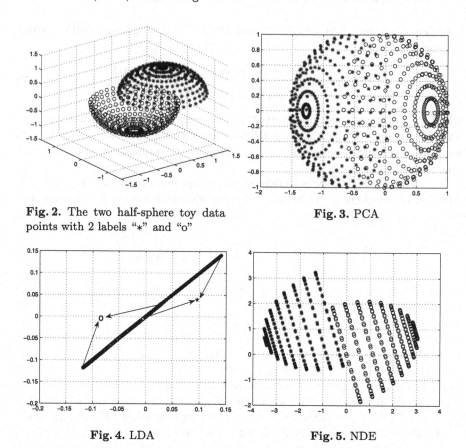

Fig. 2. The two half-sphere toy data points with 2 labels "*" and "o"

Fig. 3. PCA

Fig. 4. LDA

Fig. 5. NDE

videos. That is to run NDE on K slices $slice_k = \{\mathcal{T}_k^{(i)}\}_{i=1}^M$ (M is the total number of training video sequences), under which homogeneous keyframes belonging to synchronized and aligned clusters $\mathcal{C}_k = \{\mathcal{C}_k^{(i)}\}_i$ are input to NDE. We collect keyframes from different training videos presenting the same human identity to form one class in each slice. Ultimately, applying NDE on K slices leads to the target STEs, as well as K NDE projections $W_k \in \Re^{d \times f} (k = 1, \cdots, K)$.

4   Statistical Recognition

In the testing stage, for any unidentified video frame $\mathbf{x} \in \Re^d$, we try to compute its statistical correlation to video sequences $V^{(i)} (i = 1, \cdots, c)$ in gallery which often has one video sequence for one human subject. Let the learned spatio-temporal embedding according to $V^{(i)}$ be $\mathcal{L}^{(i)} = \{\mathbf{y}_{kj}^{(i)} = W_k^T \mathbf{e}_{kj}^{(i)} \in \Re^f | k = 1, \cdots, K, j = 1, \cdots, m\}$, and define $\mathcal{L}_k^{(i)} = \{\mathbf{y}_{kj}^{(i)} | j = 1, \cdots, m\}$. The statistical correlation is expressed as the posterior probability $p(\mathcal{L}_i | \mathbf{x})$.

Intuitively, we exploit the probabilistic fusion scheme to construct a MAP (maximum a posterior) classifier in terms of learned STEs, which settles on a solution to the image-to-video face recognition problem. The MAP classifier is derived as follows

$$\max_{i \in \{1, \cdots, c\}} p(\mathcal{L}^{(i)}|\mathbf{x}) = \max_i \sum_{k=1}^K p(\mathcal{L}^{(i)}, C_k|\mathbf{x}) = \max_i \sum_{k=1}^K \frac{p(\mathcal{L}^{(i)}, C_k, \mathbf{x})}{p(\mathbf{x})}$$

$$= \max_i \sum_{k=1}^K \frac{p(\mathcal{L}^{(i)}|\mathbf{x}, C_k)p(\mathbf{x}, C_k)}{p(\mathbf{x})}$$

$$= \max_i \sum_{k=1}^K p(\mathcal{L}_k^{(i)}|\mathbf{x}, C_k)p(C_k|\mathbf{x}). \tag{9}$$

Since $p(\mathbf{x}, C_k)$ has been modeled as eq. (3) through frame clustering on training videos, $p(C_k|\mathbf{x})$ is calculated by $p(C_k|\mathbf{x}) = p(\mathbf{x}, C_k)/\sum_k p(\mathbf{x}, C_k)$. Only the conditional probability $p(\mathcal{L}_k^{(i)}|\mathbf{x}, C_k)$ is left to be inferred. To achieve that, we start by computing the asymmetric probabilistic similarity $S_k(\mathbf{y}, \mathbf{x})$

$$S_k(\mathbf{y}, \mathbf{x}) = \exp\left(-\frac{\|\mathbf{y} - \mathbf{W}_k^T \mathbf{x})\|^2}{2\sigma_k^2}\right), \tag{10}$$

where $\mathbf{W}_k^T \mathbf{x}$ is the k-th NDE, and parameter σ_k can be predefined or computed with respect to data distribution in the embedding space. Now we can formulate $p(\mathcal{L}_k^{(i)}|\mathbf{x}, C_k)$ under the following stochastic selection rule

$$p(\mathcal{L}_k^{(i)}|\mathbf{x}, C_k) = \frac{\sum_{j=1}^m S_k(\mathbf{y}_{kj}^{(i)}, \mathbf{x})}{\sum_{t=1}^c \sum_{j=1}^m S_k(\mathbf{y}_{kj}^{(t)}, \mathbf{x})}. \tag{11}$$

Once substituting eq. (10) and eq. (11) into eq. (9), we accomplish the image-to-video recognition task. It is noticeable that $p(\mathcal{L}_k^{(i)}|\mathbf{x}, C_k)$ essentially behaves like a local analyzer $F_k(\mathbf{x}, i)$ as similarities given by eq. (10) are conducted. Specifically, $F_k(\mathbf{x}, i)$ correlates the testing frame $\mathbf{x}$ with the kth segment of spatio-temporal embedding of person i in subspace $\mathbf{W}_k$. Our recognition solution eq. (9) merges these local analyzers into a global analyzer $G(\mathbf{x}, i)$ using the probabilistic fusion model $G(\mathbf{x}, i) = \sum_k p(C_k|\mathbf{x})F_k(\mathbf{x}, i)$ which statistically fuses multiple NDEs of testing frame $\mathbf{x}$ with the probabilistic "weights" $p(C_k|\mathbf{x})$.

Naturally, we can perform the probabilistic voting strategy to recognize a video sequence $V = \{\mathbf{x}_t\}_{t=1}^N$ in the probe videos. In details, combining the recognition confidences $\{G(\mathbf{x}_t, i)\}_i$ in every frame $\mathbf{x}_t$ to decide on the person identity i^* of probe video V, we thus realize video-to-video recognition as follows

$$i^* = \arg \max_{i \in \{1, \cdots, c\}} p(\mathcal{L}^{(i)}|V)$$

$$= \arg \max_i \sum_{t=1}^N p(\mathcal{L}^{(i)}|\mathbf{x}_t) = \arg \max_i \sum_{t=1}^N G(\mathbf{x}_t, i). \tag{12}$$

5 Experiments

In this section, we conduct experiments on the XM2VTS face video database [11]. We select 294 * 4 video sequences of 294 distinct persons across four different sessions. 294 * 3 video sequences from the first three sessions are selected for training. The gallery set is composed of 294 video sequences from the first session. The probe set is composed of 294 video sequences from the fourth session. The persons in the video are asked to read two number sequences, "0 1 2 3 4 5 6 7 8 9" and "5 0 6 9 2 8 1 3 7 4".

5.1 Keyframes

In this paper we propose the Bayesian keyframe learning method for learning the temporal embeddings of videos, which complies with frame synchronization. In this section we will evaluate their performance on the XM2VTS face video database. Firstly we compare our keyframe learning method with the audio-guided keyframe extraction method proposed in [13]. The audio-guided method, called as "A-V Frame Synchronization", exploits the maximum points of audio information and strongly depends on the order of audio sentences which are spoken in video sequences. A-V synchronization extracts frames each of which corresponds to the waveform peak of audio signals.

Fig. 6(a) shows 10 cropped 72×64 keyframes learned by our method, which are the most likely frames, i.e. top-1, in $K = 10$ clusters provided by synchronized clustering on video frames without any additional information. From Fig. 6(a), we observe that keyframes extracted by our method bear rather distinct expression information, which will benefit face recognition as more expression variations are covered in the training data. An important advantage of our keyframe learning method is that it is fully automatic without relying on audio signals, which makes our recognition framework more general.

Fig. 6(b) illustrates our keyframe extraction from the audio-temporal perspective. It is surprising that these keyframes learned by our method correlate closely with the results obtained by A-V synchronization. 7 keyframes nearly lie on the peaks of audio signals, while the rest 3 frames are in the intermediate places between peaks. We thus conclude that our keyframe learning method is comparable to the audio-guided method confronted with orderly video data, but still robust to disordered video data.

5.2 Evaluate NDE

The first group of experiments is to compare the performance of the proposed NDE with the conventional LDA algorithm. For each video sequence, top-1 keyframes are selected for the experiments. So, the training set is composed of 294*3 facial images from the first three sessions. The gallery set contains 294 images from the first session and the probe set comprises 294 images from the fourth session. For the parameters z and β associated with NDE, we set $z = 1$ and $\beta = 2$ empirically.

The comparative results are shown in Fig. 7. The cumulative matching score is used for the performance measure. Instead of asking "is the top match correct",

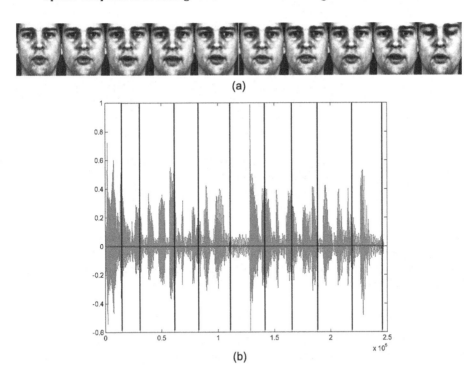

Fig. 6. Keyframes learned from one video sequence in XM2VTS. (a) Top-1 keyframes, each of which stands for a cluster in the sequence. (b) 10 keyframes shown in the temporal axis, compared with the speech signal.

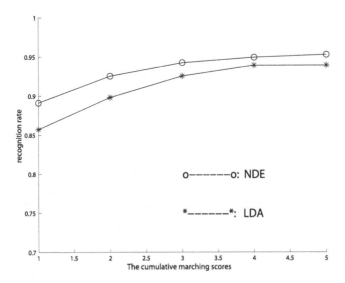

Fig. 7. NDE versus LDA

Table 2. Comparison of recognition results with existing video-based approaches

Video-Based Face Recognition Approaches	Recognition Rate
mutual subspace	79.3%
nearest frame	81.7%
nearest frame using LDA	90.9%
nearest frame using unified subspace analysis	93.2%
temporal embeddings + multi-level subspace analysis	98.0%
spatio-temporal embeddings + statistical classifier	99.3%

the cumulative matching score answers the questions of "is the correct answer in the top-n matches?", where the number n is called the rank. This lets one know how many images have to be examined to get a desired level of performance. The results clearly show the superiority of NDE over LDA.

5.3 Evaluate Statistical Recognition Performance

After 20 keyframes (top-2 keyframes from 10 clusters) are selected by means of synchronized frame clustering and Bayesian keyframe learning, we perform NDE on each slice containing 2*3*294 frames across 3 sessions from 294 persons and acquire 10 local analyzers with 6 training samples each person. Finally, based on the learned spatio-temporal embeddings (STEs), all these STE-based local analyzers are integrated using the probabilistic fusion model eq. (9) to accomplish image-to-video recognition followed by the probabilistic voting strategy eq. (12) which leads to the final video-to-video recognition results .

We compare our statistical recognition framework with existing video-based face recognition approaches. Here all approaches directly use image gray scale values as facial features. Using temporal embeddings learned by our keyframe learning method, we can perform multi-level subspace analysis proposed in our recent paper [13]. It is evident that both of our proposed approaches, temporal embeddings combined with multi-level subspace analysis and spatio-temporal embeddings incorporated into the statistical classifier, significantly outperform the existing video-based recognition approaches in Tab. 2. Further, our statistical recognition framework integrating STEs and statistical classification achieves the best recognition accuracy of 99.3%. Compared with the best performance of other recognition approaches, the error rate is still reduced by 65%, which is quite impressive and well validates the robustness and effectiveness of our framework.

6   Conclusion

This paper explores to seek a "good" spatio-temporal representation for each video sequence so that it could support the face recognition process. Considering both co-occurrence statistics and representative capability of video frames, the temporal embedding spanned by synchronized keyframes is first learned for each sequence. Furthermore, the powerful NDE enforces discriminative cues over the learned temporal embeddings. So, learning in space-time gives rise to the intrinsic spatio-temporal embeddings (STEs). In this paper, we develop a statistical framework integrating several novel techniques including Bayesian keyframe learning, NDE, and the statistical classifier, all of which depend on each other and yield a synergistic effect. The success of the framework originates from not only synchronized but also discriminative spatio-temporal representations and statistical recognition.

Acknowledgement

The work described in this paper was fully supported by grants from the Research Grants Council of the Hong Kong Special Administrative Region and a joint grant (N_CUHK409/03) from HKSAR RGC and China NSF. The work was done at the Chinese University of Hong Kong.

References

1. Baker, S., Kanade, T.: Limits on Super-Resolution and How to Break Them. *IEEE Trans. PAMI.* **24**:9 (2002) 1167-1183
2. Bar-hillel, A., Hertz, T., Shental, N., Weinshall, D.: Learning a mahalanobis metric from equivalence constraints. *J. of Machine Learning Research.* **6** (2005) 937-965
3. Belhumeur, P., Hespanha, J., Kriegman, D.: Eigenfaces vs. Fisherfaces: Recognition Using Class Specific Linear Projection. *IEEE Trans. PAMI.* **19**:7 (1997) 711-720
4. Duda, R., Hart, P., Stork, D.: Pattern Classification. Wiley, New York. (2000)
5. Fukunaga, K.: Statistical Pattern Recognition. Academic Press (1990)
6. Krueger, V., Zhou, S.: Exemplar-Based Face Recognition from Video. In *Proc. ECCV.* (2002) 732-746
7. Lee, K., Ho, J., Yang, M., Kriegman, D.: Video-Based Face Recognition Using Probabilistic Appearance Manifolds. In *Proc. IEEE Conf. CVPR.* (2003) 313-320
8. Liu, C., Shum, H., Zhang, C.: A Two-Step Approach to Hallucinating Faces: Global Parametric Model and Local Nonparametric Model. In *Proc. IEEE Conf. CVPR.* (2001) 192-198
9. Liu, X., Chen, T.: Video-Based Face Recognition Using Adaptive Hidden Markov Models. In *Proc. IEEE Conf. CVPR.* (2003) 340-345
10. Liu, W., Lin, D., Tang, X.: TensorPatch Super-Resolution and Coupled Residue Compensation. In *Proc. IEEE Conf. CVPR.* (2005) 478-484
11. Messer, K., Matas, J., Kittler, J., Luettin, J., Matitre, G.: XM2VTSDB: The Extended M2VTS Database. In *Proc. 2nd Int. Conf. Audio- and Video-Based Biometric Person Authentication.* (1999) 72-77
12. Satoh, S.: Comparative Evaluation of Face Sequence Matching for Content-based Video Access. In *Proc. IEEE Int. Conf. Automatic Face and Gesture Recognition.* (2000) 163-168

13. Tang, X., Li, Z.: Frame Synchronization and Multi-Level Subspace Analysis for Video Based Face Recognition. In *Proc. IEEE Conf. CVPR.* (2004) 902-907
14. Wang, X., Tang, X.: A Unified Framework for Subspace Face Recognition. *IEEE Trans. PAMI.* **26**:9 (2004) 1222-1228
15. Yamaguchi, O., Fukui, K., Maeda, K.: Face Recognition Using Temporal Image Sequence. In *Proc. Int. Conf. Face and Gesture Recognition* (1998) 318-323
16. Zhou, S., Krueger, V., Chellappa, R.: Probabilistic Recognition of Human Faces from Video. *Computer Vision and Image Understanding.* **91**:1 (2003) 214-245

Super-Resolution of 3D Face*

Gang Pan, Shi Han, Zhaohui Wu, and Yueming Wang

Dept. of Computer Science, Zhejiang University,
Hangzhou 310027, China
{gpan, hanshi}@zju.edu.cn

Abstract. Super-resolution is a technique to restore the detailed information from the degenerated data. Lots of previous work is for 2D images while super-resolution of 3D models was little addressed. This paper focuses on the super-resolution of 3D human faces. We firstly extend the 2D image pyramid model to the progressive resolution chain (PRC) model in 3D domain, to describe the detail variation during resolution decreasing. Then a consistent planar representation of 3D faces is presented, which enables the analysis and comparison among the features of the same facial part for the subsequent restoration process. Finally, formulated as solving an iterative quadratic system by maximizing *a posteriori*, a 3D restoration algorithm using PRC features is given. The experimental results on USF HumanID 3D face database demonstrate the effectiveness of the proposed approach.

1 Introduction

The rapid development of multimedia techniques has more impact on human life. The problem of super-resolution, arising in a number of real-world applications, has recently attracted great interest of researchers. Super-resolution literally means to generate images, 3D models, or other data representation forms of higher resolution, compared with the relatively rough inputs.

1.1 Previous Work

In real applications, the problem of resolution insufficiency generally emerges in two cases. 1) The first case is to magnify the existing images for better demonstration when only the ones of a small size are available, e.g. thumbnail images in the web pages[1]. The key issue in this case is to get rid of blur effects and fill in as many lost details as possible. There are typical approaches such as tree-based[2], level-set[3], example-based HMM[4], and neighbor embedding[1]. 2) In another case, we may require a more detailed or clearer image from a set of images or a frame sequence of poor quality, which might be obtained under noise, deformation or limitation of capturing conditions. The most widely-used model is Bayesian framework[5, 6, 7], and ML, MAP, POCS are also employed in [8, 9].

* The authors are grateful for the grants from NSF of China (60503019, 60525202) and Program for New Century Excellent Talents in University (NCET-04-0545).

A. Leonardis, H. Bischof, and A. Pinz (Eds.): ECCV 2006, Part II, LNCS 3952, pp. 389–401, 2006.

When it comes to the way in which the problem is solved, the super-resolution technique could be classified into the reconstruction-based and the learning-based methods. The reconstruction-based algorithms are based on the fundamental constraints to model the image formation process that the super-resolution image should generate the low-resolution input images when appropriately warped and down-sampled[10]. And then the process of reconstruction falls into a fusion-like problem. Therefore it is especially suitable for multi-view case as in [5, 8, 6, 9]. However, the reconstruction-based method has its theoretical limit of the magnification factor beyond which the high-resolution image deviates significantly from the ground truth, no matter how many low-resolution images are offered[10, 11]. In the other aspect, the learning-based algorithms seem to be customized for single-view case since the learned priors provide the lost details[2, 4]. It has a better performance when the training samples are similar to the target, such as human face[12, 10, 13].

1.2   Motivation

Three dimensional models are much more expressive than 2D images. Generally, images lay stress on appearance in visual spectrum while 3D models convey the additional topological and geometrical information of the object. However, super-resolution in 3D domain has been little addressed.

Super-resolution of 3D models really makes sense. Firstly, it could reduce the data volume for fast transmission over Internet. 3D models are usually of a large size, which is a big drawback restricting their application in many aspects, e.g. the web application. Although the storage is becoming a non-serious problem with the help of the large-volume storage devices, the fast transmission of 3D data over Internet still remains critical, especially under an unstable network condition. The time consumption for downloading the whole model is sometimes intolerable. Though the level-in-detail technique could reduce the response time, the total transmission time virtually is not saved if we want to view the detailed model. Therefore, we can only transfer the the simplified version of the original data and rebuild the high-resolution version at the remote end.

Secondly, super-resolution of 3D models could generate a more detailed 3D model when only the low-resolution version is available. Currently 3D acquisition is becoming easy. However the high-resolution 3D data are still hard to obtain in some cases. On the one hand, the data acquired by the cheap devices and fast acquisition systems are generally of low-resolution. On the other hand, the high-resolution data is hard to acquire when the object is not well-cooperative. And sometimes we could get only the damaged version the the original data.

Thirdly, 3D face models are playing an important role in face recognition [14, 15, 16], however, the low-resolution data, acquired under an incooperative condition, are often not suitable for the direct use of the recognition task, for detail insufficiency and incompleteness. Human faces have a lot of mutual features similar to each other on the whole, from which the learning-based algorithms benefit. The super-resolution of the 3D face models may be helpful for recognition task, with the improvement of the visual quality as well.

1.3 Problem Statement and the Proposed Approach

We propose a solution to the new problem of super-resolution of human faces in the triangulated mesh domain. Given a mesh M_L of low-resolution, we need to generate the high-resolved version M_H. In this paper, we only consider the low-resolution caused by down-sampling and blur, which are the most common cases in 3D models. Actually, other cases can be dealt with in the similar way. I.e. M_L could be either (1) blurred, which means M_L has the same topology as the original true mesh but with the distorted vertex positions, or (2) down-sampled, which means M_L has a regular topology with less number of vertices than the original mesh. In both cases, we calculate the M_H with more detailed information in order to be as similar to the original true model as possible.

In this paper we set up a Progressive Resolution Chain (PRC) model to connect M_H and M_L. The PRC between M_H and M_L acts as the relationship between the neighboring resolution levels, and provides the essential information for the subsequent restoration algorithm, described in Section 2. A consistent planar representation of 3D faces is proposed in Section 3. This procedure includes fixing the mesh boundary into the edges of the unit planar square according to the symmetrical features of the human face, and applying the intrinsic parametrization to map the ROI(region of interest) face mesh onto the plane. Then the planar parametrization establishes the correspondence among face meshes, and such correspondence is used by both the calculation of PRC features and the learning algorithm. Section 4 gives the restoration algorithm, which is to maximize a *posteriori* (MAP) by solving an iterative quadratic system based on the PRC features. Diagram of the whole approach is given in Section 5, and Section 6 shows the experimental results on the USF HumanID 3D face database. Finally the conclusion is drawn in Section 7.

2 Progressive Resolution Chain

Given high-resolution model M_H, some low-resolution version M_L could be easily figured out through a certain degenerator $Degen(\cdot)$ which is specifically designed for the specified detail level, or to emulate some information damaged effects.

$$M_L = Degen(M_H) \qquad (1)$$

But the inverse process, which is the main and key part of the high-resolution task, is much more difficult to solve, even in a simple 2D context with a linear degenerator[13]. The main difficulty is that the degeneration $Degen$ is usually an entropy losing procedure so that there is not a unique inverse regenerator $Degen^{-1}$. Even though we put restraints at the high-resolution end to restrict the solution space, it is still hard to solve since there is a huge search space.

Inspired by the pyramid model, we propose a Progressive Resolution Chain (PRC) model to describe the detail-fading procedure, which is very suitable for the learning based restoration method. The main idea is to decompose the degeneration procedure *Degen* into progressive steps, which is an iteration of some meta-degenerator *Degen*[1]. And the midway results compose a PRC, which starts from M_H and passes through M_L. Equally important, the PRC could sequentially extend beyond M_L to provide extra information for the consequent learning based method. The PRC is defined as

$$C_l(M_H) = \begin{cases} M_H & if\ l = 0 \\ Degen^1(C_{l-1}(M_H)) & if\ l > 0 \end{cases}$$

For a sub-problem, the meta-degenerator *Degen*[1] is defined accordingly. In the blur case, it could be a neighboring filter, i.e. a local linear vertex convolution:

$$Degen_b^1(M)(\mathbf{x}) = \sum_{\mathbf{u} \in Neighbor(\mathbf{x})} \frac{\|\mathbf{u} - \mathbf{x}\|^2}{S(\mathbf{x})} * M(\mathbf{u}) \tag{2}$$

$$S(\mathbf{x}) = \sum_{\mathbf{u} \in Neighbor(\mathbf{x})} \|\mathbf{u} - \mathbf{x}\|^2 \tag{3}$$

and in the down-sampling case, it could be a sampling filter. Different data formats correspond to different forms. Take the range data for example,

$$Degen_d^1(M)(x, y) = \sum_{u=sx}^{sx+s-1} \sum_{v=sy}^{sy+s-1} \frac{1}{s^2} * M(u, v) \tag{4}$$

where s is the down-sampling rate, which is 2 in this paper, and $M(x, y)$ is the depth. For other cases of low resolution, the meta-degenerator could be instanced individually, and the restoration could be dealt with in the similar way.

The restoration procedure acquires knowledge from the training set. PRC could transfer the prior knowledge of the path to the high-resolution end to reduce the search space. Figure 1 illustrates the concept of PRC.

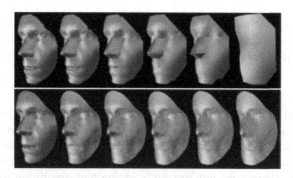

Fig. 1. Progressive Resolution Chain in six levels. The upper row is the down-sampling case, and the bottom row is the blur case.

3   Consistent Planar Representation of 3D Faces

Both PRC-building and the learning-based restoration need the correspondence among the face meshes. This task is quite similar to the traditional image alignment, but there are still some differences between them. For 2D face image, the correspondence is usually done by aligning the images in the class-based approach to fulfill the assumption that the same part of the face appears in roughly the same part of the image[17], and can be simply performed through affine warp[12]. But such a scheme could be hardly transferred smoothly into 3D mesh field, due to the irregular and loose structure of the mesh.

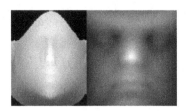

Fig. 2. The cylindrical coordinate unfolding vs the consisten planar representation

At the same time, uniformly sampling within the meshed manifold is also a problem that most fundamental sampling methods could hardly solve, even though the mesh is well-distributed. As is shown in Fig.2, the widely-used cylindrical coordinate unfolding method maps the 3D face model onto a planar area with the obvious distortion, which brings about the nonuniform sampling. Therefore the mesh parameterization methods are taken into consideration. We adopt the intrinsic parameterization method in [18], which is fast and effective. By mapping the ROI face meshes onto a unit planar square with the consistent parameterization domain, we construct the consistent planar representation of 3D faces, meanwhile establish the correspondence among the different face models.

3.1   Intrinsic Parameterization

Given a triangulated mesh S, an isomorphic planar parameterization U and the corresponding mapping $\Psi : S \mapsto U$ is defined to preserve the original, discriminative characteristic of S. The function E is defined to measure the distortion between S and U. The minimal distortion corresponds to the minimum $E(S, U)$. For compact expression, let S' be a simple patch consisting of a 1-ring neighborhood in 3D space, and U' be an planar isomorph to S' in Fig. 3. For any fixed mapping boundary, the 2D 1-ring distortion is only related to the center node u_i. Two distortion metric measures E_A and E_χ are chosen for angle-preserving and area-preserving respectively. Gray[19] shows that the minimum of Dirichlet energy E_A is attained for angle-preserving.

$$E_A = \sum_{j \in N(i)} cot\alpha_{ij} |u_i - u_j|^2 \tag{5}$$

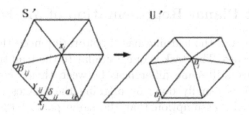

Fig. 3. Illustration of the flattening for the intrinsic parameterization

And in [18], the authalic energy E_χ is attained for area-preserving,

$$E_\chi = \sum_{j \in N(i)} \frac{cot\gamma_{ij} + cot\delta_{ij}}{|x_i - x_j|^2}(u_i - u_j)^2 \tag{6}$$

Where $|u_i - u_j|$ is the length of the edge (i, j) in U' while $|x_i - x_j|$ in S'. α, β, γ and δ are the angles shown in Fig.3.

The energy E_A and E_χ are continuous and quadratic. Thus

$$\frac{\partial E_A}{\partial u_i} = \sum_{j \in N(i)} (cot\alpha_{ij} + cot\beta_{ij})(u_i - u_j) \tag{7}$$

$$\frac{\partial E_\chi}{\partial u_i} = \sum_{j \in N(i)} \frac{(cot\gamma_{ij} + cot\delta_{ij})}{|x_i - x_j|^2}(u_i - u_j) \tag{8}$$

Then the general distortion measurement E is defined and achieves its minimum when $\partial E/\partial u_i = 0$.

$$E = \alpha E_A + (1 - \alpha)E_\chi \quad 0 \le \alpha \le 1 \tag{9}$$

Given the distortion measures above and a fixed planar boundary, the parameterization is accomplished by solving a linear system as follows,

$$MU = \begin{bmatrix} M \\ 0 \quad I \end{bmatrix} \begin{bmatrix} U_{internal} \\ U_{boundary} \end{bmatrix} = \begin{bmatrix} 0 \\ C_{boundary} \end{bmatrix}$$

where $U_{internal}$ is the variable vector of the parameterization of internal vertices in the original mesh while $U_{boundary}$ is of the boundary, and $C_{boundary}$ is the constant vector to provide a fixed planar boundary. And,

$$M = \alpha M^A + (1 - \alpha)M^\chi \quad 0 \le \alpha \le 1 \tag{10}$$

$$M^A_{ij} = \begin{cases} cot\alpha_{ij} + cot\beta_{ij} & if \ j \in N(i) \\ -\sum_{k \in N(i)} M^A_{ik} & if \ i = j \\ 0 & otherwise \end{cases}$$

$$M^\chi_{ij} = \begin{cases} (cot\gamma_{ij} + cot\delta_{ij})/|x_i - x_j|^2 & if \ j \in N(i) \\ -\sum_{k \in N(i)} M^\chi_{ik} & if \ i = j \\ 0 & otherwise \end{cases}$$

3.2 Building the Consistent Planar Representation

Calculation of ROI. To build the consistent planar representation, the region of interest (ROI) of the face model needs to be extracted first. In [12], the feature points are manually labelled on 2D images for the affine warp. However, for lack of texture information and the discrete topology of mesh representation, the manual work on 3D models is of low precision and low efficiency.

The ROI of a human face should contain the most facial features. Since the consequent mapping from the mesh field onto the planar square is conformal and authalic, we had better calculate the ROI according to the geodesic metric. Thus, we define the ROI as the region of:

$$ROI = \{p | dist(p, n) \leq R\} \tag{11}$$

where n is the nose tip, $dist(\cdot, \cdot)$ is the geodesic distance, and R is the constant radius that ensures the ROI contains the most facial features. We apply the fast marching method [20] to compute the geodesic paths on triangulated manifold.

Mapping Using Intrinsic Parametrization. We build the the consistent planar representation by mapping them onto a unit planar square. This is achieved through fixing the mesh boundary to the edges of the unit planar square and carrying out the intrinsic parameterization described above. The further alignment within the planar domain is to specify a consistent in-plane rotation. Considering the symmetry feature of the human face, we choose the symmetry axis as the y-axis and the upside direction as the positive direction. The orientation of the symmetry axis is calculated based on the symmetry metric of the depth value, which is sampled on the ROI face meshes in the polar coordinates.

4 Bayesian MAP Based Restoration

Based on the maximum a *posteriori* criterion, instead of maximizing the posterior probability $p(M_H | M_L)$, we set up an optimal solution,

$$M'_H = argmax_{M_H} p(M_L | M_H) p(M_H) \tag{12}$$

Firstly, we derive the formulation of $p(M_L | M_H)$. As mentioned above, the super-resolution image should generate the low-resolution input images when appropriately warped and down-sampled to model the image formation process[10]. We adopt this principle to define $p(M_L | M_H)$. According to the PRC model, the chain should pass through M_L. But actually M_L might be not exactly a node on the chain, and the resolution level of M_L is also unknown. So we choose the node $C_k(M_H)$ closest to M_L in the chain as the approximation of M_L. k is the supposed resolution level of M_L and therefore is not specific. We try different k values while solving the problem to find the best result. Then the similarity metric between $C_k(M_H)$ and M_L could be used to define $p(M_L | M_H)$,

$$p(M_L | M_H) = exp(-\|C_k(M_H) - M_L\|^2) \tag{13}$$
$$= exp(-\|Degen^k(M_H) - M_L\|^2) \tag{14}$$

The remaining part is to calculate $p(M_H)$. Since Equ. 14 partly determines the spacial location of vertices on M_L, here we adopt a metric based on the norm vectors, which are related to the local geometry. Let $\mathbf{n}(\mathbf{x})$ be the norm vector at $\mathbf{x}$ on the surface of M_H, while $\bar{\mathbf{n}}(\mathbf{x})$ is the reference learnt from the training samples. We define $p(M_H)$ as

$$p(M_H) = \frac{1}{V} \sum_{\mathbf{x} \in M_H} \langle \mathbf{n}(\mathbf{x}), \bar{\mathbf{n}}(\mathbf{x}) \rangle \qquad (15)$$

where V is the number of vertices on M_H and $\langle \cdot, \cdot \rangle$ is the inner product operator.

To calculate $\bar{\mathbf{n}}(\mathbf{x})$, we carry out a learning based method. And for the convenience of expression, we use the notations as follows. Given a certain mesh M, for each vertex $\mathbf{x}$ on M, let

$\mathbf{u}(\mathbf{x})$:   the parameter of $\mathbf{x}$ in the unit planar sqaure.
$\mathbf{n}(\mathbf{x})$:   the surface norm vector at $\mathbf{x}$ on mesh M.
$(\cdot)^M$:   e.g. $\mathbf{x}^M$, $\mathbf{u}^M$, $\mathbf{n}^M$, means the features of mesh M.
$(\cdot)_l$:   e.g. $\mathbf{x}_l$, $\mathbf{u}_l$, $\mathbf{n}_l$, means the features of the resolution level l.

Now we define the Tail Structure starting from level k of the PRC as

$$TS_k = (\mathbf{n}_k, \mathbf{n}_{k+1}, \mathbf{n}_{k+2}, \cdots) \qquad (16)$$

and the directed similarity metric function $S_k^{T_i}(\mathbf{x})$ between $TS_k^{M_H}$ and $TS_k^{T_i}$, which is the Tail Structure of the training sample T_i, is defined as

$$S_k^{T_i}(\mathbf{x}) = \sum_{l=k,k+1,\cdots} \langle \mathbf{n}_l^{M_H}(\mathbf{x}_l^{M_H}), \mathbf{n}_l^{T_i}(\mathbf{u}^{-1}{}_l^{T_i}(\mathbf{u}_l^{M_H}(\mathbf{x}_l^{M_H}))) \rangle^2 \qquad (17)$$

where $\langle \cdot, \cdot \rangle$ is the inner product function.

With the directed similarity metric $S_k^{T_i}(\mathbf{x})$, the learning process of calculating $\bar{\mathbf{n}}(\mathbf{x})$ is implemented with N training samples through the following loop:

for each $\mathbf{x}$ on M_H
    try i := 1 to N
        calculate $S_k^{T_i}(\mathbf{x})$ and let $j := argmax_i S_k^{T_i}(\mathbf{x})$
    let $\bar{\mathbf{n}}(\mathbf{x}) := \mathbf{n}_0^{T_j}(\mathbf{x}_0^{T_j})$

In fact, TS^{M_H} is just an abstract form and we could not get its practical value since M_H has not been calculated yet. But according to the previous analysis, we could use $TS_0^{M_L}$ for approximation of $TS_k^{M_H}$.

Thus, the original super-resolution problem is transformed into solving a system consisting of Equ. 12, 14 and 15. Considering Equ. 14 and 15 are not polynomial, we reformulate the MAP as

$$M_H^* = argmin_{M_H} \{ -\beta * ln[p(M_L|M_H)] - (1 - \beta) * p(M_H) \}, \quad 0 \le \beta \le 1 \quad (18)$$

where β is the balance weight for global optimization, and adopt an iterative method so that in each iteration the system is quadratic.

5   Algorithm Diagram

The algorithm diagram is shown in Fig.4, taking the blur case for example. We firstly extract the ROI of a severely blurred face model M_L by applying fast marching method on its supporting mesh manifold. The sequent steps are:

- Step (1): calculate the extended part beyond M_L in PRC , containing the models at lower resolution levels.
- Step (2): map the extended part of the PRC onto the unit planar squares respectively by the intrinsic parametrization.
- Step (3): the tail structure (d) of M_L mentioned in Equ. 16 is calculated.
- Step (4): the restoration using PRC features database (e) is performed according to the tail structure. There is a chosen training model for each vertex **x**. We show only the tail structure of only one of them (f) for illustration.
- Step (5): is to solve the iterative quadratic system, and get the mesh (g).
- Step (6): is for noise removal, and obtain the final super-resolved version (h).

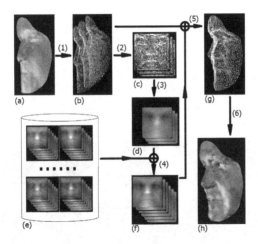

Fig. 4. Diagram of our method. (a) the input low-resolution model M_L, (b) the extended part of PRC beyond M_L, (c) the consistent planar representation of (b), (d) the extended part of PRC features of M_L, (e) the PRC features database of the training samples, (f) the PRC features selected from (e) according to (d), (g) the high-resolved version, (h) the final output. The steps (1)-(6) are described in Section 5.

6   Experimental Results

Our experiments are conducted with the USF Human ID 3D face database[21] consisting of 136 individuals with only one 3D model for each individual, which are recorded by *Cyberware* 3030PS laser scanner. There are more than 90,000 vertices and 180,000 faces for each model. It is too detailed to carry out the experiments, since the huge data amount is so time and space consuming. Thus we simplify the mesh first to reduce the load of calculation, while preserving as many essential details as possible. We use the mesh simplification method in [22] with an error tolerance of 10^{-7}.

The "leave-one-out" methodology is adopted to test the performance of our super-resolution method, i.e. for each test, one model is selected from the database as the probe, and the remainder of the database acts as the training set. Since each person has just one model in the database, for each test, the person whose model acts as the probe does not appear in the training set.

For the blur case, the blurred version is generated as the probe by applying a Gaussian filter 30 times to the 3D model (Equ. 2), and one resolution-level in PRC is defined as applying a Gaussian filter 10 times. For the down-sampling case, the 16x16 down-sampling version (Equ. 4) acts as the probe and the 64x64 down-sampling version is as the high-resolution samples. For both cases, the whole PRC consists of five levels.

Table 1. σ^2 and RMS indicate the improvements comparing the output super-resolved version with the input low-resolution meshes

		avg.	min.	max.
σ^2	*input/original*	0.749	0.664	0.810
	output/original	0.977	0.899	1.051
	output/input	1.305	1.167	1.496
RMS of distance	$|input - original|$	2.834	2.401	3.489
	$|output - original|$	2.498	1.604	4.073

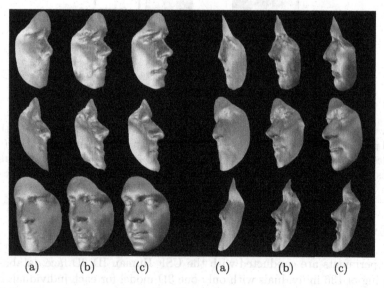

(a)   (b)   (c)   (a)   (b)   (c)

Fig. 5. Super-resolution results for the blur case, shown in the half-side view for the better illustration. (a) the blurred faces, (b) restoration by our method, (c) the true high-resolution 3D faces.

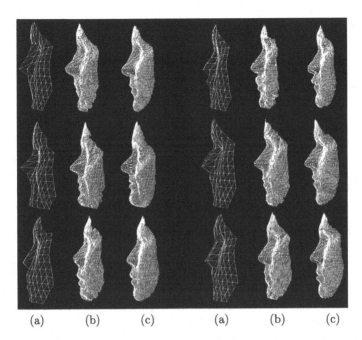

(a)   (b)   (c)   (a)   (b)   (c)

Fig. 6. Super-resolution results for the down-sampling case, shown in the half-side view for the better illustration. (a) 16x16 down-sampled face mesh, (b) restoration by our method, (c) the true high-resolution 3D faces (64x64).

We use two measurements RMS from the original model and σ^2 of the resulting surface to depict the significant improvement over the input, shown in Tab. 1. The similar σ^2 to the original model and less RMS than the input model indicate the remarkable shape and details restoration.

Some results are shown in Fig.5 and Fig.6 for the blur case and the down-sampling case respectively. In each group, the three columns are the input low resolution model (left), the super-resolved model (middle), and the original one (right). The results are all rendered in half-side view for clearly showing .

7   Conclusions and Future Work

The different data form usually represents the different underlying characteristic of the object. The image lays stress on the appearance in visual spectrum and the 3D triangulated mesh carries the additional geometrical information. In this paper, after analysis of the generality and difference of the super-resolution problems in 2D and 3D domains, we proposed an effective algorithm for the super-resolution on triangle-meshed human face models, demonstrated by the experiments on USF HumanID 3D face database.

Actually, both the PRC and the consistent planar representation method proposed in this paper are not only for 3D super-resolution. We are trying to apply them to the 3D object recognition.

It should be pointed out that in this work we do not take the texture information into consideration in our algorithm, which might trigger a new topic on the fusion of 2D and 3D super-resolution. Moreover, the investigation of contribution of the 3D super-resolution method to the 3D face recognition is an interesting issue. Both of these are ongoing in our research group.

References

1. Hong Chang, Dit-Yan Yeung and Yimin Xiong, "Super-resolution through neighbor embedding", *CVPR'04*, I:275-282, 2004.
2. C.B.Atkins, C.A.Bouman, J.P.Allebach, "Tree-Based Resolution Synthesis", *Conf. on Image Proc., Image Quality and Image Capture Sys.(PICS-99)*, pp.405-410, 1999.
3. B. S. Morse and D. Schwartzwald, "Image magnification using level-set reconstruction", *CVPR'01*, I:333-340, 2001.
4. W. T. Freeman, T. R. Jones and E. C. Pasztor, "Example-based super-resolution", *IEEE Computer Graphics and Applications*, 22(2):56-65, 2002.
5. P. Cheeseman, B. Kanefsky, R. Kraft and J. Stutz, "Super-Resolved Surface Reconstruction from Multiple Images", *NASA Technical Report*, FIA-94-12, 1994.
6. V. N. Smelyanskiy, P. Cheeseman, D. A. Maluf and R. D. Morris, "Bayesian super-resolved surface reconstruction from images", *CVPR'00*, I:375-382, June 2000.
7. J.Sun, N.-N. Zheng, H.Tao, H.-Y. Shum, "Image hallucination with primal sketch priors", *CVPR'03*, II:729-736, 2003.
8. M. Elad and A. Feuer, "Restoration of a single superresolution image from several blurred, noisy, and undersampled measured images", *IEEE Transactions on Image Processing*, 6(12):1646-1658, Dec. 1997.
9. M. Elad and Y. Hel-Or, "A fast super-resolution reconstruction algorithm for pure translational motion and common space-invariant blur", *IEEE Transactions on Image Processing*, 10(8):1187-1193, 2001.
10. S. Baker and T. Kanade, "Limits on super-resolution and how to break them", *IEEE PAMI*, 24(9):1167-1183, 2002.
11. Z.Lin and H.-Y. Shum, "Fundamental limits of reconstruction-based superresolution algorithms under local translation", *IEEE PAMI*, 26(1)83-97, 2004.
12. S. Baker and T. Kanade, "Hallucinating faces", *4th IEEE Int'l Conf. on Automatic Face and Gesture Recognition*, pp. 83-88, March 2000.
13. Ce Liu,H.-Y. Shum,C.-S. Zhang, "A two-step approach to hallucinating faces: global parametric model and local nonparametric model", *CVPR'01*, 192-198, 2001.
14. Yijun Wu, Gang Pan, Zhaohui Wu, "Face Authentication based on Multiple Profiles Extracted from Range Data", *AVBPA'03, Lecture Notes in Computer Science*, vol.2688, pp.515-522, 2003.
15. Kyong I. Chang, Kevin W. Bowyer and Partrick J. Flynn, "An evaluation of multimodal 2D+3D face biometrics", *IEEE PAMI*, 27(4):619-624, 2005.
16. Yueming Wang, Gang Pan, Zhaohui Wu et al, "Exploring Facial Expression Effects in 3D Face Recognition using Partial ICP", *ACCV'06, Lecture Notes in Computer Science, vol.3851*, pp.581-590, 2006.
17. T. Riklin-Raviv and A. Shashua, "The Quotient images: Class based recognition and synthesis under varying illumination", *CVPR'99*, pp. 566-571, 1999.

18. M. Desbrun, M. Meyer, and P. Alliez, "Intrinsic Parameterizations of Surface Meshes, *Computer Graphics Forum (Eurographics)*, 21(3):209-218, Spetember 2002.
19. A. Gray, *Modern Differential Geometry of Curves and Surfaces with Mathematica, Second Edition*, CRC Press, 1997.
20. R. Kimmel and J. A. Sethian, "Computing geodesic paths on manifolds", *Proc. Natl. Acad. Sci.* , 95:8431-8435, July 1998.
21. V. Blanz and T. Vetter, "Morphable Model for the Synthesis of 3D Faces, *SIG-GRAPH'99*, pp. 187-194, 1999.
22. H. Hoppe, T. DeRose, T. Duchamp, J. McDonald and W. Stuetzle, "Mesh optimization", *SIGGRAPH'93*, pp.19-26, 1993.

Estimating Gaze Direction from Low-Resolution Faces in Video

Neil Robertson[1,2] and Ian Reid[2]

[1] QinetiQ, St Andrews Road, Malvern, WR14 3PS, UK
[2] Oxford University, Dept. Engineering Science, Parks Road, Oxford, OX1 3PJ, UK
{nmr, ian}@robots.ox.ac.uk

Abstract. In this paper we describe a new method for automatically estimating where a person is looking in images where the head is typically in the range 20 to 40 pixels high. We use a feature vector based on skin detection to estimate the orientation of the head, which is discretised into 8 different orientations, relative to the camera. A fast sampling method returns a distribution over previously-seen head-poses. The overall body pose relative to the camera frame is approximated using the velocity of the body, obtained via automatically-initiated colour-based tracking in the image sequence. We show that, by combining direction and head-pose information gaze is determined more robustly than using each feature alone. We demonstrate this technique on surveillance and sports footage.

1   Introduction

In applications where human activity is under observation, be that CCTV surveillance or sports footage, knowledge about where a person is looking (i.e. their gaze) provides observers with important clues which enable accurate explanation of the scene activity. It is possible, for example, for a human readily to distinguish between two people walking side-by-side but who are not "together" and those who are acting as a pair. Such a distinction is possible when there is regular eye-contact or head-turning in the direction of the other person. In soccer head position is a guide to where the ball will be passed next i.e. an indicator of *intention*, which is essential for causal reasoning. In this paper we present a new method for automatically inferring gaze direction in images where any one person represents only a small proportion (the head ranges from 20 to 40 pixels high) of the frame.

The first component of our system is a descriptor based on skin colour. This descriptor is extracted for each head in a large training database and labelled with one of 8 distinct head poses. This labelled database can be queried to find either a nearest-neighbour match for a previously unseen descriptor or (as we discuss later) is non-parametrically sampled to provide an approximation to a distribution over possible head poses.

Recognising that general body direction plays an important rôle in determining where a person can look (due to anatomical limitations), we combine direction and head pose using Bayes' rule to obtain the joint distribution over head pose and direction, resulting in 64 possible gazes (since head pose and direction are discretised into 8 sectors each, shown in figure 1).

A. Leonardis, H. Bischof, and A. Pinz (Eds.): ECCV 2006, Part II, LNCS 3952, pp. 402–415, 2006.

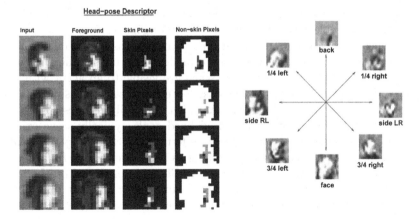

Fig. 1. The figure on the left shows the images which result from the mean-shift image patch tracker (*col. 1*) (with an additional step stabilise the descriptor by centering the head in the window), subsequent background subtraction (*col. 2*), the weight image which represents the probability that each pixel in the head is skin (*col. 3*) and non-skin (*col. 4*) (non-skin is significant as it captures proportion without the need for scaling). Thie concatenation of skin and non-skin weight vectors is our feature vector which we use to determine eight distinct head poses which are shown and labelled on the right. Varying lighting conditions are accounted for by representing the same head-pose under light from different directions in the training set. The same points on the "compass" are used as our discretisation of direction i.e. N, NE, E, etc.

The paper is organised as follows. Firstly we highlight relevant work in this, and associated, area(s). We then describe how head-pose is estimated in section 2. In section 3 we provide motivation for a Bayesian fusion method by showing intermediate results where the best head-pose match is chosen and, by contrast, where overall body-direction alone is used. Section 3 also discusses how we fuse the relevant information we have at our disposal robustly to compute a distribution over possible gazes, rejecting non-physical gazes and reliably detecting potentially significant interactions between people. Throughout the paper we test and evaluate on a number of datasets and additionally summarise comprehensive results in section 4. We conclude in section 5 and discuss potential future work in section 6.

1.1 Previous Work

Determining gaze in surveillance images is a challenging problem that has received little or no attention to date, though preliminary work in this specific problem domain was reported earlier by the authors [22].

Most closely related to our work is that of Efros *et al.* [6] for recognition of human action at a distance. That work showed how to distinguish between human activities such as walking, running etc. by comparing gross properties of motion using a descriptor derived from frame-to-frame optic-flow and performing an exhaustive search over extensive exemplar data. Head pose is not discussed in [6] but the use of a simple descriptor invariant to lighting and clothing is of direct relevance to head pose estimation and has directly inspired aspects of our approach.

Dee and Hogg [5] developed a system for detecting unusual activity which involves inferring which regions of the scene are visible to an agent within the scene. A Markov Chain with penalties associated with state transitions is used to return a score for observed trajectories which essentially encodes how directly a person made his/her way towards predefined goals, typically scene exits. In their work, gaze inference is vital, but is inferred from trajectory information alone which can lead to significant interactions being overlooked. In fact, many systems have been created to aid urban surveillance, most based on the notion of trajectories alone. For example [9] reports an entirely automated system for visual surveillance and monitoring of an urban site using agent trajectories. The same is true in the work of Buxton (who has been prominent in the use of Bayesian networks for visual surveillance) [2], Morellas et al. [17] and Makris [14]. Johnson and Hogg's work [12] is another example where trajectory information only is considered.

In contrast, there has been considerable effort to extract gaze from relatively high-resolution faces, motivated by the press for better Human/Computer Interfaces. The technical aspects of this work have often focused on detecting the eyeball primarily. Matsumoto [15] computes 3-D head pose from 2-D features and stereo tracking. Perez et al. [20] focus exclusively on the tracking of the eyeball and determination of its observed radius and orientation for gaze recognition. Gee and Cipolla's [8] gaze determination method based on the 3D geometric relationship between facial features was applied to paintings to determine where the subject is looking. Related work has tackled expression recognition using information measures. Shinohara and Otsu demonstrated that Fisher Weights can be used to recognise "smiling" in images.

While this approach is most useful in HCI where the head dominates the image and the eye orientation is the only cue to intention, it is too fine-grained for surveillance video where we must usually be content to assume that the gaze direction is aligned with the head-pose. In typical images of interest in our application area (low/medium resolution), locating significant features such as the eyes, irises, corners of the mouth, etc as used in much of the work above is regularly an impossible task. Furthermore, though standard head/face-detection techniques [24] work well in medium reolution images, they are much less reliable for detecting, say, the back of a head, which still conveys significant gaze information.

The lowest level of our approach is based on skin detection. Because of significant interest in detecting and tracking people in images and video, skin detection has naturally received much attention in the Computer Vision community [3, 10, 11]. Skin detection alone, though, is error-prone when the skin region is very small as a proportion of the image. However, contextual cues such as body-direction can help to disambiguate gaze using even a very coarse head-pose estimation. By combining this information in a principled (i.e. probabilistic,

Bayesian) fashion, gaze estimation at a distance becomes a distinct possibility as we demonstrate in this paper.

2 Head Pose Detection

2.1 Head Pose Feature Vector

Although people differ in colour and length of hair, and some people may be wearing hats, beards etc. it is reasonable to assume that the amount of skin that can be seen, the position of the skin pixels within the frame and the proportion of skin to non-skin pixels is a relatively invariant cue for a person's coarse gaze in a static image. We obtain this descriptor in a robust and automatic fashion as follows. First, a mean-shift tracker [4] is automatically initialised on the head by using naive background subtraction to locate people and subsequently modelling the person as distinct "blocks", the head and torso. Second, we centre the head within the tracker window at each time step which stabilises the descriptor ensuring consistent position within the frame for similar descriptors (the head images are scaled to the same size and, since the mean-shift tracker tracks in scale-space we have a stable, invariant, descriptor). Third, despite claims in the literature to the contrary, there is no specific region of colour-space which represents skin in all sequences and therefore it is necessary to define a skin histogram for each scenario by hand-selecting a region of one frame in the current sequence to compute a (normalised) skin-colour histogram in RGB-space. We then compute the weights for every pixel in the stabilised head images which the tracker automatically produces to indicate how likely it is that it was drawn from this predefined skin histogram[1]. Using the knowledge of the background we segment the foreground out of the tracked images. Every pixel in the segmented head image is drawn from a specific RGB bin and so is assigned the relevant weight which can be interpreted as a probability that the pixel is drawn from the skin model histograms. So for every bin i (typically we use 10 bins) in the predefined, hand-selected skin-colour histogram q the histogram of the tracked image p is a weight is computed $w_i = \sqrt{\frac{q_i}{p_i}}$. Every foreground pixel in the tracked frame falls into one of the bins according to its RGB value and the normalised weight associated with that pixel is assigned to compute the overall weight image, as shown in figure 1. The non-skin pixels are assigned a weigh that the pixel is *not* drawn from the skin histogram. This non-skin descriptor is necessary because it encodes the "proportion" of the head which is skin which is essential as people vary in size not only in the sense of scale within the but physically between one another. Each descriptor is scaled to a standard 20×20 pixel window to achieve robust comparison when the head sizes vary. Finally, in order to provide temporal context to our descriptor of head-pose we concatenate individual descriptors from 5 consecutive frames of tracker data for a particular example and this defines our instantaneous descriptor of head-pose.

---

[1] This will be recognised as a similar approximation to the Battacharyya coefficient as implemented in the meanshift algorithm [4].

Segmented targets   Heads located

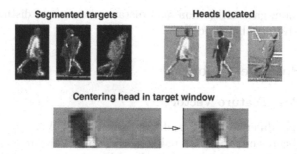

Centering head in target window

Fig. 2. Automatic location of the head is achieved by segmenting the target using simple background subtraction (*top-left*) and morphological operations with a kernel biased towards the scale of the target to identify objects. The head is taken as the top 1/7th of the entire body (*top-right*). The head is automatically centred in the bounding box at each time step to stabilise the tracking and provide an invariant descriptor for head pose, as shown in the second row.

2.2   Training Data

We assume that we can distinguish head pose to a resolution of 45°. There is no obvious benefit to detecting head orientations at a higher degree of accuracy and it is unlikely that the coarse target images would be amenable in any case. This means discretising the 360° orientation-space into 8 distinct views as shown in figure 1. The training data we select is from a surveillance-style camera position and around 100 examples of each view are selected from across a number of

Fig. 3. Detecting head pose in different scenes using the same exemplar set. The main image shows the frame with the estimated gaze angle superimposed, the pair of images directly beside each frame shows the input image that the head-pose detector uses (*top*) and the best (ML) match in the database with corresponding label (*bottom*).

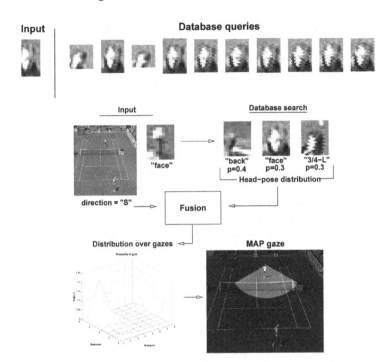

Fig. 4. (*Top*) The distribution over head-poses resulting from 10 queries of the database for this input frame is shown in the graph above. The leaf nodes of the database contain indices into matching frames and the matching frame images and assigned probabilities of a match are shown below the graph. (*Bottom*) Fusing head-pose and direction estimates improves gaze estimation. Here, the ML match for head pose would be incorrectly chosen as "back". The body-direction is identified as "S" which, since it is not possible to turn the head through 180° relative to the body, this gaze has a low (predefined) prior and is rejected as the most likely at the fusion stage. The MAP gaze is identified as "Face" which is a very good approximation to the true gaze.

different sequences and under different lighting conditions (i.e. light from left, right and above). The head was automatically tracked as described above and the example sequence labelled accordingly. The weight image for 5 consecutive frames are then computed and this feature vector stored in our exemplar set. The same example set is used in all the experiments reported (e.g. there are no footballers in the training dataset used to compute the gaze estimates presented in figure 9).

2.3   Matching Head Poses

The descriptors for each head pose are $(20 \times 20 \times 5 =)2000$ element vectors. With 8 possible orientations and 100 examples of each orientation, rapidly searching this dataset becomes an issue. We elect to structure the database using a binary-tree in which each node in the tree divides the set of exemplars below the node into roughly equal halves. Such a structure can be searched in roughly $\log n$ time to give an approximate nearest-neighbour result. We do this for two reasons: first, even for a modest database of 800 examples such as ours it *is* faster by a factor of 10; second, we wish to frame the problem of gaze detection in a probabilistic way and Sidenbladh [23] showed how to formulate a binary tree (based on the sign of the Principal Components of the data) search in a pseudo-probabilistic manner. This technique was later applied to probabilistic analysis of human activity in [21]. We achieve recognition rates of 80% (the correct example is chosen as the ML model 8/10 queries) using this pseudo-probabilistic method based on Principal Components with 10 samples. An illustrative example of such a distribution in this context is shown in figure 4. Results of sampling from this database for a number of different scenes are shown in figure 3. In order to display where the person is looking in the images angles are assigned to the discretised head-poses shown in figure 1 according to the "compass" e.g. $N : 0°$ etc. The angles are then corrected for the projection of the camera at each time step (depending on the location of the person on the ground-plane in the image) as defined in figure 5.

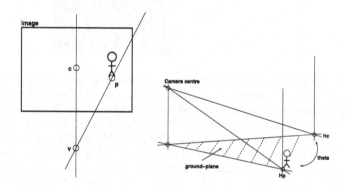

Fig. 5. When assigning angles to the matched discretised head-poses one must compensate for the camera projection since "North" (see figure 1) does not in general correspond to vertical in the image plane. In order to choose the correct frame of reference we do not perform full camera calibration but compute the projective transform ($\mathbf{H}$: image→ground-plane) by hand-selecting 4 points in the image. The vertical vanishing point ($\mathbf{v}$, *left*) is computed from 2 lines normal to the ground plane and parallel in the image. The angle *theta* between the projection of the optic-rays through the camera centre ($\mathbf{Hv}$, *right*) and the image centre ($\mathbf{Hc}$, *left*) and the point at the feet of the tracked person (($\mathbf{Hp}$, *right*) is the angle which adjusts vertical in the image to "North" in our ground plane reference frame i. e. $\cos^{-1}[(\mathbf{Hc} \times \mathbf{Hv}).(\mathbf{Hv} \times \mathbf{Hp})]$.

3   Gaze Estimation

3.1   Bayesian Fusion of Head-Pose and Direction

The naive assumption that direction of motion information is a good guide as to what a person can see has been used in figure 6. However, it is clear the crucial interaction between the two people is missed. To address this issue we compute the joint posterior distribution over direction of motion and head pose. The priors on these are initially uniform for direction of motion, reflecting the fact that for these purposes there is no preference for any particular direction in the scene, and for head pose a centred, weighted function that models a strong preference for looking forwards rather than sideways. The prior on gaze is defined using a table which lists expected (i.e. physically possible) gazes and unexpected (i.e. non-physical) gazes.

We define g as the measurement of head-pose, d is the measurement of body motion direction, G is the true gaze direction and B is the true body direction, with all quantities referred to the ground centre. We compute the joint probability of true body pose and true gaze:

$$P(B, G|d, g) \propto P(d, g|B, G)P(B, G) \tag{1}$$

Now given that the measurement of direction d is independent both true and measured gaze G, g once true body B pose is known, $P(d|B, G, g) = P(d|B)$ and similarly that the measurement of gaze g is independent of true body pose B given true gaze G, $P(g|B, G) = p(g|G)$, then we have

$$P(B, G|d, g) \propto P(g|G)P(d|B)P(G|B)P(B) \tag{2}$$

We assume that the measurement errors in gaze and direction are unbiased and normally distributed around the respective true values

$$P(g|G) = \mathcal{N}(G, \sigma_G^2), P(d|B) = \mathcal{N}(B, \sigma_B^2) \tag{3}$$

(actually, since these are discrete variables we use a discrete approximation).

The joint prior, $P(B, G)$ is factored as above into $P(G|B)P(B)$ where the first term encodes our knowledge that people tend to look straight ahead (so the distribution $P(G|B)$ is peaked around B, while $P(B)$ is taken to be uniform, encoding our belief that all directions of body pose are equally likely, although this is easily changed: for example in tennis one player is expected to be predominantly facing the camera).

While for single frame estimation this formulation fuses our measurements with prior beliefs, when analysing video data we can further impose smoothness constraints to encode temporal coherence: the joint prior at time t is in this case taken to be $P(G_t, B_t|G_{t-1}, B_{t-1}) = P(G_t|B_t, B_{t-1}, G_{t-1})P(B_t|B_{t_1})$ where we have used an assumption that the current direction is independent of previous gaze[2], and current gaze depends only on current pose and previous gaze. The former term, $P(G_t|B_t, B_{t-1}, G_{t-1})$, strikes a balance between between our belief that people tend to look where they are going, and temporal consistency of gaze via a mixture $G_t \sim \alpha\mathcal{N}(G_{t-1}, \sigma_G^2) + (1 - \alpha)\mathcal{N}(B_t, \sigma_B^2)$.

---

[2] Although we do recognise that, in a limited set of cases, this may in fact be a poor assumption since people may change their motion or pose in response to observing something interesting while gazing around.

Now we compute the joint distribution for all 64 possible gazes resulting from possible combinations of 8 head poses and 8 directions. This posterior distribution allows us to maintain probabilistic estimates without committing to a defined gaze which will be advantageous for further reasoning about overall scene behaviour. Immediately though we can see that gazes which we consider very unlikely given our prior knowledge of human biomechanics (since the head cannot turn beyond 90° relative to the torso [19]) can be rejected in addition to the obvious benefit that the quality of lower-level match can be incorporated in a mathematically sound way. An illustrative example is shown in figure 4.

4   Results

We have tested this method on various datasets (see figures 6, 7, 8, 9 and 10). The first dataset provided us with the exemplar data for use on all the test videos shown in this paper. In the first example in figure 6 we show significant improvement over using head-pose or direction alone to compute gaze. The

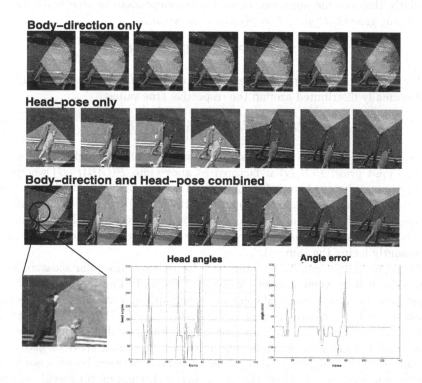

Fig. 6. In this video there is an interaction between the two people, and the fact they look at each other is the prime indicator that they are "together". On the first row we estimate gaze from body direction alone, on the second row using head-pose alone, which is improved but prone to some errors. We see that (*third row*) fusing the head-pose and body-direction estimates gives the correct result.

Fig. 7. Two people meeting could potentially be identified by each person being in the other's gaze (in addition to other cues such as proximity), as we show in this example

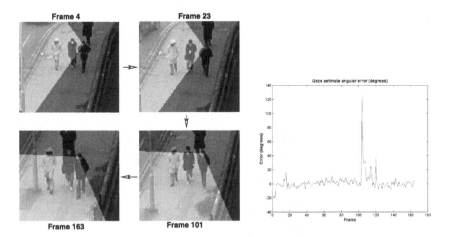

Fig. 8. Second surveillance sequence. The same training data set as used to obtain the results above is used to infer head pose in this video without temporal smoothing. The ground truth has been produced by a human user drawing the line-of-sight on the images. The mean error is 5.64^o, the median 0.5^o.

Fig. 9. This example demonstrates the method in soccer footage. The skin histogram is defined at the start of this sequence to compensate for lighting changes, but the exemplar database remains the same as that constructed initially and used on all the sequences i.e. it contains no examples from this sequence.

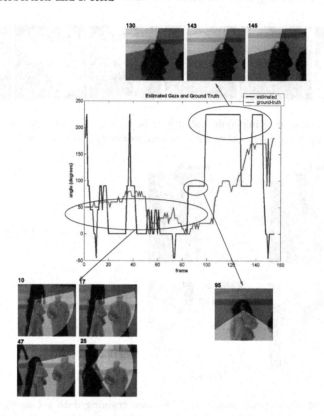

Fig. 10. This figure shows the method tested on a standard sequence (see http://groups.inf.ed.ac.uk/vision/CAVIAR/). The errors are exacerbated by our discretisation of gaze (accurate to 45°) compared to the non-discretised ground truth (computed to 10° from a hand-drawn estimate of line-of-sight which we take to be the best-estimate a human can make from low-resolution images) and tend to be isolated (the median error is 5.5°). In most circumstances it is more important that the significant head-turnings are identified, which they are here, as evidenced by the expanded frames.

crucial interaction which conveys the information that the people in the scene are together is the frequent turning of the head to look at each other. We reliably detect this interaction as can be seen from the images and the estimated head angle relative to vertical. The second example is similar but in completely different scene. The skin histogram for online skin-detection in the input images is recomputed for this video. The exemplar (training) database remains the same, however. Once more the interaction implied by the head turning to look at his companions is determined. We demonstrate the method on sports video in figure 9 and on a standard vision sequence in figure 10. It is shown in figure 7 how useful this technique can be in a causal-reasoning context where we identify two people looking at one another prior to meeting. Finally we discuss the failure mode in figure 11 which is found to be where the size of the head falls below 20 pixels and the gaze becomes ambiguous due to the small number of skin pixels.

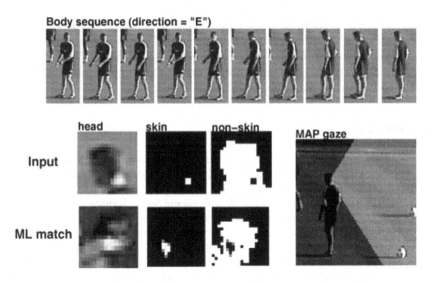

Fig. 11. We show an example here where our method can fail. The mean body direction of the player (in the frames prior to the frame for which we estimate the gaze) is East, since he is moving backwards as his head rotates. The ML match is clearly not correct because the neck has been detected and there is no representation of gaze where the neck is visible in the training dataset. Fusing the direction and head-pose estimate results in the MAP gaze "side-LR", as expected, but incorrect. The reasons for failure are clear: body direction is not a good guide to gaze in this case and there is an unusual input which results in an incorrect match. Either of these can be compensated for on their own with the Bayesian representation we devised but a scenario which combines both is likely to fail. Additional contextual information (e.g. silhouette) could improve this result, however.

5   Conclusions

In this paper we have demonstrated that a simple descriptor, readily computed from medium-scale video, can be used robustly to estimate head pose. In order to speed up non-parametric matching into an exemplar database and to maintain probabilistic estimates throughout we employed a fast pseudo-probabilistic binary search based on Principal Components. To resolve ambiguity, improve matching and reject known implausible gaze estimates we used a simple application of Bayes' Rule to fuse priors on direction-of-motion and head-pose, evidence from our exemplar-matching algorithm and priors on gaze (which we specified in advance). We demonstrated on a number of different datasets that this gives acceptable gaze estimation for people being tracked at a distance.

The Bayesian fusion method we have used in this work could be readily extended to include other contextual data. We used body direction in this paper but information such as the silhouette is equally interesting. Moreover the descriptor for head-pose could be extended to include information from multiple cameras. The work reported here would be most useful in a causal reasoning context where knowledge of where a person is looking can help solve interesting questions such as, "Is person A *following* person B?" or determine that person C looked right because a moving object entered his field-of-view. We are currently combining this advance with our reported work on human behaviour recognition [21] to aid automatic reasoning in video.

References

1. J. S. Beis and D. G. Lowe *Shape indexing using approximate nearest-neighbour search in high-dimensional space* IEEE Conf. on Computer Vision and Pattern Recognition, San Juan, PR, June 1997
2. H. Buxton *Learning and Understanding Dynamic Scene Activity* ECCV Generative Model Based Vision Workshop, Copenhagen, Denmark, 2002
3. D. Chai and K. N. Ngan *Locating facial region of a head-and-shoulders color image* Third IEEE International Conference on Automatic Face and Gesture Recognitions, Nara, Japan, pp. 124-129, April 1998
4. D. Comaniciu and P. Meer *Mean Shift Analysis and Applications* Proceedings of the International Conference on Computer Vision-Volume 2, p.1197, September 20-25, 1999
5. H. Dee and D. Hogg *Detecting Inexplicable Behaviour* Proceedings of the British Machine Vision Conference, 2004
6. A.A. Efros, A. Berg, G. Mori and J. Malik *Recognising Action at a Distance* Proceedings of the International Conference on Computer Vision, Nice, France, July 2003
7. A. Galata, N. Johnson, D. Hogg *Learning Behaviour Models of Human Activities* British Machine Vision Conference, 1999
8. A.H. Gee and R. Cipolla. *Determining the gaze of faces in images.* Image and Vision Computing, 12(10):639-647, December 1994
9. W.E.L. Grimson, C. Stauffer, R. Romano, and L. Lee. *Using Adaptive Tracking to Classify and Monitor Activities in a Site* Computer Vision and Pattern Recognition, June 23-25, 1998, Santa Barbara, CA, USA
10. K. Hidai *et al. Robust Face Detection against Brightness Fluctuation and Size Variation* International Conference on Intelligent Robots and Systems, vol. 2 pp. 1379-1384, Japan, October 2000
11. T.S. Jebara and A. Pentland *Parametrized Structure from Motion for 3D Adaptive Feedback Tracking of Faces* Proc. IEEE Computer Society Conference on Computer Vision and Pattern Recognition, San Juan, Puerto Rico, pp. 144-150
12. N. Johnson and D. Hogg. *Learning the Distribution of Object Trajectories for Event Recognition* Proc. British Machine Vision Conference, vol. 2, pp. 583-592, September 1995
13. B.D. Lucas and T. Kanade *An Iterative Image Registration Technique with Application to Stereo Vision* DARPA Image Understanding Workshop, 1981
14. D. Makris and T.Ellis *Spatial and Probabilistic Modelling of Pedestrian Behaviour* British Machine Vision Conference 2002, vol. 2, pp. 557-566, Cardiff, UK, September 2-5, 2002
15. Y. Matsumoto and A. Zelinsky *An Algorithm for Real-time Stereo Vision Implementation of Head Pose and Gaze Direction Measurement* Proceedings of IEEE Fourth International Conference on Face and Gesture Recognition, pp. 499-505, 2000

16. J. McNames *A Fast Nearest-Neighbor Algorithm Based on a Principal Axis Search Tree* IEEE Pattern Analysis and Machine Intelligence, vol. 23, September 2001, pp. 964-976 ISSN:0162-8828

17. V.Morellas, I.Pavlidis, P.Tsiamyrtzis *DETER: Detection of Events for Threat Evaluation and Recognition* Machine Vision and Applications, 15(1):29-46, October 2003

18. S. A. Nene and S. K. Nayar *A Simple Algorithm for Nearest Neighbor Search in High Dimensions* IEEE Transactions on Pattern Analysis and Machine Intelligence vol.19, September 1997, p. 989-1003

19. D. Pang, M.D. and V. Li, M.D. *Atlantoaxial Rotatory Fixation: Part 1-Biomechanics OF Normal Rotation at the Atlantoaxial Joint in Children.* Neurosurgery. 55(3):614-626, September 2004

20. A.Perez, M.L. Cordoba, A. Garcia, R. Mendez, M.L. Munoz, J.L. Pedraza, F. Sanchez *A Precise Eye-Gaze Detection and Tracking System* Proceedings of the 11th International Conference in Central Europe on Computer Graphics, Visualization and Computer Vision 2003

21. N.M. Robertson and I.D. Reid *Behaviour understanding in video: a combined method* Proceedings of the International Conference on Computer Vision, October 2005, Beijing, China

22. N.M. Robertson, I.D. Reid and J.M. Brady *What are you looking at? Gaze recognition in medium-scale images* Human Activity Modelling and Recognition, British Machine Vision Conference, Oxford, UK, September 2005

23. H. Sidenbladh M. Black, L. Sigal. *Implicit Probabilistic Models of Human Motion for Synthesis and Tracking* European Conference on Computer Vision, Copenhagen, Denmark, June 2002

24. P. A. Viola, M. J. Jones *Robust Real-Time Face Detection* International Journal of Computer Vision, 2004, 57(3) pp. 137-154

Learning Effective Intrinsic Features to Boost 3D-Based Face Recognition

Chenghua Xu[1], Tieniu Tan[1], Stan Li[1],
Yunhong Wang[2], and Cheng Zhong[1]

[1] Center for Biometrics and Security Research (CBSR)
& National Laboratory of Pattern Recognition (NLPR),
Institute of Automation, Chinese Academy of Sciences, Beijing, China
{chxu, tnt, szli, czhong}@nlpr.ia.ac.cn
http://www.cbsr.ia.ac.cn/
http://nlpr-web.ia.ac.cn/English/irds/index.html
[2] School of Computer Science and Engineering, Beihang University, Beijing, China
yhwang@buaa.edu.cn

Abstract. 3D image data provide several advantages than 2D data for face recognition and overcome many problems with 2D intensity images based methods. In this paper, we propose a novel approach to 3D-based face recognition. First, a novel representation, called **intrinsic features**, is presented to encode local 3D shapes. It describes complementary non-relational features to provide an *intrinsic representation* of faces. This representation is extracted after alignment, and is invariant to translation, rotation and scale. Without reduction, tens of thousands of intrinsic features can be produced for a face, but not all of them are useful and equally important. Therefore, in the second part of the work, we introduce a **learning** method for learning most effective local features and combining them into a strong classifier using an AdaBoost learning procedure. Experimental results are performed on a large 3D face database obtained with complex illumination, pose and expression variations. The results demonstrate that the proposed approach produces consistently better results than existing methods.

1 Introduction

Biometric identification has received much attention recent years. Face is among the most common and most accessible modality. Over the past decades, most work has been focusing on 2D images [1]. Since 2D-based face recognition suffers from variations in pose, expression, and illumination, it is still difficult to develop a robust automatic face recognition system using 2D images.

With the rapid development of 3D acquisition equipment, 3D capture is becoming easier and faster, and face recognition based on 3D information is attracting more and more attention. The existing methods mainly focus on three categories: 3D to 3D, 2D aided by 3D, and 2D combined with 3D. 3D to 3D means that the gallery and the probe examples are both 3D data, such as range images, and feature extraction and representation are both in 3D space. 2D aided

A. Leonardis, H. Bischof, and A. Pinz (Eds.): ECCV 2006, Part II, LNCS 3952, pp. 416–427, 2006.

by 3D means that 2D face recognition is done with the assistant of 3D model [9, 12]. 3D model is explored to overcome the pose, expression and illustration variations in 2D recognition. 3D combined with 2D means that features are extracted from both 3D images and 2D color or intensity images [13, 14, 15]. This paper mainly pays attention to the first category and summarizes the existing methods as follows.

Regarding feature representation, research has been focused mainly on how to extract and represent 3D features. Some earlier methods on curvature analysis [2, 3, 4] have been proposed for face recognition based on high-quality range data from laser scanners. In addition, recognition schemes based on 3D surface features have been developed. Chua et al. [5] treat face recognition as a 3D non-rigid surface matching problem and divide the human face into rigid and non-rigid regions. The rigid parts are represented by point signatures to identify an individual. They have obtained a good result in a small database (6 persons). Beumier et al. [6] propose two methods of surface matching and central/lateral profiles to compare two instances. Both of them construct some central and lateral profiles to represent an individual, and obtain the matching value by minimizing the distance of the profiles. Tanaka et al. [7] treat the face recognition problem as a 3D shape recognition problem of rigid free-form surfaces. Each face is represented as an Extended Gaussian Image, constructed by mapping principal curvatures and their directions. In more recent work, Hesher et al. [8] use a 3D scanner for generating range images and registering them by aligning salient facial features. PCA approaches are explored to reduce the dimensionality of feature vector. Lu et al. [11] use the hybrid ICP algorithm to align the reference model and the scanned data, and adopt the registration error to distinguish the different people.

Despite of the efforts mentioned above, a number of problems remain to be solved for 3D face recognition:

- Only local features have so far been used to represent unary properties of individual points. These ignore relationships between points in a reasonably large neighborhood while such relationships may play important roles in object recognition.
- These local features have been so far considered independent of each other for different points. However, they are not so in practice.
- Because these features are correlated, sophisticated and even nonlinear. Methods are needed for constructing good classifiers. The current research in 3D face recognition has not looked into this challenge.

In this work, we attempt to address the above issues. The main contributions of this paper are as follows:

- We propose a novel feature, called associative features, based on Gaussian-Hermite moments [20], to encode relationships between neighboring mesh nodes. They are combined with complementary non-relational features to provide an *intrinsic representation* of faces.
- The resulting intrinsic features are likely to be correlated for nearby nodes, and an individual face may have non-convex manifold in the features space.

We introduce a learning mechanism to deal with the problems. AdaBoost learning [22] is adopted to select most effective features and to combine these features to construct a strong classifier. This provides a new way to improve the performance of 3D face recognition.

For testing the proposed approach, we collect a large 3D face databases. The proposed approach is shown to yield consistently better results than existing methods including the benchmarking PCA methods [8, 14], the point signature based methods [5] and the curvature based method [2, 3, 4].

The rest of this paper is organized as follows. Section 2 describes associative features and the resulting intrinsic feature representation used in this work. Section 3 describes the use of AdaBoost learning for feature selection and classifier construction. Section 4 reports the experimental results and gives some comparisons with existing methods. Finally, Section 5 summarizes this paper.

2   Intrinsic Feature Representation

A vector of intrinsic features is a concatenation of scattered features and associative features. They are extracted after preprocessing.

2.1   Preprocessing

Our preprocessing includes three steps, namely, nose tip detection, alignment and meshing. We aim to exactly align the range images and approximate the original range image with a simple and regular mesh, which prepares for the feature extraction and representation.

In the facial range data, the nose is the most distinct feature. We have proposed a robust method to localize the nose tip, which is described in detail in [18]. According to the experiments in our database, the correct detection rate is over 99%. Aided by the detected nose and the classic method of the Iterative Closest Point (ICP) [21], alignment is done by our previous method [17]. We select a front 3D image as the fixed model, and all the other 3D images are rotated and translated to align with it.

The original images usually consist of considerable dense and irregular points in 3D space. It is very difficult to efficiently extract the corresponding features. Here a simple and regular mesh approximates the original range images by the multi-resolution fitting scheme. The meshing procedure is shown in Fig.1. During meshing, we only regulate the Z coordinate of each mesh node, which not only speeds up the meshing process but also keeps the correspondences of the generated meshes. In this paper, we use a mesh with 545 nodes and 1024 triangles to balance the resolution of the facial mesh and the cost of time and space. This constructed mesh is of great benefit to feature representation and extraction.

All these meshes have the same pose and corresponding nodes, which have the same position in an X-Y plane and different values along a Z-axis. Thus a vector of *depth features* can then be formed as follows

$$D = \{Z(v_1), Z(v_2), \cdots, Z(v_n)\} \tag{1}$$

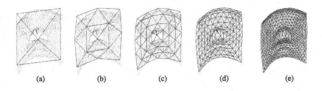

Fig. 1. The fitted meshes of different levels. (a) Basic mesh. (b)-(e) Level one to four.

where $Z(v_i)$ is the Z-coordinate of the mesh node v_i. They can be directly used for characterizing faces.

2.2 Cosine Signature Features

Here, we define a new metric, called *cosine signature* as a descriptor of local shape of each mesh node, as illustrated in Fig.2. Since a mesh well approximates the range image, we can obtain the following local information of each mesh node, p_e, that is, its spatial direct neighboring triangles, $\{T_1, T_2, \cdots, T_n\}$, its normal, N_{pe} and neighboring points in the range image within a small sphere. Due to the regularity of our mesh, the number of neighboring triangles of the common node (not the edge node) is usually six. The initial radius of the local sphere to decide the neighboring points is set as half of the length of one mesh edge in our work.

Further, the neighboring points can be classified into n categories, $\{C_1, \cdots, C_n\}$. Which category one point belongs to depends on which triangle the point's projection falls in the same direction as the normal, N_{pe}. For each class C_k, we can define its surface signal as follows:

$$d_{ek} = \frac{1}{2} + \frac{1}{2m} \sum_{i=1}^{m} cos(q_{ki} - p_e, N_{pe}) \tag{2}$$

with

$$cos(q_{ki} - p_e, N_{pe}) = \frac{(q_{ki} - p_e) \cdot N_{pe}}{\parallel q_{ki} - p_e \parallel \cdot \parallel N_{pe} \parallel} \tag{3}$$

where q_{ki} is the neighboring point belonging to class C_k, m is the number of points in C_k, and $d_{ek} \in [0, 1]$.

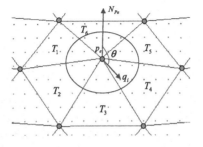

Fig. 2. Cosine signature of one mesh node

Then we can describe the local shape of each mesh node using the following vector:

$$s_e = \{d_{e1}, d_{e2}, \cdots, d_{en}\} \tag{4}$$

where d_{ek} is the surface signal. This vector describes the shape near this node, and we call it as *cosine signature*.

According to this metric, we can describe the shape of each row in the mesh with a combination of cosine signature of all nodes in this row respectively.

$$S_i = \{s_{i1}, s_{i2}, \cdots, s_{ir}\} \tag{5}$$

where S_i is the shape vector of the ith row and s_{ij} is the cosine signature of the jth vertex in the ith row. Further, from S_1 to S_n, we connect them in turn to form a long shape vector, S, in the alternate way of head and tail connection. The vector, S, is used to describe the shape of one face.

2.3   Associative Features

In the above, neither depth features or cosine signature features encode relationships in neighboring mesh nodes. In the following, we use Gaussian-Hermite moments (G-H moments) [20] to describe derivative or relational property of a local shape in a neighborhood, as a richer representation. Because such features describe the relational property of neighboring mesh nodes, we call it *associative features*.

It is well-known that moments have been widely used in pattern recognition and image processing, especially in various shape-based applications. More recently, the orthogonal moment based method has been an active research topic in shape analysis. Here, Gaussian-Hermite moments (G-H moments) are used for feature representation due to their mathematical orthogonality and effectiveness for characterizing local details of the signal [20]. They provide an effective way to quantify the signal variation. The nth order G-H moment $M_n(x, S(x))$ of a signal $S(x)$ is defined as [20]:

$$M_n(x) = \int_{-\infty}^{\infty} B_n(t) S(x+t) dt \quad n = 0, 1, 2, \cdots \tag{6}$$

with

$$Bn(t) = g(t, \sigma) H_n(t/\sigma)$$
$$H_n(t) = (-1)^n exp(t^2) \frac{d^n exp(-t^2)}{dt^n}$$
$$g(t, \sigma) = (2\pi\sigma^2)^{-1/2} exp(-x^2/2\sigma^2) \tag{7}$$

where $g(t, \sigma)$ is a Gaussian function and $H_n(t)$ is a scaled Hermite polynomial function of order n. G-H moments have many desirable properties such as insensitiveness to noise generated during differential operations.

In fact, the face surface is smooth on the whole, and high order moments usually describe the intense variation. So it is not necessary to calculate higher order moments. In our experiments, we use the 0th-2nd order G-H moment with $\sigma = 2.0$ to represent the associative features.

To the constructed shape vector in the above, S, we calculate its nth order G-H moments, thus obtaining moment vectors, SM_n, which are called nth order associative features. They describe the relational property of neighboring mesh nodes.

2.4 Intrinsic Feature Vector

A vector of intrinsic features is a concatenation of scattered features and associative features. In our work, the scattered features include depth features, D (545 dimensions), and cosine signature, S (2814 dimensions). Associative features consist of 0th-2th order moments of cosine signature features, i.e., SM_n (2814 dimensions, n=0,1,2). The total dimension of intrinsic features is 11,801. These features represent not only the non-relational features but also the relationships between the neighboring mesh nodes. They provide a complete information to reveal the intrinsic property of facial surface. Their complementarity is effective to improve recognition accuracy, which will be further proved in the following experiments. In addition, since all these features are extracted after fine alignment, they are invariant to translation, scale and rotation.

3   Feature Selection and Classification

There are a total number of 11,801 such intrinsic features for a face image. They are likely to be correlated for nearby nodes, and an individual face may have non-convex manifold in the features space. In this work, AdaBoost learning algorithm with the cascade structure [22] is used for selecting most effective features and combining them to construct a strong classification.

The AdaBoost algorithm essentially works for a two-class classification problem. While face recognition is a multi-class problem, we convert it into one of two classes using the representation of intra-personal vs. extra-personal classes, following [23]. The intra-personal examples are obtained by using difference of images of the same person whereas the extra-personal examples are obtained by using difference of images of the different persons.

After this preparation, the AdaBoost-based learning procedure in [22] is used to learn a cascade of strong classifiers with N layers, each of which contains one or multiple weak classifiers.

During recognition stage, for one given probe sample, the different with each gallery example forms the vector, x. To each vector, x, the ith layer of the strong classifier returns the similarity measure, S_i. The larger this similarity value, the more this sample belongs to the intra-personal space. If $S_i < 0$, this layer rejects the sample. According to the multiple classifiers, we can obtain its total similarity:

$$S = \sum_{i=1}^{L} S_i \qquad (8)$$

where L is the number of layers and S_i is the similarity of the ith layer. Thus we can obtain its similarity with each gallery example. Then the nearest neighbor scheme is used to decide which class the test sample belongs to.

In our training set, there are 23 persons and 33 images each person, and thus we obtain 12,144 positive examples and 275,517 negative examples. Every face image is represented as a vector of 11,801-dimensional intrinsic features, as explained above. Using the above learning procedure, we obtain a cascade of 20 classifiers with a total of 193 features.

4   Experiments

In this section, we demonstrate the excellent performance of our proposed scheme by comparing experiments in the terms of different features, different schemes and different combinations.

4.1   Databases

A large 3D face database has been collected to test the proposed algorithm. It was collected indoors during August and September 2004 using a non-contact 3D digitizer, Minolta VIVID 910, working on Fast Mode. This database contains 123 subjects, with each subject having 37 (without glasses) or 38 (with glasses) images. During the data collection, we consider not only separate variation of expressions, poses and illumination, but also combined variations of expressions under different lighting and poses under different expressions.

For the following experiments, images with large facial pose (80-90 degrees) and with glasses are excluded. The reasons are the following: (1) Our focus here is to compare different algorithms with images of approximate front faces whereas side view face recognition is too challenging for any methods. (2) The range scan quality was bad at glasses areas. Therefore, the actual database contains a total of 4059 images.

The database of 4059 images is divided into three subsets, that is, the training set, the gallery set and the probe set. The last 23 of the 123 subjects are used as the training set. The first images of the other 100 subjects (under the condition of front view, office lighting, and neutral expression) are used as the gallery set. The other images of the 100 subjects are used as the probe set.

There are 3200 images in the probe set. They are further divided into seven subsets:

- IV (400 images): illumination variations.
- EV (500 images): expression variations, including smile, laugh, anger, surprise and eye closed.
- EVI (500 images): expression variations under right lighting.
- PVS (700 images): small pose variations, views of front, left/right 20-30 degrees, up/down 20-30 degrees and tilt left/right 20-30 degrees.
- PVL (200 images): large pose variations, views of left/right 50-60 degrees.
- PVSS (700 images): small pose variations under smile.
- PVSL (200 images): large pose variations under smile.

4.2   Experiments with Different Features

In this experiment, we test the recognition performance using the different features. The considered features include surface curvature (SC) [2, 3, 4], point signature (PS) [5], COSMOS shape index (CO) [10, 11] and three kinds of features used in this paper, that is, depth features (DEP), cosine signature (COS) and associative features (ASS).

In our experiment, after the regular mesh is constructed following the schemes in Section 2.1, the different features are extracted for each node to characterize an individual. Then, we use one simple classifier to test the recognition performance, that is, PCA for reducing dimension and Euclidian distance for similarity measure. Table 1 shows the rank-one recognition accuracy (CCR, Correct Classification Rate) in different probe sets. In this table, the best recognition accuracy is emphasized. Fig.3 shows CMS (Cumulative Match Score) curves in the EV probe set.

From these result, we can obtain the following conclusion. (1) On the whole, the three features that we used have better performance than the other three; (2) In the probe sets related to expression and illumination variations, the

Table 1. CCR(%) using different features in the different probe sets (100 persons)

Probe sets	SC	PS	Co	DEP	COS	ASS
IV	97.6	87.0	89.0	98.5	**99.0**	**99.0**
EV	71.9	66.0	53.3	85.0	81.4	**85.2**
EVI	74.6	65.9	56.6	85.0	86.4	**87.0**
PVS	79.1	61.2	67.1	**85.1**	83.0	84.7
PVL	51.6	38.2	41.1	**70.0**	51.0	51.5
PVSS	63.7	53.3	44.5	**81.9**	75.4	76.9
PVSL	47.2	34.6	26.8	**65.0**	43.0	46.5

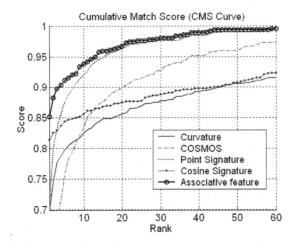

Fig. 3. CMS curves using different features in the EV probe set

proposed associative feature are more robust than depth information. This may be reasonably explained by the following reason. Depth information using the absolute range value is prone to shape variation, such as expression, whereas associative features use the relative information between reference nodes. These results also encourage us to improve the recognition performance by combining these complementary information.

4.3 Experiments with Different Schemes

In this section, we will test the different performances when using different classification methods, i.e., fusion scheme and AdaBoost learning.

Scattered features and associative features are of the different properties. Fusion rules [16] and AdaBoost learning [22] are two kinds of method to combine them. We test their performance by experiments. Using depth features, cosine signature and associative features, we construct the three single classifiers, respectively. After obtaining the matching score from each single classifier, the weighted sum rule [14] is used to combine them. The first row in Table 2 shows the rank-one recognition accuracy. In other way, from the intrinsic features consisting of scattered features and associative features, one cascade classifier is built following the scheme in Section 3. The CCR is shown in the second row in Table 2.

Table 2. CCR(%) of the different test sets in our face database (100 persons)

Probe sets	IV	EV	EVI	PVS	PVL	PVSS	PVSL
Fusion	99.5	88.0	90.2	96.1	73.5	**88.3**	67.5
AdaBoost	99.5	90.8	90.6	96.7	76.5	**87.9**	70.0

Comparing this result with Table 1, we can see that the recognition accuracy is better when combining the different features using the fusion scheme or AdaBoost learning. This verifies the conclusion in the last section.

From this result of Table 2, we also see that AdaBoost learning outperforms the fusion rule in all probe sets except the PVSS set. Further, we test the verification performance when using these two methods. Compared with single classifiers, the classifier by AdaBoost learning largely decreases the EER (Equal Error Rate) in all the probe sets. However, the classifier using the fusion scheme decreases the EER weakly. Fig.4 shows the ROC curves using single classifiers, fusion rule and AdaBoost learning in the EV probe set. On the whole, AdaBoost learning distinctly outperforms the fusion scheme.

4.4 Experiments with Different Combination

In [14], they evaluate the recognition performances of different combination of 2D and 3D images and draw the conclusion that multi-modal 2D+3D has the best performance. Their conclusion is very limited since they only explore the depth

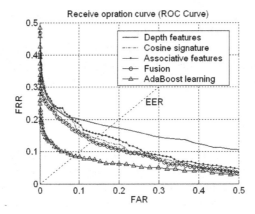

Fig. 4. ROC curves using single classifiers, fusion scheme and AdaBoost learning in the EV Probe set

Table 3. Rank-one recognition accuracy (%) with different combination (100 persons)

Probe sets	IV	EV	EVI	PVS	PVL	PVSS	PVSL
Depth+ intensity	97.0	84.6	89.0	85.6	**86.0**	82.9	**73.5**
Intrinsic features	99.5	90.8	90.6	96.7	**76.5**	87.9	**70.0**

information of 3D images. Here, we compare the recognition performance using the different combination, that is, depth+intensity vs. scattered+associative.

After registration of different 3D images, depth and intensity images are generated. Using AdaBoost learning [22], a strong classifier is constructed based on depth and intensity images. The rank-one recognition accuracy is showed in the first row of Table 3. Another classifier is constructed using intrinsic features by AdaBoost learning (see Section 3). The CCR is showed in the bottom row of Table 3.

From this result, we can see that combination of intrinsic features outperform the combination of depth and intensity in five probe sets. This result suggests that it is a promising way to extract 3D shape information for improving recognition information. Some effective 3D shape features even have better performance than multi-modal 2D+3D. In addition, it is noted that the latter is more robust than the former in large pose variations.

5   Conclusions

Personal identification based on 3D information has recently been gaining more and more interest. We have proposed a novel representation, called associative features, based on Gaussian-Hermite moments, to encode relationships between neighboring mesh nodes. It is integrated by complementary non-relational features to provide an *intrinsic representation* of faces. Then, a powerful learning algorithm, i.e., AdaBoost, is used for feature selection and classification. One large 3D face database with complex illumination, expression and pose variations has been collected to test the proposed algorithm. The experimental results and the comparisons with some existing methods have demonstrated the excellent performance of the proposed method for 3D face recognition.

Acknowledgment

The authors are grateful to Dr L. Quan for valuable discussions and proofreading this paper. This work is supported by research funds from the Natural Science Foundation of China (Grant No. 60121302 and 60332010), the Outstanding Overseas Chinese Scholars Fund of CAS (Grant No. 2001-2-8), and the National 973 Program (Grant No. 2004CB318100).

References

1. W. Zhao, R. Chellappa, P.J. Phillips, and A. Rosenfeld, "Face Recognition: A Literature Survey", ACM Computing Surveys archive, Vol.35, No.4, pp.399-458, 2003.
2. J.C. Lee, and E. Milios, "Matching Range Images of Human Faces", Proc. ICCV'90, pp.722-726, 1990.
3. G.G. Gordon, "Face Recognition Based on Depth and Curvature Features", Proc. CVPR'92, pp.108-110, 1992.
4. Y. Yacoob and L.S. Davis, "Labeling of Human Face Components from Range Data", CVGIP: Image Understanding, 60(2):168-178, 1994.
5. C.S. Chua, F. Han, and Y.K. Ho, "3D Human Face Recognition Using Point Signiture", Proc. FG'00, pp.233-239, 2000.
6. C. Beumier and M. Acheroy, "Automatic 3D Face Authentication", Image and Vision Computing, 18(4):315-321, 2000.
7. H.T. Tanaka, M. Ikeda and H. Chiaki, "Curvature-based Face Surface Recognition Using Spherical Correlation", Proc. FG'98, pp.372-377, 1998.
8. C. Hesher, A. Srivastava, and G. Erlebacher, "A Novel Technique for Face Recognition Using Range Imaging", Inter. Multiconference in Computer Science, 2002.
9. V. Blanz, and T. Vetter, "Face Recognition Based on Fitting a 3D Morphable Model", IEEE Trans. on PAMI, 25(9):1063-1074, 2003.
10. C. Dorai and A.K. Jain, "COSMOS-A Representation Scheme for 3-D Free-Form Objects", IEEE Trans. on PAMI, 19(10):1115-1130, 1997.
11. X. Lu, D. Colbry, and A.K. Jain, "Three-dimensional Model Based Face Recognition", Proc. ICPR'04, pp.362-365, 2004.
12. M.W. Lee, and S. Ranganath, "Pose-invariant Face Recognition Using a 3D Deformable Model", Pattern Recognition, Vol.36, pp.1835-1846, 2003.
13. Y. Wang, C. Chua, and Y. Ho, "Facial Feature Detection and Face Recognition from 2D and 3D Images", Pattern Recognition Letters, Vol.23, pp.1191-1202, 2002.
14. K.I. Chang, K.W. Bowyer, and P.J. Flynn, "An Evaluation of Multi-model 2D+3D Biometrics", IEEE Trans. on PAMI, 27(4):619-624, 2005.
15. A.M. Bronstein, M.M. Bronstein, and R. Kimmel, "Expression-Invariant 3D Face Recognition", Proc. AVBPA'03, LCNS 2688, pp.62-70, 2003.

16. L.I. Kuncheva, J.C. Bezdek, and R.P.W. Duin, "Decision Templates for Multiple Classifier Fusion: an Experimental Comparon", Patter Recognition, Vol.34, pp.299-314, 2001.

17. C. Xu, Y. Wang, T. Tan, L. Quan, "Automatic 3D Face Recognition Combining Global Geometric Features with Local Shape Variation Information", Proc. FG'04, pp.308-313, 2004.

18. C. Xu, Y. Wang, T. Tan, L. Quan, "Robust Nose Detection in 3D Facial Data Using Local Characteristics", Proc. ICIP'04, pp.1995-1998, 2004.

19. P.J. Phillips, H. Moon, S.A. Rizvi, and P.J. Rauss, "The Feret Evaluation Methodology for Face-Recognition Algorithm", IEEE Trans. on PAMI, 22(10):1090-1104, 2000.

20. J. Shen, W. Shen and D. Shen, "On Geometric and Orthogonal Moments", Inter. Journal of Pattern Recognition and Artificial Intelligence, 14(7):875-894, 2000.

21. P.J. Besl, and N.D. Mckay, "A Method for Registration of 3-D shapes", IEEE Trans. on PAMI, 14(2):239-256, 1992.

22. P. Viola, and M. Jones, "Robust Real-time Object Detection", Proc. 2nd Inter. Workshop on Statistical Computational Theories of Vision, 2001.

23. B. Moghaddam, and A. Pentland, "Beyond Euclidean Eigenspaces: Bayesian Matching for Vision recognition", Face Recognition: From Theories to Applications, ISBN 3-540-64410-5, pp.921, 1998.

Human Detection Using Oriented Histograms of Flow and Appearance

Navneet Dalal, Bill Triggs, and Cordelia Schmid

GRAVIR-INRIA, 655 avenue de l'Europe, Montbonnot 38330, France
Firstname.Lastname@inrialpes.fr
http://lear.inrialpes.fr

Abstract. Detecting humans in films and videos is a challenging problem owing to the motion of the subjects, the camera and the background and to variations in pose, appearance, clothing, illumination and background clutter. We develop a detector for standing and moving people in videos with possibly moving cameras and backgrounds, testing several different motion coding schemes and showing empirically that orientated histograms of differential optical flow give the best overall performance. These motion-based descriptors are combined with our Histogram of Oriented Gradient appearance descriptors. The resulting detector is tested on several databases including a challenging test set taken from feature films and containing wide ranges of pose, motion and background variations, including moving cameras and backgrounds. We validate our results on two challenging test sets containing more than 4400 human examples. The combined detector reduces the false alarm rate by a factor of 10 relative to the best appearance-based detector, for example giving false alarm rates of 1 per 20,000 windows tested at 8% miss rate on our Test Set 1.

1 Introduction

Detecting humans in video streams is a challenging problem owing to variations in pose, body shape, appearance, clothing, illumination and background clutter. Moving cameras or backgrounds make it even harder. Potential applications include film and television analysis, on-line pedestrian detection for smart vehicles [8] and video surveillance. Although single-image appearance based detectors have made considerable advances in recent years (*e.g.* [3, 13, 15]), they are not yet reliable enough for many practical applications. On the other hand, certain kinds of movement are very characteristic of humans, so detector performance can potentially be improved by including motion information. Most existing work in this area assumes that the camera and the background are essentially static. This greatly simplifies the problem because the mere presence of motion already provides a strong cue for human presence. For example, Viola *et al.* [23] find that including motion features markedly increases the overall performance of their system, but they assume a fixed surveillance camera viewing a largely static scene. In our case, we wanted a detector that could be used to analyse film and TV content, or to detect pedestrians from a moving car – applications in which the camera and the background often move as much as the people in the scene, if not more. The main challenge is thus to find a set of features that characterize human motion well, while remaining resistant to camera and background motion.

A. Leonardis, H. Bischof, and A. Pinz (Eds.): ECCV 2006, Part II, LNCS 3952, pp. 428–441, 2006.

Fig. 1. Sample images from our human motion database, which contains moving people with significant variation in appearance, pose, clothing, background, illumination, coupled with moving cameras and backgrounds. Each pair shows two consecutive frames.

This paper introduces and evaluates a number of motion-based feature sets for human detection in videos. In particular it studies oriented histograms of various kinds of local differences or differentials of optical flow as motion features, evaluating these both independently and in combination with the Histogram of Oriented Gradient (HOG) appearance descriptors that we originally developed for human detection in static images [3]. The new descriptors are designed to capture the relative motion of different limbs while resisting background motions. Combining them with the appearance descriptors reduces the false alarm rate by an order of magnitude in images with movement while maintaining the performance of the original method [3] in stationary images.

The detectors are evaluated on two new and challenging feature film based data sets, giving excellent results. Fig. 1 shows some typical image pairs from our '*Test Set 1*' (see § 7).

Contents. § 2 briefly reviews the state-of-art in human detection in static and moving images. § 3 describes the overall system architecture. § 4–7 respectively describe the appearance descriptors, the motion descriptors, the optical flow methods and the training and test data sets that we used. § 8 studies the effect of representation choices and parameter settings on performance, and § 9 summarizes the results.

2   Previous Work

We will only mention a few of the more recent works on human detection here – see Gavrilla's survey [7] for older references. A polynomial SVM based pedestrian detector (upright whole-body human detector) using rectified Haar wavelets as input descriptors is described in [17] , with a parts (subwindow) based variant in [16]. The pedestrian detector of Gavrila & Philomen [9] takes a more direct approach, extracting edge images and matching them to a set of learned exemplars using chamfer distance. This has recently been extended to a practical real-time pedestrian detection system [8]. The success of SIFT appearance descriptors [14] for object recognition has motivated several recent approaches. Mikolajczyk *et al.* [15] use position-orientation histograms of binary image edges as image features, combining seven "part" (subwindow) detectors to build a static-image detector that is robust to occlusions. Our own static detector [3] uses a dense grid of SIFT-like blocks with a linear SVM for static-image person detection, giving false alarm rates 1–2 orders of magnitude lower than [17]. Leibe *et al.* [13] developed an effective static-image pedestrian detector for crowded scenes by coding local image patches against a learned codebook and combining the resulting bottom up labels with top-down refinement.

Regarding person detectors that incorporate motion descriptors, Viola *et al.* [23] build a detector for static-camera surveillance applications, using generalized Haar wavelets and block averages of spatiotemporal differences as image and motion features and a computationally efficient rejection chain classifier [1,22,21] trained with AdaBoost [19] feature selection. The inclusion of motion features increases the performance by an order of magnitude relative to a similar static detector. Other surveillance based detectors include the flow-based activity recognition system of Haritaoglu *et al.* [10]. Efros *et al.* [4] used appearance and flow features in an exemplar based detector for long shots of sports players, but quantitative performance results were not given.

3   Overall Architecture

This paper focuses on developing effective motion features so we have adopted a single relatively simple learning framework as a baseline in most of our experiments. For simplicity, we concentrate on detecting people who are upright and fully or almost fully visible. However they may be stationary or moving, against a background that may be stationary or moving. Linear SVM's [20] are used as a baseline classifier. They offer good performance relative to other linear classifiers and they are fast to run, providing at least a prospect of reliable real time detection. Three properties make them valuable for comparative testing work: reliable, repeatable training; the ability to handle large data sets gracefully; and good robustness to different choices of feature sets and parameters. Nonlinear SVM's typically achieve slightly lower error rates, but this comes at the cost of greatly increased run time and in practice we find that the main conclusions about feature sets remain unchanged.

Our person detector combines appearance descriptors extracted from a single frame of a video sequence with motion descriptors extracted from either optical flow or spatiotemporal derivatives against the subsequent frame. It scans a 64×128 pixel window across the image at multiple scales, running a linear SVM classifier on the descriptors extracted from each resulting image window. The classifier is trained to make person/no-person decisions using a set of manually labeled training windows. Fig. 2 gives an overview of the feature extraction process. Image gradient vectors are used to produce weighted votes for local gradient orientation and these are locally histogrammed to produce an appearance descriptor (SIFT / HOG process) [3]. Differentials of optical flow are fed to a similar oriented voting process based on either flow orientation or oriented

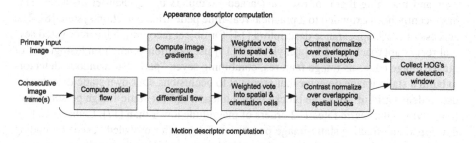

Fig. 2. The feature extraction process for our combined detector

spatial gradients of flow components. Each descriptor set is normalized over local, overlapping blocks of spatial cells, and the resulting normalized histograms are concatenated to make the detection window descriptor vector used in the detector.

For the learning process we use a method similar to that of [3]. We start with a set of training images (here consecutive image pairs so that flow can be used) in which all of the positive training windows (ones containing people) have been manually marked. A fixed set of initial negative training windows was selected by randomly sampling the negative images. A preliminary classifier is trained on the marked positives and initial negatives, and this is used to search the complete set of negative images exhaustively for false alarms. As many of these "hard negatives" as will fit into the available RAM are selected randomly and added to the training set, and the final classifier is trained. Each classifier thus has its own set of hard negatives. This retraining procedure significantly increases the performance of every detector that we have tested. Additional rounds of search for hard negatives make little difference, so are not used. In most of the experiments below the RAM is limited to 1.5 GB, so the larger the descriptor vector, the smaller the number of hard examples that can be included. We think that this is fair as memory is typically the main resource limitation during training.

In use, the algorithm runs a detection window across the image at all positions and scales, giving a detection score at each point. Negative scores are zeroed and a 3D position-scale mean shift process [2] is run to identify significant local peaks in the resulting score. If above threshold, these are declared as detections. Currently there is no attempt to enforce temporal continuity of detections: the detector runs independently in each pair of images.

4   Appearance Descriptors

The static-image part of our descriptor set [3] uses Histogram of Oriented Gradient grids (HOG) – a close relation of the descriptor in Lowe's SIFT approach [14] – to code visual appearance. Briefly, the HOG method tiles the detector window with a dense grid of cells, with each cell containing a local histogram over orientation bins. At each pixel, the image gradient vector is calculated and converted to an angle, voting into the corresponding orientation bin with a vote weighted by the gradient magnitude. Votes are accumulated over the pixels of each cell. The cells are grouped into blocks and a robust normalization process is run on each block to provide strong illumination invariance. The normalized histograms of all of the blocks are concatenated to give the window-level visual descriptor vector for learning. To reduce aliasing, spatial and angular linear interpolation, and in some cases Gaussian windowing over the block, are used during voting. The blocks overlap spatially so that each cell appears several times with different normalizations, as this typically improves performance. See [3] for further details and a study of the effects of the various parameters. The same default parameter settings are used here.

5   Motion Descriptors

To use motion for human detection from moving cameras against dynamic backgrounds we need features that characterize human movements well while remaining resistant to typical camera and background motions. Most of the existing motion descriptors, such as the phase based features of Fleet & Jepson [5] and the generalized wavelet features of Viola *et al.* [23], use absolute motions and hence work well only when the camera and background are largely static. Nor do these representations take into account the lessons learned from the SIFT / HOG family of descriptors [14,15,3]. This section introduces descriptors that use differential flow to cancel out most of the effects of camera motion and HOG like oriented histogram voting to obtain robust coding.

First note that the image flow induced by camera rotation (pan, tilt, roll) varies smoothly across the image irrespective of 3D depth boundaries, and in most applications it is locally essentially translational because significant camera roll is rare. Thus, any kind of local differential or difference of flow cancels out most of the effects of camera rotation. The remaining signal is due to either depth-induced motion parallax between the camera, subject and background, or to independent motion in the scene. Differentials of parallax flows are concentrated essentially at 3D depth boundaries, while those of independent motions are largest at motion boundaries. For human subjects, both types of boundaries coincide with limb and body edges, so flow differentials are good cues for the outline of a person. However we also expect internal dynamics such as relative limb motions to be quite discriminant for human motions and differentials taken within the subject's silhouette are needed to capture these. Thus, flow-based features can focus either on coding motion (and hence depth) boundaries, or on coding internal dynamics and relative displacements of the limbs.

Notation. $\mathcal{I}^x, \mathcal{I}^y$ denote images containing the x (horizontal) and y (vertical) components of optical flow, $\mathcal{I}^w = (\mathcal{I}^x, \mathcal{I}^y)$ denote the 2D flow image ($w = (x, y)$), and $\mathcal{I}^x_x, \mathcal{I}^x_y, \mathcal{I}^y_x, \mathcal{I}^y_y$ denote the corresponding x- and y-derivative differential flow images. E.g., $\mathcal{I}^x_y = \frac{d}{dy}\mathcal{I}^x$ is the y-derivative of the x component of optical flow.

5.1 Motion Boundary Based Coding

For motion boundary coding it is natural to try to capture the local orientations of motion edges by emulating the static-image HOG descriptors [3]. The simplest approach is to treat the two flow components $\mathcal{I}^x, \mathcal{I}^y$ as independent 'images', take their local gradients separately, find the corresponding gradient magnitudes and orientations, and use these as weighted votes into local orientation histograms in the same way as for the standard gray scale HOG. We call this family of schemes *Motion Boundary Histograms (MBH)* (see Fig. 3). A separate histogram can be built for each flow component, or the two channels can be combined, *e.g.* by the winner-takes-all voting method used to handle color channels in [3]. We find that separate histograms are more discriminant. As with standard gray scale HOG, it is best to take spatial derivatives at the smallest possible scale ($[1, 0, -1]$ mask) without any form of smoothing.

5.2 Internal / Relative Dynamics Based Coding

One could argue that the static appearance descriptor already captures much of the available boundary information, so that the flow based descriptor should focus more on capturing complementary information about internal or relative motions. This suggests that flow differences should be computed between pairs of nearby, but not necessarily

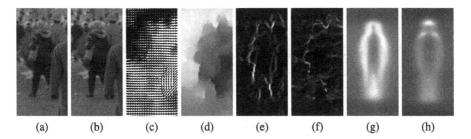

(a)   (b)   (c)   (d)   (e)   (f)   (g)   (h)

Fig. 3. Illustration of the MBH descriptor. (a,b) Reference images at time t and $t+1$. (c,d) Computed optical flow, and flow magnitude showing motion boundaries. (e,f) Gradient magnitude of flow field $\mathcal{I}^x$, $\mathcal{I}^y$ for image pair (a,b). (g,h) Average MBH descriptor over all training images for flow field $\mathcal{I}^x$, $\mathcal{I}^y$.

neighboring, points, and that angular voting should be based on the direction of the flow difference vector, not the direction of the spatial derivative displacement. So in opposition to MBH, we use $(\mathcal{I}^x_x, \mathcal{I}^y_x)$ and $(\mathcal{I}^x_y, \mathcal{I}^y_y)$ as the pairs for angular voting, and the simple x, y derivatives are replaced by spatial differences taken at larger scales, perhaps in several different directions. We will call this family of schemes Internal Motion Histograms (IMH). Ideally, IMH descriptors would directly capture the relative movements of different limbs, *e.g.* left *vs.* right leg, but choosing the necessary spatial displacements for differencing would require reliable part detectors. Instead we test simple variants based on fixed spatial displacements, as follows:

IMHdiff is the simplest IMH descriptor. It takes fine-scale derivatives, using $(\mathcal{I}^x_x, \mathcal{I}^y_x)$ and $(\mathcal{I}^x_y, \mathcal{I}^y_y)$ to create two relative-flow-direction based oriented histograms. As with MBH, using separate orientation histograms for the x- and y-derivatives is better than combining them. Variants of IMHdiff use larger (but still central) spatial displacements for differencing – 5 pixels apart ($[1, 0, 0, 0, -1]$ mask), or even 7 – and take spatial differencing steps along several different directions, *e.g.* including diagonal axes.

IMHcd uses the blocks-of-cells structure of the HOG descriptors differently. It uses $3{\times}3$ blocks of cells, in each of the 8 outer cells computing flow differences for each pixel relative to the corresponding pixel in the central cell and histogramming to give an orientation histogram[1]. Figure 4(a) illustrates. The resulting 8 histograms are normalized as a block. The motivation is that if the person's limb width is approximately the same as the cell size, IMHcd can capture relative displacements of the limbs w.r.t. to the background and nearby limbs. The results in § 8 support this hypothesis.

IMHmd is similar to IMHcd, but instead of using the corresponding pixel in the central cell as a reference flow, it uses the average of the corresponding pixels in all 9 cells. The resulting 9 histograms are normalized as a block.

IMHwd is also similar to IMHcd but uses Haar wavelet like operators rather than non-central differences, as shown in Fig. 4(b).

---

[1] IMHcd uses non-central cell-width spatial differences that access only pixels within the block, whereas IMHdiff uses central differences and in the boundary cells it accesses pixels that lie outside the block.

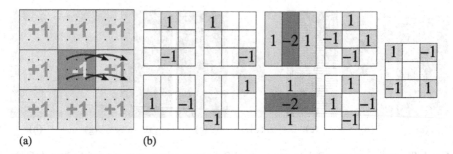

(a)   (b)

Fig. 4. Different coding schemes for IMH descriptors. (a) One block of IMHcd coding scheme. The block is partitioned into cells. The dots in each cell represent the cell pixels. The arrows emerging from the central cell show the central pixel used to compute differences for the corresponding pixel in the neighbouring cell. Similar differences are computed for each of the 8 neighbouring cells. Values +1 and −1 represent the difference weights. (b) The wavelet operators used in the IMHwd motion coding scheme.

ST Diff. We also evaluated a scheme inspired by Viola *et al.* [23] based on simple spatiotemporal differencing rather than flow. For each pixel, its 3×3 stride-8 neighborhood at the next time step is taken and its image intensity is subtracted from each of these 9 pixels. The absolute values are accumulated over each cell to make a 9 bin histogram for the cell, which then undergoes the usual block normalization process.

5.3   Descriptor Parameters

For the combined flow and appearance detectors with the optimal cell size of 8×8 pixels, memory constraints limit us to a total of about 81 histogram bins per cell. (Increasing the histogram size beyond this is possible, but it reduces the number of hard negatives that can be fitted into memory during re-training to such an extent that performance suffers). In the experiments below, we test: MBH with 9 gradient orientations, 2 separate flow components, and 4× block overlap; IMHdiff with 2 displacements (horizontal and vertical $[1, 0, -1]$ masks), 9 flow orientations and 4× block overlap; and IMHcd, IMHwd and IMHmd with eight 8-pixel displacements and 6 flow orientations.

All of the methods use orientation histograms with votes weighted by vector modulus followed by a block-level normalization – essentially the same scheme as the original HOG descriptor [3]. We tested various different bin sizes, normalization schemes, *etc.* with similar conclusions to [3]. For both MBH and IMHdiff, fine (9 bin) orientation coding with 2×2 blocks of 8×8 pixel cells seem to be best. 3 × 3 blocks of cells (9× block overlap) perform better for the flow-only MBH classifier, but for the combined detectors the performance of this combination drops owing to the increased feature size. Changing the cell size from 8 × 8 to 6 × 6 only reduces the performance slightly. Good normalization of the blocks is critical and for the flow descriptors Lowe's hysteresis-based L2 normalization seems to do significantly better than L2 or L1-sqrt normalization. We tried larger displacement masks (3- and 5- pixel displacement) for MBH but found that the performance drops. For the IMHcd/wd/md schemes, 6 and 9 orientation bins give the same performance (we use 6 below), and Lowe's hysteresis based L2 normalization still works best, but only by a small margin.

We also evaluated variants that use the least squares image prediction error of the estimated flow as a flow quality metric, down-weighting the histogram vote in proportion to $\exp(-|e|/\sigma)$, where e is the fitting error over the local 5×5 window. This very slightly ($\lesssim 1\%$) improves the performance provided that σ is not set too small.

We also tested various motion descriptors that do not use orientation voting (*e.g.* based simply on the modulus of velocity), but the results were significantly worse.

6   Optical Flow Estimation

We tried several optical flow methods. Our initial testing was done with the Otago implementation [6] of the Proesmans *et al.* [18] multi-scale nonlinear diffusion based algorithm. This gives dense high-quality sub-pixel motion estimates but it is computationally expensive (15 seconds per frame). Also, motion boundaries are critical for human detection and we recently began to suspect that the Otago flows were over-regularized for this application. To test this we implemented a simple but fast flow method based on the constant brightness assumption [11]. Flow is found top-down in a multi-scale approach, with initial flow estimates made at a coarse scale propagated downwards and refined in fine scale steps. The flow $\mathbf{w}$ is estimated *independently* at each pixel by solving a damped Linear Least Squares equation $\mathbf{w} = (\mathbf{A}^\top \mathbf{A} + \beta \mathbf{I})^{-1} \mathbf{A}^\top \mathbf{b}$ over a small $N \times N$ neighborhood, where $\mathbf{b}$ is an N^2 column vector encoding the temporal image differences, $\mathbf{A}$ is an $N^2 \times 2$ matrix of spatial gradients $[\mathcal{I}_x, \mathcal{I}_y]$, and β is a damping factor included to reduce numerical issues arising from singular $\mathbf{A}^\top \mathbf{A}$. The model does not include any explicit spatial regularization or smoothing and its flow estimates are visibly less accurate than the Otago ones, but our experiments show that using it in the combined detector reduces false positives by a factor of more than 3 at 8% miss rate. In fact, any regularization aimed at improving the flow smoothness appears to reduce the detector performance. Our method is also much faster than the Otago one, running in 1 second on DVD resolution 752×396 images, with $N = 5$ and a scale refinement step of 1.3. The new method is used in all of the experiments in § 8 unless otherwise noted.

We also tested motion descriptors based on an MPEG-4 block matcher taken from the www.xvid.org codec. No attempt was made to enforce motion continuity between blocks. Even though the matching estimates were visually good, the detection results were not competitive. We think that there are several reasons for this. Firstly, block matching provides only one vote for each cell, whereas with optical flow each pixel provides a separate vote into the histogram. Secondly, the block matching flow estimates do not have deep sub-pixel accuracy. Experiments on rounding the flow values from the Otago code showed that even 1/10 of a pixel of rounding causes the performance to drop significantly (the need for accurate orientation voting is one reason for this). Thirdly, 8×8 MPEG blocks are too large for the best results.

7   Data Sets

To train our detectors, we selected shots from various movie DVDs and personal digital camera video sequences and annotated the humans in them. Our main training set, '*Training Set 1*', was obtained from 5 different DVDs. It contains a total of 182 shots with 2781 human examples (5562 including left-right reflections). We created two test sets. *'Test Set 1'* contains 50 shots and 1704 human examples from unseen shots from the DVDs used in *Training Set 1*. *Test Set 2* is more challenging, containing 2700 human examples from 128 shots from 6 new DVDs.

We have also used the static-image training and test sets from [3] (available at http://pascal.inrialpes.fr/data/human/). In this paper, we call these the *'Static Training/Test Sets'*. They contain respectively 2416 training and 1132 test images. Even though the *Static Training Set* has no (zero) flow, we find that including it along with *Training Set 1* significantly improves the performance of both the static and the combined detectors (see § 8). More precisely, the detector performance on *Test Set 1* improves, without changing that of the static detector on the *Static Test Set*. This is perhaps because the *Set 1* images contain many poses that do not appear in the *Static* sets – notably running and other rapid actions.

8   Experiments

To quantify the performance of the various detectors we plot Detection Error Tradeoff (DET) curves, *i.e.* Miss Rate $(1 - \text{Precision or } N_{\text{FalseNeg}}/(N_{\text{FalseNeg}} + N_{\text{TruePos}}))$ versus False Positives Per Window tested (FPPW) on logarithmic scales. DET plots present the same information as Receiver Operating Characteristic (ROC) curves in a more readable form. Lower curves are better.

We begin by comparing the results of the motion descriptors introduced above, trained and tested on Set 1. Figure 5(a,b) give results respectively for detectors learned with the motion descriptors alone, and for detectors that include both these features and the HOG appearance descriptors. The oriented histogram of differential flow schemes MBH and IMHdiff with the Proesmans flow method dominate the motion-only results. In fact for the video test sets (which do contain many frames without much visible movement) these motion features alone are within an order of magnitude of the static HOG detector and significantly better than the static Haar wavelet detector. When motion and appearance features are combined, neither the Proesmans flow method nor the MBH descriptors perform so well and it is IMHcd and IMHmd computed using our flow method that are the leaders. Below we use SHOG + IMHcd as the default combined detector, although SHOG + IMHmd would lead to similar conclusions.

Fig. 5 shows that motion-only results are not a good guide to the performance of the combined detector. The reduced spread of the results in the combined case suggests that there is a considerable degree of redundancy between the appearance and motion channels. In particular, IMHdiff and MBH are the schemes with the smallest spatial strides and thus the greatest potential for redundancy with the human boundary cues used by the appearance based descriptors – factors that may explain their reduced performance after combination. Similarly, the strong regularization of the Proesmans' flow estimates may make them effective cues for motion (and hence occlusion) boundaries, while the unregularized nature of ours means that they capture motion within thin limbs more accurately and hence provide information that is more complementary to the appearance descriptors.

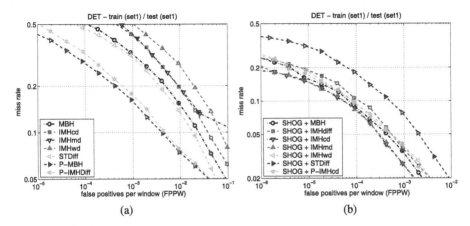

Fig. 5. A comparison of the different motion descriptors, trained on *Training Set 1* and tested on *Test Set 1*, using: (a) the motion feature set alone; and (b) the motion feature set combined with the SHOG appearance descriptor. The prefix 'P' in the MBH and IMH legends denotes the same methods using Proesmans' flow estimates.

Figure 6 demonstrates the overall performance of a selection of our detectors on several different test sets. Unless otherwise noted, the detectors are trained on the combined *Set 1* and *Static* Training Sets. The static (appearance based) detectors shown are: SHOG – the HOG detector of [3]; SHOG (static) – SHOG trained on the *Static Training Set* alone, as in [3]; and Wavelet – our version of the static Haar wavelet based detector of [17]. Two combined detectors are also shown: SHOG + IMHcd – SHOG combined with the IMHcd flow feature (8-pixel steps in 8-neighbor directions); and SHOG + ST Diff – SHOG combined with Viola *et al.* spatiotemporal differences [23].

Again the good performance of the SHOG + IMHcd combination is apparent. The absolute results on Test Set 2 are an order of magnitude worse than on Test Set 1 owing to the more challenging nature of the images, but the relative rankings of the different methods are remarkably stable. Overall, on video data for which motion estimates are available, the false alarm rates of the best combined detectors are an order of magnitude lower than those for the best static-appearance-based ones.

Given that we want methods that can detect people reliably whether or not they are moving, we were concerned that the choice of method might be sensitive to the relative proportion of moving and of static people in the videos. To check this, we tested the detectors not only on the pure video *Test Sets 1* and *2*, but also on the combination of these with the *Static Test Set* (again with static image flows being zero). The results are shown in fig. 6(c–d). Diluting the fraction of moving examples naturally reduces the advantage of the combined methods relative to the static ones, but the relative ranking of the methods remains unchanged. Somewhat surprisingly, table 1 shows that when used on entirely static images for which there is no flow, the best combined detectors do marginally *better* the best static one. The images here are from the *Static Test Set*, with the detectors trained on *Training Set 1* plus the *Static Training Set* as before.

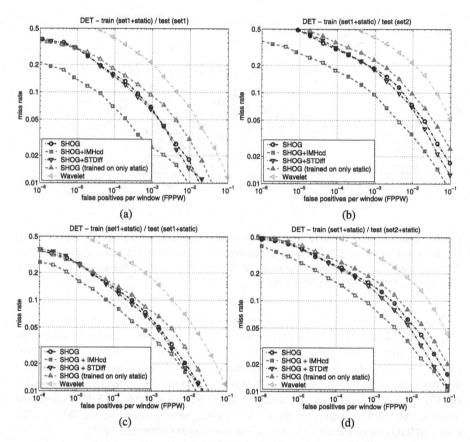

Fig. 6. An overview of the performance of our various detectors. All detectors are trained on *Training Set 1* combined with the *Static Training Set* with flow set to zero. They are tested respectively on: (a) *Test Set 1*; (b) *Test Set 2*; (c) *Test Set 1* plus the *Static Test Set*; (d) *Test Set 2* plus the *Static Test Set*.

Table 1. The miss rates of various detectors trained on Set 1 + Static images and tested on purely Static images. Despite the complete lack of flow information, the combined detectors provide slightly better performance than the static one.

FPPW	10^{-3}	10^{-4}	10^{-5}
SHOG	6.2%	11.4%	19.8%
SHOG + IMHcd	5.8%	11.0%	19.8%
SHOG + ST Diff	5.7%	10.5%	19.7%

Figure 7 shows some sample detections of the combined detector (SHOG + IMHcd trained on Set 1 + Static) on images from *Test Set 2*. *Set 2* contains challenging images taken from different films from the training images. Here there are shots of people in Indian costume, some dance sequences, and people in crowds that are different from anything seen in the training images.

Fig. 7. Sample detections on *Test Set 2* from the combined SHOG + IMHcd detector trained on *Set 1 + Static*. Note the variations in pose, appearance, background and lightning.

The experiments shown here use linear SVMs. Informal tests with Gaussian kernel SVMs suggest that these would reduce false positives by an additional factor of about 2, at a cost of a 5000-fold increase in run time.

Mixture of Experts. The combined-feature detectors above are *monolithic* – they concatenate the motion and appearance features into a single large feature vector and train a combined classifier on it. We have also tested an alternative *Mixture of Experts* architecture. In this, separate detectors are learned from the appearance features and from the motion features, and a second stage classifier is then trained to combine the (real valued scalar) outputs of these to produce a combined detector. In our case the second stage classifier is a linear SVM over a 2D feature space (the appearance score and the motion score), so the final system remains linear in the input features. This approach keeps the feature space dimensions relatively low during training, thus allowing more hard negatives to be included at each stage. (Indeed, for the 2D second stage classifier there can be millions of them). In our experiments these effects mitigate the losses due to separate training and the linear Mixture of Experts classifier actually performs slightly better than the best monolithic detector. For now the differences are marginal (less than 1%), but the Mixture of Experts architecture provides more flexibility and may ultimately be preferable. The component classifiers could also be combined in a more sophisticated way, for example using a rejection cascade [1, 22, 21] to improve the runtime.

9   Summary and Conclusions

We have developed a family of high-performance detectors for fully visible humans in videos with moving people, cameras and backgrounds. The detectors combine gradient based appearance descriptors with differential optical flow based motion descriptors in a linear SVM framework. Both motion and appearance channels use oriented histogram voting to achieve a robust descriptor. We studied various different motion coding schemes but found that although there are considerable performance differences between them when motion features alone are used, the differences are greatly reduced when the features are used in combination with static appearance descriptors. The best combined schemes used motion descriptors based on oriented histogramming of differences of unregularized multiscale flow relative to corresponding pixels in adjacent cells (IMHcd) or to local averages of these (IMHmd).

Acknowledgments. This work was supported by the European Union research projects ACEMEDIA and PASCAL. SVMLight [12] proved reliable for training large-scale SVM's. We thank Matthijs Douze for his comments on the manuscript.

References

[1] S. Baker and S. Nayar. Pattern rejection. In *Proceedings of the Conference on Computer Vision and Pattern Recognition, San Francisco, California, USA*, 1996.

[2] D. Comaniciu. An algorithm for data-driven bandwidth selection. IEEE *Transactions on Pattern Analysis and Machine Intelligence*, 25(2):281–288, 2003.

[3] N. Dalal and B. Triggs. Histograms of oriented gradients for human detection. In *Proceedings of the Conference on Computer Vision and Pattern Recognition, San Diego, California, USA*, pages 886–893, 2005.

[4] A. Efros, A. Berg, G. Mori, and J. Malik. Recognizing action at a distance. In *Proceedings of the 9th International Conference on Computer Vision, Nice, France*, pages II:726–733, 2003.

[5] D. Fleet and A. Jepson. Stability of phase information. IEEE *Transactions on Pattern Analysis and Machine Intelligence*, 15(12):1253–1268, 1993.

[6] B. Galvin, B. McCane, K. Novins, D. Mason, and S. Mills. Recovering motion fields: An evaluation of eight optical flow algorithms. In *Proceedings of the ninth British Machine Vision Conference, Southampton, England*, 1998. http://www.cs.otago.ac.nz/research/vision.

[7] D. M. Gavrila. The visual analysis of human movement: A survey. *Computer Vision and Image Understanding*, 73(1):82–98, 1999.

[8] D. M. Gavrila, J. Giebel, and S. Munder. Vision-based pedestrian detection: the protector+ system. In *Proc. of the IEEE Intelligent Vehicles Symposium, Parma, Italy*, 2004.

[9] D. M. Gavrila and V. Philomin. Real-time object detection for smart vehicles. In *Proceedings of the Conference on Computer Vision and Pattern Recognition, Fort Collins, Colorado, USA*, pages 87–93, 1999.

[10] I. Haritaoglu, D. Harwood, and L. Davis. W4: Real-time surveillance of people and their activities. IEEE *Transactions on Pattern Analysis and Machine Intelligence*, 22(8):809–830, 2000.

[11] K.P. Horn and G. Schunck. Determining optical flow. *Artificial Intelligence*, 17:185–203, 1981.

[12] T. Joachims. Making large-scale svm learning practical. In B. Schlkopf, C. Burges, and A. Smola, editors, *Advances in Kernel Methods - Support Vector Learning*. The MIT Press, Cambridge, MA, USA, 1999.

[13] B. Leibe, E. Seemann, and B. Schiele. Pedestrian detection in crowded scenes. In *Proceedings of the Conference on Computer Vision and Pattern Recognition, San Diego, California, USA*, pages 876–885, June 2005.

[14] D. G. Lowe. Distinctive image features from scale-invariant keypoints. *International Journal of Computer Vision*, 60(2):91–110, 2004.

[15] K. Mikolajczyk, C. Schmid, and A. Zisserman. Human detection based on a probabilistic assembly of robust part detectors. In *Proceedings of the 8th European Conference on Computer Vision, Prague, Czech Republic*, volume I, pages 69–81, 2004.

[16] A. Mohan, C. Papageorgiou, and T. Poggio. Example-based object detection in images by components. IEEE *Transactions on Pattern Analysis and Machine Intelligence*, 23(4): 349–361, April 2001.

[17] C. Papageorgiou and T. Poggio. A trainable system for object detection. *International Journal of Computer Vision*, 38(1):15–33, 2000.

[18] M. Proesmans, L. Van Gool, E. Pauwels, and A. Oosterlinck. Determination of optical flow and its discontinuities using non-linear diffusion. In *Proceedings of the 3rd European Conference on Computer Vision, Stockholm, Sweden*, volume 2, pages 295–304, 1994.

[19] R. E. Schapire. The boosting approach to machine learning, an overview. In *MSRI Workshop on Nonlinear Estimation and Classification*, 2002.

[20] Bernhard Schölkopf and Alex Smola. *Learning with Kernels*. The MIT Press, Cambridge, MA, USA, 2002.

[21] J. Sun, J.M. Rehg, and A. Bobick. Automatic cascade training with perturbation bias. In *Proceedings of the Conference on Computer Vision and Pattern Recognition, Washington, DC, USA*, pages II:276–283, 2004.

[22] P. Viola and M. Jones. Rapid object detection using a boosted cascade of simple features. In *Proceedings of the Conference on Computer Vision and Pattern Recognition, Kauai, Hawaii, USA*, volume I, pages 511–518, 2001.

[23] P. Viola, M. J. Jones, and D. Snow. Detecting pedestrians using patterns of motion and appearance. In *Proceedings of the 9th International Conference on Computer Vision, Nice, France*, volume 1, pages 734–741, 2003.

Cyclostationary Processes on Shape Spaces for Gait-Based Recognition

David Kaziska[1] and Anuj Srivastava[2]

[1] Department of Mathematics and Statistics,
Air Force Institute of Technology, Dayton, OH
[2] Department of Statistics, Florida State University, Tallahassee, FL

Abstract. We present a novel approach to gait recognition that considers gait sequences as cyclostationary processes on a shape space of simple closed curves. Consequently, gait analysis reduces to quantifying differences between statistics underlying these stochastic processes. The main steps in the proposed approach are: (i) off-line extraction of human silhouettes from IR video data, (ii) use of piecewise-geodesic paths, connecting the observed shapes, to smoothly interpolate between them, (iii) computation of an average gait cycle within class (i.e. associated with a person) using average shapes, (iv) registration of average cycles using linear and nonlinear time scaling, (iv) comparisons of average cycles using geodesic lengths between the corresponding registered shapes. We illustrate this approach on infrared video clips involving 26 subjects.

1 Introduction

We study the problem of analyzing videos of humans walking, with a goal of recognizing them using an analysis of their gait. Gait analysis closely relates to statistical analysis of shapes of objects. Assuming that one focuses on silhouettes of human beings, as they are walking, gait analysis becomes the problem of analyzing sequences of shapes of closed curves. In this sense gait analysis is an extension of shape analysis; shape analysis deals with comparisons of individual shapes, while gait analysis deals with comparisons of sequences of shapes. A gait sequence can be considered as a stochastic process on the shape space, with finite, noisy measurements. Therefore, gait analysis can be considered as the science of analyzing stochastic processes on shape manifolds. Furthermore, considering the repetitive nature of a gait sequence, one can restrict to the family of cyclo-stationary processes, i.e. processes whose statistics repeat themselves periodically.

An an application of gait analysis, we will focus on infrared (IR) image sequences as the observed data, an example is shown in Figure 1. Depending on the quality of infrared image detector, and ambient conditions such as temperature, humidity, windchill, etc, the task of gait analysis using IR sequences is somewhat more complicated than that using visual spectrum video sequences. Essentially, the task of extracting shapes, or silhouettes, automatically becomes more difficult in this application. However, in this paper we avoid that issue by

A. Leonardis, H. Bischof, and A. Pinz (Eds.): ECCV 2006, Part II, LNCS 3952, pp. 442–453, 2006.

working with a good quality IR camera and known backgrounds. The main focus here is on a statistical analysis of shape processes for gait analysis.

1.1   Challenges and Past Work

What are the different components and issues associated with gait-based recognition of human beings? To develop a comprehensive system, one needs to develop the following components:

1. Representation: First, one needs to choose a representation of human appearance in images that lends itself to gait analysis. The chosen representation should highlight differences in walking styles between people, and should suppress the variations in walking style of a person. Also, a practical need is to be able to extract these representations from video sequences fast, and in presence of noise, clutter and partial obscuration. It is important to point out that very few of the existing approaches, including the one proposed here, utilize real-time, automated extraction of representations from video data. In other words, the focus in the recent literature is on the methodology and not on issue of real-time extraction of features/representations. Several representations have been suggested in the past: binary images or silhouettes [4, 2, 10, 11], width of silhouettes [4], shapes of configurations of landmarks [9], systems of articulate parts, etc. Each has its advantages and disadvantages. A survey of different ideas currently used in gait analysis is presented in [8].

2. Models: Once the representations are chosen, the next issue is to impose models for analyzing gait. Several papers have studied parametric dynamic models or state equations for analyzing gait processes [9, 1]. In the interest of computational efficiency, one would like to use parametric models while the nonparametric models provide a broad generality to the approach. A more general approach is to consider gaits as stochastic processes in a certain representation space; then one needs a stochastic model to characterize these processes. As noted earlier, a good model highlights interclass variability while suppressing intra-class variability.

3. Classification: Given probability models governing the evolution of a gait process, the process of human identification or classification is simply that of hypothesis testing. Some papers reduce this problem to the choice of metric between gait representations, and use a distance-based classifier, e.g. the nearest neighbor classifier, to perform recognition.

1.2   Our Approach

Our approach is to represent a human appearance using the shape of its boundary. We consider this boundary as a closed curve in the image plane, and analyze its shape during gait analysis. An important point here is that curves are considered in continuum and not just a collection of landmarks as is done in classical shape analysis [3]. The shapes of all closed curves form a shape space $\mathcal{S}$ and shape variation due to human motion forms a stochastic process on $\mathcal{S}$. Furthermore, due to the periodicity of human walk the resulting process becomes cyclostationary. Any two gait observations can be considered as two sample paths on

S, and our goal is to quantify differences between them. We accomplish this by registering two paths on S and then comparing corresponding points along the two paths; these points are actually shapes of two closed curves and to compare them we use geodesics connecting them on S. In other words, geodesic lengths quantify differences between individual silhouettes. In order to remove intra-class variability, i.e. variability associated with different gait observations of the same human being, we compute average gait processes and use them for recognition, rather than using single sample paths. Another important step is to register the observed gait cycles using either linear or nonlinear time scaling before they can be averaged. This often requires interpolating between observed shapes to obtain the same number of shapes in all cycles. We form piecewise-geodesic paths between observed shapes for this interpolation. The main strengths of this approach are:

1. It chooses the boundaries of human silhouettes to analyze gait; **analysis of curves is computationally faster** and more immune to noise than analysis of full images even if they are binary.
2. It removes shape-preserving transformations – translation, rotation, and scale – from representations of human appearances, making gait analysis relatively immune to viewing angles and imaging distances. It is **easier to remove these transformations for curves** than for binary images.
3. Several papers have pointed out the use of gait cycles as the basic units for comparisons. Modeling gaits as **cyclostationary processes on a shape space provides a formal, nonparametric framework** for a quantitative study of gaits.
4. Computation of mean cycles, on an appropriate shape space, removes the intra-class variability. Similarly, the use of **geodesics on shape spaces provides natural tools** for: (i) interpolating between shapes during registration of gait cycles, and (ii) comparison of individual shapes during comparisons of cycles. These tools may not be available in other approaches.

2 Experimental Setup and Data Generation

In our experiments described later we have used two IR cameras: (i) Raytheon PalmIR Pro with a spectral range of 7-14 μm, using an uncooled BST, producing images of 320 × 240 pixels, and having a field of view of 36 × 27°. (ii) FLIR Systems' Thermovision A40V. It uses a focal plane array, made of uncooled microbolometer and produces images and video of 320 × 240 pixels. It has a thermal sensitivity of 80mK at 30°C, a spectral range of 7.5 - 13 μm and a field of view of 24 × 10° at 0.3m. The first camera uses an older technology provides noisy images with low sensitivity, while the second is a new generation with higher thermal sensitivity and thus lower noise. Sample images from A40 are shown in Figure 1 top row.

We need to extract the boundaries of human silhouettes in the observed images for gait analysis. For PalmIR camera, with noisy images, the automated methods have not been successful and we resorted to manual extraction of the

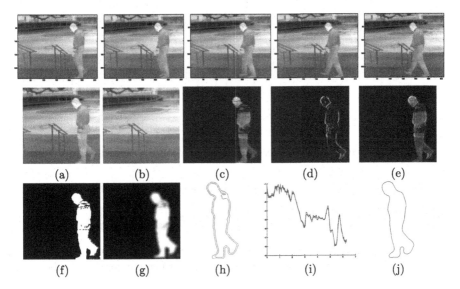

Fig. 1. Top row: A portion of IR sequence. Middle row: (a) Original frame, (b) background frame, (c) image after background subtraction, (d) edge estimation using motion, (e) composite image. Bottom row: (f) binary image after a low threshold, (g) smoothed using a Gaussian filter, (h) level sets, (i) direction functions of outermost level – before and after wavelet denoising, and (j) the final shape.

required curves. However, for the high contrast A40 camera, the process of automated boundary extraction works better and uses background subtraction and simple ideas from motion estimation. Shown in Figure 1 is an illustration of the automated extraction process. Figure 1(a) and (b) show the original IR image with and without the subject. Panel (c) shows the difference image and panel (d) shows the motion-based edge detection. In this case, this frame is simply an absolute difference of two successive image frames. A convex combination of images in (c) and (d) is used to extract the contour via thresholding, wavelet smoothing, and level set extraction. The final curve is shown in the panel (j).

3   A Framework for Gait Analysis

Let $\mathcal{S}$ be the space of shapes defined later. We are interested in studying a stochastic process $X(t) \in \mathcal{S}$ whose statistics repeat themselves in time. More formally, we will focus on a family of cyclostationary stochastic processes in $\mathcal{S}$.

Definition 1 (Cylostationary). *A stochastic process is called cyclostationary with a period τ if the joint probability distribution of the random variables $X(t_1), X(t_2), \ldots, X(t_n)$ is same as that of $X(t_1 + \tau), X(t_2 + \tau), \ldots, X(t_n + \tau)$, for all $t_1, t_2, \ldots, t_n$ and for all n. In particular, the random quantities $X(t)$ and $X(t + \tau)$ have the same probability distribution.*

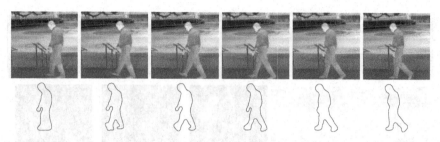

Fig. 2. Sequence of silhouettes extracted automatically as described in Figure 1

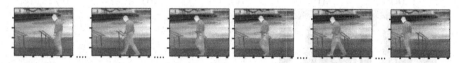

Fig. 3. The sequence from legs together to right leg forward to legs together is the first half-cycle. The sequence from legs-together to left leg forward to legs together is the second half cycle.

Therefore, in our notation we generally consider the time t to be modulo τ so that $t \in [0, \tau)$.

In the context of gait analysis, we consider a *full cycle* as the period starting from when legs and hands are all together to the time of return to a similar state. The top row of Figure 3 shows the first half-cycle where the left foot goes forward and the right foot catches up, and the bottom row shows the second half-cycle where the right foot moves first. We will assume that gait sequence associated with a person is a cyclostationary process on a shape space. The duration of a full cycle corresponds to the period τ of the process. Like any cyclostationary process, it suffices to study statistics of a gait sequence in $[0, \tau]$.

Given two stochastic processes, our goal is to quantify differences between them. Let $X(t)$ and $Y(t)$ be two gait processes on the shape space $\mathcal{S}$, with periods τ_x and τ_y, respectively, our goal is to develop a metric $d(X, Y)$, with certain desired properties. A simple idea is to use the mean squared distance:

$$d_p(X, Y) = \underset{\kappa \in [0, \tau_y], \phi}{\operatorname{argmin}} E \left[\left(\int_0^{\tau_x} d(X(t), Y(\kappa + \phi(t)))^2 dt \right) \right], \quad (1)$$

where E denotes expectation, $d(\cdot, \cdot)$ denotes a metric defined on an appropriate shape space, ϕ denotes a mapping between $[0, \tau_x]$ and $[0, \tau_y]$ that registers the two cycles, and κ denotes a possible relative time-shift between the two paths. An alternate form is to use squared distance of the mean cycles:

$$d_p(X, Y) = \underset{\kappa \in [0, \tau_y], \phi}{\operatorname{argmin}} \left(\int_0^{\tau_x} d(E[X(t)], E[Y(\kappa + \phi(t))])^2 dt \right),$$

where the expectations $E[X(t)$ and $E[Y(t)]$ are computed on the shape space $\mathcal{S}$ in a suitable fashion. We choose this later quantity and use its discrete form:

$$d_p(X,Y) = \operatorname*{argmin}_{\kappa \in [0,\tau_y], \phi} \left(\sum_{t=1}^{T} d(\overline{X}(t), \overline{Y}(\kappa + \phi(t)))^2 \right), \qquad (2)$$

where $\overline{X}$ and $\overline{Y}$ are sample Karcher means of the processes X and Y at times $t = 1, \ldots, T$. Next we specify our choices of $\mathcal{S}$, $d(\cdot, \cdot)$, Karcher mean, and ϕ.

3.1   Analysis of Silhouettes' Shapes

For comparing shapes of planar curves, a recent emphasis has been on using functions, such as direction function or curvature function, for representing curves, and add a closure condition to analyze shapes [5]. One extension is to allow for shapes to stretch and compress, in order for a better matching of feature points [7], as follows. A parameterized curve in $\mathbb{R}^2$ of length 2π, denoted by α, is represented by a pair of function (ϕ, θ) such that at any point $s \in [0, 2\pi]$, we have $\alpha'(s) = \exp(\phi(s)) \exp(j\theta(s))$, where $j = \sqrt{-1}$. ϕ is called the *log-speed function* and θ is called the *direction function* of the curve α. Consider the space $\mathcal{C}$ of all closed curves of length 2π, and average direction π, in $\mathbb{R}^2$ given by:

$$\mathcal{C} = \{(\phi, \theta)| \int_0^{2\pi} e^{\phi(s)} e^{j\theta(s)} ds = 0, \int_0^{2\pi} e^{\phi(s)} ds = 0, \int_0^{2\pi} \theta e^{\phi(s)} ds = \pi \}.$$

Note that the variability generated by shape-preserving transformations (rotation, translation, and scale) are already removed, but the variability resulting from different placements of origin on α, and different re-parameterizations of $[0, 2\pi]$ remain. The former variability results from the group action of $\mathbb{S}^1$, the unit circle, and the latter results from the group action of $\mathcal{D}$, the set of all automorphisms $\{\gamma : [0, 2\pi] \mapsto [0, 2\pi]\}$. Therefore, the shape space is defined to be a quotient space $\mathcal{S} = \mathcal{C}/(\mathbb{S}^1 \times \mathcal{D})$.

An efficient technique for quantifying shape differences is to compute a geodesic path in $\mathcal{S}$ connecting the two shapes, and then use its length to quantify shape differences. An integral part of this computation is to find an optimal matching of points across shapes. That is, given two shapes (ϕ_1, θ_1) and (ϕ_2, θ_2), we are interested in finding a re-parametrization γ of (ϕ_2, θ_2) such that it minimizes the matching cost: $\int_0^{2\pi} \left(\lambda \|(\phi_1(s), \theta_1(s)) - (\phi_2(s), \theta_2(s)) \circ \gamma\|^2 + (1 - \lambda)|\gamma'(s)|^2 \right) ds$. Here, λ is a parameter that balances between stretching and bending. Shown in Figure 4 are some examples of this matching. Note that the matching process works well whether the legs are apart or together, hands are visible or not, etc. The computation of a geodesic is based on a shooting method [5]. To illustrate this idea by example, shown in Figure 5 are some examples of geodesic paths between shapes of human silhouettes. Intermediate shapes denote equally-spaced points along geodesics connecting the end shapes. For any two shapes (ϕ_1, θ_1) and (ϕ_2, θ_2), the length of geodesic path between them forms a natural tool to compare them and is denoted by $d((\phi_1, \theta_1), (\phi_2, \theta_2))$. Also, we will use the function $\Psi(t)$ to denote the geodesic path, so that $\Psi(0) = (\phi_1, \theta_1)$ and $\Psi(1) = (\phi_2, \theta_2)$.

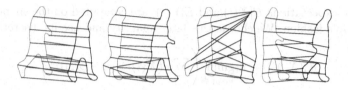

Fig. 4. Each pair shows an optimal registration of points, the lines connect the matched points across the shapes

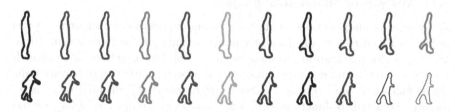

Fig. 5. Examples of geodesic paths between human shapes in S

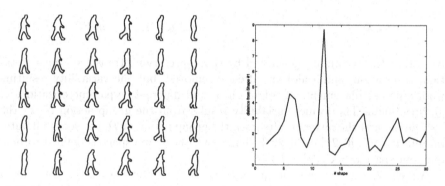

Fig. 6. Left: an ordered sequence of silhouettes. Right: a plot of $d(X(1), X(t))$ versus t. The peaks at shapes $t = 5, 12, 18,$ and 25 determine beginnings and ends of cycles.

3.2 Detection of Gait Cycles

We seek automated techniques for detecting cycles from ordered sequences of extracted shapes. For this, we utilize the fact that silhouettes with the arms and legs together are far away, in terms of geodesic distances, from the silhouettes where the limbs are extended. We begin with a silhouette with the limbs extended and compute geodesic distances from that first shape to all the following shapes. This distance attains peaks at the shapes with the limbs together, and we detect the beginning and end of cycles by looking for these peaks. An example is shown in Figure 6.

3.3 Interpolation Between Observed Shapes

An important tool in our approach to gait recognition is the ability to interpolate on $\mathcal{S}$. In Eqn. 2, the evaluation of $X(t)$ and $Y(\kappa + \phi(t))$ for the same t is an issue as the two paths may not have been observed at corresponding times. One needs an ability to "fill in" shapes using the observed shapes. To estimate a shape that occurs between any two observed shapes, we use geodesics paths to interpolate on the shape space $\mathcal{S}$. We compute these interpolated points as $\Psi(t)$ for some $t \in (0,1)$, as illustrated in Figure 7. The silhouettes in the top row were obtained at eight uniformly-spaced points in time, which we shall denote $t = 0$ to $t = 7$. In case we need resample them at six time points, we obtain silhouettes at $t = 0, \frac{7}{5}, \frac{14}{5}, \frac{21}{5}, \frac{28}{5}, 7$ via interpolation. For example, to get a point at time $t = \frac{7}{5}$, we compute the geodesic path Ψ from the shape at $t = 1$ to the shape at $t = 2$ and an estimate of the shape at $t = \frac{7}{5}$ is given by $\Psi(0.2)$. The remaining shapes in the second row of Figure 7 are computed similarly.

Fig. 7. Geodesic Interpolation. Top: a sequence of eight shapes. Bottom: interpolation of this sequence to sampled uniformly at six points.

3.4 Registration of Gait Cycles

The next issue in comparison and recognition of gait is the registration of points along any two cycles. In other words, given samples of shapes along two observed walks, which shapes should be compared with each other. Even though the shapes form an ordered sequence, there may be a time scaling, time warping, and/or time shifting between the two sequences. Shown in Figures 8 are examples of observed gait cycles for two people. One cycle contains 10 shapes while the other contains eight shapes. In order to compare these two sequences, we need to

Fig. 8. Observed gait cycles for two different people. They need to be registered before their comparison.

register the two cycles. As earlier, let τ_x and τ_y be the periods of gait sequences X and Y, and let $\phi : [0, \tau_x] \mapsto [0, \tau_y]$ be a map that is invertible, and both ϕ and ϕ^{-1} have piecewise continuous derivatives. Our first goal is to find κ and ϕ that minimize energy given in Eqn. 1. However, once the cycles have been detected, the need to estimate κ is no more. The problem of finding ϕ is addressed as follows:

1. Nonlinear time scaling: Several authors have used the idea of using dynamic programming, often called dynamic time warping (DTW), earlier in different contexts. This solves for $\hat{\phi} = \mathrm{argmin}_\phi \int_0^{\tau_x} d(X(t), Y(\phi(t)))^2 dt$ (see [9] for example.) An example of dynamic time warping is given in Figure 9.

2. Linear time scaling: Another idea to consider ϕ simply as a linear time scaling, $\phi(t) = \beta dt$, where $\beta > 0$ is a scalar. In case the end points of the two cycles are known, then β is simply τ_y / τ_x, otherwise both κ and β can be jointly estimated from the observed gait sequences according to: $(\hat{\kappa}, \hat{\beta}) = \mathrm{argmin}_{(\kappa, \beta)} \int_0^{\tau_x} d(X(t), Y(\kappa + \beta t))^2 dt$. An example of linear time scaling is given in Figure 7.

3.5   Computation of Mean Gait Cycles

To utilize Eqn. 2 for comparing gait sequences, we need to estimate the mean shape $E[X(t)]$ for relevant times in a gait cycle. Assuming that we have multiple observations of a person's gait cycle, the task here is to first register the shapes across cycles, as described above, and then to compute means of corresponding shapes across sequences. The mean shape $E[X(t)]$ is defined to be the sample Karcher mean shape at time t as follows. Given a set of sample shapes $(\phi_1, \theta_1) \ldots, (\phi_n, \theta_n) \in \mathcal{S}$, the sample Karcher variance is a function of $(\phi, \theta) \in \mathcal{S}$, and is given by $V(\phi, \theta) = \sum_{k=1}^n d((\phi, \theta), (\phi_k, \theta_k))^2$, where the metric d denotes the metric on $\mathcal{S}$ denoting the shortest geodesic path between points. The Karcher mean set of $(\phi_1, \theta_1), \ldots, (\phi_n, \theta_n) \in \mathcal{S}$ is the set of minimizers of $V(\phi, \theta)$. Klassen

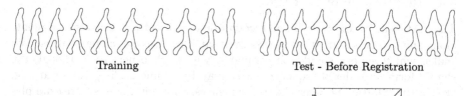

Training   Test - Before Registration

Test - After Registration   optimal ϕ

Fig. 9. Dynamic Time Warping. Top left: a sequence of ten silhouettes from a training sequence. Top right: a test sequence to be registered to the training sequence. Bottom left: the test sequence after registration and the plot shows the function ϕ, found by dynamic programming, used in the registration.

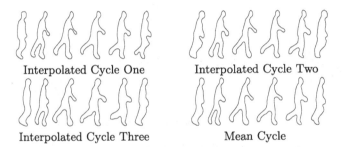

Interpolated Cycle One   Interpolated Cycle Two

Interpolated Cycle Three   Mean Cycle

Fig. 10. Computation of a mean cycle. The first three sets consist of gait cycles registered using linear interpolation. The mean cycle is shown in the fourth set. Each shape in the fourth row is the Karcher mean of the three corresponding shapes.

et al. [5] present an algorithm for computation of the sample Karcher mean. An example of calculation of a mean gait cycle is shown in Figure 10.

4   Experimental Results

Our experimental results are based on a collection of IR video clips of 26 people. We collected at least two video clips of each person, and formed disjoint training and tests. We performed a gait matching experiment, following these steps:

- For each of the training and test sequences we extracted three half-cycles, performed registration using linear time scaling, then computed an average gait cycle.
- For each test sequence, we computed the metric in Eqn. 2 for each training sequence and sought the nearest match.

The results are summarized in Table 1 under Method 1. Under the nearest neighbor criterion, we obtain a successful match for 17 of the 26 test sequences. For 21 of the 26 test sequences, the correct match in the training set was among the top three choices. An example of a correct match is show in the top row of Figure 11, while an incorrect match is shown in the bottom row.

For comparison we studied a simpler method, called the *mean-shape approach*. Some papers suggest that gait recognition can be achieved using merely a mean shape of the cycle, rather than using the full cycle [6, 11]. For each person in

Table 1. This table shows the number of test data, out of 26, for which the correct class is in top i-classes, plotted against i

i	1	2	3	4	5	6	7	8	9	10
Our Approach	17	20	21	21	21	22	22	23	24	24
Mean-Shape Approach	13	14	16	19	19	20	20	20	20	22
Landmark-Based Approach	10	11	14	17	19	19	20	20	21	22

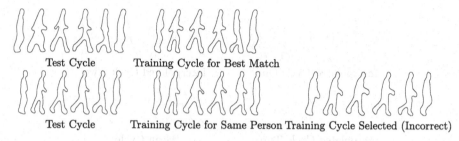

Fig. 11. Top: Example of a correct match. Bottom: An example of an incorrect match.

the training set, these methods compute a single mean shape. Then for a test sequence, a single mean shape is computed and then the best match in the training set is sought. Surprisingly, a decent performance has been reported with this simplified method. In Table 1, results are summarized for this approach for our dataset. Finally, we also compute recognition performance using the landmark-based shape analysis of boundary curves. Although the general approach here is same as our method, the choices of shape space S, geodesic length $d(\cdot, \cdot)$, Karcher means, etc are different [3]. Recognition results based on this method are reported in Table 1.

5   Summary

In this work we present a novel framework for gait recognition, considering gait as a cyclostationary process on a shape space of simple closed curves. Geometric tools enable us to perform: (i) interpolation between shapes, (ii) registration of gait cycles, (ii) averaging of gait cycles, and (iv) comparisons of gait cycles for human recognition. An important note is that comparison of mean cycles, rather than the cycles themselves, help suppress intra-class variability and improve the classification performance.

Acknowledgements

This research was supported in part by grants ARO W911NF-04-1-0268, ARO W911NF-04-1-0113, and CCF-0514743.

References

1. B. Bhanu and J. Huan. Individual recognition by kinematic-based gait analysis. In *Proceedings of the 16 th International Conference on Pattern Recognition*, volume 3, pages 30343–46, 2002.
2. D. Cunado, M. S. Nixon, and J. N. Carter. Automatic extraction and description of human gait models for recognition purposes. *Computer Vision and Image Understanding*, 90(1):1–41, 2003.

3. I. L. Dryden and K. V. Mardia. *Statistical Shape Analysis*. John Wiley & Son, 1998.
4. A. Kale, A. Sundaresan, A. N. Rajagopalan, N. P. Cuntoor, A. K. Roy-Chowdhury, V. Kruger, and R. Chellappa. Identification of humans using gait. *IEEE Transactions on Image Processing*, 13(9):1163–1173.
5. E. Klassen, A. Srivastava, W. Mio, and S. Joshi. Analysis of planar shapes using geodesic paths on shape spaces. *IEEE Patt. Analysis and Machine Intell.*, 26(3):372–383, March, 2004.
6. Z. Liu and S. Sarkar. Simplest representation yet for gait recognition: Averaged silhouette. In *Proc. of IEEE International Conference on Pattern Recogntion*, 2004.
7. W. Mio and A. Srivastava. Elastic string models for representation and analysis of planar shapes. In *Proc. of IEEE Computer Vision and Pattern Recognition*, 2004.
8. S. Sarkar, P. J. Phillips, Z. Liu, I. R. Vega, P. Grother, and K. W. Bowyer. The humanid gait challenge problem: data sets, performance, and analysis. *IEEE Trans. Pattern Analysis and Machine Intelligence*, 27(2):162–177, 2005.
9. A. Veeraghavan, A. Roy-Chowdhury, and R. Chellappa. Role of shape and kinematics in human movement analysis. In *Processings of CVPR*, volume 01, pages 730–737, 2004.
10. I. R. Vega and S. Sarkar. Statistical motion model based on the change of feature relationships: human gait-based recognition. *IEEE Trans. Pattern Analysis and Machine Intelligence*, 25(10):1323–1328, 2003.
11. L. Wang, T. Tan, H Ning, and W. Hu. Silhouette analysis-based gait recognition for human identification. *IEEE Trans. Pattern Analysis and Machine Intelligence*, 25(12):1505–1518, 2003.

Multiclass Image Labeling
with Semidefinite Programming

Jens Keuchel

Institute of Computational Science, ETH Zurich, 8092 Zurich, Switzerland
Jens.Keuchel@inf.ethz.ch

Abstract. We propose a semidefinite relaxation technique for multiclass image labeling problems. In this context, we consider labeling as a special case of supervised classification with a predefined number of classes and known but arbitrary dissimilarities between each image element and each class. Using Markov random fields to model pairwise relationships, this leads to a global energy minimization problem. In order to handle its combinatorial complexity, we apply Lagrangian relaxation to derive a semidefinite program, which has several advantageous properties over alternative methods like graph cuts. In particular, there are no restrictions concerning the form of the pairwise interactions, which e.g. allows us to incorporate a basic shape concept into the energy function. Based on the solution matrix of our convex relaxation, a suboptimal solution of the original labeling problem can be easily computed. Statistical ground-truth experiments and several examples of multiclass image labeling and restoration problems show that high quality solutions are obtained with this technique.

1 Introduction

Classification of extracted image elements (e.g. pixels, patches, objects) or in short *image labeling* is a fundamental issue in computer vision. Based on a *predefined number* of classes, the goal is to assign each image element to one of these classes according to some suitable criterion. Not considering the corresponding problem of learning adequate class representations here, we assume that *fixed dissimilarity values* between each image element in comparison to the different classes are given in advance. Depending on the application, these dissimilarities may be based on previously known class prototypes, resulting in an *image restoration problem* (the image features are noisy measurements of the given prototypes), or on class representations that can be estimated from training data (by making certain assumptions about the distribution of the image features).

As illustrating examples consider the images given in Figure 1: based on the observed values, we want to either restore the original image by determining the 'true' intensity for each pixel, or classify the pixels according to some measured feature (like texture). To this end, a compromise between two competing forces is usually sought [1]: on the one hand, we look for classifications that best conform to the observed feature values, while on the other hand — assuming that natural

A. Leonardis, H. Bischof, and A. Pinz (Eds.): ECCV 2006, Part II, LNCS 3952, pp. 454–467, 2006.
© Springer-Verlag Berlin Heidelberg 2006

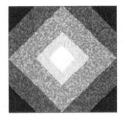

Fig. 1. Multiclass image restoration/labeling. Restore a gray-value image from noisy measurements (left). Label image parts according to their texture (right).

images are mostly smooth, except for occasional region boundaries — spatially neighboring pixels should receive similar labels.

In order to find a labeling which captures this trade-off, we seek to minimize a global energy function which involves pairwise relationships among the objects. This kind of problem has a long history in the literature, in particular as it arises naturally from the well-studied theory of *Markov random fields*, a statistical framework that builds the core of many image processing applications [1, 2, 3, 4].

Using integer variables x_i to indicate the label for each image element i, the resulting problem can be formulated as minimizing an energy functional of the following general form [5]:

$$E(x) = \sum_i C_i(x_i) + \sum_{\langle i,j \rangle} V_{ij}(x_i, x_j) \,, \tag{1}$$

where the second term sums over all pairwise interacting image elements. The energy (1) comprises two terms familiar from many regularization approaches: a data-fitting term and a smoothness term modeling spatial context. In more detail, the data-fitting term measures the dissimilarity $C_i(x_i)$ between element i and class x_i (*assignment costs*), while the smoothness term evaluates the disagreement $V_{ij}(x_i, x_j)$ of the labels for related pairs i, j (*separation costs*).

Due to the integer constraint on the variables x_i the optimization problems obtained from (1) are much more difficult than standard regularization problems. In fact, apart from a few special cases, they are in general NP-hard [5]. Accordingly, different methods have been proposed to find good minimizers of (special instances of) the energy (1) efficiently, like the ICM-algorithm [3], the graduated non-convexity approach [6], different versions of annealing procedures [2, 7], local search heuristics based on graph cuts [5], or linear programming relaxations [8].

Recently, a semidefinite relaxation approach was presented to approximate the minimal solution of the energy (1) for the special case of *binary* labeling problems [9]. At the cost of an increased but still moderate computational complexity, the tightness of this relaxation method results in high quality combinatorial solutions. This fact along with the recent success of semidefinite relaxation for other combinatorial optimization problems [10, 11, 12] motivated us to extend the approach from [9] to image labeling problems involving *multiple classes*. In contrast to other methods [5, 8, 13] the resulting approximation technique needs *no special assumptions* with respect to the pairwise interactions between variables given by $V_{ij}(x_i, x_j)$ in (1), so that it is applicable to a very general class of problems. In particular, each pair of image elements can have its own distinct, arbitrary interaction function, which will allow us to include basic 'shape' information into the labeling problem (see Section 4). Although recent efforts show that e.g. graph cut methods can also be adapted to less restricted problems [14, 15], they are not able to deal with the energy (1) in the general case.

Other favorable properties of our approach include: As it yields a convex semidefinite program (SDP), the global optimum of the relaxation can be computed to arbitrary precision in polynomial time, without the need to heuristically optimize any tuning parameters (cf. [16]). Like the LP relaxation presented in [8], we obtain probabilities for each point-label pair, which allows us to define sophisticated rounding schemes. Moreover, the SDP relaxation gives a lower bound on the optimal objective value that can be used to estimate the per-instance approximation error.

2   Problem Formulation

In order to apply semidefinite relaxation to the image labeling problem, we first derive a trace formulation of the energy functional (1). To this end, let k denote the number of possible classes present in the image. Furthermore, we indicate the class membership of each image element i by a vector $x_i \in \{e_1, \ldots, e_k\}$ taking as value one of the k standard unit vectors from $\mathbb{R}^k$. Assuming that the image contains n elements, the indicator vectors form the rows of the labeling matrix $X \in \mathbb{R}^{n \times k}$.

Using these definitions, and denoting the trace of a matrix A by $\mathrm{Tr}(A) = \sum_i A_{ii}$, we obtain the following formulation of the energy functional (1):

$$E(x) = \sum_{i=1}^{n} \sum_{a=1}^{k} C_i(a) x_{ia} + \sum_{\langle i,j \rangle} \sum_{a=1}^{k} \sum_{b=1}^{k} V_{ij}(a,b) x_{ia} x_{jb}$$
$$= \mathrm{Tr} \left(C X^\top + \sum_{a,b} V(a,b) X I^{ab} X^\top \right), \tag{2}$$

where $C \in \mathbb{R}^{n \times k}$ contains the costs $C_{ia} = C_i(a)$ for assigning object i to class a, $V(a,b) \in \mathbb{R}^{n \times n}$ comprises the separation costs of related objects for a fixed label pair (a,b), and $I^{ab} \in \mathbb{R}^{k \times k}$ is the matrix with the only non-zero entry $I^{ab}_{ab} = 1$.

For many image labeling problems, the separation costs in (1) can be decomposed into two factors:

$$V_{ij}(x_i, x_j) = P_{ij} D(x_i, x_j), \tag{3}$$

where the weight P_{ij} indicates the strength of the relation between image elements i, j, and $D(x_i, x_j)$ measures the distance between the two labels x_i, x_j. In this case, the trace formulation of the energy functional (2) simplifies to:

$$E(x) = \mathrm{Tr} \left(C X^\top + P X D X^\top \right), \tag{4}$$

with matrices $P \in \mathbb{R}^{n \times n}$ and $D \in \mathbb{R}^{k \times k}$. A typical example is the discontinuity preserving model of metric Potts interaction penalties [5], which are defined as

$$P_{ij}D(x_i, x_j) = \lambda \|x_i - x_j\|^2 = 2\lambda(1 - x_i^\top x_j) \qquad (5)$$

for associated (neighboring) image elements i, j. Controlling the desired smoothness by the fixed parameter $\lambda \in \mathbb{R}^+$, seperation costs of this form encourage image regions with constant labels without penalizing sharp boundaries too much. As can be verified easily, in terms of the trace formulation (4) the Potts interactions are expressed by symmetric matrices P with non-zero entries $P_{ij} = \lambda$ for associated objects i, j, and $D = E - I$, where E and I are the matrix of all ones and the identity matrix, respectively.

However, in contrast to other image labeling methods [5, 8] our semidefinite relaxation approach will not require any specific form of the separation costs; in fact, they are allowed to be non-symmetric or may vary depending on the labels for a fixed object pair. Putting everything together, we consider the following optimization problem for *multiclass image labeling*:

$$
\begin{aligned}
z^* := \min_{X \in \mathbb{R}^{n \times k}} \ &\mathrm{Tr}\left(CX^\top + \sum_{a,b} V(a,b)XI^{ab}X^\top\right) \\
\text{s.t.} \quad &Xe^k = e^n \\
&X_{ia} \in \{0,1\} \qquad \forall\, 1 \le i \le n, 1 \le a \le k\,,
\end{aligned}
\qquad (6)
$$

where $e^j \in \mathbb{R}^j$ denotes the vector of all ones of appropriate size. The first constraint in (6) requires each row of X to sum to one, which in connection with the second constraint ensures that each row corresponds to a unit vector $e_i \in \mathbb{R}^k$.

This combinatorial optimization problem resembles the generalized *quadratic assignment problem* (QAP, see, e.g., [17]), which has the objective to optimally place n given activities at n given locations by minimizing a cost function of the form $\mathrm{Tr}(AXBX^\top - 2CX^\top)$ over the set of permutation matrices $X \in \mathbb{R}^{n \times n}$ (with $A, B, C \in \mathbb{R}^{n \times n}$). In fact, we can interpret (6) as an *uncapacitated* version of a general QAP where multiple activities are allowed to be placed at the same location [8]. In the context of solving the NP-hard QAP, semidefinite relaxation approaches have attracted considerable interest [10, 18]. In the next section, we will show how these methods can be generalized to also find approximate solutions for our less restricted labeling problem (6).

3   Semidefinite Relaxation

Following the QAP relaxation presented in [10], we apply Lagrangian relaxation to the image labeling problem (6). For ease of notation, we use the simplified form (4) of the energy here; the result for the more general case (2) is derived analogously and will be stated later. As a first step, we represent the constraints in (6) in quadratic form, which results in the following equivalent problem:

$$z^* = \min_{X \in \mathbb{R}^{n \times k}} \mathrm{Tr}\left(PXDX^\top + CX^\top\right)$$

$$\text{s.t.} \quad \|Xe^k - e^n\|^2 = 0 \tag{7}$$

$$X_{ia}^2 - X_{ia} = 0 \quad \forall i, a .$$

Using the Lagrange multipliers $W \in \mathbb{R}^{n \times k}$ and $u_0 \in \mathbb{R}$, we add the constraints to the objective function, and perform relaxation by virtue of the "minimax inequality" [12]:

$$z^* = \min_X \max_{W,u_0} \mathrm{Tr}\left(PXDX^\top + CX^\top\right) + \sum_{i,a} W_{ia}(X_{ia}^2 - X_{ia})$$

$$+ u_0(Xe^k - e^n)^\top(Xe^k - e^n)$$

$$\geq \max_{W,u_0} \min_X \mathrm{Tr}\left(PXDX^\top + CX^\top\right) + \mathrm{Tr}\left(W(X \circ X - X)^\top\right)$$

$$+ u_0 \mathrm{Tr}\left(XE_kX^\top - 2E_{n \times k}X^\top\right) + u_0 n$$

$$= \max_{W,u_0} \min_X \mathrm{Tr}\left(PXDX^\top + W(X \circ X)^\top + X(u_0E_k)X^\top\right.$$

$$\left. + (C - W - 2u_0E_{n \times k})X^\top\right) + u_0 n .$$

Here, $X \circ X$ denotes the Hadamard (elementwise) product of two matrices, and E_k and $E_{n \times k}$ are matrices of all ones of appropriate dimension.

Next we homogenize the objective function by multiplying X with a constrained scalar $x_0 = \pm 1$, which increases the dimension of the problem by one. The additional constraint is then inserted into the objective function by introducing the Lagrange multiplier $w_0 \in \mathbb{R}$:

$$z^* \geq \max_{W,u_0} \min_{X,x_0^2=1} \mathrm{Tr}\left(PXDX^\top + W(X \circ X)^\top + X(u_0E_k)X^\top\right.$$

$$\left. + x_0(C - W - 2u_0E_{n \times k})X^\top\right) + u_0 n x_0^2$$

$$\geq \max_{W,u_0,w_0} \min_{X,x_0} \mathrm{Tr}\left(PXDX^\top + W(X \circ X)^\top + X(u_0E_k)X^\top\right.$$

$$\left. + x_0(C - W - 2u_0E_{n \times k})X^\top\right) + u_0 n x_0^2 + w_0 x_0^2 - w_0 =: s_d^* .$$

Transforming the problem variables x_0 and X into a vector by defining $y := \binom{x_0}{\mathrm{vec}(X)}$, we obtain

$$s_d^* = \max_{W,u_0,w_0} \min_y y^\top \left(L_{P,D,C} + A_{W,w_0} + u_0 F\right)y - w_0 , \tag{8}$$

with

$$L_{P,D,C} := \begin{pmatrix} 0 & \frac{1}{2}\mathrm{vec}(C)^\top \\ \frac{1}{2}\mathrm{vec}(C) & D \otimes P \end{pmatrix} , \tag{9}$$

$$A_{W,w_0} := \begin{pmatrix} w_0 & -\frac{1}{2}\mathrm{vec}(W)^\top \\ -\frac{1}{2}\mathrm{vec}(W) & \mathrm{Diag}(\mathrm{vec}(W)) \end{pmatrix} , \tag{10}$$

$$F := \begin{pmatrix} n & -(e^{nk})^\top \\ -e^{nk} & E_k \otimes I \end{pmatrix} . \tag{11}$$

Here, $\text{vec}(X)$ is the vector containing the stacked columns x_i of X, $\text{Diag}(w)$ is the diagonal matrix formed from the vector w, and $A \otimes B$ denotes the Kronecker product of two matrices.

There is a hidden semidefinite constraint in (8): the inner minimization is bounded below only if the matrix in the quadratic term is positive semidefinite, in which case the corresponding minimum becomes zero (cf. [10]). Indicating positive semidefiniteness of a matrix by $X \succeq 0$, this finally yields the following relaxation of (6):

$$
\begin{aligned}
s_d^* = \max_{W, u_0, w_0} \quad & -w_0 \\
\text{s.t.} \quad & L_{P,D,C} + A_{W,w_0} + u_0 F \succeq 0 .
\end{aligned}
\tag{12}
$$

To obtain a direct semidefinite relaxation of (6), we derive the Lagrangian dual of (12). To this end, first observe that the matrix in (10) can be split into $A_{W,w_0} = \sum_{i=0}^{nk} w_i A_i$ by defining $w := \text{vec}(W)$ and sparse symmetric, $nk + 1$-dimensional matrices A_i with the only non-zero entries $(A_i)_{i+1,i+1} = 1$ and (for $i \neq 0$) $(A_i)_{1,i+1} = (A_i)_{i+1,1} = -\frac{1}{2}$. Using the dual positive semidefinite matrix variable $Y \in \mathbb{R}^{nk+1 \times nk+1}$, we get

$$
s_d^* = \max_{w_0, w, u_0} \min_{Y \succeq 0} -w_0 + \text{Tr}\left(Y\left(L_{P,D,C} + \sum_{i=0}^{nk} w_i A_i + u_0 F\right)\right)
$$

$$
\leq \min_{Y \succeq 0} \max_{w_0, w, u_0} \text{Tr}(L_{P,D,C} Y) + w_0\left(\text{Tr}(A_0 Y) - 1\right) + \sum_{i=1}^{nk} w_i \, \text{Tr}(A_i Y)
$$

$$
+ u_0 \, \text{Tr}(FY) \quad =: s_p^* .
$$

As the inner maximization is unconstrained, this minimization problem is finite valued only if all the factors in the last three terms are zero. Using this hidden constraint, we finally obtain the following semidefinite program (SDP) as the dual of (12):

$$
\begin{aligned}
s_p^* = \min_{Y \succeq 0} \quad & \text{Tr}(L_{P,D,C} Y) \\
\text{s.t.} \quad & \text{Tr}(A_0 Y) = 1 \\
& \text{Tr}(A_i Y) = 0 \quad \forall 1 \leq i \leq nk \\
& \text{Tr}(FY) = 0 .
\end{aligned}
\tag{13}
$$

The connection of this semidefinite relaxation with the original integer problem (6) now becomes obvious: the binary labeling matrix $X \in \mathbb{R}^{n \times k}$ is first transformed into a vector $\text{vec}(X)$ and then lifted into the higher, $(nk + 1)^2$-dimensional space of positive semidefinite matrices by setting

$$
Y := \begin{pmatrix} 1 \\ \text{vec}(X) \end{pmatrix} \left(1, \text{vec}(X)^\top\right) .
\tag{14}
$$

The relaxation consists in discarding the intractable rank one constraint on this matrix Y, and minimizing over the more general space of $nk + 1$-dimensional, positive semidefinite matrices instead (cf. [9]). Besides the A_0-constraint, which is an artificial one to enable the homogenization of the objective function, the other constraints in (13) directly correspond to the constraints in the original problem formulation (6): the A_i-constraints guarantee that the diagonal and the first row (and column) of Y are identical, thus modeling the $\{0,1\}$-constraint on the entries of X, whereas the F-constraint is derived from the sum-one-constraint on the indicator vectors constituting the rows of X.

Regarding the more general case of the energy functional (2), the only difference during the relaxation process occurs in the derivation of (8): instead of the matrix $L_{P,D,C}$ from (9), the term $\sum_{a,b} V(a,b)XI^{ab}X^\top$ in (2) yields the matrix

$$L_{V,C} := \begin{pmatrix} 0 & \frac{1}{2}\mathrm{vec}(C)^\top \\ \frac{1}{2}\mathrm{vec}(C) & \sum_{a,b} I^{ab} \otimes V(a,b) \end{pmatrix} = \begin{pmatrix} 0 & \frac{1}{2}\mathrm{vec}(C)^\top \\ \frac{1}{2}\mathrm{vec}(C) & V \end{pmatrix}, \quad (15)$$

with $V \in \mathbb{R}^{nk \times nk}$ being composed blockwisely of the $V(a,b)$-matrices. Hence, we obtain the corresponding general semidefinite relaxation of (6) by simply replacing $L_{P,D,C}$ with $L_{V,C}$ in (12) and (13).

Concerning the solvability of the SDP relaxation (13), we have the following lemma (cf. [10]):

Lemma 1. *A feasible solution matrix Y for (13) is singular, with at least n of its eigenvalues being equal to zero.*

Proof. The constraint matrix $F \neq 0$ is positive semidefinite: as can easily be calculated, its non-zero eigenvalues are $\lambda_{nk+1} = n+k$ and $\lambda_{n(k-1)+2} = \cdots = \lambda_{nk} = k$. As Y is also positive semidefinite, the constraint $\mathrm{Tr}(FY) = \mathrm{Tr}(YF) = 0$ in (13) directly implies that YF has to be the null-matrix [19, Lemma 2.9]. Hence, $YF_i = 0$ for each column F_i, which shows the singularity of Y. As exactly n columns F_i of F are linearly independent (namely $i = 2, \ldots, n+1$), the dimension of the null space $\ker(Y)$ is at least n. $\qquad\square$

Lemma 1 implies that the semidefinite program (13) has no strictly interior point. On the other hand, we can always define a strictly interior point for the corresponding dual SDP (12) by setting $u_0 = 0$ and choosing w_0 and the entries of W large enough to make the diagonal of the matrix $L_{P,D,C} + A_{W,w_0}$ as dominant as necessary to yield a positive definite matrix. Hence, the Slater condition holds for the dual, so that by the strong duality theorem for SDP [19], there is no duality gap: $s_p^* = s_d^*$ (for more details about the elegant duality theory for SDP, we refer to [16]).

Due to Lemma 1, however, it is not guaranteed that the optimal value of the dual SDP (12) is attained. Therefore, interior point methods can suffer from instability when solving the SDP relaxation and may not converge. One possibility to circumvent this problem is to project the SDP (13) onto a lower dimensional face of the semidefinite cone [10]. However, as we only need the optimal solution of the primal SDP (and not the dual), we revert to a non-interior point algorithm to solve the SDP relaxation instead: the PENNON SDP solver [20] is based on a generalized version of the augmented Lagrangian method, and therefore does not need to compute the optimum of the dual SDP (12).

4   Experimental Results

In this section, we experimentally investigate the performance of the SDP relaxation for one- and two-dimensional labeling problems. In this context, we need to derive a feasible integer solution of the original combinatorial problem (6) based on the solution matrix Y^* of the primal SDP relaxation (13). Since the first column of Y^* originally corresponds to $Y_1 = \binom{1}{\mathrm{vec}(X)}$ (cf. (14)), we obtain an approximation $\tilde{Y}$ of the binary matrix X by reshaping Y_1 appropriately: starting with the second entry, the columns of $\tilde{Y}$ are formed by blocks of length n in Y_1. As in particular, the constraints on Y in (13) ensure that each row $\tilde{y}_i$ of $\tilde{Y}$ sums to one, the entries can be interpreted as probabilities of assigning the different labels. This suggests to define the label of object i (and thus the position of the one-entry in the corresponding class indicator vector x_i) by simply seeking the largest value in $\tilde{y}_i$. However, the difference $\Delta\tilde{y}_i$ between the two highest probability values in $\tilde{y}_i$ may be quite small for some objects. To take such 'doubtful labelings' into account, we follow a slightly different idea to obtain the final solution: In a first step, the labeling is fixed to the most likely class only for those objects i where the difference $\Delta\tilde{y}_i$ is bigger than a threshold $\Delta_{\min}$. In subsequent steps, the current labeling and the remaining probabilities $\tilde{y}_i$ are combined into the matrix $\tilde{X}$, and modified contributions $\tilde{z}_i^\top = 2P_i\tilde{X}D + C_i$ to the objective value are calculated for the remaining objects. Seeking the smallest value $\tilde{z}_{ja}$ within all vectors $\tilde{z}_i$, we then fix the label for the corresponding object j to a. In this way, the strong labels are taken into account when setting the doubtful labelings according to the objective function.

Statistical Ground Truth. As a first experiment, we measure the performance of the multiclass SDP relaxation (13) statistically. To this end, we perform the following binary ($k = 2$) ground-truth experiment (cf. [9]): A synthetic one-dimensional signal (Figure 2, top left) is first distorted by adding Gaussian white

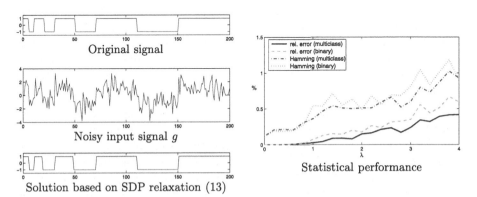

Original signal

Noisy input signal g

Solution based on SDP relaxation (13)

Statistical performance

Fig. 2. One-dimensional restoration. The original signal (top left) is distorted by Gaussian white noise (middle left) and restored based on the SDP relaxation (13). Giving relative errors mostly below 1%, our multiclass SDP relaxation in general performs slightly better in comparison to the binary SDP relaxation presented in [9] (right).

noise and then restored with the SDP relaxation approach — see Figure 2 (left) for a representative example. The energy $E(x)$ in this case is defined by Potts interaction penalties (5) and assignment costs

$$C_i(a) = (u_a - g_i)^\top (u_a - g_i) \,, \tag{16}$$

where g_i denotes the local measurement at point i and $u_1 = 1, u_2 = -1$ are the two prototypical class labels. As each signal element is only connected to its two neighbors, the optimal solution X^* of (6) can be found easily in this case (for fixed smoothness parameter λ), e.g. by dynamic programming. Comparing X^* with the combinatorial solution obtained with the SDP relaxation, we then calculate the relative error of the objective value and the corresponding relative Hamming distance (percentage of misclassified elements).

In order to derive some significant statistics, we perform this experiment for 100 different noisy versions of the original signal, and calculate the corresponding mean errors. The results obtained for a variety of fixed λ-values are depicted in Figure 2, right. They show that the solutions based on the SDP relaxation approach are remarkably good: the average relative error of the objective value and the average relative Hamming distance both are below 1.5%, with standard deviations below 0.9% (objective error) and 1.5% (Hamming distance), respectively. Note that in this experiment, we do not measure the quality of the restoration, which also depends on picking a suitable value λ, but the performance of the SDP relaxation approach in relation to the optimal solution.

For comparison, we also performed the same statistical experiment for the *direct binary* SDP relaxation technique presented in [9]. Although the experiments reveal that the objective values s_p^* of both relaxations coincide (meaning that they are equally tight), a slightly better performance of the multiclass SDP relaxation approach can be observed (see Figure 2, right). This difference indicates that the randomized hyperplane technique used in [9] to obtain a combinatorial solution performs worse than the more sophisticated method used here to find the indicator vectors from the first column Y_1 of the solution of the multiclass relaxation (13). However, the larger problem size of the multiclass SDP relaxation (401×401 compared to 201×201 for binary relaxation) increases the computational requirements: whereas the solution of the direct binary SDP relaxation is calculated in less than a second, it takes 6–7 seconds to solve the multiclass relaxation (13).

Multiclass Image Labeling. Figure 3 indicates the main characteristics of our SDP relaxation approach for image labeling with a first synthetic example: the restoration of a noisy image originally comprising multiple blocks of different gray-values. For this and all the following two-dimensional experiments, we use a second-order neighborhood structure (horizontally, vertically and diagonally adjacent points are connected), and define separation costs based on Potts interactions penalties (5) with distance weighted values $P_{ij} = \frac{1}{dist(i,j)} \lambda$. Moreover, assignment costs of type (16) are used, based on suitable prototypes $u_1, \ldots, u_k \in \mathbb{R}^m$ for each class that are fixed in advance. As this type of energy function satisfies the requirements given in [13], we also compare our results

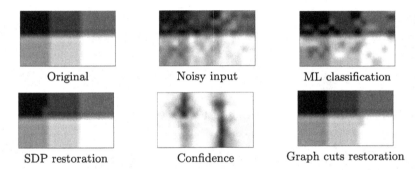

Fig. 3. Multiclass image labeling result. The original image (top left) of 10×18 pixels is degraded by adding Gaussian white noise (top middle). Without spatial relations, ML classification yields a noisy restoration (top right). In contrast, the result of the reconstruction obtained with SDP relaxation (with $\lambda = 0.01$) is almost perfect: only two pixels are classified incorrectly (bottom left), with high confidence for most pixel labels (bottom middle). This result is comparable to the corresponding restoration obtained with graph cuts (bottom right).

with the corresponding restorations achieved with the expansion move graph cuts algorithm from [5].

The reconstruction obtained with the SDP relaxation method for the small image in Figure 3 is very promising: for this example comprising $k = 6$ classes, only two of 180 pixels are labeled incorrectly. Hence, it is of the same quality as the corresponding graph cuts restoration, which also mislabels two pixels. In contrast to that, a simple maximum likelihood (ML) classification (which does not use spatial context) yields a much noisier result (see Figure 3). Interpretation of the solution values y_i as probabilities allows us to compute confidence values of the pixel labels by subtracting the two highest probabilities from each other: the results show that only some boundary points receive uncertain labels (dark pixels in Figure 3, bottom middle). Finally, we note that the lower bound s_p^* on the objective value of (6) computed by the relaxation (13) permits to estimate the performance of the labeling method: comparison with the value z_{sdp} of the final combinatorial solution indicates that the relative error of the result is at most $\frac{z_{sdp} - z^*}{z^*} \leq \frac{z_{sdp} - s_p^*}{s_p^*} = 0.064$ for this instance.

Figure 4 depicts more results obtained for different types of image labeling problems. Due to the involved problem sizes (see below), we restrict the algorithm to smaller patches of the original images here. The first row shows the reconstruction of a noisy grayvalue image taken from [5]. Whereas the ML classification is very noisy due to its local behaviour, both the SDP relaxation and graph cuts produce nearly optimal restorations. The example given in the second row demonstrates how the SDP relaxation approach can be applied to natural color images: using the three main colors from the noisy patch as prototypes, a satisfactory classification is obtained (as the original image comprises more than three colors, this cannot be called a 'restoration'). Color differences are calculated in the perceptually uniform L*u*v* space in this case.

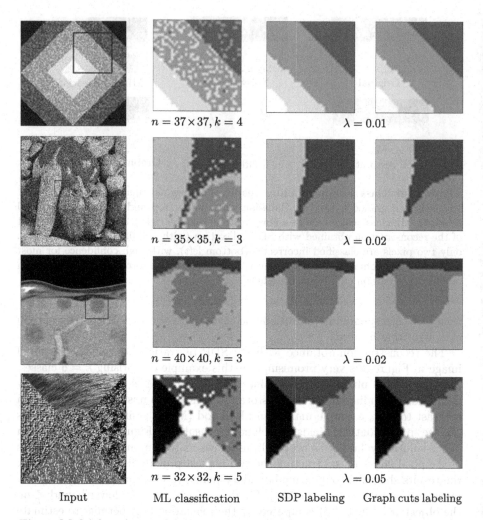

$n = 37 \times 37, k = 4$ $\lambda = 0.01$

$n = 35 \times 35, k = 3$ $\lambda = 0.02$

$n = 40 \times 40, k = 3$ $\lambda = 0.02$

$n = 32 \times 32, k = 5$ $\lambda = 0.05$

Input   ML classification   SDP labeling   Graph cuts labeling

Fig. 4. Multiclass image labeling results. Patches of larger noisy images are restored (rows 1–3) resp. labeled according to texture (row 4) with the SDP relaxation approach. While getting superior results in comparison to a simple maximum likelihood classification, the labelings are of the same quality as those obtained with graph cuts.

The third row of Figure 4 indicates an application of our image labeling method for segmenting tumors in noisy medical images. In this case, prototypes are calculated directly from the image by choosing representative points for each class and averaging the gray values over their neighborhoods. The SDP relaxation then yields a corresponding smooth labeling of the pixels. The last row shows that our SDP relaxation can also successfully be applied for texture classification: dividing the original image into patches of size 16 × 16, we compute feature vectors for each patch by averaging the absolute log-Gabor filter convolutions of the corresponding pixels. We then pick representative patches for each class, and additionally calculate a diagonal covariance matrix Σ from the distribution of filter responses within these patches to obtain more robust assignment costs $C_i(a) = (u_a - g_i)^\top \Sigma^{-1}(u_a - g_i)$. Again, the SDP relaxation results in a smooth classification of the same quality as the corresponding graph cuts labeling.

The good performance of the SDP relaxation is also confirmed by the estimates of the relative error obtained from the lower bounds s_p^*, which range between 1%–4% for the examples in Figure 4. On the other hand, solving the SDP relaxation is more involved than applying graph cuts: the problem size increases quadratically with nk, which results in computation times of up to 4 hours for the examples in Figure 4 in comparison to about one second for finding the corresponding graph cuts solutions. However, these increased computational requirements also make the approach less restrictive, as we will show next.

Image Labeling with Basic Shape Knowledge. In order to demonstrate the generality of our SDP relaxation, we apply it to an image labeling task that in general cannot be handled by other approaches like graph cuts [13]. Assuming that some specific information is available on the arrangement of certain label pairs, it is possible to incorporate a basic concept of 'shape' into the labeling problem. For example, it may be known that two labels a, b cannot be neighbored vertically. This information is easily included into the general energy functional (1) by setting $V_{ij}(a, b)$ to a high value whenever i and j are vertical neighbors, and to a small value otherwise. Note that besides preventing the application of methods that rely on a decomposition (3) of the interaction terms [8] (which do not permit *label dependent* penalties for different neighbor constellations), this might also result in violations of the triangle inequality-type requirements on the interactions necessary e.g. for the expansion move graph cuts algorithm [13].

Figure 5 shows some illustrative examples. To obtain a perfect reconstruction for the image from Figure 3, we simply increase separation costs $V_{ij}(a, b)$ by multiplying them with $\alpha = 3$ for vertically neighboring pixels i, j for all three label pairs a, b contained in the top part of the image. In this way, horizontal label changes are preferred over vertical ones, which efficiently prevents the wrong classification of the two pixels in the top left block. The second example is handled similarly, but this time we need to modify interactions differently according to the label constellations: denoting the labels of the left part as a and of the right part as b_1, b_2, respectively, the penalties $V_{ij}(a, b_r)$ are increased for vertical neighbors i, j, while $V_{ij}(b_1, b_2)$ is increased for horizontal neighbors. Although not perfect, the result clearly demonstrates the influence of these priors.

The last row of Figure 5 indicates how the classification can be restricted to find rectangular shapes: dividing the background into two classes a_1 and a_2 neighbored vertically and horizontally to the shape class b, respectively, we generally decrease $V_{ij}(a_1, a_2)$ to allow pixels to vary from one background class to the other (without changing the assignment costs $C_i(a_1) = C_i(a_2)$), but increase vertical penalties $V_{ij}(b, a_2)$ and $V_{ij}(a_1, a_2)$ and horizontal penalties $V_{ij}(b, a_1)$ to model the general label arrangement. The result clearly demonstrates that these modified separation costs successfully restrict the labeling to a rectangular shape, whereas the original interaction values give an inferior reconstruction.

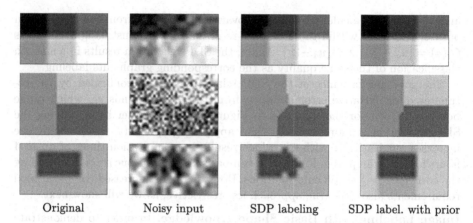

| Original | Noisy input | SDP labeling | SDP label. with prior |

Fig. 5. Image labeling with basic 'shape' concept. Including simple information about preferred label arrangements results in better reconstructions of heavily noisy images. The slightly varying background color in the bottom right image visualizes the artificially enforced splitting into two different background classes.

5   Conclusion

We have presented a method for multiclass image labeling that is able to find approximate solutions of high quality for a very general class of combinatorial optimization problems. Applying the mathematically fundamental concept of Lagrangian relaxation, we obtain a semidefinite program which due to its convexity can be solved in polynomial time without having to optimize any tuning parameters. In fact, besides defining the classes, only the parameter λ controlling the smoothness of the result needs to be adjusted. In comparison to other approaches like graph cuts, our SDP relaxation method is not restricted to special types of the energy function, and additionally gives a lower bound on the optimal solution value that can be used to estimate the relative error of the result for each problem instance.

The generality of our method enables us to incorporate a basic concept of shape into the labeling process. It will be interesting to further investigate this idea to see whether more complex shape information can be included.

However, this generality of the multiclass SDP relaxation approach has its price: since the problem size increases quadratically with the product of the number of image elements and the number of classes, the application of this method is (yet) restricted to small optimization problems consisting of only few different classes. In order to remedy this drawback one could perform labeling successively on different scales: Extracting larger image objects, a corresponding coarse scale classification is computed in a first step. Afterwards, the labeling can be refined by applying fine scale classification to those objects that received low confidence values. In this way, instead of having to compute the solution for one large problem instance, a sequence of smaller problems that can be solved more efficiently needs to be considered.

Finally, we note that it is often possible to tighten Lagrangian relaxations by incorporating additional constraints that are redundant for the original problem (cf. [10]). Future work will show whether this is useful in our case to find better approximative solutions.

References

1. Winkler, G.: Image Analysis, Random Fields and Dynamic Monte Carlo Methods. Volume 27 of Appl. of Mathematics. Springer (1995)
2. Geman, S., Geman, D.: Stochastic relaxation, Gibbs distributions, and the Bayesian restoration of images. IEEE Trans. PAMI **6** (1984) 721–741
3. Besag, J.: On the statistical analysis of dirty pictures. Journal of the Royal Statistical Society, Series B **48** (1986) 259–302
4. Li, S.Z.: Markov Random Field Modeling in Image Analysis. Springer (2001)
5. Boykov, Y., Veksler, O., Zabih, R.: Fast approximate energy minimization via graph cuts. IEEE Trans. PAMI **23** (2001) 1222–1239
6. Blake, A., Zisserman, A.: Visual Reconstruction. MIT Press (1987)
7. Hofmann, T., Buhmann, J.: Pairwise data clustering by deterministic annealing. IEEE Trans. PAMI **19** (1997) 1–14
8. Kleinberg, J., Tardos, E.: Approximation algorithms for classification problems with pairwise relationships: Metric labeling and Markov random fields. Journal of the ACM **49** (2002) 616–639
9. Keuchel, J., Schnörr, C., Schellewald, C., Cremers, D.: Binary partitioning, perceptual grouping, and restoration with semidefinite programming. IEEE Trans. PAMI **25** (2003) 1364–1379
10. Zhao, Q., Karisch, S.E., Rendl, F., Wolkowicz, H.: Semidefinite programming relaxations for the quadratic assignment problem. J. Combinat. Optim. **2** (1998) 71–109
11. Wolkowicz, H., Anjos, M.F.: Semidefinite programming for discrete optimization and matrix completion problems. Discr. Appl. Math. **123** (2002) 513–577
12. Laurent, M., Rendl, F.: Semidefinite programming and integer programming. In Aardal, K., Nemhauser, G.L., Weismantel, R., eds.: Discrete Optimization. Volume 12 of Handbooks in Op. Res. and Man. Sci. Elsevier (2005)
13. Kolmogorov, V., Zabih, R.: What energy functions can be minimized via graph cuts? IEEE Trans. PAMI **26** (2004) 147–159
14. Rother, C., Kumar, S., Kolmogorov, V., Blake, A.: Digital tapestry. In: Proceedings CVPR (1). (2005) 589–596
15. Raj, A., Zabih, R.: A graph cut algorithm for generalized image deconvolution. In: Proc. 10th Int. Conf. Computer Vision (ICCV). (2005) 1048–1054
16. Wolkowicz, H., Saigal, R., Vandenberghe, L., eds.: Handbook of Semidefinite Programming. Volume 27 of International Series in Operations Research & Management Science. Kluwer Acad. Publ., Boston (2000)
17. Çela, E.: The Quadratic Assignment Problem: Theory and Algorithms. Kluwer Acad. Publishers, Dordrecht (1998)
18. Brixius, N., Anstreicher, K.: Solving quadratic assignment problems using convex quadratic programming relaxations. Optim. Methods Software **16** (2001) 49–68
19. Alizadeh, F.: Interior point methods in semidefinite programming with applications to combinatorial optimization. SIAM J. Optimization **5** (1995) 13–51
20. Kočvara, M., Stingl, M.: PENNON - a code for convex nonlinear and semidefinite programming. Optimization Methods and Software **18** (2003) 317–333

Automatic Image Segmentation by Positioning a Seed*

Branislav Mičušík and Allan Hanbury

Pattern Recognition and Image Processing Group,
Institute of Computer Aided Automation,
Vienna University of Technology,
Favoritenstraße 9/1832, A-1040 Vienna, Austria
{micusik, hanbury}@prip.tuwien.ac.at

Abstract. We present a method that automatically partitions a single image into non-overlapping regions coherent in texture and colour. An assumption that each textured or coloured region can be represented by a small template, called the seed, is used. Positioning of the seed across the input image gives many possible sub-segmentations of the image having same texture and colour property as the pixels behind the seed. A probability map constructed during the sub-segmentations helps to assign each pixel to just one most probable region and produce the final pyramid representing various detailed segmentations at each level. Each sub-segmentation is obtained as the min-cut/max-flow in the graph built from the image and the seed. One segment may consist of several isolated parts. Compared to other methods our approach does not need a learning process or a priori information about the textures in the image. Performance of the method is evaluated on images from the Berkeley database.

1 Introduction

Image segmentation can be viewed as a partitioning of an image into regions having some similar properties, e.g. colour, texture, shape, etc, or as a partitioning of the image into semantically meaningful parts (as people do). A common problem is that it is difficult to objectively measure the goodness of a segmentation produced for such a task. Obtaining absolute ground truth is almost impossible since different people produce different manual segmentations of the same images [1].

Recently, a method combining image segmentation, the detection of faces, and the detection and reading of text in an integrated framework has appeared [2]. It is one of the first attempts to look at segmentation as a knowledge-driven task. At the beginning of the whole face/text recognition task a pre-segmentation of the image is performed which is then iteratively improved by the recognition results. It turns out that the knowledge-based approach using good initial segmentation leads to a reasonable result towards recognition of the objects in images. Similarly, in [3] it is shown that the image segmentation is an important first step in automatic annotation of pictures.

In this paper we concentrate on finding an initial segmentation without any a priori knowledge such as an object database. The image is split automatically into regions

---

* This work was supported by the Austrian Science Foundation (FWF) under grant SESAME (P17189-N04), and the European Union Network of Excellence MUSCLE (FP6-507752).

A. Leonardis, H. Bischof, and A. Pinz (Eds.): ECCV 2006, Part II, LNCS 3952, pp. 468–480, 2006.
© Springer-Verlag Berlin Heidelberg 2006

Fig. 1. Automatic segmentation of the zebra image shown at the left. The three images on the right show three dominant textures as three different regions produced by the proposed method.

having similar properties in terms of colour and texture. See Fig. 1, where zebras were segmented due to different texture and colour to the grass background. This should be useful in a cognitive vision system leading towards the understanding of an image, as in [2, 3]. As psychophysics experiments have shown [4], at the beginning of the human procedure leading to scene understanding, some pre-segmentation using boundaries and regions is performed as well. Finally, humans use a huge object database in their brains to tune the segmentation. Usually, even with large occlusions, strong shadows and geometric distortions, humans still are able to recognize objects correctly.

There are many papers dealing with automatic segmentation. We have to mention the well known work of Shi & Malik [5] based on normalized cuts which segments an image into non-overlapping regions. They introduced a modification of graph cuts, namely normalized graph cuts, and provided an approximate closed-form solution. However, the boundaries of detected regions often do not follow the true boundaries of the objects. The work [6] is a follow-up to [5] where the segmentation is improved by doing it at various scales.

The normalized cuts method has often been used with success in combination with methods computing pixel neighborhood relations through brightness, colour and texture cues [7, 8, 9, 10]. See results [11] showing what automatic segmentation without knowledge database using affinity functions [8] which were fed to an eigensolver to cluster the image can achieve. In our experiments we used the same image dataset [12] to easily compare the results.

There is another direction in image segmentation by using Level Set Methods [13, 14]. The boundary of a textured foreground object is obtained by minimization (through the evolution of the region contour) of energies inside and outside the region.

The main contribution of this paper lies in showing how a small image patch can be used to automatically drive the image segmentation based on graph cuts resulting in colour- and texture-coherent non-overlapping regions. Moreover, a new illumination invariant similarity measure between histograms is designed. For finding min-cut/max-flow in the graph we applied the algorithm [15] used for the user-driven image segmentation for grayscale non-textured images [15, 16, 17] augmented to colour and textured images in [18].

The proposed method works very well for images containing strong textures like natural images, see Fig. 1. Compared to other methods our approach does not need a learning process [8] or a priori information about the textures in the image [13]. The method positions a circular patch, called the seed, to detect the whole region having the same properties as the area covered by the seed. Many sub-segmentations produced during the positioning of the seed are then merged together based on proposed similarity measures. To obtain semantically correct regions composed often of many segments with different textures and colours some knowledge-based method would have to be applied which, however, is out of the scope of this paper.

A similar idea for establishing seeds at salient points based on a spectral embedding technique and min-cut in the graph appeared in [19]. However, we provide another more intuitive solution to this problem.

The structure of the paper is as follows. The segmentation method is first explained for one seed in Sec. 2 and then for multiple seeds together with combining and merging partial segmentations yielding the final segmentation pyramid in Sec. 3, outlined in steps in Sec. 4. Finally an experimental evaluation and summary conclude the paper.

2   One Seed Segmentation

We use a seed segmentation technique [18] taking into account colour and texture based on the interactive graph cut method [15]. The core of the segmentation method is based on an efficient algorithm [16] for finding the min-cut/max-flow in a graph. At first we very briefly outline the boundary detection and then the construction and segmentation of the graph representing an image.

2.1   Boundary Detection

Our main emphasis is put on boundaries at the changes of different textured regions and not local changes inside a single texture. However, there are usually large responses of edge detectors inside textures. Therefore, in this paper we use as a cue the colour and texture gradients introduced in [7,9] to produce the *combined boundary probability* image, see Fig. 5(b).

2.2   Graph Representing the Image

The general framework for building the graph is depicted in Fig. 2 (left). The graph is shown here for a 9 pixel image and an 8-point neighborhood $\mathcal{N}$. In general, the graph has as many nodes as pixels plus two extra nodes labeled F, B. In addition, the pixel neighborhood is larger, e.g. we use a window of size 21×21 pixels.

The neighborhood penalty between two pixels is defined as follows

$$W_{\mathbf{q},\mathbf{r}} = \left(e^{-\frac{g(\mathbf{q},\mathbf{r})^2}{\sigma_2}} \right)^2, \qquad g(\mathbf{q},\mathbf{r}) = p_b(\mathbf{q}) + \max_{\mathbf{s} \in \mathcal{L}_{\mathbf{q},\mathbf{r}}} p_b(\mathbf{s}), \qquad (1)$$

where σ_2 is a parameter (we used $\sigma_2 = 0.08$ in all our experiments), $p_b(\mathbf{q})$ is the combined boundary probability (Sec. 2.1) at point $\mathbf{q}$ and $\mathcal{L}_{\mathbf{q},\mathbf{r}} = \{\mathbf{x} \in \mathbb{R}^2 : \mathbf{x} = \mathbf{q} + k(\mathbf{r} - \mathbf{q}), k \in (0,1)\}$ is a set of points on a discretized line from the point $\mathbf{q}$ (exclusive) to the point $\mathbf{r}$ (inclusive).

Each node in the graph is connected to the two extra nodes F, B. This allows the incorporation of the information provided by the seed and a penalty for each pixel being foreground or background to be set. The penalty of a point as being foreground $\mathcal{F}$ or background $\mathcal{B}$ is defined as follows

$$R_{\mathcal{F}|\mathbf{q}} = -\ln p(\mathcal{B}|\mathbf{c}_\mathbf{q}), \qquad R_{\mathcal{B}|\mathbf{q}} = -\ln p(\mathcal{F}|\mathbf{c}_\mathbf{q}), \qquad (2)$$

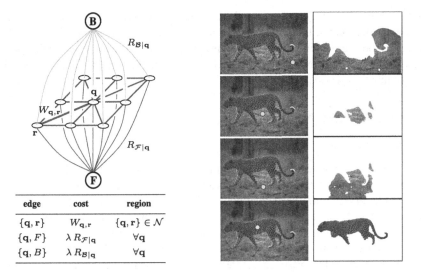

edge	cost	region
$\{\mathbf{q}, \mathbf{r}\}$	$W_{\mathbf{q}, \mathbf{r}}$	$\{\mathbf{q}, \mathbf{r}\} \in \mathcal{N}$
$\{\mathbf{q}, F\}$	$\lambda\, R_{\mathcal{F}|\mathbf{q}}$	$\forall \mathbf{q}$
$\{\mathbf{q}, B\}$	$\lambda\, R_{\mathcal{B}|\mathbf{q}}$	$\forall \mathbf{q}$

Fig. 2. Left: Graph representation for a 9 pixel image and a table defining the costs of graph edges. Symbols are explained in the text. Right: Four binary image segmentations using various positions of the seed.

where $\mathbf{c_q} = (c_L,\ c_a,\ c_b)^\top$ is a vector in $\mathbb{R}^3$ of CIELAB values at the pixel $\mathbf{q}$. The CIELAB colour space has the advantage of being approximately perceptually uniform. Furthermore, Euclidean distances in this space are perceptually meaningful as they correspond to colour differences perceived by the human eye. Another reason for the good performance of this space could be that in calculating the colour probabilities below, we make the assumption that the three colour channels are statistically independent. This assumption is better in the CIELAB space than in the RGB space. The posterior probabilities are computed as

$$p(\mathcal{B}|\mathbf{c_q}) = \frac{p(\mathbf{c_q}|\mathcal{B})}{p(\mathbf{c_q}|\mathcal{B}) + p(\mathbf{c_q}|\mathcal{F})},\tag{3}$$

where the prior probabilities are

$$p(\mathbf{c_q}|\mathcal{F}) = f^L(c_L) \cdot f^a(c_a) \cdot f^b(c_b), \quad \text{and} \quad p(\mathbf{c_q}|\mathcal{B}) = b^L(c_L) \cdot b^a(c_a) \cdot b^b(c_b),$$

and $f^{\{L,a,b\}}(i)$, resp. $b^{\{L,a,b\}}(i)$, represents the foreground, resp. the background histogram of each colour channel separately at the ith bin smoothed by a Gaussian kernel. We used 64 bins. The foreground histograms $f^{\{L,a,b\}}$ are computed from all pixels behind the seed. The background histograms $b^{\{L,a,b\}}$ are computed from all pixels in the image. See [18] for more details. λ in the table in Fig. 2 controls the importance of foreground/background penalties against colour+texture penalties and was set to 1000.

After the graph is built the min-cut/max-flow splitting the graph and also the image into two regions is found by the algorithm [16].

See segmentations resulting from various seed positions in Fig. 2 (right). It can be seen that segmented foreground region has similar properties to the pixels behind the seed. Due to illumination changes, shadows and perspective distortion changing the resolution of textures, the whole texture region is usually not marked as one region. However, the segmented regions representing the same texture overlap which we use in the procedure described in the next section to merge them and to build a probability map yielding the segmentation.

3   Multiple Seed Segmentation

3.1   Seed Positioning

Each seed position gives one binary segmentation of the image, see Fig. 2(right). To obtain image segmentation we move the seed across the image as follows.

A regular grid of initial seed positions is created, marked as black dots on small white patches in Fig. 3(a). Using seeds at regular grid positions would segment two textured regions as one segment. Since we want to find segments with a constant inner structure we avoid cases where the seed crosses a strong response in the combined boundary probability map in Fig. 5(b). Therefore we create a local neighborhood around each initial position in the grid and the position of the seed which minimizes the sum of values of pixels behind the seed in the combined probability map is looked for, i.e.

$$\mathbf{u}^* = \operatorname*{argmin}_{\mathbf{u} \in \mathcal{A}} \sum_{\mathbf{v} \in \mathcal{S}_\mathbf{u}} p_b(\mathbf{v}), \tag{4}$$

where $\mathbf{u}$ is a 2 element vector with $(x, y)^\top$ image coordinates, $\mathcal{S}_\mathbf{u}$ is the seed (in our case circular) area centered at the point $\mathbf{u}$ and $\mathcal{A}$ is a neighborhood rectangle around the initial grid point. The neighborhood rectangles should not overlap to avoid the case of identical seed positions having different initial points. We find the minimum in Eq. (4) by brute force, i.e. the error is evaluated at all possible positions of the seed in the neighborhood $\mathcal{A}$ because of low computational demand.

For each initial grid position, one $\mathbf{u}^*$ is found and the segmentation method described in Sec. 2 is applied using a seed positioned at $\mathbf{u}^*$ to obtain a binary sub-segmentation. The positions $\mathbf{u}^*$ of the seeds for the leopard image are shown in Fig. 3(a).

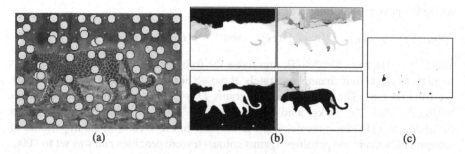

(a)   (b)   (c)

Fig. 3. (a) The input image with automatically positioned seeds. (b) Probability maps for four possible segments. Black corresponds to the higher probability, white to the lowest one. (c) Unassigned pixels.

3.2   Combining Partial Segmentations

The sub-segmentations corresponding to the seeds are grouped together w.r.t. the size of the mutual common area with other sub-segmentations. At the beginning of moving the seed an empty list of potential segments is created. After the first run (first position of the seed) the sub-segmentation is assigned to the first segment in the list. After each consecutive run the actual sub-segmentation is compared to segments already stored in the list. If there is any segment in the list overlapping with a specified fraction (we use 80%) of pixels then the sub-segmentation is *summed* to this segment. Otherwise a new segment in the list is created.

Summing the sub-segmentations produces the probability with which each pixel belongs to each of the possible segments. The sum of values of pixels lying at the same position in different segments in the list is used for normalization to get the value range from 0 to 1. Fig. 3(b) shows an example of a four segment list obtained by applying segmentations using seeds depicted in Fig. 3(a). There may still remain pixels which were not assigned to any segment, see Fig. 3(c), which are treated in the merging stage described later.

3.3   From Probability Map to Segments

The probability map constructed in the previous sub-section can be used to obtain the a priori probability of each possible segment. Assuming that each segment is equally important and no penalizations are applied, the decision following Bayes theorem leads to choosing for each pixel the segment which has the highest support by sub-segmentations, i.e. has highest a priori probability. For example, the tail of the leopard is present in three segments, see Fig. 3(b). However, in the segment containing the whole leopard the pixels corresponding to the tail have the highest probability to be assigned to this segment. See Fig. 4 for the result. The list of segments $\mathcal{L}$ is represented by binary matrices L_i, i.e.

$$\mathcal{L} = \{L_i \in \{0,1\}^{n \times m} : 0 \leq i \leq S\},$$

where S is the number of segments. The matrix L_0 stands for the segment containing unassigned pixels.

For the leopard image after this stage we could be satisfied since the segmentation captures the main regions. One possible region (top right in Fig. 3(b)) disappeared as no pixels remained assigned to this segment after incorporating probabilities. However, the non-overlapping segments having similar properties can sometimes be split due to illumination changes. To observe this, look at the grass or the bear head in the bear image

Fig. 4. Segmentation after assigning the most probable segment to each pixel. The rightmost image corresponds to unassigned pixels.

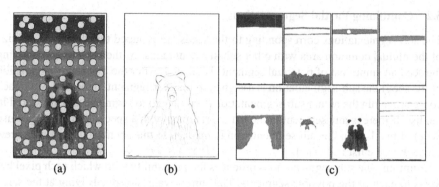

Fig. 5. (a) The bear image with automatically positioned seeds. (b) Combined boundary probability image. (c) Possible segments. The last one corresponds to unassigned pixels.

segmentation in Fig. 5. Therefore, we incorporate a shadow-invariant colour space and merge similar segments into one using a newly designed similarity measure described in the following subsections.

3.4   Elimination of Unassigned Segments

We convert an input image into the $c_1 c_2 c_3$ illumination invariant colour space [20]. Comparison and evaluation of various colour models in the sense of their invariance can be found in [20]. The conversion from RGB to $c_1 c_2 c_3$ colour space is done as follows

$$c_1 = \arctan \frac{R}{\max\{G, B\}}, \quad c_2 = \arctan \frac{G}{\max\{R, B\}}, \quad c_3 = \arctan \frac{B}{\max\{R, G\}}.$$

We compute colour histograms $h_i^{\{c_1, c_2, c_3\}}$ from pixels marked in segment L_i by 1's for $1 \leq i \leq S$. We used 64 bins and smoothed the histograms by a Gaussian kernel.

We label an unassigned segment stored in the binary matrix L_0 to separate all regions in this image. For each region $\mathcal{R}_j$ in the segment L_0, if its area is larger than some threshold (we use 200 pixels), the new segment L_{S++} is added into the list of all segments $\mathcal{L}$. Otherwise, if the area is below the threshold, the region $\mathcal{R}_j$ is assigned to the most probable segment i^* in the list $\mathcal{L}$ w.r.t. to the following criterion

$$i^*(j) = \underset{1 \leq i \leq S}{\operatorname{argmax}} \sum_{\mathbf{u} \in \mathcal{R}_j} h_i^{c_1}(\mathbf{I(u)}_{c_1}) \cdot h_i^{c_2}(\mathbf{I(u)}_{c_2}) \cdot h_i^{c_3}(\mathbf{I(u)}_{c_3}), \tag{5}$$

where $\mathbf{I(u)}_{\{c_1, c_2, c_3\}}$ are c_1, c_2, c_3 values of an image point at the position $\mathbf{u}$. By this step all pixels/regions in the unassigned segment L_0 are eliminated, however, the number of segments in the list $\mathcal{L}$ can increase.

3.5   Merging Segments

We observed that the change of illumination on the same surface does not change the shape of the histograms, however, it causes their mutual shift. This motivated us to design a new illumination invariant similarity function between histograms based on evaluating the shift.

At first, compute the cross-correlation between histograms of segments for each colour channel separately and find the maximum values of cross-correlation in some range $\langle t_1, t_2 \rangle$, i.e.

$$\mathbf{r}(i,j) = \begin{pmatrix} \operatorname{argmax}_{t_1 \leq t \leq t_2} (h_i^{c_1} \star h_j^{c_1})(t) \\ \operatorname{argmax}_{t_1 \leq t \leq t_2} (h_i^{c_2} \star h_j^{c_2})(t) \\ \operatorname{argmax}_{t_1 \leq t \leq t_2} (h_i^{c_3} \star h_j^{c_3})(t) \end{pmatrix}, \tag{6}$$

where $\star$ stands for cross-correlation. We show in Fig. 6 the cross-correlation of third segment histograms with each of the other segments, i.e. $(h_3^{c\{1,2,3\}} \star h_j^{c\{1,2,3\}})(t)$, for the segments shown in Fig. 5(c). As can be seen the cross-correlations have single maxima which can easily be detected. If there is no peak inside the interval bounded by t_1, t_2, the distance is set to Inf. We use $t_2 = -t_1 = 20$. The interval should be reasonably narrow since comparison of the same colours affected by shadows yields only small displacement of the maxima. In contrast, comparison of different colours yields more significant displacement and the distance between maxima is meaningless.

Let three elements of $\mathbf{r}(i,j)$ be sorted in a vector $\mathbf{s} = (s_1, s_2, s_3)^\top$ such that $s_1 \leq s_2 \leq s_3$. The squared distance of two histograms i, j is then evaluated as

$$d(i,j) = (s_1 - s_2)^2 + (s_3 - s_2)^2. \tag{7}$$

The histogram distance in Eq. (7) computed for all pairs of segments is used for finding most similar segment(s) in the list $\mathcal{L}$. The segments which mutually match to each other are merged together if the distance is below some threshold d_{thr}. The level of merging can be controlled by this threshold. Depending on the value various levels in the final segmentation pyramid are created, see for example the three-level pyramid in Fig. 7. In this case d_{thr} was increasing from 10 to 200 while three levels were obtained.

From Fig. 6 it is evident that the grass segment (third segment in Fig. 5(c)) is most similar to other green segments. The same happens to the bear's head which is at first

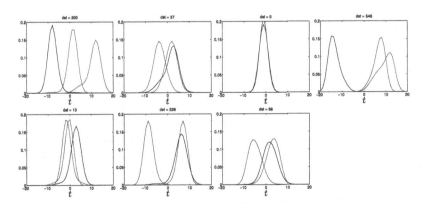

Fig. 6. Histogram cross-correlation $(h_3^{c\{1,2,3\}} \star h_j^{c\{1,2,3\}})(t)$ for $j = 1..7$. Red, green, blue colour of the curves in each graph corresponds to the c_1, c_2, c_3 colour channel respectively.

Fig. 7. Three-level pyramid of the bear image. Top row: First pyramid level with six segments. Bottom row: Second level (five segments on the left) and third level (two rightmost segments).

divided into two parts in Fig. 5(c), however, at some level in the pyramid is merged together.

4   Algorithm

We shortly summarize all the steps leading to the final single image segmentation:

1. Convert the image from the RGB colour space to the CIELAB space.
2. Compute the combined boundary gradient based on [7, 9] of the image.
3. Make a regular initial grid of seeds. For each initial seed position find a new optimal position, Sec. 3.1, and compute a binary segmentation based on the min-cut/max-flow in the graph, Sec. 2.
4. Combine segmentations yielding a probability map, Sec. 3.2, and create a list of segments $\mathcal{L}$, Sec. 3.3.
5. Eliminate unassigned pixels, Sec. 3.4, and merge similar segments based on the illumination invariant similarity measure described in Sec. 3.5.
6. Depending on the chosen distance threshold d_{thr} in the similarity measure, the degree of segmentation coarseness is controlled and the final segmentation pyramid is obtained.

5   Experimental Evaluation

To benchmark the results of the algorithms, we made use of the Berkeley segmentation benchmark described in [1]. Two measures of the difference between two segmentations S_1 and S_2 are introduced in this paper, the Global and Local Consistency Errors (GCE and LCE). As the GCE is a more demanding measure, we make use of only this measure. There are other possibilities for benchmarking such as to use precision/recall curves as in [19, 9].

We used the 200 colour images in the test group of the Berkeley Segmentation Dataset [12] as well as the corresponding human segmentations. For each of the images, at least 5 segmentations produced by different people are available. For each image, the GCE of the segmentation produced by the tested algorithm with respect to each of the

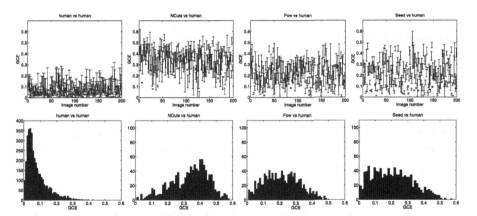

Fig. 8. Global Consistency Error (GCE) for human, normalized cuts (ncuts), Fowlkes et al. [8] (fow) and our proposed method (seed) (from left). The top row shows variance of the GCE for each image in the dataset. The bottom row shows the histogram of the GCE.

available human segmentations for that image was calculated. The mean of these values gives the mean GCE per image, which was plotted in a histogram, see Fig. 8. The global GCE was calculated as the mean of these 200 mean GCE values.

We compared human segmentations to each other and then with the normalized cuts algorithm (ncuts) [5], Fowlkes et al. algorithm (fow) [8] and our seed algorithm (seed). Comparison of human vs. human produces a very low GCE value which indicates the consistency of the human segmentations. The "ncuts" and "fow" methods were applied to the same combined boundary images as we used, mentioned in Sec. 2.1. Using the same boundary gradient implies that the performance of the various methods is compared using the same starting condition.

The implementation of the "ncuts" used (provided on the authors' web page) requires that the number of regions required be passed as a parameter. We used 5 as the average number of segments per image for our seed segmentation was 4.3. There is a version of the "ncuts" which determines the number of regions automatically [7], but we currently have no implementation of it. The segmentations for the "fow" method were provided directly by the author. In this segmentation, the average number of segments was 13. See Tab. 1 for the results.

Table 1. Comparison of the methods. The first column contains the acronyms of the methods. The second column corresponds to the average number of segments per image. The third column shows the mean GCE error over all segmentations.

method	# of reg	GCE
hum	17	0.080
seed	4	0.209
fow	13	0.214
ncuts	5	0.336

Usually as the number of regions per image grows it appears that the images become more over-segmented. As is mentioned in [1] the GCE measure does not penalize an over-segmentation. Our method and the "fow" method produce comparable GCE, however, the average number of segments of our method is less, approximately one third. In some cases it means that our method does not split coherent regions.

Our segmentation method was implemented in MATLAB. Some of the most time consuming operations (such as creating the graph edge weights) were implemented in C and interfaced with MATLAB through mex-files. We used the online available C++ implementations of the min-cut algorithm [16] and some MATLAB code for colour and texture gradient computation [7].

The method is relatively slow, for one 375x250 image with 96 seeds it needs on average 15 minutes on a Pentium 4@2.8 GHz. However, the computation can easily be parallelized as each sub-segmentation can be done independently on many computers. The building of the weight matrix W representing the graph (which is done only once per image) needs approximately 50 seconds. Once the graph is built, finding the min-cut for one seed position takes 2 – 10 seconds.

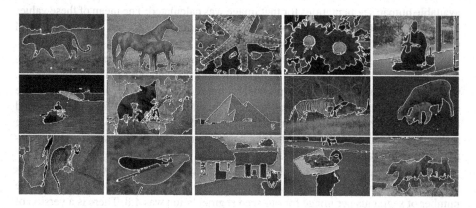

Fig. 9. Some segmentation results on images from the Berkeley dataset

You may look at the results of the "fow" method [11] and our method[1] to visually compare their performance. In general, both methods perform comparably, however, one method performs better on some images, the second one on others. This gives an option to combine the methods in some further processing to choose the better result. Some segmentations using our method can be seen in Fig. 9. The results shown here correspond to the threshold d_{thr} equal to 10. The whole pyramid was built by changing the d_{thr} from 10 to 200. Each new level of pyramid is created when the number of segments increases according to the previous level. Usually, 4 levels is the maximum.

Constants (number of histogram bins, sigmas, etc.) which appear in the text are tuned experimentally on real images to obtain reasonable performance on large data.

---

[1] http://www.prip.tuwien.ac.at/Research/muscle/Images/ECCV06res

6   Conclusion

The paper proposes a method for image segmentation into texture and colour coherent segments. The segmentation combines known algorithms for computing combined boundary gradient and for finding min-cut/max-flow in the graph. The novelty is in introducing the positioning of the seed, and collecting and merging similar segments yielding the segmentation pyramid. Moreover, an illumination invariant similarity measure is introduced.

We show that our method gives comparable results to the state-of-the-art methods based on normalized graph cuts on the Berkeley dataset. We cannot say if the proposed method outperforms existing methods since quantitative comparison of segmentations is still an open problem. However, visual comparison as well as GCE comparison indicate reasonable and useful results.

References

1. Martin, D., Fowlkes, C., Tal, D., Malik, J.: A database of human segmented natural images and its application to evaluating segmentation algorithms and measuring ecological statistics. In: Proc. ICCV. (2001) 416–425
2. Tu, Z., Chen, X., Yuille, A., Zhu, S.: Image parsing: Unifying segmentation, detection, and recognition. IJCV **63**(2) (2005) 113–140 *Marr Prize*.
3. Barnard, K., Duygulu, P., de Freitas, N., Forsyth, D., Blei, D., Jordan, M.I.: Matching words and pictures. Journal of Machine Learning Research **3** (2003) 1107–1135
4. Wolfson, S., Landy, M.: Examining edge- and region-based texture analysis mechanisms. Vision Research **38**(3) (1998) 439–446
5. Shi, J., Malik, J.: Normalized cuts and image segmentation. PAMI **22**(8) (2000) 888–905
6. Stella, X.Y.: Segmentation using multiscale cues. In: Proc. CVPR. (2004) I: 247–254
7. Malik, J., Belongie, S., Leung, T., Shi, J.: Contour and texture analysis for image segmentation. IJCV **43**(1) (2001) 7–27
8. Fowlkes, C., Martin, D., Malik, J.: Learning affinity functions for image segmentation: Combining patch-based and gradient-based approaches. In: Proc. CVPR. (2003) II: 54–61
9. Martin, D.R., Fowlkes, C.C., Malik, J.: Learning to detect natural image boundaries using local brightness, color, and texture cues. PAMI **26**(5) (2004) 530–549
10. Zabih, R., Kolmogorov, V.: Spatially coherent clustering using graph cuts. In: Proc. CVPR. (2004) II:437–444
11. (http://www.cs.berkeley.edu/~fowlkes/BSE/cvpr-segs)
12. (http://www.cs.berkeley.edu/projects/vision/grouping/segbench)
13. Paragios, N., Deriche, R.: Geodesic active regions and level set methods for supervised texture segmentation. IJCV **46**(3) (2002) 223–247
14. Osher, S., Paragios, N., eds.: Geometric Level Set Methods in Imaging, Vision and Graphics. Springer-Verlag (2003)
15. Boykov, Y., Jolly, M.P.: Interactive graph cuts for optimal boundary & region segmentation of objects in N-D images. In: Proc. ICCV. (2001) 105–112
16. Boykov, Y., Kolmogorov, V.: An experimental comparison of min-cut/max-flow algorithms for energy minimization in vision. PAMI **26**(9) (2004) 1124–1137
17. Kolmogorov, V., Zabih, R.: What energy functions can be minimized via graph cuts? PAMI **26**(2) (2004) 147–159

480   B. Mičušík and A. Hanbury

18. Mičušík, B., Hanbury, A.: Supervised texture detection in images. In: Proc. Conference on Computer Analysis of Images and Patterns (CAIP). (2005) 441–448
19. Estrada, F.J., Jepson, A.D.: Quantitative evaluation of a novel image segmentation algorithm. In: Proc. CVPR. (2005) II: 1132–1139
20. Gevers, T., Smeulders, A.: Color-based object recognition. Pattern Recognition **32**(3) (1999) 453–64

Patch-Based Texture Edges and Segmentation

Lior Wolf[1], Xiaolei Huang[2], Ian Martin[1], and Dimitris Metaxas[2]

[1] Center for Biological and Computational Learning,
The McGovern Institute for Brain Research and dept. of Brain & Cognitive Sciences,
Massachusetts Institute of Technology, Cambridge, MA
[2] Division of Computer and Information Sciences,
Rutgers University, New Brunswick, NJ

Abstract. A novel technique for extracting texture edges is introduced. It is based on the combination of two ideas: the patch-based approach, and non-parametric tests of distributions.

Our method can reliably detect texture edges using only local information. Therefore, it can be computed as a preprocessing step prior to segmentation, and can be very easily combined with parametric deformable models. These models furnish our system with smooth boundaries and globally salient structures.

1 Introduction

The detection of image edges has been one of the most explored domains in computer vision. While most of the effort has been aimed at the detection of intensity edges, the study of color edges and the study of texture edges are also well developed fields.

The dominant approach in texture edge analysis is to construct a description of the local neighborhood around each pixel, and then to compare this descriptor to the descriptors of nearby points. This approach is often referred to as "patch-based" since a fragment around each pixel is used in order to compute the outputs of the filters. In this work, however, the term "patch-based" is quite distinguishable from the above: it means that the gray values of the patch are used as-is, and that the basic operation on patches is the comparison of two patches using image correlation measures, such as normalized cross correlation between the gray values, or their Euclidean distance.

What makes this approach novel for texture edge detection is that since texture is a stochastic property, this kind of descriptor would traditionally be considered unfit. In other words, since the gray values of two neighboring patches from the same texture could be very different, most methods rely on more elaborate descriptors. This is in contrast to the dominant trend in current texture synthesis research, where patches of the original texture are stitched together in order to generate a new texture image – a trend that seems to be much more successful than the best descriptor based methods.

The main idea of this work is simple to grasp: if a point lies on the left-hand side of a texture edge, the distribution of similarities of the patch centered at this point to the patches on its left is different from the distribution of similarities to

A. Leonardis, H. Bischof, and A. Pinz (Eds.): ECCV 2006, Part II, LNCS 3952, pp. 481–493, 2006.
© Springer-Verlag Berlin Heidelberg 2006

the patches on its right. Detection of the texture edges can therefore be achieved by examining these differences in the similarity distributions.

As this paper will show, sampling from the distributions of similarities can be done very efficiently. In order to estimate whether the distributions are the same, we use a non-parametric test called the Wilcoxon Mann-Whitney Test [38]. It is similar to the t-test but performs well even for small sample sizes with unknown distributions.

In contrast to intensity edges, which have many uses in computer vision, texture edges have been used primarily for image segmentation. In order to make this work complete, we couple it with a segmentation scheme. Since texture edges are often gapped, we use a hybrid deformable model to capture the image contour. This hybrid deformable model is an adaptation of the general class of Metamorphs Deformable models [19]. This type of deformable model borrows the best features from traditional parametric deformable models [20, 35] and geometric level-set based deformable models [7, 22], and enjoys the advantage of bridging over gaps in contours, topology freedom during evolution, and fast convergence. In particular, the model shape is implicitly represented in a higher dimensional space of distance transforms as a distance map "image", and model deformations are efficiently parameterized using a space warping technique: the Free Form Deformations (FFD) [1, 3] based on cubic B-splines.

2   Previous Work

Below we discuss traditional texture segmentation approaches, the emerging patch-based techniques, and explain the background for our statistical test.

Feature-Based Texture Edge Detection and Segmentation. Traditional methods for texture analysis are often grouped into three major categories: statistical, structural and spectral. In the statistical approach, texture statistics (e.g., moments of the gray-value histogram, or co-occurrence matrices) serve as texture descriptors. In structural approaches, the structure is analyzed by constructing a set of rules that generates the texture. In spectral approaches, the texture is analyzed in the frequency domain. In contrast to the wealth of approaches suggested in the past, the last decade has been dominated by the filter bank approach, to which we will suggest an alternative.

> "There is an emerging consensus that for texture analysis, an image should first be convolved with a bank of filters tuned to various orientations and spatial frequencies."[11]

Of the many studies that employ banks of filters, the most common set of filters used seems to be the Gabor filters [10, 16, 17, 11, 23, 32]. We would like to specifically mention the work of [32] which, like our work, emphasizes the detection of texture edges, not texture segmentation. In relation to our work, we would also like to point out that non-parametric tests have been used in the past for texture segmentation, [16, 17], where nearby blocks of the image were grouped together if the distributions of filter outputs in those blocks were not statistically distinguishable. Similar to our work, the statistical distinguishability has been measured using non parametric tests: [16] used the Kolmogorov-Smirnov distance and [17] used the χ^2 statistic.

On a more abstract level, we find relation to the work of [14] in which characteristics of small segments in the image are used as part of the texture description in addition to filter banks. We conjecture that, similar to the move in object recognition from semantic-object-parts to patches at random locations [36], patches from textured areas may be similar in strength to identified subsegments for texture segmentation.

Patch Based Methods. The filter bank approach was popular in the field of texture synthesis as well (e.g., [15, 28]), up until the advent of the patch based methods. In the few years since its publication [9, 21], the patch-based method has dominated the field of texture synthesis.

The basic use of the patch for texture synthesis consists of stitching together small overlapping patches of the input texture, such that their boundaries overlap (i.e., the gray value differences at the boundaries are minimal). This results in a new texture image, which seems to match the original texture in appearance, and has similar statistical properties. A similar approach was used for super-resolution [13] and for class-based edge detection [5]. The success of the patch-based methods has been extended to image completion [8] and to image denoising [2]. Patch-based methods were also shown to be extremely successful in object recognition [36].

Non-parametric Statistical Tests. Non-parametric statistical tests are preferred over their parametric counterparts, when certain assumptions about the data cannot be made. For example, the t-test assumes that the difference between the two independent samples it is applied to is normally distributed, while its non-parametric analog, the Wilcoxon Mann-Whitney Test [38], does not.

The WMW Test is one of the most powerful of the non-parametric tests for comparing two samples. It is used to test the null hypothesis that two samples have identical distribution functions against the alternative hypothesis that the two distribution functions differ only with respect to location (median), if at all.

This test has several advantages that make it especially suitable for our application. First, it is valid for data from any distribution and is robust to outliers. Second, it reacts to differences both in the location of the distributions (i.e., to the difference of their median), and to the shape of the distributions. The test is well known, however, since it is uncommon in Computer Vision circles, and in order to keep this paper self-contained, we describe it in Fig. 1.

Deformable Models for Segmentation. Deformable models or Active Contours are curves and surfaces that move toward edges under the influence of internal smoothness forces and external image forces. In traditional deformable models, the external image forces come from image gradient or intensity edge information, which are not reliable guides for texture segmentation. Region Competition [41] performs texture segmentation by combining region growing and active

Given two vectors of samples v_a and v_b, of lengths n_a and n_b we wish to find a measure for the similarity of the underlying distributions.

1. Combine the samples into one vector of length $n_a + n_b$ and sort this vector.
2. Each observation in the combined vector has a rank. The first observation has a rank of 1, the second has a rank of 2, etc.
3. Let w_a be the sum of all of the ranks of elements originating from the vector v_a, and let w_b be a similar sum for v_b.
4. Use the statistic $w = min(w_a, w_b)$ to determine if the two distributions are different. Very low values of w suggest they are.

Fig. 1. The Wilcoxon Mann-Whitney Test

contours using multi-band input after applying a set of gabor filters. The method assumes multivariate Gaussian distributions on the filter-response vector inputs. Geodesic Active Regions [27] deals with supervised texture segmentation in a frame partition framework using level-set deformable model implementation; the assumptions of the method are that the number of regions in an image are known beforehand and statistics of each region are learned offline. The active unsupervised texture segmentation approach proposed in [31] uses feature channels extracted based on structure tensor and nonlinear diffusion to discriminate different texture regions, the statistics of these features are then incorporated in a level set based deformable model segmentation process to partition the image into a foreground and a background region. Another level-set based algorithm proposed in [33] detects texture edges by applying multiple gabor transforms and an vector valued active contour model; the method supports both supervised and unsupervised forms of the model, although it is limited by the selection of proper gabor filter parameters and the Gaussian assumption on filter responses within each region. Our unsupervised segmentation method overcomes the difficulties faced by these methods by decomposing the problem into the two stages of an initial local texture edge detection and a follow-up segmentation using a hybrid deformable model that smoothly bridges over the missing gaps.

Work Related on an Abstract Level. In this work we detect discontinuities (edges) by comparing distributions to the left and to the right of each point. This idea can be tracked back to [40]. Comparing gray values of adjusted curves was used in [39] in order to classify hand marked edges into the occluding contour or the cast shadow types, in a manner that has faint similarities to our method.

3   Patch Based Texture Edge Detection

Our method is straightforward and is illustrated in Fig. 2(a). In essence, it tests whether a point (x, y) in the image is near a texture edge. Assume a situation where (x, y) is not near a texture edge. Then the similarities between the patch surrounding (x, y) and the nearby patches to its left and right are drawn from the same distribution. In our experiments we measure similarities by simply computing the Euclidean distance between the patch at (x, y) and the nearby

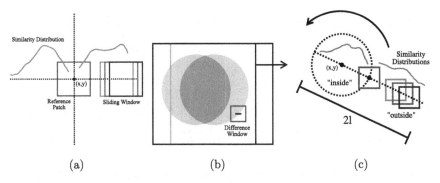

Fig. 2. (a) An illustration of the grid method, in which the patches near the center patch are used in order to compute the similarity distributions. Four distributions are sampled: D_{up}, D_{down}, D_{left} and D_{right}. The pixel at the center would be considered to lie on a texture edge if, according to the Wilcoxon Mann Whitney test, the distribution D_{up} is determined to be different from the distribution D_{down}, or if D_{left} is determined to be different from D_{right}. (b) An illustration of the efficient method to sample the four distributions, using vector operations. To simultaneously sample all of the differences between all of the patches in the image, and all of the patches which are Δx pixels to the right or to the left, a copy of the image is translated Δx pixels left, and then subtracted from the original image. The difference is squared, and then summed at each 5x5 patch in the image, which is a separable operation. (c) An alternative architecture using the flux idea. A pixel would not be on a texture edge if the similarity of points along a circle around it are as likely to be similar to points inside the circle, as they are to points outside the circle. For each point on the circle of radius r, the similarity of the patch around it is compared to patches along the line of length $2l$, which passes through the center point, the point on the circle, and outside of the circle.

patches. Our use of the actual image patch as a template, instead of a predefined filter bank, has the potential to be very sensitive to changes in the local texture.

Let D_{right}, D_{left} be the distributions of similarities between the patch surrounding (x, y) and the nearby patches. If there is a texture edge on the left side of (x, y), it is natural to expect the distributions D_{right} and D_{left} to be different. For example, it might be reasonable to assume larger similarities within D_{right}.

In order to determine whether the two distributions are the same, we sample patches slightly to the left and to the right of the point (x, y). In the experiments we used a maximum distance of 15 pixels, and sampled at each pixel, therefore sampling 15 similarities from each distribution.

As mentioned above, we use the Wilcoxon Mann-Whitney Test, which excels for samples small in size, and assumes very little about the nature of the distributions. The horizontal texture edge points are those points for which the test determines that the two distributions D_{right} and D_{left} are different. The same process is then applied vertically, and two similar distributions D_{up} and D_{down} are compared. For our application we combine the two edge directions by taking the minimum value returned from the two tests.

Note, that since measurements from patches as far as 15 pixels away affect the distribution, we can expect the test score to change gradually. Moreover,

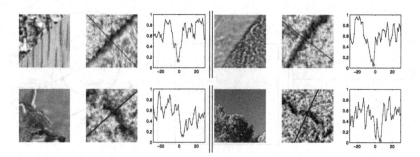

Fig. 3. Profile of the edges we obtain by using our method. Left of each triplet: the original part of the image. Middle: the texture edge we get. Right: the profile as a 2D plot. Note that the profile has a double edge effect, but it is rather minimal.

when (x, y) lies exactly on a texture edge, the patch around it is a hybrid patch, composed of two textures, and we expect the difference between the distributions to be lower exactly at the edge, this could create a double edge. It turns out that for the small patch size we used in the experiments (5×5 pixels), these concerns did not affect the texture edges dramatically. This is demonstrated in Fig. 3 with plots of several edge profiles (See also Fig. 2(c), for an brief illustration of a method developed to solve the double edge problem).

Another important implementation detail is the way ties are handled inside the non-parametric test [29]. While, in general, this question has a critical effect on the results, and should be addressed with caution, exact ties in patch similarity scores obtained from images are rare. An exception is when applying our method to areas where the gray value is exactly fixed. Adding a negligible amount of random noise to the Euclidean distances solves this problem by producing a random order in such cases.

3.1   Efficient Computation

Every pixel in the image contributes to many patches, which are in turn compared with many overlapping patches. A naïve implementation might compute the difference of the same two pixels multiple times. Another important facet of efficiency is that in some programming environments or hardware configurations (e.g., Matlab, designated graphics hardware) vector computations are done more efficiently than the repeated index-by-index computation.

The implementation we suggest is illustrated in Fig. 2(b), and is based on computing all of the patch comparisons to patches at a distance of Δx in either the vertical or horizontal direction at once. In order to do so, one only needs to translate the image Δx pixels in either the horizontal or vertical direction, and subtract the resulting image from the original image. Since we are interested in the Euclidean distance, we square each value in the difference image, and we then sum across all patches in the difference image. Since the summing operation is separable (can be done first horizontally, and then vertically), the procedure can be made extremely efficient.

4   Segmentation Using Hybrid Deformable Models

The detected texture edges can be coupled with a hybrid deformable model that moves in the manner of free form deformations to achieve segmentation over the entire image domain. The Euclidean distance transform is used to implicitly embed an evolving model as the zero level set of a higher dimensional distance function [25]. If we denote the model as $\mathcal{M}$, and the implicit model representation as a distance map $\Phi_{\mathcal{M}}$, then the shape defines a partition of the image domain: the region enclosed by $\mathcal{M}$, $[\mathcal{R}_{\mathcal{M}}]$; the background region $[\Omega - \mathcal{R}_{\mathcal{M}}]$; and the model itself, $[\partial \mathcal{R}_{\mathcal{M}}]$, which corresponds to the zero level set. Such a model shape representation provides a feature space in which objective functions that are optimized using a gradient descent method are stable enough to use.

The deformations that a model can undergo are defined using a space warping technique: the Free Form Deformations (FFD) [34]. In essence, FFD deforms an object by manipulating a regular control lattice $F = \{(F_{m,n}^x, F_{m,n}^y)\}$ of $M \times N$ control points overlaid on top of a region Γ in the volumetric embedding space that contains the object (below we use $\Gamma = \{(x,y)|1 \le x \le X, 1 \le y \le Y\}$ in the object-centered coordinate system). In the Incremental Free Form Deformations (IFFD) formulation used in [19], the deformation parameters, $\mathbf{q}$, are the deformations of the control points in both x and y directions:

$$\mathbf{q} = \{(\delta F_{m,n}^x, \delta F_{m,n}^y)\}; \ (m,n) \in [1,M] \times [1,N].$$

When the control lattice deforms from F^0 to $F = F^0 + \delta F$, the deformed position of a pixel $\mathbf{x} = (x,y)$ is given by $D(\mathbf{q}; \mathbf{x})$, which is defined in terms of a tensor product of Cubic B-spline polynomials:

$$D(\mathbf{q}; \mathbf{x}) = \sum_{k=0}^{3} \sum_{l=0}^{3} B_k(u) B_l(v)(F_{i+k,j+l}^0 + \delta F_{i+k,j+l}) \tag{1}$$

where $i = \lfloor \frac{x}{X} \cdot (M-1) \rfloor + 1$, $j = \lfloor \frac{y}{Y} \cdot (N-1) \rfloor + 1$.

To find texture region boundaries given a simple-shape model initialized around a seed point, the dynamics of the free-form deformable model are derived from edge energy terms. Instead of intensity edges, which fail to separate textured regions, we use the texture edges computed using our patch-based method above. The result of our patch-based filtering is a texture edge map (e.g., Fig. 3, middle columns), on which true edges between different texture regions correspond to low values. Denote the texture edge map as I_t, the boundary data term E_b below encourages model deformations that map the model boundary to the pixel locations with the smallest values on I_t.

$$E_b = \frac{1}{V(\partial \mathcal{R}_{\mathcal{M}})} \iint_{\partial \mathcal{R}_{\mathcal{M}}} \left(I_t(D(\mathbf{q}; \mathbf{x}))\right)^2 d\mathbf{x} \ ,$$

where $V(\mathcal{R})$ represents the volume of a region $\mathcal{R}$. The above boundary term E_b can help the model to converge to the exact edge location where the difference between two neighboring texture patches is maximized. However, it may cause the model to get stuck in local minima when the model is initialized far-away from the true boundary. To address this problem, we compute a binary edge map by thresholding on the texture edge map I_t. The threshold is computed automatically using Otsu's method [26]; the method selects the threshold that minimizes the weighted sum of within-group variances on the histogram of the texture edge map. Given the binary edge map, we encode information from this binary edge map by computing its un-signed distance transform. The resulting distance map image is denoted by Φ_e. The data term E_e below aims to minimize the sum-of-squared-differences between the implicit shape representation values both on the model and inside the model and the underlying distance values on Φ_e at corresponding deformed positions.

$$E_e = \frac{1}{V(\mathcal{R})} \iint_{\mathcal{R}} \left(\Phi_{\mathcal{M}}(\mathbf{x}) - \Phi_e(D(\mathbf{q}; \mathbf{x})) \right)^2 d\mathbf{x},$$

where $\mathcal{R} = \mathcal{R}_{\mathcal{M}} \cup \partial\mathcal{R}_{\mathcal{M}}$. During optimization, when the model is still far-away from the true edges, this term serves as a two-way ballooning force that expands or shrinks the model along the gradient direction of Φ_e. At an edge with small gaps, this term also constrains the model to follow the "geodesic" path (i.e., the shortest smooth path connecting the two open ends of a gap).

Combining the two data terms – the boundary term E_b and the thresholded edge term E_e, the overall energy functional is: $E = E_b + kE_e$, where k is a constant balancing the contributions from the two terms [1]. Both terms are differentiable with respect to the free-form-deformation parameters $\mathbf{q}$, and a gradient-descent based method is used to derive the model evolution equation for each element $\mathbf{q}_i$ in $\mathbf{q}$:

$$\frac{\partial E}{\partial \mathbf{q}_i} = \frac{\partial E_b}{\partial \mathbf{q}_i} + k \frac{\partial E_e}{\partial \mathbf{q}_i}, \tag{2}$$

where

$$\frac{\partial E_b}{\partial \mathbf{q}_i} = \frac{1}{V(\partial\mathcal{R}_{\mathcal{M}})} \iint_{\partial\mathcal{R}_{\mathcal{M}}} 2I_t(D(\mathbf{q}; \mathbf{x})) \cdot (\nabla I_t(D(\mathbf{q}; \mathbf{x})) \cdot \frac{\partial}{\partial \mathbf{q}_i} D(\mathbf{q}; \mathbf{x})) d\mathbf{x}$$

$$\frac{\partial E_e}{\partial \mathbf{q}_i} = \frac{\iint_{\mathcal{R}_{\mathcal{M}} \cup \partial\mathcal{R}_{\mathcal{M}}} 2(\Phi_{\mathcal{M}}(\mathbf{x}) - \Phi_e(D(\mathbf{q}; \mathbf{x}))) \cdot (-\nabla \Phi_e(D(\mathbf{q}; \mathbf{x})) \cdot \frac{\partial}{\partial \mathbf{q}_i} D(\mathbf{q}; \mathbf{x})) d\mathbf{x}}{V(\mathcal{R}_{\mathcal{M}} \cup \partial\mathcal{R}_{\mathcal{M}})}.$$

In the above formulas, the partial derivatives $\frac{\partial}{\partial \mathbf{q}_i} D(\mathbf{q}; \mathbf{x})$ can be easily derived from the model deformation formula in Eq. 1.

The whole image is processed in the following manner: the first region is segmented by starting a deformable model at the center of the image. Another point well outside the first region is then used to initialize a second model, and a second region is segmented. The process continues until almost all of the points in the image are segmented. In the case where a new region grows into an old region, the two regions are joined together.

---

[1] We are able to omit an explicit model smoothness term here because of the strong implicit smoothness constraints imposed by FFD.

5   Experiments

Comparing Methods for Texture Edge Detection. The main purpose of these experiments is to demonstrate that Gabor based filter bank methods cannot be used directly in *local* methods of deriving texture edges. Indeed, in [16,17] a global clustering method was used to combine regions based on the filter bank descriptors; in [32] a method based on anisotropic diffusion in the direction of the global principle direction was suggested; in [14] the filter bank output was integrated along a region and was modified with statistics on the shape of small segments. One can also refer to the text of [32,14], where the limitations of the local filter bank measurements are discussed.

In Fig. 4, we compare our method, Canny edge detection, and a method based on [17], in which, for each pixel we plot the maximum difference (using the original parameters and distance measure) of the block around it to the nearest four blocks (the results are similar if using Wilcoxon Mann Whitney instead of χ^2). As can be seen, this "alternative" is not doing well. A verification of this can be found in Fig. 4(a) of [32].

Experiments on Texture Mosaics. In Fig. 5, we show examples results on the texture mosaic images of [17], available online at http://www-dbv.cs.uni-bonn.de/image/mixture.tar.gz. This data set contains mosaics generated from a set of 86 micro-patterns from the Brodatz album [6].

Real Image Experiments. In Fig. 6 we present experiments on images taken from the first 25 gray level testing images of the *Berkeley Segmentation Dataset*

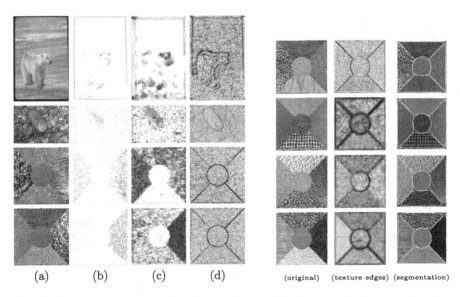

(a)   (b)   (c)   (d)   (original)   (texture edges) (segmentation)

Fig. 4. Comparison of edge detection performed on the original gray images (a), using the Canny edge detector (b), using the filter bank dissimilarity based on [17](c), and using our method (d)

Fig. 5. Results of our edge detection and texture segmentation methods on several mosaics constructed by the authors of [17]

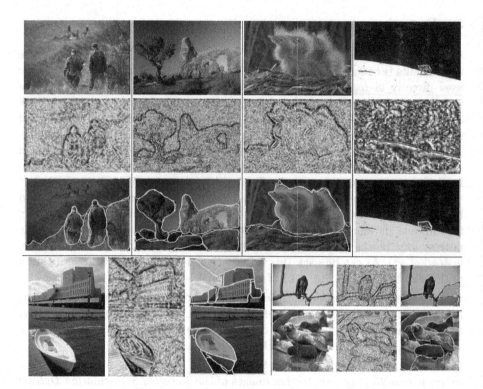

Fig. 6. Results of our edge detection and texture segmentation methods on several real images taken from the *Berkeley Segmentation Dataset*, including the original images, the recovered texture edges, and the resulting segmentation. The images in the lower right demonstrate the detection of texture edges that also constitute intensity edges.

(`http://www.cs.berkeley.edu/projects/vision/grouping/segbench/`). We did not use any dedicated intensity edges method, but as can be seen in the image of the bird, edges between regions of uniform but different intensities, are detected.

6 Summary and Conclusions

The patch based technologies, which are based on local gray value representations and correlations between gray values, have proven to be successful in many computer vision domains, and suggest an appealing alternative to filter bank approaches. While there is no doubt that their recent proliferation is partly due to the increasing computational power available, the representation itself seems inherently powerful. In this work, we use patches in order to compute texture edges. The edge representation (as opposed to a representation of regions using some form of descriptor) is powerful in that it can be readily combined with global optimization based-segmentation (e.g., "snakes"). Most energy-based methods do not deal with texture edges. Attempts that have been made in the past to incorporate texture into these methods used simple texture descriptors such as mean intensity of a region or the variance of the intensity in that region [27, 30], and were computationally expensive.

By using our patch based texture edge detection technique, combined with Free-Form Deformations, we are able to suggest a tractable solution, which enjoys both rich texture information, and the advantages of a global solution. These advantages include the detection of a smooth boundary, which is globally salient. In this work we focused solely on texture edges, but it had not escaped us that in our framework one can easily add the traditional energy terms for intensity edges and color edges, thus making our framework complete for image segmentation. This completeness was available in the affinity based approaches, but not in the energy based methods.

Acknowledgments

The research was done collaboratively at the Center for Biological & Computational Learning (CBCL), which is in the McGovern Institute for Brain Research at MIT, as well as in the Dept. of Brain & Cognitive Sciences, and which is affiliated with the Computer Sciences & AI Laboratory (CSAIL), and at the Center for Computational Biomedicine, Imaging and Modeling (CBIM) at Rutgers University, which is part of the CS and BME departments . This research was sponsored by CBCL grants from: Office of Naval Research (DARPA) Contracts No. MDA972-04-1-0037 and No. N00014-02-1-0915, National Science Foundation-NIH (CRCNS) Contract No. EIA-0218506, and National Institutes of Health (Conte) Contract No. 1 P20 MH66239-01A1. Additional CBCL support was provided by: Central Research Institute of Electric Power Industry (CRIEPI), Daimler-Chrysler AG, Eastman Kodak Company, Honda Research Institute USA, Inc., Komatsu Ltd., Merrill-Lynch, NEC Fund, Oxygen, Siemens Corporate Research, Inc., Sony, Sumitomo Metal Industries, Toyota Motor Corporation, and the Eugene McDermott Foundation. The research was also supported by CBIM grants NSF 0205671, NSF 0313184, NSF 0428231, AFOSR and ONR.

References

1. A.A. Amini, Y. Chen, M. Elayyadi, and P. Radeva. Tag surface reconstruction and tracking of myocardial beads from SPAMM-MRI with parametric b-spline surfaces. IEEE Transactions on Medical Imaging, 20(2), 2001.
2. S. Awate and R. Whitaker, Image Denoising with Unsupervised, Information-Theoretic, Adaptive Filtering. University of Utah TR, UUCS-04-013, 2004.
3. E. Bardinet, L.D. Cohen, and N. Ayache. A parametric deformable model to fit unstructured 3D data. Computer Vision and Image Understanding, 71(1), 1998.
4. S. Bouix, K. Siddiqi and A. Tannenbaum. Flux Driven Automatic Centerline Extraction. Medical Image Analysis, 2004.
5. E. Borenstein, and S. Ullman. Class-specific, top-down segmentation. ECCV2002.
6. P. Brodatz. Textures:A Photographic Album for Artists and Designers. Dover, '66.
7. V. Caselles, R. Kimmel, and G. Sapiro. Geodesic active contours.ICCV'95.

8. I. Drori, D. Cohen-Or and H. Yeshurun. Fragment-based image completion. SIG-GRAPH, 2003.
9. A. Efros, and W.T. Freeman, Image quilting for texture synthesis and transfer. In *SIGGRAPH*, 2001.
10. I. Fogel and D. Sagi. Gabor Filters as Texture Discriminator,Bio.Cybernetics '89.
11. C. Fowlkes, D. Martin, J. Malik. Learning Affinity Functions for Image Segmentation: Combining Patch-based and Gradient-based Approaches. *CVPR*, 2003.
12. W.T. Freeman, E.C. Pasztor, and O.T. Carmichael. Learning low-level vision. *IJCV* 40(1), 2000.
13. W.T. Freeman, T.R. Jones, and E. Pasztor. Example-based super-resolution. *IEEE Computer Graphics and Applications*, 2002.
14. M. Galun, E. Sharon, R. Basri, A. Brandt. Texture Segmentation by Multiscale Aggregation of Filter Responses and Shape Elements. In *ICCV*, 716-723, 2003.
15. D.J. Heeger and J.R. Bergen. Pyramid-based texture analysis/synthesis. SIG-GRAPH, 1995.
16. T. Hofmann, J. Puzicha and J.M. Buhmann. Unsupervised Segmentation of Textured Images by Pairwise Data Clustering. ICIP, 1996.
17. T. Hofmann, J. Puzicha and J.M. Buhmann. An Optimization Approach to Unsupervised Hierarchical Texture Segmentation. ICIP, 1997.
18. T. Hofmann, J. Puzicha and J.M. Buhmann. Unsupervised Texture Segmentation in a Deterministic Annealing Framework PAMI, 1998.
19. X. Huang, D. Metaxas, and T. Chen. Metamorphs: Deformable Shape and Texture Models. CVPR, 2004.
20. M. Kass, A. Witkin, and D. Terzopoulos. Snakes: Active contour models. International Journal of Computer Vision, 1, 1987.
21. L. Liang, C. Liu, Y. Xu, B. Guo, and H.Y. Shum. Real-time texture synthesis by patch-based sampling. MSR-TR-2001-40,Microsoft Research, 2001.
22. R. Malladi, J. A. Sethian, and B. C. Vemuri. Shape modelling with front propagation: a level set approach. In TPAMI, 17(2):158-175, 1995.
23. J. Malik and P. Perona. Preattentive Texture Discrimination with Early Vision Mechanisms. J. Optical Soc. Am., vol. 7, no. 2, pp. 923- 932, 1990.
24. D. Martin, C. Fowlkes, J. Malik, Learning to Detect Natural Image Boundaries Using Local Brightness, Color and Texture Cues, TPAMI 26 (5), 2004.
25. S. Osher and J. Sethian. Fronts propagating with curvature-dependent speed : Algorithms based on the Hamilton-Jacobi formulation. *J. of Comp. Physics*, 1988.
26. N. Otsu. A threshold selection method from gray level histograms. *IEEE. Trans. Systems, Man and Cybernetics*, 9:62–66, 1979.
27. N. Paragios and R. Deriche. Geodesic active regions and level set methods for supervised texture segmentation. IJCV, 2002.
28. J. Portilla and E.P. Simoncelli. A parametric texture model based on joint statistics of complex wavelet coefficients. IJCV, 40(1), 2000.
29. J. C. W. Rayner and D. J. Best, A Contingency Table Approach to Nonparametric Testing.Chapman & Hall/CRC, 2001.
30. M. Rousson and R. Deriche. A variational framework for active and adaptive segmentation of vector valued images. Motion and Video Computing, 2002.
31. M. Rousson, T. Brox and R. Deriche. Active Unsupervised Texture Segmentation on a Diffusion Based Feature Space. Proc. of CVPR, Vol. 2, pages 699-704, 2003.
32. Y. Rubner and C. Tomasi. Coalescing Texture Descriptors. Proc. of the ARPA Image Understanding Workshop, 1996.
33. B. Sandberg, T. Chan and L. Vese. A level-set and Gabor based active contour algorithm for segmenting textured images. UCLA Math. Report, 02-39, July 2002.

34. T. W. Sederberg and S. R. Parry. Free-form deformation of solid geometric models. In *Proc. Annual Conference on Computer Graphics*, 1986.
35. L.H. Staib and J.S. Duncan. Boundary finding with parametrically deformable models. TPAMI, 14(11), 1992.
36. S. Ullman, E. Sali. Object Classification Using a Fragment-Based Representatio. BMVC 2000, Proc. Lecture Notes in CS 1811 Springer, 73-87, 2000.
37. H. Voorhees and T. Poggio. Computing Texture Boundaries from Images. Nature, 333, 364-367, 1988.
38. F. Wilcoxon. Individual Comparisons by Ranking Methods. Biometrics 1, 1945.
39. A. W. Witkin. Intensity-based Edge Classification. Proc. AAAI-82, 1982.
40. Y. Leclerc. Computing the Local Structure in Two Dimensions. Readings in Computer Vision: issues, problems, principles and paradigms, 1987.
41. S.C. Zhu, A. Yuille. Region Competition: Unifying snakes, region growing and Bayes/MDL for multiband image segmentation. PAMI, 18, pages 884-900, 1996.

Unsupervised Texture Segmentation with Nonparametric Neighborhood Statistics

Suyash P. Awate, Tolga Tasdizen, and Ross T. Whitaker

Scientific Computing and Imaging Institute, School of Computing,
University of Utah, Salt Lake City, UT 84112, USA

Abstract. This paper presents a novel approach to unsupervised texture segmentation that relies on a very general nonparametric statistical model of image neighborhoods. The method models image neighborhoods directly, without the construction of intermediate features. It does not rely on using specific descriptors that work for certain kinds of textures, but is rather based on a more generic approach that tries to adaptively capture the core properties of textures. It exploits the fundamental description of textures as images derived from stationary random fields and models the associated higher-order statistics nonparametrically. This general formulation enables the method to easily adapt to various kinds of textures. The method minimizes an entropy-based metric on the probability density functions of image neighborhoods to give an optimal segmentation. The entropy minimization drives a very fast level-set scheme that uses threshold dynamics, which allows for a very rapid evolution towards the optimal segmentation during the initial iterations. The method does not rely on a training stage and, hence, is unsupervised. It automatically tunes its important internal parameters based on the information content of the data. The method generalizes in a straightforward manner from the two-region case to an arbitrary number of regions and incorporates an efficient multi-phase level-set framework. This paper presents numerous results, for both the two-texture and multiple-texture cases, using synthetic and real images that include electron-microscopy images.

1   Introduction

Image segmentation is one of the most extensively studied problems in computer vision. The literature gives numerous approaches based on a variety of criteria including intensity, color, texture, depth, and motion. This paper addresses the problem of segmenting textured images. Textured regions do not typically adhere to the piecewise-smooth or piecewise-constant assumptions that characterize most intensity-based segmentation problems. Julesz [13] pioneered the statistical analysis of textures and characterized textures as possessing regularity in the higher-order intensity statistics. This establishes the description of a textured image, or a Julesz ensemble, as one derived from stationary random fields [21]. This principle forms the foundation of the approach in this paper.

In recent years, researchers have advanced the state-of-the-art in texture segmentation in several important directions. An important direction relates to

A. Leonardis, H. Bischof, and A. Pinz (Eds.): ECCV 2006, Part II, LNCS 3952, pp. 494–507, 2006.

the mechanism used to model or quantify the regularity in image textures. Researchers have developed progressively richer descriptions of local image geometry and thereby captured more complex and subtle distinctions between textures [2, 23, 24]. In another direction, researchers have expressed the dissimilarity between textures through sophisticated statistically-based metrics [4, 15, 19, 14, 22]. Furthermore, research in texture segmentation, like image segmentation in general, has focused on more robust mechanisms for enforcing geometric smoothness in the segmented-region shapes. This is usually done via the construction of a patchwork of regions that simultaneously minimize a set of geometric and statistical criteria [26].

This paper advances the state-of-the-art in texture segmentation by exploiting the principle characteristics of a texture coupled with the generality of nonparametric statistical modeling. The method relies on an information-theoretic metric on the statistics of image neighborhoods that reside in high-dimensional spaces. The nonparametric modeling of the statistics of the stationary random field imposes very few restrictions on the statistical structure of neighborhoods. This enables the method to easily adapt to a variety of textures. The method does not rely on a training stage and, hence, is unsupervised. These properties make it is easily applicable to a wide range of texture-segmentation problems. Moreover, the method incorporates relatively recent advances in level-set evolution strategies that use threshold dynamics [11, 10].

The rest of the paper is organized as follows. Section 2 discusses recent works in texture segmentation and their relationship to the proposed method. Section 3 describes the optimal formulation with an entropy-based energy on higher-order image statistics. Entropy optimization entails the estimation of probability density functions. Hence, Section 4 describes a nonparametric multivariate density estimation technique. It also describes the general problems associated with density estimation in high-dimensional spaces and provides some intuition behind the success of the proposed method in spite of these difficulties. Section 5 gives the optimization strategy using a very fast level-set scheme that uses threshold dynamics, along with the associated algorithm. Section 6 addresses several important practical issues pertaining to nonparametric statistical estimation and its application to image neighborhoods. Section 7 gives experimental results on numerous real and synthetic images, including electron-microscopy medical images. Section 8 summarizes the contributions of the paper and presents ideas for further exploration.

2   Related Work

Much of the previous work in texture segmentation employs filter banks, comprising both isotropic and anisotropic filters, to capture texture statistics. For instance, researchers have used Gabor-filter responses to discriminate between different kinds of textures [19, 23, 24]. Gabor filters are a prominent example of a very large class of oriented multiscale filters [4, 3]. This approach emphasizes the extraction of appropriate features for discriminating between specific textures, which is typically a non-trivial task. The proposed method, on the other hand, does not rely on using specific descriptors that work for certain kinds of textures, but is based on a more generic approach that tries to adaptively capture the core properties of a wide variety of textures.

Researchers have also investigated using more compact sets of texture features. For instance, Bigun *et al.* [2] use the structure tensor (a second-order moment matrix used, e.g., to analyze flow-like patterns [32]) to detect local orientation. Rousson *et al.* [22] refine this strategy by using vector-valued anisotropic diffusion, instead of Gaussian blurring, on the feature space formed using the components of the structure tensor. This strategy requires the structure tensors to have a sufficient degree of homogeneity within regions as well as sufficient dissimilarity between regions. However, as the coming paragraphs explain, not all images meet these criteria.

Other approaches use the intensity (or grayscale) histograms to distinguish between textures [15, 14]. However, the grayscale intensity statistics (i.e. 1D histograms), may fail to capture the *geometric* structure of neighborhoods, which is critical for distinguishing textures with similar 1D histograms. The proposed method exploits higher-order image statistics, modeled nonparametrically, to adaptively capture the geometric regularity in textures.

Figure 1(a) shows two textures that are both *irregular* (in addition to having similar means and gradient-magnitudes) that would pose a challenge for structure-tensor-based approaches such as [2, 22]. In Figure 1(b) the textures differ *only in scale*. Approaches based on structure tensors at a single scale would fail to distinguish such cases, as reported in [22]. Approaches solely using intensity histograms would also fail here. In Figure 1(c) the textures have identical histograms, identical scale, and an almost-identical set of structure-tensor matrix components. In this case, the above-mentioned approaches [2, 22] would face a formidable challenge. The proposed method, on the other hand, incorporating

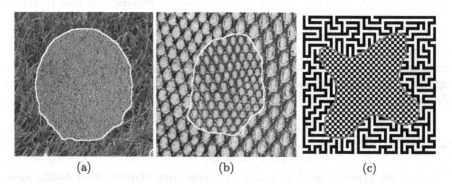

(a)   (b)   (c)

Fig. 1. Segmentations with the proposed approach (depicted by white/gray outlines) for (a) Brodatz textures for sand and grass— both *irregular* textures with similar gradient magnitudes, (b) Brodatz textures differing *only in scale*, and (c) synthetic textures with identical histograms, identical scales, and an almost-identical set of structure-tensor matrix components

a fundamentally richer texture description, produces successful segmentations (depicted by white/gray outlines) for all the images in Figure 1.

Recently, researchers have investigated more direct approaches towards modeling image statistics. For instance, the dynamic-texture segmentation approach by Doretto *et al.* [6] uses a Gauss-Markov process to model the relationships among pixels within regions and over time. However, that approach assumes a Gaussian process for image intensities, a restrictive assumption that cannot easily account for complex or subtle texture geometries [6, 22, 4]. Rousson *et al.* [22] use nonparametric statistics for one of the channels (the image-intensity histogram) in their feature space to counter this restriction and the proposed method generalizes that strategy to the complete higher-order image statistics.

Popat *et al.* [20] were among the first to use nonparametric Markov sampling in images. Their method takes a *supervised* approach for learning neighborhood relationships. They attempt to capture the higher-order nonlinear image statistics via cluster-based nonparametric density estimation and apply their technique for texture classification. Varma and Zisserman [28] used a similar training-based approach to classify textures based on a small Markov neighborhood that was demonstrably superior to filter based approaches. Indeed, researchers analyzing the statistics of 3×3 patches in images, in the corresponding high-dimensional spaces, have found the data to be concentrated in clusters and low-dimensional manifolds exhibiting nontrivial topologies [16, 5]. The proposed approach also relies on the principle that textures exhibit regularity in neighborhood structure, but this regularity is discovered for each texture individually in a nonparametric manner. The proposed method builds on the work in [1], which lays down the essentials for unsupervised learning of higher-order image statistics. That work, however, focuses on image restoration.

The literature dealing with texture synthesis also sheds some light on the proposed method. Texture synthesis algorithms rely on texture statistics from an input image to construct novel images that exhibit a qualitative resemblance to the input texture [9, 31]. This paper describes a very different application, but the texture-synthesis work demonstrates the power of neighborhood statistics in capturing the essential aspects of texture.

Lastly, this paper also borrows from a rather extensive body of work on variational methods for image segmentation [26], in particular the Mumford-Shah model [18], its extensions to motion, depth, and texture, and its implementation via level-set flows [29]. The proposed method employs the very fast approximation proposed by Esedoglu and Tsai [11, 10] based on threshold dynamics, and extends it to include multiple regions within the variational framework.

3   Neighborhood Statistics for Texture Segmentation

This section introduces the random-field texture model, along with the associated notation, and then describes the optimal segmentation formulation based on entropy minimization.

3.1   Random Field Texture Model

A random field [7] is a family of random variables $X(\Omega; T)$, for an index set T, where, for each fixed $T = t$, the random variable $X(\Omega; t)$, or simply $X(t)$, is defined on the sample space Ω. If we let T be a set of points defined on a discrete Cartesian grid and fix $\Omega = \omega$, we have a realization of the random field called the *digital image*, $X(\omega, T)$. In this case $\{t\}_{t \in T}$ is the set of pixels in the image. For two-dimensional images t is a two-vector. We denote a specific realization $X(\omega; t)$ (the image), as a deterministic function $x(t)$.

If we associate with T a family of pixel neighborhoods $N = \{N_t\}_{t \in T}$ such that $N_t \subset T$, and $s \in N_t$ if and only if $t \in N_s$, then N is called a neighborhood system for the set T and points in N_t are called neighbors of t. We define a random vector $Z(t) = \{X(t)\}_{t \in N_t}$, denoting its realization by $z(t)$, corresponding to the set of intensities at the neighbors of pixel t. We refer to the statistics of the random vector Z as *higher-order* statistics. Following the definition of texture as a Julesz ensemble [13, 21], we assume that the intensities in each texture region arise out of a stationary ergodic random field.

3.2   Optimal Segmentation by Entropy Minimization on Higher-Order Statistics

Consider a random variable $L(t)$, associated with each pixel $t \in T$, that gives the region the pixel t belongs to. For a good segmentation, knowing the neighborhood intensities (z) tells us the unique pixel class (k). Also, knowing the pixel class gives us a good indication of what the neighborhood is. This functional dependence is captured naturally in the concept of mutual information. Thus, the optimal segmentation is one that maximizes the mutual information between L and Z:

$$I(L, Z) = h(Z) - h(Z|L) = h(Z) - \sum_{k=1}^{K} P(L = k) h(Z|L = k), \qquad (1)$$

where $h(\cdot)$ denotes the entropy of the random variable. The entropy of the higher-order PDF associated with the entire image, $h(Z)$, is a constant for an image and is irrelevant for the optimization. Let $\{T_k\}_{k=1}^{K}$ denote a mutually-exclusive and exhaustive decomposition of the image domain T into K texture regions. Let $P_k(Z(t) = z(t))$ be the probability of observing the image neighborhood $z(t)$ given that the center pixel of the neighborhood belongs to the texture region k. We define the energy associated with the set of K texture probability density functions (PDFs), i.e.

$$E = \sum_{k=1}^{K} P(L = k) h(Z|L = k). \qquad (2)$$

The entropy

$$h(Z|L = k) = -\int_{\Re^m} P_k(Z(t_k) = z(t_k)) \log P_k(Z(t_k) = z(t_k)) dz, \qquad (3)$$

where $m = |N_t|$ is the neighborhood size and t_k is any pixel belonging to region k—for any $t_k \in T_k$ the PDF $P_k(\cdot)$ remains the same due to the assumed stationarity. Let $R_k : T \rightarrow \{0, 1\}$ denote the indicator function for region T_k, i.e. $R_k(t) = 1$ for $t \in T_k$ and $R_k(t) = 0$ otherwise. Considering the intensities in each region as derived from a stationary ergodic random field to approximate entropy, and using $P(L = k) = |T_k|/|T|$, gives

$$E \approx -\sum_{k=1}^{K} \left(\frac{P(L = k)}{|T_k|} \sum_{t \in T} R_k(t) \log P_k(z(t)) \right) \qquad (4)$$

$$= \frac{-1}{|T|} \sum_{k=1}^{K} \sum_{t \in T} R_k(t) \log P_k(z(t)). \qquad (5)$$

Thus, the optimal segmentation is the set of functions R_k for which E attains a minimum. The strategy in this paper is to minimize the total entropy given in (4) by manipulating the regions defined by R_k. This rather-large nonlinear optimization problem potentially has many local minima. To regularize the solution, variational formulations typically penalize the boundary lengths of the segmented regions [18]. The objective function, after incorporating this penalty using a Lagrange multiplier, now becomes

$$E + \alpha \sum_{k=1}^{K} \sum_{t \in T} \| \nabla_t R_k(t) \|, \qquad (6)$$

where α is the regularization parameter and ∇_t denotes a discrete spatial-gradient operator. In this framework, the critical issue lies in the estimation of $P_k(z(t))$, and the next section focuses on addressing this issue.

4 Nonparametric Multivariate Density Estimation

Entropy optimization entails the estimation of higher-order conditional PDFs. This introduces the challenge of high-dimensional, scattered-data interpolation, even for modest sized image neighborhoods. High-dimensional spaces are notoriously challenging for data analysis (regarded as the *the curse of dimensionality* [27, 25]), because they are so sparsely populated. Despite theoretical arguments suggesting that density estimation beyond a few dimensions is impractical, the empirical evidence from the literature is more optimistic [25, 20]. The results in this paper confirm that observation. Furthermore, stationarity implies that the random vector Z exhibits identical marginal PDFs, and thereby lends itself to more accurate density estimates [25, 27]. We also rely on the neighborhoods in natural images having a lower-dimensional topology in the multi-dimensional feature space [16, 5]. Therefore, *locally* (in the feature space) the PDFs of images are lower dimensional entities that lend themselves to better density estimation.

We use the Parzen-window nonparametric density estimation technique [8] with an n-dimensional Gaussian kernel $G_n(z, \Psi_n)$, where $n = |N_t|$. We have no a priori information on the structure of the PDFs, and therefore we choose an isotropic Gaussian, i.e. $\Psi_n = \sigma^2 I_n$, where I_n is the $n \times n$ identity matrix. For a stationary ergodic random field, the multivariate Parzen-window estimate is

$$P_k(Z(t) = z(t)) \approx \frac{1}{|A_{k,t}|} \sum_{s \in A_{k,t}} G_n(z(t) - z(s), \Psi_n), \qquad (7)$$

where the set $A_{k,t}$ is a small subset of T_k chosen randomly, from a uniform PDF, for each t. This results in a *stochastic* estimate of the entropy that helps alleviate the effects of spurious local maxima introduced in the Parzen-window density estimate [30]. We refer to this sampling strategy as the *global-sampling* strategy. Selecting appropriate values of the kernel-width σ is important for success, and Section 6 presents a data-driven strategy for the same.

5 Fast Level-Set Optimization Using Threshold Dynamics

The level-set framework [26] is an attractive option for solving the variational problem defined by (6), because it does not restrict either the shapes or the topologies of regions. However, classical level-set evolution schemes for front-tracking based on narrow-band strategies entail some significant computational costs—in particular, the CFL condition for numerical stability [26] limits the motion of the moving wavefront (region boundaries) to one pixel per iteration.

Recently, Esedoglu and Tsai introduced a fast level-set algorithm based on threshold dynamics [11, 10] for minimizing Mumford-Shah type energies. The proposed method adopts their approach for the level-set evolution but relies on a *multiphase extension* of the basic formulation to enable multiple-texture segmentation [17, 29]. In this method, the embeddings, one for each phase, are maintained as piecewise-constant binary functions. This method, essentially, evolves the level-set by first updating the embeddings using the PDE-driven force, and then regularizing the region boundaries by Gaussian smoothing the embedding followed by re-thresholding. This approach needs to neither keep track of points near interfaces nor maintain distance transforms for embeddings. At the same time it allows new components of a region to crop up at remote locations. We have found that this last property allows for very rapid level-set evolution when the level-set location is far from the optimum.

We now let $\{R_k\}_{k=1}^K$ be a set of level-set functions. The segmentation for texture k is then defined as $T_k = \{t \in T | R_k(t) > R_j(t), \forall j \neq k\}$. It is important to realize that coupling (6) and (7) creates nested region integrals that introduce extra terms in the gradient flow associated with the level-set evolution [15, 22]. The shape-derivative tool [12], specifically designed to handle such situations, gives the level-set speed term for minimizing the energy defined in (6) as

$$\frac{\partial R_k(t)}{\partial \tau} = \log P_k(z(t)) + \frac{1}{|T_k|} \sum_{s \in T_k} \frac{G_n(z(s) - z(t), \Psi_n)}{P_k(z(s))} + \alpha \nabla_t \cdot \left(\frac{\nabla_t R_k(t)}{\| \nabla_t R_k(t) \|} \right),$$

$$(8)$$

where τ denotes the time-evolution variable [15, 22].

To obtain an initial segmentation $\{R_k^0\}_{k=1}^K$, the proposed method uses randomly generated regions, as shown in Section 7, based on the following algorithm.

1. Generate K images of uniform random noise, one for each R_k^0.
2. Convolve each R_k^0 with a chosen Gaussian kernel.
3. $\forall k, t$ do: if $R_k^0(t) > R_j^0(t), \forall j \neq k$ then set $R_k^0(t) = 1$, otherwise set $R_k^0(t) = 0$.

The iterations in Esedoglu and Tsai's fast level-set evolution scheme [11, 10], given a segmentation $\{R_k^m\}_{k=1}^K$ at iteration m, proceed as follows.

1. $\forall k, t$ do:
   (a) Estimate $P_k(z(t))$ nonparametrically, as described in Section 4.
   (b) $R_k'(t) = R_k^m(t) + \beta \left(\log P_k(z(t)) + \frac{1}{T_k} \sum_{s \in T_k} \frac{G_n(z(s) - z(t), \Psi_n)}{P_k(z(s))} \right)$
2. Compute $R_k'' = R_k' \otimes \mathbb{N}(0, \gamma^2)$, where $\otimes$ denotes convolution and $\mathbb{N}(0, \gamma^2)$ is a Gaussian kernel with zero mean and standard deviation γ.
3. $\forall k, t$ do: if $R_k''(t) > R_j''(t), \forall j \neq k$ then set $R_k^{m+1}(t) = 1$, otherwise set $R_k^{m+1}(t) = 0$.
4. Stop upon convergence, i.e. when $\| R_k^{m+1} - R_k^m \|_2 < \delta$, a small threshold.

For a detailed discussion on the relationship between the new parameters γ, β, and the parameter α in the traditional level-set framework, we refer the reader to [11, 10]. In short, increasing β corresponds to increasing the PDE-driven force on the level-set evolution and increasing γ results in smoother region boundaries.

6   Important Implementation Issues

This section discusses several practical issues that are crucial for the effectiveness of the entropy reduction scheme. The work in [1] presents a detailed discussion on these issues.

Data-driven choice for the Parzen-window kernel width: Using appropriate values of the Parzen-window parameters is important for success, and that can be especially difficult in the high-dimensional spaces associated with higher-order statistics. The best choice depends on a variety of factors including the sample size $|A_{k,t}|$ and the natural variability in the data. To address this issue we fall back on our previous work for automatically choosing the optimal values [1]. In that work, which focused on image restoration, we choose σ to minimize the entropy of the associated PDF via a Newton-Raphson optimization scheme. We have found that such a σ, i.e. one minimizing the entropy of Z, can be too discriminative for the purpose of texture segmentation, splitting the image into many more regions than what may be appropriate. Hence, in this paper, we set σ to be 10 times as large. The choice of the precise value of this multiplicative factor is not critical and we have found that the algorithm is quite robust to small changes in this parameter.

Data-driven choice for the Parzen-window sample size: Our experiments show [1] that for sufficiently large $|A_{k,t}|$ additional samples do not significantly affect the estimates of entropy and σ, and thus $|A_{k,t}|$ can also be selected automatically from the input data. For the Parzen-windowing scheme we choose 500 samples, i.e. $|A_{k,t}| = 500$, uniformly distributed over each region.

Neighborhood size and shape: The quality of the results also depend on the neighborhood size. We choose the size relative to the size of the textures in the image. Bigger neighborhoods are generally more effective but increase the computational cost. To obtain rotationally invariant neighborhoods, we use a metric in the feature space that controls the influence of each neighborhood pixel so that the distances in this space are less sensitive to neighborhood rotations [1]. In this way, feature space dimensions close to the corners of the square neighborhood shrink so that they do not significantly influence the filtering. Likewise, image boundaries are handled through such anisotropic metrics so that they do not distort the neighborhood statistics of the image.

7   Experiments and Results

This section presents results from experiments with real and synthetic data. The number of regions K is a user parameter and should be chosen appropriately. The neighborhood size, in the current implementation, is also a user parameter. This can be improved by using a multi-resolution scheme for the image representation and constitutes an important area of future work. We use 9×9 neighborhoods, $\beta = 2$, and $\gamma = 3$ for all examples, unless stated otherwise. Each iteration of the proposed method takes about 3 minutes for a 256×256 image on a standard Pentium workstation. Figure 2(a) shows a level-set initialization $\{R_k^0\}_{k=1}^K$ as a randomly generated image with $K = 2$ regions.

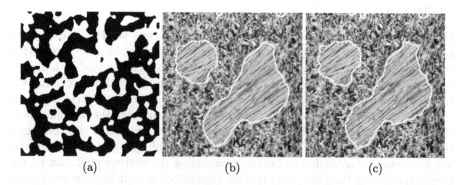

(a)   (b)   (c)

Fig. 2. Two-texture segmentation. (a) Random initial segmentation for an image having two Brodatz textures for grass and straw. The black and white intensities denote the two regions. (b) Segmentation after stage 1; *global* samples only (see text). (c) Segmentation after stage 2; *local* and *global* samples (see text).

The level-set scheme using threshold dynamics, coupled with the *global-sampling* strategy as explained in Section 4, makes the level sets evolve very fast towards the optimal segmentation. We have found that, starting from the random initialization, just a few iterations (less than 10) are sufficient to reach an almost-optimal segmentation. However, this sampling strategy is sometimes unable to give very accurate boundaries. This is because, in practice, the texture boundaries present neighborhoods overlapping both textures and exhibiting subtleties that may not be captured by the global sampling. Moreover, the joining of intricate textures may inherently make the boundary location significantly fuzzy so that it may be impossible even for humans to define the true segmentation. Figure 2(b) depicts this behavior. In this case, for each point t, selecting a larger portion of the samples in $A_{k,t}$ from a region close to t would help. Hence, we propose a second stage of level-set evolution that incorporates *local* sampling, in addition to global sampling, and is initialized with the segmentation resulting from the first stage. We found that such a scheme consistently yields better segmentations. Figure 2(c) shows the final segmentation. We have used about 250 local samples taken from a Gaussian distribution, with a variance of 900, centered at the concerned pixel. Furthermore, we have found that the method performs well for any choice of the variance such that the Gaussian distribution encompasses more than several hundred pixels. Note that given this variance, both $|A_{k,t}|$ and the Parzen-window σ are computed automatically in a data-driven manner, as explained before in Section 6.

Figure 3 gives examples dealing with multiple-texture segmentation. Figure 3(a) shows a randomly generated initialization with three regions that leads to the final segmentation in Figure 3(b). In this case the proposed algorithm uses a multi-phase extension of the fast threshold-dynamics based scheme [11, 10]. Figure 3(c) shows another multiple-texture segmentation with four textures.

Figure 4 shows electron-microscopy images of cellular structures. Because the original images severely lacked contrast, we preprocessed them using adaptive

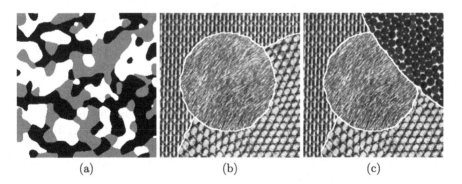

(a)	(b)	(c)

Fig. 3. Multiple-texture segmentation. (a) Random initial segmentation containing three regions for the image in (b). (b) Final segmentation for an image with three Brodatz textures, including both irregular and regular textures. (c) Final segmentation for an image with four Brodatz textures.

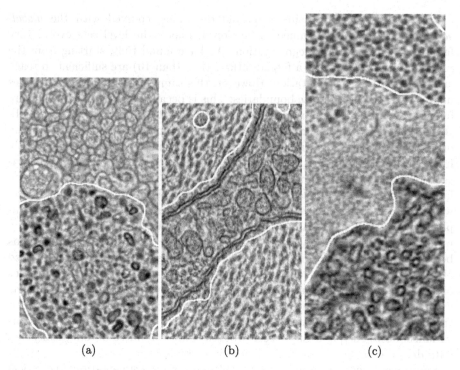

(a)   (b)   (c)

Fig. 4. Final segmentations for electron-microscopy images of rabbit retinal cells for (a),(b) the two-texture case, and (c) the three-texture case

histogram equalization before applying the proposed texture-segmentation method. Figure 4 shows the enhanced images. These images are challenging to segment using edge or intensity information because of reduced textural homogeneity in the regions. The discriminating feature for these cell types is their subtle textures formed by the arrangements of sub-cellular structures. To capture the large-scale structures in the images we used larger neighborhood sizes of 13×13. We combine this with a higher γ for increased boundary regularization. Figure 4(a) demonstrates a successful segmentation. In Figure 4(b) the two cell types are segmented to a good degree of accuracy; however, notice that the membranes between the cells are grouped together with the middle cell. A third texture region could be used for the membrane, but this is not a trivial extension due to the thin, elongated geometric structure of the membrane and the associated difficulties in the Parzen-window sampling. The hole in the region on the top left forms precisely because the region contains a large elliptical patch that is identical to such patches in the other cell. Figure 4(c) shows a successful three-texture segmentation for another image.

Figure 5(a) shows a zebra example that occurs quite often in the texture-segmentation literature, e.g. [23, 22]. Figures 5(b) and 5(c) show other zebras. Here, the proposed method performs well to differentiate the striped patterns, with varying orientations and scales, from the irregular grass texture. The grass

Fig. 5. Final segmentations for real images of Zebras

Fig. 6. Final segmentations for real images of Leopards. Note: The segmentation outline for image (b) is shown in gray.

texture depicts homogeneous statistics. The striped patterns on the Zebras' body, although incorporating many variations, change gradually from one part of the body to another. Hence, neighborhoods from these patterns form one continuous manifold in the associated high-dimensional space, which is captured by the method as a single texture class.

Figure 6(a) shows the successful segmentation of the Leopard with the random sand texture in the background. Figure 6(b) shows an image that actually contains three different kinds of textures, where the background is split into two textures. Because we constrained the number of regions to be two, the method grouped two of the background textures into the same region.

8 Conclusions and Discussion

This paper presents a novel approach for texture segmentation exploiting the higher-order image statistics that principally define texture. The proposed method adaptively learns the image statistics via nonparametric density estimation and does not rely on specific texture descriptors. It relies on the information content of input data for setting important parameters, and does not require significant parameter tuning. Moreover, it does not rely on any kind of training and, hence, is easily applicable to a wide spectrum of texture segmentation tasks. The paper applies the proposed method to segment different cell types in electron-microscopy medical images, giving successful segmentations. It also demonstrates the effectiveness of the method on real images of Zebras and Leopards, as well as numerous examples with Brodatz textures. The method incorporates a very fast multiphase level-set evolution framework using threshold dynamics [11, 10].

The algorithmic complexity of the method is $O(K|T||A_{k,t}|S^D)$ where D is the image dimension and S is the extent of the neighborhood along a dimension. This grows exponentially with D, and our current results are limited to 2D images. The literature suggests some improvements, e.g. reduction in the computational complexity via the improved fast-gauss transform [33]. In the current implementation, the neighborhood size is chosen manually and this is a limitation. This can be improved by defining a feature space comprising neighborhoods at multiple scales. These are important areas for future work.

Acknowledgments

We thank support from the NSF EIA0313268, NSF CAREER CCR0092065, NIH EB005832-01, NIH EY002576, and NIH EY015128 grants. We are grateful to Prof. Robert Marc and Prof. Bryan Jones from the John A. Moran Eye Center, University of Utah for providing the electron-microscopy retinal images.

References

1. S. P. Awate and R. T. Whitaker. Unsupervised, Information-Theoretic, Adaptive Image Filtering for Image Restoration. *IEEE Trans. Pattern Anal. Mach. Intell. (PAMI)*, 28(3):364–376, March 2006.
2. J. Bigun, G. H. Granlund, and J. Wiklund. Multidimensional orientation estimation with applications to texture analysis and optical flow. *IEEE Trans. Pattern Anal. Mach. Intell.*, 13(8):775–790, 1991.
3. R. Boomgaard and J. Weijer. Robust estimation of orientation for texture analysis. In *2nd Int. Workshop on Texture Analysis and Synthesis*, 2002.
4. J. S. de Bonet and P. Viola. Texture recognition using a non-parametric multiscale statistical model. In *Proc. IEEE Conf. on Comp. Vision and Pattern Recog.*, pages 641–647, 1998.
5. V. de Silva and G. Carlsson. Topological estimation using witness complexes. *Symposium on Point-Based Graphics*, 2004.
6. G. Doretto, D. Cremers, P. Favaro, and S. Soatto. Dynamic texture segmentation. In *Proc. Int. Conf. Computer Vision*, pages 1236–1242, 2003.
7. E. Dougherty. *Random Processes for Image and Signal Processing.* Wiley, 1998.
8. R. Duda, P. Hart, and D. Stork. *Pattern Classification.* Wiley, 2001.
9. A. A. Efros and T. K. Leung. Texture synthesis by non-parametric sampling. In *Int. Conf. Computer Vision*, pages 1033–1038, 1999.
10. S. Esedoglu, S. Ruuth, and R. Tsai. Threshold dynamics for shape reconstruction and disocclusion. In *Proc. Int. Conf. Image Processing*, pages 502–505, 2005.
11. S. Esedoglu and Y.-H. R. Tsai. Threshold dynamics for the piecewise constant mumford-shah functional. Number CAM-04-63, 2004.

12. S. Jehan-Besson, M. Barlaud, and G. Aubert. Dream2s: Deformable regions driven by an eulerian accurate minimization method for image and video segmentation. In *Proc. European Conf. on Computer Vision-Part III*, pages 365–380, 2002.
13. B. Julesz. Visual pattern discrimination. *IRE Trans. Info. Theory*, IT(8):84–92, 1962.
14. T. Kadir and M. Brady. Unsupervised non-parametric region segmentation using level sets. In *Proc. of IEEE Int. Conf. Comp. Vision*, pages 1267–1274, 2003.
15. J. Kim, J. W. Fisher, A. Yezzi, M. Cetin, and A. S. Willsky. Nonparametric methods for image segmentation using information theory and curve evolution. In *Proc. IEEE Int. Conf. on Image Processing*, pages 797–800, 2002.
16. A. Lee, K. Pedersen, and D. Mumford. The nonlinear statistics of high-contrast patches in natural images. *Int. J. Comput. Vision*, 54(1-3):83–103, 2003.
17. B. Merriman, J. K. Bence, and S. Osher. Motion of multiple junctions: A level set approach,. Technical Report CAM-93-19, Dept. Mathematics, UCLA, 1993.
18. D. Mumford and J. Shah. Optimal approximations by piecewise smooth functions and associated variational problems. *Com. Pure and App. Math.*, 42:577–685, 1989.
19. N. Paragios and R. Deriche. Geodesic active regions and level set methods for supervised texture segmentation. *Int. J. Comput. Vision*, 46(3):223–247, 2002.
20. K. Popat and R. Picard. Cluster based probability model and its application to image and texture processing. *IEEE Trans. Image Processing*, 6(2):268–284, 1997.
21. J. Portilla and E. Simoncelli. A parametric texture model based on joint statistics of complex wavelet coefficients. *Int. J. Comput. Vision*, 40(1):49–70, 2000.
22. M. Rousson, T. Brox, and R. Deriche. Active unsupervised texture segmentation on a diffusion based feature space. In *Proc. IEEE Conf. on Computer Vision and Pattern Recognition*, pages 699–706. IEEE Computer Society, 2003.
23. C. Sagiv, N. A. Sochen, and Y. Y. Zeevi. Texture segmentation via a diffusion segmentation scheme in the gabor feature space. In *2nd Int. Workshop on Texture Analysis and Synthesis*, 2002.
24. B. Sandberg, T. Chan, and L. Vese. A level-set and gabor-based active contour algorithm for segmenting textured images. Technical Report CAM-02-39, Dept. Mathematics, UCLA, 2002.
25. D. W. Scott. *Multivariate Density Estimation*. Wiley, 1992.
26. J. Sethian. *Level Set Methods and Fast Marching Methods*. Cambridge Univ. Press, 1999.
27. B. Silverman. *Density Estimation for Statistics and Data Analysis*. Chapman and Hall, 1986.
28. M. Varma and A. Zisserman. Texture classification: Are filter banks necessary ? In *Proc. IEEE Conf. on Comp. Vision and Pattern Recog.*, pages 691–698, 2003.
29. L. Vese and T. Chan. A multiphase level set framework for image segmentation using the mumford and shah model. Technical Report CAM-01-25, Dept. Mathematics, UCLA, 2001.
30. P. Viola and W. Wells. Alignment by maximization of mutual information. In *Int. Conf. Comp. Vision*, pages 16–23, 1995.
31. L. Wei and M. Levoy. Order-independent texture synthesis. *Stanford University Computer Science Department Tech. Report TR-2002-01*, 2002.
32. J. Weickert. Coherence-enhancing diffusion filtering. *Int. J. Comp. Vis.*, 31: 111–127, 1999.
33. C. Yang, R. Duraiswami, N. Gumerov, and L. Davis. Improved fast gauss transform and efficient kernel density estimation. In *Int. Conf. Comp. Vision*, pages 464–471, 2003.

Detecting Symmetry and Symmetric Constellations of Features

Gareth Loy* and Jan-Olof Eklundh

Computational Vision & Active Perception Laboratory,
Royal Institute of Technology (KTH), Sweden
{gareth, joe}@nada.kth.se

Abstract. A novel and efficient method is presented for grouping feature points on the basis of their underlying symmetry and characterising the symmetries present in an image. We show how symmetric pairs of features can be efficiently detected, how the symmetry bonding each pair is extracted and evaluated, and how these can be grouped into symmetric constellations that specify the dominant symmetries present in the image. Symmetries over all orientations and radii are considered simultaneously, and the method is able to detect local or global symmetries, locate symmetric figures in complex backgrounds, detect bilateral or rotational symmetry, and detect multiple incidences of symmetry.

1   Introduction

Symmetry is an intrinsic phenomenon in the world around us, occurring both naturally and in artefacts and architecture. Symmetry is attractive, both aesthetically and as a cue directing visual attention [2, 8, 15, 27]. Not only does it give balance and form to appearance, but it ties together features that can otherwise seem diffuse. With the recent success of feature point methods in computer vision [9, 16, 21, 22] it is useful to establish mechanisms for grouping the features generated, and symmetry provides a natural means of doing so.

The contribution of this paper is a simple and effective method for grouping symmetric constellations of features and detecting symmetry in the image plane. Modern feature-based methods (such as [9, 16]) are used to establish pairs of symmetric point matches from which either bilateral symmetry axes or centres of rotational symmetry can be analytically determined. These pairs are grouped into symmetric constellations of features about common symmetry foci, identifying both the dominant symmetries present and a set features associated with each foci. The method is independent of the feature detector and descriptor used, requiring only robust, rotation-invariant matching and an orientation measure for each feature. Symmetries over all orientations and radii are considered simultaneously, and the method can also detect multiple axes of symmetry, rotational symmetry and symmetric figures in complex backgrounds.

The remainder of this paper is organised as follows, Section 2 reviews previous work, Section 3 describes the method, Section 4 presents experimental results and discusses the performance of the method, and Section 5 presents our conclusions.

---

* This work was carried out during the tenure of a MUSCLE Internal fellowship.

A. Leonardis, H. Bischof, and A. Pinz (Eds.): ECCV 2006, Part II, LNCS 3952, pp. 508–521, 2006.

2   Background

Symmetry has fascinated people since ancient times, and in the computer vision literature there is a significant body of work dealing with the detection of symmetry in images dating back to the 1970's (e.g. [3, 10, 17, 19, 20, 24, 30, 31, 35, 37]). Symmetry detection has been used for numerous applications, including facial image analysis [23], vehicle detection [12, 38], reconstruction [1, 6, 14, 34], visual attention [17, 24, 27] indexing of image databases [28], completion of occluded shapes [36], object detection [19, 37] and detecting tumours in medical imaging [18]. The problem of symmetry detection amounts to trying to find an image region of unknown size that, when flipped about an unknown axis or rotated about an unknown point, is sufficiently similar to another image region an unknown distance away. With so many unknown parameters it is not surprising that symmetry detection is a complex task.

Some researchers have taken a global approach to the problem, treating the entire image as a signal from which symmetric properties are inferred, often via frequency analysis. Marola [19] proposed a method for detecting symmetry in symmetric and "almost symmetric" images, where the axis of symmetry intersects or passes near the centroid. Keller and Shkolnisky [10] took an algebraic approach and employed Fourier analysis to detect symmetry, and Sun [31] showed that the orientation of the dominant bilateral symmetry axis could be computed from the histogram of gradient orientations. However, these global approaches have two key shortcomings: they are limited to detecting a single incidence of symmetry, and are adversely influenced by background structure.

An alternative to the global approach is to use local features such as edge features, contours or boundary points, to reduce the problem to one of grouping symmetric sets of points or lines. Scott and Longuet-Higgins [26] grouped symmetric sets of dot-patterns extracted from the wing markings of a butterfly using the eigenvectors of a proximity matrix. Masuda *et al.* [20] adopted an image similarity measure based on the directional correlation of edge features and proceeded to detect rotational and reflectional symmetry. This required an exhaustive search of all congruent transformations (consisting of translation, rotation and reflection) of an image to identify any such transformations under which parts of the image were close to invariant.

Zabrodsky *et al.* [37] proposed the *symmetry distance* as a continuous measure of the amount of symmetry present in a shape. This distance was defined as the minimum mean squared distance required to move points of the original shape to obtain a perfectly symmetrical shape, and enabled a comparison of the "amount" of symmetry present in different shapes. Given the location and orientation of a symmetry axis, this method was used in conjunction with active contours to extract symmetric regions such as faces. However, this method required the foci of symmetry to be known a priori.

Tuytelaars *et al.* [32] detected regular repetitions of planar patterns under perspective skew using a geometric framework. The approach detected all planar homologies[1] and could thus find reflections about a point, periodicities, and mirror symmetries. By considering perspective skew this method dealt with a much more general and complex problem than detection of two-dimensional symmetries within an image. Whilst this

---

[1] A plane projective transformation is a planar homology if it has a line of fixed points (called the axis), together with a fixed point (called the vertex) not on the line [5].

approach could indeed detect mirror symmetries in the image plane, it was a slow and involved means of doing so, and as posed was unable to detect rotational symmetries. This method built clusters of matching points that were evaluated for symmetry, by contrast the new method forms pairs of matching features whose symmetry can be rapidly assessed from their embedded orientation and scale information.

Lazebnik *et al.* [13] also noted that clusters of features could be matched within an image to detect symmetries. However, the use of rotationally invariant descriptors (providing no orientation information) restricted this, like [32], to a cluster-based approach.

Shen *et al.* [29] used an affine invariant representation to detect skewed symmetries in cleanly segmented contours. A set of ordered feature points is sampled around a contour and an affine invariant feature vector is constructed for each feature point. A similarity matrix is then constructed describing the similarities between the features, a threshold is applied to the matrix, and symmetries are identified as diagonal lines in the binarized similarity matrix. The method is able to detect skew symmetries and rotational symmetries, but is only suitable for pre-segmented objects and requires a strict ordering of feature points around the object contour.

Motivated by the ease with which humans and other creatures (even bees) detect symmetries, Scognamillo *et al.* [25] constructed a biologically plausible model for symmetry detection. A 2D local energy function was calculated defining a salience map of the image. The symmetry of this map was evaluated via convolution with a broad Gaussian filter oriented approximately perpendicular to the proposed axis of symmetry. Maxima were then detected in the filtered direction, and were expected to lie close to the axis of symmetry for a symmetric figure. If multiple maxima were detected the average location was used, and consequentially the method became unsuitable for detecting symmetric figures in complex backgrounds, where maxima can occur that are unrelated to the symmetric object.

Kiryati and Gofman [11] combined local and global approaches to detect the dominant reflective symmetry axis in an image. They used a symmetry measure similar to Marola [19] and applied this to assess symmetry in local circular regions parameterised by their location, size and symmetry axis orientation (x, y, s, θ). The global maximum of this measure was then determined using a probabilistic genetic algorithm which was typically able to find the global maximum of the local symmetry measure in around 1,000 iterations. As posed the method detects only a single axis of symmetry, although it is feasible to extend the genetic algorithm approach to detect multiple symmetries. However, owing to the parameterisation the method is limited to detecting circular regions of symmetry.

3   Symmetry from Feature Constellations

Our approach is based on the simple idea of matching symmetric pairs of feature points. This is achieved efficiently and robustly using modern feature point methods. The "amount" of symmetry exhibited by each pair is quantified by the relative location, orientation and scale of the features in the pair. These pair-wise symmetries are then accumulated in a Hough-style voting space to determine the dominant symmetries present in the image.

Modern feature point methods [9, 16, 21, 22] provide a proven robust means for generating dense sets of feature points and matching these between images, however, little use has been made of matching points *within* a single image. Feature point methods typically define the orientation and scale of each feature, and normalise with respect to these parameters to compute matches independent of orientation and scale. The distinctiveness of the matches obtained, together with their invariance to rotation make these methods well suited to detecting pairs of symmetric features. Rotational and translational symmetric pairs can be detected by directly matching the feature points within an image, and potential mirror symmetric matches can be obtained by constructing a set of *mirrored feature descriptors* and matching these against the original feature descriptors. Mirrored feature descriptors are defined as descriptors of mirrored copies of the local image patches associated with the original feature points (the choice of mirroring axis is arbitrary).

Matching pairs of features, mirrored or otherwise, generates a collection of matched pairs of feature points. Each feature can be represented by a point vector describing its location in x, y co-ordinates, its orientation ϕ and scale s. Symmetry can then be computed directly from these pairs of point vectors.

The remainder of this section discusses the details of this procedure for detecting bilateral and rotational symmetries.

3.1 Defining Feature Points

A set of feature points $\mathbf{p}_i$ are determined using any rotationally invariant method, such as SIFT [16], that detects distinctive points with good repeatability. Whilst a scale-invariant detection method can be used, this is not necessary. The point vector $\mathbf{p}_i = (x_i, y_i, \phi_i, s_i)$ assigned to each feature point describes its location, orientation and (optionally) scale. Scale need only be determined if a scale-invariant feature detection method is used. Orientation, however, must be determined as it is central to the evaluation of symmetry.

Next a feature descriptor $\mathbf{k}_i$ is generated for each feature point, encoding the local appearance of the feature after its orientation (and scale) have been normalised. Any feature descriptor suitable for matching can be used, see [21] for a review of leading techniques. The experiments in this paper use the SIFT descriptor [16], which gives $\mathbf{k}_i$ as a 128 element vector.

3.2 Bilateral Symmetry

A set of mirrored feature descriptors $\mathbf{m}_i$ is generated. Here $\mathbf{m}_i$ describes a mirrored version of the image patch associated with feature $\mathbf{k}_i$. The choice of mirroring axis is arbitrary owing to the orientation normalisation in the generation of the descriptor.

The mirrored feature descriptors can be generated in one of two ways. The simplest, which allows the feature detection and matching to be treated entirely as a "black box", is to flip the original image about the y (or x) axis, and compute the feature point descriptors for the mirrored image. Each mirrored feature point is then assigned to the corresponding feature point in the original image, so that $\mathbf{m}_i$ is the mirrored version of $\mathbf{k}_i$. The second, more efficient, yet slightly more involved approach requires knowledge of the configuration of the feature descriptor $\mathbf{k}_i$, and generates the mirrored feature

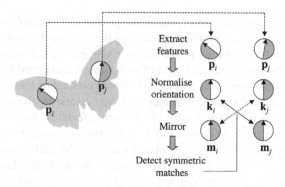

Fig. 1. Schematic illustrating the extraction and matching of a pair of symmetric features

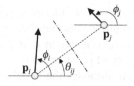

Fig. 2. A pair of point vectors $\mathbf{p}_i$ and $\mathbf{p}_j$ under scrutiny for mirror symmetry

points $\mathbf{m}_i$ by directly modifying this feature descriptor. For example, in the case of Lowe's SIFT descriptor [16] this can be achieved simply by reordering the elements of the descriptor vector so they represent the original image patch flipped about the axis aligned with the dominant orientation.

Matches are then sort between the features $\mathbf{k}_i$ and the mirrored features $\mathbf{m}_j$ to form a set of $(\mathbf{p}_i, \mathbf{p}_j)$ pairs of potentially symmetric features. Figure 1 shows a schematic of the process of extracting and matching a pair of symmetric features from an image. Each pair of symmetric features generates two matching pairs, but as these matches are equivalent only one need be recorded.

The symmetry of each pair is quantified as a function of the relative location, orientation and scale of $\mathbf{p}_i$ and $\mathbf{p}_j$. An angular symmetry weighting $\Phi_{ij} \in [-1, 1]$ (adapted from the first component of Reisfeld's [24] phase weighting function) is computed as

$$\Phi_{ij} = 1 - \cos(\phi_i + \phi_j - 2\theta_{ij}), \tag{1}$$

where the angles are defined as shown in Figure 2. A scale weighting $S_{ij} \in [0, 1]$ quantifying the relative similarity in scale of the two vectors is computed as

$$S_{ij} = \exp\left(\frac{-|s_i - s_j|}{\sigma_s(s_i + s_j)}\right)^2 \tag{2}$$

where σ_s controls the amount of scale variation accepted, $\sigma_s = 1$ was used in our experiments. Lastly an optional Gaussian distance weighting function $D_{ij} \in [0, 1]$ can be introduced to reward matching pairs that are closer to the symmetry axis. This agrees with psychophysical findings that symmetric features close to the symmetry axis contribute more to human symmetry perception than features further away [33]. However, from a computer vision perspective introducing a distance weighting is only appropriate if a bound can be given for the diameter of symmetry to be detected, i.e., how far symmetry detection should extend perpendicular to the symmetry axis. Given such a bound σ_d the distance weighting is defined as

$$D_{ij} = \exp\left(\frac{-d^2}{2\sigma_d^2}\right) \tag{3}$$

where d is the distance separating the feature pair, otherwise $D_{ij} = 1$. Our experiments used $D_{ij} = 1$, imposing no constraint on the diameter of symmetry detected.

All these weightings are combined to form a *symmetry magnitude* for each $(\mathbf{p}_i, \mathbf{p}_j)$ pair defined by

$$M_{ij} = \begin{cases} \Phi_{ij} S_{ij} D_{ij} & \text{if } \Phi_{ij} > 0 \\ 0 & \text{otherwise} \end{cases} \tag{4}$$

The symmetry magnitude M_{ij} quantifies the "amount" of symmetry exhibited by an individual pair of point vectors. We now accumulate the symmetries exhibited by all individual pairs in a voting space to determine the dominant symmetries present in the image.

Each pair of matching points defines a potential axis of symmetry passing perpendicularly through the mid-point of the line joining $\mathbf{p}_i$ and $\mathbf{p}_j$, shown by the dash-dotted line in Figure 2. These potential symmetry axis lines can be represented using the standard $r\theta$ polar co-ordinate parameterisation with

$$r_{ij} = x_c \cos\theta_{ij} + y_c \sin\theta_{ij}$$

where (x_c, y_c) are the image centred co-ordinates of the mid-point of the line joining $\mathbf{p}_i$ and $\mathbf{p}_j$, and θ_{ij} is the angle this line subtends with the x-axis.

The linear Hough transform can then be used to find dominant symmetry axes. Each symmetric pair $(\mathbf{p}_i, \mathbf{p}_j)$ casts a vote (r_{ij}, θ_{ij}) in Hough space weighted by its symmetry magnitude M_{ij}. The resulting Hough space is blurred with a Gaussian and the maxima extracted and taken to describe the dominant symmetry axes. The points lying in the neighbourhood of these maxima in Hough space indicate the symmetric pairs that are associated with this particular axis of symmetry. The spatial extent of each symmetry axis in the image is bounded by the convex hull of the population of pairs associated with the axis.

Figure 3 shows the steps involved in computing symmetry in an example image containing a symmetric figure in a cluttered background.

This method can be adapted to detect translational symmetry by replacing the mirrored feature points with unmirrored ones and modifying the assessment of the angular symmetry weighting in Equation 1 to $\Phi_{ij} = \cos(\phi_i - \phi_j)$.

3.3 Rotational Symmetry

Unlike bilateral symmetry detection, detecting rotational symmetry does not require the manufacture of additional feature descriptors, and is detected by simply matching the features $\mathbf{k}_i$ against each other. Each match defines a pair of point vectors $(\mathbf{p}_i, \mathbf{p}_j)$. If

514   G. Loy and J.-O. Eklundh

(a)   (b)   (c)

(d)   (e)   (f)

Fig. 3. Example. (a) 254×254 original image, (b) 946 feature points detected, (c) axes of symmetry associated with the 254 reflective matches obtained, intensity is proportional to symmetry magnitude M_{ij}, (d) symmetry axes in Hough space, (e) 22 symmetric features associated with the dominant symmetry axis, (f) dominant axis of symmetry and associated symmetric features.

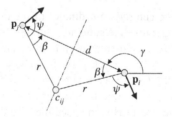

Fig. 4. Centre of rotation c_{ij} defined by point vectors $\mathbf{p}_i$ and $\mathbf{p}_j$

these vectors are parallel they do not exhibit rotational symmetry, but if they are not parallel their exists a point about which they are rotationally symmetric.

Formally, given a pair of non-parallel point vectors $\mathbf{p}_i$ and $\mathbf{p}_j$ in general position there exists a point c_{ij} a distance r from $\mathbf{p}_i$ and $\mathbf{p}_j$ about which $\mathbf{p}_i$ can be rotated to become precisely aligned and coincident with $\mathbf{p}_j$.

Figure 4 shows two such point vectors. The rotation centre c_{ij} is given by

$$c_{ij} = \begin{pmatrix} x_i \\ y_i \end{pmatrix} + \begin{pmatrix} r\cos(\beta + \gamma) \\ r\sin(\beta + \gamma) \end{pmatrix} \tag{5}$$

where x_i, y_i are the Cartesian co-ordinates of $\mathbf{p}_i$, γ is the angle the line joining $\mathbf{p}_i$ and $\mathbf{p}_j$ makes with the x-axis. By Pythagoras

$$r^2 = \left(\frac{d}{2}\right)^2 + \left(\frac{d}{2}\tan\beta\right)^2 \implies r = \frac{d\sqrt{1+\tan^2\beta}}{2},$$

where d is the distance between $\mathbf{p}_i$ and $\mathbf{p}_j$. Denoting the orientations of the point vectors $\mathbf{p}_i$ by ϕ_i, it can be seen from Figure 4 that

$$\left.\begin{array}{l}\phi_i = \gamma + \beta + \psi \\ \phi_j = \gamma + \pi - \beta + \psi\end{array}\right\} \implies \beta = \frac{\phi_i - \phi_j + \pi}{2}$$

which solves for all unknowns in Equation 5 and analytically specifies the centre of rotation of two non-parallel point vectors.

Once the centres of rotational symmetry have been determined for every matching feature pair the *rotational symmetry magnitude* R_{ij} is computed for each pair,

$$R_{ij} = S_{ij}D_{ij} \tag{6}$$

where S_{ij} is defined by Equation 2 or can be set to unity if all features have the same scale, and D_{ij} is defined by Equation 3 or is set to unity if no restriction on the size of symmetric objects to be detected is given.

Finally, the dominant centres of rotational symmetry are determined by accumulating the centres of rotation c_{ij} in a vote image the same size as the input image. Each vote is weighted by its rotational symmetry magnitude R_{ij}. The result is blurred with a Gaussian and the maxima identified as dominant centres of rotational symmetry. All centres of rotation close to a maxima are associated with that maxima.

If desired, the order of rotational symmetry can be estimated by examining the histogram of angles of rotation between matched features about each centre of rotation. Each order of rotation n defines an set of rotation angles $A = \{\frac{2\pi k}{n} : k = 1, 2, ..., n-1\}$ which should occur frequently in the angular histogram if this order of rotation is present. A simple measure of the prevalence of different rotational orders can be obtained by calculating the mean number of rotations in some vicinity q of the the angles in A and subtracting the mean number of rotations that are $\frac{2\pi(k-1)}{n}$ out of phase with these angles. This gives the order estimation function

$$O(n) = \frac{1}{n-1}\sum_{k=1}^{n-1}\sum_{-q}^{q}\left(h(\tfrac{2\pi k}{n}+q) - h(\tfrac{2\pi(k-1)}{n}+q)\right)$$

Figure 5 shows the stages towards computing rotational symmetry in an example image containing a rotationally symmetric region, (f) shows the order estimation function $O(n)$ with a clear peak at $n = 10$, and (e) shows the angular histogram with the shaded areas above and below the axis indicating the regions sampled when determining $O(n)$ for $n = 10$ (here $q = \frac{\pi}{18}$). Figure 5 (d) shows the correctly detected rotational symmetry foci of order 10, note the stray match lying off the wheel was introduced by allowing more than one match per feature, this is discussed in Section 3.4.

3.4 Matching

A similarity matrix is constructed quantifying the similarity between feature points. There are numerous ways to measure the similarity between feature vectors, for our experiments we used the Euclidean distance between the SIFT descriptors. The similarity

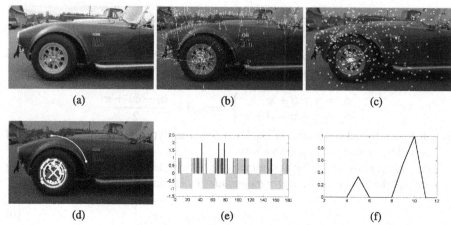

Fig. 5. Example. (a) original image, (b) feature points detected, (c) centres of rotation of matched feature pairs, (d) dominant centre of rotational symmetry and associated rotationally symmetric features, (e) histogram of angles of rotation (black) and mask applied when assessing order 10 symmetry, (f) response to detection of order of symmetry, order 10 detected.

matrix is symmetric, and as we are not interested in matching features with themselves or their mirrored equivalents, we only need to calculate the upper off-diagonal portion of the matrix. We can also limit the necessary comparisons by only attempting to match features whose scales are sufficiently similar for them to exhibit significant symmetry.

The number of matches per feature is not limited by the algorithm. Using only one match per feature works well in most situations. However, when there are repeated objects in the scene, or when searching for rotational symmetry of order greater than two there are obvious reasons to allow more than one match per feature. There is little additional computational load to generate several matching pairs per feature — the comparisons have been computed already — the only extra work is determining the symmetry for the additional pairs, which is extremely fast.

Allowing more than one match per feature allows the feature matching some degree of leeway when finding the correct match, however, it also increases the chance that incorrect "fluke" matches will be found that align with a dominant symmetry foci and are incorrectly grouped into a symmetric constellation. For our experiments we allowed one match per feature when detecting bilateral symmetry and four matches per feature when detecting rotational symmetry.

4   Performance

The new method was implemented in Matlab, with feature points detected and described using Lowe's SIFT code [16], and applied to detect bilateral and rotational symmetries in a diverse range of real images. Bilateral symmetry detection results are shown in Figure 6 and rotational symmetry detection results are shown in Figure 7.

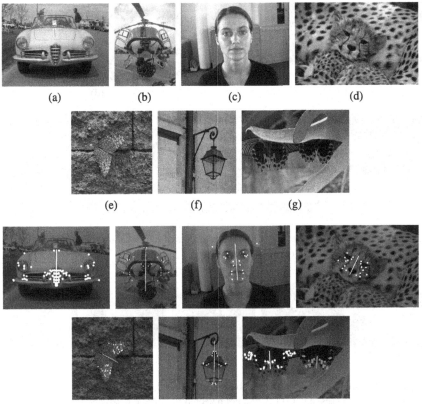

Fig. 6. Bilateral symmetry detection

Many objects and creatures exhibit a high degree of bilateral symmetry, especially when viewed from the front or rear, this is particularly common for moving objects (and creatures) whose dynamics benefit from symmetry about their direction of motion. In Figure 6 we see examples of this with the detection of vehicles (a) and (b), and faces of a person (c) and a cheetah (d). The symmetry axes detected together with the pairs of reflective feature points contributing to the symmetry axis are illustrated. Figure 6 (d) and (e) show creatures being detected with significant background clutter, (e) is particularly interesting as the subject appears partially camouflaged to a human eye. Many static artefacts also exhibit symmetry such as the street lamp in Figure 6 (f). Figure 6 (g) demonstrates the method detecting multiple axes of symmetry. When multiple axes are drawn the brightness indicates the relative symmetry magnitudes of the constellations.

Figure 7 shows five images containing rotationally symmetric objects. The second row shows the centres of rotational symmetry detected in each image, the feature points associated with each centre of rotation, and arcs indicating the rotations linking matching feature pairs. Figures 7 (a) and (b) illustrate the algorithm's ability to detect rotationally symmetric objects in cluttered scenes, (c) and (d) show the method applied to

Fig. 7. Rotational symmetry detection. Estimated orders of rotational symmetry for detected centres: (a) 5 and 5, (b) 2, (c) 10, (d) 4, and (e) 8.

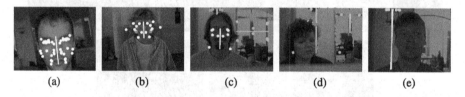

Fig. 8. Some results from the BioID database where the bilateral symmetry of the face was detected in 95.1% of cases, e.g. (a)-(c), and not detected in 4.9%, e.g. (d) and (e)

images with global and almost-global rotational symmetry, and (e) shows the method detecting rotational symmetry under partial occlusion. The orders of symmetry detected are also shown. Note that the order detected for (d) is 4 not 12, this is due to the cropping of the symmetric figure by the square image border which has left numerous features in the corners of the image with order 4 rotation.

To give an indication of the method's robustness it was applied to detect axes of symmetry in 1521 images from the BioID face database[2]. Ground truth symmetry axes were determined from 20 facial feature points manually annotated on each image[3]. Up to five symmetry axes were detected per image, and the axis of facial symmetry was deemed detected if the (r, θ) values of at least one detected axis lay within ± 5 pixels and $\pm 5°$ of the ground truth respectively. Figure 8 shows some results. The symmetry axes of the faces were correctly identified in 95.1% of the images. The 4.9% of cases where the symmetry of the faces were not detected (e.g. Figure 8 (d) and (e)) were attributed to the non-symmetric appearance of facial features in some of the images, or insufficient feature points on the face due to lack of contrast. Note that other (non-facial) axes of symmetry detected in the images still exhibited a degree of symmetry.

---

[2] http://www.bioid.com/downloads/facedb

[3] FGNet Annotation of the BioID Dataset http://www-prima.inrialpes.fr/FGnet/

The performance of the new algorithm is closely linked to the matching capability of the feature method used, and it is important to generate a substantial number of feature points on a symmetric object for it to be reliably detected. In essence our method is matching instances of locally symmetric texture, so it works very well when applied to detailed two-dimensional symmetric patterns such as butterfly wings (Figure 3 and Figure 6 (e) and (g)), however, it works equally well for three-dimensional features when these features form symmetric patterns in an image, such as the face, lamp and vehicles in Figure 6. The method works less well for smooth textureless objects where the number of feature points diminishes. It is feasible, however, that a shape-based descriptor, such as [7], could provide sufficient features in such circumstances.

The new method is simple and fast with the majority of time consumed in computing features and performing the matching. The computational order for matching n feature points is $O(n^2)$, although the number of computations is reduced by only matching across similar scales. If a non-unity distance weighting D_{ij} (Equation 3) is used the squared distance between pairs can be used to further limit the number of comparisons necessary. This would be useful when searching for relatively small symmetric objects in large scenes. The image can then be divided into grid squares as wide as the maximum expected symmetry diameter and features need only be matched against features in the same or adjacent grid regions. However, at present with no such constraints, and running unoptimised Matlab code on a 2.8 GHz Pentium 4, the method is quite fast, e.g. it takes less than 1.5 seconds to compute symmetry in the image in Figure 6 (c) with 314 feature points, and under 7 seconds to compute the symmetry in Figure 3 with 946 feature points. The majority of time is spent generating and matching the features, for Figure 3 this takes 1 and 5.5 seconds respectively (SIFT feature generation is done by calling Lowe's pre-compiled C code [16]).

There is a great deal of opportunity to extend the approach presented here. The symmetric constellations of features, together with the accurate characterisation of symmetry foci, provide a strong basis for segmenting the symmetric regions. One possibility is to generate additional feature points in the vicinity of the symmetric matches, verify their symmetry and grow symmetric regions, in a similar fashion to Ferrari *et al.*'s object segmentation approach [4]. Segmenting the symmetric regions would also provide a more accurate measure of the extent of the axes of symmetry in the image.

5   Conclusions

A method has been presented that finds symmetric constellations of features in images and allows efficient computation of symmetries in the image plane. Its performance has been demonstrated on a diverse range of real images. The method simultaneously considers symmetries over all locations, scales and orientations, and was shown to reliably detect both bilaterally and rotationally symmetric figures in complex backgrounds, and handle multiple occurrences of symmetry in a single image. The method relies on the robust matching of feature points generated by modern feature techniques such as SIFT [16]. However, it is not restricted to any one such technique, rather, it provides a means to compute symmetry from features, with the requirements that these features facilitate orientation invariant matching and have an associated orientation measure.

The pair-wise matching underpinning this approach accounts for its efficiency, allowing symmetric pairs to "vote" for symmetry foci rather than having to search the space of all possible symmetries. Symmetric features are grouped into constellations based on their underlying symmetry, characterising both the symmetries present and identifying the features associated with each incidence of symmetry.

References

1. Stefan Carlsson. Symmetry in perspective. In *ECCV (1)*, pages 249–263, 1998.
2. Steven C. Dakin and Andrew M. Herbert. The spatial region of integration for visual symmetry detection. *Proc of the Royal Society London B. Bio Sci*, 265:659–664, 1998.
3. Larry S. Davis. Understanding shape, ii: Symmetry. *SMC*, 7:204–212, 1977.
4. V. Ferrari, T. Tuytelaars, and L. Van Gool. Simultaneous object recognition and segmentation from single or multiple model views. *Int. J. of Comp. Vis.*, 2005.
5. R. I. Hartley and A. Zisserman. *Multiple View Geometry in Computer Vision*. Cambridge University Press, ISBN: 0521540518, second edition, 2004.
6. W. Hong, A. Y. Yang, K. Huang, and Y. Ma. On symmetry and multiple-view geometry: Structure, pose, and calibration from a single image. *Int. J. of Comp. Vis.*, 2004.
7. F. Jurie and C. Schmid. Scale-invariant shape features for recognition of object categories. In *CVPR*, 2004.
8. L. Kaufman and W. Richards. Spontaneous fixation tendencies of visual forms. *Perception and Psychophysics*, 5(2):85–88, 1969.
9. Yan Ke and Rahul Sukthankar. Pca-sift: A more distinctive representation for local image descriptors. In *CVPR (2)*, pages 506–513, 2004.
10. Yosi Keller and Yoel Shkolnisky. An algebraic approach to symmetry detection. In *ICPR (3)*, pages 186–189, 2004.
11. N. Kiryati and Y. Gofman. Detecting symmetry in grey level images: The global optimization approach. *Int. J. of Comp. Vis.*, 29(1):29–45, August 1998.
12. Andreas Kuehnle. Symmetry-based recognition of vehicle rears. *Pattern Recognition Letters*, 12(4):249–258, 1991.
13. S. Lazebnik, C. Schmid, and J. Ponce. Semi-local affine parts for object recognition. In *BMVC*, 2004.
14. J. Liu, J. Mundy, and A. Zisserman. Grouping and structure recovery for images of objects with finite rotational symmetry. In *ACCV*, volume I, pages 379–382, 1995.
15. P. Locher and C Nodine. Symmetry catches the eye. In J. O'Regan and A Lévy-Schoen, editors, *Eye Movements: from physiology to cognition*. Elsevier, 1987.
16. David G. Lowe. Distinctive image features from scale-invariant keypoints. *Int. J. of Comp. Vis.*, 60(2):91–110, 2004.
17. Gareth Loy and Alexander Zelinsky. Fast radial symmetry for detecting points of interest. *IEEE Trans Pat. Rec. & Mach. Int.*, 25(8):959–973, August 2003.
18. M. Mancas, B. Gosselin, and B. Macq. Fast and automatic tumoral area localisation using symmetry. In *Proc. of the IEEE ICASSP Conference*, 2005.
19. G. Marola. On the detection of the axes of symmetry of symmetric and almost symmetric planar images. *IEEE Trans Pat. Rec. & Mach. Int.*, 11(1):104–108, January 1989.
20. T. Masuda, K. Yamamoto, and H. Yamada. Detection of partial symmetry using correlation with rotated-reflected images. *Pattern Recognition*, 26(8):1245–1253, August 1993.
21. K. Mikolajczyk and C. Schmid. A performance evaluation of local descriptors. *IEEE Trans Pat. Rec. & Mach. Int.*, pages 1615–1630, October 2005.

22. K. Mikolajczyk, T. Tuytelaars, C. Schmid, A. Zisserman, J. Matas, F. Schaffalitzky, T. Kadir, and L. Van Gool. A comparison of affine region detectors. *Int. J. of Comp. Vis.*, 2006.
23. S. Mitra and Y. Liu. Local facial asymmetry for expression classification. In *CVPR*, 2004.
24. D. Reisfeld, H. Wolfson, and Y. Yeshurun. Context free attentional operators: the generalized symmetry transform. *Int. J. of Comp. Vis.*, 14(2):119–130, 1995.
25. R. Scognamillo, G. Rhodes, C. Morrone, and D. Burr. A feature-based model of symmetry detection. *Proc R Soc Lond B Biol Sci*, 270:1727–33, 2003.
26. G. Scott and H. C. Longuet-Higgins. Feature grouping by "relocalisation" of eigenvectors of the proximity matrix. In *BMVC*, pages 103–108, 1990.
27. Gal Sela and Martin D. Levine. Real-time attention for robotic vision. *Real-Time Imaging*, 3:173–194, 1997.
28. D. Sharvit, J. Chan, H. Tek, and B. B. Kimia. Symmetry-based indexing of image databases. In *Proc. IEEE Workshop on Content-Based Access of Image and Video Libraries*, 1998.
29. D. Shen, H.H.S. Ip, and E.K. Teoh. Robust detection of skewed symmetries. In *ICPR*, volume 3, pages 1010–1013, 2000.
30. D.G. Shen, H.H.S. Ip, and E.K. Teoh. Affine invariant detection of perceptually parallel 3d planar curves. *Pattern Recognition*, 33(11):1909–1918, November 2000.
31. C. Sun and D. Si. Fast reflectional symmetry detection using orientation histograms. *Journal of Real Time Imaging*, 5(1):63–74, February 1999.
32. Tinne Tuytelaars, Andreas Turina, and Luc J. Van Gool. Noncombinatorial detection of regular repetitions under perspective skew. *IEEE Trans Pat. Rec. & Mach. Int.*, 25(4):418–432, 2003.
33. C. W. Tyler, L. Hardage, and R. T. Miller. Multiple mechanisms for the detection of mirror symmetry. *Spatial Vision*, 9(1):79–100, 1995.
34. A.Y. Yang, S. Rao, K. Huang, W. Hong, and Y. Ma. Geometric segmentation of perspective images based on symmetry groups. In *ICCV*, pages 1251–1258, 2003.
35. R.K.K. Yip. A hough transform technique for the detection of reflectional symmetry and skew-symmetry. *Pattern Recognition Letters*, 21(2):117–130, February 2000.
36. H. Zabrodsky, S. Peleg, and D. Avnir. Completion of occluded shapes using symmetry. In *CVPR*, pages 678–679, 1993.
37. Hagit Zabrodsky, Schmuel Peleg, and David Avnir. Symmetry as a continuous feature. *IEEE Trans Pat. Rec. & Mach. Int.*, 17(12):1154–1166, December 1995.
38. T. Zielke, M. Brauckmann, and W. von Seelen. Intensity and edge-based symmetry detection with an application to car-following. *CVGIP: Image Underst.*, 58(2):177–190, 1993.

Discovering Texture Regularity as a Higher-Order Correspondence Problem

James Hays, Marius Leordeanu, Alexei A. Efros, and Yanxi Liu

School of Computer Science,
Carnegie Mellon University,
Pittsburgh, PA, USA
{jhhays, manudanu, efros, yanxi}@cs.cmu.edu

Abstract. Understanding texture regularity in real images is a challenging computer vision task. We propose a higher-order feature matching algorithm to discover the lattices of near-regular textures in real images. The underlying lattice of a near-regular texture identifies all of the texels as well as the global topology among the texels. A key contribution of this paper is to formulate lattice-finding as a correspondence problem. The algorithm finds a plausible lattice by iteratively proposing texels and assigning neighbors between the texels. Our matching algorithm seeks assignments that maximize both pair-wise visual similarity and higher-order geometric consistency. We approximate the optimal assignment using a recently developed spectral method. We successfully discover the lattices of a diverse set of unsegmented, real-world textures with significant geometric warping and large appearance variation among texels.

1 Introduction

Texture is all around us, taking up a large part of our visual world. However, human perception is so well-tuned to detecting regularity (both structural as well as statistical) that the casual observer often takes texture for granted, blind to its actual complexity (see Figure 1a). But scientifically, texture analysis has been a long-standing and surprisingly difficult problem. Interest in visual texture predates computer vision, going back at least to J.J. Gibson [1], who pointed out its importance for the perception of surface orientation (i.e. shape-from-texture). Later, Bela Julesz developed a theory of human texture discrimination based on matching Nth order texture statistics [2]. Both researchers speak of a *texture element* (texel or texton)[1], as the basic building block which defines a particular texture. This notion of a texture element turned out to be extremely useful in

---

[1] Although now most researchers use *texel* and *texton* interchangeably, we believe that there is a useful distinction to be made. Texels, by analogy with pixels, define a partitioning (or tiling) of the texture, with each texel having a finite, non-overlapping spatial extent. On the other hand, Julesz's textons serve the role of statistical features, and (as operationalized by Malik et al. [3]) are computed at every pixel, without concern for overlap. In this paper, we are primarily interested in *texels*.

A. Leonardis, H. Bischof, and A. Pinz (Eds.): ECCV 2006, Part II, LNCS 3952, pp. 522–535, 2006.

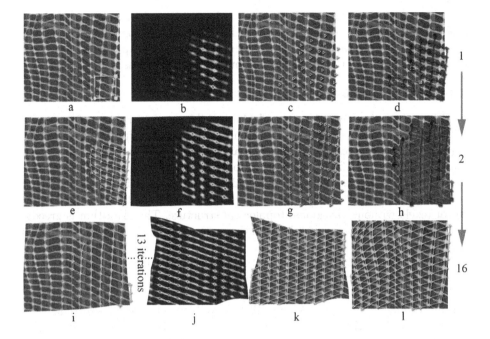

Fig. 1. The stages of our algorithm, one iteration per row. (a) is the input image, (l) is the final result. The leftmost column shows (potentially warped) input images with the current, refined lattice overlaid. The second column is the correlation map, calculated from valid texels, used to propose the potential texels in (c) and (g). (d) and (h) show assignments made from these potential texels before they are refined into the lattices of (e) and (i), respectively. (k) shows the lattice with the highest a-score after 16 iterations, and (l) is that lattice mapped back to input image coordinates. The input image (a) is a challenge posed by David Martin at the Lotus Hill workshop, 2005. Best seen in color.

approaching a number of problems, including shape-from-texture [4, 5, 6], texture segmentation [7, 3], texture recognition [8, 9], as well as texture editing and resynthesis [10, 11, 12, 13]. However, finding texels in real images has proved to be an extremely difficult task. (In this paper, we are not concerned about highly stochastic textures with no easily identifiable texels.) For textures with well defined texture elements, most existing automatic texel detection algorithms appear too brittle, severely constraining the applicability of algorithms such as shape-from-texture to the very limited class of "easy" textures. For the same reason, in computer graphics literature, automatic approaches have been largely unsuccessful, typically replaced by the user identifying texels by hand [13].

Why is finding repeated texture elements such a difficult problem? The answer is that texture is inherently a *global process*. Texture, by definition, exists only over a large spatial extent. It is meaningless to talk about a single texel in isolation, since it only becomes a texel when it is repeated. Only when consideration is given to the persistent re-appearance of deformed, noisy versions of the same texel in a texture, does the structure of the texture have a chance to overcome its local noise and emerge as a global solution. In fact, texel finding is an instance of the notoriously hard Gestalt grouping problem. Therefore, local approaches alone are doomed to fail due to their inherent computational brittleness.

1.1   Finding Repeated Elements

In the now classic paper, Leung and Malik [14] pose the problem of detecting and grouping texture elements in the language of tracking. After being initialized through corner features, potential texels are spatially "tracked" to nearby image locations under the affine deformation model. Texels that have a high similarity with their neighbors are deemed good and are stitched together. This algorithm iterates until no more texture elements can be added, resulting in a connected set of texels without any global topological structure. The algorithm is greedy, with no mechanism to fix mistakes and there is no method to evaluate groupings produced from different initializations.

Lobay and Forsyth [6, 12] address these concerns by building a global texel model, based on clustering SIFT descriptors. The authors model texture regularity as a "marked point process" that ignores the geometric arrangement of texture elements and assumes that all texture elements are foreshortened, rotated, and differently illuminated versions of an identical canonical texel. The advantage of this model is that the appearance deformations of the different instances of the same texel provide useful information about surface orientation without having to reason about their geometric or topological relationship.

The above approaches place strong requirements on the appearance of each individual texel (e.g. it must be distinctive enough to be matched), but make no strict assumptions about the spatial relationships between the texels. Schaffalitzky et al. [15] and Turina et al. [16] take the opposite view by assuming a very strong transformation model. In particular, they assume that the texture is completely regular and planar, and that it has undergone a global projective transformation. Under such strong assumptions, it is possible to locate texels even if they are not very distinctive. However, such restrictive assumptions limit the applicability of these methods.

1.2   The Case for Lattice Estimation

Previous work on discovering repeated texture elements can be viewed as two extremes: one focusing on individual texels (or local neighborhoods) with no regard to their global organization or regularity [14, 12]; the other placing very strict requirements on the overall image structure (i.e. planar regular texture under global perspective transformation) [15, 16]. The former can handle a wide range of textures but at the cost of relying entirely on the appearance of individual texels. The latter uses the overall arrangement of the texels to its advantage, but is only applicable to a limited subset of textures.

In this paper, we would like to consider the middle ground – an algorithm that uses the underlying structure of the texture, but does not place undue restrictions on the allowable deformations. For this paper we will consider a class of near-regular textures (NRT) [13] that are regular textures under locally smooth geometric and appearance deformations. Although this somewhat restricts the types of textures we can handle (e.g. randomly distributed polka dots are probably out), NRT can model a broad set of real-world textures (see Result Section for examples). The most useful property of near-regular texture is that it can be completely characterized by an underlying 2D lattice.

We can formally define a near-regular texture P as a deformed regular texture P_r through a multi-modal, multi-dimensional mapping d: $P = d(P_r)$. Wallpaper group theory [17] states that all translationally symmetric textures P_r can be generated by a pair of shortest (among all possible) vectors t_1, t_2. The *orbits* of this pair of generators form a 2D *quadrilateral lattice*, which simultaneously defines all 2D texels (partitions the space into smallest generating regions) and a topological structure among all texels. A regular texture can be expressed by a single pair of t_1, t_2, while an NRT is uniquely determined by its location-varying lattice under actions $t_1(x, y), t_2(x, y)$.

Two important observations on the lattice are worth noting: (1) the lattice topology for all different types of wallpaper patterns remains the same: quadrilateral; (2) while NRT may suffer large geometry and appearance variations locally or globally, its lattice topology remains invariant. Therefore, automatically discovering the lattice of an NRT is a well-defined and conceptually feasible task. Understanding and explicitly searching for lattice structures in real world textures enables us to develop more powerful texture analysis algorithms that are not totally dependent on specific image features [14, 12], and to approach a much broader set of textures than could be covered in [15, 16].

1.3   Lattice Estimation as Correspondence

Our main contribution in this paper is the formulation of texel lattice discovery as an instance of the general *correspondence problem*. Correspondence problems come up in computer vision whenever there are two disjoint sets of features that require a one-to-one assignment (e.g. stereo correspondence, non-rigid shape matching [18], etc). Here, however, we propose to assign a set of potential texels *to itself*, with constraints to avoid self-assignments and other degeneracies. While this formulation might seem counterintuitive, by phrasing lattice finding as a correspondence problem we can leverage powerful matching algorithms that will allow us to reason *globally* about regularity. Robustness is key because there is no foolproof way to identify texels before forming a lattice – the two must be discovered simultaneously.

But how can 2D lattice discovery (where each texel is connected to a spatial neighborhood) be formulated in terms of pairwise correspondence? Our solution is to perform two semi-independent correspondence assignments, resulting in each texel being paired with two of its neighbors along two directions, which turn out to be precisely the t_1 and t_2 directions discussed earlier. Combining all these pairwise assignments into a single graph will produce a consistent texture lattice, along with all its constituent texels. Thus, the overall correspondence procedure will involve: 1) generating a set of potential texels in the form of visual descriptors and their locations, and 2) using a matching algorithm to discover the inherent regularity in the form of a lattice and to throw out the potentially numerous false positives.

Correspondence problems in computer vision are commonly constructed as a "bipartite matching." One can use the Hungarian algorithm or integer linear programming to find, in polynomial time, the global optimum assignment based on any such bipartite, pairwise matching costs. But texture regularity is not a pairwise phenomenon – it is inherently higher-order. Consider the following scenario: a texel, in trying to decide who his neighbors are, can see that he looks very much like many other potential texels. This is necessarily the case in a repeating texture. This leaves a great deal of ambiguity about who his t_1 and t_2 neighbors should be. But the texel knows that whatever assignment he makes should be consistent with what other texels are picking as their neighbors – i.e. his t_1 vector should be similar to everyone else's. This compels us to adopt a higher order assignment scheme in which the "goodness" of an assignment can be conditioned not just on pairwise features and one-to-one assignment, but on higher-order relationships between potential assignments. We can thus encourage assignments that are geometrically consistent with each other.

Unfortunately finding a global optimum in a situation like this is NP-complete. One can try to coerce bipartite matching to approximate the process by rolling the higher-order considerations (e.g. consistency with the some t_1 and t_2) into the pairwise costs. However, this is a tall order, effectively requiring us to estimate the regularity of a texture *a priori*. Fortunately there are other efficient ways to approximate the optimal assignments for higher order correspondence [19, 20]. We use the method presented in [20] because of its speed and simplicity.

2   Approach

Our algorithm proceeds in four stages: 1) *Proposal of texels*, in which new candidate texels will be proposed based on an interest point detector, correlation with a random template, or a lattice from a previous iteration. 2) *Lattice assignment*, in which potential texels will be assigned t_1 and t_2 neighbors based on their pairwise relationships to each other as well as higher-order relationships between assignments. 3) *Lattice refinement*, in which the assignments are interpreted so as to form a meaningful lattice and discard the outlier texels. 4) *Thin-plate spline warping*, in which the texture is regularized based on our deformed lattice and a corresponding regular lattice. Our algorithm will iterate through these four stages based on several random initializations and pick the best overall lattice.

2.1   Initial Texel Proposal

Our task in initialization is to propose a set of potential texels from an input texture that can be passed to the assignment procedure. Without initial knowledge of the nature of the regularity in a texture our initial estimates of texels are necessarily crude. Our approach is therefore to avoid making commitments until the global assignment procedure can discover the true regularity and separate the "true" texels from the "false."

Many previous regular texture analysis approaches [14, 15, 16, 12] use some manner of interest point detector or corner detector to propose initial texel locations. All of these methods use a grouping or verification phase, analogous to our assignment phase, in order to confirm their proposed texels. Likewise, we propose a set of potential texels with MSER[21], which we found to be the most effective interest point detector for structured textures.

However, for about half of the textures in our test set the interest points were so poorly correlated with the regularity that not even a partial lattice could be formed through any subset of the interest points. If such a failure occurs, our algorithm falls back to a texel proposal method based on normalized cross correlation (NCC). We pick a patch at random location and radius from our image (figure 1a) and correlate it at all offsets within 5 radii of its center (Figure 1b). We then find peaks in this correlation score map using the Region of Dominance method [22]. In a highly deformed near-regular texture it is likely that NCC will not be effective at identifying all similar texels. However, we find that it can do a reasonable job *locally* so long as textures vary smoothly.

2.2 Higher-Order Matching

The use of higher-order matching to discover a lattice from potential texels is the core of our algorithm. We assign each potential texel a t_1 neighbor and then a t_2 neighbor. Figures 1d and 1h show the assignments from the potential texels 1c and 1g, respectively, during the first and second iteration of our lattice finding.

In order to employ the machinery of higher-order assignment, we need to answer two questions: 1) what is the affinity between each *pair of texels*. 2) what is the affinity between each *pair of assignments*. The former are pairwise affinities and the latter are higher-order affinities. Because our higher-order matching problem is NP-complete, we must engineer our answers such that they are amenable to approximation by the specific algorithm that we have chosen [20].

To calculate pairwise affinities we will consider all of the information that a pair of texels can draw upon to decide if they are neighbors. The most obvious and vital source of pairwise information is visual similarity– how similar do these two texels appear? Other factors must be considered as well– how near are the two texels? Would the angle of this assignment compromise the independence of t_1 and t_2? To calculate the higher-order affinities, we will focus on geometric consistency – how geometrically similar are these two potential pairs of assignments? By rewarding the selection of t_1, t_2 vectors that agree with each other we encourage the assignment algorithm to discover a globally consistent lattice. The higher-order affinities also prevent geometrically inconsistent false positives from being included in the lattice, even if they are visually indistinguishable from the true texels.

Taken together, these affinities should prefer visually and geometrically consistent lattices which are made up of true texels while the false texels are left unassigned or assigned to each other. Before getting into further detail about the calculation of these affinities we must first discuss the mechanics of our matching algorithm as they will influence our precise metrics.

Estimating the Optimal Higher-Order Assignment. The higher-order assignment algorithm we adopt from [20] is a spectral method which will infer the correct assignments based on the dominant eigenvector of an affinity matrix M. M is symmetric and strictly non-negative, containing affinities between all possible assignments. Therefore, M is n^2-by-n^2, where n is the number of potential texels found in section 2.1, for a total of n^4 elements. Each element $M(a,b)$, where $a = (i,i')$ and $b = (j,j')$, describes the affinity between the assignment from texel i to i' with the assignment from texel j to j'. Where $a = b$ on the diagonal of the affinity matrix lie what could be considered the lower-order affinities. Clearly, M will need to be extremely sparse.

The correspondence problem now reduces to finding the cluster C of assignments (i,i') that maximizes the intra-cluster score $S = \sum_{a,b \in C} M(a,b)$ such that the one to one mapping constraints are met. We can represent any cluster C by an indicator vector x, such that $x(a) = 1$ if $a \in C$ and zero otherwise. We can rewrite the total intra-cluster score as $S = \sum_{a,b \in C} M(a,b) = x^T M x$ and thus the optimal assignment x^* is the binary vector that maximizes the score, given the mapping constraints: $x^* = argmax(x^T M x)$. Finding this optimal x^* is NP-Hard so Leordeanu and Hebert[20] approximate the optimal assignment by relaxing the integral constraints on x^*. Then by Raleigh's ratio theorem the x^* that maximizes $x^* = argmax(x^T M x)$ is the principal eigenvector of M. The principal eigenvector x^* is binarized in order to satisfy the mapping constraints by iteratively finding the maximum value of the eigenvector, setting it to 1, and zeroing out all conflicting assignments. The magnitude of each value of the eigenvector before binarization roughly equates to the confidence of the corresponding assignment.

Specifying the Affinities. The lower-order, pairwise affinities A are calculated as follows:

$$A(i,i') = NCC(Patch(i), Patch(i')) * \theta(i,i',t_1) * \lambda(i,i') \qquad (1)$$

NCC is normalized cross correlation, clamped to [0,1], where $Patch(i)$ is the image region centered at the location of potential texel i. $\theta(i,i',t_1)$ is the angular distance between the vector from i to i' and the t_1 vector (or its opposite) previously assigned at i (if i is in the process of assigning t_1 then this term is left out). The θ term is necessary to prevent t_1 and t_2 connecting in the same direction. $\lambda(i,i') = \sqrt{1/(Length(i,i') + C_l)}$ is a penalty for Euclidean distance between two potential texels. The λ term is necessary to encourage a texel to connect to its nearest true neighbor instead of a farther neighbor which would otherwise be just as appealing based on the other metrics. C_l is a constant used to prevent λ from going to infinity as a potential assignment becomes degenerately short.

The higher-order affinity G is a scale-invariant measure of geometric distortion between each pair of potential t vectors.

$$G(i,i',j,j') = max(1 - C_d * Distance(i,i',j,j')/Length(i,i',j,j'), 0) \qquad (2)$$

This term gives affinity to pairs of assignments that would produce similar t vectors. $Distance(i, i', j, j')$ is the Euclidean distance between the vectors from i to i' and j to j'. $Length(i, i', j, j')$ is the average length of the same vectors. Multiplying the lengths of these vectors by some constant has no effect on the G. This is desirable– we wouldn't expect resizing a texture to change the distortion measured in the potential assignments. C_d controls how tolerant to distortion this metric is.

Logically, we could place the lower-order affinities on the diagonal of M and place the higher-order affinities on the off-diagonal of M. But by keeping these affinities distinct in M, x^* could be biased towards an assignment with very large lower-order affinity but absolutely no higher-order support (or vice versa). Since we are looking for $x^* = argmax(x^T M x)$, by placing the lower-order and higher-order affinities separately in M the two sets of affinities are additive. We want a more conservative affinity measure which requires both lower-order and higher-order affinities to be reasonable. Therefore we multiply the lower-order affinities onto the higher-order affinities and leave the diagonal of M empty. Assignments without lower-order (appearance) agreement or without higher-order (geometric) support will not be allowed.

Combining all of the previously defined terms, we build the affinity matrix M as follows:

$$M((i, i'), (j, j')) = A(i, i') * A(j, j') * G(i, i', j, j')$$
$$\text{for all } i, i', j, j' \text{such that } i \neq i' \text{ and } j \neq j' \text{ and } i \neq j \text{ and } i' \neq j' \qquad (3)$$

The restrictions on which (i, i', j, j') tuples are visited are based on the topology of the lattice– no self assignments ($i = i'$ or $j = j'$) or many-to-one assignments ($i = j$ or $i' = j'$) are given affinity. We avoid cycles (both $i = j'$ and $i' = j$) as well. It would still be computationally prohibitive to visit all the remaining (i, i', j, j') tuples, but we skip the configurations which would lead to zero affinity. For a given (i, i'), the geometric distortion measure G will only be non-zero for (j, j') that are reasonably similar. In practice, this will be the case for several hundred choices of (j, j') out of the hundred thousand or so possible assignments. We therefore build a kd-tree out of all the vectors implied by all assignments and only calculate affinity between assignments whose vectors fall inside a radius (implied by C_d) where they can have non-zero G score. Affinities not explicitly calculated in M are 0. In practice, M is commonly 99.99% sparse. Lastly, this affinity metric is symmetric (as required by [20]), so we only need to visit the lower diagonal.

2.3   Lattice Refinement / Outlier Rejection

The matching algorithm produces a one-to-one assignment of texels to texels, both for t_1 and t_2, but the assignments do not directly define a proper lattice. A lattice has topological constraints that are of higher-order than a second-order correspondence algorithm can guarantee. We enforce three distinct topological constraints: 1) border texels don't necessarily have two t_1 or t_2 neighbors, 2) the lattice is made up of quadrilaterals, and 3) the lattice is connected and non-overlapping. Because the higher-order assignment algorithm has chained the true texels into a coherent lattice, these simple heuristics tend to discard most of the false positive texels.

Non-assignments. Our first refinement of the lattice is performed based on the "confidences" found during the assignment phase above. By keeping only assignments whose eigenvector value is above a certain threshold, we can find all border nodes or unmatched texels. We use a threshold of 10^{-2} to distinguish these "non-assignments" from the real assignments. Non-assignments have low confidences because they cannot find a match that is geometrically consistent with the dominant cluster of assignments. In figures 1d and 1h these non-assignments are shown as blue "stubs." An alternative approach is to use dummy nodes as proposed in [18], but we find our method more effective in conjunction with the higher-order approximation we use.

Quadrilaterals. Our second refinement requires that the lattice be composed entirely of quadrilaterals. A texel is included in the lattice only if, by going to its t_1 neighbor and then that neighbor's t_2 neighbor, you arrive at the same texel as taking t_2 and then t_1 links. We also require all four texels encountered during such a test to be distinct in order to discard cycles and self-assignments. All quadrilaterals that pass this test are shown with a beige line through their diagonal in figures 1d and 1h.

Maximum Connected Component. If false positive texels appear in an organized fashion either by coincidence or by poor thresholding in the texel proposal phase, these false positives will self-connect into a secondary, independent quadrilateral lattice. Two such texels can be seen in the upper right of figure 1d. It is not rare to see large secondary lattices which are the dual of the primary lattice. These secondary lattices are perfectly valid but redundant. We reduce the final lattice to a single, connected lattice by finding the maximum connected component of the valid texels.

2.4   Regularized Thin-Plate Spline Warping

The result of the previous section is a connected, topologically valid lattice that can be unambiguously corresponded to a "regular" lattice. Inspired by work in shape matching [18], we use this correspondence to parameterize a regularized thin-plate spline coordinate warp to invert whatever geometric distortions are present in our texture. At each texel in the lattice, we specify a warp to the corresponding texel in a regular lattice which is constructed from uniform t_1 and t_2 vectors that are the mean of the t_1 and t_2 vectors observed in the deformed lattice. We use a strong regularization parameter which globalizes the un-warping and prevents a few spurious, incorrectly included or wrongly shaped texels from distorting the image too much. We use the same affine regularization term as in [18].

Unwarping the texture makes the true texels easier to recognize. For instance, in figure 2 the unwarping flattens the seams in the lower half of the image where the distortion would otherwise be too strong to detect the texels. Figures 1 and 3

Fig. 2. From left to right: input, warp specified at each texel after the second iteration, flattened texture after nine iterations, and the final lattice

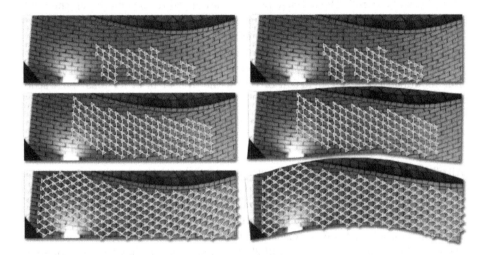

Fig. 3. From top to bottom: Iterations 1, 3, and 9 of our lattice finding procedure. On the left is the final lattice overlaid onto the original image. On the right one can observe the effects of successive thin-plate spline warps to regularize the image.

show the effect of thin-plate spline warping through several iterations. Figures 1e and 1i show the combined effects of lattice refinement and thin-plate spline warping on the assignments returned from the matching algorithm (shown in figure 1d and 1h). The warping effects may seem subtle because of the strong regularization parameter but by later iterations the effect is pronounced. (See figure 1k)

2.5   Iterative Refinement

One of the keys of our approach is the idea of incrementally building and refining a lattice by trusting the texels that have been kept as inliers through the assignment and refinement steps. At the end of each iteration we allow texels to "vote" on a new set of potential texels. We extract each texel from the final, warped lattice and correlate it locally just as we did with our initial patch in section 2.1. These local correlation maps for each texel are then summed up at the appropriate offsets for the combined correlation map (see figures 1b, 1f, 1j). This voting process prevents a few false texels from propagating to future iterations since they are overridden by the majority of true texels.

2.6   Evaluation: The A-Score

With an iterative, randomly initialized lattice-finding procedure we need a way to reason about the relative quality of the many lattices we will discover. For this purpose we adopt a modified version of the "a-score" from [13]:

$$\text{A-score} = \frac{\sum_{i=1}^{m} std(T_1(i), T_2(i), \ldots, T_n(i))}{m * \sqrt{n}} \tag{4}$$

where n is the number of final texels, and m is the number of pixels in each aligned texel T_n. This score is the average per-pixel standard deviation among the final, aligned texels. Texel alignment is achieved with a perspective warp which aligns the corner points of each texel with the mean sized texel. This alignment is required because the regularized thin-plate spline does not necessarily bring the texels into complete alignment, although it will tend to do so given enough iterations. Our modification is the inclusion of $\sqrt{n}$ in the divisor in order bias the a-score toward more complete lattices.

3   Results

All of the results shown in this paper were generated with the same parameters and constants ($C_l = 30$ and $C_d = 3$). Each texture was randomly initialized and run for 20 iterations. This procedure was repeated 5 times with different initializations and the best result was chosen based on the a-score. For bad initializations, it takes less than a minute to propose texels, run them through matching, and realize that there is no meaningful lattice. A full 20 iterations can take half an hour for some textures as the number of texels increases.

For our experiments, we used textures from the *CMU Near-regular Texture Database* (http://graphics.cs.cmu.edu/data/texturedb/gallery). Some qualitative results of our algorithm are presented in Figures 4, 5, and 6. Quantitatively, the algorithm was evaluated on about 60 different textures. The full lattices were discovered in about 60% of the cases, with about 20-30% producing partially-complete lattices (as in Figure 6 upper left), and the rest being miserable failures.

Fig. 4. From left to right: input, final lattice, warped texture, and extracted texels

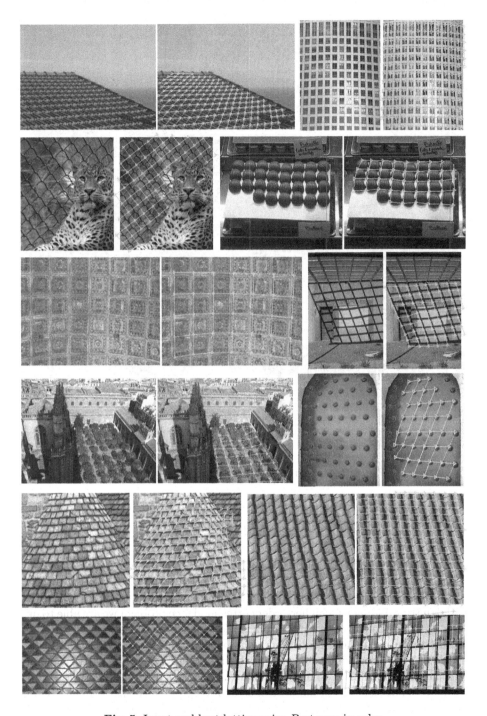

Fig. 5. Input and best lattice pairs. Best seen in color.

534 J. Hays et al.

Fig. 6. Input and best lattice pairs. Best seen in Color.

Failure is typically due to the low-level visual features rather than the matching algorithm.

4 Conclusions

We have presented a novel approach for discovering texture regularity. By formulating lattice finding as a higher-order correspondence problem we are able to obtain a globally consistent solution from the local texture measurements. With our iterative approach of lattice discovery and post-warping we recover the structure of extremely challenging textures. Our basic framework of higher-order matching should be applicable to discovering regularity with any set of features. While there does not exist any standard test sets for comparing the performance of our method against the others, we demonstrate that our algorithm is able to handle a wide range of different textures as compared to previous approaches.

Acknowledgements. This research was funded in part by an NSF Graduate Fellowship to James Hays and NSF Grants IIS-0099597 and CCF-0541230.

References

1. Gibson, J.J.: The Perception of the Visual World. Houghton Mifflin, Boston, Massachusetts (1950)
2. Julesz, B.: Visual pattern discrimination. IRE Transactions on Information Theory **8** (1962) 84–92
3. Malik, J., Belongie, S., Shi, J., Leung, T.: Textons, contours and regions: Cue integration in image segmentation. In: ICCV. (1999) 918–925
4. Garding, J.: Surface orientation and curvature from differential texture distortion. ICCV (1995) 733–739
5. Malik, J., Rosenholtz, R.: Computing local surface orientation and shape from texture for curved surfaces. In: Int. J. Computer Vision. (1997) 149–168
6. Forsyth, D.A.: Shape from texture without boundaries. In: ECCV. (2002) 225–239
7. Puzicha, J., Hofmann, T., Buhmann, J.: Non-parametric similarity measures for unsupervised texture segmentation and image retrieval. In: CVPR. (1997) 267–72
8. Leung, T., Malik, J.: Recognizing surfaces using three-dimensional textons. In: ICCV. (1999)
9. Varma, M., Zisserman, A.: Texture classification: Are filter banks necessary? In: CVPR. (2003) 691–698
10. Brooks, S., Dodgson, N.: Self-similarity based texture editing. In: SIGGRAPH '02, New York, NY, USA, ACM Press (2002) 653–656
11. Cohen, M.F., Shade, J., Hiller, S., Deussen, O.: Wang tiles for image and texture generation. ACM Trans. Graph. **22** (2003) 287–294
12. Lobay, A., Forsyth, D.A.: Recovering shape and irradiance maps from rich dense texton fields. In: CVPR. (2004) 400–406
13. Liu, Y., Lin, W.C., Hays, J.: Near-regular texture analysis and manipulation. In: ACM Transactions on Graphics (SIGGRAPH). (2004)
14. Leung, T.K., Malik, J.: Detecting, localizing and grouping repeated scene elements from an image. In: ECCV, London, UK, Springer-Verlag (1996) 546–555
15. Schaffalitzky, F., Zisserman, A.: Geometric grouping of repeated elements within images. In: Shape, Contour and Grouping in Computer Vision. (1999) 165–181
16. Turina, A., Tuytelaars, T., Gool, L.V.: Efficient grouping under perspective skew. In: CVPR. (2001) pp. 247–254
17. Grünbaum, B., Shephard, G.C.: Tilings and Patterns. W. H. Freeman and Company, New York (1987)
18. Belongie, S., Malik, J., Puzicha, J.: Shape matching and object recognition using shape contexts. PAMI **24** (2002) 509–522
19. Berg, A.C., Berg, T.L., Malik, J.: Shape matching and object recognition using low distortion correspondence. In: CVPR. (2005)
20. Leordeanu, M., Hebert, M.: A spectral technique for correspondence problems using pairwise constraints. In: ICCV. (2005)
21. Matas, J., Chum, O., Urban, M., Pajdla, T.: Robust wide baseline stereo from maximally stable extremal regions. In: British Machine Vision Conference. (2002)
22. Liu, Y., Collins, R., Tsin, Y.: A computational model for periodic pattern perception based on frieze and wallpaper groups. PAMI **26** (2004) 354–371

Exploiting Model Similarity for Indexing and Matching to a Large Model Database

Yi Tan, Bogdan C. Matei, and Harpreet Sawhney

Sarnoff Corporation,
201 Washington Road, CN5300, Princeton, NJ 08543-5300
{ytan, bmatei, hsawhney}@Sarnoff.com

Abstract. This paper proposes a novel method to exploit model similarity in model-based 3D object recognition. The scenario consists of a large 3D model database of vehicles, and rapid indexing and matching needs to be done without sequential model alignment. In this scenario, the competition amongst shape features from similar models may pose serious challenge to recognition. To solve the problem, we propose to use a metric to quantitatively measure model similarities. For each model, we use similarity measures to define a model-centric class (MCC), which contains a group of similar models and the pose transformations between the model and its class members. Similarity information embedded in a MCC is used to boost matching hypotheses generation so that the correct model gains more opportunities to be hypothesized and identified. The algorithm is implemented and extensively tested on 1100 real LADAR scans of vehicles with a model database containing over 360 models.

1 Introduction

1.1 Background

In a model-based 3D object recognition system, two model-related issues are challenging for the recognition performance: the number of models in the database and the degree of similarity amongst the models. In an indexing based recognition system that employs shape features for indexing, as the number of models increases, so does the number of the model features. As more features need to be searched, the recognition process may become inefficient. When a large number of similar models exist in a database, features from these models will compete with each other, the matching uncertainty may result in missing the correct target model. Numerous methods have been proposed to solve the first problem, such as the locality sensitivity hashing (LSH) techniques [2], which result in sublinear efficiency in feature search. There are, however, far fewer methods proposed to solve the model similarity problem in order to improve the recognition performance.

In this paper, we propose a new approach to tackle the model similarity issue in a model-based 3D object indexing system to improve the object indexing performance. Our indexing system takes the 3D object data obtained from a LADAR sensor, searches through the model database, and outputs a short list of models with high likelihood of matching to the scene target. Our application is vehicle recognition. A large

A. Leonardis, H. Bischof, and A. Pinz (Eds.): ECCV 2006, Part II, LNCS 3952, pp. 536–548, 2006.

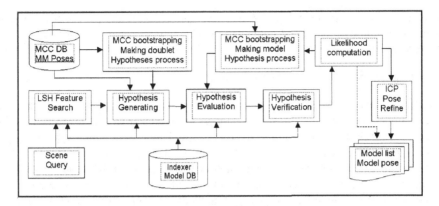

Fig. 1. The model-based 3D object indexing system

model database is built which contains several hundred commercial and military vehicles, of which about 2/3rd are sedans, pickup trucks, minivans and SUVs.

In our previous work [14], as shown in middle-row blocks in Figure 1, we have developed a method of coarse alignment and hypothesis testing by using linear model hashing and batch RANSAC for rapid and accurate model indexing. Facet models are converted into point clouds, and a set of shape signatures, the spin images [3], in the form of high-dimensional shape vectors is computed for each model and stored in the database. During the indexing process, the set of shape signatures is computed from a scene object and matched to the models features in the database. Features matched between the scene and models are used to generate indexing hypotheses. These hypotheses are verified by using the geometrical correspondence between the scene and model signatures, and the final matching likelihood is computed for each matched model. The indexer outputs a list of matched models with high likelihood value, as well as the model pose estimates.

1.2 Issues

As discussed above, the matched scene and model features are used to generate matching hypotheses. Based on indexing with shape signatures, for efficiency, the method tests for a limited number of pose hypotheses generated through the feature-pair of spin image matches. The method works well on diversified and mixed models. However, shape signatures tend to be alike if they are generated from the same location among the similar models. With the constraint of limited number of hypotheses, when the number of similar models increases in the model database, the best-matched model features may not come from the right model, but from models that are similar to the right one. This may result in the target model not being hypothesized and tested through the indexing process. The problem gets worse when large model database is indexed and many similar models present with quite severe ambiguities.

To alleviate the similar model indexing problem, in this paper we discuss a new approach to (1) measure the model similarity, (2) define the model-centric class to make use of model similarity, (3) use the model similarity to bootstrap model hypothesis to increase indexing and matching performance, and (4) use ICP for pose refining to improve likelihood computation. The new approach is shown in top-row blocks in Figure 1.

1.3 Related Work

Model similarity has been addressed in 2D/3D model retrieval applications, where on a given query of a model, the similar models are searched and retrieved from a domain specific database or from the Internet [4, 5]. The most common approaches for estimating model shape similarity is to establish the correspondence between two models and then to define the measure of similarity in terms of the mean-squared distance between pairs of points in correspondence [6]. 3D pose estimation between two 3D objects is well studied and a variety of methods were proposed [10, 11, 12, 13].

In recent years, instead of direct matching model raw points, a wide range of shape descriptors, in form of high-dimensional feature vectors, either global or semi-local, such as spin image [3] or shape context [7, 17], were introduced to represent 3D models. In shape descriptor or signature representations, model similarity measures become distance measurement between two sets of shape description vectors [2, 3, 7, 8, 9]. Point-based methods measure the local features; it is highly sensitive to precision of model alignment and to noise – if in the case the similarity is measured between a model and a scene object. Shape descriptors are, in general, more global or semi-local, and more immune to noise. The approach is generally invariant to viewing point transformations, which enables the computing the model similarity without using alignment. In [15] Sharp et al proposed the combination of shape and point-based methods for refining the ICP registration in the ICPIF algorithm.

Similarity measures between models were employed in [16] to define part based classes of 3D models, however the similarity was obtained using shape signatures only and the measures obtained were relative to the models used in the database. Thus, if several models were added to the database, the similarity between two models would change.

One of the approaches in dealing with similar models is to categorize models into classes and compose the model prototypes to represent the classes. Recognition process starts with matching on class prototypes, and then matching the individual models in the selected classes [18]. While the method sounds efficient, there are certain unresolved problems with such scheme. One is how to select the class prototypes such that they can well represent a model class? Bad prototyping will sure fail the recognition in the classification stage. The second is what if the right class prototype misses the matching at the first place? The continuing identification process inside classes using wrong prototypes will guarantee to generate wrong results.

Our work does not use class prototypes explicitly. However, the way the LSH process organizing the model features implies that the similar model features are grouped for scene-model match. Since such grouping is performed in model feature space, certain bad feature matches would not have fatal impact to the final recognition – because of large number of features used for each model (>1500).

1.4 Notation

In this paper, models are represented by a group of shape descriptor features. Each feature, $F=(s, x, n, m_{id})$, consists of four elements: s – the shape signature, e.g. a spin image defined w.r.t. a locally planar coordinate system; x – the 3D coordinate of the shape signature origin; n – the local surface normal, and m_{id} – the model ID. Match from scene object to model is represented by transformation $\Phi(R, T)$, where R is a 3x3 rotation matrix and T is 3x1 translation vector. We call a model the *target model* if the model is the ground truth for the scene object. The similarity between model i and j is represented by S_{ij}, with the value in the range of [0, 1]; 0 means completely dissimilar, 1 means identical. S_{ij} also has the property of symmetry, i.e. $S_{ij} = S_{ji}$.

The remainder of this paper is organized as follows: In Section 2, we discuss how to quantitatively measure the model similarity, which provides the basis for using model similarity in 3D object indexing. We then propose a novel concept to define a model class for each model by using similarities, which is different from the conventional model-clustering methods. We then propose a new method to use our definition of model class to improve the matching hypothesizing process so that the target models gain more chances to be indexed. In Section 3, we discuss the models and database used in the experiments, and present the results from extensive testing on real LADAR vehicle data to show the performance improvement.

2   Our Approach

2.1   Quantitative Measure for Model Similarities

We use the distance measures between a pair of models to evaluate their similarity S. Two sets of data are used for the measurement: the raw model point clouds and the shape signatures extracted from the sampled positions. Prior to the measurement, two models are aligned to obtain their relative pose by using the Iterative Closest Point (ICP) algorithm [6]. The pose alignment is initiated by feeding one of the models into the indexing system, which generates coarse alignment between this model and the one in the database. The similarity is calculated by a weighted sum of point-to-point distance and shape signature differences, as shown in Eq. 1, in which, x is a 3D point, s is the shape signature at point x. The α's are used to weight the contribution from each component. The value of S is normalized between [0, 1]. Figure 2 shows the overlap a 1995 Toyota Tercel (white) aligned with a 1995 BMW 318i (black). The alignment and match measure show that the difference between the two is very small.

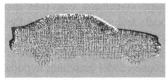 

Fig. 2. The overlap of model 1995 Toyota Tercel (white pixels) with 1995 BMW 318i (black pixels) shows the small shape difference between the two vehicles

$$S(M_1, M_2) = \exp\left(-\alpha_1 \frac{1}{N_x} \sum_i \left\|\vec{x}_{1,i} - \vec{x}_2(\vec{x}_{1,i})\right\|^2 - \alpha_2 \frac{1}{N_s} \sum_{\vec{x} \in S} \left\|s_1(\vec{x}) - s_2(\vec{x})\right\|^2\right). \qquad (1)$$

2.2 Model-Centric Class

For each model, we define a class, the model-centric class (MCC), to specify the association of a model with its class members. The MCC_i for model m_i contains a group of models which have the highest similarities to model m_i. For a given database containing N models, the similarities S_{ij} between m_i and rest of N-1 models are calculated. Models satisfying the following criterion are defined as a member in MCC_i:

$$m_j \in MCC_i \quad iff \quad S_{ij} \geq S_{threshold} \ (i \neq j) . \qquad (2)$$

MCC_i also includes the pose transformation Φ_{ij} between model m_i and m_j, which is obtained in similarity computation process.

MCC has the following properties: (1) a model can be a class member in multiple MCCs, (2) the number of class members can vary in different MCCs, and (3) if model m_j is a member of MCC_i, then model m_i must be a member in MCC_j.

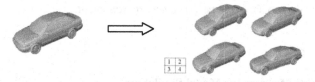

Fig. 3. 1995 Toyota Tercel (right) and a group of models with high similarity values: (1) 1996 Nissan Sentra-GXE s=0.79, (2) 1999 Volkswagon Passat s=0.76, (3) 1999 Toyota Corolla s=0.75, and (4) 1996 BMW 318i s=0.75

For instance, in Figure 3 if $S_{threshold}$ set to be 0.7, all four models as shown will be the members of MCC for the 1999 Toyota Tercel. By property #3, under the same similarity threshold, 1999 Toyota Tercel is also the member of MCCs of these 4 vehicle models.

Model similarity association within MCC provides a convenient way to bootstrap the matching hypothesis from a model to its class members without involving an expensive correspondence search and pose computation process.

2.3 Generate Matching Hypotheses

As mentioned in Introduction section, we use shape signatures, e.g. spin images, augmented with 3D positions to represent both models and scene objects. In the feature search process, Q best-matched model features are obtained for each of the scene object's features. The Q features can belong to P different models. A data-driven method, described in [14], is used to generate the scene-model matching hypotheses. In the method, a feature pair (doublet) is randomly generated from the scene data and the corresponding model doublet, sampled from the matched model feature list Q, is

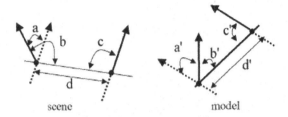

Fig. 4. Scene-model doublets are used to generate the matching hypothesis. Geometrical constraints are applied to ensure the goodness of matching.

selected. This doublet of features, if passes all the geometrical constraints, is used to generate a scene-model matching hypothesis, i.e. the R and T transformation, as shown in Figure 4.

For Q model features matched to each scene feature, the maximum number of doublets to be generated is Q^2. In our case, scene data usually contains 2000 features. If we match each scene feature to $Q=100$ model features, then, the potential matches to be generated could be $C^2_{2000} \times 100^2 \sim 10^{10}$, which is clearly impractical. To make the matching process efficient, scene features are checked to make sure they are salient before use; matched model features are sorted to make sure the best-matched ones are first used. A sequence of geometrical constraints are applied between the matched doublets, such as that $|d| > d_{min}$, $|d\text{-}d\text{'}| \leq \varepsilon$, $|a\text{-}a\text{'}| < \eta$, $|b\text{-}b\text{'}| < \eta$, and $|c\text{-}c\text{'}| < \eta$, to ensure choosing good hypotheses. After all checks have passed, it is checked if the best-matched model doublet belongs to the same model. Otherwise, the matching cannot be established.

At the end of the hypothesis generating process, we find that it may never guarantee to generate good hypotheses, if any, for the target model, largely due to (1) The features of target model never get in the Q list, (2) even though they get in Q list, there is a chance that they never get sampled, (3) even though they get sampled and used to form the matching doublet hypothesis, the constraint checks as discussed above may fail the match.

2.4 Use MCC to Enhance Matching Hypothesis

As discussed, we have the problem that when two best-matched model features in a doublet do not belong to the same model, no matching hypothesis will be generated. In such case, if one of the features belongs to the target model, then the target model may be missed in hypothesis generation process.

To solve this problem, we propose to use information in MCC to boost the hypothesis making process. It is observed that (1) the best set of model features matched to the scene largely comes from models that are similar to the scene object, and (2) most of these models are similar to the target model. The proposed idea is, if two best-matched features belong to two models that are similar to each other, we can use $\varPhi$ in MCC to transform a feature from the location of one model to the corresponding location of the other, and then use the transformed features to generate hypothesis. This is illustrated in Figure 5. The method is stated as follows:

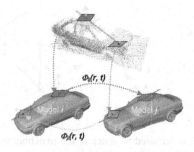

Fig. 5. Two matched features belong to two similar models, as indicated by solid-line patches. Features can be mapped to the same location from one model to the other by using MCC, as indicated by dashed-line patches. Thus for each model, a feature doublet, a solid-dashed pair, can be constructed.

For two best matched model features, $F_i(s_i, x_i, n_i, m_i)$ and $F_j(s_j, x_j, n_j, m_j)$ where $i{\neq}j$, if the following conditions are met:

$$m_j \in MCC_i \text{ and } S_{ij} \geq S_{threshold}.$$
$$or \quad m_i \in MCC_j \text{ and } S_{ji} \geq S_{threshold}. \tag{3}$$

Then, the two new features, one for each model, can be generated:

$$F'_i(s_i(\Phi_{ji}(x_j)), \ \Phi_{ji}(x_j), \ n(\Phi_{ji}(x_j)), \ m_i).$$
$$F'_j(s_j(\Phi_{ij}(x_i)), \ \Phi_{ij}(x_i), \ n(\Phi_{ij}(x_i)), \ m_j). \tag{4}$$

A hypothesis can be generated for each model by using two original best-matched features and two newly generated features:

For model i: $[F_i(s_i, x_i, n_i, m_i), \ F'_i(s_i(\Phi_{ji}(x_j)), \ \Phi_{ji}(x_j), \ \Phi_{ji}(n_j), \ m_i)].$
For model j: $[F_j(s_j, x_j, n_j, m_j), \ F'_j(s_j(\Phi_{ij}(x_i)), \ \Phi_{ij}(x_i), \ \Phi_{ij}(n_i), \ m_j)].$

These new hypotheses are added to the hypothesis list of the corresponding model and evaluated by feature alignment and matching.

2.5   Use MCC to Bootstrap Poses for Similar Models

The goal of the indexer is to produce a pruned short list of potential matching models. Indexer fails if the target model is not in the output list. To increase the chance of target model match, we use MCC to bootstrap new pose hypotheses for un-hypothesized models, evaluate the newly generated hypotheses, and increase the probability of target model detection. The idea is again based on two observations: (1) models in the indexer's output list are typically the good matches to the scene object; (2) the target model should ideally be in the list or at least be similar to some of the models in the list. The method is described as follows.

We begin by examining the top K $(m_1, m_2, ..., m_k)$ highest ranked models from the indexer output. For each of these models m_i, we look at its MCC_i and perform the following operation: for each model m_j in MCC_i, if $S_{ij} \geq S_{threshold}$, we generate a new matching hypothesis for model m_j:

$$\Phi_{sj}(m_j) = \Phi_{si} \bullet \Phi_{ij}. \tag{5}$$

Where Φ_{si} is the pose transformation from scene to model m_i, Φ_{ij} is the relative pose transformation from model m_i to its class model m_j, and Φ_{sj} is the new matching hypothesis generated for m_j. This idea is depicted in Figure 6.

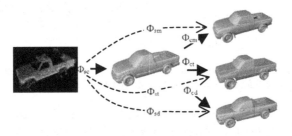

Fig. 6. Scene object (leftmost column) matches to model 1998 Chevrolet_S10 (mc) (middle column), which has a list of similar models in MCC: right top - 1999 Mazda B2500 (mm) , right middle - 1988 Toyota SR5 (mt), and right bottom - 1997 Dodge Dakota (md). Using scene-to-model and model-to-model transformations in MCC$_c$, new matching hypotheses are generated for the three similar models, indicated by the dashed arrows. The final best-matched model is 1988 Toyota SR5 (right middle), which is the true model.

The pose bootstrapping process generates a new set of matching hypotheses, which are evaluated through the verification process, and added to the previously generated pruned model list. The final indexer output is generated by ranking the likelihoods of the models in the expanded list.

2.6 ICP for Scene-Model Pose Refinement

Point distance between aligned scene and model is used for likelihood computation. It is observed that the accuracy of the likelihood computation heavily depends on the fine pose alignment between the model and the scene. This is especially critical when many similar models exist in the hypothesis list; in such case, a slight misalignment may cause the target model to be ranked low in the candidate list. To ensure that the target model will prevail in competing with its similar rivals, the pose of scene-model alignment is refined by using ICP algorithm on both model and scene point cloud data. The final model candidates is sorted on the likelihood values and constrained by top K threshold.

3 Experimental Results

3.1 Model Database and Similarity Distribution

We generated a 3D model database containing 366 vehicle models, of which most are civilian vehicles, such as sedans, SUVs, pickups trucks etc. Samples of vehicle models in the model database are shown in Figure 7(a). Similar models are commonly seen in database.

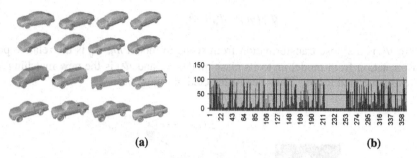

Fig. 7. (a) Sample models in model database; (b) Model similarity distribution on 366 model database (Sthreshold=0.5), and most models in the database are sedans

Figure 7(b) shows the similar model distribution for 366 models in the database with the similarity threshold, $S_{threshold}$ set at 0.5. Each model, on average, contains 35 similar models. There are over 127 models containing more than 50 similar models in their MCCs. These models are all sedans. On the other hand, most of construction or military vehicles, located between models 211 and 253 in Figure 7(b), have very few similar models since their geometrical shapes are unique.

Facet model data are processed to generate point clouds. Spin images are generated on evenly sampled locations around the model point clouds. Model features are built by combining the spin image, its 3D location, the local surface normal, and the model ID. A 366x366 model similarity matrix is computed. MCC for each model is extracted from the similarity matrix. Model database consists of nearly 1,000,000 shape features and 366 MCCs.

3.2 Real LADAR Scene Data and Pre-processing

We used three sets of LADAR data collected from high-lift on ground, airship, and helicopter platforms. About 250 real vehicles, both civilian and military, situated in the natural settings (urban, suburban) were scanned by Laser Terrain Mapper. Vehicles range from cars, SUVs, minivans, to trucks and construction utilities. More than 1000 volume of interest (VOIs) containing scene targets were extracted and used for testing. Note that typically each VOI contains only partial "views" of an object since only 2 or at most 3 sides of vehicles are scanned by the LADAR and that the point density is quite non-uniform. Scene data input to indexer are noisy with 5-10 cm standard deviation, contain ground plane and tree-like clutter, are sparse at times, may have articulations (doors, hood, trunk may open), and may be partially occluded.

Data from multiple views covering approximately 90° of viewing angle (2-3 sides) are registered to form the input scene object. Prior to feature computation, ground plane is removed through automated pre-processing. The input VOI in Figure 11 shows that with high degree of noise, fine features from vehicle data are lost. This increases the challenge for indexing process.

3.3 Experimental Results

We used data from all three collections and the 366-models database to test indexing system with and without using the new algorithm. For each input VOI query, the indexer outputs a variable length of ranked models (from 1 up to 25) as the best-matched model candidates. The probability of correct identification (P_{id}) is computed by comparison with the ground truth. We use the precision vs. the recall (ROC) curve to present the performance.

The first set testing is on 344 vehicles' VOI from ground high-lift data collection. The results are shown in Figure 8, where the triangle curve indicates the indexing performance with using the new algorithm; the diamond curve shows the performance without using the new algorithm. It shows that the new method increases the indexing performance on P_{id} by about 15%.

The second set testing is on 210 vehicles' VOI from airship data collection. The results are shown in Figure 9. Again, the triangle curve indicates the indexing performance with using the new algorithm; the diamond curve shows the performance without. It shows that the new algorithm increases the indexing performance by up to 20% on airship data.

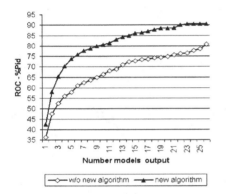 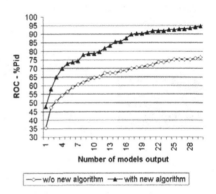

Fig. 8. Testing results on 344 highlift vehicles   **Fig. 9.** Testing results on 210 airship vehicles

The last set of testing is on 548 vehicles' VOI from helicopter data collection. The results are shown in Figure 10 (a). Again, the triangle curve indicates the indexing performance by using the new algorithm; the diamond curve shows the performance without using the new algorithm. It shows that the new algorithm increases the indexing performance by up to 30% on helicopter data collection.

Overall, the indexing performance improvement with using new algorithm is significant on the large model database and large data collection sets. Indexer performs better on helicopter data collection is due to better data density in VOI, though the noise level (up to 10 cm) in this data set is larger than in other two data collections.

Together with ranked model output, indexer also outputs the pose alignment for each candidate model to the scene. Figure 10 (b) shows indexing results with scene-model poses; dark pixels are for scene data, light pixels are for matched models.

In general, for scene targets that have distinctive 3D shape, the target model will appear on top of the output list. In the case the 3D shape of input data can match to many models, the top K list will automatically expand to have the target model included. If the target model does not rank on top of the output list, the models ranked

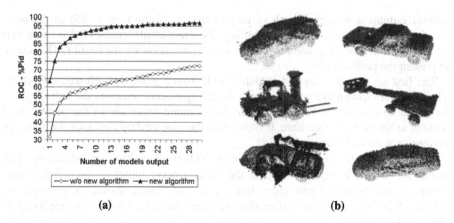

(a)   (b)

Fig. 10. (a) Results on 548 helicopter collection data; (b) Examples of scene-model pose alignment output from indexing process. In the image, dark pixels are for scene, light pixels are for matched models.

Fig. 11. Input query "1987 Honda Accord" and its top 10 best matched models: 1) 1994 Nissan_Sentra, 2) 1995 Oldsmobile_Cutlass-Ciera, 3) 1994 Ford_Tempo, 4) 1995 Geo_Prizm, 5) 1987 Ford_Escort, 6) 1992 Mazda_626, 7) 1984 Ford_Tempo, 8) 1987 Honda_Accord, 9) 1999 Dodge_Neon, and 10) 1991 Honda_Prelude-SI. High noise data and model similarity pushed the target model to rank 8. In the image, dark pixels are for scene, light pixels are for models.

above it are mostly very similar to the target model. Figure 11 shows an example of 1989 Honda Accord scene data and the top 10 best-matched models. The target model is ranked at 8, but the 7 models above it are very similar in shape and all match well with the scene.

To further distinguish among fine differences in indexed similar models needs to use model saliency features for fine verification. We discuss the issue in a separate paper [19].

The indexing runs on a PC with a 2.0 GHz CPU and 2 GB memory, on Windows and Linux OS. The entire process takes about 100 seconds on a 366 models database.

4 Conclusion

In this paper, we present a new method to solve the model similarity problem encountered in model-based 3D object recognition. We use a new metric to quantitatively measure model similarities on both shape signatures and 3D points. We use the similarity measures to define a model-centric class, the MCC, for each model. MCC contains a group of similar models and the pose transformation between the model and its class members. Similarity information embedded in MCC is used to boost matching hypotheses generation so that the target model gains more opportunity to be hypothesized and identified through the indexing process. The algorithm is implemented and extensively tested in a 3D object indexing system with a large model database containing 366 vehicle models, among which many similar models exist. Over 1000 real LADAR data from vehicle scans with noise up to 10cm standard deviation are used to test the new method. Our test results show that the target recognition performance improved by 15% to 30% in correct target identification with the new approach.

References

[1] Y. Lamdan and H. Wolfson, Geometric hashing: a general and efficient model-based recognition scheme, *Proc. 2nd Intl. Conf. on Comp. Vision*, pp. 238-249, 1988.

[2] A. Gionis, P. Indyk, and R. Motwani, Similarity search in high dimensions via hashing. In *Proceedings of the 25th International Conference on Very Large Data Bases (VLDB99)*, pages 518–529, 1999.

[3] Andrew E. Johnson and Martial Hebert, Using spin images for efficient object recognition in cluttered 3D scenes. *IEEE Trans. Pattern Analysis and Machine Intelligence (PAMI)*, 21(5):433–449, 1999.

[4] Johan W.H. Tangelder and Remco C. Veltkamp, A Survey of Content Based 3D Shape Retrieval Methods", *IEEE International Conf. on Shape Modeling and Applications*, 2004.

[5] T. Funkhouser, P. Min, M. Kazhdan, J. Chen, A. Halderman, D. Dobkin, and D. Jacobs. *A search engine for 3d models*, ACM Transacions on Graphics, pp83-105, 2003.

[6] P. Besl, N. McKay, A method for registration of 3D shapes. *IEEE PAMI*, 14:239-256, 1992.

[7] S. Belongie and J. Malik, Matching with Shape Contexts. *IEEE Workshop on Content-based access of Image and Video-Libraries*, 2000.

[8] G. Mori, S. Belongie, and H. Malik. Shape contexts enable efficient retrieval of similar shapes. *Computer Vision and Pattern Recognition*, 1:723-730, 2001.

[9] R.C. Veltkamp. Shape matching: Similarity measures and algorithms. In *Shape Modeling International*, pp188-197, May 2001.

[10] R. M. Haralick, H. Joo, C.N. Lee, X. Zhuang, V.G. Vaidya, & M.B. Kim, "Pose estimation from corresponding point data", *IEEE Trans. on Systems, Man, and Cybernetics.* Aug. 1989.

[11] R. Campbell and P. Flynn, A survey of free-form object represent and recognition techniques, *Computer Vision & Image Understanding*, 81(2):166-210, 2001.

[12] D.G. Lowe, "Object recognition from local scale-invariant features", in *International Conf. on Computer Vision*, (ICCV99) 1999, pp. 525-531.

[13] F. Stein and G. Medioni, "Structural indexing: Efficient three dimensional object recognition," *IEEE Trans. Pattern Analysis and Machine Intelligence (PAMI)*, vol. 14, no. 2, pp 125-145, 1992.

[14] Y. Shan, B. Matei, H.S. Sawhney, R. Kumar, D. Huber, M. Hebert, Linear model hashing and batch RANSAC for rapid and accurate object recognition, *IEEE Conf. on CVPR 2004.*

[15] Gregory C. Sharp, Sang W. Lee, & David K. Wehe, ICP Registration Using Invariant Features, *IEEE Trans. Pattern Analysis and Machine Intelligence (PAMI),* 24(1):90-102, 2002.

[16] D. Huber, A. Kapuria, R. R. Donamukkala and M. Hebert, Part-based 3D object classification, *Proceedings of the IEEE Conference on Computer Vision and Pattern Recognition (CVPR 04),* June, 2004.

[17] Andrea Frome, Daniel Huber, Ravi Kolluri, Thomas Bülow, Jitendra Malik: Recognizing Objects in Range Data Using Regional Point Descriptors. ECCV (3) 2004: 224-237.

[18] Ronen Basri, Recognition by Prototypes, International Journal of Computer Vision, 19(2): 147–168, 1996.

[19] B. Matei, H. Sawhney, and C. Spence, Identification of highly similar 3D objects using model saliency, *ECCV,* May 2006.

Shift-Invariant Dynamic Texture Recognition

Franco Woolfe[1] and Andrew Fitzgibbon[2]

[1] Yale University, New Haven, CT
franco.woolfe@yale.edu
http://www.yale.edu
[2] Microsoft Research, Cambridge, UK
awf@microsoft.com
http://www.research.microsoft.com/~awf

Abstract. We address the problem of recognition of natural motions such as water, smoke and wind-blown vegetation. Such dynamic scenes exhibit characteristic stochastic motions, and we ask whether the scene contents can be recognized using motion information alone. Previous work on this problem has considered only the case where the texture samples have sufficient overlap to allow registration, so that the visual content of the scene is very similar between examples. In this paper we investigate the recognition of entirely non-overlapping views of the same underlying motion, specifically excluding appearance-based cues.

We describe the scenes with time-series models—specifically multivariate autoregressive (AR) models—so the recognition problem becomes one of measuring distances between AR models. We show that existing techniques, when applied to non-overlapping sequences, have significantly lower performance than on static-camera data. We propose several new schemes, and show that some outperform the existing methods.

1 Recognition from Motion

Motion is a powerful cue for visual recognition of scenes and objects. Johansson's moving dot displays [1] show that objects which are highly ambiguous from a single view are readily recovered once motion is supplied. In computer vision, the classification of scenes from motion information has seen considerable research, summarized in the recent survey of Chetverikov and Péteri [2]. In this paper, we focus on classification of objects using the class of state-space *dynamic texture* models introduced by Doretto and Soatto [3, 4] and Fitzgibbon [5].

Dynamic textures are image sequences of moving scenes which exhibit characteristic stochastic motion. Examples include natural scenes such as water, wind-blown flowers and fire. State-space models [5, 4] view a dynamic texture as a realization of a time-series model such as an autoregressive process. By determining the model parameters for such sequences, we can hope to recognize similar motions by comparing the models represented by the parameters. Our goal in this paper is to define a distance measure between pairs of image sequences which is low for models representing the same motion (or motion class), and high for models derived from motions of different classes. Such distance

A. Leonardis, H. Bischof, and A. Pinz (Eds.): ECCV 2006, Part II, LNCS 3952, pp. 549–562, 2006.
© Springer-Verlag Berlin Heidelberg 2006

measures can be used in kernel-based or nearest-neighbour classifiers; and as the basis of clustering algorithms for the unsupervised learning of dynamic texture classes. Some of the distance measures we propose are based on feature vectors extracted from the state-space models, and are thus also suitable for density estimation or regression.

Two important new aspects of our work are that we require shift invariance, and that we want to investigate recognition using motion alone, for reasons we now explain.

Shift invariance. Previous authors [6, 7] have investigated only the case where the temporal sequences are captured by a camera at a single viewpoint, so that the same area of the scene is viewed in (part of) each sequence. In some cases [5, 8] the camera is panning across the scene, or the textures compared are in overlapping tiles [9], but there remains the constraint of overlap between the textures. However, in order to separate the appearance and dynamic components of recognition we compare images of the scene where there is no spatial overlap between the example dynamic textures. Recognition rates for this configuration are much lower than for the single-viewpoint case, but are significantly higher than either baseline methods or chance, and thus confirm that motion can provide a useful cue for recognition.

Recognition from motion alone. As noted by Chan and Vasconcelos [7], much of the recognition performance on typical test data may be attributed to appearance cues. Thus comparisons between the recognition schemes conflate appearance and motion, and this conflation is of a form that is hard to disentangle. Furthermore, the appearance component of these schemes is not representative of the current state of the art in appearance-based recognition, being based essentially on a principal components analysis of the image sequence. Thus a practical scheme for recognition including motion should combine a state-of-the-art appearance-based scheme and the best possible motion-based scheme. By considering motion-only schemes, we hope to allow this selection to be more carefully performed, and to allow the balance between motion and appearance to depend on the training set for any given real-world system.

The remainder of the paper is structured as follows: a discussion of the state of the art also serves to introduce the DT model and the notation of the paper. We then discuss the construction of motion-based distance measures between such models, and introduce some novel measures. We conduct experiments comparing these and existing distance measures in section 4, and conclude with a discussion of the relative merits of the various models.

2 Background

General-purpose automated recognition of motions in video sequences may be attributed to Polana and Nelson, who considered two classes: stochastic motions and "activities". For activities they considered periodicity measures on edges in xyt slices [10]. Subsequent research on activity recognition has been considerable, using optical flow [11], features in the spatiotemporal volume [12, 13],

Fig. 1. Single frames from the database sequences. Although many of the sequences are easily distinguished using colour information, the goal of this paper is to explore how well they can be distinguished using motion information alone.

spatiotemporal correlation [14], parametrized models [15] and exemplars [16]. In addition, models of videotextures [17] may be considered to be related to activity models. These perform well for regular motions, but are less well suited to stochastic motions of the types we consider.

Stochastic models of temporal texture may be divided into local and global: local models include Polana and Nelson's co-occurrence statistics of optical flow vectors [18]; and the spatiotemporal autoregressive models of Szummer and Picard [19], which model stochastic regularity by expressing each pixel of the sequence as a linear combination of its spatial and temporal neighbours. By fitting the model to an example sequence, and assuming the AR model parameters are constant over the sequence, each temporal texture is represented by a small number of model parameters. Comparison of such parameters may be achieved using the methods reviewed in the current paper. Fablet and Bouthemy [20] first quantize certain motion-related per-pixel measurements, and then model the spatiotemporal cooccurrence of the quantized labels as a Gibbs distribution. A model is learned for each class to be recognized and recognition proceeds by measuring the likelihood of the labels of a novel sequence under each class model. These local models allow robust classification, but strongly bind together the appearance and motion of the texture, limiting their applicability to textures which are both spatially and temporally stationary; yet offering limited shift and viewpoint invariance.

State-space models [3, 5] on the other hand, model the image sequence more globally, and have been used for recognition [6], image segmentation [21, 9, 8], image registration [5] and videotexture synthesis [4, 5]. The core of such models is a spatiotemporal autoregressive (AR) model, and recognition depends on computing the similarity of pairs of AR models. Saisan *et al.* [6] propose the Martin distance between AR model parameters, and Chan and Vasconcelos [7] measure the Kullback-Leibler (KL) divergence between the realization distributions defined by the models. In both of these previous cases however, the sequence appearance plays an important role in the recognition performance, and indeed, as we show, swamps the motion-based results.

2.1   The State-Space Model

Dynamic texture models [4, 5] represent the image using a state-space model. Images are represented by column vectors $\mathbf{y}$. A sequence of T images is the matrix $\mathtt{Y} = [\mathbf{y}_1, ..., \mathbf{y}_T]$. Under the state-space model of such a sequence, each $\mathbf{y}_t$ is assumed to be a linear projection of a low-dimensional state vector $\mathbf{x}_t \in \mathbb{R}^N$, with typical values of N in the range 5 to 35. The observed $\mathbf{y}$ are corrupted with zero-mean Gaussian noise with covariance matrix $\mathtt{R}$, yielding

$$\mathbf{y}_t = \mathtt{C}\mathbf{x}_t + \mathbf{w}_t, \qquad \mathbf{w}_t \sim \mathcal{N}(\mathbf{0}, \mathtt{R}) \tag{1}$$

The matrix $\mathtt{C}$ is sometimes termed the *output matrix*. The temporal evolution of $\mathbf{x}_t$ is modelled by the first-order time-series, or autoregressive (AR) model,

$$\mathbf{x}_{t+1} = \mathtt{A}\mathbf{x}_t + \mathbf{v}_t, \qquad \mathbf{v}_t \sim \mathcal{N}(\mathbf{0}, \mathtt{Q}) \tag{2}$$

where $\mathtt{A}$ is the $N \times N$ *state matrix*, and $\mathtt{Q}$ is the $N \times N$ *driving noise covariance matrix*. The model from which a given sequence is drawn will be represented by its parameters $\theta = (\mathtt{C}, \mathtt{A}, \mathtt{Q})$, where C models the sequence *appearance* and A and Q its *motion*. A sequence such as $\mathtt{Y}$ which is generated from the model is called a *realization* of the model. Figure 2 shows some example trajectories.

2.2   Fitting the Model

Given an example sequence $\mathtt{Y}$, we would like to estimate the parameters $\theta = (\mathtt{C}, \mathtt{A}, \mathtt{Q})$ of the model of which it is a realization. We adopt the approach of [4, 5], described here for completeness.

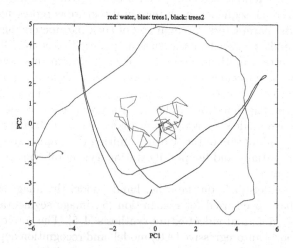

Fig. 2. Example 2D state-space trajectories $\mathbf{x}_{1..T} \subset \mathbb{R}^2$ for three example sequences. Red: water flowing over stone; Black and Blue: tree blowing in the wind. We characterize the sequences using auto-regressive models, and wish to compare the model parameters to identify similar models. Any distance metric must be invariant to changes of basis in the state space (see §2.3).

We ensure that input sequences have zero mean $\sum_t \mathbf{y}_t = 0$, by subtracting the mean from each frame. The matrix C is determined via principal components analysis of the sequence, i.e. assuming Y is much taller than it is wide, compute the eigendecomposition $\mathsf{Y}^\top \mathsf{Y} = \mathsf{VDV}^\top$ and set $\mathsf{C} = \mathsf{YVD}^{-\frac{1}{2}}$. From this we may immediately obtain estimates of the state vectors

$$\mathbf{x}_t = \mathsf{C}^\top \mathbf{y}_t, \quad t = 1 \ldots T \tag{3}$$

The state matrix A is found as the minimizer

$$\mathsf{A} = \operatorname*{argmin} \sum_{t=2}^{T} \|\mathbf{x}_t - \mathsf{A}\mathbf{x}_{t-1}\|^2 \tag{4}$$

which is easily computed. Finally the driving covariance Q is approximated as the sample covariance of the residuals $\mathbf{r}_t = \mathbf{x}_t - \mathsf{A}\mathbf{x}_{t-1}$, given by

$$\mathsf{Q} = \frac{1}{T-1} \sum_{t=2}^{T} \mathbf{r}_t \mathbf{r}_t^\top \tag{5}$$

As we are interested in recognition schemes which depend only on motion, and not appearance, we shall not be required to estimate R.

2.3   Comparing State-Space Models

For recognition, we will need to determine whether two models $\theta = (\mathsf{C}, \mathsf{A}, \mathsf{Q})$ and $\theta' = (\mathsf{C}', \mathsf{A}', \mathsf{Q}')$ represent the same dynamic texture. It is not sufficient to check for equality of the parameters, because a given sequence may be generated by an equivalence class of models [3]. Specifically, for any invertible $N \times N$ matrix M the model

$$(\mathsf{CM}^{-1}, \mathsf{MAM}^{-1}, \mathsf{MQM}^\top) \tag{6}$$

generates image sequences drawn from the same distribution as $(\mathsf{C}, \mathsf{A}, \mathsf{Q})$. Thus any metric for comparing AR models must be invariant to this class of transformations of the model parameters. In this paper we explore three classes of distance measure which (sometimes approximately) obey this property: measures of divergence between the distributions of the model realizations [7], spectral methods [6], and techniques which operate directly on invariant functions of the AR model parameters. Each of these will now be discussed.

2.4   Time-Series Spectrum

Several of the distance measures previously proposed in the literature, as well as those we introduce, may be expressed in terms of the Fourier transform of the autocovariance of the time series, or its spectral density [22, Ch3]. For an infinite time-series $(\mathsf{C}, \mathsf{A}, \mathsf{Q})$, the spectral density matrix is a matrix function of frequency ν, $\mathsf{F}(\nu) \in \mathbb{C}^{N \times N}$ defined as

$$F(\nu) = (I - Ae^{-2\pi i\nu})^{-1}Q(I - Ae^{2\pi i\nu})^{-1}.$$

and for a finite time-series of length T it will suffice to evaluate this on the finite set $\nu_k = k/T$, $k = 0, ..., T - 1$. Thus the spectral density of a length T time-series is a set of T matrices. We refer to this method for estimating the spectral density matrices as the AR method, since it is computed from the auto-regressive model parameters. We may also directly estimate the spectrum $F(\nu_k)$ using the fast Fourier transform of the raw time-series as follows. Given the $N \times T$ matrix of state values X, compute the componentwise FFT f_k (i.e. FFT each component $f(i,:) = \text{fft}(X(i,:))$, and set $f_k = f(:,k)$.) Then compute the periodogram $G_k = f_k f_k^*$. The spectrum is then given by smoothing G with a window of size $2H + 1$, yielding $F(\nu_k) = \sum_{i=k-H}^{k+H} G_k$. We refer to this as the time-series or TS method, and show that it can give better results than the AR method for appropriate choices of smoothing parameter H.

3   Distance Measures Between Dynamic Textures

We are now in a position to define distance measures between dynamic textures. We consider distances of three forms. The first class compares the probability densities over all possible sequences generated by the time-series under comparison. We present a new formulation of the KL metric and introduce the Chernoff distance. The second class of measure is based on a multivariate definition of the Cepstrum. The final class is based on computing a set of features from the fitted AR model parameters.

3.1   Distances Between Realization Distributions

We consider the set of all possible realizations of time-series generated by the AR model (C, A, Q). Following [7], it suffices to consider only sequences of a certain length T. This is a probability density over the set of sequences Y, which we may write as $p(Y)$ or $p(y_T, ..., y_1)$. As the y_t are linear transformations of x_t, it is sufficient to characterize the distribution of the x_t, written $p(X) = p(x_T, ..., x_1)$. From (2), this is exactly $p(x_T|x_{T-1})p(x_{T-1}|x_{T-2})\cdots p(x_2|x_1)p(x_1)$ where each term in the product is Gaussian, so that the joint distribution is a Gaussian, whose covariance matrix may be computed from the model parameters A and Q. Thus any sequence X drawn from the model is a draw from a Gaussian distribution whose parameters depend only on the model parameters. Comparing two AR models then amounts to comparing two Gaussian distributions, i.e. measuring their *divergence*. We consider two possible definitions: the Kullback-Leibler divergence and the Chernoff distance.

Given two probability distributions over X with pdfs f_1 and f_2, the Kullback Leibler divergence is

$$I_{KL}(f_1, f_2) = E_1\left[\frac{f_1(X_1)}{f_2(X_1)}\right]. \tag{7}$$

A generalization of this is the Chernoff distance, given by

$$I_{CH}(f_1, f_2) = -\ln E_2 \left[\left(\frac{f_2(X_1)}{f_1(X_1)} \right)^\alpha \right],$$ (8)

where $0 < \alpha < 1$ is a parameter. It was found in experiments that for our task, the success rate did not depend sensitively on α near the middle of the interval $(0, 1)$. Thus we often took $\alpha = 0.5$, yielding Bhattacharya's symmetric divergence.

In order to compute the KL divergence of our dynamic texture model, suppose we have two movies $(C_j, A_j, Q_j)_{j=1,2}$. Compute the spectral densities $F_j(\nu_k)$ as above. From this definition, we can compute the Kullback Leibler distance from (C_1, A_1, Q_1) to (C_2, A_2, Q_2) by [22, p459]

$$I_{KL}(F_1, F_2) = \sum_{0 < \nu_k < 1/2} \left[\text{trace} \left\{ F_1(\nu_k) F_2^{-1}(\nu_k) \right\} - \ln \frac{|F_1(\nu_k)|}{|F_2(\nu_k)|} - N \right].$$ (9)

The Chernoff distance may also be expressed in terms of the spectral density as follows [22, p461].

$$I_{CH}(\alpha, F_1, F_2) = \frac{1}{2} \sum_{0 < \nu_k < 1/2} \left[\ln \frac{|\alpha F_1(\nu_k) + (1 - \alpha) F_2(\nu_k)|}{|F_2(\nu_k)|} - \alpha \ln \frac{|F_1(\nu_k)|}{|F_2(\nu_k)|} \right].$$ (10)

Note that these distance measures are not invariant to transformations of the form described in §2.3, so Chan and Vasconcelos suggest resolving the ambiguity by projecting A_2 into the space of A_1 using the appearance matrices C_1, C_2.

3.2   Distances Based on the Cepstrum

The cepstrum of a time series may be thought of as being derived from the frequency domain representation in the same way that this comes from the time domain. Intuitively, peaks in the cepstrum correspond to "echoes" in the signal. The cepstrum coefficients are powerful features for characterizing speech and music signals, so it is of interest to see how they may apply to repetitive video signals. In this section, we give the conventional univariate definition of cepstrum and apply it to dynamic texture recognition via cepstral distance. We suggest three extensions of the cepstrum to the case of multivariate time series.

Univariate case. For a general univariate time series (x_t) the cepstrum, written $(\hat{x}_t)$, is defined as [23] the inverse z-transform of the logarithm of the z-transform of (x_t). In symbols:

$$(x_t) \rightarrow \sum_{t \in \mathbb{Z}} x_t z^{-t} = X(z) : \text{the z transform}$$ (11)

$$\rightarrow \log X(z)$$ (12)

$$= \sum_{t \in \mathbb{Z}} \hat{x}_t z^{-t}$$ (13)

$$\rightarrow (\hat{x}_t) : \text{the complex cepstrum.}$$ (14)

If the time series (x_t) above is drawn from an autoregressive model of order K the above definition gives rise to a characterization of the cepstrum in terms of poles. Assume (x_t) comes from such an $AR(K)$ model, that is:

$$x_t + a_1 x_{t-1} + ... + a_K x_{t-K} = w_t; w_t \sim N(0, \sigma^2). \tag{15}$$

Define the model's poles as $p_i \in \mathbb{C}$ where the system function is:

$$H(z)^{-1} = 1 + a_1 z^{-1} + ... + a_K z^{-K} = \prod_{i=1}^{K}(1 - p_i z^{-1}). \tag{16}$$

The cepstral coefficients $\hat{x}_t$ are then given by

$$\hat{x}_t = 0, \text{ for } t \leq 0 \tag{17}$$

$$= \frac{1}{t}\sum_{i=1}^{K} p_i^t \text{ for } t > 0.$$

The cepstral distance between two univariate time series (x_t) and (x_t'), with cepstra $(\hat{x}_t)$ and $(\hat{x}_t')$, is then [23]

$$\sum_{t=0}^{\infty}|\hat{x}_t - \hat{x}_t'|^2. \tag{18}$$

Note the similarity to the Martin distance [4, 24] where the weighting of higher degree cepstral coefficients is increased linearly:

$$\sum_{t=0}^{\infty} t\,|\hat{x}_t - \hat{x}_t'|^2. \tag{19}$$

For practical computation, in our application, the sum may be terminated at about $t = 20$. Performance (i.e. success rate in the classification task of §4, figure 4) rises quickly for $t < 20$ and then plateaus.

Multivariate case. There is no consensus definition in the literature of either cepstra or cepstral distance for multivariate time series, to the best of our knowledge. We present three such definitions, which are mutually incompatible, and use them to construct distances for classifying dynamic textures.

Summed univariate distances. One simple extension of the univariate definitions is to fit univariate $AR(K)$ models to each component of the series $(\mathbf{x}_t)$ independently. The distance is simply the sum of the per-component distances. Although this ignores correlations between the components, the fact that C is obtained by projection onto a PCA space will have the effect of somewhat decorrelating the components, and thus this technique can provide good results, as we shall see.

Fig. 3. Crop regions. In order to test the invariance of recognition to shifts of the image, all comparisons are between cropped sub-sequences. This figure indicates the two crops of the test dataset used. Note that the appearance of the tree varies considerably (globally—local texture measures will be similar) between the two regions, so that motion is the main recognition cue, even for schemes which include some appearance modelling.

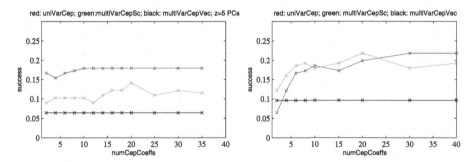

Fig. 4. Performance of cepstral distances for two values of N, the number of principal components. The abscissa is the upper bound on the summations in (18). Left: $N = 5$, Right: $N = 15$. The three distances tested are (red) summed univariate distances, (green) state matrix eigenvalues, (black) DFT. The DFT method is uniformly outperformed by the other two.

State matrix eigenvalues. This definition is by analogy to (17). The state equation for a dynamic texture is $\mathbf{x}_t = \mathbf{A}\mathbf{x}_{t-1} + \mathbf{v}_t$; $\mathbf{v}_t \sim N(0, \mathbf{Q})$, that is a multivariate AR(1) process. Let the system function be

$$H(z) = (\mathbf{I} - \mathbf{A}z^{-1})^{-1}, \ z \in \mathbb{C}. \tag{20}$$

Let the poles be solutions of $|\mathbf{I} - \mathbf{A}p_i^{-1}| = 0$, that is to say eigenvalues of $\mathbf{A}$. Now define the cepstrum by analogy with (17) as

$$\hat{x}_t = 0, \ \text{for } t \leq 0 \tag{21}$$

$$= \frac{1}{t} \sum_{i=1}^{N} p_i^t \ \text{for } t > 0.$$

Note that the cepstral coefficients of a multivariate time series are scalars, according to this definition. The multivariate cepstral distance is again given here by (18).

Discrete Fourier transform. Here we let the cepstrum of a multivariate time series $(x_t)_{t=1}^T$ be the inverse DFT of the logarithm of the DFT of (x_t):

$$(\hat{x}_t)_{t=1}^T = \text{IDFT}(\ln(\text{DFT}((x_t)_{t=1}^T))). \tag{22}$$

Here the DFT of a sequence of vectors is taken componentwise. Thus, the cepstral coefficients of a multivariate time series are vectors. The cepstral distance is then

$$\sum_{t=1}^n \|\hat{x}_t - \hat{y}_t\|. \tag{23}$$

3.3   Distances Based on Feature Extraction

In this section we measure discrepancy between dynamic textures by Euclidean distances between feature vectors. A feature vector is some vector function of the sequence parameters (C, A, Q) which we hope characterizes a movie.

The choice of feature vectors is subject to two constraints, for the purposes of this paper. Firstly we restrict ourselves only to consider motion. So the state matrix A and driving noise covariance matrix Q are both allowed, but we may not examine the output matrix C or the movie frames y_t. Secondly, recall that we aim to measure distances between observationally equivalent classes of dynamic textures. Thus any property of A we examine should be invariant under a change of basis $A \rightarrow M^{-1}AM$. Similarly, any property of Q we use should be invariant under $Q \rightarrow M^\top QM$.

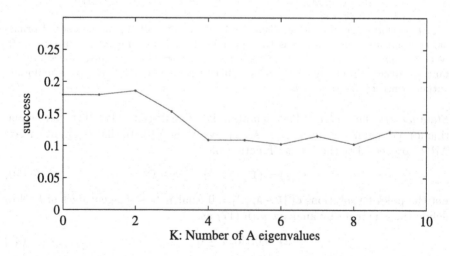

Fig. 5. Feature-based distance. Each sequence is characterized by a feature vector comprising K eigenvalues of Q and $(N - K)$ eigenvalues of A.

A typical feature vector consists of some eigenvalues of A and some eigenvalues of Q. From the above considerations, eigenvalues of A seem valid choices for feature vectors, and we note that the set of eigenvalues of A already appears in the definition of multivariate cepstrum above. Eigenvalues of Q are invariant under $Q \rightarrow M^\top Q M$ when M is orthogonal, but not otherwise, in general. Nevertheless, experiments suggest there is some information to be gained from the eigenvalues of Q.

Specifically, denote by α_i the eigenvalues of A with $|\alpha_i| > |\alpha_{i+1}|$, and denote by σ_i^2 the eigenvalues of Q, again in descending order. Generate the feature vector $\mathbf{v}(K) = [\alpha_1, ..., \alpha_K, \sigma_1^2, ..., \sigma_{N-K}^2]$. Figure 5 shows performance of this feature vector as a function of K.

4   Experimental Results

In order to compare the distance measures on experimental data, we tested classification performance on the UCLA test database [6]. The UCLA database comprises 50 sets of four sequences of a dynamic texture scene, for a total of 200 sequences. The movies are 75-frame sequences of size 110×160, and were converted to grayscale before any computation. In each category, the four movies are captured from the same camera viewpoint, and thus recognition performance is dominated by the sequence appearance. Indeed simply using the mean frame of each sequence, and performing a 1-vs-all classification using a 1-nearest neighbor classifer (described in more detail below) yields a 60% classification rate. Existing dynamic texture recognition algorithms quote performance figures of 90% on this dataset.

In order to more rigorously test the performance of motion-based classification, we have cropped the test data to remove the effects of identical viewpoint. The sequences were cropped into a pair of 48×48 subsequences, denoted "L" and "R" for left and right crop windows (illustrated in figure 3). Comparisons between sequences were only ever performed between different crop locations. From the 51 categories in the UCLA database, we discarded 12 which violated the assumption of spatial stationarity (e.g. "candle", "fire", "fountain", in all of which the "L" cropping viewed stationary background, while the "R" cropping viewed the motion). Retaining these sequences would be expected to yield similar results, but with a reduced success rate on all algorithms. There were thus 39 categories. The introduction of this cropping reduces the performance of state-of-the-art metrics from a quoted 90% to about 15%. Note that this is still well above the performance of random guessing, which is expected to be about 1%.

In all experiments we considered a nearest-neighbour classifier—classifiers with stronger priors on the density could be considered, such as a support vector machine using these distance metrics as a kernel [7], but the NN classifier makes the fewest assumptions about the parameter distribution, and generally performs competitively with a wide range of classifiers [25], providing a useful baseline.

The experimental procedure may be defined as follows. Index the $m = 36 \times 4$ test sequences by i, with the sequence category given by $c(i)$. For each sequence, fit models $\theta_{iL} = (C_L, A_L, Q_L)$ and $\theta_{iR} = (C_R, A_R, Q_R)$ to the left and right

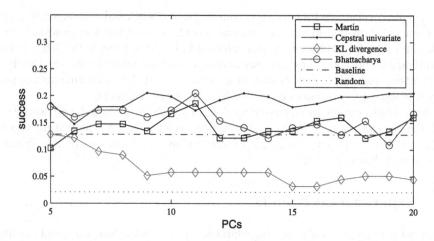

Fig. 6. Performance of distance metrics as a function of state-space dimension (i.e. nu mber of principal components) N. The state of the art is represented by the "Martin" and "KL" schemes, which are generally outperformed by the new cepstral univari- ate scheme. The Bhattacharya metric performs comparably to the Martin distance. The "Baseline" metric simply compares the mean frames of the (greyscale) sequences. Note that all performance figures are low—best achieved performance is about 20%— reflecting the difficulty of the dataset when cropping is introduced.

croppings. For a distance metric $d(\theta, \phi)$ between AR models, define the distance between sequences i and j as

$$d_{ij} = \min\{d(\theta_{iL}, \theta_{jR}), d(\theta_{iR}, \theta_{jL})\}. \qquad (24)$$

One-NN classification performance is then computed as

$$\text{success} = \sum_i \delta(c(i), c(\text{argmin}_{j \neq i}\, d_{ij}))$$

where $\delta(x, y) = 1/m$ for $x = y$, zero otherwise. Figure 6 summarizes the primary result. The tuning parameter common to all techniques is N, the number of principal components used to characterize the sequence, and the figure plots performance against N. The graph shows that for a wide range of values, the leading performers were the Bhattacharya distribution comparison (Chernoff information with $\alpha = 0.5$) and the summed univariate cepstral distances of §3.2.

5 Conclusion

This paper has introduced a new and challenging recognition problem: shift- invariant dynamic texture recognition. We have shown that existing dynamic texture recognition algorithms, when applied to classification problems where there is a difference in camera viewpoint, show a significant drop in performance. Several new similarity measures have been proposed, and some have been shown to outperform the state of the art. In particular, the use of the cepstrum appears to be a natural tool for the comparison of AR models.

The investigation has concentrated on defining distance metrics between AR models, rather than modelling the distributions of model parameters in a learning framework. This allows us to test classification without requiring a large labelled training set, and provides insight into the behaviour of these model parameters which may be useful in feature selection for distributional approaches.

The reader will note that we are quoting absolute performance figures of the order of 20%, which may appear unusually low. We comment that the absolute performance figures are not relevant, providing that performance is significantly different from random, which is true here. The absolute performance figures can be increased by further pruning of the dataset, but relative performance of the algorithms is expected to remain unchanged. In a real-world system, of course, we would not expect to use cues based on motion alone—distinguishing grass from water is rendered artificially difficult if colour is removed from consideration. It is our contention however, that when testing metrics for motion-based recognition, it is valuable to exclude textural cues as much as possible.

The paper has concentrated on global modelling approaches in order to capture large-scale correlations in the motion sequences. However, the relatively small size of our crop windows may be thought of as positioning the technique between local and global strategies. It may be valuable to further explore this tradeoff, and build a multi-scale strategy.

References

1. Johansson, G.: Visual perception of biological motion and a model for its analysis. Perception and Psychophysics **14** (1973) 201–211
2. Chetverikov, D., Peteri, R.: A brief survey of dynamic texture description and recognition. In: Intl. Conf. on Computer Recognition Systems. (2005) 223–230
3. Doretto, G., Chiuso, A., Wu, Y.N., Soatto, S.: Dynamic textures. IJCV **51** (2003) 91–109
4. Soatto, S., Doretto, G., Wu, Y.N.: Dynamic textures. In: Proc. ICCV. (2001) 439–446
5. Fitzgibbon, A.W.: Stochastic rigidity: Image registration for nowhere-static scenes. In: Proc. ICCV. Volume 1. (2001) 662–670
6. Saisan, P., Doretto, G., Wu, Y.N., Soatto, S.: Dynamic texture recognition. In: Proc. CVPR. Volume 2. (2001) 58–63
7. Chan, A.B., Vasconcelos, N.: Probabilistic kernels for the classification of autoregressive visual processes. In: Proc. CVPR. (2005) 846–851
8. Vidal, R., Ravichandran, A.: Optical flow estimation and segmentation of multiple moving dynamic textures. In: Proc. CVPR. (2005)
9. Doretto, G., Soatto, S.: Towards plenoptic dynamic textures. In: Proc. Intl. Workshop on Texture Analysis and Synthesis. (2003)
10. Polana, R., Nelson, R.: Detecting activities. In: Proc. CVPR. (1993) 2–7
11. Black, M.J.: Explaining optical flow events with parameterized spatio-temporal models. In: Proc. CVPR. (1999) 1326–1332
12. Niyogi, A.A.: Analyzing and recognizing walking figures in xyt. In: Proc. CVPR. (1994) 469–474

13. Laptev, I., Lindeberg, T.: Space-time interest points. In: Proc. ICCV. (2003) 432–439
14. Shechtman, E., Irani, M.: Space-time behavior based correlation. In: Proc. CVPR. (2005) 405–412
15. Yacoob, Y., Black, M.J.: Parameterized modeling and recognition of activities. In: CVIU. (1999) 232–247
16. Efros, A.A., Berg, A.C., Mori, G., Malik, J.: Recognizing action at a distance. In: Proc. ICCV. (2003)
17. Schodl, A., Szeliski, R., Salesin, D.H., Essa, I.: Video textures. In: Proc. ACM SIGGRAPH. (2000) 489–498
18. Polana, R., Nelson, R.: Recognition of motion from temporal texture. In: Proc. CVPR. (1992) 129–134
19. Szummer, M.: Temporal texture modeling. Master's thesis, MIT Media Lab, Cambridge MA (1995)
20. Fablet, R., Bouthemy, P.: Motion recognition using nonparametric image motion models. IEEE PAMI **25** (2003) 1619–1624
21. Doretto, G., Cremers, D., Favaro, P., Soatto, S.: Dynamic texture segmentation. In: Proc. ICCV. (2003) 1236–1242
22. Shumway, R.H., Stoffer, D.S.: Time Series Analysis and its Applications. Springer (2000)
23. Manolakis, D.G., Ingle, V.K., Kogon, S.M.: Statistical and Adaptive Signal Processing. McGraw-Hill, Boston (2000)
24. Martin, R.: A metric for ARMA processes. IEEE Trans. on Signal Processing **48** (2000) 1164–1170
25. Ripley, B.D.: Why do nearest-neighbour algorithms do so well? SIMCAT (Similarity and Categorization), Edinburgh (1997)

Modeling 3D Objects from Stereo Views and Recognizing Them in Photographs

Akash Kushal[1] and Jean Ponce[1,2]

[1] Department of Computer Science,
University of Illinois at Urbana Champaign, USA
[2] Département d'Informatique,
Ecole Normale Supérieure, Paris, France
{kushal, ponce}@cs.uiuc.edu

Abstract. Local appearance models in the neighborhood of salient image features, together with local and/or global geometric constraints, serve as the basis for several recent and effective approaches to 3D object recognition from photographs. However, these techniques typically either fail to explicitly account for the strong geometric constraints associated with multiple images of the same 3D object, or require a large set of training images with much overlap to construct relatively sparse object models. This paper proposes a simple new method for automatically constructing 3D object models consisting of *dense* assemblies of small surface patches and affine-invariant descriptions of the corresponding texture patterns from *a few* (7 to 12) stereo pairs. Similar constraints are used to effectively identify instances of these models in highly cluttered photographs taken from arbitrary and unknown viewpoints. Experiments with a dataset consisting of 80 test images of 9 objects, including comparisons with a number of baseline algorithms, demonstrate the promise of the proposed approach.

1   Introduction

This paper addresses the problem of recognizing three dimensional (3D) objects in photographs taken from arbitrary viewpoints. Recently, object recognition approaches based on local viewpoint invariant feature matching ([1], [2], [3], [4]) have become increasingly popular. The local nature of these features provides tolerance to occlusions and their viewpoint invariance provides tolerance to changes in object pose. Most methods (for example [5],[6]) match each of the training images of the object to the test image independently and use the highest matching score to detect the presence/absence of the object in the test image. This essentially reduces object recognition to a wide-baseline stereo matching problem. Only a few previous approaches ([2], [7], [8]) exploit the relationships among the model views. Lowe [2] clusters the training images into model views and links matching features in adjacent clusters. Each test image feature matched to some feature f in a model view v votes for v and its neighbors linked to f. This helps to model feature appearance variation since different model views provide slightly different pictures of the features they share, yet features' votes do not

A. Leonardis, H. Bischof, and A. Pinz (Eds.): ECCV 2006, Part II, LNCS 3952, pp. 563–574, 2006.

get dispersed among competing model views. Ferrari *et al.* [7] integrate the information contained in successive images by constructing *region tracks* consisting of the same region of the object seen in multiple views. They introduce the notion of a group of aggregated matches (*GAM*) which is a collection of matched regions on the same surface of the object. The region tracks are then used to transfer matched GAMs from one model view to another, and their consistency is checked using a heuristic test. The problem with this (as with all other methods that do not explicitly exploit 3D constraints) is that geometric consistency can only be *loosely* enforced. Also, for both [2] and [7] there is no way to determine consistency among matched regions which are not seen together in any model view. Rothganger *et al.* [8] use multiple images to build a model encoding the 3D structure of the object, and the much tighter constraints associated with the 3D projection of the model patches are used to guide matching during recognition. In this case, the 3D model explicitly integrates the various model views, but the determination of the 3D position and orientation of a patch on the object requires it to be visible in three or more training images [8], and hence requires a large number of closely separated training images for modeling the object. Also, [8] only makes use of patches centered at interest points, so the model constructed is sparse and does not encode all the available information in the training images. We tackle these issues by using calibrated stereo pairs to construct partial 3D object models and then register these models together to form a full model.[1] This allows the use of a sparse set of stereo training views (7 to 12 pairs in our experiments) for the modeling. We also extend to 3D object models the idea proposed in [6] in the image matching domain, and augment the model patches associated with interest points of [8] (called *primary* patches from now on) with more general *secondary* patches. This allows us to cover the object densely, utilize all the available texture information in the training images, and effectively handle clutter and occlusion in recognition tasks.

The paper is organized as follows. In section 2 we discuss the detection and representation of affine invariant patches as well as give an overview of our approach. The construction of the partial models and their inter-registration to generate the full model is explained in section 3. The details of the recognition phase of the algorithm are provided in section 4. In section 5 we show recognition results using the proposed approach and summarize in section 6.

2   An Overview of Our Approach

We use an implementation of the *affine region* detector developed by Mikolajczyk and Schmid [3] for low-level image description. The detector is initialized with the Harris-Laplacian interest point detector and the Difference of Gaussian (DoG) operator similar to [9]. The two detectors find complementary type of points. The Harris-Laplacian detector tends to find corners and points at which significant intensity changes occur while the DoG operator detects blob like features in the image. The output of the interest point detection/rectification process is

---

[1] This is for modeling only of course; individual photographs are used for recognition.

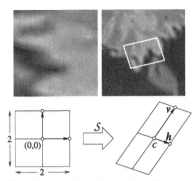

(a) Affine regions found in an image of a teddy bear. Only a subset of the patches detected is shown for clarity.

(b) The inverse transformation S maps the rectified square associated with an affine region back onto the image

Fig. 1. Affine regions and inverse rectification

a set of parallelogram-shaped image patches together with the corresponding affine *rectifying* transformations mapping these onto a square with edge length 2 centered at the origin. We represent each detected region by the 2×3 affine transformation matrix S that maps the rectified texture patch back onto its position in the image as shown in Fig. 1(b) (after [8]).

We use calibrated stereo for determining the 3D structure of the object and building the model mentioned in the previous section. Potential *primary matches* between the affine regions found in each stereo pair are first filtered using photometric and geometric consistency constraints, and then augmented with additional *secondary matches* for dense coverage of the object, as proposed in [6] in the 2D case. The 3D location and shape of the patches is determined using standard stereo to generate partial models which are later combined to form a complete model of the object. The 3D patches that correspond to primary (or secondary) matches are called primary (or secondary) model patches.

A similar scheme is followed during recognition. First, the primary patches in the model are matched to the affine regions found in the test image. These primary patches are then used as guides for matching nearby secondary patches. The object is recognized based on the number of matched patches.

3   Stereo Modeling

We start by acquiring a few (7 to 12) stereo pairs that are roughly equally spaced around the equatorial ring of the object for modeling. The stereo views are taken against a uniform background to allow for easy segmentation. Then, a standard stereo matching algorithm that searches for matching patches along corresponding epipolar lines is used to determine an initial set of tentative matches. We use a combination of SIFT [5] and the color histogram descriptor described in [10] to compute the initial matches. The matches are then refined to obtain the correct alignment of the patches in the left and right images. Only matches with normalized correlation greater than a pre-refinement threshold (kept at 0.75) are considered for the refinement step for efficiency reasons. The refinement process employs nonlinear optimization to affinely deform the right image patch until the correlation with its match in the left image is maximized. Matches with normalized correlation greater than a post-refinement threshold (equal to 0.9 in this paper) are kept for subsequent processing.

The matches are filtered by using a neighborhood constraint which removes a match if its neighbors are not consistent with it. More precisely, for every match m we look at its K closest neighbors in the left image ($K = 5$ in our implementation) and, for every triple out of these, we calculate the barycentric coordinates of the center of the left and right patches of m with respect to the triangle formed by the centers of the patches of the triple in the left and right images respectively. We then count the number of triples for which these barycentric coordinates agree (the sum of squared differences is smaller than a tolerance limit $\mathcal{L} = 0.5$). We repeat the process using the K closest neighbors of m in the right image and add up both the counts. Finally, the matches with a count smaller than a threshold T are dropped. Setting $T = 2\binom{K-1}{3}$ ensures that a correct match with one bad nearby match out of the K still survives after this test. This gives us a set Γ of reliable matches. Note that these matches are based only on the primary patches associated with salient affine regions detected in the stereo training images and hence, only cover the object sparsely. To get a dense coverage of the object we use an expansion technique similar to [6] to spread these initial matches in Γ.

Expansion Technique

We use the fact that the training views are taken against a uniform background to segment the object and cover it with a grid Ω of partially overlapping square-shaped patches in the left image (Fig. 2(a)). For every match m_i in Γ, we

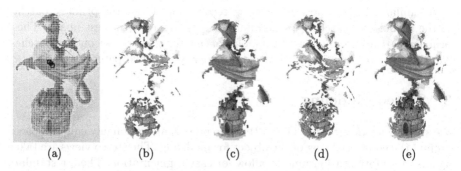

| (a) | (b) | (c) | (d) | (e) |

Fig. 2. (a) Left image in a stereo pair, covered with a grid of patches (three of the overlapping patches are shown in black for clarity). (b) Partial model constructed from primary matches before expansion. (c) Model constructed using only the secondary patches found during expansion. (d) Model containing the primary patches after expansion. (e) Model containing all the patches after expansion.

compute the affine transformation $\mathcal{T} = \mathcal{S}_{R_i}\mathcal{S}_{L_i}^{-1}$ between the corresponding patches L_i and R_i in the left and right images. Here $\mathcal{S}_{L_i}$ and $\mathcal{S}_{R_i}$ are the inverse rectification matrices for L_i and R_i respectively. We use $\mathcal{T}$ to predict the location $\mathcal{S}_{R_j} = \mathcal{T}\mathcal{S}_{L_j}$ of the right matches of the yet unmatched patches L_j in Ω that are close to (within one side length of) the center of L_i. Then, a refinement process is used to align the predicted patch correctly in the right image. Again, if the match has sufficient correlation after refinement, it is accepted as a valid match and added to Γ. Since the patches that form these matches are not associated with interest points, we call these secondary matches. The expansion process iterates by expanding around the newly added matches to Γ until no more matches can be added. This process usually covers the entire object surface densely with matches. Figure 2(c) shows the secondary patches on a partial model of the dragon constructed from a single stereo pair.

We then use the secondary matches to locate additional primary matches associated with salient affine regions. Even though the corresponding part of the object surface may already be covered (with secondary matches), this is useful because it is the primary matches that can be repeatably detected, and will later be required for the initial matching to the test image as well as for the alignment of the partial models. This is accomplished by finding unmatched affine regions in the left (respectively right) image, and using close-by secondary matches to predict the position of the corresponding patches in the right (respectively left) image. Again, a refinement process is used to adjust the alignment of the right (respectively left) image patch. If there is sufficient correlation (again 0.9) between the left and right patches, the match is added to Γ. Figures 2(d) and 2(e) respectively show the expanded primary patches and the union of the primary and secondary patches in the partial model of the dragon.

Model Construction

The dense matches constructed as discussed above are used for building the 3D model. First, we solve for the patch centers in 3D by using standard calibrated stereo triangulation. Then, we reconstruct the edges of the corresponding parallelograms using a first-order approximation to the perspective projection equations in the vicinity of the patch centers as proposed by Rothganger [10]. This gives us a partial 3D model of the object for each stereo pair. The next task is to combine these partial models into a complete model.

The first step in combining the models is to find appearance-based matches between the primary model patches in adjacent partial models. Again, SIFT and color histogram descriptors are used to facilitate the initial matching. Next, a variant of the expansion scheme described earlier is used to propagate these initial matches between 3D patches to neighboring model patches as follows (Fig. 3). Let the two partial models being registered be M_P and M_Q. For each initial match $\mathcal{M}_i$ between the 3D patches $\mathcal{P}_i$ in M_P and $\mathcal{Q}_i$ in M_Q, we consider the 2D patch p_i (resp. q_i) corresponding to $\mathcal{P}_i$ (resp. $\mathcal{Q}_i$) in the left stereo image of M_P (resp. M_Q). We calculate the affine transformation $\mathcal{T}$ that maps the patch p_i onto q_i. Then, we consider the yet unmatched patches P_j in M_P whose 2D

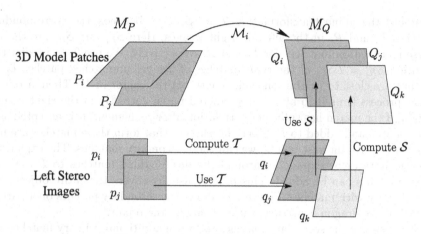

Fig. 3. Expansion during registration

projection p_j in the left stereo image lies within a small distance limit of the center of p_i. These patches p_j are then projected to q_j in the left stereo image of M_Q using $\mathcal{T}$. A refinement process (similar to the one described earlier) is then used to align the projected patch q_j correctly. The match is removed from consideration if the final correlation between p_j and q_j's normalized representation is less than a threshold (again kept at 0.9). If the match passes this test we find the patch Q_k in M_Q whose projection q_k into the left stereo image of M_Q is closest to q_j's center point. An estimate of the position of the 3D patch Q_j that corresponds to the 2D patch q_j can then be obtained, assuming that Q_j lies on the same plane π_k as Q_k. An affine transformation $\mathcal{S}$ that maps the 2D patch q_k to the 3D patch Q_k on π_k is calculated and then Q_j is estimated by projecting q_j onto π_k using $\mathcal{S}$. This new match between P_j and Q_j is then added to the set of matches and is used for finding other matches. This expansion step has proven to be very useful while registering models with small overlap.

Finally, all the matches are filtered through a RANSAC procedure that finds the matches consistent with a rigid transformation. This provides an estimate of the pairwise rigid transformations. Since these pairwise estimates may not in general be consistent with each other (the product of the rotations between the consecutive models must be the identity), we use a process similar to [11] to find a consistent solution: It is initialized using the pairwise transformation estimates and these estimates are refined by looping through all the partial models and updating the position of the current model to align it best with its neighbors. More formally, we search for the rigid transformation that minimizes the sum of squared distances between the centers of the matched patches in the current model and its neighbors. The positions of these neighbors are kept fixed while the position of the current partial model is calculated via linear least squares [11]. The above process is iterated until a local minimum of the error is reached. Figure 4(c) shows a plot of the mean squared error after each iteration of the refinement process for three of the models used for experimentation. Finally the rigid transformations estimated are used to bring all the partial models into a

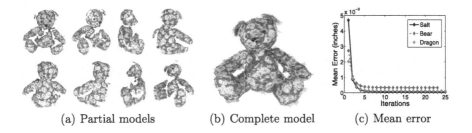

(a) Partial models   (b) Complete model   (c) Mean error

Fig. 4. Registration of partial models

common euclidean coordinate frame and a complete model is constructed by taking the union of these transformed partial models. The partial models and the complete model formed after registration for a teddy bear are shown in Figs. 4(a) and 4(b) respectively.

4   Recognition

The recognition starts by matching the repeatable primary patches in the 3D model to the interest points detected in the test image. Again, we use both SIFT descriptors and color histograms to characterize the appearance of the patches and compute the initial matches. The refinement process is then employed to affinely deform the matched test image patch so as to maximize the its correlation with its corresponding model patch. Matches with correlation smaller than a threshold (again taken as 0.9) are dropped before further processing. The remaining matches are used as seeds for the subsequent match expansion stage.

Expansion Process

This process is similar in spirit to the expansion technique used during the initial modeling but the expansion here happens on the surface of the 3D model instead of the stereo images. For this, we first preprocess the model M to build an undirected graph G_M that represents the adjacency information of the patches in M. We add an edge e between two patches if their centers lie within a distance limit of each other. This limit is set to be such that the average degree of a vertex is around 20. We now spread the matches along the edges of this graph using the following steps.

Expansion using images (Fig. 5(a)): This expansion step is similar to the expansion during modeling. For each previously matched model patch P we calculate the affine transformation S that maps its projection in the left training image of the stereo pair from which it originates into the test image. Then we look at every unmatched neighbor Q of P that is part of the same partial model (and so shares the same left stereo image) and use S to predict its location in the test image. This predicted position is then refined as before and the match is accepted if the correlation is sufficiently large (again 0.9). This expansion scheme does not allow expanding matches from one partial model to another.

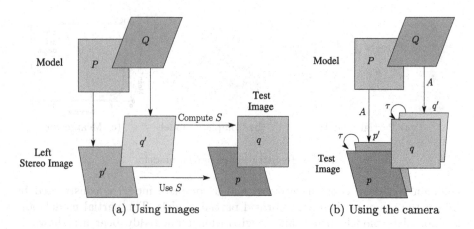

(a) Using images   (b) Using the camera

Fig. 5. Expansion during recognition

Geometric consistency test (Algorithm 1): A *"greedy"* RANSAC-like algorithm is used to extract a set of geometrically consistent matches and estimate the camera for the test image. The test image camera is modeled as a weak-perspective camera with zero skew and square pixels.

Expansion using the camera (Fig. 5(b)): This step is used after the matches have been filtered through the above geometric consistency test and the camera A associated with the test image has been estimated. A is used to project a base 3D patch P (which is already matched to a patch p in the test image) and some adjacent patch Q into the test image. Let the 2D projected patches be p' and q' respectively. A correcting affine transformation τ is computed that aligns the projection p' of the base 3D match exactly with its correct location p. τ is then applied to the projection q' of the adjacent patch to obtain a corrected prediction q of its position. The prediction is then refined as before to maximize the normalized correlation between the patches corresponding to the match and accepted only if it has high correlation (greater than 0.9). This expansion step allows for moving smoothly from one partial model to another and hence provides an advantage over the pure 2D expansion technique of [6].

For extending matches to parts of the object that are not directly connected to the initial matches in the test image (possibly due to occlusion) the reconstructed test camera is used to project unmatched primary patches from the model into the test image. Affine regions detected in the test image close to these projected positions are then matched to the corresponding model patch. Again, the refinement process is used to correctly align the patch in the test image and the match is accepted if the correlation exceeds a threshold (again, 0.9).

The two expansion steps also allow us to reject false matches by simply removing those that do not have enough support. More precisely, if the expansion step from a base match tries to expand to a large number of neighbors and none of

---

Input: A set M of possible matches.
Output: A set S of trusted matches, camera for the test image C

   for $i = 1$ to *numIter* **do**

- Pick a match $m_i \in M$ at random.
- Select the most compatible match $m_i' \in M \setminus \{m_i\}$ to m_i.
- Initialize $S_i = \{m_i, m_i'\}$ and C_i to the camera estimated using S_i.
- Select $m_{best} \in M \setminus S_i$ with minimum reprojection error $\mathcal{E}_{best}$ using C_i

   while $|S_i| < K$ and $\mathcal{E}_{best} < \tau$ **do**

- $S_i \Leftarrow S_i \cup \{m_{best}\}$.
- Update C_i with the camera estimated using S_i
- Select $m_{best} \in M \setminus S_i$ with minimum reprojection error $\mathcal{E}_{best}$ using C_i

   end while

- Add all matches $m \in M \setminus S_i$ with reprojection error $\mathcal{E}_m < \tau$ to S_i.

   end for

- Set S to the S_i with the largest cardinality.
- Estimate the camera C for the test image using S.

Algorithm 1. Geometric consistency test

these succeeds in forming an acceptable match, the base match is removed. The above cycle consisting of the two expansion steps and the geometric consistency test is iterated until the number of matches does not increase any more. This process usually takes only 3 iterations.

5   Results

We have evaluated the proposed method on a dataset consisting of 9 objects and 80 test images. The object models, constructed from 7 to 12 stereo views each, are shown in Fig. 6. The objects vary from simple shapes (e.g., the salt container) to quite complex ones (e.g., the two dragons and the chest buster model).

The test images contain the objects in different orientations and under varying amounts of occlusion and clutter. The total number of occurrences of the objects in the test image dataset is 129 since some images contain more than one object. Figure 7(a) shows the ROC plot between the true positive (detection) rate and the false positive rate. To assess the value of the expansion step of our approach, we have simply removed the secondary patches and the extra primary patches added during this stage of modeling from our models, and used these sparse models for recognition (this is similar in spirit to the algorithm proposed by Rothganger et al. [8], but includes the expansion step during the recognition phase which was absent in [8]). The corresponding recognition performance is depicted by the blue ROC curve. Our experiments clearly demonstrate the benefit of using dense models as opposed to sparse ones for our dataset. We have also implemented recognition as wide-baseline stereo matching to assess the power of using explicit 3D constraints as opposed to simple epipolar ones. Each test image is matched to all the 168 training images (both left and right images for each stereo pair) for every object separately, making a total of $168 \times 80 = 13440$

582 A. Kushal and J. Ponce

(a) Bournvita (8)   (b) Ball (12)   (c) Yogurt (8)

(d) Vase (8)   (e) Chest Buster (7)   (f) Bear (8)

(g) Small Dragon (12)   (h) Salt (8)   (i) Dragon (12)

Fig. 6. Object models. The number of stereo views used is given in parenthesis.

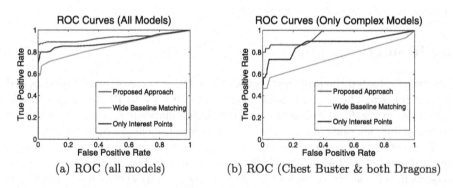

(a) ROC (all models)   (b) ROC (Chest Buster & both Dragons)

Fig. 7. Comparison ROC plots

image pairs to be compared. The maximum number of matches corresponding to each object is recorded and used to construct the ROC curve. As expected, our method clearly outperforms this simple baseline approach. The detection rates for zero false positives and the equal error rates for the different methods are shown in Fig. 5.

The proposed approach also performs well on the highly complex geometric objects like the dragons and the chest buster model. Figure 7(b) shows the comparison of the ROC plots on the dataset restricted to only these 3 models. The variation in appearance of the features due to small viewpoint changes is

Method	Detection Rate (zero false positives)	Equal Error Rate
Proposed Approach	86.8%	89.1%
Primary patches only	69.8%	84.9%
Wide Baseline	58.1%	77.1%

Fig. 8. Error rate comparison

larger for these models since the surface of the models is not smooth. Because the proposed approach combines the different views of the features together (when the different partial models are merged) its performance is less severely affected on the restricted dataset. On the other hand, the performance of the wide-baseline matching scheme drops by a significant amount.

Finally, Fig. 9 gives a qualitative illustration of the performance of our algorithm with a gallery of recognition results on some test images which contain the objects under heavy occlusion, viewpoint and scale variation, as well as extensive clutter. The dataset used in this paper is available at the following URL: http://www-cvr.ai.uiuc.edu/ponce_grp/data/stereo_recog_dataset/

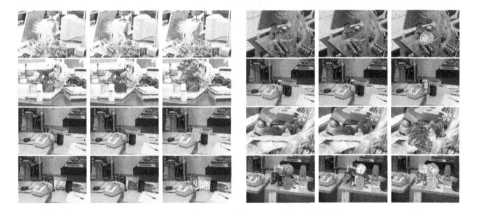

Fig. 9. Results: test image (left), matched patches (center), predicted location (right)

6 Conclusions and Summary

We have proposed an approach to efficiently build dense 3D euclidean models of objects from stereo views and use them for recognizing these objects in cluttered photographs taken from arbitrary viewpoints. At this point there are many directions for future work.

- Extending the approach to handle non rigid deformations
- Recognizing objects in a cluttered scene using a pair of calibrated stereo images of the scene.

Also, it would be desirable to do a comparison with the native implementations of other state-of-the-art recognition methods such as those proposed by Ferrari et al. [7], Lowe [2], and Rothganger et al. [8].

Acknowledgments

This research was supported in part by the National Science Foundation under grants IIS 03-12438, IIS 03-08087 and IIS 05-35152 and the Beckman Institute.

References

1. Tuytelaars, T., Van Gool, L.J.: Content-based image retrieval based on local affinely invariant regions. In: Visual Information and Information Systems. (1999) 493–500
2. Lowe, D.G.: Local feature view clustering for 3d object recognition. In: Conference on Computer Vision and Pattern Recognition. (2001)
3. Mikolajczyk, K., Schmid, C.: An affine invariant interest point detector. In: European Conference on Computer Vision. Volume I. (2002) 128–142
4. Matas, J., Chum, O., Urban, M., Pajdla, T.: Robust wide baseline stereo from maximally stable extremal regions. In: British Machine Vision Conference. Volume I. (2002) 384–393
5. Lowe, D.G.: Object recognition from local scale-invariant features. In: International Conference on Computer Vision, Corfu, Greece (1999) 1150–1157
6. Ferrari, V., Tuytelaars, T., Van Gool, L.: Simultaneous object recognition and segmentation by image exploration. In: European Conference on Computer Vision. (2004)
7. Ferrari, V., Tuytelaars, T., Gool, L.V.: Integrating multiple model views for object recognition. In: Conference on Computer Vision and Pattern Recognition. (2004)
8. Rothganger, F., Lazebnik, S., Schmid, C., Ponce, J.: 3d object modeling and recognition using affine-invariant patches and multi-view spatial constraints. In: Conference on Computer Vision and Pattern Recognition. Volume II. (2003) 272–277
9. Rothganger, F., Lazebnik, S., Schmid, C., Ponce, J.: 3d object modeling and recognition using local affine-invariant image descriptors and multi-view spatial constraints. International Journal of Computer Vision (In press, 2005)
10. Rothganger, F.: 3D object modeling and recognition in photographs and video. PhD thesis, University of Illinois, Urbana Champaign (2004)
11. Raouf Benjemaa, F.S.: A solution for the registration of multiple 3d point sets using unit quaternions. In: European Conference on Computer Vision. (1998)

A Boundary-Fragment-Model for Object Detection

Andreas Opelt[1], Axel Pinz[1], and Andrew Zisserman[2]

[1] Vision-based Measurement Group, Inst. of El. Measurement
and Meas. Sign. Proc. Graz, University of Technology, Austria
{opelt, axel.pinz}@tugraz.at
[2] Visual Geometry Group, Department of Engineering Science,
University of Oxford
az@robots.ox.ac.uk

Abstract. The objective of this work is the detection of object classes, such as airplanes or horses. Instead of using a model based on salient image fragments, we show that object class detection is also possible using only the object's boundary. To this end, we develop a novel learning technique to extract class-discriminative boundary fragments. In addition to their shape, these "codebook" entries also determine the object's centroid (in the manner of Leibe et al. [19]). Boosting is used to select discriminative combinations of boundary fragments (weak detectors) to form a strong "Boundary-Fragment-Model" (BFM) detector. The generative aspect of the model is used to determine an approximate segmentation.

We demonstrate the following results: (i) the BFM detector is able to represent and detect object classes principally defined by their shape, rather than their appearance; and (ii) in comparison with other published results on several object classes (airplanes, cars-rear, cows) the BFM detector is able to exceed previous performances, and to achieve this with less supervision (such as the number of training images).

1 Introduction and Objective

Several recent papers on object categorization and detection have explored the idea of learning a codebook of appearance parts or fragments from a corpus of images. A particular instantiation of an object class in an image is then composed from codebook entries, possibly arising from different source images. Examples include Agarwal & Roth [1], Vidal-Naquet & Ullman [27], Leibe et al. [19], Fergus et al. [12, 14], Crandall et al. [9], Bar-Hillel et al. [3]. The methods differ on the details of the codebook, but more fundamentally they differ in how strictly the geometry of the configuration of parts constituting an object class is constrained. For example, Csurka et al. [10], Bar-Hillel et al. [3] and Opelt et al. [22] simply use a "bag of visual words" model (with no geometrical relations between the parts at all), Agarwal & Roth [1], Amores et al. [2], and Vidal-Naquet and Ullman [27] use quite loose pairwise relations, whilst Fergus et al. [12] have a strongly parametrized geometric model consisting of a joint Gaussian over the

A. Leonardis, H. Bischof, and A. Pinz (Eds.): ECCV 2006, Part II, LNCS 3952, pp. 575–588, 2006.
© Springer-Verlag Berlin Heidelberg 2006

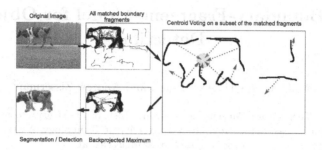

Fig. 1. An overview of applying the BF model detector

centroid position of *all* the parts. The approaches using no geometric relations are able to categorize images (as containing the object class), but generally do not provide location information (no detection). Whereas the methods with even loose geometry are able to detect the object's location.

The method of Leibe *et al.* ([19], [20]) has achieved the best detection performance to date on various object classes (e.g. cows, cars-rear (Caltech)). Their representation of the geometry is algorithmic – all parts vote on the object centroid as in a Generalized Hough transform. In this paper we explore a similar geometric representation to that of Leibe *et al.* [19] but use only the *boundaries* of the object, both internal and external (silhouette). In our case the codebook consists of *boundary-fragments*, with an additional entry recording the location of the object's centroid. Figure 1 overviews the idea. The boundary represents the shape of the object class quite naturally without requiring the appearance (e.g. texture) to be learnt. For certain categories (bottles, cups) where the surface markings are very variable, approaches relying on consistency of these appearances may fail or need considerable training data to succeed. Our method, with its stress on boundary representation, is highly suitable for such objects. The intention is not to replace appearance fragments but to develop complementary features. As will be seen, in many cases the boundary alone performs as well as or better than the appearance and segmentation masks (mattes) used by other authors (e.g. [19, 27]) – the boundary is responsible for much of the success.

The areas of novelty in the paper include: (i) the manner in which the boundary-fragment codebook is learnt – fragments (from the boundaries of the training objects) are selected to be highly class-distinctive, *and* are stable in their prediction of the object centroid; and (ii) the construction of a strong *detector* (rather than a classifier) by Boosting [15] over a set of weak detectors built on boundary fragments. This detector means that it is not necessary to scan the image with a sliding window in order to localize the object.

Boundaries have been used in object recognition to a certain extent: Kumar *et al.* [17] used part outlines in their application of pictorial structures [11]; Fergus *et al.* [13] used boundary curves between bitangent points in their extension of the constellation model; and, Jurie and Schmid [16] detected circular arc features from boundary curves. However, in all these cases the boundary features are segmented independently in individual images. They are not flexibly selected

Fig. 2. Example training images for the cows category

Fig. 3. Examples of detecting multiple objects in one test image

to be discriminative over a training set, as they are here. Bernstein and Amit [4] do use discriminative edge maps. However, theirs is only a very local representation of the boundary; in contrast we capture the global geometry of the object category. Recently, and independently, Shotton *et al.* [24] presented a method quite related to the Boundary-Fragment-Model presented here. The principal differences are: the level of segmentation required in training ([24] requires more); the number of boundary fragments employed in each weak detector (a single fragment in [24], and a variable number here); and the method of localizing the detected centroid (grid in [24], mean shift here).

We will illustrate BFM classification and detection for a running example, namely the object class cows. For this we selected cow images as [7, 19] which originate from the videos of Magee and Boyle [21]. The cows appear at various positions in the image with just moderate scale changes. Figure 2 shows some example images. Figure 3 shows detections using the BFM detector on additional, more complex, cow images obtained from Google image search.

2   Learning Boundary Fragments

In a similar manner to [19], we require the following data to train the model:

- A training image set with the object delineated by a bounding box.
- A validation image set labelled with whether the object is absent or present, and the object's centroid (but the bounding box is not necessary).

The training images provide the candidate boundary fragments, and these candidates are optimized over the validation set as described below. For the results of this section the training set contains 20 images of cows, and the validation set contains 25 cow images (the positive set) and 25 images of other objects (motorbikes and cars – the negative set).

Given the outlines of the training images we want to identify boundary fragments that:

(i) discriminate objects of the target category from other objects, and
(ii) give a precise estimate of the object centroid.

A candidate boundary fragment is required to (i) match edge chains often in the positive images but not in the negative, *and* (ii) have a good localization of the centroid in the positive images. These requirements are illustrated in figure 4. The idea of using validation images for discriminative learning is motivated by

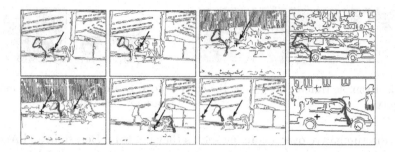

Fig. 4. Scoring boundary fragments. The first row shows an example of a boundary fragment that matches often on the positive images of the validation set, and less often on the negative images. *Additionally* it gives a good estimate of the centroid position on the positive images. In contrast, the second row shows an example of an unsuitable boundary fragment. The cross denotes the estimate of the centroid and the asterisk the correct object centroid.

Sali and Ullman [23]. However, in their work they only consider requirement (i), the learning of class-discriminate parts, but not the second requirement which is a geometric relation. In the following we first explain how to score a boundary fragment according to how well it satisfies these two requirements, and then how this score is used to select candidate fragments from the training images.

2.1 Scoring a Boundary Fragment

Linked edges are obtained in the training and validation set using a Canny edge detector with hysteresis. We do not obtain perfect segmentations – there may be gaps and false edges. A linked edge in the training image is then considered as a candidate boundary fragment γ_i, and scoring cost $C(\gamma_i)$ is a product of two factors:

1. $c_{match}(\gamma_i)$: the matching cost of the fragment to the edge chains in the validation images using a Chamfer distance [5, 6], see (1). This is described in more detail below.
2. $c_{loc}(\gamma_i)$: the distance (in pixels) between the true object centroid and the centroid predicted by the boundary fragment γ_i averaged over all the positive validation images.

with $C(\gamma_i) = c_{match}(\gamma_i)c_{loc}(\gamma_i)$. The matching cost is computed as

$$c_{match}(\gamma_i) = \frac{\sum_{i=1}^{L^+} distance(\gamma_i, P_{v_i})/L^+}{\sum_{i=1}^{L^-} distance(\gamma_i, N_{v_i})/L^-} \tag{1}$$

where L^- denotes the number of negative validation images N_{v_i} and L^+ the number of positive validation images P_{v_i}, and $distance(\gamma_i, I_{v_i})$ is the distance to the best matching edge chain in image I_{v_i}:

$$distance(\gamma_i, I_{v_i}) = \frac{1}{|\gamma_i|} \min_{\gamma_i \subset I_{v_i}} \sum_{t \in \gamma_i} DT_{I_{v_i}}(t) \tag{2}$$

where $DT_{I_{v_i}}$ is the distance transform. The Chamfer distance [5] is implemented using 8 orientation planes with an overlap of 5 degrees. The orientation of the edges is averaged over a length of 7 pixels by orthogonal regression. Because of background clutter the best match is often located on highly textured background clutter, i.e. it is not correct. To solve this problem we use the $N = 10$ best matches (with respect to (2)), and from these we take the one with the best centroid prediction. Note, images are scale normalized for training.

2.2 Selecting Boundary Fragments

Having defined the cost, we now turn to selecting candidate fragments. This is accomplished by optimization. For this purpose seeds are randomly distributed on the boundary of each training image. Then at each seed we extract boundary fragments. We let the size of each fragment grow and at every step we calculate the cost $C(\gamma_i)$ on the validation set. Figure 5(a) shows three examples of this growing of boundary fragments (the length varies from 20 pixels in steps of 30 pixels in both directions up to a length of 520 pixels). The cost is minimized over the varying length of the boundary fragment to choose the best fragment. If no length variation meets some threshold of the cost we reject this fragment and proceed with the next one. Using this procedure we obtain a codebook of boundary fragments each having the geometric information to vote for an object centroid.

To reduce redundancy in the codebook the resulting boundary fragment set is merged using agglomerative clustering on medoids. The distance function is $distance(\gamma_i, \gamma_j)$ (where I_{v_i} in (2) is replaced by the binary image of fragment γ_j) and we cluster with a threshold of $th_{cl} = 0.2$. Figure 5(b) shows some examples of resulting clusters. This optimized codebook forms the basis for the next stage in learning the BFM.

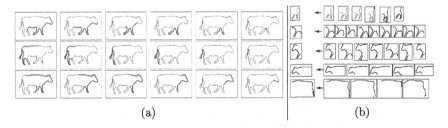

(a)   (b)

Fig. 5. Learning boundary fragments. (a) Each row shows the growing of a different random seed on a training image. (b) Clusters from the optimized boundary fragments. The first column shows the chosen codebook entries. The remaining columns show the boundary fragments that also lie in that cluster.

3   Training an Object Detector Using Boosting

At this stage we have a codebook of optimized boundary fragments each carrying additional geometric information on the object centroid. We now want to combine these fragments so that their aggregated estimates determine the centroid and increase the matching precision. In the case of image fragments, a single region can be used to determine a unique correspondence (e.g. see [19]). In contrast, boundary fragments are not so discriminating, but a combination of several such fragments (for example distributed around the actual object boundary) is characteristic for an object class.

We combine boundary fragments to form a weak detector by learning combinations which fit well on all the positive validation images. We then learn a strong detector from these weak detectors using a standard Boosting framework which is adapted to learn detection rather than classification. This learning of a strong detector chooses boundary fragments which model the whole distribution of the training data (whereas the method of the previous section can score fragments highly if they have low costs on only a subset of the validation images).

3.1   Weak Detectors

A weak detector is composed of k (typically 2 or 3) boundary fragments. We want a detector to fire ($h_i(I) = 1$) if (i) the k boundary fragments match image edge chains, (ii) the centroid estimates concur, and, in the case of positive images, (iii) the centroid estimate agrees with the true object centroid. Figure 6(a) illustrates a positive detection of an image (with $k = 2$ and the boundary fragments named γ_a and γ_b). The classification output $h_i(I)$ of detector h_i on an image I is defined as:

$$h_i(I) = \begin{cases} 1 & \text{if } D(h_i, I) < th_{h_i} \\ 0 & \text{otherwise} \end{cases}$$

with th_{h_i} the learnt threshold of each detector (see section 3.2), and where the distance $D(h_i, I)$ of h_i (consisting of k boundary fragments γ_j) to an image I is defined as:

$$D(h_i, I) = \frac{1}{m_s^2} \cdot \sum_{j=1}^{k} distance(\gamma_j, I) \tag{3}$$

The $distance(\gamma_j, I)$ is defined in (2) and m_s is explained below. Any weak detector where the centroid estimate misses the true object centroid by more than d_c (in our case 15 pixels), is rejected.

Figure 6(b) shows examples of matches of weak detectors on positive and negative validation images. At these positions as shown in column 2 of figure 6(a) each fragment also estimates a centroid by a circular uncertainty window. Here the radius of the window is $r = 10$. The compactness of the centroid estimate is measured by m_s (shown in the third column of figure 6(a)). $m_s = k$ if the circular uncertainty regions overlap, and otherwise a penalty of $m_s = 0.5$ is allocated. Note, to keep the search for weak detectors tractable, the number

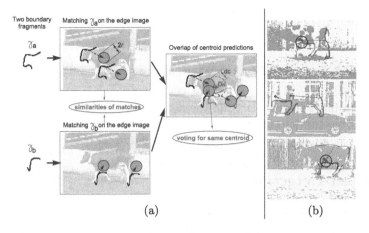

(a)   (b)

Fig. 6. Learning a weak detector. (a) The combination of boundary fragments to form a weak detector. Details in the text. (b) Examples of matching the weak detector to the validation set. Top: a weak detector with $k = 2$, that fires on a positive validation image because of highly compact centre votes close enough to the true object centre (black circle). Middle: a negative validation image where the same weak detector does not fire (votings do not concur). Bottom: the same as the top with $k = 3$. In the implementation $r = 10$ and $d_c = 15$.

of used codebook entries (before clustering, to reduce the effort already in the clustering procedure) is restricted to the top 500 for $k = 2$ and 200 for $k = 3$ (determined by the ranked costs $C(\gamma_i)$). Also, each boundary fragment is matched separately and only those for which $distance(\gamma_j, I) < 0.2$ are used.

3.2   Strong Detector

Having defined a weak detector consisting of k boundary fragments and a threshold th_{h_i}, we now explain how we learn this threshold and form a strong detector H out of T weak detectors h_i using AdaBoost. First we calculate the distances $D(h_i, I_j)$ of all combinations of our boundary fragments (using k elements for one combination) on all (positive and negative) images of our validation set $I_1 \ldots I_v$. Then in each iteration $1 \ldots T$ we search for the weak detector that obtains the best detection result on the current image weighting (for details see AdaBoost [15]). This selects weak detectors which generally (depending on the weighting) "fire" often on positive validation images (classify them as correct and estimate a centroid closer than d_c to the true object centroid) and not on the negative ones. Figure 7 shows examples of learnt weak detectors that contribute to the strong detector. Each of these weak detectors also has a weight w_{h_i}. The output of a strong detector on a whole test image is then:

$$H(I) = sign(\sum_{i=1}^{T} h_i(I) \cdot w_{h_i}). \tag{4}$$

Fig. 7. Examples of weak detectors, left for $k = 2$, and right for $k = 3$

The sign function is replaced in the detection procedure by a threshold t_{det}, where an object is detected in the image I if $H(I) > t_{det}$ and no evidence for the occurrence of an object if $H(I) \leq t_{det}$ (the standard formulation uses $t_{det} = 0$).

4 Object Detection

Detection algorithm and segmentation: The steps of the detection algorithm are now described and qualitatively illustrated in figure 8. First the edges are detected (step 1) then the boundary fragments of the weak detectors, that form the strong detector, are matched to this edge image (step 2). In order to detect (one or more) instances of the object (instead of classifying the whole image) each weak detector h_i votes with a weight w_{h_i} in a Hough voting space (step 3). Votes are then accumulated in a circular search window ($W(x_n)$) with radius d_c around candidate points x_n (represented by a Mean-Shift-Mode estimation [8]). The Mean-Shift modes that are above a threshold t_{det} are taken as detections of object instances (candidate points). The confidence in detections at these candidate points x_n is calculated using probabilistic scoring (see below). The segmentation is obtained by backprojection of the boundary fragments (step 3) of weak detectors which contributed to that centre to a binary pixel map. Typically, the contour of the object is over-represented by these fragments. We obtain a closed contour of the object, and additional, spurious contours (seen in figure 8, step 3). Short segments (< 30 pixels) are deleted, the contour is filled (using Matlab's 'filled area' in regionprops), and the final segmentation matte is obtained by a morphological opening, which removes thin structures (votes from

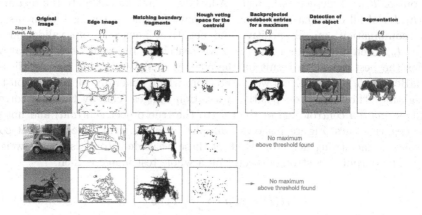

Fig. 8. Examples of processing test images with the BFM detector

outliers that are connected to the object). Finally, each of the objects obtained by this procedure is represented by its bounding box.

Probabilistic scoring: At candidate points x_n for instances of an object category c, found by the strong detector in the test image I_T we sum up the (probabilistic) votings of the weak detectors h_i in a 2D Hough voting space which gives us the probabilistic confidence:

$$conf(x_n) = \sum_i^T p(c, h_i) = \sum_i^T p(h_i)p(c|h_i) \tag{5}$$

where $p(h_i) = \frac{1}{\sum_{q=1}^M score(h_q, I_T)} \cdot score(h_i, I_T)$ describes the pdf of the effective matching of the weak detector with $score(h_i, I_T) = 1/D(h_i, I_T)$ (see (3)). The second term of this vote is the confidence we have in each specific weak detector and is computed as:

$$p(c|h_i) = \frac{\#fires_{correct}}{\#fires_{total}} \tag{6}$$

where $\#fires_{correct}$ is the number of positive and $\#fires_{total}$ is the number of positive and negative validation images the weak detector fires on. Finally our confidence of an object appearing at position x_n is computed by using a Mean-Shift algorithm [8] (circular window $W(x_n)$) in the Hough voting space defined as: $conf(x_n|W(x_n)) = \sum_{X_j \in W(x_n)} conf(X_j)$.

5   Detection Results

In this section we compare the performance of the BFM detector to published state-of-the-art results, and also give results on new data sets. Throughout we use fixed parameters ($T = 200$, $k = 2$, $t_{det} = 8$) for our training and testing procedure unless stated otherwise. An object is deemed correctly detected if the overlap of the bounding boxes (detection vs ground truth) is greater than 50%.

Cows: First we give quantitative results on the cow dataset. We used 20 training images (validation set 25 positive/25 negative) and tested on 80 unseen images, half belonging to the category cows and half to counter examples (cars and motorbikes). In table 2 we compare our results to those reported by Leibe et al. [19] and Caputo et al. [7] (Images are from the same test set – though the authors do not specify which ones they used). We perform as well as the result in [19], clearly demonstrating that in some cases the contour alone is sufficient for excellent detection performance. Kumar et al. [17] also give an RPC curve for cow detection with an ROC-equal-error rate of 10% (though they use different test images). Note, that the detector can identify multiple instances in an image, as shown in figure 3.

Variation in performance with number of training images: The results on the cow dataset reported above have been achieved using 20 training images. Figure 9 shows how the number of training images influences the performance of

584   A. Opelt, A. Pinz, and A. Zisserman

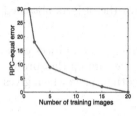 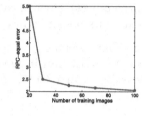 

Fig. 9. Error depending on the number of training images for the cow dataset

Fig. 10. Error depending on the number of training images for Cars-Rear

Fig. 11. Example of BFM detections for horses showing computed bounding boxes and segmentations

the BFM detector. Even with five images our model achieves detection results of better than 10% RPC-equal-error rate. The performance saturates at twenty in this case, but this number is dependent on the degree of within class variation (e.g. see fig.10).

Caltech datasets: From the widely used Caltech datasets we performed experiments on the category Cars-Rear and Airplanes. Table 1 shows our results compared with other state of the art approaches on the same test images as reported in [12]. First we give the detection results (BFM-D) and compare them to the best (as far as we know) results on detection by Leibe *et. al* [18, 19, 20] (scale changes are handled as described in section 6). We achieve superior results – even though we only require the bounding boxes in the training images (and not foreground segmentation as in [24], for example). For the classification results an image is classified, in the manner of [12], if it contains the object, but localization by a bounding box is not considered. Compared to recently published results on this data we again achieve the best results. Note that the amount of supervision varies over the methods where e.g. [26] use labels and bounding boxes (as we do); [2, 3, 12, 22] use just the object labels; and Sivic *et al.* [25] use no supervision. It should be pointed out, that we use just 50 training images and 50 validation images for each category, which is less than the other approaches use. Figure 10 shows the error rate depending on the number of training images (again, the same number of positive and negative validation images are used). However, it is known that the Caltech images are now not sufficiently demanding, so we next consider further harder situations.

Table 1. Comparison of the BFM detector to other published results on the Caltech dataset (Cars-Rear and Airplanes). The first two columns give the actual object detection error (BFM-D) and the remaining columns the categorization of the images (BFM-C) given by the ROC-equal error rates.

Cat.	BFM-D	[18]	BFM-C	[12]	[22]	[25]	[2]	[3]	[14]	[26]	[28]
Cars-Rear	**2.25**	6.1	**0.05**	8.8	8.9	21.4	3.1	2.3	1.8	9.8	-
Airplanes	**7.4**	-	**2.6**	6.3	11.1	3.4	4.5	10.3	-	17.1	5.6

Table 2. Comparison of the BFM detector to other published results on the cows

Method	RPC-err.
Caputo *et al.* [7]	2.9%
Leibe *et al.* [19]	0.0%
Our approach	0.0%

Table 3. The first 3 rows show the failures made by the three different models (FP=false positive, FN=false negative, M=multiple detection). The last row shows the RPC-equal-error rate for each model.

-	cow	horse1	horse2
FP	0	3	0
FN	0	13	12
M	0	1	2
RPC-err	0%	23%	19%

Horses and Cow/horse discrimination: To address the topic of how well our method performs on categories that consist of objects that have a similar boundary shape we attempt to detect and discriminate horses and cows. We use the horse data from [16] (no quantitative comparison as the authors could not report their exact test set because of lost data). In the following we compare three models. In each case they are learnt on 20 training images of the category and a validation set of 25 positive and 25 negative images that is different for each model. The first model for cows (cow-BFM) is learnt using no horses in the negative validation set (13 cars, 12 motorbikes). The second model for horses (horse1-BFM) is learnt using also cows in the negative validation set (8 cars, 10 cows, 7 motorbikes). Finally we train a model (horse2-BFM) which uses just cow images as negative validation images (25 cows). We now apply all three models on the same test set, containing 40 images of cows and 40 images of horses (figure 11 shows example detection results). Table 3 shows the failures and the RPC-equal error rate of each of these three models on this test set. The cow model is very strong (no failures) because it needs no knowledge of another object class even if its boundary shape is similar. Horse1-BFM is a weaker model (this is a consequence of greater variations of the horses in the training and test images). The model horse2-BFM obviously gains from the cows in the negative validation images, as it does not have any false positive detections. Overall this means our models are good at discriminating classes of similar boundary shapes.

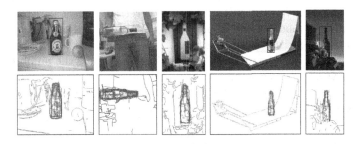

Fig. 12. Example of BFM detections for bottles. The first row shows the bounding box of the detection and the second row shows the backprojected boundary fragments for these detections.

Still, categories with higher intra-class variability (like horses compared to cows) are harder to learn and might need more training data to generalize over the whole distribution.

Bottles: To show the advantage of an approach relying on the shape of an object category we set up a new dataset of bottle images. This consists of 118 images collected using Google Image Search. Negative images are provided by the Caltech background image set. We separated the images in test/training/validation-set (64/24/30) and added the same amount of negative images in each case. We achieve an RPC-equal error rate of 9%. Figure 12 shows some detection examples.

6   Invariance to Scale, Rotation and Viewpoint

This section briefly discusses the topic of invariance of the BFM with respect to scale, rotation and changes in viewpoint.

Search over scale: A scaled codebook representation is used. Additionally we normalize the parameters in the detection procedure with respect to scale, for example the radius for centroid estimation, in the obvious way. The Mean-Shift modes are then aggregated over the set of scales, and the maxima explored as in the single scale case. Results on Cars-rear, airplanes and bottles of section 5 were obtained by this method.

Rotation: To achieve in-plane rotation invariance we use rotated versions of the codebook (see figure 12 second column for an example). The BFM is invariant to small rotations in plane due to the orientation planes used in the Chamfer-matching. This is a consequence of the nature of our matching procedure. For many categories the rotation invariance up to this degree may be sufficient (e.g. cars, cows) because they have a favoured orientation where other occurrences are quite unnatural.

Changes in viewpoint: For natural objects (e.g. cows) the perceived boundary is the visual rim. The position of the visual rim on the object will vary with pose but the shape of the associated boundary fragment will be valid over a range of poses. We performed experiments under controlled conditions on the ETH-80 database. With a BFM learnt for a certain aspect we could still detect a prominent mode in the Hough voting space up to 45 degrees rotation in both directions (horizontal and vertical). Thus, to extend the BFM to various aspects this invariance to small viewpoint changes reduces the number of necessary positions on the view-sphere to a handful of aspects that have to be trained separately. Our probabilistic formulation can be straightforwardly extended to multiple aspects.

7   Discussion and Conclusions

We have described a Boundary Fragment Model for detecting instances of object categories. The method is able to deal with the partial boundaries that typically are recovered by an edge detector. Its performance is similar to or outperforms state-of-the-art methods that include image appearance region fragments. For classes where the texture is very variable (e.g. bottles, mugs) a BFM may be preferable. In other cases a combination of appearance and boundary will have superior performance.

It is worth noting that the BFM once learnt can be implemented very efficiently using the low computational complexity method of Felzenszwalb & Huttenlocher[11].

Currently our research is focusing on extending the BFM to multi-class and multiple aspects of one class.

Acknowledgements

This work was supported by the Austrian Science Foundation FWF, project S9103-N04, ECVision and Pascal Network of Excellence.

References

1. S. Agarwal, A. Awan, and D. Roth. Learning to detect objects in images via a sparse, part-based representation. *IEEE PAMI*, 26(11):1475–1490, Nov. 2004.
2. J. Amores, N. Sebe, and P. Radeva. Fast spatial pattern discovery integrating boosting with constellations of contextual descriptors. In *Proc. CVPR*, volume 2, pages 769–774, CA, USA, June 2005.
3. A. Bar-Hillel, T. Hertz, and D. Weinshall. Object class recognition by boosting a part-based model. In *Proc. CVPR*, volume 2, pages 702–709, June 2005.
4. E. J. Bernstein and Y. Amit. Part-based statistical models for object classification and detection. In *Proc. CVPR*, volume 2, pages 734–740, 2005.
5. G. Borgefors. Hierarchical chamfer matching: A parametric edge matching algorithm. *IEEE PAMI*, 10(6):849–865, 1988.
6. H. Breu, J. Gil, D. Kirkpatrick, and M. Werman. Linear time Euclidean distance transform algorithms. *IEEE PAMI*, 17(5):529–533, May. 1995.
7. B. Caputo, C. Wallraven, and M. Nilsback. Object categorization via local kernels. In *Proc. ICPR*, pages 132–135, 2004.
8. D. Comaniciu and P. Meer. Mean shift: A robust approach towards feature space analysis. In *IEEE PAMI*, volume 24(5), pages 603–619, 2002.
9. D. Crandall, P. Felzenszwalb, and D. Huttenlocher. Spatial priors for part-based recognition using statistical models. In *Proc. CVPR*, pages 10–17, 2005.
10. G. Csurka, C. Bray, C. Dance, and L. Fan. Visual categorization with bags of keypoints. In *ECCV04. Workshop on Stat. Learning in Computer Vision*, pages 59–74, 2004.
11. P. Felzenszwalb and D. Huttenlocher. Pictorial structures for object recognition. *Intl. Journal of Computer Vision*, 61(1):55–79, 2004.
12. R. Fergus, P. Perona, and A. Zisserman. Object class recognition by unsupervised scale-invariant learning. In *Proc. CVPR*, pages 264–271, 2003.
13. R. Fergus, P. Perona, and A. Zisserman. A visual category filter for google images. In *Proc. ECCV*, pages 242–256, 2004.

14. R. Fergus, P. Perona, and A. Zisserman. A sparse object category model for efficient learning and exhaustive recognition. In *Proc. Proc. CVPR*, 2005.
15. Y. Freund and R. Schapire. A decision theoretic generalisation of online learning. *Computer and System Sciences*, 55(1):119–139, 1997.
16. F. Jurie and C. Schmid. Scale-invariant shape features for recognition of object categories. In *Proc. of CVPR*, pages 90–96, 2004.
17. M. Kumar, P. Torr, and A. Zisserman. Extending pictural structures for object recognition. In *Proc. BMVC*, 2004.
18. B. Leibe. *Interleaved Object Categorization and Segmentation*. PhD thesis, Swiss Federal Institute of Technology, 2004.
19. B. Leibe, A. Leonardis, and B. Schiele. Combined object categorization and segmentation with an implicit shape model. In *ECCV04. Workshop on Stat. Learning in Computer Vision*, pages 17–32, May 2004.
20. B. Leibe and B. Schiele. Scale-invariant object categorization using a scale-adaptive mean-shift search. In *DAGM'04*, pages 145–153, Aug. 2004.
21. D. Magee and R. Boyle. Detecting lameness using re-sampling condensation and multi-steam cyclic hidden markov models. *Image and Vision Computing*, 20(8):581–594, 2002.
22. A. Opelt, M. Fussenegger, A. Pinz, and P. Auer. Weak hypotheses and boosting for generic object detection and recognition. In *Proc. ECCV*, pages 71–84, 2004.
23. E. Sali and S. Ullman. Combining class-specific fragments for object classification. In *Proc. BMVC*, pages 203–213, 1999.
24. J. Shotton, A. Blake, and R. Cipolla. Contour-based learning for object detection. In *Proc. ICCV*, pages 503–510, 2005.
25. J. Sivic, B. Russell, A. Efros, A. Zisserman, and W. Freeman. Discovering objects and their location in images. In *Proc. ICCV*, 2005.
26. J. Thureson and S. Carlsson. Appearance based qualitative image description for object class recognition. In *Proc. ECCV*, pages 518–529, 2004.
27. M. Vidal-Naquet and S. Ullman. Object recognition with informative features and linear classification. In *Proc. ICCV*, volume 1, pages 281–288, 2003.
28. W. Zhang, B. Yu, G. Zelinsky, and D. Samaras. Object class recognition using multiple layer boosting with heterogenous features. In *Proc. CVPR*, pages 323–330, 2005.

Region Covariance: A Fast Descriptor for Detection and Classification

Oncel Tuzel[1,3], Fatih Porikli[3], and Peter Meer[1,2]

[1] Computer Science Department,
[2] Electrical and Computer Engineering Department,
Rutgers University, Piscataway, NJ 08854
{otuzel, meer}@caip.rutgers.edu
[3] Mitsubishi Electric Research Laboratories,
Cambridge, MA 02139
fatih@merl.com

Abstract. We describe a new region descriptor and apply it to two problems, object detection and texture classification. The covariance of d-features, e.g., the three-dimensional color vector, the norm of first and second derivatives of intensity with respect to x and y, etc., characterizes a region of interest. We describe a fast method for computation of covariances based on *integral images*. The idea presented here is more general than the image sums or histograms, which were already published before, and with a series of integral images the covariances are obtained by a few arithmetic operations. Covariance matrices do not lie on Euclidean space, therefore we use a distance metric involving generalized eigenvalues which also follows from the Lie group structure of positive definite matrices. Feature matching is a simple nearest neighbor search under the distance metric and performed extremely rapidly using the integral images. The performance of the covariance features is superior to other methods, as it is shown, and large rotations and illumination changes are also absorbed by the covariance matrix.

1   Introduction

Feature selection is one of the most important steps for detection and classification problems. Good features should be discriminative, robust, easy to compute and efficient algorithms are needed for a variety of tasks such as recognition and tracking.

The raw pixel values of several image statistics such as color, gradient and filter responses are the simplest choice for image features, and were used for many years in computer vision, e.g., [1, 2, 3]. However, these features are not robust in the presence of illumination changes and nonrigid motion, and efficient matching algorithms are limited by the high dimensional representation. Lower dimensional projections were also used for classification [4] and tracking [5].

A natural extension of raw pixel values are via histograms where a region is represented with its nonparametric estimation of joint distribution. Following [6], histograms were widely used for nonrigid object tracking. In a recent study [7],

A. Leonardis, H. Bischof, and A. Pinz (Eds.): ECCV 2006, Part II, LNCS 3952, pp. 589–600, 2006.
© Springer-Verlag Berlin Heidelberg 2006

fast histogram construction methods were explored to find a global match. Besides tracking, histograms were also used for texture representation [8,9], matching [10] and other problems in the field of computer vision. However, the joint representation of several different features through histograms is exponential with the number features.

The *integral image* idea is first introduced in [11] for fast computation of Haar-like features. Combined with cascaded AdaBoost classifier, superior performances were reported for face detection problem, but the algorithm requires long training time to learn the object classifiers. In [12] scale space extremas are detected for keypoint localization and arrays of orientation histograms were used as keypoint descriptors. The descriptors are very effective in matching local neighborhoods but do not have global context information.

There are two main contributions within this paper. First, we propose to use the covariance of several image statistics computed inside a region of interest, as the region descriptor. Instead of the joint distribution of the image statistics, we use the covariance as our feature, so the dimensionality is much smaller. We provide a fast way of calculating covariances using the integral images and the computational cost is independent of the size of the region. Secondly, we introduce new algorithms for object detection and texture classification using the covariance features. The covariance matrices are not elements of the Euclidean space, therefore we can not use most of the classical machine learning algorithms. We propose a nearest neighbor search algorithm using a distance metric defined on the positive definite symmetric matrices for feature matching.

In Section 2 we describe the covariance features and explain the fast computation of the region covariances using integral image idea. Object detection problem is described in Section 3 and texture classification problem is described in Section 4. We demonstrate the superior performance of the algorithms based on the covariance features with detailed comparisons to previous methods and features.

2   Covariance as a Region Descriptor

Let I be a one dimensional intensity or three dimensional color image. The method also generalizes to other type of images, e.g., infrared. Let F be the $W \times H \times d$ dimensional feature image extracted from I

$$F(x, y) = \phi(I, x, y) \tag{1}$$

where the function ϕ can be any mapping such as intensity, color, gradients, filter responses, etc. For a given rectangular region $R \subset F$, let $\{\mathbf{z}_k\}_{k=1..n}$ be the d-dimensional feature points inside R. We represent the region R with the $d \times d$ covariance matrix of the feature points

$$\mathbf{C}_R = \frac{1}{n-1} \sum_{k=1}^{n} (\mathbf{z}_k - \boldsymbol{\mu})(\mathbf{z}_k - \boldsymbol{\mu})^T \tag{2}$$

where $\boldsymbol{\mu}$ is the mean of the points.

There are several advantages of using covariance matrices as region descriptors. A single covariance matrix extracted from a region is usually enough to match the region in different views and poses. In fact we assume that the co-variance of a distribution is enough to discriminate it from other distributions. If two distributions only vary with their mean, our matching result produces perfect match but in real examples these cases almost never occur.

The covariance matrix proposes a natural way of fusing multiple features which might be correlated. The diagonal entries of the covariance matrix represent the variance of each feature and the nondiagonal entries represent the correlations. The noise corrupting individual samples are largely filtered out with an average filter during covariance computation.

The covariance matrices are low-dimensional compared to other region descriptors and due to symmetry $\mathbf{C}_R$ has only $(d^2 + d)/2$ different values. Whereas if we represent the same region with raw values we need $n \times d$ dimensions, and if we use joint feature histograms we need b^d dimensions, where b is the number of histogram bins used for each feature.

Given a region R, its covariance $\mathbf{C}_R$ does not have any information regarding the ordering and the number of points. This implies a certain scale and rotation invariance over the regions in different images. Nevertheless, if information regarding the orientation of the points are represented, such as the norm of gradient with respect to x and y, the covariance descriptor is no longer rotationally invariant. The same argument is also correct for scale and illumination. Rotation and illumination dependent statistics are important for recognition/classification purposes and we use them in Sections 3 and 4.

2.1 Distance Calculation on Covariance Matrices

The covariance matrices do not lie on Euclidean space. For example, the space is not closed under multiplication with negative scalers. Most of the common machine learning methods work on Euclidean spaces and therefore they are not suitable for our features. The nearest neighbor algorithm which will be used in the following sections, only requires a way of computing distances between feature points. We use the distance measure proposed in [13] to measure the dissimilarity of two covariance matrices

$$\rho(\mathbf{C}_1, \mathbf{C}_2) = \sqrt{\sum_{i=1}^{n} \ln^2 \lambda_i(\mathbf{C}_1, \mathbf{C}_2)} \tag{3}$$

where $\{\lambda_i(\mathbf{C}_1, \mathbf{C}_2)\}_{i=1...n}$ are the generalized eigenvalues of $\mathbf{C}_1$ and $\mathbf{C}_2$, computed from

$$\lambda_i \mathbf{C}_1 \mathbf{x}_i - \mathbf{C}_2 \mathbf{x}_i = 0 \qquad i = 1...d \tag{4}$$

and $\mathbf{x}_i \neq 0$ are the generalized eigenvectors. The distance measure ρ satisfies the metric axioms for positive definite symmetric matrices $\mathbf{C}_1$ and $\mathbf{C}_2$

1. $\rho(\mathbf{C}_1, \mathbf{C}_2) \geq 0$ and $\rho(\mathbf{C}_1, \mathbf{C}_2) = 0$ only if $\mathbf{C}_1 = \mathbf{C}_2$,
2. $\rho(\mathbf{C}_1, \mathbf{C}_2) = \rho(\mathbf{C}_2, \mathbf{C}_1)$,
3. $\rho(\mathbf{C}_1, \mathbf{C}_2) + \rho(\mathbf{C}_1, \mathbf{C}_3) \geq \rho(\mathbf{C}_2, \mathbf{C}_3)$.

The distance measure also follows from the Lie group structure of positive definite matrices and an equivalent form can be derived from the Lie algebra of positive definite matrices. The generalized eigenvalues can be computed with $O(d^3)$ arithmetic operations using numerical methods and an additional d logarithm operations are required for distance computation, which is usually faster than comparing two histograms that grow exponentially with d. We refer the readers to [13] for a detailed discussion on the distance metric.

2.2   Integral Images for Fast Covariance Computation

Integral images are intermediate image representations used for fast calculation of region sums [11]. Each pixel of the integral image is the sum of all the pixels inside the rectangle bounded by the upper left corner of the image and the pixel of interest. For an intensity image I its integral image is defined as

$$\text{Integral Image } (x', y') = \sum_{x<x', y<y'} I(x, y). \tag{5}$$

Using this representation, any rectangular region sum can be computed in constant time. In [7], the integral images were extended to higher dimensions for fast calculation of region histograms. Here we follow a similar idea for fast calculation of region covariances.

We can write the (i, j)-th element of the covariance matrix defined in (2) as

$$C_R(i, j) = \frac{1}{n-1} \sum_{k=1}^{n} (z_k(i) - \mu(i))(z_k(j) - \mu(j)). \tag{6}$$

Expanding the mean and rearranging the terms we can write

$$C_R(i, j) = \frac{1}{n-1} \left[\sum_{k=1}^{n} z_k(i) z_k(j) - \frac{1}{n} \sum_{k=1}^{n} z_k(i) \sum_{k=1}^{n} z_k(j) \right]. \tag{7}$$

To find the covariance in a given rectangular region R, we have to compute the sum of each feature dimension, $z(i)_{i=1...n}$, as well as the sum of the multiplication of any two feature dimensions, $z(i)z(j)_{i,j=1...n}$. We construct $d + d^2$ integral images for each feature dimension $z(i)$ and multiplication of any two feature dimensions $z(i)z(j)$.

Let P be the $W \times H \times d$ tensor of the integral images

$$P(x', y', i) = \sum_{x<x', y<y'} F(x, y, i) \qquad i = 1...d \tag{8}$$

and Q be the $W \times H \times d \times d$ tensor of the second order integral images

$$Q(x', y', i, j) = \sum_{x<x', y<y'} F(x, y, i)F(x, y, j) \qquad i, j = 1...d. \tag{9}$$

In [11], it is shown that integral image can be computed in one pass over the image. In our notation, $\mathbf{p}_{x,y}$ is the d dimensional vector and $\mathbf{Q}_{x,y}$ is the $d \times d$ dimensional matrix

$$\mathbf{p}_{x,y} = [P(x,y,1)\ldots P(x,y,d)]^T$$

$$\mathbf{Q}_{x,y} = \begin{pmatrix} Q(x,y,1,1) & \ldots & Q(x,y,1,d) \\ & \vdots & \\ Q(x,y,d,1) & \ldots & Q(x,y,d,d) \end{pmatrix}. \tag{10}$$

Note that $\mathbf{Q}_{x,y}$ is a symmetric matrix and $d + (d^2 + d)/2$ passes are enough to compute both P and Q. The computational complexity of constructing the integral images is $O(d^2 W H)$.

Let $R(x', y'; x'', y'')$ be the rectangular region, where (x', y') is the upper left coordinate and (x'', y'') is the lower right coordinate, as shown in Figure 1. The covariance of the region bounded by $(1,1)$ and (x', y') is

$$\mathbf{C}_{R(1,1;x',y')} = \frac{1}{n-1}\left[\mathbf{Q}_{x',y'} - \frac{1}{n}\mathbf{p}_{x',y'}\mathbf{p}_{x',y'}^T\right] \tag{11}$$

where $n = x' \cdot y'$. Similarly, after a few manipulations, the covariance of the region $R(x', y'; x'', y'')$ can be computed as

$$\mathbf{C}_{R(x',y';x'',y'')} = \frac{1}{n-1}\left[\mathbf{Q}_{x'',y''} + \mathbf{Q}_{x',y'} - \mathbf{Q}_{x'',y'} - \mathbf{Q}_{x',y''}\right. \tag{12}$$

$$\left. -\frac{1}{n}\left(\mathbf{p}_{x'',y''} + \mathbf{p}_{x',y'} - \mathbf{p}_{x',y''} - \mathbf{p}_{x'',y'}\right)\left(\mathbf{p}_{x'',y''} + \mathbf{p}_{x',y'} - \mathbf{p}_{x',y''} - \mathbf{p}_{x'',y'}\right)^T\right]$$

where $n = (x'' - x') \cdot (y'' - y')$. Therefore, after constructing integral images the covariance of any rectangular region can be computed in $O(d^2)$ time.

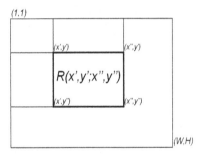

Fig. 1. Integral Image. The rectangle $R(x', y'; x'', y'')$ is defined by its upper left (x', y') and lower right (x'', y'') corners in the image, and each point is a d dimensional vector.

3   Object Detection

In object detection, given an object image, the aim is to locate the object in an arbitrary image and pose after a nonrigid transformation. We use pixel locations (x,y), color (RGB) values and the norm of the first and second order derivatives of the intensities with respect to x and y. Each pixel of the image is converted to a nine-dimensional feature vector

$$F(x,y) = \begin{bmatrix} x & y & R(x,y) & G(x,y) & B(x,y) \end{bmatrix}$$

$$\left| \frac{\partial I(x,y)}{\partial x} \right| \left| \frac{\partial I(x,y)}{\partial y} \right| \left| \frac{\partial^2 I(x,y)}{\partial x^2} \right| \left| \frac{\partial^2 I(x,y)}{\partial y^2} \right| \Bigg]^T \tag{13}$$

where R, G, B are the RGB color values, and I is the intensity. The image derivatives are calculated through the filters $[-1\ 0\ 1]^T$ and $[-1\ 2\ -1]^T$. The covariance of a region is a 9×9 matrix. Although the variance of pixel locations (x,y) is same for all the regions of the same size, they are still important since their correlation with the other features are used at the nondiagonal entries of the covariance matrix.

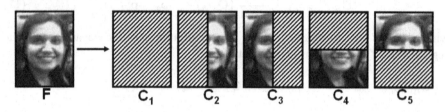

Fig. 2. Object representation. We construct five covariance matrices from overlapping regions of an object feature image. The covariances are used as the object descriptors.

We represent an object with five covariance matrices of the image features computed inside the object region, as shown in Figure 2. Initially we compute only the covariance of the whole region, $\mathbf{C}_1$, from the source image. We search the target image for a region having similar covariance matrix and the dissimilarity is measured through (3). At all the locations in the target image we analyze at nine different scales (four smaller, four larger) to find matching regions. We perform a brute force search, since we can compute the covariance of an arbitrary region very quickly. Instead of scaling the target image, we just change the size of our search window. There is a 15% scaling factor between two consecutive scales. The variance of the x and y components are not the same for regions with different sizes and we normalize the rows and columns corresponding to these features. At the smallest size of the window we jump three pixels horizontally or vertically between two search locations. For larger windows we jump 15% more and round to the next integer at each scale.

We keep the best matching 1000 locations and scales. At the second phase we repeat the search for 1000 detected locations, using the covariance matrices $\mathbf{C}_{i=1...5}$. The dissimilarity of the object model and a target region is computed

$$\rho(O,T) = \min_j \left[\sum_{i=1}^{5} \rho(\mathbf{C}_i^O, \mathbf{C}_i^T) - \rho(\mathbf{C}_j^O, \mathbf{C}_j^T) \right] \tag{14}$$

where $\mathbf{C}_i^O$ and $\mathbf{C}_i^T$ are the object and target covariances respectively, and we ignore the least matching region covariance of the five. This increases robustness

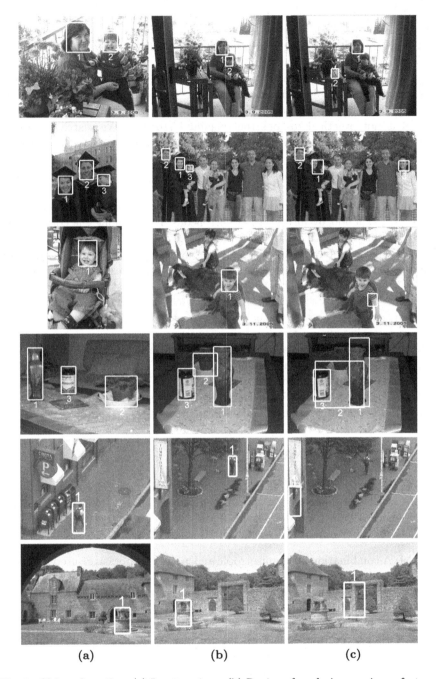

Fig. 3. Object detection. (a) Input regions. (b) Regions found via covariance features. (c) Regions found via histogram features.

towards possible occlusions and large illumination changes. The region with the smallest dissimilarity is selected as the matching region.

We present the matching results for a variety of examples in Figure 3 and compare our results with histogram features. We tested histogram features both with the RGB and HSV color spaces. With the RGB color space the results were much worse in all of the cases, therefore we did not present these results. We construct three separate 64 bin histograms for hue, saturation and value since it is not practical to construct a joint histogram. We search the target image for the same locations and sizes, and fast construction of histograms are performed through integral histograms [7]. We measure the distance between two histograms through Bhattacharyya distance [6] and sum over three color channels.

Covariance features can match all the target regions accurately whereas most of the regions found by histogram are erroneous. Even among the correctly detected regions with both methods we see that covariance features better localize the target. The examples are challenging since there are large scale, orientation and illumination changes, and some of the targets are occluded and have nonrigid motion. Almost perfect results indicate the robustness of the proposed approach. We also conclude that the covariances are very discriminative since they can match the correct target in the presence of similar objects, as seen in the face matching examples.

Covariance features are faster than the integral histograms since the dimensionality of the space is smaller. The search time of an object in a color image with size 320×240 is 6.5 seconds with a MATLAB 7 implementation. The performance can be improved by a factor of 20-30 with a C++ implementation which would yield to near real time performance.

4   Texture Classification

Currently, the most successful methods for texture classification are through textons which are cluster centers in a feature space derived from the input. The feature space is built from the output of a filter bank applied at every pixel and the methods differ only in the employed filter bank.

- **LM:** A combination of 48 anisotropic and isotropic filters were used by Leung and Malik [8]. The feature space is 48 dimensional.
- **S:** A set of 13 circular symmetric filters was used by Schmid [14]. The feature space is 13 dimensional.
- **M4, M8:** Both representations were proposed by Varma and Zissermann [9]. Original filters include both rotationally symmetric and oriented filters but only maximum response oriented filters are included to feature vector. The feature space is 4 and 8 dimensional respectively.

To find the textons, usually the k-means clustering algorithm is used, although it was shown that it might not be the best choice [15]. The most significant textons are aggregated into the texton library and the texton histograms are used as texture representation. The χ^2 distance [8] is used to measure the similarity of two histograms and the training image with the smallest distance from the test image determines the class of the latter. The process is computationally expensive since the images are convolved with large filter banks and in most cases requires clustering in high dimensional space.

4.1 Random Covariances for Texture Classification

We present a new approach to texture classification problem without using textons. We start with extracting several features from each pixel. For texture classification problem we use image intensities and norms of first and second order derivatives of intensities in both x and y direction. Each pixel is mapped to a $d = 5$ dimensional feature space

$$F(x,y) = \left[I(x,y) \left| \frac{\partial I(x,y)}{\partial x} \right| \left| \frac{\partial I(x,y)}{\partial y} \right| \left| \frac{\partial^2 I(x,y)}{\partial x^2} \right| \left| \frac{\partial^2 I(x,y)}{\partial y^2} \right| \right]^T. \tag{15}$$

We sample s random square regions from each image with random sizes between 16×16 and 128×128. Using integral images we compute the covariance matrix of each region. Each texture image is then represented with s covariance matrices and we have u training texture images from each texture class, a total of $s \cdot u$ covariance matrices. Texture representation process is illustrated in Figure 4. We repeat the process for the c texture classes and construct the representation for each texture class in the same way.

Given a test image, we again extract s covariance matrices from randomly selected regions. For each covariance matrix we measure the distance (3) from all the matrices of the training set and the label is predicted according to the majority voting among the k nearest ones (kNN algorithm). This classifier performs as a weak classifier and the class of the texture is determined according to the maximum votes among the s weak classifiers.

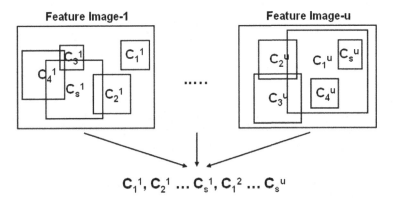

Fig. 4. Texture representation. There are u images for each texture class and we sample s regions from each image and compute covariance matrices $\mathbf{C}$.

4.2   Texture Classification Experiments

We perform our tests on the Brodatz texture database which consists of 112 textures. Because of the nonhomogeneous textures inside the database, classification is a challenging task. We duplicate the test environment of [15]. Each 640×640 texture image is divided into four 320×320 subimages and half of the images are used for training and half for testing.

We compare our results with the results reported in [15] in Table 1. Here we present the results for k-means based clustering algorithm. The texture representation through texton histograms has 560 bins. The results vary from 85.71% to 97.32% depending on the filter bank used.

In our tests we sample $s = 100$ random covariances from each image, both for testing and training, and we used $k = 5$ for the kNN algorithm. For $d = 5$ dimensional features, the covariance matrix is 5×5 and has only 15 different values compared to 560 bins before. Our result, 97.77%, is better than all of the previous results and faster. Only 5 images out of 224 is misclassified which is close to the upper limit of the problem. We show two of the misclassified images in Figure 5 and the misclassification is usually in nonhomogeneous textures.

To make the method rotationally invariant, we used only three rotationally invariant features: intensity and the magnitude of the gradient and Laplacian. The covariance matrices are 3×3 and have only 6 different values. Even with this very simple features the classification performance is 94.20%, which is as good as or even better than other rotationally invariant methods (**M4**, **M8**, **S**) listed in Table 1. Due to random sized window selection our method is scale invariant. Although the approach is not completely illumination invariant, it is more robust than using features (intensity and gradients) directly. The variances of intensity and gradients inside regions change less than intensity and gradients themselves in illumination variations.

In the *second experiment* we compare the covariance features with other possible choices. We run the proposed texture classification algorithm with the raw intensity values and histograms extracted from random regions.

For raw intensities we normalize each random region to 16×16 square region and use Euclidean distance to compute distances for kNN classification, which is similar to [3]. The feature space is 256 dimensional. The raw intensity values are very noisy therefore only in this case we sample $s = 500$ regions from each image.

We perform two tests using histogram features: intensity only, and intensity and norms of first and second order derivatives together. In both cases the dissimilarity is measured with Bhattacharyya distance [6]. We use 256 bins for intensity only and $5 \cdot 64 = 320$ bins for intensity and norm of derivatives together. It is not practical to construct the joint intensity and norm of derivatives histograms, due to computational and memory requirement.

Table 1. Classification results for the Brodatz database

	M4	M8	S	LM	Random Covariance
Performance	85.71	94.64	93.30	97.32	97.77

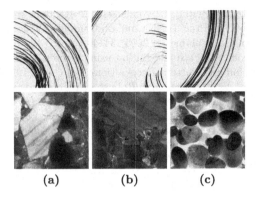

(a)   (b)   (c)

Fig. 5. Misclassified samples. (a) Test examples. (b) Samples from the same class. (c) Samples from the predicted texture class.

Table 2. Classification results for different features

	Raw Inten.	Inten. Hist.	Inten./Deriv. Hist.	Covariance
Performance	26.79	83.35	96.88	97.77

We sample $s = 100$ regions from each texture image. The results are shown in Table 2. The only result close to covariance is the 320 dimensional intensity and derivative histograms together. This is not surprising because our covariance features are the covariances of the joint distribution of the intensity and derivatives. But with covariance features we achieve a better performance in a much faster way.

5 Conclusion

In this paper we presented the covariance features and related algorithms for object detection and texture classification. Superior performance of the covariance features and algorithms were demonstrated on several examples with detailed comparisons to previous techniques and features. The method can be extended in several ways. For example, following automatical detection of an object in a video, it can be tracked in the following frames using this approach. As the object leaves the scene, the distance score will increase significantly which ends the tracking. Currently we are working on classification algorithms which use the Lie group structure of covariance matrices.

References

1. Rosenfeld, A., Vanderburg, G.: Coarse-fine template matching. IEEE Trans. Syst. Man. Cyb. **7** (1977) 104–107
2. Brunelli, R., Poggio, T.: Face recognition: Features versus templates. IEEE Trans. Pattern Anal. Machine Intell. **15** (1993) 1042 – 1052

3. Marée, R., Geurts, P., Piater, J., Wehenkel, L.: Random subwindows for robust image classification. In: Proc. IEEE Conf. on Computer Vision and Pattern Recognition, San Diego, CA. Volume 1. (2005) 34–40
4. Turk, M., Pentland, A.: Face recognition using eigenfaces. In: Proc. IEEE Conf. on Computer Vision and Pattern Recognition, Maui, HI. (1991) 586–591
5. Black, M., Jepson, A.: Eigentracking: Robust matching and tracking of articulated objects using a view-based representation. Intl. J. of Comp. Vision 26 (1998) 63–84
6. Comaniciu, D., Ramesh, V., Meer, P.: Real-time tracking of non-rigid objects using mean shift. In: Proc. IEEE Conf. on Computer Vision and Pattern Recognition, Hilton Head, SC. Volume 1. (2000) 142–149
7. Porikli, F.: Integral histogram: A fast way to extract histograms in cartesian spaces. In: Proc. IEEE Conf. on Computer Vision and Pattern Recognition, San Diego, CA. Volume 1. (2005) 829 – 836
8. Leung, T., Malik, J.: Representing and recognizing the visual appearance of materials using three-dimensional textons. Intl. J. of Comp. Vision 43 (2001) 29–44
9. Varma, M., Zisserman, A.: Statistical approaches to material classification. In: Proc. European Conf. on Computer Vision, Copehagen, Denmark. (2002)
10. Georgescu, B., Meer, P.: Point matching under large image deformations and illumination changes. IEEE Trans. Pattern Anal. Machine Intell. 26 (2004) 674–688
11. Viola, P., Jones, M.: Rapid object detection using a boosted cascade of simple features. In: Proc. IEEE Conf. on Computer Vision and Pattern Recognition, Kauai, HI. Volume 1. (2001) 511–518
12. Lowe, D.: Distinctive image features from scale-invariant keypoints. Intl. J. of Comp. Vision 60 (2004) 91–110
13. Förstner, W., Moonen, B.: A metric for covariance matrices. Technical report, Dept. of Geodesy and Geoinformatics, Stuttgart University (1999)
14. Schmid, C.: Constructing models for content-based image retreival. In: Proc. IEEE Conf. on Computer Vision and Pattern Recognition, Kauai, HI. (2001) 39–45
15. Georgescu, B., Shimshoni, I., Meer, P.: Mean shift based clustering in high dimensions: A texture classification example. In: Proc. 9th Intl. Conf. on Computer Vision, Nice, France. (2003) 456–463

Affine-Invariant Multi-reference Shape Priors for Active Contours

Alban Foulonneau[1], Pierre Charbonnier[1], and Fabrice Heitz[2]

[1] ERA 27 LCPC, Laboratoire des Ponts et Chaussées 11 rue Jean Mentelin,
B.P. 9, 67035 Strasbourg, France
`Alban.Foulonneau@equipement.gouv.fr`,
`Pierre.Charbonnier@equipement.gouv.fr`
[2] Laboratoire des Sciences de l'Image, de l'Informatique et de la Télédétection,
UMR 7005 CNRS, Strasbourg I University, Bd Sébastien Brandt,
67400 Illkirch, France
`heitz@lsiit.u-strasbg.fr`

Abstract. We present a new way of constraining the evolution of a region-based active contour with respect to a set of reference shapes. The approach is based on a description of shapes by the Legendre moments computed from their characteristic function. This provides a region-based representation that can handle arbitrary shape topologies. Moreover, exploiting the properties of moments, it is possible to include intrinsic affine invariance in the descriptor, which solves the issue of shape alignment without increasing the number of d.o.f. of the initial problem and allows introducing geometric shape variabilities. Our new *shape prior* is based on a distance between the *descriptors* of the evolving curve and a reference shape. The proposed model naturally extends to the case where multiple reference shapes are simultaneously considered. Minimizing the *shape energy*, leads to a geometric flow that does not rely on any particular representation of the contour and can be implemented with any contour evolution algorithm. We introduce our prior into a two-class segmentation functional, showing its benefits on segmentation results in presence of severe occlusions and clutter. Examples illustrate the ability of the model to deal with large affine deformation and to take into account a set of reference shapes of different topologies.

1 Introduction

Incorporating global shape constraints into deformable models, which traces back to pioneering works such as [1, 2], has recently received an increasing attention in the context of active contours (see e.g. [3], [4], [5], [6], [7] and references therein). The standard approach consists in defining an additional *prior* term, based on a similarity measure between the evolving shape and a *reference* one. A first important issue that must be dealt with is the question of shape *alignment*. Pose transformations (rotation, translation and scaling) are generally taken into account in an explicit fashion, which increases the number of d.o.f. of the problem, and leads to systems of coupled partial differential equations (PDE's). A second

A. Leonardis, H. Bischof, and A. Pinz (Eds.): ECCV 2006, Part II, LNCS 3952, pp. 601–613, 2006.
© Springer-Verlag Berlin Heidelberg 2006

issue is the question of *variability*. Variations of the shape away from a reference template are, in the majority of existing works, handled using statistical models, even if a framework that accounts for geometric transformations of the reference shape has recently been proposed in [6].

In this paper, we introduce a novel approach for image segmentation, which combines a parametric representation of shapes with curve evolution theory to constrain the geometry of an evolving active contour toward a given reference shape or a set of reference shapes. More specifically, we consider a parametric description based on Legendre moments computed from the characteristic function of a shape. Such a representation is region-based, does not depend on implementation considerations and allows taking into account arbitrary topologies. Based on this shape description, we define a shape prior as a distance between the evolving curve and a reference shape. This framework naturally extends to the multi-reference case, i.e. when multiple reference shapes are simultaneously considered. Moreover, we exploit the fact that moments convey all geometric information about shape to define a *canonical* representation, i.e. a configuration in which two shapes differing by an affine transformation have identical *descriptors*. Our shape prior is thus intrinsically affine-invariant. This naturally avoids the pose estimation problem and allows the model to handle geometrical variabilities. Finally, a unique evolution equation for the active contour is derived using the formalism of shape derivative and classical differentiation rules as proposed in [8] by Aubert *et al.* Thanks to the ability of the model to change topology during evolution, automatic initialization of the active contour is also possible, whatever the topology of the final target shape.

The reminder of the paper is structured as follows. In Sec. 2, we introduce our new multi-reference, affine-invariant moment-based shape prior. The associated evolution equation is given in Sec. 3. In Sec. 4, we illustrate the benefits of the new prior on the segmentation of objects with various topologies, undergoing large affine transformations, in presence of occlusions and clutter.

2   An Affine-Invariant, Multi-reference Shape Prior

2.1   Encoding Shapes with Moments

Denoting by Ω_{in} the inside region of a shape, the *regular* or *geometric* moments of its characteristic function (which is binary) are defined as:

$$M_{p,q} = \iint_{\Omega_{in}} x^p y^q dx dy \tag{1}$$

where $(p, q) \in \mathbb{Z}^2$, and $(p + q)$ is called the order of the moment. Any shape, discretized on a sufficiently fine grid, may be reconstructed from its infinite set of moments. Hence, when computed from the characteristic function, moments naturally provide region-based *shape descriptors*. However, as is well-known [9], a more tractable representation for reconstruction purposes is obtained by using an orthogonal basis, such as Legendre polynomials:

$$\lambda_{p,q} = C_{pq} \iint_{\Omega_{in}} P_p(x)P_q(y)dxdy, \tag{2}$$

for $(x,y) \in [-1,1]^2$, where $C_{pq} = (2p+1)(2q+1)/4$ is a normalizing constant, and for $x \in [-1,1]$:

$$P_p(x) = \sum_{k=0}^{p} a_{pk}x^k = \frac{1}{2^p p!}\frac{d^p}{dx^p}(x^2-1)^p. \tag{3}$$

Note that there is a linear relationship between Legendre moments and regular moments:

$$\lambda_{p,q} = C_{pq} \sum_{u=0}^{p}\sum_{v=0}^{q} a_{pu}a_{qv}M_{u,v}. \tag{4}$$

In practice we limit this representation to a finite order N and we define the shape descriptor as the D-dimensional vector of Legendre moments: $\boldsymbol{\lambda} = \{\lambda_{p,q}, p+q \leq N\}$, where $D = (N+1)(N+2)/2$. Note that this compact description can take into account arbitrary shape topologies.

2.2 Shape Prior Based on Legendre Shape Descriptors

Let us first consider the case where the evolving active contour, Γ, is constrained to evolve toward a *single* reference shape. It is natural to define a shape constraint as a distance d in terms of shape descriptors. Equivalently, in a probabilistic framework, we define a shape prior energy as:

$$J_{prior} = -\log\left(\mathcal{P}(\boldsymbol{\lambda})\right), \tag{5}$$

with:

$$\mathcal{P}(\boldsymbol{\lambda}) \propto \exp\left(-d(\boldsymbol{\lambda}(\Omega_{in}),\boldsymbol{\lambda}^{ref})\right), \tag{6}$$

where Ω_{in} is the inside region of Γ, and $\boldsymbol{\lambda}^{ref}$ is the set of moments of the reference object. In the simplest case d is a quadratic distance. Of course, more elaborate expressions can be used to model arbitrarily complex priors. For example, when N_{ref} reference shapes are simultaneously considered, the above model is extended by defining $\mathcal{P}(\boldsymbol{\lambda})$ as a mixture of pdf's. When d is quadratic and all shapes are equiprobable, this leads to a mixture-of-Gaussians:

$$\mathcal{P}(\boldsymbol{\lambda}) = \frac{1}{N_{ref}}\frac{1}{\sigma\sqrt{2\pi}}\sum_{k=1}^{N_{ref}}\exp\left(-\frac{\|\boldsymbol{\lambda}(\Omega_{in})-\boldsymbol{\lambda}^{ref}_{(k)}\|^2}{2\sigma^2}\right). \tag{7}$$

In this paper, we will consider multiple-reference models involving different *fixed* shapes. Let us notice that eq. (7) is very close to the classical Parzen density estimator, thus the model readily extends to the definition of *statistical shape variabilities*, in the spirit of [10].

2.3 Handling Pose and Geometric Variabilities

Dealing with affine transformations allows to solve the alignment problem since translation, scaling and rotation are included in this group. Moreover, since transformations such as skewing and reflection are also included, this allows the introduction of geometrical variabilities in the model. For this purpose, we define what we call a *canonical* representation. This is, in fact, a change of variables in which two original shapes, differing by a certain transformation, are represented by the same set of moments. Then, using such a representation for both the reference and the evolving shape straightforwardly makes the model invariant w.r.t. the transformation in question. The advantage of this approach is that the change of variable is defined by closed-form expressions involving only geometric moments, i.e. the data at hand during the optimization stage. No additional optimization over pose parameters is necessary.

For example, in the case of scaling and translation, the canonical representation of a shape is obtained by aligning its centroid, $(\bar{x}, \bar{y})$, with the center of the domain and normalizing its area, $|\Omega_{in}|$, to a constant, $1/\beta$. This amounts to using the *normalized central moments* $\eta_{p,q}$ instead of the $M_{p,q}$'s in (4), as proposed in [11].

$$\eta_{p,q} = \iint_{\Omega_{in}} \frac{(x - \bar{x})^p (y - \bar{y})^q}{(\beta |\Omega_{in}|)^{(p+q+2)/2}} \, dx\, dy, \tag{8}$$

$$\text{with} \quad \bar{x} = \frac{M_{1,0}}{M_{0,0}}, \ \bar{y} = \frac{M_{0,1}}{M_{0,0}} \ \text{and} \ |\Omega_{in}| = M_{0,0}. \tag{9}$$

In the more general case of affine invariance, our approach is inspired by the *image normalization* procedure [12]. Consider the so-called *compaction* algorithm, which consists first in aligning the ellipse-of-inertia of the shape with the axes of the coordinate system, then, in applying a non-isotropic scaling to make this ellipse circular. It can be shown [12] that two shapes differing by an affine transformation yield the same *compact* shape, up to a rotation. Compensating for this rotation, we obtain a *normalized* shape, which is identical for all affinely-related shapes. Hence, *image normalization* naturally provides our *canonical* representation. Image normalization itself amounts to an affine transformation, i.e. a translation followed by a linear transformation which can be decomposed as:

$$\begin{bmatrix} \cos\gamma & \sin\gamma \\ -\sin\gamma & \cos\gamma \end{bmatrix} \cdot \begin{bmatrix} l_1 & 0 \\ 0 & l_2 \end{bmatrix} \cdot \begin{bmatrix} \cos\theta & \sin\theta \\ -\sin\theta & \cos\theta \end{bmatrix} \tag{10}$$

As already mentioned, the parameters of the *canonical* representation are given by closed-form expressions involving geometric moments. Following [9] and [12], we have:

$$\theta = \frac{1}{2}\text{atan2}\left(\frac{2\nu_{1,1}}{\nu_{2,0} - \nu_{0,2}}\right) \tag{11}$$

where atan2 is the usual four-quadrant inverse tangent,

$$l_{1/2} = \frac{(\nu_{2,0} + \nu_{0,2}) \pm \sqrt{(\nu_{2,0} - \nu_{0,2})^2 + 4\nu_{1,1}^2}}{2} \tag{12}$$

where the $\nu_{u,v}$'s are the second-order central moments of the original shape, and

$$\gamma = \tan^{-1}\left(-\frac{M^c_{1,2} + M^c_{3,0}}{M^c_{0,3} + M^c_{2,1}}\right) + (1 - \text{sign}(M^c_{0,3} + M^c_{2,1}))\frac{\pi}{2} \qquad (13)$$

where the $M^c_{u,v}$'s are the central moments of the *compact* shape. Image *normalization*, however, does not handle reflection. Since reflection only affects the sign of moments for p odd (reflection w.r.t. y axis) or for q odd (reflection w.r.t. x axis), we choose, without loss of generality, to fix the sign of the third-order moments. *Affine-invariant* moments, yielding the desired *canonical* representation, are finally defined in the following equations:

$$\eta^A_{u,v} = \left(\text{sign}\left(\widehat{\eta}^A_{3,0}\right)\right)^u \cdot \left(\text{sign}\left(\widehat{\eta}^A_{0,3}\right)\right)^v \cdot \widehat{\eta}^A_{u,v}. \qquad (14)$$

where:

$$\widehat{\eta}^A_{u,v} = \frac{(l_1.l_2)^{\frac{u+v}{4}}}{(\beta|\Omega_{in}|)^{(u+v+2)/2}}$$
$$\times \iint_{\Omega_{in}} \left(\frac{((x-\overline{x})\cos\theta + (y-\overline{y})\sin\theta)}{\sqrt{l_1}}\cos\gamma + \frac{((y-\overline{y})\cos\theta - (x-\overline{x})\sin\theta)}{\sqrt{l_2}}\sin\gamma\right)^u$$
$$\times \left(\frac{((y-\overline{y})\cos\theta - (x-\overline{x})\sin\theta)}{\sqrt{l_2}}\cos\gamma - \frac{((x-\overline{x})\cos\theta + (y-\overline{y})\sin\theta)}{\sqrt{l_1}}\sin\gamma\right)^v dxdy.$$
$$(15)$$

Note that a simpler model, that only handles rigid transformations may readily be obtained by setting $\gamma = 0$ and $l_1 = l_2 = 1$ in (15) [1].

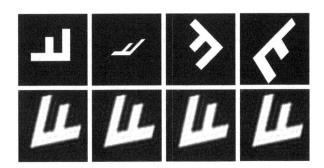

Fig. 1. Reconstruction of shapes from their affine-invariant moments (see text)

Replacing $M_{p,q}$ by $\eta^A_{p,q}$ in (4), we obtain an affine-invariant descriptor that we will denote by λ^A. Fig. (1) shows examples of reconstruction of four shapes from their affine-invariant descriptor up to the 45th order. The four initial letters

---

[1] Handling reflection is still necessary in that case, to avoid ambiguity in the determination of θ.

F shown on the upper row are similar up to affine transformations. As it can be seen on the lower row, the four reconstructed shapes are the same. This corresponds to the *canonical* representation and illustrates the invariance of the proposed descriptor.

Using $\boldsymbol{\lambda}^A$ instead of $\boldsymbol{\lambda}$ in (5), we define a shape prior which benefits from the affine invariance of the descriptor. This shape constraint, based on the characteristic function, handles complex topologies, does not rely on a particular implementation and is intrinsically invariant w.r.t. affine transformations: the prior has a closed-form expression depending only on moments.

3 Active Contour Evolution Equation

The evolution equation for the boundary of Ω_{in} can be derived from the minimization of J_{prior} using the shape derivative framework [8].

3.1 Single-Reference Model

Let us first focus on the case where the shape constraint is a quadratic distance to as single reference shape, described by $\boldsymbol{\lambda}^{ref}$, i.e.:

$$J_{prior}(\Omega_{in}(t)) = \sum_{p,q}^{p+q\leq N} (\lambda_{p,q}(\Omega_{in}(t)) - \lambda_{p,q}^{ref})^2. \tag{16}$$

When the descriptor is invariant w.r.t. translation and scaling, $\boldsymbol{\lambda}$ and $\boldsymbol{\lambda}^{ref}$ are computed from normalized central moments (8), i.e.:

$$\lambda_{p,q} = C_{pq} \sum_{u=0}^{p} \sum_{v=0}^{q} a_{pu} a_{qv} \eta_{u,v}. \tag{17}$$

Applying the strategy described in [8] in order to minimize J_{prior} leads, in this particular case, to the following flow (see [13] for details):

$$\frac{\partial \Gamma}{\partial t} = \underbrace{\sum_{u,v}^{u+v\leq N} A_{uv} \left(H_{uv}(x,y,\Omega_{int}) + \sum_{i=0}^{2} B_{uvi}.L_i(x,y) \right) \mathcal{N}}_{V_{prior}}, \tag{18}$$

where $\mathcal{N}$ is the inward unit normal vector of Γ and:

$$A_{uv} = 2 \sum_{p,q}^{p+q\leq N} (\lambda_{p,q} - \lambda_{p,q}^{ref}) C_{pq} a_{pu} a_{qv}, \tag{19}$$

$$H_{uv}(x,y,\Omega_{in}) = \frac{(x-\bar{x})^u (y-\bar{y})^v}{|\beta \Omega_{in}|^{(u+v+2)/2}}, \tag{20}$$

$$B_{uv0} = \frac{u.\bar{x}.\eta_{u-1,v} + v.\bar{y}.\eta_{u,v-1}}{\beta^{\frac{1}{2}} |\Omega_{in}|^{\frac{3}{2}}} - \frac{(u+v+2).\eta_{u,v}}{2|\Omega_{in}|}, \tag{21}$$

$$B_{uv1} = \frac{-u.\eta_{u-1,v}}{\beta^{\frac{1}{2}} |\Omega_{in}|^{\frac{3}{2}}}, \quad B_{uv2} = \frac{-v.\eta_{u,v-1}}{\beta^{\frac{1}{2}} |\Omega_{in}|^{\frac{3}{2}}}, \tag{22}$$

$$L_0 = 1, \quad L_1 = x, \quad L_2 = y. \tag{23}$$

When taking into account affine invariance in the prior, i.e. using $\boldsymbol{\lambda}^A$, we obtain (see [13] for details):

$$\frac{\partial \Gamma}{\partial t} = \underbrace{\sum_{u,v}^{u+v \leq N} A_{uv}^A \cdot \left(\text{sign} \left(\widehat{\eta}_{3,0}^A \right) \right)^u \cdot \left(\text{sign} \left(\widehat{\eta}_{0,3}^A \right) \right)^v \cdot \left(H_{uv}^A + \sum_{i=0}^{9} \widehat{B}_{uvi}^A \cdot L_i \right)}_{V_{prior}} \mathcal{N}, \quad (24)$$

where the expressions of $\widehat{B}_{u,v,i}^A$ are given in [13] and:

$$A_{uv}^A = 2 \sum_{p,q}^{p+q \leq N} (\lambda_{p,q}^A - \lambda_{p,q}^{Aref}) \cdot C_{pq} a_{pu} a_{qv}, \quad (25)$$

$$H_{uv}^A = \frac{(l_1 \cdot l_2)^{\frac{u+v}{4}}}{(|\beta \Omega_{in}|)^{(u+v+2)/2}}$$

$$\times \left(\frac{((x-\bar{x}) \cos \theta + (y-\bar{y}) \sin \theta)}{\sqrt{l_1}} \cos \gamma + \frac{((y-\bar{y}) \cos \theta - (x-\bar{x}) \sin \theta)}{\sqrt{l_2}} \sin \gamma \right)^u . \quad (26)$$

$$\times \left(\frac{((y-\bar{y}) \cos \theta - (x-\bar{x}) \sin \theta)}{\sqrt{l_2}} \cos \gamma - \frac{((x-\bar{x}) \cos \theta + (y-\bar{y}) \sin \theta)}{\sqrt{l_1}} \sin \gamma \right)^v$$

$$L_0 = 1, \ L_1 = x, \ L_2 = y, \quad (27)$$

$$L_3 = x^2, \ L_4 = y^2, \ L_5 = xy, \quad (28)$$

$$L_6 = x^3, \ L_7 = y^3, \ L_8 = x^2 y, \ L_9 = xy^2. \quad (29)$$

3.2 Multi-reference Model

Let us now consider the multi-reference case. For the sake of conciseness, we present the case of translation and scale invariance, the case of affine invariance being similar. Taking the log in eq. (7) and differentiating leads to an expression similar to (18), but with a different $A_{u,v}$ factor:

$$\frac{\partial \Gamma}{\partial t} = \underbrace{\sum_{u,v}^{u+v \leq N} A_{uv}^{multi} \left(H_{uv}(x,y,\Omega_{int}) + \sum_{i=0}^{2} B_{uvi} \cdot L_i(x,y) \right)}_{V_{prior}} \mathcal{N}, \quad (30)$$

where the expressions of H_{uv}, B_{uvi} and L_i are given by equations (20) to (23). The $A_{u,v}^{multi}$ factor is a weighted average of the individual factors, $A_{(k)uv}$ computed for each reference shape descriptor $\boldsymbol{\lambda}_{(k)}^{ref}$ from (19):

$$A_{uv}^{multi} = \frac{1}{2\sigma^2 \sum_{k=1}^{N_{ref}} \exp \left(\frac{-||\boldsymbol{\lambda} - \boldsymbol{\lambda}_{(k)}^{ref}||^2}{2\sigma^2} \right)} \sum_{k=1}^{N_{ref}} A_{(k)uv} \exp \left(\frac{-||\boldsymbol{\lambda} - \boldsymbol{\lambda}_{(k)}^{ref}||^2}{2\sigma^2} \right). \quad (31)$$

In other words, the force induced by the minimization of J_{prior} in the multi-reference case is a weighted average of the individual forces directed towards each reference shape. Note that the weights decay exponentially with the distance in terms of shape descriptors between the evolving curve and the reference shape.

3.3   Implementation

Both the models and the derivation of the active contour evolution equation
are independent from any implementation consideration. Consequently, (18) or
(24) may be implemented using either a parametric approach, such as spline-
snakes [14], or the non-parametric level set formalism [15]. We use here the latter,
which naturally handles changes of topology.

4   Application to Image Segmentation

We now address the general problem of two-class segmentation. Our purpose
being to illustrate the behavior of the novel prior term, we choose a standard
data functional, which was first introduced by Chan and Vese in [16]:

$$J_{data}(\Omega_{in}, \Omega_{out}) = \iint_{\Omega_{in}} (I(x,y) - \mu_{in})^2 dxdy + \iint_{\Omega_{out}} (I(x,y) - \mu_{out})^2 dxdy, \quad (32)$$

where μ_{in} (resp. μ_{out}) is the (unknown) average intensity in the inside (resp. outside) domain, Ω_{in} (resp. Ω_{out}), and $I(x,y)$ is the intensity value of the pixel. Its
differentiation may be cast in the general framework presented in [8]. Minimizing
the total energy:

$$J(\Omega_{in}, \Omega_{out}) = J_{data}(\Omega_{in}, \Omega_{out}) + \alpha J_{prior}(\Omega_{in}), \quad (33)$$

we obtain:

$$\frac{\partial \Gamma(t)}{\partial t} = \underbrace{((I - \mu_{in})^2 - (I - \mu_{out})^2}_{V_{data}} + \alpha V_{prior}) \mathcal{N}, \quad (34)$$

where V_{prior} is defined in (18), (24) or (30) and μ_{in}, μ_{out} are computed after
each iteration [16].

4.1   Single-Reference Model

We illustrate the behavior of our algorithm on the real image of a partially
occluded rabbit against a cluttered background (Fig. 3). We first evolve the
curve with the region-based energy (32) and an additional standard curvature
component. The result (Fig. 3b) is clearly sensitive to the presence of clutter
and occlusion. We then refine this result, replacing the curvature term by the
shape prior invariant w.r.t. translation and scaling, i.e. evolving according to
(34) with V_{prior} given by (18). We obtain the final result shown in Fig. 3c. The
order of the model, N, is chosen such that the Normalized Mean Squared Error
(NMSE) between the reference shape, shown in Fig. 2 (leftmost image), and the
reconstruction from its descriptor, given by $\sum_{p=0}^{N} \sum_{q=0}^{p} \lambda_{p-q,q}^{ref} P_{p-q}(x) P_q(y)$, is
less than 10%. In the present case, we obtain $N = 40$.

We next consider topologically more complex objects (Fig. 2) against cluttered
background and with occlusions (Fig. 4). As in the previous experiment, we first
evolve the curve with the region-based energy, then we introduce the shape prior.

Fig. 2. Reference shapes used with the single reference model, eq. (6)

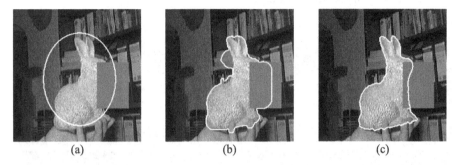

        (a)   (b)   (c)

Fig. 3. Segmentation results on real data (test image: by courtesy of D. Cremers [3]): (a) initial contour, (b) segmentation result without shape prior (standard curvature component used), (c) segmentation result using the single-reference prior (moments up to the 40th-order)

Fig. 4. Segmentation of topologically non-trivial shapes. First row: initial contours (note that they are of different kinds). Second row: results without shape constraint; a curvature term is used for the mug only. Third row: final results, adding the single-reference prior up to the order 40 for the mug and the *stop* sign, up to the order 43 for the *triangle* sign.

The reference shapes are presented on Fig. 2 and the shape prior used in this case is invariant w.r.t. translation and scaling, i.e. V_{prior} is given by (18). Considering for example the third column of Fig. 4, we can see that our prior improves the segmentation result, for a complex shape (the *stop* sign) with important data missing and in presence of noise. Fig. 4 also illustrates the flexibility of our approach w.r.t. the kind of initial curve that is used. Moreover, using the shape constraint, it is possible to overcome the absence of regularization term during the first step of the segmentation.

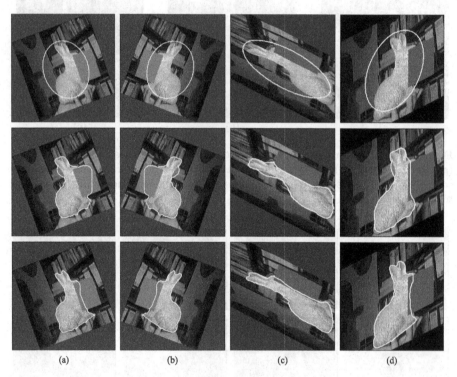

      (a)   (b)   (c)   (d)

Fig. 5. Segmentation of objects with affine deformations. First row: initial contours. Second row: results without shape constraint (standard curvature component used). Third row: final results, adding the single-reference prior up to the order 40. (a) and (b): the prior is invariant w.r.t. translation, rotation, scaling and reflection. (c) and (d): the full affine model is used.

| A | B | C | D | E | F | G | H | I | J | K | L | M |
| N | O | P | Q | R | S | T | U | V | W | X | Y | Z |

Fig. 6. Set of reference shapes used with the multi-reference model, eq. (7)

Finally, results presented Fig. 5 show the ability of our constraint to deal with large affine deformations of the shape. We use here the flow (24) to regularize the segmentation result. The reference shape is the same as in the experiment presented Fig. 3.

4.2   Multi-reference Model

We now illustrate how the model can take into account several reference shapes in a segmentation application. We consider five images (Fig. 7, first row), each one representing a partially occluded letter. The five segmentation results on the fourth row are obtained with the same curve evolution equation for the contour (34), with V_{prior} given by eq. (30). The constraint is invariant w.r.t. translation and scale. The set of reference shapes, shown Fig. 6, consists of 26 letters. The parameter σ is computed from the set $\{\lambda_{(k)}^{ref}\}$ in order to bound the

Fig. 7. Segmentation of five images of letters featuring large occlusions. First row: original images. Second row: initialization. Third row: results without shape constraint (no standard curvature component). Fourth row: final results, adding the multi-reference prior up to the order 40. The same set of parameters is used for the whole experiments.

612 A. Foulonneau, P. Charbonnier, and F. Heitz

classification error probability, $\mathcal{P}_e$, between the two closest reference shapes in terms of descriptors, where:

$$\mathcal{P}_e = \frac{1}{2} \ \text{erfc} \left(\min_{k \neq l} \frac{\sqrt{||\lambda_{(k)}^{ref} - \lambda_{(l)}^{ref}||^2}}{2\sigma\sqrt{2}} \right) \tag{35}$$

In practice, σ is chosen so that $\mathcal{P}_e < 3\%$.

5 Conclusion

In this paper, we have considered Legendre moments to define affine-invariant shape descriptors. Experimental results show that the obtained evolution equation is able to constrain an active contour to evolve toward a reference shape, and provides robustness to clutter and occlusions in image segmentation. The proposed approach also naturally handles pose variations, affine deformations and complex changes of topology. Moreover, it naturally extends to the multiple-reference case, which paves the way for further extensions to the modeling of statistical shape variabilities.

References

1. Terzopoulos, D., Metaxas, D.: Dynamic 3D models with local and global deformations: Deformable superquadrics. IEEE Transactions on Pattern Analysis and Machine Intelligence **13**(7) (1991) 703–714
2. Cootes, T., Cooper, D., Taylor, C., Graham, J.: Active shape models - their training and application. Computer Vision and Image Understanding **61**(1) (1995) 38–59
3. Cremers, D., Kohlberger, T., Schnörr, C.: Shape statistics in kernel space for variational image segmentation. Pattern Recognition : Special Issue on Kernel and Subspace Methods in Computer Vision **36**(9) (2003) 1929–1943
4. Leventon, M., Grimson, W., Faugeras, O.: Statistical shape influence in geodesic active contours. In: Proc. of IEEE Conference on Computer Vision and Pattern Recognition, Hilton Head Island, Southern Carolina, USA (2000) 1316–1323
5. Rousson, M., Paragios, N.: Shape priors for level set representations. In: Proc. of 7th European Conference on Computer Vision, Lecture Notes in Computer Science. Volume 2351., Copenhaguen, Denmark (2002) 78–93
6. Riklin-Raviv, T., Kiryati, N., Sochen, N.: Unlevel-sets : geometry and prior-based segmentation. In: Proc. of the 8th European Conference on Computer Vision, Lecture Notes in Computer Science. Volume 3024., Prague, Czech (2004) 50–61
7. Tsai, A., Yezzi, A., Wells, W., Tempany, C., Tucker, D., Fan, A., Grimson, W., Willsky, A.: A shape-based approach to the segmentation of medical imagery using level sets. IEEE Transactions on Medical Imaging **22**(2) (2003) 137–154
8. Aubert, G., Barlaud, M., Faugeras, O., Jehan-Besson, S.: Image segmentation using active contours: calculus of variations or shape gradients? SIAM, Journal on Applied Mathematics **63**(6) (2003) 2128–2154
9. Teague, M.: Image analysis via the general theory of moments. Journal of the Optical Society of America **70**(8) (1980) 920–930

10. Cremers, D., Osher, S., Soatto, S.: Kernel density estimation and intrinsic alignment for knowledge-driven segmentation: Teaching level sets to walk. In C. Rasmussen et al., ed.: Pattern Recognition Symposium, Springer, Lecture Notes in Computer Science. Volume 3175., Tübingen, Germany (2004) 36–44

11. Foulonneau, A., Charbonnier, P., Heitz, F.: Geometric shape priors for region-based active contours. In: Proc. of IEEE Conference on Image Processing. Volume 3., Barcelona, Spain (2003) 413–416

12. Pei, S., Lin, C.: Image normalization for pattern recognition. Image and Vision Computing **13**(10) (1995) 711–723

13. Foulonneau, A., Charbonnier, P., Heitz, F.: Affine-invariant geometric shape priors for region-based active contours. Technical Report RR-AF01-2005, LRPC ERA 27 LCPC/LSIIT UMR 7005 CNRS (2005) Available online: http://lsiit-miv.u-strasbg.fr/lsiit/perso/Charbonnier.htm.

14. Precioso, F., Barlaud, M.: B-spline active contour with handling of topology changes for fast video segmentation. Eurasip Journal on Applied Signal Processing, special issue: image analysis for multimedia interactive services - PART II **2002**(6) (2002) 555–560

15. Osher, S., Sethian, J.: Fronts propagating with curvature-dependent speed: algorithms based on Hamilton-Jacobi formulations. Journal of Computational Physics **79**(1) (1988) 12–49

16. Chan, T., Vese, L.: Active contours without edges. IEEE Transactions on Image Processing **10**(2) (2001) 266–277

Figure/Ground Assignment in Natural Images

Xiaofeng Ren, Charless C. Fowlkes, and Jitendra Malik

Computer Science Division,
University of California at Berkeley,
Berkeley, CA 94720, USA

Abstract. Figure/ground assignment is a key step in perceptual organization which assigns contours to one of the two abutting regions,
providing information about occlusion and allowing high-level processing to focus on non-accidental shapes of figural regions. In this paper,
we develop a computational model for figure/ground assignment in complex natural scenes. We utilize a large dataset of images annotated with
human-marked segmentations and figure/ground labels for training and
quantitative evaluation.

We operationalize the concept of *familiar configuration* by constructing prototypical local shapes, i.e. *shapemes*, from image data. Shapemes
automatically encode mid-level visual cues to figure/ground assignment
such as convexity and parallelism. Based on the shapeme representation,
we train a logistic classifier to locally predict figure/ground labels. We
also consider a global model using a *conditional random field* (CRF) to
enforce global figure/ground consistency at T-junctions. We use loopy
belief propagation to perform approximate inference on this model and
learn maximum likelihood parameters from ground-truth labels.

We find that the local shapeme model achieves an accuracy of 64%
in predicting the correct figural assignment. This compares favorably to
previous studies using classical figure/ground cues [1]. We evaluate the
global model using either a set of contours extracted from a low-level
edge detector or the set of contours given by human segmentations. The
global CRF model significantly improves the performance over the local model, most notably when using human-marked boundaries (78%).
These promising experimental results show that this is a feasible approach to bottom-up figure/ground assignment in natural images.

1 Introduction

Figure/ground organization, as pioneered by Edgar Rubin [2], is a step of
perceptual organization which assigns a contour to one of the two abutting regions. It is commonly thought to follow region segmentation, it is an essential
step in forming our perception of surfaces, shapes and objects, as vividly demonstrated by the pictures in Figure 1. These pictures are highly ambiguous and we
may perceive either side as the figure and "see" its shape. We always perceive
the ground side as being shapeless and extended behind the figure, never seeing
both shapes simultaneously.

Figure/ground organization is a classical topic in Gestalt psychology, and over
the years many factors have been discovered which play a role in determining

A. Leonardis, H. Bischof, and A. Pinz (Eds.): ECCV 2006, Part II, LNCS 3952, pp. 614–627, 2006.
© Springer-Verlag Berlin Heidelberg 2006

Fig. 1. The figure/ground assignment problem. We perceive that each boundary belongs to one, but not both, of the two abutting regions. The figure side has a "shape" and the ground side is "shapeless", extending behind the figure.

what regions are seen as figural [3]. The most important of these factors include *size, convexity, symmetry, parallelism, surroundedness* and *lower-region* as well as *familiar configuration*. Recent studies in psychophysics show that familiar configurations of contours provide a powerful cue for figure/ground [4], which often dominates more generic cues.

In computer vision, partly due to its lack of immediate applications, figure/ground organization has received little attention. Nevertheless, a few influential studies on figure/ground persist: many focusing on modeling and exploiting global structure such as T-junctions (e.g. [5, 6, 7, 8, 9]), others studying the use of local cues such as convexity (e.g. [10]). Typically such approaches have only been demonstrated on a limited set of images, mostly synthetic.

Fig. 2. Examples from the figure/ground dataset of natural scenes. Each image is first segmented by a human subject; then two human subjects assign figure/ground labels to each boundary in the segmentation. Here the white boundary indicates the figure side and black the ground side. Blue boundaries indicate contours labeled by subjects as not having a clear figure/ground assignment (e.g. surface markings).

In this work we utilize a large dataset of natural images where human subjects provide segmentations as well as figure/ground labels (the Berkeley Figure/Ground Dataset [1]). Figure 2 shows a few images from this dataset, each annotated with a segmentation and corresponding figure/ground labels. The purpose of this work is to address the challenges of figure/ground assignment in such complex natural scenes, in the presence of hierarchical object structure, arbitrary occlusion and texture as well as background clutter and imaging noise.

We propose a two-step approach: a local model using prototypical local shapes to represent context; and a global model using a random field to enforce consistency along contours and junctions. We train both models with human-marked groundtruth data and quantitatively evaluate their performance.

2   Figure/Ground Assignment in Natural Images

A standard view in perceptual organization is that images are first grouped into smooth contours, regions and junctions. Then each contour is assigned to one of the two abutting regions, after which shape analysis and object recognition happen. Recently this theory of sequential processing has been brought into question. Psychophysical experiments suggest that recognition of familiar contour configurations is a powerful figure/ground cue and may occur prior to figure/ground assignment [4]. On the other hand, studies from neurophysiology indicate that figure/ground organization may occur early in the visual pathway [11, 12], long before grouping is completed.

There is, of course, nothing contradictory between these findings and the traditional Gestalt emphasis on global processing. It could well be that informative cues (including familiar shape) are available in the local context of each contour independently extracted quite early. After this initial step, more global structure, such as T-junctions, may be constructed and used to enforce consistency between local figure/ground assignments.

This is the philosophy behind our approach, which is outlined in Figure 3. Starting from an image, first we compute its edge map using the **Pb** (Probability of Boundary) operator [13]. Then we use Geometric Blur [14], a local shape descriptor, to represent the local context around each image location. The representation is in terms of its similarity to set of prototypical local shapes, or **shapemes**, that we find in advance from clustering training data. These similarity terms are then combined using a linear classifier to predict the figure/ground label at each image location. We show that the shapeme-based classifier performs much better than a baseline model using size/convexity.

Next we develop a global figure/ground model which enforces labeling consistency at junctions. First we integrate local figure/ground cues over continuous

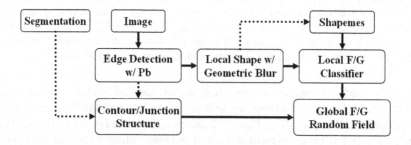

Fig. 3. Summary of our two-stage approach. First we use the **Pb** operator [13] to compute a soft edge map. The Pb map is used to compute local shape descriptors using Geometric Blur [14]. These shape descriptors are clustered into prototypical shapes, or shapemes, which encode rich mid-level visual information. Our local figure/ground model is a logistic classifier based on the shapeme representation. Our global figure/ground model uses a conditional random field to enforce global consistency by learning junction frequency and continuity. It operates either on a human-marked segmentation or thresholded Pb boundaries.

contour segments. We consider the following two cases separately: (1) if we assume that a segmentation is available, we obtain a contour/junction structure from a human-marked segmentation; or (2) if we don't assume to have a segmentation, a contour/junction structure is constructed from bottom-up based on thresholded Pb edges.

We use a *conditional random field* model [15, 16] to build a joint probabilistic model over the figure/ground labels on the complete set of contours segments. Empirical frequencies of junction types (such as valid or invalid T-junction labels), along with continuity of foreground contours, are exploited to correct locally ambiguous labelings. Inference is done with loopy belief propagation. We learn maximum likelihood model parameters with gradient descent.

We quantify the performance of our models by testing them against groundtruth labels. In the case of using human segmentations, each pixel on a human-marked boundary has a figure/ground label, and we count the percentage of figure/ground labels correctly predicted. In the case of bottom-up contour detection, we use the Canny's hysteresis to threshold Pb boundaries and apply a bipartite matching process to "assign" groundtruth labels to each pixel on the Pb boundaries. We then count the percentage of correct predictions of our models on these transferred labels.

3 Local Figure/Ground Model with Shapemes

Many of the classical figure/ground cues are *mid-level* cues. Unlike edge detection, which measures contrast at a point, visual cues such as convexity, parallelism and symmetry are about the relations between points or elements. On the other hand, these cues can still be estimated within a moderately sized neighborhood, without requiring a complete segmentation or recognition of objects.

Such mid-level cues are not trivial to operationalize. Parallelism, symmetry and convexity have precise mathematical definitions but models constructed from mathematical/geometric analysis are seldom flexible enough to cope with the variety of natural phenomenon including noise, texture and clutter. Another challenge with natural scenes is that they often contain multiple objects/parts and hence have a complex junction structure which is impossible to reliably detect using local operators[17].

3.1 Shapemes: Prototypical Shapes

Instead of seeking a mathematical definition for every local figure/ground cue, we take an empirical approach, using a generic shape descriptor to discover **shapemes**, or prototypical shapes, from data. This is in the spirit of Wertheimer's *familiar configuration* and Brunswik's *ecological theory* of Gestalt principles.

We use the Geometric Blur operator [14] to describe local shape. Let I be an input image and E an edge map. The *geometric blur* centered at location x, $GB_x(y)$, is a linear operator applied to E whose value is another image given by the "convolution" of E with a spatially varying Gaussian. GB_x has the property that points farther away from x are more blurred, making the descriptor robust

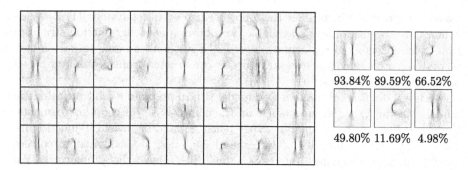

93.84% 89.59% 66.52%

49.80% 11.69% 4.98%

Fig. 4. Shapemes, or clusters of local shapes from a set of human-marked boundaries of baseball players. Shown here are the average shapes in each cluster. We find that shapemes encode rich contextual information, such as parallelism (row 1, col 1), convexity (row 1, col 2), sharp corners (row 2, col 3) or straight lines (row 2, col 5). On the right we show a few shapemes and the percentage of the shapes in each cluster that have the left side as figure. Empirical data confirm that mid-level cues such as parallelism or convexity are very useful for figure/ground assignment; figure/ground labelings are heavily biased in such cases.

to affine distortions. The value $GB_x(y)$ is the inner product of E with a Gaussian centered at y whose standard deviation is $\alpha|y - x|$. We rotate the blurred image GB_x so that the locally estimated contour orientation at x is always vertical. We choose $\alpha = 0.5$ and sample the blurred and rotated image GB_x at 4 different radii (increasing by a factor of $\sqrt{2}$) and 12 orientations, to obtain a feature vector of length 48.

We then cluster these Geometric Blur descriptors to find prototypical shapes, or shapemes. The use of shapemes was first introduced in [18] as a means to efficiently index and retrieve object specific shapes. Here we use shapemes in a rather different way, as a representation derived from data to capture mid-level cues. Our shapemes also differ in that they are orientation-independent, as we align them to local boundary orientations. This allows us to encode rich contextual information with a small set of shapemes.

To illustrate the concept, Figure 4 visualizes 32 shapemes constructed (using k-means) from a simpler database containing silhouettes of baseball player photos [19]. We find that mid-level cues such as convexity and parallelism are implicitly captured in the shapemes, making it an appealing representation for figure/ground organization.

For experiments on the more complex Berkeley Figure/Ground Dataset, we use 64 shapemes constructed from Pb edge maps and modeled as a mixture of Gaussians. For each local shape, we use the mixture of Gaussian to obtain a feature vector f of dimension 64, which is the log posterior probability of each component mixture. We use these features to predict a binary label $Y \in \{-1, 1\}$ indicating which side is figure and which side is ground, a binary classification problem. A logistic classifier is fit to the human-marked labels using standard iteratively re-weighted least squares.

4   Global Figure/Ground Model with Conditional Random Fields

Although local shape is quite informative, figure/ground organization is not a local phenomenon. Contour form parts of object boundaries in the scene, and they interact through junctions and regions. One classical problem in the early days of computer vision is the labeling of line drawings. There, T-junctions are probably the most important cue in interpreting objects and scenes. Following this tradition, many previous studies focus on the global inference of figure/ground relations through junctions [5, 6, 7, 8, 9].

In the previous section we have shown that shapemes encode rich mid-level cues and can be used to construct a local model for figure/ground organization. To combine local cues and enforce global consistency, we assume that we have a discrete graph structure of the image, as shown in Figure 5(a), where edge pixels form contours and contours join to form junctions. This structure may either come from a human-marked segmentation or, as we will show in the next section, from a thresholded edge map.

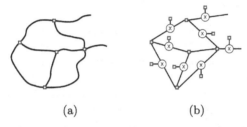

(a)   (b)

Fig. 5. Global inference of figure/ground assignments. Suppose we have a discrete contour/junction structure as in (a), which comes either from a human-marked segmentation or from thresholded Pb edge maps. We use a conditional random field to enforce global consistency of the figure/ground labels on individual edges. (b) shows the factor graph of our probabilistic model corresponding to the edge structure in (a). Edge potentials combine evidence from the local figure/ground model. Junction potentials ensure that the figure/ground labels are consistent with one another, forming valid junctions.

We use a *conditional random field* (CRF) model for global figure/ground inference on this discrete structure. Conditional random fields were first introduced by [15] for natural language processing, and have been shown to outperform traditional Markov Random Fields in many domains. It has been previously applied to image labeling [20, 21], as well as contour completion [16].

For every contour e in the image, the local model provides us with an estimate p_e, the probability that the "left" side of e is figure (averaged over all pixels on e). We associate with e a ternary variable X_e, where $X_e = 1$ if the "left" side of e is figure, $X_e = -1$ if the "right" side is figure, or $X_e = 0$ if neither (e.g. a surface marking). Let X_V be the collection of variables for all contours which join at a junction V in the graph. We consider an exponential family distribution over the collection of edges of the form

$$P(X|I,\Theta) = \frac{1}{Z(I,\Theta)} \exp \left\{ \sum_e \phi(X_e|I,\Theta) + \sum_V \psi(X_V|I,\Theta) \right\} \qquad (1)$$

where ϕ is a unary potential function on each contour e, ψ a potential function on each junction X_V, and Θ is the collection of model parameters. An example factor graph, showing the conditional independence structure of our CRF model, is illustrated in Figure 5(b).

The contour potential ϕ incorporates local figure/ground evidence, defined as $\phi(X_e) = \beta X_e log(\frac{p_e}{1-p_e})$, where p_e is the local estimate that the "left" side of e is figure.

The junction potential ψ assigns a weight to each distinctive "junction type". Suppose a junction V contains k contours $\{e_1, \cdots, e_k\}$, sorted in a clock-wise way, with a figure/ground label assignment X_V (we do not consider any contour with a label $X_e = 0$). The type of the junction V can be represented by a vector of dimension k: $T(X_V) = \{X_{e_1}, \cdots, X_{e_k}\}$. We define

$$\psi(X_V) = \sum_{t \in T_a} \alpha_t \cdot 1_{\{T(X_V)=t\}} + \sum_{t \in T_c} \gamma \cdot \theta(X_V) \cdot 1_{\{T(X_V)=t\}} \qquad (2)$$

where T_a is the set of all possible junction types, and T_c is a subset of junction types on which a continuity term θ may be defined (explained below).

Figure 6 shows a few examples of junction types. Intuitively, junction types (a) and (d) are sensible junction labelings, (a) being a continuation of contours, and (d) being a classical T-junction; while junction types (b) and (c) seem highly unlikely. We can count the empirical frequencies of these junction types; and indeed we find that type (a) and (d) are much more common than (b) and (c).

In order to analyze junctions, we need to know the geometric configuration in addition to its type. For example, in a T-junction, we need to know which two contours form the "top" of the "T". This is accomplished by defining a continuity term between a pair of contours. For junction type (d), we know from

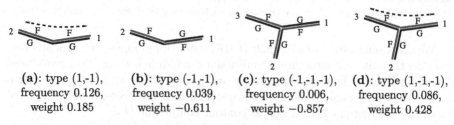

(a): type (1,-1), frequency 0.126, weight 0.185

(b): type (-1,-1), frequency 0.039, weight −0.611

(c): type (-1,-1,-1), frequency 0.006, weight −0.857

(d): type (1,-1,-1), frequency 0.086, weight 0.428

Fig. 6. A number of junction types, red indicating the figure side and blue the ground. Each type is represented by its set of figure/ground labels collected in a clockwise way. The empirical frequencies of these junction types confirm that type (a) and (d) are common junction labelings but (b) and (c) are uncommon. This is encoded into the CRF model parameters by maximum likelihood learning. For type (a) and (d), we may define a continuity term θ, which is the angle between the two contours that belong to the foreground.

the figure/ground labels that the contours 1 and 3 form the boundary of the foreground object, while the contour 2 is an occluded contour in the background. Therefore the continuity of this junction is the angle between the contours 1 and 3. We also use continuity in junction type (a) by measuring the angle between the two contours.

Because the contour/junction graph typically contains many loops, exact inference on the CRF model is intractable. We perform approximate inference using loopy belief propagation to estimate marginal posterior distributions of the figure/ground labels X_e. We then assign a binary figure/ground label to a contour e (hence all the pixels on e), the figure being on its "left" side if $P(X_e = 1) > P(X_e = -1)$, or otherwise the "right" side. In our experiments, we find loopy belief propagation converges quickly (< 10 iterations) to a reasonable solution.

We fit the model parameters $\Theta = \{\alpha, \beta, \gamma\}$ using maximum likelihood criterion. The partial derivatives of the log-likelihood take on a simple form as the difference between two expectations. For example,

$$\frac{\partial}{\partial \alpha_t} \log \left(\frac{1}{Z(I, \Theta)} \exp \left\{ \sum_e \phi(X_e | I, \Theta) + \sum_V \psi(X_V | I, \Theta) \right\} \right)$$

$$= \sum_V \mathbf{1}_{\{T(X_V)=t\}} - \left\langle \sum_V \mathbf{1}_{\{T(X_V)=t\}} \right\rangle_{P(X|I,\Theta)}$$

where the first term is the empirical frequency of junction type t, and the second term is the frequency of type t under the current parameter setting. Learning parameters with simple gradient descent converges quickly (< 500 iterations).

5   Figure/Ground Assignment Without Segmentation

The figure/ground models we have introduced are based on the assumption that figure/ground organization occurs after region grouping. Using human-marked segmentations, these models provide valuable insights into the figure/ground process, such as relative powers of the local and global cues involved. To utilize these cues in a practical algorithm, however, we need to compute a segmentation first. Unfortunately, segmentation is a hard problem itself and requires the use of all available visual information, potentially including figure/ground cues.

In this section we replace the human segmentation with a bottom-up grouping process based directly on edge detection. There are two main questions that need to be addressed:

1. The groundtruth labels in the dataset are all given on human-marked boundaries. How do we transfer these labels to a set of (potentially mislocalized) edges, so that we may train and test our models as before?
2. The global conditional random field model requires a discrete contour/ junction graph structure. How do we construct such a structure from the image?

To transfer groundtruth labels, we run a bipartite matching between pixels on human-marked boundaries and pixels on Pb edge maps, illustrated in Figure 7 (a). For each Pb edge pixel, we have an estimate of the local orientation at that location. We then look at the matched pixel on human-marked boundary, compute its figure/ground label at that particular orientation, and transfer it to the Pb pixel. Figure 7(b) shows a few examples from this matching process.

(a)   (b)

Fig. 7. Transferring groundtruth labels to Pb edge maps. (a) a bipartite matching establishes the correspondence between thresholded Pb edges and human-marked boundaries. This correspondence determines the figure/ground label on each Pb pixel, at its local orientation. (b) examples of the transferred groundtruth labels. White indicates that "left" is the figure side, black the ground side; blue pixels are either not matched, or matched to a boundary with no figure/ground labels (not used in evaluation).

To construct a discrete junction structure on which our conditional random field model can be applied, we use Canny's hysteresis thresholding to trace salient contours in Pb edge maps. Junctions are discovered during the process when two or more contours join. A heuristic is used which merges two vertices when they are sufficiently close to each other.

Pb edge maps have nice non-maximum suppression properties so a naive contour tracing approach suffices most of the time. Figure 8 shows an example of the resulting contour/junction graph, alongside the human-marked segmentation. Our conditional random field model can directly apply to either of these discrete structures.

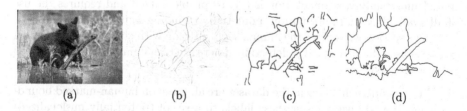

(a)   (b)   (c)   (d)

Fig. 8. Constructing contour/junction structure (c) from thresholded Pb edge maps (b). Contours are marked in black and junctions in red. Such a discrete structure allows global inference on junction consistencies. However, bottom-up contours are much more fragmented and not nearly as clean (and useful) as the human-marked boundaries (d).

6   Experimental Results

The figure/ground dataset we use for both training and testing include 200 Corel images of size 321×481. Human subjects provide one segmentation for each image as well as two sets of figure/ground labels. We use 100 images for training and 100 for testing.

We test the performance of four models: a baseline size/convexity model, the local shapeme model, the local shapeme model averaged on continuous contours, and the global conditional random field model. Each model provides a binary figure/ground label on boundary pixels, and we count the percentage of correct predictions. Surface markings are excluded in these experiments. The models are evaluated in two cases, with or without using human-marked segmentations. Chance is 50%. Since each image is labeled by multiple human subjects, we can measure the labeling consistency between human subjects. For this dataset the self-consistency is 88%.

The baseline size/convexity model is constructed in the following way. Given a segmentation, suppose p is a pixel on a contour c between two segments S_1 and S_2. Let D be a disk around p with a radius r. We can measure the area of overlap $A_1 = |D \cap S_1|$ and $A_2 = |D \cap S_2|$: if the area $A_1 < A_2$, then we label S_1

Table 1. Performance evaluation based on human-marked segmentations. The baseline size/convexity model has difficulties around junctions. Its performance slowly increases with scale/radius, capped at 55.6%. The shapeme model, incorporating convexity, parallelism and textureness, performs much better than the baseline. Averaging local cues over human-marked boundaries proves to suppress noise and significantly increase the performance. The global CRF model, by enforcing labeling consistency at T-junctions, performs the best, achieving 78.3% accuracy.

Chance	Size/ Convexity	Local Shapeme	Averaging Shapemes on Contours	Global CRF	Dataset Consistency
50%	55.6%	64.8%	72.0%	78.3%	88%

Table 2. Performance evaluation based on Pb boundaries. Without the knowledge of a segmentation, the baseline size/convexity model cannot be applied. The local shapeme model, based solely on local image-based descriptors, performs as good as in the case with human-marked boundaries. The global models, however, are severely handicapped without a perfect segmentation. The contour/junction structure constructed from edge maps is useful at enforcing global consistencies (4% improvement); but as it is much more fragmented and noisy than the set of human-marked boundaries, the benefit of global integration is much smaller. Clearly, a more sophisticated contour/region grouping algorithm is needed here to produce better junction structures.

Chance	Size/ Convexity	Local Shapeme	Averaging Shapemes on Contours	Global CRF	Dataset Consistency
50%	n/a	64.9%	66.5%	68.9%	88%

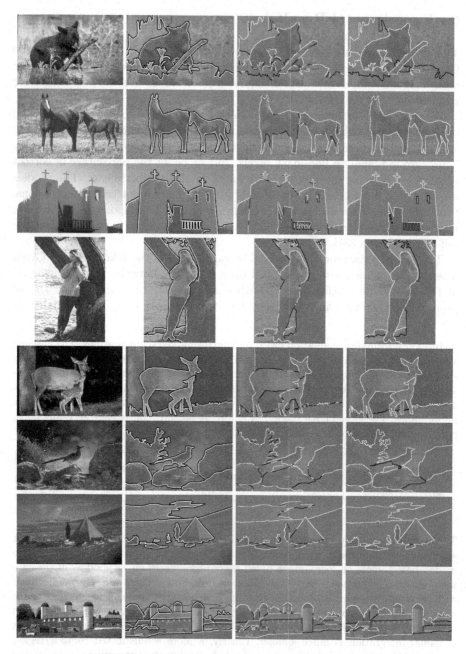

Fig. 9. Results based on human-marked boundaries. Shown here are the images, the groundtruth labels (white being the figure, black the ground, blue neither), figure/ground labels from the local shapeme model (white being correct, black incorrect; average accuracy 64.8%), and labels from the global CRF model (average accuracy 78.3%). The global model performs well in most cases, suggesting that figure/ground assignment in natural images is a feasible problem, if a good segmentation is available.

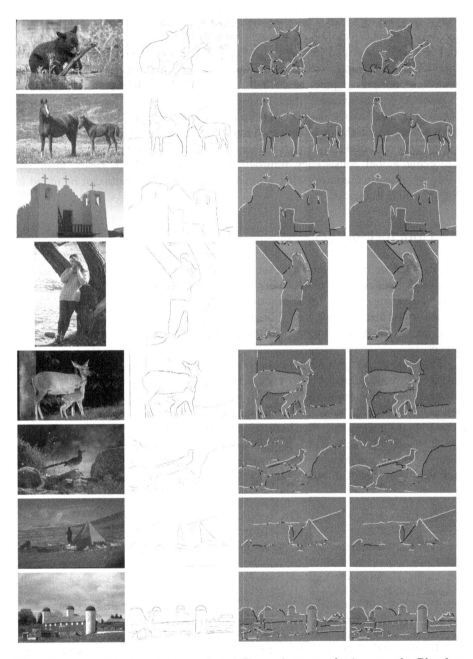

Fig. 10. Results based on Pb boundaries. Shown here are the images, the Pb edge map, figure/ground labels from the local shapeme model (average accuracy 64.9%), and labels from the global CRF model (average accuracy 68.9%). Without using human-marked segmentations, the results are more noisy and less consistent. Nevertheless the local shapeme model applies without any difficulty, and global inference on a bottom-up contour/junction structure still significantly improves performance.

as figure, and vice versa. This simple size cue is closely correlated with convexity (convex regions typically have a smaller size, if the boundary is smooth enough) and has been shown to perform well on this dataset without interference with junctions [1]. This cue, however, relies on the availability of a segmentation and performs poorly near junctions.

Table 1 lists the average labeling accuracy for the case of using human-marked segmentations. Table 2 lists the results in the case of bottom-up contour detection. We find that the local shapeme model performs well in both cases, achieving an accuracy of 64.8%, much higher than the baseline size/convexity model. Enforcing global consistency improves performance in both cases, most notably when using human-marked segmentations. Sample results can be found in Figure 9 and Figure 10.

7 Conclusion

In this work we have developed a model for figure/ground assignment in natural images using shapemes to represent context and a conditional random field to enforce labeling consistency at junctions. We train and test our models on a large dataset of natural images with human-marked groundtruth data, using either a high-quality segmentation or a bottom-up edge detector to determine junction structure.

The local figure/ground prediction based on shapemes performs well in both cases, comparing favorably to previous studies using classical Gestalt figure/ground cues. Shapemes automatically discover contextual cues such as parallelism or convexity, and are robust to complex variability in natural images. The global CRF model significantly improves the performance, most notably when using human-marked boundaries. Experimental results suggest that figure/ground assignment in natural images is a feasible problem and a good segmentation algorithm would greatly facilitate figure/ground organization.

References

1. Fowlkes, C., Martin, D., Malik, J.: On measuring the ecological validity of local figure/ground cues. In: ECVP. (2003)
2. Rubin, E.: Visuell wahrgenommene figuren. In: Kobenhaven: Glydenalske boghandel. (1921)
3. Palmer, S.: Vision Science: Photons to Phenomenology. MIT Press (1999)
4. Peterson, M.A., Gibson, B.S.: Must figure-ground organization precede object recognition? an assumption in peril. Psychological Science 5 (1994) 253–259
5. Kienker, P.K., Sejnowski, T.J., Hinton, G.E., Schumacher, L.E.: Separating figure from ground with a parallel network. Perception 15 (1986) 197–216
6. Heitger, F., von der Heydt, R.: A computational model of neural contour processing: figure-ground segregation and illusory contours. In: ICCV, Berlin, Germany (1993) 32–40
7. Geiger, D., Kumaran, K., Parida, L.: Visual organization for figure/ground separation. In: CVPR. (1996) 155–160

8. Saund, E.: Perceptual organization of occluding contours of opaque surfaces. CVIU Special Issue on Perceptual Organization (1999) 70–82
9. S. Yu, T.L., Kanade, T.: A hierarchical markov random field model for figure-ground segregation. In: EMM CVPR 01. (2001) 118–133
10. Pao, H.K., Geiger, D., Rubin, N.: Measuring convexity for figure/ground separation. In: ICCV. (1999) 948–955
11. Lamme, V.A.F.: The neurophysiology of figure-ground segregation in primary visual cortex. Journal of Neuroscience 15 (1995) 1605–1615
12. Zhou, H., Friedman, H.S., von der Heydt, R.: Coding border ownership in monkey visual cortex. Journal of Neuroscience 20 (2000) 6594–6611
13. Martin, D., Fowlkes, C., Malik, J.: Learning to detect natural image boundaries using brightness and texture. In: Advances in Neural Information Processing Systems 15. (2002)
14. Berg, A., Malik, J.: Geometric blur for template matching. In: CVPR. (2001)
15. Lafferty, J., McCallum, A., Pereira, F.: Conditional random fields: Probabilistic models for segmenting and labeling sequence data. In: Proc. 18th International Conf. on Machine Learning. (2001)
16. Ren, X., Fowlkes, C., Malik, J.: Scale-invariant contour completion using conditional random fields. In: ICCV. (2005)
17. McDermott, J.: Psychophysics with junctions in real images. Perception 33 (2004) 1101–1127
18. Mori, G., Belongie, S., Malik, J.: Shape contexts enable efficient retrieval of similar shapes. In: CVPR. Volume 1. (2001) 723–730
19. Mori, G., Ren, X., Efros, A., Malik, J.: Recovering human body configurations: Combining segmentation and recognition. In: CVPR. Volume 2. (2004) 326–333
20. Kumar, S., Hebert, M.: Discriminative random fields: A discriminative framework for contextual interaction in classification. In: ICCV. (2003) 1150–1159
21. He, X., Zemel, R., Carreira-Perpinan, M.: Multiscale conditional random fields for image labelling. In: CVPR. Volume 2. (2004) 695–702

Background Cut

Jian Sun, Weiwei Zhang, Xiaoou Tang, and Heung-Yeung Shum

Microsoft Research Asia, Beijing, P.R. China
{jiansun, weiweiz, xitang, hshum}@microsoft.com

Abstract. In this paper, we introduce *background cut*, a high quality and real-time foreground layer extraction algorithm. From a single video sequence with a moving foreground object and stationary background, our algorithm combines background subtraction, color and contrast cues to extract a foreground layer accurately and efficiently. The key idea in background cut is *background contrast attenuation*, which adaptively attenuates the contrasts in the background while preserving the contrasts across foreground/background boundaries. Our algorithm builds upon a key observation that the contrast (or more precisely, color image gradient) in the background is dissimilar to the contrast across foreground/background boundaries in most cases. Using background cut, the layer extraction errors caused by background clutter can be substantially reduced. Moreover, we present an adaptive mixture model of global and per-pixel background colors to improve the robustness of our system under various background changes. Experimental results of high quality composite video demonstrate the effectiveness of our background cut algorithm.

1 Introduction

Layer extraction [2, 20] has long been a topic of research in computer vision. In recent work [8], Kolmogorov et al. showed that the foreground layer can be very accurately and efficiently (near real time) extracted from a binocular stereo video in a teleconferencing scenario. One application of foreground layer extraction is high quality live background substitution. The success of their approach arises from a probabilistic fusion of multiple cues, i.e, stereo, color, and contrast.

In real visual communication scenario, e.g., teleconferencing or instant messaging, however, most users have only a single web camera. So, can we achieve a similar quality foreground layer extraction using a single web camera? For an arbitrary scene (e.g. non-static background), automatically foreground layer extraction is still a monumental challenge to the current state of the art [21, 23]. To facilitate progress in this area, we address a somewhat constrained but widely useful real world problem in this paper — high quality, real-time foreground extraction (or background removal) from a single camera with a known, stationary background.

To address this problem, the most efficient approach is background subtraction. Background subtraction detects foreground objects as the difference between the current image and the background image. Nevertheless, there are two issues in background subtraction: 1) the threshold in background subtraction is very sensitive to noise and background illuminance changes. A larger threshold detects fewer foreground pixels and vice versa. 2) foreground color and background color might be

A. Leonardis, H. Bischof, and A. Pinz (Eds.): ECCV 2006, Part II, LNCS 3952, pp. 628–641, 2006.

very similar, resulting in holes in detected foreground object. More sophisticated techniques [7, 22, 1, 6, 17, 16, 14, 11, 12, 18] have been proposed to overcome these problems. But the results are still error-prone and not accurate enough for high quality foreground extraction required in our application because most of these methods make local decisions. Figure 2 (b) shows a background subtraction result. Postprocessing (e.g, morphological operations) may help but cannot produce an accurate and coherent foreground.

Recent interactive image and video segmentation techniques [15, 10, 19, 9] have shown the powerful effectiveness of the color/contrast based model proposed by Boykov et al. [3]. The color/contrast based model considers both color similarity to manually obtained foreground/background color models and contrast (or edge) strength along the segmentation boundary. The final foreground layer is globally determined using the min-cut algorithm. But, as demonstrated in [8], using only color and contrast cues is insufficient.

Therefore, a straightforward solution is to combine the above two techniques - building foreground and background color models from background subtraction and then applying the color/contrast based model. Because the background image is known and stationary, the background color model can be modeled as a mixture of a global color model and a more accurate per-pixel color model, as done in [8] and [19]. This combination can produce a more accurate segmentation result. We refer to this as the basic model.

However, there are still problems in the basic model. Since the basic model considers both color and contrast simultaneously, the final segmentation boundary will inevitably be snapped or attracted to high contrast edges in a cluttered background, more or less as shown in Figure 2 (c). Though this kind of error may be small around the boundary

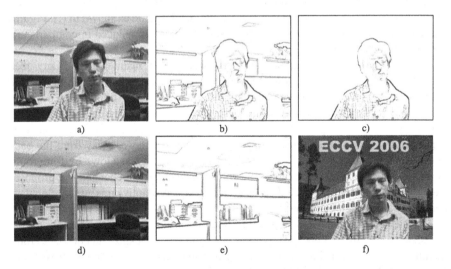

a)   b)   c)

d)   e)   f)

Fig. 1. Background Cut. (a) an image I in a video sequence. (b) contrast map of I. (c) attenuated contrast map by our approach. (d) the background image I^B. (e) contrast map of I^B. (f) our final foreground extraction result using attenuated contrast map.

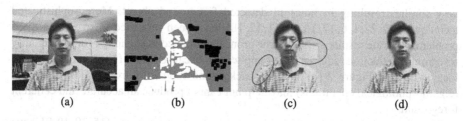

       (a)   (b)   (c)   (d)

Fig. 2. Foreground layer extraction by different approaches. (a) an image in a video sequence. (b) background subtraction result. Threshold is set to a conservative value to avoid classifying more pixels to foreground. (c) color/contrast-based segmentation result. Red circles indicate notable segmentation errors. (d) our result.

or only occur in partial frames, the flickering artifact in the video due to this error can be very distractive and unpleasant in the final composite video.

In this paper, we propose an new approach, "background cut", to address the above issue in the basic model. The novel component in background cut is "background contrast attenuation" which can substantially reduce the segmentation errors caused by high contrast edges in the clutter background. Background contrast attenuation is based on an key observation that the contrast from background is dissimilar to the contrast caused by foreground/background boundaries in most cases. Figure 1 (b) and (e) show contrast maps of current image and background image respectively. Notice that most contrasts caused by foreground/background boundaries in (b) is not consistent with the contrasts in (e). Based on this observation, background contrast attenuation adaptively modified the contrast map in (b) to produce an attenuated contrast map in (c). Most contrasts from background are removed while contrasts caused by foreground/background boundaries are well preserved. Using this attenuated contrast map, background cut can extract high quality foreground layer from clutter background as shown in (f). Figure 2 (d) also shows that segmentation errors can be significantly reduced in comparison to the basic model.

Another challenge in real scenarios is background maintenance. Many techniques [7, 22, 1, 6, 17, 16, 14, 11, 12, 18] have been proposed to handle various changes in the background, e.g, gradual and sudden illuminance change (light switch in office), small moving objects in the background (e.g, moving curtain), casual camera shaking (e.g, webcame on laptop), sleeping object (an object moves into the background and then becomes motionless), waking object (an object that moves away from the background and reveals new parts of the background), and cast shadows by foreground. To make our system more practical and robust to background changes, we propose a background maintenance scheme based on modeling an adaptive mixture of global and per-pixel background color model.

The paper is organized as follows. In Section 2, we give notations and introduce the basic model. In Section 3, we present our approach - background cut. Background maintenance is described in Section 4 and experimental results are shown in Section 5. Finally, we discuss the limitations of our current approach and give conclusions in Section 6.

2   Notation and Basic Model

Let I^B be the known background image and I be the image at the current timestep that is to be processed. I_r^B and I_r are color values of pixel r in I^B and I respectively. Let $\mathcal{V}$ be the set of all pixels in I and $\mathcal{E}$ be the set of all adjacent pixel pairs (4 neighbors or 8 neighbors) in I. Foreground/background segmentation can be posed as a binary *labeling* problem — to assign a unique label x_r to each pixel $r \in \mathcal{V}$, i.e. $x_r \in \{\text{foreground}(= 1), \text{background}(= 0)\}$. The labeling variables $X = \{x_r\}$ can be obtained by minimizing a Gibbs energy $E(X)$ [3]:

$$E(X) = \sum_{r \in \mathcal{V}} E_1(x_r) + \lambda \sum_{(r,s) \in \mathcal{E}} E_2(x_r, x_s), \qquad (1)$$

where $E_1(x_i)$ is the color term, encoding the cost when the label of pixel r is x_r, and $E_2(x_r, x_s)$ is the contrast term, denoting the cost when the labels of adjacent nodes r and s are x_r and x_s respectively. The parameter λ balances the influences of the two terms.

2.1   Basic Model

Color term. To model the likelihood of each pixel r belonging to foreground or background, a foreground color model $p(I_r|x = 1)$ and a background color model $p(I_r|x = 0)$ are learned from samples. Both models are represented by spatially global Gaussian mixture models (GMMs).

The global background color model $p(I_r|x = 0)$ can be directly learned from the known background image I^B:

$$p(I_r|x = 0) = \sum_{k=1}^{K_b} w_k^b N(I_r|\mu_k^b, \Sigma_k^b), \qquad (2)$$

where $N(\cdot)$ is a Gaussian distribution and $(w_k^b, \mu_k^b, \Sigma_k^b)$ represents the weight, the mean color, and the covariance matrix of the kth component of the background GMMs. The typical value of K_b is 10-15 for the background. For stationary background, a per-pixel single isotopic Gaussian distribution $p_B(I_r)$ is also used to model the background color more precisely:

$$p_B(I_r) = N(I_r|\mu_r^B, \Sigma_r^B), \qquad (3)$$

where $\mu_r^B = I_r^B$ and $\Sigma_r^B = \sigma_r^2 I$. The per-pixel variance σ_r^2 is learned from a background initialization phase. The per-pixel color model is more precise than the global color model but is sensitive to noise, illuminance change, and small movement of background. The global background color model is less precise but more robust. Therefore, an improved approach is to mix the two models:

$$p_{mix}(I_r) = \alpha \cdot p(I_r|x = 0) + (1 - \alpha) \cdot p_B(x_r) \qquad (4)$$

where α is a mixing factor for the global and per-pixel background color models.

The global foreground color model is learned from background subtraction. With a per-pixel background color model, we can mark the pixel that has a very low background probability as "definitely foreground". Let B, F, U represent "definitely background", "definitely foreground" and "uncertainty region" respectively, we have:

$$I_r = \begin{cases} B & p_B(I_r) > t_b \\ F & p_B(I_r) < t_f \\ U & otherwises \end{cases} \tag{5}$$

where t_b and t_f are two thresholds. Then, the global foreground color model $p(I_r|x_r = 1)$ is learned from the pixels in F. In order to enforce temporal coherence, we also sample the pixels from the intersection of F and the labeled foreground region (after segmentation) in the frame at the previous timestep. The component number in the global foreground color model is set to 5 in our experiments because foreground colors are usually simpler than background colors.

Finally, the color term is defined as:

$$E_1(x_r) = \begin{cases} -\log p_{mix}(I_r) & x_r = 0 \\ -\log p(I_r|x_r = 1) & x_r = 1 \end{cases} . \tag{6}$$

Contrast term. For two adjacent pixels r and s, the contrast term $E_2(x_r, x_s)$ between them is defined as:

$$E_2(x_r, x_s) = |x_r - x_s| \cdot \exp(-\beta d_{rs}), \tag{7}$$

where $d_{rs} = ||I_r - I_s||^2$ is the L_2 norm of the color difference, which we call *contrast* in this paper. β is a robust parameter that weights the color contrast, and can be set to $\beta = (2\langle||I_r - I_s||^2\rangle)^{-1}$ [15], where $\langle \cdot \rangle$ is the expectation operator. Note that the factor $|x_r - x_s|$ allows this term to capture the contrast information only along the segmentation boundary. In other words, the contrast term E_2 is the penalty term when adjacent pixels are assigned with different labels. The more similar the colors of the two adjacent pixels are, the larger contrast term E_2 is, and thus the less likely the edge is on the object boundary.

To minimize the energy $E(X)$ in Equation (1), we use the implementation of the min-cut algorithm in [4].

3   Background Cut

The basic model usually produces good results in most frames. However, when the scene contains background clutter, notable segmentation errors around the boundary often occur. This generates flickering artifacts in video. The top row of Figure 3 shows several frames in a video and the third row shows segmentation results by the basic model. Notable segmentation errors are marked by red circles. Why does this happen? The reason is that the basic model contains two terms for both color and contrast. Inevitably, high contrasts (strong edges) from the background will bias the final segmentation result. The second row in Figure 3 shows the corresponding contrast maps[1] of input frames. Notice that most incorrect segmentation boundaries pass strong edges in background. These errors are mainly caused by the contrast term in the basic model:

$$E_2(x_r, x_s) = |x_r - x_s| \cdot \exp(-\beta \cdot d_{rs}). \tag{8}$$

How to fix this bias? More specifically, can we remove or attenuate the contrasts in the background to obtain more accurate segmentation results?

---

[1] For display, the contrast for each pixel r is computed as $\sqrt{d_{r,r_x} + d_{r,r_y}}$, where r_x and r_y are two adjacent pixels on the left and above pixel r.

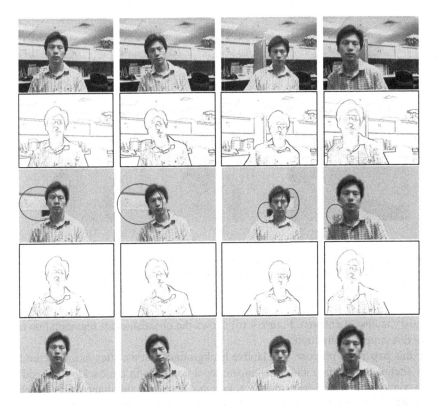

Fig. 3. Background contrast attenuation. Top row: several frames from a video. Second row: contrast maps. Third row: segmentation results by the basic model. Red circles indicate notable segmentation errors. Fourth row: attenuated contrast maps. Last row: segmentation result using attenuated contrast map.

3.1 Background Contrast Attenuation

Because the background is known, a straightforward idea is to subtract the contrast of the background image I^B from the contrast of the current image I. To avoid hard thresholding and motivated by anisotropic diffusion [13], we attenuate the contrast between two adjacent pixels (r, s) in image I from $d_{rs} = ||I_r - I_s||^2$ to d'_{rs} by the contrast $||I_r^B - I_s^B||^2$ in the background image:

$$d'_{rs} = ||I_r - I_s||^2 \cdot \frac{1}{1 + \left(\frac{||I_r^B - I_s^B||}{K}\right)^2}, \qquad (9)$$

where K is a constant to control the strength of attenuation. The larger the contrast $||I_r^B - I_s^B||^2$ is in the background, the more attenuation is applied on the contrast $||I_r - I_s||^2$ in image I. Figure 4 (a) and (c) show the contrast maps before and after this soft contrast subtraction. Unfortunately, the contrast caused by the foreground/background

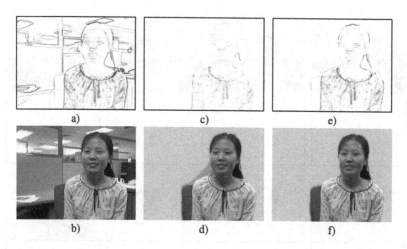

a)   c)   e)

b)   d)   f)

Fig. 4. Adaptive contrast attenuation. (a) contrast map of image I. (b) an image I in a video sequence. (c) and (d) attenuated contrast map and segmentation result using Equation (9). (e) and (f) adaptively attenuated contrast map and segmentation result using Equation (10).

boundary is also attenuated. Figure 4 (d) shows the unsatisfactory segmentation result using this simple subtraction.

In this paper, we propose an adaptive background contrast attenuation method. An ideal attenuation method should attenuate most contrasts in the background and preserve contrasts along the foreground/background boundary simultaneously. To achieve this goal, we define the following method to adaptively preform background contrast attenuation:

$$d''_{rs} = ||I_r - I_s||^2 \cdot \frac{1}{1 + \left(\frac{||I_r^B - I_s^B||}{K}\right)^2 \exp(-\frac{z_{rs}^2}{\sigma_z})}, \qquad (10)$$

where z_{rs} measures the dissimilarity between pixel pair (I_r, I_s) in image I and (I_r^B, I_s^B) in background image I^B. A Hausdorff distance-like definition for z_{rs} is:

$$z_{rs} = \max\{||I_r - I_r^B||, ||I_s - I_s^B||\}. \qquad (11)$$

If z_{rs} is small, the pixel pair (I_r, I_s) has a high probability of belonging to the background, and the attenuation strength should be large $(\exp(-z_{rs}^2/\sigma_z) \to 1)$. Otherwise, it probably belongs to the contrast caused by the foreground/background boundary, and the attenuation strength should be small $(\exp(-z_{rs}^2/\sigma_z) \to 0)$. Figure 4 (e) shows the contrast map after adaptive background contrast attenuation by Equation (10). Clearly, most contrasts in the background are greatly attenuated and most contrasts along the foreground object boundary are well preserved. Figure 4 (f) shows the corresponding segmentation result. The last two rows of Figure 3 also show the attenuated contrast maps and good segmentation results.

Figure 5 shows attenuation results using different values for parameters K and z_{rs}. Figure 5 (b) shows that a large K will decrease the attenuation strength. A small

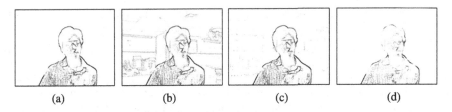

Fig. 5. Parameter settings. (a) $K = 5, \sigma_z = 10$. (b) $K = 500, \sigma_z = 10$. (c) $K = 5, \sigma_z = 1$. (d) $K = 5, \sigma_z = 50$.

z_{rs} will leave more contrasts in the image (Figure 5 (c)) and vise versa (Figure 5 (d)). In all our experiments, we set the default values of K and z_{rs} to 5 and 10 respectively to obtain good segmentation results on average, as shown in Figure 5 (a). These values are quite stable — there is no notable change in segmentation results when we change K and z_{rs} within the ranges $(2.5, 10)$ and $(5, 20)$ respectively.

This adaptive attenuation method works very well in most cases if there is no large illuminance change in the background image. In order to make our background contrast attenuation more robust, we also propose a measure z_{rs} which is not sensitive to large illuminance change:

$$z_{rs} = \left|\left| \vec{\mathbf{V}}(I_r, I_s) - \vec{\mathbf{V}}(I_r^B, I_s^B) \right|\right|, \tag{12}$$

where $\vec{\mathbf{V}}(a, b)$ is a vector from point a to point b in RGB color space. z_{rs} is illuminance-invariant if we assume the color changes of two adjacent pixels to be the same.

4 Background Maintenance

4.1 Adaptive Mixture of Global and Per-pixel Background Color Model

As mentioned in section 2.1, for the color term, there is a tradeoff between the global background color model (more robust to background change) and the per-pixel background color model (more accurate). In previous works [8] and [19], the mixing factor α in Equation (4) is a fixed value. To maximize robustness, an ideal system should adaptively adjust the mixing factor: if the foreground colors and background colors can be well separated, it should rely more on the global color model such that the whole system is robust to various changes of background; otherwise, it should rely on both the global and per-pixel color models. To achieve this goal, we adaptively mix two models based on the discriminative capabilities of the global foreground and background color models. In this paper, we adopt an approximation of the Kullback-Liebler (KL) divergence between two GMMs models [5]:

$$KL_{fb} = \sum_{k=0}^{K} w_k^f \min_i (KL(N_k^f || N_i^b) + \log \frac{w_k^f}{w_i^b}), \tag{13}$$

where N_k^f and N_i^b are the kth component of foreground GMMs and the ith component of background GMMs respectively. The KL-divergence between N_k^f and N_i^b can be computed analytically. Our adaptive mixture for the background color model is:

$$p'_{mix}(I_r) = \alpha' p(I_r|x=0) + (1-\alpha')p_B(I_r) \tag{14}$$

$$\alpha' = 1 - \frac{1}{2}\exp(-KL_{fb}/\sigma_{KL}), \tag{15}$$

where σ_{KL} is a parameter to control the influence of KL_{fb}. If the foreground and background color can be well separated, i.e., KL_{fb} is large, the mixing factor α' is set to be large to rely more on the global background color model. Otherwise, α' is small (minimum value is 0.5) to use both the global and per-pixel background color models.

4.2 Background Maintenance Scheme

Because visual communication (e.g., video chat) usually last a short period, sudden illuminance change is the main issue to be considered due to auto gain/white-balance control of the camera, illumination by fluorescent lamps (asynchronous with frame capture in the camera), and light switching. In addition, we also consider several background change events, i.e., small movement in background, casual camera shaking, sleeping and waking object. The following is our background maintenance scheme based on the above adaptive mixture of global and per-pixel background color model.

Sudden illuminance change. Illuminance change caused by auto gain/white-balance control of a camera or illumination by a fluorescent lamp is usually a small global change. We adopted histogram specification to adjust the background image globally. After segmentation at each timestep, we compute a histogram transformation function between two histograms from the labeled background regions in I and I^B. Then we apply this transformation to update the whole background image I^B. This simple method works well for small global illuminance or color changes. The large sudden illuminance change is detected by using frame differences. If the difference is above a predefined threshold, we trigger the following process:

Before segmentation: the background image I^B is updated by histogram specification and the global background color model is rebuilt. The foreground threshold t_f is increased to $3t_f$ to avoid introducing incorrect samples. A background uncertainty map $U^B = \{u_r^B = 1\}$ is initialized. The mixture for the background color model is modified as:

$$p'_{mix}(I_r|x=0) = \alpha' p(I_r|x=0) + (1-u_r^B)\cdot(1-\alpha')p_B(I_r). \tag{16}$$

After segmentation: the color, variance, and uncertainty of each pixel in the labeled background region is updated as follows:

$$I_{r,t}^B = (1-\rho)I_{r,t}^B + \rho I_{r,t} \tag{17}$$

$$\sigma_{r,t}^2 = (1-\rho)\sigma_{r,t}^2 + \rho(I_{r,t}-I_{r,t}^B)^T(I_{r,t}-I_{r,t}^B) \tag{18}$$

$$u_r^B = (1-\rho)u_r^B + \rho(1-\exp(-||I_{r,t}-I_{r,t}^B||/2\sigma_{r,t}^{-2})), \tag{19}$$

where $\rho = \beta N(I_{r,t}|I_{r,t}^B, \sigma_{r,t}^2)$ and β (typically 0.2) is the learning rate. Note that the uncertainty of the hidden pixel behind the foreground will never be decreased because we have no information about it.

Movement in background. We handle moving backgrounds using two mechanisms: 1) if the foreground colors and background colors can be well separated, our model will automatically self adjust to rely on the global background color model which is robust to small movements or dynamic motions (e.g., moving curtain) in background. 2) if there is no intersection between a moving object and the foreground, we can keep the biggest connected component in the segmentation result as foreground object. Otherwise, our system will treat the moving object as foreground if there is no higher-level sematic information available.

Sleeping and waking object. Both cases are essentially the same - a sleeping object is a new static object in the background and a waking object reveals new background areas. We should absorb these new pixels into background when they do not intersect with the foreground. After segmentation, the small connected components far from the foreground (largest connected component) are identified as new pixels. If these pixels and their neighboring pixels are labeled as background for a sufficient time period, we trigger background maintenance processing (Equation (17-19)) to absorb these pixels into the background.

Casual camera shaking. Camera shaking often occurs for a laptop user. We detect camera translation between the current and previous frames. If the translation is small (<4 pixels), a Gaussian blurred (standard variance 2.0) background image is applied and the weight of the per-pixel color model is decreased because global background color model is insensitive to camera shaking. If the translation is large, we disable the per-pixel color model. We will investigate motion compensation in the next step.

We show our background maintenance and segmentation results on the above mentioned background changing cases in the next section.

5   Experimental Results

All videos in our experiments are captured by consumer level web cameras (Logitech QuickCam@ Pro 5000 and Logitech QuickCam@ for Notebooks Deluxe) and we leave all parameters in the web cameras at the default settings (auto gain control and auto white balance). The frame rate is about 12-15 frames/seconds for a 320x240 video on a 3.2GHz desktop PC, with our 2-level multi-scale implementation (the result at the fine level is computed in a narrow band (20 pixels width) around the result at the coarse level). The opacity around the object boundary is obtained by a feathering operation.

Comparison with "Bi-layer segmentation". We quantitatively evaluate the accuracy of our approach on "AC" video which is a stereo video sequence for the evaluation of "Bi-layer segmentation" [8]. The ground truth foreground/background segmentation is provided every 5 frames. The segmentation error is measured as the percentage of bad pixels with respect to the whole image. We only use the video of the left view to test our approach (static background image is obtained by image mosaicing). Figure 6 (a) shows

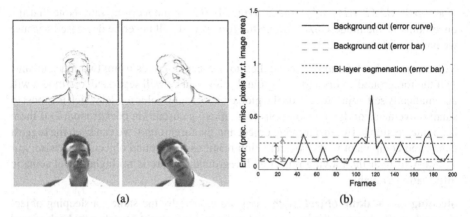

(a)   (b)

Fig. 6. Comparison with "Bi-layer segmentation" on "AC" video. (a) Background cut results (attenuated contrast map and final segmentations). (b) Error statistics. The solid blue line and two green dash lines are error curve and 1 standard error bar of background cut. Two red dotted lines is 1 standard variance error bar of "Bi-layer segmentation". The original video and ground truth segmentation are obtained from (http://research.microsoft.com/vision/cambridge/i2i/DSWeb.htm).

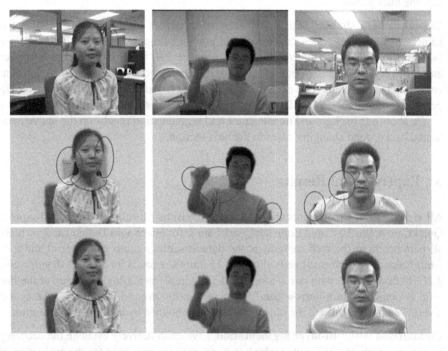

Fig. 7. Comparison with the basic model. Top row: a frame in a video sequence. Second row: result by the basic model. Red circles indicate notable segmentation errors. Last row: result by background cut.

two attenuated contrast maps and segmented foreground layers in the video. Figure 6 (b) plots an error curve (blue solid line) and 1 std error bar (two green dash lines) for our approach, and 1 std error bar (two red dotted lines) for "Bi-layer segmentation". Without using stereo information, the accuracy of our approach is still comparable.

Comparison with "basic model". We compare our approach with the basic model. Figure 7 shows the results produced by the basic model (2nd row) and background cut (last row), respectively. Using the attenuated contrast map, our approach can

Fig. 8. "Light1", "Curtain", and "Sleeping" examples (from top to bottom). In each example, the upper row shows input images and the lower row shows our segmentation results.

substantially reduce the errors caused by background contrast. Notice that the error of the basic model often results in temporal flickering artifacts around the boundary. For side-by-side comparisons, we highly recommend the reader to view our videos online (http://research.microsoft.com/~jiansun/).

Background maintenance. Figure 8 shows partial examples to demonstrate our background maintenance scheme. In the "Light1" example, there are two sudden illuminance changes in the 20th frame (first light off) and 181th frame (second light off). The system detected these changes and triggered the background maintenance process. The segmentation results in the 2nd row of Figure 8 shows that good segmentation results can still be obtained during maintenance process. The updated background image sequence is shown in the accompanying video. The "Curtain" example shows a moving curtain in the background. The system adaptively adjusted the mixture of global and per-pixel background color models to handle movements in the background. In the "Sleeping" example, a cloth is put into the background in the 50th frame. Then, it becomes motionless from the 100th frame. The system identified this event and gradually absorbed the cloth into the background. The right most image in the last row of Figure 8 shows correct segmentation when the foreground is interacting with this "sleeping" object. More examples containing sudden illuminance change, casual camera shaking and waking object are shown in our accompanying videos.

6   Discussion and Conclusion

In this paper, we have proposed a high quality, real-time foreground/background layer extraction approach called background cut, which combines background subtraction, color and contrast cues. In background cut, background subtraction is not only done on image color but also on image contrast — *background contrast attenuation* which reduces segmentation errors significantly. Our system is also robust to various background changes in real applications.

The current system still has some limitations. First, when the foreground and background colors are very similar or the foreground object contains very thin structures with respect to image size, high quality segmentation usually is hard to be obtain with our current algorithm. Enforcing more temporal coherence of the foreground boundary may improve the result to a certain extent. Second, in the current system, we assume a static background is obtained in an initialization phase. Automatically initialization of the background image is also important in real applications. Last, we misclassified the moving object which is interacting with the foreground. To solve this ambiguity, high level priors should be integrated into the system.

References

1. D. Harwood A. Elgammal and L. Davis. Non-parametric model for background subtraction. In *Proceedings of ECCV*, pages 751–767, 2000.
2. J.R. Bergen, P.J. Burt, R. Hingorani, and S. Peleg. A three-frame algorithm for estimating two-component image motion. In *IEEE Trans. on PAMI*, volume 14, pages 886–896, 1992.

3. Y. Boykov and M. Pi. Jolly. Interactive graph cuts for optimal boundary & region segmentation of objects in n-d images. In *Proceedings of ICCV*, pages 105–112, 2001.
4. Yuri Boykov and Vladimir Kolmogorov. An experimental comparison of min-cut/max-flow algorithms for energy minimization in vision. In *Energy Minimization Methods in CVPR*, 2001.
5. J. Goldberger, S. Gordon, and H. Greenspan. An efficient image similarity measure based on approximations of kl-divergence between two gaussian mixtures. In *Proceedings of CVPR*, pages 487–494, 2004.
6. W. E. L. Grimson, C. Stauffer, R. Romano, and L. Lee. Using adaptive tracking to classify and monitor activities in a site. In *Proceedings of CVPR*, pages 22–29, 1998.
7. D. Koller, J. Weber, and J. Malik. Robust multiple car tracking with occlusion reasoning. In *Proceedings of ECCV*, pages 189–196, 1993.
8. V. Kolmogorov, A. Criminisi, A. Blake, G. Cross, and C. Rother. Bi-layer segmentation of binocular stereo video. In *Proceedings of CVPR*, pages 1186–1193, 2005.
9. Y. Li, J. Sun, and H. Y. Shum. Video object cut and paste. In *Proceedings of ACM SIG-GRAPH*, pages 595–600, 2005.
10. Y. Li, J. Sun, C. K. Tang, and H. Y. Shum. Lazy snapping. In *Proceedings of ACM SIG-GRAPH*, 2004.
11. A. Mittal and N. Paragios. Motion-based background subtraction using adaptive kernel density estimation. In *Proceedings of CVPR*, pages 302–309, 2004.
12. A. Monnet, A. Mittal, N. Paragios, and V. Ramesh. Background modeling and subtraction of dynamic scenes. In *Proceedings of ICCV*, pages 1305–1312, 2005.
13. P. Perona and J. Malik. Scale-space and edge detection using anisotropic diffusion. In *IEEE Tran. on PAMI*, volume 12, pages 629–63, 1990.
14. Y. Ren, C. S. Chua, and Yeong-Khing HO. Motion detection with non-stationary background. In *Machine Vision and Applications.*, pages 332–343, 2003.
15. C. Rother, A. Blake, and V. Kolmogorov. Grabcut - interactive foreground extraction using iterated graph cuts. In *Proceedings of ACM SIGGRAPH*, pages 309–314, 2004.
16. Y. Sheikh and M. Shah. Bayesian object detection in dynamic scenes. In *Proceedings of CVPR*, pages 1778–1792, 2005.
17. K. Toyama, J. Krumm, B. Brumitt, and B. Meyers. Wallflower: principles and practice of background maintenance. In *Proceedings of ICCV*, pages 255–261, 1999.
18. O. Tuzel, F. Porikli, and Peter Meer. A bayesian approach to background modeling. In *IEEE Workshop on Machine Vision for Intelligent Vehicles*, 2005.
19. J. Wang, P. Bhat, R. A. Colburn, M. Agrawala, and M. F. Cohen. Interactive video cutout. In *Proceedings of ACM SIGGRAPH*, pages 585–594, 2005.
20. J. Y. A. Wang and E. H. Adelson. Layered representation for motion analysis. In *Proceedings of CVPR*, pages 361–366, 1993.
21. J. Wills, S. Agarwal, and S. Belongie. What went where. In *Proceedings of CVPR*, pages 37–44, 2003.
22. C. Wren, A. Azarbayejani, T. Darrell, and A. Pentland. Pfinder: Real-time tracking of the human body. In *IEEE Tran. on PAMI*, volume 19, pages 780–785, 1997.
23. J. J. Xiao and M. Shah. Motion layer extraction and alpha matting. In *Proceedings of CVPR*, pages 698–703, 2005.

PoseCut: Simultaneous Segmentation and 3D Pose Estimation of Humans Using Dynamic Graph-Cuts*

Matthieu Bray, Pushmeet Kohli, and Philip H.S. Torr

Dept. of Computing, Oxford Brookes University
{mbray, pushmeet.kohli, philiptorr}@brookes.ac.uk

Abstract. We present a novel algorithm for performing integrated segmentation and 3D pose estimation of a human body from multiple views. Unlike other related state of the art techniques which focus on either segmentation or pose estimation individually, our approach tackles these two tasks together. Normally, when optimizing for pose, it is traditional to use some fixed set of features, e.g. edges or chamfer maps. In contrast, our novel approach consists of optimizing a cost function based on a Markov Random Field (MRF). This has the advantage that we can use all the information in the image: edges, background and foreground appearances, as well as the prior information on the shape and pose of the subject and combine them in a Bayesian framework. Previously, optimizing such a cost function would have been computationally infeasible. However, our recent research in dynamic graph cuts allows this to be done much more efficiently than before. We demonstrate the efficacy of our approach on challenging motion sequences. Note that although we target the human pose inference problem in the paper, our method is completely generic and can be used to segment and infer the pose of any specified rigid, deformable or articulated object.

1 Introduction

Human pose inference is an important problem in computer vision standing at the crossroads of various applications ranging from Human Computer Interaction (HCI) to surveillance. The importance and complexity of this problem can be guaged by observing the number of papers which have tried to deal with it [1, 2, 3, 4, 5, 6]. In the last few years, several techniques have been proposed for tackling the pose inference problem, some of which have obtained decent results. In particular, the work of Agarwal and Triggs [1] using relevance vector machines and that of Shakhnarovich et al. [3] based on parametric sensitive hashing induced a lot interest and have been shown to give good results.

Most algorithms which perform pose estimation require the segmentation of humans as an essential introductory step [1, 2, 3]. This precondition limits the

* This work was supported by the EPSRC research grant GR/T21790/01(P) and the IST Programme of the European Community, under the PASCAL Network of Excellence, IST-2002-506778.

A. Leonardis, H. Bischof, and A. Pinz (Eds.): ECCV 2006, Part II, LNCS 3952, pp. 642–655, 2006.

use of these techniques to scenarios where good segmentations are made available by enforcing strict studio conditions like blue-screening. Otherwise a preprocessing step must be performed in an attempt to segment the human, such as [7]. These approaches however cannot overcome the complexity of the problem of producing good segmentations for the general case of complex foreground and backgrounds (as will be seen in section 4), and where there are multiple objects in the scene or the camera/background is not stationary. Some pose inference methods exist which do not need segmentations. These rely on features such as chamfer distance [4], appearance [5], or edge and intensity [6]. However, none of these methods is able to efficiently utilize all the information present in an image and fail if the feature detector they are using fails. This is partly because the feature detector is not coupled to the knowledge of the pose of the object.

The question is then, how to simultaneously obtain the segmentation and human pose using all available information contained in the images?

Some elements of the answer to this question have been described by Kumar *et al.* [8]. Addressing the object segmentation problem, they report that the *"samples from the Gibbs distribution defined by the MRF very rarely give rise to realistic shapes"*. As an illustration of this statement, figure 1(*b*) shows the segmentation result corresponding to the maximum a posteriori (MAP) solution of the Markov random Field (MRF) incorporating information about the image edges and appearances of the object and background. It can be clearly seen that this result is nowhere close to the ground truth.

Shape priors and segmentation. In recent years, a number of papers have tried to couple MRFs used for modelling the image segmentation problem, with information about the nature and shape of the object to be segmented [8, 10, 11]. One of the initial methods for combining MRFs with a shape prior was proposed by Huang *et al.* [10]. They incrementally found the MAP solution of an extended MRF[1] integrated with a probabilistic deformable model. By using belief propagation in the area surrounding the contour of this deformable model in an iterative manner, they were able to obtain a refined estimate of the contour. Their work however did not address the crucial problem of obtaining a object-like segmentation using prior information about the object which was later addressed by [8, 11].

The problem however was still far from being completely solved since objects in the real world change their shapes constantly and hence it is difficult to ascertain what would be a good choice for a prior on the shape. This complex and important problem was addressed by the work of Kumar *et al.* [8]. They modelled the segmentation problem by combining MRFs with layered pictorial structures (LPS) which provided them with a realistic shape prior described by a set of latent shape parameters. Their cost function was a weighted sum of the energy terms for different shape parameters (samples). The weights of this energy function were obtained by optimizing the labelling solution (background/foreground) using the Expectation-Maximization (EM) algorithm. During this optimization

---

[1] It is named an *extended* MRF due to the presence of an extra layer in the MRF to cope with the shape prior.

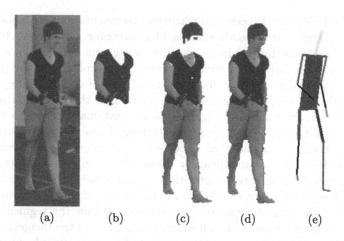

(a)   (b)   (c)   (d)   (e)

Fig. 1. Segmentation results corresponding to MRFs incorporating increasingly more information. (a) Original image. (b) The segmentation obtained corresponding to the MAP solution of a MRF consisting of colour likelihood and contrast terms as described in [9]. We give the exact formulation of this MRF in section 2.2. (c) The result obtained when the likelihood term of the MRF also takes into account the Gaussian Mixture Models (GMM) of individual pixel intensities as described in section 2.2. (d) Segmentation obtained after incorporating a 'pose-specific' shape prior in the MRF as explained in Section 2.3. The prior is represented as the distance transform of a stickman which guarantees a human-like segmentation. (e) The stickman model after optimization of its 3D pose (see Section 3). Observe how incorporating the individual pixel colour models in the MRF (c) gives a considerably better result than the one obtained using the standard appearance and contrast based representation (b). However the segmentation still misses the face of the subject. The incorporation of a stickman shape prior ensures a human-like segmentation (d) and provides simultaneously (after optimization) the 3D pose of the subject (e).

procedure, a graph cut had to be computed in order to obtain the segmentation score each time any parameter of the MRF was changed. This made their algorithm extremely computationally expensive.

Although their approach produced good results, it had some shortcomings. It was focused on obtaining good segmentations and did not furnish the pose of the object explicitly. Moreover, a lot of effort had to be spent to learn the exemplars for different parts of the LPS model. In the next section we will describe how we overcome the second limitation by using a simple articulated stickman model, which is not only efficiently renderable, but also provides a robust human-like segmentation and accurate pose estimate. To make our algorithm further computationally efficient we use the dynamic graph cut algorithm which was recently proposed in [12]. This new algorithm enables multiple graph cut computations, each computation taking a fraction of the time taken by the conventional graph cut algorithm if the change in the problem is small.

Solving markov random fields using dynamic graph cuts. A MRF is defined by its parameters and the observed data. A change in any of the two thus causes a change in the MRF. If these changes are minimal, then intuitively the change in the MAP solution of the MRF should also be small. We made this observation and showed how dynamic graph cuts can be used to efficiently find the MAP solutions for MRFs that vary minimally from one time instant to the next [12]. The underlying idea of our paper was that of dynamic computation, where an algorithm solves a problem instance by dynamically updating the solution of the previous problem instance. Its goal is to be more efficient than a re-computation of the problem solution after every change from scratch. In the case of enormous problem instances and few changes, dynamic computation yields a substantial speed-up.

Overview of the paper. The paper proposes a novel algorithm for performing integrated segmentation and 3D pose estimation of a human body from multiple views. We do not require a feature extraction step but use all the data in the image. We formulate the problem in a Bayesian framework building on the object-specific MRF [8] and provide an efficient method for its solution called POSECUT. We include a human *pose-specific* shape prior in the MRF used for image segmentation, to obtain high quality segmentation results. We refer to this integrated model as a *pose-specific* MRF. As opposed to Kumar *et al.* [8], our approach does not require the laborious process of learning exemplars. Instead we use a simple articulated stickman model, which together with an MRF is used as our shape prior. Our experimental results show that this model suffices to ensure human-like segmentations.

Given an image, the solution of the pose-specific MRF is used to measure the quality of a 3D body pose. This cost function is then optimized over all pose parameters using dynamic graph cuts to provide both a object-like segmentation and the pose. The astute reader will notice that although we focus on the human pose inference problem, our method is in-fact general and can be used to segment and/or infer the pose of any object. We believe that our methodology is completely novel and we are not aware of any published methods which perform simultaneous segmentation and pose estimation. To summarize, the novelties of our approach include:

- An efficient method for combined object segmentation and pose estimation (POSECUT).
- Integration of a simple 'stickman prior' based on the skeleton of the object in a MRF to obtain a *pose-specific* MRF which helps us in obtaining high quality object pose estimate and segmentation results.

In the next section we give an intuitive insight into our framework. The pose-specific MRF and the different terms used in its construction are introduced in the same section. In section 3 we formulate the pose inference problem and describe the use of dynamic graph cuts for optimization in our problem construction. We present the experimental results obtained by our methods in section 4. These include comparison of our segmentation results with those obtained by some state of the art methods. We also show some results of simultaneous 3D pose estimation and segmentation. Our conclusions and the directions for future work are listed in Section 5.

2   Pose Specific MRF for Image Segmentation

In this section, we define an MRF-based energy function that gives the cost of any pose of a subject. We will optimize over this MRF using the Powell [13] minimization algorithm to infer the pose, and graph cuts to solve the segmentation as described in Section 3. The optimization of the energy is made efficient by the use of the dynamic graph cut algorithm [12].

Image segmentation has always remained an iconic problem of computer vision. The past few years have seen rapid progress made on it driven by the emergence of powerful optimization algorithms such as graph cuts. The early methods for performing image segmentation worked by coupling colour appearance information about the object and background with the edges present in an image to obtain good segmentations. However, this framework does not always guarantee good results. In particular, it fails in cases where the colour appearance models of the object and background are not discriminative as seen in figure 1(b). The problem becomes even more pronounced in the case of humans where we have to deal with the various idiosyncracies of human clothing.

A semi-automated solution to this problem was explored by Boykov and Jolly [9] in their work on interactive image segmentation. They showed how users could refine segmentation results by specifying additional constraints. This can be done by labelling particular regions of the image as 'object' or 'background' and then computing the MAP solution of the MRF again. From their work, we made the following interesting observations: *Simple user supplied shape cues used as rough priors for the object segmentation problem produced excellent results. The exact shape of the object can be induced from the edge information embedded in the image.* Taking these into consideration, we hypothesized that the accurate exemplars used in [8] to generate shape priors were in-fact an overkill and could be replaced by a much simpler model.

Stickman model. Motivated by the observations made above, we decided against using a sophisticated shape prior. Instead, we used a simple articulated stickman model (shown in figure 1(e)) to generate a rough pose-specific shape prior on the segmentation. As can been seen from the segmentation results in figure 1(d), the stickman model helped us to obtain excellent segmentation results. The model has 26 degrees of freedom consisting of parameters defining absolute position and orientation of the torso, and the various joint angle values. There were no constraints or joint-limits incorporated in our model.

We now formally describe how the image segmentation problem can be modeled using a *pose-specific* MRF.

2.1   Markov Random Fields

A random field comprises of a set of discrete random variables $\{X_1, X_2, \ldots, X_n\}$ defined on the index set $\mathcal{V}$, such that each variable X_v takes a value x_v from the label set $\mathcal{X} = \{\mathcal{X}_1, \mathcal{X}_2, \ldots, \mathcal{X}_l\}$ of all possible labels. We represent the set of all values $x_v, \forall v \in \mathcal{V}$ by the vector $\mathbf{x}$ which takes values in $\mathcal{X}^n$, and is referred to as the configuration of the MRF. Further, we use $\mathcal{N}_v$ to denote the set consisting of indices of all variables which are neighbours of the random variable X_v in the graphical model. This random field is said to be a MRF with respect to a neighborhood system $\mathcal{N} = \{\mathcal{N}_v | v \in \mathcal{V}\}$ if and only if it satisfies the positivity property: $\Pr(\mathbf{x}) > 0 \;\; \forall \mathbf{x} \in \mathcal{X}^n$, and the Markovian property:

$$\Pr(x_v | \{x_u : u \in \mathcal{V} - \{v\}\}) = \Pr(x_v | \{x_u : u \in \mathcal{N}_v\}) \qquad \forall v \in \mathcal{V}. \qquad (1)$$

Here we refer to $\Pr(X = \mathbf{x})$ by $\Pr(\mathbf{x})$ and $\Pr(X_i = x_i)$ by $\Pr(x_i)$. The MAP-MRF estimation problem can be formulated as an energy minimization problem where the energy corresponding to configuration $\mathbf{x}$ is the negative log likelihood of the joint posterior probability of the MRF and is defined as

$$E(\mathbf{x}) = -\log \Pr(\mathbf{x}|\mathbf{D}) + \text{const.} \qquad (2)$$

where $\mathbf{D}$ is the observed data.

2.2   Image Segmentation as MAP-MRF Inference

In the context of image segmentation, $\mathcal{V}$ corresponds to the set of all image pixels, $\mathcal{N}$ is a neighbourhood defined on this set[2], the set $\mathcal{X}$ comprises of the labels representing the different image segments (which in our case are 'foreground' and 'background'), and the value x_v denotes the labeling of the pixel v of the image. Every configuration $\mathbf{x}$ of such an MRF defines a segmentation. The image segmentation problem can thus be solved by finding the least energy configuration of the MRF. The energy corresponding to a configuration $\mathbf{x}$ consists of a likelihood and a prior term as:

$$\Psi_1(\mathbf{x}) = \sum_{i \in \mathcal{V}} \left(\phi(\mathbf{D}|x_i) + \sum_{j \in \mathcal{N}_i} \psi(x_i, x_j) \right) + \text{const}, \qquad (3)$$

where the prior $\psi(x_i, x_j)$ takes the form of a Generalized Potts model:

$$\psi(x_i, x_j) = \begin{cases} K_{ij} & \text{if } x_i \neq x_j, \\ 0 & \text{if } x_i = x_j. \end{cases} \qquad (4)$$

The MRF used to model the image segmentation problem also contains a contrast term which favours pixels with similar colour having the same label [9, 14]. This is incorporated in the energy function by reducing the cost within the Potts model for two labels being different in proportion to the difference in intensities of their corresponding pixels. In our experiments, we use the term:

$$\gamma(i, j) = \lambda \exp\left(\frac{-g^2(i, j)}{2\sigma^2} \right) \frac{1}{\text{dist}(i, j)}, \qquad (5)$$

---

[2] In this paper, we have used the standard 8-neighbourhood i.e. each pixel is connected to the 8 pixels surrounding it.

where $g^2(i,j)$ measures the difference in the RGB values of pixels i and j and dist(i,j) gives the spatial distance between i and j. This is a likelihood term (not prior) as it is based on the data, and hence has to be added separately from the smoothness prior. The energy function of the MRF now becomes

$$\Psi_2(\mathbf{x}) = \sum_{i \in \mathcal{V}} \left(\phi(\mathbf{D}|x_i) + \sum_{j \in \mathcal{N}_i} (\phi(\mathbf{D}|x_i, x_j) + \psi(x_i, x_j)) \right) \qquad (6)$$

The contrast term of the energy function is defined as

$$\phi(\mathbf{D}|x_i, x_j) = \begin{cases} \gamma(i,j) & \text{if } x_i \neq x_j \\ 0 & \text{if } x_i = x_j. \end{cases} \qquad (7)$$

The term $\phi(\mathbf{D}|x_i)$ in the MRF energy is the data log likelihood which imposes individual penalties for assigning any label $\mathcal{X}_k$ to pixel i. If we only take the appearance model into consideration, the likelihood is given by

$$\phi(\mathbf{D}|x_i) = -\log \Pr(i \in \mathcal{V}_k | \mathcal{H}_k) \qquad \text{if } x_i = \mathcal{X}_k \qquad (8)$$

where $\mathcal{H}_k$ is the RGB (or for grey scale images, the intensity value) distribution for $\mathcal{S}_k$, the segment denoted by label $\mathcal{X}_k{}^3$. The probability of a pixel belonging to a particular segment i.e. $\Pr(i \in \mathcal{S}_k | \mathcal{H}_k)$ is proportional to the likelihood $\Pr(I_i | \mathcal{H}_k)$, where I_i is the colour intensity of the pixel i. As can be seen from figure 2(b), this term is rather undiscriminating as the colours (grey intensity values in this case) included in the foreground histogram are similar to the ones included in the background histogram.

Modeling pixel intensities as GMMs. The MRF defined above for image segmentation performs poorly when segmenting images in which the appearance models of the foreground and background are not highly discriminative. When working on video sequences, we can use a background model developed using the Grimson-Stauffer [7] algorithm to improve our results. This algorithm works by representing the colour distribution of each pixel position in the video as a Gaussian Mixture Model (GMM). The likelihoods of a pixel for being background or foreground obtained by this technique are integrated in our MRF. Figure 1(c) shows the segmentation result obtained after incorporating this information in our MRF formulation.

2.3   Incorporating the Pose-Specific Shape Prior

Though the results obtained from the above formulation look decent, they are not perfect. Note that there is no prior on the segmentation to look human like. Intuitively, incorporating such a constraint in the MRF would improve the final result obtained. In our case, this prior should be *pose-specific* as it depends on what pose the object (the human) is in. Kumar *et. al.* [8] in their work on

---

[3] In our problem, we have only 2 segments i.e. the foreground and the background.

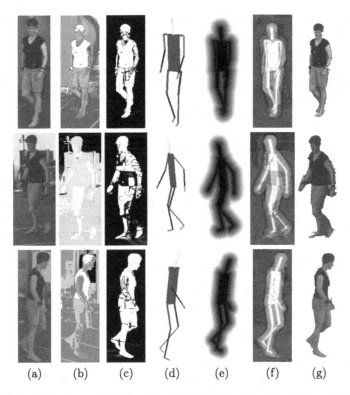

(a)   (b)   (c)   (d)   (e)   (f)   (g)

Fig. 2. (a) Original image. (b) The ratios of the likelihoods of pixels being labelled foreground/background ($\phi(\mathbf{D}|\mathbf{x}_i = \text{'fg'}) - \phi(\mathbf{D}|\mathbf{x}_i = \text{'bg'})$). These values are derived from the colour intensity histograms (see Section 2.2). (c) The segmentation results obtained by using the GMM models of pixel intensities. (d) The stickman in the optimal pose (see Sections 2.3 and 3). (e) The shape prior (distance transform) corresponding to the optimal pose of the stickman. (f) The ratio of the likelihoods of being labelled foreground/background using all the energy terms (colour histograms defining appearance models, GMMs for individual pixel intensities, and the pose-specific shape prior (see Sections 2.2, 2.2 and 2.3)) $\Psi_3(x_i = \text{'fg'}, \mathbf{\Theta}) - \Psi_3(x_i = \text{'bg'}, \mathbf{\Theta})$. (g) The segmentation result obtained from our algorithm which is the MAP solution of the energy Ψ_3 of the pose-specific MRF.

interleaved object recognition and segmentation, used the result of the recognition to develop a shape prior over the segmentation. This prior was defined by a set of latent variables which favoured segmentations of a specific pose of the object. They called this model the Object Category Specific MRF, which had the following energy function:

$$\Psi_3(\mathbf{x}, \mathbf{\Theta}) = \sum_i (\phi(\mathbf{D}|x_i) + \phi(x_i|\mathbf{\Theta}) + \sum_j (\phi(\mathbf{D}|x_i, x_j) + \psi(x_i, x_j))) \quad (9)$$

with posterior $p(\mathbf{x}, \mathbf{\Theta}|\mathbf{D}) = \frac{1}{Z_3} \exp(-\Psi_3(\mathbf{x}, \mathbf{\Theta}))$. Here $\mathbf{\Theta}$ is used to denote the vector consisting of the object pose parameters. The shape-prior term of the energy function for a particular pose of the human is shown in figure 2(e). This is a distance transform generated from the stick-man model silhouette using the fast implementation of Felzenszwalb and Huttenlocher [15].

The function $\phi(x_i|\Theta)$ was choosen such that given an estimate of the location and shape of the object, pixels falling near to that shape were more likely to be labelled as 'foreground' and vice versa. It has the form: $\phi(x_i|\Theta) = -\log p(x_i|\Theta)$. We follow the formulation of [8] and define $p(x_i|\Theta)$ as

$$p(x_i = \text{figure}|\Theta) = 1 - p(x_i = \text{ground}|\Theta) = \frac{1}{1 + \exp(\mu * (d(i, \Theta) - d_r))}, \quad (10)$$

where $d(i, \Theta)$ is the distance of a pixel i from the shape defined by Θ (being negative if inside the shape). The parameter d_r decides how 'fat' the shape should be, while parameter μ determines the ratio of the magnitude of the penalty that points outside the shape have to face compared to the points inside the shape.

2.4   MAP-MRF Inference Using Graph Cuts

Energies like the one defined in (9) can be solved using graph cuts if they are *sub-modular* [16]. The condition for sub-modularity is given as:

$$E(0,0) + E(1,1) \leq E(0,1) + E(1,0) \quad (11)$$

which implies that the energy for two labels taking similar values should be less than the energy for them taking different values. In our case, this is indeed the case and thus we can find the optimal configuration $\mathbf{x}^* = \min_{\mathbf{x}} \Psi_3(\mathbf{x}, \Theta)$ using a single graph cut. The labels of the latent variable in this configuration give the segmentation solution.

3   Formulating the Pose Inference Problem

Since the segmentation of an object depends on its estimated pose, we would like to make sure that our shape prior reflects the actual pose of the object. This takes us to our original problem of finding the pose of the human in an image. In order to solve this, we start with an initial guess of the object pose and optimize it to find the correct pose. When dealing with videos, a good starting point for this process would be the pose of the object in the previous frame. However, more sophisticated methods could be used based on object detection [17] at the expense of increasing the computation time.

One of the key contributions of this paper is to show how given an image of the object, the pose inference problem can be formulated in terms of a optimization problem over the MRF energy given in (9). Specifically, we solve the problem:

$$\Theta_{\text{opt}} = \arg \min_{\Theta}(\min_{\mathbf{x}} \Psi_3(\mathbf{x}, \Theta)). \quad (12)$$

Fig. 3 shows how $\min_{\mathbf{x}} \Psi_3(\mathbf{x}, \Theta)$ changes with rotation and translation of our shape prior. It can be clearly seen that the energy surface is uni-modal and hence can

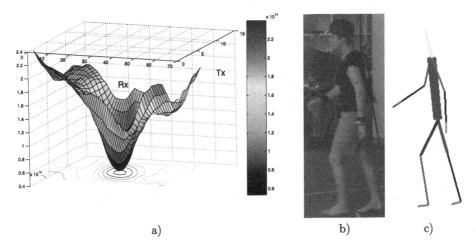

a)   b)   c)

Fig. 3. a) The values of $\min_x \Psi_3(\mathbf{x}, \Theta)$ obtained by varying the global translation and rotation of the shape prior in the x-axis. b) Original image. c) The pose obtained corresponding to the global minimum of the energy.

be optimized using any standard optimization algorithm like gradient descent. However, for more subtle joint angles, the energy is multi-modal, containing local minima. In our experiments, we used the Powell minimization [13] algorithm for optimization. When dealing with multiple views we solve the problem:

$$\Theta_{\text{opt}} = \arg \min_{\Theta} (\min_{\mathbf{x}} \sum_{\text{views}} (\Psi_3(\mathbf{x}, \Theta)). \tag{13}$$

Minimizing energies using dynamic graph cuts. As explained earlier global minima of energies like the one defined in (9) can be found by graph cuts [16]. The time taken for computing a graph cut for a reasonably sized MRF is of the order of seconds. This would make our optimization algorithm extremely slow since we need to compute the global optimum of $\Psi_3(\mathbf{x}, \Theta)$ with respect to $\mathbf{x}$ multiple number times for different values of Θ. The graph cut computation can be made significantly faster by using the dynamic graph cut algorithm proposed recently in [12]. This algorithm works by using the solution of the previous graph cut computation for solving the new instance of the problem. We obtained a speed-up in the range of 15-20 times by using the dynamic graph cut algorithm.

4 Experiments

We now discuss the results obtained by POSECUT.

Segmentation. In order to demonstrate the performance of our method, we compare our segmentation results with those obtained by using the methods proposed in [7] and [18]. Bhatia *et al.* [18] learn a pixelwise background model

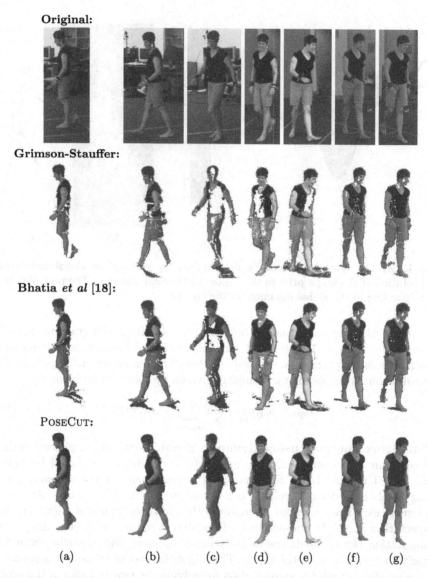

Fig. 4. Segmentation results obtained by Grimson-Stauffer, the method proposed by Bhatia *et al* [18] and POSECUT

represented by 3 Gaussians whose parameters are estimated by the Expectation-Maximization algorithm. They assume a uniform distribution for the likelihood of foreground pixels. It can be seen from the results in figure 4 that the segmentations obtained by using the methods of [7] and [18] are not accurate: They contain "speckles" and often segment the shadows of the feet as foreground. This is expected as they use only a pixelwise term to differentiate the background from the foreground and do not incorporate any spatial term which could offer a

Camera 2   **Camera 3**

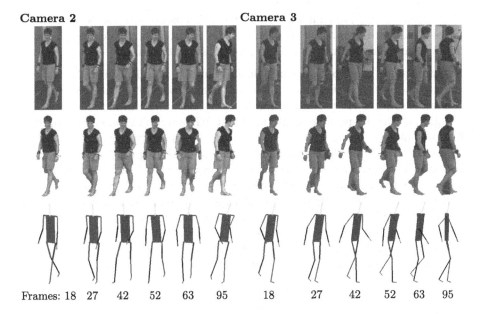

Frames: 18   27   42   52   63   95   18   27   42   52   63   95

Fig. 5. Segmentation (middle) and pose estimation (bottom) results from POSECUT

Camera 2   **Camera 3**

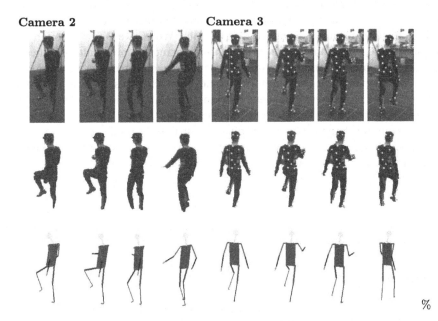

%

Fig. 6. Segmentation (middle row) and pose estimation (bottom row) results obtained by POSECUT. Observe that although the foreground and background appearances are similar, our algorithm is able to obtain good segmentations.

better "smoothing". In contrast, POSECUT which uses a pairwise potential term (as any standard graph cut approach) and a shape prior (which guarantees a human-like segmentation), is able to provide accurate results.

Segmentation and pose estimation. Figures 5 and 6 present the segmentations and the pose estimates obtained using POSECUT. The first data set comprises of three views of human walking circularly. The time needed for computation of the 3D pose estimate, on a PM 2GHz machine, when dealing with 644×484 images, is about 50 seconds per view[4]. As shown in these figures, the pose estimates match the original images accurately. In Figures 5 and 6, it should be noted that the appearance models of the foreground and background are quite similar: for instance, in Figure 6, the clothes of the subject are black in colour and the floor in the background is rather dark. The accuracy of the segmentation obtained in such challenging conditions demonstrates the robustness of POSECUT. An interesting fact to observe in Figure 5 about frame 95 is that the torso rotation of the stickman does not exactly conform with the original pose of the object. However, the segmentation of these frames is still accurate.

5   Conclusions and Future Work

The paper sets out a novel method for performing simultaneous segmentation and 3D pose estimation (POSECUT). The problem is formulated in a Bayesian framework which has the capability to utilize all information available (prior as well as observed data) to obtain good results. We showed how a rough pose-specific shape prior could be used to improve segmentation results significantly. We also gave a new formulation of the pose inference problem as an energy minimization problem and showed how it could be efficiently solved using dynamic graph cuts. The experiments demonstrate that our method is able to obtain excellent segmentation and pose estimation results.

It is common knowledge that the set of all human poses constitutes a low-dimensional manifold in the complete pose space. Optimizing over a parametrization of this low dimensional space instead of the 26D pose vector would intuitively improve both the accuracy and computation efficiency of our algorithm. Thus the use of dimensionality reduction algorithms is an important area to be investigated. The directions for future work also include using an appearance model per limb, which being more discriminative could help provide more accurate segmentations and pose estimates.

References

1. Agarwal, A., Triggs, B.: 3d human pose from silhouettes by relevance vector regression. In: CVPR. Volume II. (2004) 882–888
2. Kehl, R., Bray, M., Van Gool, L.: Full body tracking from multiple views using stochastic sampling. In: CVPR. Volume II. (2005) 129 – 136

---

[4] However, this could be speed up by computing the parameters of the MRF in an FPGA (Field-programmable gate array).

3. Shakhnarovich, G., Viola, P., Darrell, T.: Fast pose estimation with parameter-sensitive hashing. In: ICCV. (2003) 750–757
4. Gavrila, D., Davis, L.: 3D model-based tracking of humans in action: a multi-view approach. In: CVPR. (1996) 73–80
5. Sidenbladh, H., Black, M.J., Fleet, D.J.: Stochastic tracking of 3D human figures using 2D image motion. In: ECCV. (2000) 702–718
6. Sminchisescu, C., Triggs, B.: Covariance scaled sampling for monocular 3D body tracking. In: CVPR. (2001) 447–454
7. Stauffer, C., Grimson, W.: Adaptive background mixture models for real-time tracking. In: CVPR. (1999) 246–252
8. Kumar, M., Torr, P., Zisserman, A.: Obj cut. In: CVPR. Volume I. (2005) 18–25
9. Boykov, Y., Jolly, M.: Interactive graph cuts for optimal boundary and region segmentation of objects in n-d images. In: ICCV. (2001) 105–112
10. Huang, R., Pavlovic, V., Metaxas, D.: A graphical model framework for coupling mrfs and deformable models. In: CVPR. Volume II. (2004) 739–746
11. Freedman, D., Zhang, T.: Interactive graph cut based segmentation with shape priors. In: CVPR. Volume I. (2005) 755–762
12. Kohli, P., Torr, P.: Efficiently solving dynamic markov random fields using graph cuts. In: ICCV. (2005)
13. Press, W., Flannery, B., Teukolsky, S., Vetterling, W.: Numerical recipes in C. Cambridge Uni. Press (1988)
14. Blake, A., Rother, C., Brown, M., Pérez, P., Torr, P.: Interactive image segmentation using an adaptive gmmrf model. In: ECCV. Volume I. (2004) 428–441
15. Felzenszwalb, P., Huttenlocher, D.: Distance transforms of sampled functions. Technical Report TR2004-1963, Cornell University (2004)
16. Kolmogorov, V., Zabih, R.: What energy functions can be minimized via graph cuts? In: ECCV. Volume III. (2002) 65 ff.
17. Stenger, B., Thayananthan, A., Torr, P., Cipolla, R.: Filtering using a tree-based estimator. In: ICCV. (2003) 1063–1070
18. Bhatia, S., Sigal, L., Isard, M., Black, M.: 3d human limb detection using space carving and multi-view eigen models. In: ANM Workshop. Volume I. (2004) 17

Author Index

Lecture Notes in Computer Science

For information about Vols. 1–3848

please contact your bookseller or Springer